PRINCIPLES OF
INCIDENT RESPONSE AND
DISASTER RECOVERY

PRINCIPLES OF INCIDENT RESPONSE AND DISASTER RECOVERY

Dr. Michael E. Whitman, CISSP
Herbert J. Mattord, CISSP
Kennesaw State University

THOMSON
COURSE TECHNOLOGY

Australia • Canada • Mexico • Singapore • Spain • United Kingdom • United States

THOMSON
COURSE TECHNOLOGY

Principles of Incident Response and Disaster Recovery

Dr. Michael E. Whitman, CISSP
Herbert J. Mattord, CISSP
Kennesaw State University

Managing Editor:
William Pitkin III

Product Manager:
Nick Lombardi

Production Editor:
Kristen Guevara

Editorial Assistant:
Allison Murphy

Marketing Manager:
Guy Baskaran

Cover Designer:
Abby Scholz

Manufacturing Coordinator:
George Morrison

Compositor:
GEX Publishing Services

Copy Editor:
Mark Goodin

Indexer:
Sharon Hilgenberg

TABLE OF CONTENTS

AS GLOBAL NETWORKS CONTINUE TO EXPAND, the interconnections between them become ever more vital to the smooth operation of communication and computing systems. However, escalating incidences of virus and worm attacks and the success of criminal attackers illustrate the weaknesses in current information technologies and the need for heightened system security.

In attempting to secure current systems and networks, organizations must draw on the pool of current information security practitioners. These same organizations will count on the next generation of professionals to have the correct mix of skills and experiences to develop more secure computing environments in the future. Students of technology must learn to recognize and plan for the threats and vulnerabilities present in existing systems. They must also learn how to design and develop the secure systems that will address these threats in the future.

The purpose of this textbook is to fill the increasing need for a quality academic textbook in the discipline of Information Security and its associated areas of Contingency Operations. While there are dozens of quality publications on information security and assurance oriented to the practitioner, there are fewer textbooks that provide the student with a focus on the managerial issues associated with planning for and reacting to events, incidents, disasters, and crises. By creating a book specifically oriented toward students of information systems management, we hope to close this gap. Specifically, there is a clear need for disciplines such as Information Systems, Criminal Justice, Political Science, and Accounting Information Systems to understand the foundations of contingency operations and the development of managerial plans to deal with them. The fundamental tenet of this textbook is that information security in the modern organization is a management problem, and not one that technology alone can answer; it is a problem that has important economic consequences and for which management is accountable.

Approach

The book provides an overview of contingency operations – including its components and a thorough treatment of the administration of the planning process for incident response, disaster recovery, and business continuity planning. It can be used to support course delivery for information-security-driven programs targeted at Information Technology students as well as support IT management and technology management curricula aimed at business or technical management students.

Chapter Scenarios—Each chapter opens with a short story that follows the same fictional company as it encounters various contingency planning or operational issues. The scenario also offers a few discussion questions. These questions give the student and the instructor an opportunity to discuss the issues that underlie the content.

Ongoing Case Sidebars—These sections highlight an ongoing case in which a hypothetical organization deals with the challenges in preparation for and reacting to events that become incidents, disasters, and crises. The boxes put the human face to the theoretical context and constructs presented, allowing students to experience the challenges and stress of dealing with the issues associated with contingency operations.

Technical Details Sidebars—These sections highlight specific technical issues, allowing the student to explore these topics in greater detail.

Boxed Examples—These sections include other examples, not associated with the ongoing case study which are included to illustrate key learning objectives or show extended examples of plans and policies.

Hands-On Learning—At the end of each chapter, students will find a Chapter Summary and Review Questions, as well as Exercises, which give them the opportunity to examine the contingency planning arena outside the classroom. Using the Exercises, the student can research, analyze, and write to reinforce learning objectives and deepen their understanding of the text.

Author Team

Michael Whitman and Herbert Mattord have jointly developed this text to merge knowledge from the world of academic study with practical experience from the business world.

Michael Whitman, Ph.D., CISSP is a Professor of Information Systems in the Computer Science and Information Systems Department at Kennesaw State University, Kennesaw, Georgia, where he is also the Director of the KSU Center for Information Security Education (*infosec.kennesaw.edu*), and the Coordinator of the Bachelor of Science in Information Security and Assurance. Dr. Whitman teaches graduate and undergraduate courses in Information Security and Data Communications. He and Herbert Mattord are the authors of *Principles of Information Security, Management of Information Security, Readings and Cases in the Management of Information Security,* and *the Hands-On Informaion Security Lab Manual,* all from Course Technology. Dr. Whitman is an active researcher in Information Security, Fair and Responsible Use Policies, Ethical Computing, and Information Systems Research Methods. He has published articles in the top journals in his field, including *Information Systems Research*, the *Communications of the ACM, Information and Management*, the *Journal of International Business Studies*, and the *Journal of Computer Information Systems*. He is the chair of the Human Firewall Council and a member of the Metro Atlanta Information Systems Security Association, the Computer Security Institute, the Association for Computing Machinery and the Association for Information Systems.

Herbert Mattord, MBA, CISSP recently completed 24 years of IT industry experience as an application developer, database administrator, project manager, and information security practitioner to join the faculty at Kennesaw State University. He and Michael Whitman are the authors of *Principles of Information Security, Management of Information Security, Readings and Cases in the Management of Information Security,* and *the Hands-On Information Security Lab Manual* from Course Technology. During his career as an IT practitioner, he has been an adjunct professor at Kennesaw State University, Southern Polytechnic State University in Marietta, Georgia, Austin Community College in Austin, Texas, and Texas State University: San Marcos. He currently teaches undergraduate courses in Information Security, Data Communications, Local Area Networks, Database Technology, Project Management, and Systems Analysis and Design. He was formerly the Manager of Corporate Information Technology Security at Georgia-Pacific Corporation, where much of the practical knowledge found in this and his other textbooks was acquired.

Structure

The textbook is organized into sections based on the functions associated with the various facets of Contingency Planning: Business Impact Analysis, Incident Response Planning,

Disaster Recovery Planning, Business Continuity Planning, and Crisis Management Planning, and consists of eleven chapters and several Appendixes. The text also includes hands-on laboratory exercises included in the Instructor's Resource Kit.

SECTION I—INTRODUCTION

Chapter 1. Introduction and Overview of Contingency Planning

This chapter introduces the student to the concept of Contingency Planning, and defines the constituent components of Business Impact Analysis, Incident Response Planning, Disaster Recovery Planning, Business Continuity Planning, and Crisis Management Planning. The chapter provides an overview of integrated planning for contingencies and defines the responsibilities of each community of interest and stakeholder in the process.

SECTION II—ORGANIZATIONAL READINESS AND THE BUSINESS IMPACT ANALYSIS

Chapter 2. Planning for Organizational Readiness

This chapter shows how organizational readiness and a Business Impact Analysis (BIA) lay the foundation for all contingency planning and operations. The BIA is essentially an analysis of the threats facing the organization, focusing on the attacks that could occur and the damage that could result from those attacks. This information can then be used to support Incident Response, Disaster Recovery, Business Continuity, and Crisis Management planning.

SECTION III—INCIDENT RESPONSE

Chapter 3. Incident Response: Preparation, Organization, and Prevention

This chapter introduces the phases associated with the preparation and organization of incident response operations and tasks the organization can implement, or use to prevent incidents from occurring. It examines the necessary communications and planning that the organization undertakes to prevent, detect, and react to these disruptions in operations.

Chapter 4. Incident Response: Detection, Decision, and Notification

This chapter continues the discussion of incident response, providing additional insight into the mechanisms and plans the organization uses to detect an incident. It also discusses the decision challenges the organization must face in determining what course of action to pursue. It concludes with discussion on internal and external organizational communications, informing management and other stakeholders as to what happened.

Chapter 5. Incident Response: Recovery and Maintenance

The chapter concludes the discussion of incident response by focusing on response activities the organization must undertake to conclude a specific incident response action. It also describes the ongoing management activities necessary to keep the organization ready to respond, including plan maintenance and rehearsal and testing strategies.

SECTION IV—CONTINGENCY STRATEGIES

Chapter 6. Contingency Strategies for Disaster Recovery and Business Continuity

This chapter introduces a series of strategies that serve both the disaster recovery and business continuity efforts. These strategies include exclusive options like hot, warm, and cold sites, as well as shared functions like time-shares, mutual agreements, and service bureaus, as well as other options. The chapter also examines data backup and recovery strategies, which, if effectively implemented, assist both disaster recovery and business continuity efforts in recovering and reestablishing operations after the respective plans have been activated.

SECTION V—DISASTER RECOVERY

Chapter 7. Disaster Recovery: Preparation and Implementation

This chapter begins the examination of disaster through an examination of the tasks associated with formulating the disaster recovery team, developing the disaster recovery plan, and preparing for a disaster. It specifies the individual and team responsibilities during a disaster and presents the tasks that must be performed to assist in disaster recovery efforts.

Chapter 8. Disaster Recovery: Operation and Maintenance

This chapter continues the discussion of disaster recovery through an examination of the operations during a disaster as covered in the disaster recovery plan. It examines the actions of the team during each of the key phases of a disaster, including preparation, response, resumption, recovery, and restoration.

SECTION VI—BUSINESS CONTINUITY

Chapter 9. Business Continuity Preparation and Implementation

This chapter introduces the subject of business continuity, and overviews the necessary steps to prepare for business continuity operations. It covers the process of developing a business continuity plan and describes the components critical to its success. The chapter also discusses the design and preparation of a business continuity team, and presents the roles and responsibilities associated with it.

Chapter 10. Business Continuity Operations and Maintenance

This chapter continues the discussion of business continuity by discussing the actions of the business continuity team during an actual implementation. The chapter provides insight into the planning and efforts that must occur to make a business continuity effort a success, and examines the impact of business continuity on the organization workflow.

SECTION V—CRISIS MANAGEMENT

Chapter 11. Crisis Management and Human Factors

The final chapter examines the special requirements associated with dealing with crises—incidents or disasters that have directly impacted human safety and life. The special requirements for preparing to deal with crises and the challenges associated with crises are also presented and discussed.

Instructor Resources

A variety of teaching tools have been prepared to support this textbook and offer many options to enhance the classroom learning experience:

Electronic Instructor's Manual—The Instructor's Manual includes suggestions and strategies for using this text, such as suggestions for lecture topics. The Instructors Manual also includes answers to the review questions and suggested solutions to the exercises at the end of each chapter.

Figure Files—Figure Files allow instructors to create their own presentations using figures taken from the text.

PowerPoint Presentations—This book comes with Microsoft PowerPoint slides for each chapter. These are included as a teaching aid for classroom presentation, to make available to students on the network for chapter review, or to be printed for classroom distribution. Instructors can add their own slides for additional topics they introduce to the class.

Lab Manual Content—The Instructor's Resource Kit contains a set of laboratory exercises specifically designed to assist in student understanding of the challenges in preparing for and reacting to incidents. These exercises are provided for use in hands-on computer labs by the instructor, and include setup and use guides. This information will be incorporated into future issues of the *Hands-On Information Security Lab Manual*, also published by Course Technology.

Curriculum Model for Programs of Study in Information Security and Assurance—In addition to the texts authored by this team, a curriculum model for programs of study in Information Security and Assurance is available from the Kennesaw State University Center for Information Security Education (*http://infosec.kennesaw.edu*). This document provides details on designing and implementing security coursework and curricula in academic institutions, as well as guidance and lessons learned from the authors' perspective.

ExamView—ExamView®, the ultimate tool for objective-based testing needs. ExamView® is a powerful objective-based test generator that enables instructors to create paper, LAN or Web-based tests from testbanks designed specifically for their Course Technology text. Instructors can utilize the ultra-efficient QuickTest Wizard to create tests in less than five minutes by taking advantage of Course Technology's question banks, or customize their own exams from scratch.

ACKNOWLEDGMENTS

The authors would like to thank their families for their support and understanding for the many hours dedicated to this project, hours taken in many cases from family activities. Special thanks to Carola Mattord, postgraduate student of English at Georgia State University. Her reviews of early drafts and suggestions for keeping the writing focused on the students resulted in a more readable manuscript.

Contributors

Two Kennesaw State University students also assisted in the preparation of the textbook, and we thank them for their contributions:

Dan Martin

Matthew North

Reviewers

We are indebted to the following individuals for their respective contributions of perceptive feedback on the initial proposal, the project outline, and the chapter-by-chapter reviews of the text:

Rose Ellis Dr.

Bob Gehling

Gary Kessler

Special Thanks

The authors wish to thank the Editorial and Production teams at Course Technology. Their diligent and professional efforts greatly enhanced the final product.

In addition, several professional and commercial organizations and individuals have aided the development of the textbook by providing information and inspiration, and the authors wish to acknowledge their contribution:

Bernstein Crisis Management

Continuity Central

The Human Firewall Council

Information Systems Security Associations

The Institute for Crisis Management

The National Institute of Standards and Technology

Onecle, Inc.

Purdue University

Rothstein Associates, Inc-SunGard

Our colleagues in the Department of Computer Science and Information Systems, Kennesaw State University Professor Merle King, Chair of the Department of Computer Science and Information Systems, Kennesaw State University

Our Commitment

The authors are committed to serving the needs of the adopters and readers. We would be pleased and honored to receive feedback on the textbook and its supporting materials. You can contact us through Course Technology at *mis@course.com*.

CHAPTER 1

CONTINGENCY PLANNING WITHIN INFORMATION SECURITY

An ounce of prevention is worth a pound of cure

—The New Dictionary of Cultural Literacy

OPENING SCENARIO

Paul Alexander and his boss, Amanda Wilson, were sitting in her office discussing the upcoming year's budget when they heard a commotion in the hall. Upon hearing his name, Paul stuck his head out the door and saw Jonathon Jasper, or JJ to his friends, walking quickly toward him.

"*Paul!*" Jonathan called again. He was relieved to see him waiting in Amanda's office.

"Hi, Amanda," JJ said, then to Paul, "We have a problem." JJ was one of the system administrators for Hierarchical Access LTD (HAL), an Internet service provider operating out of Marietta, Georgia.

Paul stepped into the hall, closing Amanda's door behind him. "What's up, JJ?"

"I think we've got someone sniffing around the e-mail server." JJ replied. "I just looked at the log files, and there are an unusual number of failed login attempts on accounts that normally just don't have that many, like *yours!*"

Paul paused, "But the e-mail server's proxied, which means it would have to be an internal probe."

"Yeah, that's why it's a problem. We haven't gotten this kind of thing since we installed the proxy and moved the Web and e-mail servers inside the DMZ. It's got to be someone in-house." JJ looked exasperated. "And after all that time I spent conducting awareness training!"

"Don't worry just yet." Paul responded. "Let's make a few calls, and we'll go from there. Grab your incident response book and meet me in the conference room in 10 minutes. Grab Tina in network operations on the way."

Questions for Discussion:

- Who should Paul invite to this meeting?
- What other information can Paul and his team use to track down this incident?

LEARNING OBJECTIVES

Upon completion of this material, you should be able to:

- Define and explain information security
- Define and explain the basic concepts of risk management
- Identify and define the components of contingency planning
- Know and understand the role of information security policy in the development of contingency plans

INTRODUCTION

This book is about being prepared for the unexpected, being ready for events such as incidents and disasters. These are topics that most organizations generally don't think about when conducting day-to-day business; thus, such organizations are often not well prepared to offer the proper response to a disaster or security incident. At the end of 2004, ClickZ, a marketing statistics firm, estimated that there were over 934 million people online. The projections for 2005 are over 1 billion, and 1.35 billion users are estimated by 2007.[1] Each one of those online users is a threat to any online system. The vast majority of those users will not intentionally probe, monitor, attack, or attempt to access an organization's information without authorization; however, that potential does exist. Even if less than one-tenth of one percent of online users become a threat, that would still result in almost a million potential attackers.

In the weeks that followed the September 11, 2001, attacks in New York, Pennsylvania, and Washington D.C., the media reported on the disastrous losses organizations suffered. While the loss of life was horrific, many organizations were able to continue to conduct business. Why? Because they had prepared for the unexpected. The 2001 disaster was not the first attack on the WTC complex. On February 26, 1993, a car bomb exploded beneath one of the WTC towers, killing six and injuring over 1000. The attack was limited in its devastation only because the attackers ran out of resources to acquire components for the bomb and a coordinated cyanide gas attack that was to occur simultaneously.[2] This attack was a wake-up call for the hundreds of organizations that conducted business in the WTC. Many began asking the question, "What would we have done if the attack had been more successful?" As a direct result, many of the organizations occupying the WTC on September 11, 2001, had developed contingency plans. Though thousands of people lost their lives in the attack, many were able to evacuate, and many organizations were prepared to resume their businesses in the aftermath of the devastation.

A 2004 report in *Information Week* examining downtime and business continuity in organizations found that 25% of organizations surveyed had to invoke their disaster recovery or business continuity plans in 2003, with 70% reporting the disaster as severe or extremely severe.[3] Considering almost 80% of businesses affected by a major incident either never reopen or close within 18 months, having a disaster recovery and business continuity plan are vital to sustaining operations when disasters strike.[4] With these odds against the average organization, it is imperative that management create, implement, and test effective plans to deal with incidents and disasters. For this reason, the field of information security has been steadily growing and is taken seriously by more and more organizations, not only in the United States, but throughout the world.

It should be understood that *information security* is an umbrella term for many programs and activities that assure the availability of information used by organizations. This includes steps to assure the confidentiality, integrity, and, in the case of contingency planning, availability of organizational information systems. Because information security is a complex subject, it is important to have an overview of the entire field and an understanding of the major components that make up its hierarchy. Contingency planning is an important element of information security, but before management can plan for contingencies, it should have an overall strategic plan for information security in place. That way the risk management processes are in place to guide the appropriate managerial and technical controls. The following chapter serves as an overview of information security and its terminology with special consideration given to risk management and the role contingency planning plays in the overall information security hierarchy.

INFORMATION SECURITY

Information security is defined by the Committee on National Security Systems (CNSS) as the protection of information and its critical elements, including the systems and hardware that use, store, and transmit that information. See Figure 1-1 to learn more about the CNSS model that underlies this definition. The CNSS model of information security evolved from a concept developed by the computer security industry known as the C.I.A. triangle. The **C.I.A. triangle** has been the industry standard for computer security since the development of the mainframe. The C.I.A. triangle is based on three of the most critical characteristics of information that give it value when used within information systems: confidentiality, integrity, and availability. Information has the characteristic of **confidentiality** when disclosure or exposure to unauthorized individuals or systems is prevented. Confidentiality ensures that only those with the rights and privileges to access information are able to do so. When unauthorized individuals or systems can view information, confidentiality is breached. The integrity of information is threatened when the information is exposed to corruption, damage, destruction, or other disruption of its authentic state. The threat of corruption can occur while information is being stored or transmitted. **Integrity** is the prevention of that corruption. Information has integrity when it is whole, complete, and uncorrupted. **Availability** enables authorized users—persons or computer systems—to access information without interference or obstruction, and to receive it in the required format.

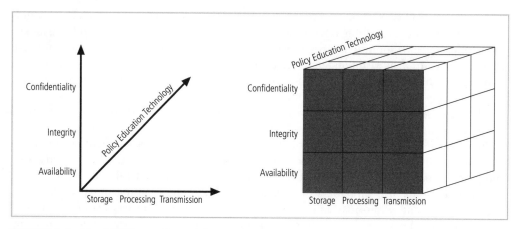

FIGURE 1-1 The CNSS security model

In summary, **information security** (often abbreviated to **InfoSec**) is the protection of the confidentiality, integrity, and availability of information, whether in storage, during processing, or in transmission. Such protection is accomplished through the application of policy, education and training, and technology.

Key Information Security Concepts

In general, a **threat** is a category of objects, persons, or other entities that pose a potential risk of loss to an **asset**—the organizational resource that is being protected. An asset can be logical, such as a Web site, information, or data; or an asset can be physical, such as a person, computer system, or other tangible object. A threat can become the basis for an **attack** on information—an intentional or unintentional attempt to cause damage to or otherwise compromise the information or the systems that support it. Threats are usually obvious when they can be seen or when the knowledge of their arrival is well known. The **threat-agent** is a specific and identifiable instance of a general threat. A threat-agent exploits vulnerabilities present in the controls that protect the asset. A **vulnerability** is a weakness or fault in the protection mechanisms that are intended to protect information and information assets from attack or damage. Vulnerabilities that have been examined, documented, and published are referred to as **well-known vulnerabilities**. Some vulnerabilities are latent, and thus are not revealed until they are discovered and made known. There are two common uses of the term **exploit** in security. First, threat-agents may attempt to exploit a system or information asset by using it illegally for their personal gains. Second, an exploit can be a targeted solution to misuse a specific hole or vulnerability, usually in software, that an attacker creates to formulate an attack. Defenders try to prevent attacks by applying a **control, a safeguard,** or a **countermeasure**: these terms, all synonymous with *control*, represent security mechanisms, policies, or procedures that can successfully counter attacks, reduce risk, resolve vulnerabilities, and generally improve the security within an organization.

A recent study collected and categorized the identifiable threats to information security and is shown in Table 1-1.

TABLE 1-1 Threats to information security[5]

Threat	Example
Act of human error or failure	Accidents, employee mistakes
Compromises to intellectual property	Piracy, copyright infringement
Deliberate acts of trespass	Unauthorized access and data collection
Deliberate acts of information extortion	Blackmail for information disclosure
Deliberate acts of sabotage or vandalism	Destruction of systems or information
Deliberate acts of theft	Illegal confiscation of equipment or information
Deliberate software attacks	Viruses, worms, macros, denial of service
Forces of nature	Fire, flood, earthquake, lightning
Deviations in quality of service by service providers	Power and WAN quality-of-service issues service providers
Technical hardware failures or errors	Equipment failure
Technical software failures or errors	Bugs, code problems, unknown loopholes
Technological obsolescence	Antiquated or outdated technologies

©2003 ACM, Inc. Included here by permission.

The threat categories described in the study by Whitman are explained in detail in the following sections.

Acts of Human Error or Failure

This category of threats includes acts performed without intent or malicious purpose by an authorized user. When people use information systems, sometimes mistakes happen. Inexperience, improper training, making incorrect assumptions, or other circumstances can cause these misfortunes. But, harmless mistakes can produce extensive damage with catastrophic results.

Compromises to Intellectual Property

Many organizations create or support the development of intellectual property as part of their business operations. **Intellectual property** is defined as "the ownership of ideas and control over the tangible or virtual representation of those ideas. Use of another person's intellectual property may or may not involve royalty payments or permission, but should always include proper credit to the source."[6] Intellectual property includes trade secrets, copyrights, trademarks, and patents. Employees may have access privileges to the various types of IP, and may be required to use the IP to conduct day-to-day business. Once intellectual property (IP) has been defined and properly identified, breaches in the controls that have been placed around the IP constitute a threat to the security of this information.

Frequently an organization purchases or leases the IP of other organizations, and must abide by the purchase or licensing agreement for its fair and responsible use. The most common IP breach is the unlawful use or duplication of software-based intellectual property, more commonly known as software piracy. Because most software is licensed to a particular purchaser, its use is restricted to a single user or to a designated user in an organization. If the user copies the program to another computer without securing another license or transferring the license, he or she has violated the copyright. Software licenses are strictly enforced by several regulatory and private organizations, and software publishers use several control mechanisms to prevent copyright infringement. In addition to the laws surrounding software piracy, two watchdog organizations investigate allegations of software abuse: the Software & Information Industry Association (SIIA) at *www.siia.net* (formerly known as the Software Publishers Association), and the Business Software Alliance (BSA) at *www.bsa.org*.

Deliberate Acts of Trespass

Deliberate acts of trespass are a well-known and broad category of electronic and human activities that can breach the confidentiality of information. When an unauthorized individual gains access to the information an organization is trying to protect, that act is categorized as a deliberate act of trespass. In the opening scenario of this chapter, the IT staff at HAL was more disappointed than surprised to find someone poking around their mail server looking for a way in. Acts of trespass can lead to unauthorized real or virtual actions that enable information gatherers to enter premises or systems they have not been authorized to enter. The classic perpetrator of deliberate acts of espionage or trespass is the hacker. The most common definition of **hackers** is "people who use and create computer software [to] gain access to information illegally."[7] In the gritty world of reality, a hacker uses skill, guile, or fraud to attempt to bypass the controls placed around information that is the property of someone else.

Deliberate Acts of Information Extortion

The threat of information extortion is the possibility of an attacker or trusted insider stealing information from a computer system and demanding compensation for its return or for an agreement to not disclose the information. Extortion is common in credit card number theft.

Deliberate Acts of Sabotage or Vandalism

Another frequently encountered threat is the assault on the electronic face of an organization—its Web site. This category of threat involves the deliberate sabotage of a computer system or business or acts of vandalism to either destroy an asset or damage the image of an organization. These acts can range from petty vandalism by employees to organized sabotage against an organization.

A much more sinister form of hacking is cyberterrorism. **Cyberterrorists** hack systems to conduct terrorist activities through network or Internet pathways. The United States and other governments are developing security measures intended to protect the critical computing and communications networks as well as the physical and power utility infrastructures.

Deliberate Acts of Theft

The threat of theft—the illegal taking of another's property—is a constant problem. Within an organization, property can be physical, electronic, or intellectual. The value of information suffers when it is copied and taken away without the owner's knowledge. The category of theft also includes acts of espionage, because an attacker is often looking for information to steal. Any breach of confidentiality of information can technically be construed as an act of theft. Attackers can use many different methods to access the information stored in an information system. However, some information-gathering techniques are quite legal, for example, research. Legal information-gathering techniques are called, collectively, *competitive intelligence*. When information gatherers employ techniques that cross the legal or ethical threshold, they are conducting industrial espionage.

Deliberate Software Attacks

Perhaps the most familiar threat is the software attack. Deliberate software attacks occur when an individual or group designs software to attack a system. Most of this software is referred to as *malicious code*, *malicious software*, or sometimes **malware**. These software components or programs are designed to damage, destroy, or deny service to the target systems. Some of the more common instances of malicious code are viruses and worms, Trojan horses, logic bombs, and backdoors. Equally prominent among the recent incidences of malicious code are the denial-of-services attacks conducted by attackers on popular e-commerce sites. A denial-of-service (DoS) attack seeks to deny legitimate users access to services by either tying up a server's available resources or causing it to shut down. A variation on the DoS attack is the distributed DoS (DDoS) attack, in which an attacker compromises several systems, and then uses these systems (called *zombies*) to attack an unsuspecting target.

A point of confusion for many when it comes to threats posed by malicious code comes from the difference between the *method of propagation* (worm versus virus), the *payload* (what the malware does once it is in place, such as deny service or install a backdoor), and the *vector of infection* (how the code is transmitted from system to system, whether it is by making a person perform an action through social engineering or using a technical means such as an open network share). Some of the concepts surrounding the topic of malicious code are discussed in the following sections.

Viruses   Computer viruses are segments of code that perform malicious actions. The code attaches itself to an existing program and takes control of that program's access to the targeted computer. The virus-controlled target program then carries out the virus's plan by replicating itself into additional targeted systems.

Opening an infected e-mail or performing some other seemingly trivial action can cause anything from random messages popping up on a user's screen to the complete destruction of entire hard drives of data. Viruses are passed from machine to machine via physical media, e-mail, or other forms of computer data transmission. When these viruses infect a machine, they may immediately scan the local machine for e-mail applications, or even send themselves to every user in the e-mail address book.

There are several types of viruses. One is the macro virus, which is embedded in automatically executing macrocode, common in word-processed documents, spreadsheets, and database applications. Another type, the boot virus, infects the key operating systems files located in a computer's boot sector.

Worms   Named for the tapeworm in John Brunner's novel *The Shockwave Rider*, worms are malicious programs that replicate themselves constantly without requiring another program to provide a safe environment for replication. Worms can continue replicating themselves until they completely fill available resources, such as memory, hard drive space, and network bandwidth. These complex behaviors can be invoked with or without the user downloading or executing the file. Once the worm has infected a computer, it can redistribute itself to all e-mail addresses found on the infected system. Further, a worm can deposit copies of itself onto all Web servers that the infected system can reach, so that users who subsequently visit those sites become infected themselves. Worms also take advantage of open shares found on the network in which an infected system is located, placing working copies of the worm code onto the server so that users of those shares are likely to become infected.

Backdoors and Trapdoors   A virus or worm can have a payload that installs a backdoor or trapdoor component in a system, which allows the attacker to access a system at will, with special privileges. Examples of these kinds of payloads include Subseven and Back Orifice.

Polymorphism   One of the biggest problems in fighting viruses and worms is the recent development of polymorphic threats. A polymorphic threat is one that changes its apparent shape over time, making it undetectable by techniques that look for preconfigured signatures. These viruses and worms actually evolve, changing their size and appearance to elude detection by antivirus software programs. This means that an e-mail generated by the virus may not match previous examples, making detection more of a challenge.

Propagation Vectors   The ways that malicious code is spread from one system to another can vary widely. One favorite is the social engineering attack—getting the computer user to perform an action that enables the infection. A favorite method to accomplish this is the Trojan horse, often simply called a *Trojan*. A Trojan is something that looks like a desirable program or tool, but that is in fact a malicious entity. Other propagation vectors do not require human interaction, leveraging open network connections, file shares, or software vulnerabilities to spread themselves.

Virus and Worm Hoaxes   As frustrating as viruses and worms are, perhaps more time and money is spent on resolving virus hoaxes. Well-meaning people can disrupt the harmony and flow of an organization when they send random e-mails warning of dangerous viruses that are fictitious. When this happens and individuals fail to follow procedures, the network becomes overloaded, and much time and energy is wasted as everyone forwards the message to everyone they know, posts the message on bulletin boards, and begins updating antivirus protection software.

Forces of Nature

Forces of nature, *force majeure*, or acts of God, pose some of the most dangerous threats imaginable, because they can be unexpected and occur with very little warning. These threats can disrupt not only the lives of individuals, but also the storage, transmission, and use of information, and include fire, flood, earthquake, and lightning as well as volcanic eruption and insect infestation.

Deviations in Quality of Service, by Service Providers

This category of threats covers situations in which a product or service is not delivered to the organization as expected. Utility companies, service providers, and other value-added organizations form a vast web of interconnected services. The organization's information system depends on the successful operation of many interdependent support systems, including power grids, telecom networks, parts suppliers, service vendors, and even the janitorial staff and garbage haulers. Any one of these support systems can be interrupted by storms, employee illnesses, or other unforeseen events. Threats in this category are seen in attacks such as a backhoe taking out a fiber-optic link for an ISP. The backup provider may be online and in service, but may be able to supply only a fraction of the bandwidth the organization needs for full service. This degradation of service is a form of availability disruption. Internet service, communications, and power irregularities can dramatically affect the availability of information and systems.

Technical Hardware Failures or Errors

Technical hardware failures or errors occur when a manufacturer distributes equipment containing a known or unknown flaw. These defects can cause the system to perform outside of expected parameters, resulting in unreliable service or lack of availability. Some errors are terminal; they result in the unrecoverable loss of the equipment. Some errors are intermittent; they only periodically manifest themselves, resulting in faults that are not easily repeated. For example, equipment can sometimes stop working, or work in unexpected ways. Murphy's Law says that if something can possibly go wrong, it will. In other words, it's not if something *will* fail, but *when*.

Technical Software Failures or Errors

This category of threats comes from purchasing software with unknown hidden faults. Large quantities of computer code are written, debugged, published, and sold before all bugs are detected and resolved. Sometimes, combinations of certain software and hardware reveal new bugs. These failures range from bugs to untested failure conditions. Sometimes, these are not errors, but rather purposeful shortcuts left by programmers for benign or malign reasons. Collectively, shortcut access routes into programs that bypass security checks are called trap doors and can cause serious security breaches.

Software bugs in general are so commonplace that entire Web sites are dedicated to documenting them. Among the most often used is Bugtraq, found at *www.securityfocus.com*. It provides up-to-the-minute information on the latest security vulnerabilities, as well as a very thorough archive of past bugs.

Technological Obsolescence

The final threat category from the Whitman study describes how antiquated or outdated infrastructure leads to unreliable and untrustworthy systems. Management must recognize that when technology becomes outdated, there is a risk of loss of data integrity from attacks. Management's strategic planning should always include an analysis of the technology currently in use. Ideally, proper planning by management should prevent the risks from technology obsolesce, but when obsolescence is identified, management must take immediate action. IT professionals play a large role in the identification of probable obsolescence.

Other Listings of Threats

Another popular study also examines threats to information security. The Computer Security Institute in cooperation with the Federal Bureau of Investigation conducts an annual study of computer crime. The CSI/FBI Survey presented in Table 1-2 shows the results of this study from the last seven years.

Virus attacks continue to be the source of most financial loss. In the CSI/FBI study, the most frequently cited type of attack continues to be from malicious code with an aggregate reported loss of over $42 million. Over 70 percent of respondents noted that they had experienced one or more virus attacks in the 12-month reporting period. Whether a company catches an attack and is then willing to report the attack is another matter entirely. In any case, the fact is, almost every company has been attacked. Whether or not that attack was successful depends on the company's security efforts.

TABLE 1-2 CSI/FBI survey results for types of attack or misuse (1999–2005)[8]

Types of Attack or Misuse in Percentages		2005	2004	2003	2002	2001	2000	1999
1.	Virus	74	78	82	85	94	85	90
2.	Insider abuse of net access	48	59	80	78	91	79	97
3.	Laptop/mobile theft	48	49	59	55	64	60	69
4.	Denial of service	32	39	36	40	40	25	30
5.	Unauthorized access to information	32	37	45	38	49	71	55
6.	System penetration	14	17	42	40	36	27	31
7.	Abuse of wireless	17	15	New category in 2004				

TABLE 1-2 CSI/FBI survey results for types of attack or misuse (1999–2005)[8] (continued)

Types of Attack or Misuse in Percentages	2005	2004	2003	2002	2001	2000	1999
8. Theft of proprietary information	9	10	21	20	26	20	25
9. Misuse of public Web applications	5	10	New category in 2004				
10. Web site defacement	5	7	New category in 2004				
11. Sabotage	2	5	21	8	18	17	13
12. Financial fraud	7	10	15	12	12	11	14
13. Telecom fraud	10	10	10	9	10	11	17
14. Telecom eavesdropping		Dropped in 2004	6	6	10	7	14
15. Active wiretap		Dropped in 2004	1	1	2	1	2

OVERVIEW OF RISK MANAGEMENT

As part of information security, risk management is the process used to identify and then control risks to an organization's information assets. While this process is an expected responsibility for managers in all organizations, information security managers are usually tasked with many of the risk management responsibilities in the information technology areas of an organization's operations. Very often, the CIO of an organization delegates many accountabilities for risk management to the CISO. It is almost certain that the CIO involves the information security function of the organization in IT risk management activities.

Contingency planning is usually considered to be part of the risk management program process. Before moving on to more detailed coverage of contingency planning, it is useful to first explore the broader topic of risk management.

The formal process of identifying and controlling the risks facing an organization is called *risk management*. This process is made up of two major undertakings: risk identification and risk control. The first of these, **risk identification**, is the process of examining and documenting the security posture of an organization's information technology and the risks it faces. Risk assessment is the documentation of the results of risk identification. The second major undertaking, **risk control**, is the process of applying controls to reduce the risks to an organization's data and information systems. The various components of risk management and their relationships to each other are shown in Figure 1-2.

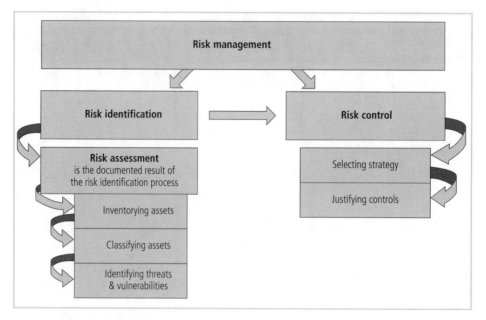

FIGURE 1-2 Components of risk management

As an aspiring information security professional, you have a key role to play in risk management. Among the communities of interest, the general management of the organization must structure the IT and information security functions to lead a successful defense of the organization's information assets—information and data, hardware, software, procedures, and people. The IT community must serve the information technology needs of the broader organization and at the same time leverage the special skills and insights of the information security community. The information security team must lead the way with skill, professionalism, and flexibility as it works with the other communities of interest to appropriately balance the usefulness and security of the information system.

Risk management is the process of identifying vulnerabilities in an organization's information systems and taking carefully reasoned steps to ensure the confidentiality, integrity, and availability of all the components in the organization's information system. Each of the three elements in the C.I.A. triangle are an essential part of every IT organization's ability to sustain long-term competitiveness. When an organization depends on IT-based systems to remain viable, information security and the discipline of risk management move beyond theoretical discussions and become an integral part of the economic basis for making business decisions. These decisions are based on trade-offs between the costs of applying information systems controls and the benefits realized from the operation of secured, available systems.

An observation made over 2400 years ago by Chinese General Sun Tzu has direct relevance to information security today:

> If you know the enemy and know yourself, you need not fear the result of a hundred battles. If you know yourself but not the enemy, for every victory gained you will also suffer a defeat. If you know neither the enemy nor yourself, you will succumb in every battle.[9]

Consider for a moment the similarities between information security and warfare. Information security managers and technicians are the defenders of information. The many threats mentioned earlier are constantly attacking the defenses surrounding information assets. Defenses are built in layers, by placing safeguard upon safeguard. You attempt to prevent, protect, detect, and recover from attack after attack after attack. Moreover, organizations are legally prevented from switching to offense, and the attackers themselves have no need to expend their resources on defense. To be victorious, you must, therefore, know yourself and know the enemy.

Know Yourself

First, you must identify, examine, and understand the information and systems currently in place within your organization. This is self-evident. To protect assets, which are defined here as information and the systems that use, store, and transmit information, you must understand what they are, how they add value to the organization, and to which vulnerabilities they are susceptible. Once you know what you have, you can identify what you are already doing to protect it. Just because you have a control in place to protect an asset does not necessarily mean that the asset is protected. Frequently, organizations implement control mechanisms, but then neglect the necessary periodic review, revision, and maintenance. The policies, education and training programs, and technologies that protect information must be carefully maintained and administered to ensure that they are still effective.

Know the Enemy

Informed of your organization's assets and weaknesses, you move on to Sun Tzu's second step: know the enemy. This means identifying, examining, and understanding the *threats* facing the organization. You must determine those threat aspects that most directly affect the organization and the security of the organization's information assets. You can then use your understanding of these aspects to create a list of threats prioritized by how important each asset is to the organization.

It is essential that all stakeholders conduct periodic management reviews. The first focus of management review is asset inventory. On a regular basis, management must verify the completeness and accuracy of the asset inventory. In addition, organizations must review and verify the threats and vulnerabilities that have been identified as dangerous to the asset inventory, as well as the current controls and mitigation strategies. The cost effectiveness of each control should be reviewed as well and the decisions on deployment of controls revisited. Further, managers of all levels must regularly verify the ongoing effectiveness of every control deployed. For example, a sales manager might assess control procedures by going through the office before the workday starts and picking up all the papers from every desk in the sales department. When the workers show up, the manager could inform them that a fire had been simulated and all of their papers had been destroyed and that each worker must now follow the disaster recovery procedures to assess the effectiveness of the procedures and suggest corrections.

The first phase of risk management is risk identification and is discussed in the following section.

Risk Identification

A risk management strategy calls on information security professionals to know their organization's information assets through identifying, classifying, and prioritizing them. Assets are the targets of various threats and threat agents, and the goal is to protect the assets from the threats. Once the organizational assets have been identified, a threat identification process is undertaken. The setting and circumstances of each information asset are examined to identify vulnerabilities. When vulnerabilities are found, controls are identified and assessed as to their capability to limit possible losses in the event of attack.

The subsequent components of this process are shown in Figure 1-3.

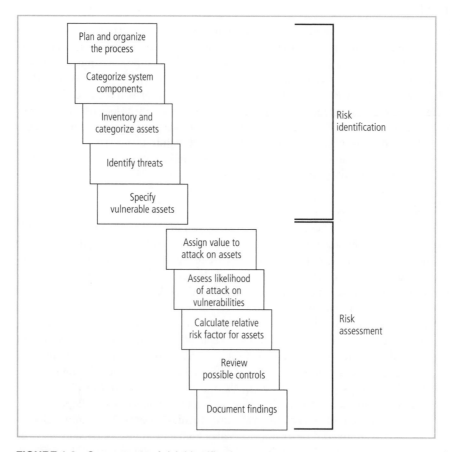

FIGURE 1-3 Components of risk identification

Asset Identification and Valuation

The iterative process of identifying assets and assessing their value begins with the identification of assets, including all of the elements of an organization's system, such as people, procedures, data and information, software, hardware, and networking elements. Then, you classify and categorize the assets, adding details as you dig deeper into the analysis. These assets include all the elements of an information system: people; procedures and data; software; hardware; and networks.

Information Asset Classification   In addition to identifying the assets used in a system, it is advisable to add another dimension to represent the sensitivity and security priority of the data and the devices that store, transmit, and process the data. Examples of these kinds of classifications are confidential data, internal data, and public data. The other side of the data classification scheme is the personnel security clearance structure, which determines the level of information individuals are authorized to view based on what each person needs to know.

No matter how an organization chooses to identify the various components of systems, it is most important that the classification of components be specific enough to allow determination of priority levels. This is necessary because the next step is to rank the components based on criteria established by the categorization. It is also important that the categories be comprehensive and mutually exclusive. *Comprehensive* means that all information assets must fit in the list somewhere, and *mutually exclusive* means that an information asset should fit in only one category. Using a purely technical standard, an analysis team could categorize the certificate authority in the asset list as software, and within the software category as either an application or a security component. To simplify the categorization of elements that could be placed in a number of slots, it is essential to establish a clear and comprehensive set of categories.

Information Asset Valuation   As each asset is assigned to its category, posing several questions assists in developing the weighting criteria to be used for information asset valuation or impact evaluation. As each question is asked and answered, you should document your answers for later analysis. Before beginning the inventory process, the organization should determine which criteria is best suited to establish the value of the information assets.

Among the criteria to be considered are:

- Which information asset is the most critical to the success of the organization?
- Which information asset generates the most revenue?
- Which information asset generates the most profitability?
- Which information asset would be the most expensive to replace?
- Which information asset would be the most expensive to protect?
- Which information asset would be the most embarrassing or cause the greatest liability if revealed?

In addition to those just listed, there are other company-specific criteria that may add value to the asset evaluation process. They should be identified, documented, and added to the process. To finalize this step of the information asset identification process, each organization should assign a weight to each asset based on the answers to the various chosen questions.

Once the process of inventorying and assessing value is complete, you can calculate the relative importance of each asset using a straightforward process known as *weighted factor analysis*, as shown in Table 1-3. In this process, each information asset is assigned a score for each critical factor. In the example shown, these scores range from 0.1 to 1.0, which is the range of values recommended by NIST SP800-30, a document published by the National Institute of Standards and Technology (NIST) and titled *Risk Management Guide for Information Technology Systems*. In addition, each critical factor is also assigned a weight (ranging from 1 to 100), to show that criteria's assigned importance for the organization.

TABLE 1-3 Example of a weighted factor analysis worksheet

Information Asset	Criteria 1: Impact to Revenue	Criteria 2: Impact to Profitability	Criteria 3: Public Image Impact	Weighted Score
Criterion Weight (1–100) Must total 100	30	40	30	
EDI Document Set 1— Logistics BOL to outsourcer (outbound)	0.8	0.9	0.5	75
EDI Document Set 2— Supplier orders (outbound)	0.8	0.9	0.6	78
EDI Document Set 2— Supplier fulfillment advice (inbound)	0.4	0.5	0.3	41
Customer order via SSL (inbound)	1.0	1.0	1.0	100
Customer service request via e-mail (inbound)	0.4	0.4	0.9	55

Notes: EDI: Electronic Data Interchange
             SSL: Secure Sockets Layer

Data Classification and Management

Corporate and military organizations use a variety of classification schemes. Georgia-Pacific Corporation uses a corporate **data classification scheme** throughout the company that helps secure confidentiality and integrity of information. Information owners are responsible for classifying the information assets for which they are responsible. At least once a year, information owners must review information classifications to ensure the information is still classified correctly and the appropriate access controls are in place.

The military has some specialized classification ratings, ranging from Public to For Official Use Only, to Confidential, to Secret, and Top Secret. Most organizations do not need the detailed level of classification used by the military or federal agencies. However, organizations may find it necessary to classify data to provide protection. A simple scheme can allow an organization to protect sensitive information such as marketing or research data, personnel data, customer data, and general internal communications. Or, a scheme such as the following could be adopted:

- Public: Information for general public dissemination, such as an advertisement or public release
- For Official Use Only: Information that is not particularly sensitive, but not for public release, such as internal communications
- Sensitive: Information important to the business that could embarrass the company or cause loss of market share if revealed
- Classified: Information of the utmost secrecy to the organization, disclosure of which could severely impact the well-being of the organization

The other side of the data classification scheme is the personnel **security clearance** structure. In organizations that require security clearances, each user of data must be assigned a single authorization level that indicates the level of classification he or she is authorized to view. This is usually accomplished by assigning each employee to a named role, such as data entry clerk, development programmer, information security analyst, or even CIO. Most organizations have a set of roles and the accompanying security clearances associated with each role. Overriding an employee's security clearance is the fundamental principle of **need-to-know**. Regardless of security clearance, employees are not simply allowed to view any and all data that falls within their level of clearance. Before someone can access a specific set of data, the need-to-know requirement must be met. This extra level of protection ensures that the confidentiality of information is properly maintained.

Threat Identification

After identifying and performing a preliminary classification of an organization's information assets, the analysis phase moves on to an examination of the threats facing the organization. An organization and its information and information systems face a wide variety of threats. The realistic threats need to be investigated further while the unimportant threats are set aside. If you assume every threat can and will attack every information asset, the project scope quickly becomes so complex it overwhelms the ability to plan.

Each of the threat categories that were identified in Table 1-1 must be considered to assess its potential to endanger the organization. This examination is known as a **threat assessment**. You can address each threat with a few basic questions, as follows:

- Which threats present a danger to an organization's assets in the given environment?
- Which threats represent the most danger to the organization's information?
- How much would it cost to recover from a successful attack?
- Which of the threats require the greatest expenditure to prevent?

By posing and answering these questions, you establish a framework for the discussion of threat assessment. This list of questions may not cover everything that affects the information security threat assessment. If an organization has specific guidelines or policies, these should influence the process and require the posing of additional questions. This list can be easily expanded to include additional requirements.

Vulnerability Identification

Once you have identified the organization's information assets and documented some criteria for beginning to assess the threats they face, you then review each information asset for each threat it faces and create a list of vulnerabilities. Now, examine how each of the threats that are possible or likely to be perpetrated, and list the organization's assets and their vulnerabilities. The list is usually long and shows all the vulnerabilities of the information assets. Some threats manifest themselves in multiple ways, yielding multiple vulnerabilities for that threat. The process of listing vulnerabilities is somewhat subjective and is based on the experience and knowledge of the people creating the list. Therefore, the process works best when groups of people with diverse backgrounds within the organization work iteratively in a series of brainstorming sessions. For instance, the team that reviews the vulnerabilities for networking equipment should include the networking specialists, the systems management team that operates the network, the information security risk specialist, and even technically proficient users of the system.

At the end of the risk identification process, you have a list of assets and their vulnerabilities. This list, along with any supporting documentation, is the starting point for the next step, risk assessment.

Risk Assessment

Now that you have identified the organization's information assets and the threats and vulnerabilities of those assets, you can assess the relative risk for each of the vulnerabilities. This is accomplished by a process called **risk assessment**. Risk assessment assigns a risk rating or score to each information asset. While this number does not mean anything in absolute terms, it is useful in gauging the relative risk to each vulnerable information asset and facilitates the development of comparative ratings later in the risk control process.

Figure 1-4 shows the factors that go into the risk-rating estimate for each of the vulnerabilities.

It is important to note that the goal at this point is to create a method for evaluating the relative risk of each of the listed vulnerabilities. There are many detailed methods to determine accurate and detailed costs of each of the vulnerabilities. Likewise, there are models that can be used to estimate expenses for the variety of controls that can reduce the risk for each vulnerability. However, it is often more useful to use a simpler risk model such as the one described in Figure 1-4 to evaluate the risk for each information asset. The next section presents the factors that are used to calculate the relative risk for each vulnerability.

Likelihood

Likelihood is the probability that a specific vulnerability within an organization will be successfully attacked.[10] In risk assessment, you assign a numeric value to the likelihood of a vulnerability being successfully exploited. Likelihood vulnerabilities could be assigned a number between 0.1 for low and 1.0 for high, or assigned a number between 1 and 100, but zero is not used, because vulnerabilities with a zero likelihood have been removed from the asset/vulnerability list. Whatever rating system you decide to use for assigning likelihood, use professionalism, experience, and judgment—and use the rating model you select consistently. Whenever possible, use external references for likelihood values that have

Risk is
the **likelihood** of the occurrence of a vulnerability
multiplied by
the **value** of the information asset
minus
the percentage of risk mitigated by **current controls**
plus
the **uncertainty** of current knowledge of the vulnerability

FIGURE 1-4 Factors of risk

been reviewed and adjusted for your specific circumstances. Many asset/vulnerability combinations have sources for likelihood. For example:

- The likelihood of a fire has been estimated actuarially for each type of structure.
- The likelihood that any given e-mail contains a virus or worm has been researched.
- The number of network attacks can be forecast based on how many network addresses the organization has assigned.

Valuation of Information Assets

Using the information obtained during the information asset identification steps, you can now assign weighted scores to each information asset's value to the organization. The actual number used can vary with the needs of the organization. Some groups use a scale of 1 to 100, with 100 reserved for those information assets, which if lost, the company would stop operations within a few minutes. Other scales use assigned weights in broad categories, assigning all important assets a value of 100, all low-criticality assets a value of 1, and all others a medium value of 50. Still other groups use a scale of 1 to 10, or assigned values of 1, 3, and 5 to represent low, medium, and high-valued assets. You can also create weight values for your specific needs. To be effective, the values must be assigned by asking the questions described earlier:

- Which threats present a danger to an organization's assets in the given environment?
- Which threats represent the most danger to the organization's information?

- How much would it cost to recover from a successful attack?
- Which of the threats would require the greatest expenditure to prevent?

After reevaluating these questions, you must use the background information from the risk identification process and illuminate that information by posing one additional question: which of the questions posed earlier for each information asset is the most important to the protection of the organization's information?

This question helps to set priorities in the assessment of vulnerabilities. Which is the most important to the organization, the cost to recover from a threat attack, the cost to protect against a threat attack—or generally, which of the threats has the highest probability of successful attack? Additional questions may also be asked. Again, you are looking at threats the organization faces in its current state; however, this information will be valuable in later stages as you begin to design the final security solution. Once these questions are answered, you move to the next step in the process: examining how current controls can reduce the risk faced by specific vulnerabilities.

If a vulnerability is fully managed by an existing control, it no longer needs to be considered for additional controls and can be set aside. If it is partially controlled, estimate what percentage of the vulnerability has been controlled.

It is impossible to know everything about each vulnerability, such as how likely it is to occur, or how great an impact a successful attack would have. The degree that a current control can reduce risk is also subject to estimation error. You must apply judgment when adding factors into the equation to allow for an estimation of the uncertainty of the information.

Risk Determination

For the purpose of relative risk assessment, risk *equals* likelihood of vulnerability occurrence *times* value (or impact) *minus* percentage risk already controlled *plus* an element of uncertainty. As an example, consider that information asset A has a value score of 50 and has one vulnerability that has a likelihood of 1.0 with no current controls; and the estimate is that assumptions and data are 90% accurate (or have a 10% uncertainty). The resulting risk ratings based on these assumptions show that Asset A's vulnerability is rated as 55 from the calculation of (50 [being the value] × 1.0 [being the likelihood of occurrence]) – 0% [being the percent of risk currently controlled] + 10% [being the uncertainty of our assumptions], where:

$$55 = (50 \times 1.0) - ((50 \times 1.0) \times 0.0) + ((50 \times 1.0) \times 0.1)$$
$$55 = 50 - 0 + 5$$

Identify Possible Controls

For each threat and its associated vulnerabilities that have residual risk, create a preliminary list of control ideas. **Residual risk** is the risk that remains to the information asset even after the existing control has been applied.

Controls, safeguards, and countermeasures are terms used to represent security mechanisms, policies, and procedures that are used to reduce the risk from operating information systems. These mechanisms, policies, and procedures counter attacks, reduce risk, resolve vulnerabilities, and otherwise improve the general state of security within an organization. The three general categories of controls according to the CNSS model are: policies, programs, and technologies. Policies are documents that specify an organization's approach to security. There are three types of security policies: the enterprise information security policy, issue-specific policies, and systems-specific policies. The enterprise information security policy is an executive-level document that outlines the organization's approach and attitude toward information security and relates the strategic value of information security within the organization. This document, typically created by the CIO in conjunction with the CEO and CISO, sets the tone for all subsequent security activities. Issue-specific policies address the specific implementations or applications of which users should be aware. These policies are typically developed to provide detailed instructions and restrictions associated with security issues. Examples include policies for Internet use, e-mail, and access to the building. Finally, systems-specific policies address the particular use of certain systems. This could include firewall configuration policies, systems access policies, and other technical configuration areas. Programs are activities performed within the organization to improve security. These include security education, training, and awareness programs. Security technologies are implementations of the policies defined by the organization using technology-based mechanisms, such as firewalls or intrusion detection systems.

Risk Control Strategies

When organizational management has determined that risks from information security threats are creating a competitive disadvantage, they empower the information technology and information security communities of interest to control the risks. Once the project team for information security development has created the ranked vulnerability worksheet, the team must choose one of four basic strategies to control each of the risks that result from these vulnerabilities. The four strategies are as follows:

- Apply safeguards that eliminate or reduce the remaining uncontrolled risks for the vulnerability (avoidance).
- Transfer the risk to other areas or to outside entities (transference).
- Reduce the impact should the vulnerability be exploited (mitigation).
- Understand the consequences and accept the risk without control or mitigation (acceptance).

Avoidance

Avoidance is the risk control strategy that attempts to prevent the exploitation of the vulnerability. This is the preferred approach, and is accomplished by means of countering threats, removing vulnerabilities in assets, limiting access to assets, and adding protective safeguards.

There are three common methods of risk avoidance: avoidance through application of policy, avoidance through application of training and education, and avoidance through application of technology.

The application of policy allows management to mandate that certain procedures are always followed. For example, if the organization needs to control password use more tightly, a policy requiring passwords on all IT systems can be implemented. Note that policy alone may not be enough, and effective management always couples changes in policy with training and education or the application of technology, or both. Policy must be communicated to employees. In addition, new technology often requires training. Awareness, training, and education are essential if employees are to exhibit safe and controlled behavior.

In the real world of information security, technical solutions are often required to assure that risk is reduced. To continue the earlier example, passwords can be used with most modern operating systems, but some system administrators may not configure systems to use passwords. If, however, policy requires passwords, and the administrators are both aware of the requirement and trained to implement it, the technical control is successfully used.

Risks may be avoided by countering the threats facing an asset or by eliminating the exposure of a particular asset. Eliminating a threat is a difficult proposition, but it is possible. Another method of risk management that falls under the category of avoidance is the implementation of security controls and safeguards to deflect attacks on systems and therefore minimize the probability that an attack will be successful. An organization with dial-in access vulnerability, for example, may choose to implement a control or safeguard for that service, or the organization may choose to eliminate the dial-in system and service to avoid the potential risk.

Transference

Transference is the control approach that attempts to shift the risk to other assets, other processes, or other organizations. This may be accomplished through rethinking how services are offered, revising deployment models, outsourcing to other organizations, purchasing insurance, or implementing service contracts with providers.

When an organization does not have the correct balance of information security skills, it should consider hiring or making outsourcing arrangements with individuals or firms that provide such expertise. This allows the organization to transfer the risks associated with the management of these complex systems to another organization that has experience in dealing with those risks. A side benefit of specific contract arrangements is that the provider is responsible for disaster recovery and through service-level agreements is responsible for guaranteeing server and Web site availability.

Outsourcing, however, is not without its own risks. It is up to the owner of the information asset, IT management, and the information security team to ensure that the disaster recovery requirements of the outsourcing contract are sufficient and have been met *before* they are needed for recovery efforts. If the outsourcer has failed to meet the contract terms, the consequences may be far worse than expected.

Mitigation

Mitigation is the control approach that attempts to reduce the impact caused by the exploitation of vulnerability through planning and preparation. This approach includes contingency planning and its four functional components: the business impact analysis, the incident response plan, the disaster recovery plan, and the business continuity plan. Each of these components of the contingency plan depends on the ability to detect and respond to an attack as quickly as possible and relies on the existence and quality of the other plans. Mitigation begins with the early detection that an attack is in progress and the ability of the organization to respond quickly, efficiently, and effectively. Each of these is described later in this chapter and explored in depth in later chapters of the book.

Acceptance

In contrast to mitigation, **acceptance** of risk is the choice to do nothing to protect a vulnerability, and to accept the outcome of its exploitation. This may or may not be a conscious business decision. The only industry-recognized valid use of this strategy occurs when the organization has:

- Determined the level of risk
- Assessed the probability of attack
- Estimated the potential damage that could occur from attacks
- Performed a thorough cost-benefit analysis
- Evaluated controls using each appropriate type of feasibility
- Decided that the particular function, service, information, or asset did not justify the cost of protection

This control, or rather lack of control, is based on the conclusion that the cost of protecting an asset does not justify the security expenditure. In this case, management may be satisfied with taking its chances and saving the money that would normally be spent on protecting this asset. If every vulnerability identified in the organization is handled through acceptance, it may reflect an organization's inability to conduct proactive security activities and an apathetic approach to security in general.

CONTINGENCY PLANNING AND ITS COMPONENTS

A key role for all managers is planning. Managers in IT in general and information security in particular usually provide strategic planning for an organization to assure the continuous availability of information systems. Unfortunately for managers, the probability that some form of attack will occur is very high, whether from inside or outside, intentional or accidental, human or nonhuman, annoying or catastrophic factors. Thus, managers from each community of interest within the organization must be ready to act when a successful attack occurs.

There are various types of plans for events of this type, and they all fall under the general definition of contingency planning. A **contingency plan (CP)** is prepared by the organization to anticipate, react to, and recover from events that threaten the security of information and information assets in the organization, and, subsequently, to restore the organization to normal modes of business operations. The discussion of the CP begins with an explanation of the differences among its various elements and an examination of the points at which each element is brought into play.

Contingency planning involves four subordinate functions:

- Business impact assessment
- Incident response planning
- Disaster recovery planning
- Business continuity planning

Each of these is described in the following sections, and discussed in greater detail in later chapters.

As the individual components of the CP are described, you may notice that contingency planning has many similarities with the risk management process. The CP is a microcosm of risk management activities, and it focuses on the specific steps required to return all information assets to the level at which they were functioning before the incident or disaster. As a result, the planning process closely emulates the process of risk management.

Business Impact Analysis

The entire planning process begins with an assessment of the risks associated with these contingencies. The first function in the development of the CP process is the **business impact analysis (BIA)**. A BIA is an investigation and assessment of the impact that various attacks can have on the organization. The BIA takes up where the risk assessment process leaves off. It begins with the prioritized list of threats and vulnerabilities identified in the risk management process and adds critical information. The BIA is a crucial component of the initial planning stages because it provides detailed scenarios of the potential impact each attack could have on the organization.

Incident Response Plan

The actions an organization can and perhaps should take while the incident is in progress should be defined in a document referred to as the **incident response (IR) plan**. An **incident** is any clearly identified attack on the organization's information assets that would threaten the assets' confidentiality, integrity, or availability. The IR plan deals with the identification, classification, response, and recovery from an incident. The IR plan provides answers to questions victims might pose in the midst of an incident, for example, "What do I do now?" As was noted in the opening scenario, the IT organization was ready to respond to the unusual events that had alerted JJ to an unusual situation. In that example, a simple process is used, based on documented procedures that were prepared in advance. For another example, a systems administrator may notice that someone is copying information from the server without authorization, signaling violation of policy by a potential hacker or an unauthorized employee. What should the administrator do first? Whom should they contact? What should they document? The IR plan supplies the answers.

For example, in the event of a serious virus or worm outbreak, the IR plan may be used to assess the likelihood of imminent damage and to inform key decision makers in the various communities of interest (IT, information security, organization management, and users). The IR plan also enables the organization to take coordinated action that is either predefined and specific, or ad hoc and reactive. The intruders that, in some instances, cause the incidents, constantly scan for new weaknesses in operating systems, network services, and protocols. According to the Carnegie Mellon Software Engineering Institute, "[Intruders] actively develop and use sophisticated programs to rapidly penetrate systems. As a result, intrusions, and the damage they cause, are often achieved in a matter of seconds."[11]

The same source also reports that organizations "will not know what to do in the event of an intrusion if the necessary procedures, roles, and responsibilities have not been defined and exercised in advance. The absence of systematic and well-defined procedures can lead to:

- Extensive damage to data, systems, and networks due to not taking timely action to contain an intrusion. This can result in increased costs, loss of productivity, and loss of business.
- The possibility of an intrusion affecting multiple systems both inside and outside your organization because staff did not know who else to notify and what additional actions to take
- Negative exposure in the news media that can damage your organization's stature and reputation with your shareholders, your customers, and the community at large
- Possible legal liability and prosecution for failure to exercise an adequate standard of due care when your systems are inadvertently or intentionally used to attack others."[12]

Disaster Recovery Plan

The most wisely implemented form of mitigation strategy is the disaster recovery plan. A **disaster recovery (DR) plan** deals with the preparation for and recovery from a disaster, whether natural or man-made. Although media backup strategies are an integral part of the disaster recovery plan, the overall program includes the entire spectrum of activities used to recover from an incident. The DR plan can include strategies to limit losses before and during the disaster. These strategies are fully deployed once the disaster has stopped. DR plans usually include all preparations for the recovery process, strategies to limit losses during the disaster, and detailed steps to follow when the smoke clears, the dust settles, or the floodwaters recede.

The DR planning and IR planning (IRP) development processes overlap to a degree. In many regards, the DR plan is the subsection of the IR plan that covers disastrous events. The IR plan is also flexible enough to be useful in situations that are near disasters but still require coordinated, planned actions. While some DRP and IRP decisions and actions are the same, their urgency and results can differ dramatically. DRP focuses more on preparations completed before and actions taken after the incident, whereas IRP focuses on intelligence gathering, information analysis, coordinated decision making, and urgent, concrete actions.

Business Continuity Plan

The third type of planning within the mitigation strategy is business continuity planning (BCP). A **business continuity (BC) plan** is a document that expresses how an organization ensures that critical business functions continue at an alternate location while the organization recovers its ability to function at the primary site if a catastrophic incident or disaster occurs. The BC plan is the most strategic and long term of the three plans. It encompasses the continuation of business activities if a catastrophic event occurs, such as the loss of an entire database, building, or operations center. The BCP development process includes planning the steps necessary to ensure the continuation of the organization when the scope or scale of a disaster exceeds the ability of the DR plan to restore operations. Many companies offer services as a contingency against disastrous events such as fires, floods, earthquakes, and most natural disasters.

Another concept that is emerging into widespread awareness in the world of contingency planning is that of **business resumption planning (BRP)**. This phrase reflects the fact that disaster recovery and business continuity are closely related functions, and it is used to describe an approach that merges the capabilities of both subsets of contingency planning. In fact, in a growing number of organizations, all of the subordinate functions of the CP might be handled as a single planning process and result in a single document. In large, complex organizations, each of these named plans may represent separate but related planning functions that differ in scope, applicability, and design. In a small organization, the security administrator (or systems administrator) may have one simple plan that consists of a straightforward set of media backup and recovery strategies, and a few service agreements from the company's service providers. But the sad reality is that many organizations have a level of planning that is woefully deficient.

Contingency Planning Timeline

A brief review of the steps in CP reveals:

1. The IR plan focuses on immediate response, but if the attack escalates or is disastrous (such as a fire, flood, earthquake, or total blackout) the process moves on to disaster recovery and business continuity.
2. The DR plan typically focuses on restoring systems at the original site after disasters occur, and as such is closely associated with the BC plan.
3. The BC plan runs concurrently with DRP when the damage is major or long term, requiring more than simple restoration of information and information resources. The BC plan establishes critical business functions at an alternate site.

Some organizations treat the DR plan and BC plan as so closely linked that they are indistinguishable. However, each has a distinct role and planning requirement. The following sections detail the tasks necessary for each of these three types of plans. You can also further distinguish among the three types of planning by examining when each comes into play during the life of an incident. Figure 1-5 shows a sample sequence of events and the overlap between when each plan comes into play. Disaster recovery activities typically continue even after the organization has resumed operations at the original site.

The major project work modules as described later in this book are performed by the contingency planning project team and are shown in Figure 1-6. While Figure 1-6 is not explained in full detail at this time, it provides a useful overview to the process and the component parts shown in the figure will be fully explained in later chapters. Many of the components of upcoming chapters correspond to the steps depicted in the diagram.

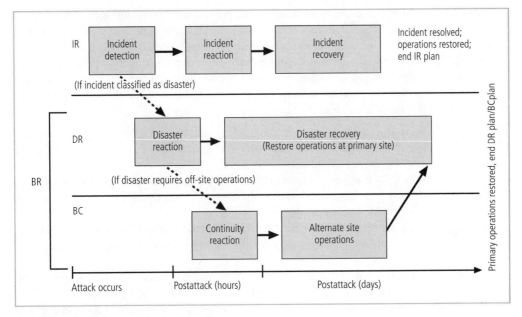

FIGURE 1-5 Contingency planning timeline

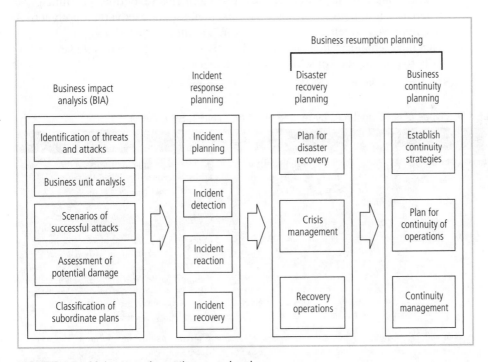

FIGURE 1-6 Major steps in contingency planning

According to NIST there are seven steps in the NIST-sanctioned contingency planning process. In that model, CP involves much more than the IRP, DRP, and BCP, although many of their components fall under one of these categories. As noted in NIST SP 800-61:

The [CP] document also defines the following seven-step contingency process that an agency may apply to develop and maintain a viable contingency planning program for its IT systems. These seven progressive steps are designed to be integrated into each stage of the system development life cycle.

1. Develop the contingency planning policy statement: A formal department or agency policy provides the authority and guidance necessary to develop an effective contingency plan.
2. Conduct the business impact analysis (BIA): The BIA helps to identify and prioritize critical IT systems and components. A template for developing the BIA is also provided to assist the user.
3. Identify preventive controls: Measures taken to reduce the effects of system disruptions can increase system availability and reduce contingency life cycle costs.
4. Develop recovery strategies: Thorough recovery strategies ensure that the system may be recovered quickly and effectively following a disruption.
5. Develop an IT contingency plan: The contingency plan should contain detailed guidance and procedures for restoring a damaged system.
6. Plan testing, training, and exercises: Testing the plan identifies planning gaps, whereas training prepares recovery personnel for plan activation; both activities improve plan effectiveness and overall agency preparedness.
7. Plan maintenance: The plan should be a living document that is updated regularly to remain current with system enhancements.

The NIST plans that support these processes are summarized in Table 1-4.

TABLE 1-4 Types of NIST contingency-related plans (from NIST, SP 800-61)

Plan	Purpose	Scope
Business continuity (BC) plan	Provide procedures for sustaining essential business operations while recovering from a significant disruption	Addresses business processes; IT addressed based only on its support for business process
Business recovery (BR) (or resumption) plan	Provide procedures for recovering business operations immediately following a disaster	Addresses business processes; not IT focused; IT addressed based only on its support for business process
Continuity of operations plan (COOP)	Provide procedures and capabilities to sustain an organization's essential, strategic functions at an alternate site for up to 30 days	Addresses the subset of an organization's missions that are deemed most critical; usually written at headquarters level; not IT focused
Continuity of support plan/IT contingency plan	Provide procedures and capabilities for recovering a major application or general support system	Same as IT contingency plan; addresses IT system disruptions; not business process focused

TABLE 1-4 Types of NIST contingency-related plans (from NIST, SP 800-61) (continued)

Plan	Purpose	Scope
Crisis communications plan	Provides procedures for disseminating status reports to personnel and the public	Addresses communications with personnel and the public; not IT focused
Cyberincident response plan	Provide strategies to detect, respond to, and limit consequences of malicious cyberincident	Focuses on information security responses to incidents affecting systems and/or networks
Disaster recovery (DR) plan	Provide detailed procedures to facilitate recovery of capabilities at an alternate site	Often IT focused; limited to major disruptions with long-term effects
Occupant emergency plan (OEP)	Provide coordinated procedures for minimizing loss of life or injury and protecting property damage in response to a physical threat	Focuses on personnel and property particular to the specific facility; not business process or IT system functionality based

Figure 1-7 shows how the various plans referenced in SP 800-61 relate to each other.

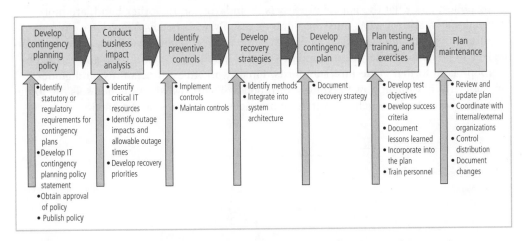

FIGURE 1-7 Interrelationship of emergency preparedness plans (from NIST, SP 800-61)

INFORMATION SECURITY POLICY IN DEVELOPING CONTINGENCY PLANS

Much of what must be done in CP should be guided by, and reinforce, organizational information security policies. In fact, the outcome of the typical CP process often results in new policy. This reinforces the need for proactive planning for the employees and the organization. It also identifies that policy is needed to enforce certain requirements necessary for the protection of information before, during, and after any situation requiring a contingency plan. To better understand this relationship, a brief review of the key elements of the policy-making process is in order.

Quality security programs begin and end with policy.[13] Because information security is primarily a management problem, not a technical one, policy obliges personnel to function in a manner that adds to the security of information assets, rather than as a threat to those assets. Security policies are the least expensive control in that they involve only the time and effort of the management team to create, approve, and communicate, but they are the most difficult to implement *properly*. Shaping policy is difficult because it must never conflict with laws, it must stand up in court if challenged, and be properly administered through dissemination and documented acceptance.

Key Policy Definitions

Before examining the various types of information security policies, it is important to understand exactly what policy is and how it can and should be used.

A **policy** is a plan or course of action used by an organization to convey instructions from its senior-most management to those who make decisions, take actions, and perform other duties on behalf of the organization. Policies are organizational laws in that they dictate acceptable and unacceptable behavior within the context of the organization's culture. Like laws, policies must define what is right, what is wrong, what the penalties are for violating policy, and what the appeal process is. **Standards**, on the other hand, are more detailed statements of what must be done to comply with policy. They have the same requirements for compliance as policies. The level of acceptance of standards may be informal, as in **de facto standards**, or standards may be published, scrutinized, and ratified by a group, as in formal or **de jure standards**. Finally, practices, procedures, and guidelines effectively explain how to comply with policy. Figure 1-8 shows policies as the force that drives standards, which in turn drive practices, procedures, and guidelines.

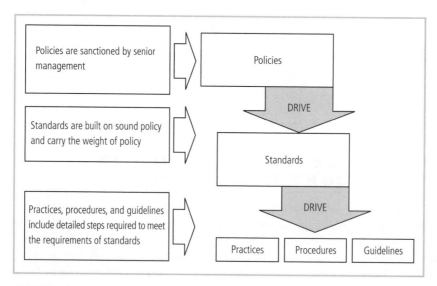

FIGURE 1-8 Policies, standards, and practices

Policies are written to support the mission, vision, and strategic planning of an organization. The **mission** of an organization is a written statement of an organization's purpose. The **vision** of an organization is a written statement about the organization's goals—where will the organization be in five years? In 10 years? **Strategic planning** is the process of moving the organization toward its vision.

To be effective, a policy must be disseminated by all means possible, including printed personnel manuals, organization intranets, and periodic supplements. All members of the organization must read, understand, and agree to the policies. At the same time, policies should be considered living documents, in that they require constant modification and maintenance as the needs of the organization evolve.

In general, a security policy is a set of rules that protect an organization's assets. An **information security policy** provides rules for the protection of the information assets of the organization. According to the National Institute of Standards and Technology's Special Publication 800-14, management must define three types of security policy: the enterprise security policy, issue-specific security policies, and systems-specific security policies.

Enterprise Information Security Policy

An **enterprise information security policy (EISP)** is also known as a general security policy, IT security policy, or information security policy. The EISP is based on and directly supports the mission, vision, and direction of the organization and sets the strategic direction, scope, and tone for all security efforts. The EISP is an executive-level document, usually drafted by, or in cooperation with, the chief information officer of the organization. This policy is usually two to ten pages long and shapes the philosophy of security in the IT environment. The EISP does not usually require continuous modification, unless there is a change in the strategic direction of the organization.

The EISP guides the development, implementation, and management of the security program. It contains the requirements to be met by the information security blueprint or framework. It defines the purpose, scope, constraints, and applicability of the security program in the organization. It also assigns responsibilities for the various areas of security, including systems administration, maintenance of the information security policies, and the practices and responsibilities of the users. Finally, it addresses legal compliance. According to the National Institute of Standards, the EISP typically addresses compliance by documenting the organizational structures put into place, describing the programs that have been developed and reviewing the assignment of responsibilities, and/or the use of specified penalties and disciplinary actions.[14]

When the EISP has been developed, the CISO (or chief information security officer) begins forming the security team and initiating the necessary changes to the information security program.

Issue-Specific Security Policy

As an organization executes various technologies and processes to support routine operations, guidelines are needed to instruct employees to use these technologies and processes properly. In general, the **issue-specific security policy (ISSP)** addresses specific areas of technology, requires frequent updates, and contains a statement on the organization's position on a specific issue.[15]

There are a number of approaches to creating and managing ISSPs within an organization. Three of the most common are to create the following types of ISSP documents:

- Independent ISSP documents, each tailored to a specific issue
- A single comprehensive ISSP document covering all issues
- A modular ISSP document that unifies policy creation and administration, while maintaining each specific issue's requirements

Table 1-5 is an outline of a sample ISSP, which can be used as a model. An organization should add to this structure the specific details that dictate security procedures not covered by these general guidelines.

TABLE 1-5 Elements of an issue-specific security policy[16]

1. Statement of policy
   a. Scope and applicability
   b. Definition of technology addressed
   c. Responsibilities
2. Authorized access and usage of equipment
   a. User access
   b. Fair and responsible use
   c. Protection of privacy
3. Prohibited usage of equipment
   a. Disruptive use or misuse
   b. Criminal use
   c. Offensive or harassing materials
   d. Copyrighted, licensed, or other intellectual property
   e. Other restrictions
4. Systems management
   a. Management of stored materials
   b. Employer monitoring
   c. Virus protection
   d. Physical security
   e. Encryption
5. Violations of policy
   a. Procedures for reporting violations
   b. Penalties for violations
6. Policy review and modification
   a. Scheduled review of policy and procedures for modification
7. Limitations of liability
   a. Statements of liability or disclaimers

© 2003 ACM, Inc. Included here by permission.

The components of each of the major categories presented in the sample issue-specific policy shown in Table 1-5 are discussed in the following sections. Even though the details may vary from policy to policy and some sections of a modular policy may be combined, it is essential for management to address and complete each section.

Statement of Policy

The policy should begin with a clear statement of purpose and outline these topics: What is the scope of this policy? Who is responsible and accountable for policy implementation? What technologies and issues does it address?

Authorized Access and Usage of Equipment

This section of the policy statement addresses *who* can use the technology governed by the policy, and *what* it can be used for. This section defines "fair and responsible use" of equipment and other organizational assets, and should also address key legal issues, such as protection of personal information and privacy.

Prohibited Usage of Equipment

While the policy section described above detailed what the issue or technology *can* be used for, this section outlines what it *cannot* be used for. Unless a particular use is clearly prohibited, the organization cannot penalize its employees for misuse. The following can be prohibited: personal use, disruptive use or misuse, criminal use, offensive or harassing materials, and infringement of copyrighted, licensed, or other intellectual property.

Systems Management

The systems management section of the ISSP policy statement focuses on the users' relationship to systems management. It is important that all such responsibilities are designated as belonging to either the systems administrator or the users; otherwise, both parties may infer that the responsibility belongs to the other party.

Violations of Policy

This section of the policy statement should contain not only the specifics of the penalties for each category of violation but also instructions on how individuals in the organization can report observed or suspected violations without fear of recrimination or retribution.

Policy Review and Modification

The policy should contain procedures and a timetable for periodic review. This section should contain a specific methodology for the review and modification of the policy to ensure that users do not begin circumventing it as it grows obsolete.

Limitations of Liability

The final consideration listed in Table 1-5 is a general statement of liability or set of disclaimers. The policy should state that if employees violate a company policy or any law using company technologies, the company will not protect them, and the company is not liable for their actions.

Systems-Specific Policy

While issue-specific policies are formalized as written documents to be distributed to users and agreed to in writing, **systems-specific security policies (SysSPs)** are frequently codified as standards and procedures to be used when configuring or maintaining systems. Systems-specific policies can be organized into two general groups:

- **Access control lists (ACLs)**: Lists, matrices, and capability tables governing the rights and privileges of a particular user to a particular system
- **Configuration rules:** The specific configuration codes entered into security systems to guide the execution of the system when information is passing through it

ACL Policies

Most modern network operating systems (NOS) translate ACLs into sets of configurations that administrators use to control access to their respective systems. ACLs allow a configuration to set restrictions for a particular user, computer, time, duration—even a particular file. In general, ACLs regulate the who, what, when, and where of access:

- *Who* can use the system
- *What* authorized users can access
- *When* authorized users can access the system
- *Where* authorized users can access the system from

In some systems, these lists of ACL rules are known as *capability tables, user profiles*, or *user policies*. They specify what the user can and cannot do on the resources within that system.

Rule Policies

Rule policies are more specific to the operation of a system than ACLs and may or may not deal with users directly. Many security systems require specific configuration scripts that tell the systems what actions to perform on each set of information they process. Examples of these systems include firewalls, intrusion detection systems, and proxy servers.

Policy Management

Policies are dynamic documents that must be managed and nurtured, as they constantly change and grow. These documents must be properly disseminated (distributed, read, understood, and agreed to) and managed. To remain viable, security policies must have the following:

- An individual (like a policy administrator) responsible for the creation, revision, distribution, and storage of the policy; this individual should solicit input from all communities of interest in policy development
- A schedule of reviews to ensure currency and accuracy, and to demonstrate due diligence
- A mechanism by which individuals can comfortably make recommendations for revisions, preferably anonymously
- A policy and revision date and possibly a "sunset" expiration date
- Optionally, policy management software to streamline the steps of writing policy, tracking the workflow of policy approvals, publishing policy once it is written and approved, and tracking when individuals have read the policy

Chapter Summary

- Information security is defined by the Committee on National Security Systems (CNSS) as the protection of information and its critical elements, including the systems and hardware that use, store, and transmit that information.

- The CNSS model of information security evolved from a concept developed by the computer security industry known as the C.I.A. triangle, which has been the industry standard for computer security since the development of the mainframe.

  - Confidentiality ensures that only those with the rights and privileges to access information are able to do so.

  - Information has integrity when it is whole, complete, and uncorrupted.

  - Availability enables authorized users to access information when and where needed.

- A threat is a category of objects, persons, or other entities that pose a potential for loss to an asset.

- An asset can be logical, such as a Web site, information, or data; or an asset can be physical, such as a person, computer system, or other tangible object.

- A vulnerability is a weakness or fault in the protection mechanisms that are intended to protect information and information assets from attack or damage.

- Risk management is the process of identifying vulnerabilities in an organization's information systems and taking carefully reasoned steps to ensure the confidentiality, integrity, and availability of all the components in the organization's information system.

- Risk management is made up of two major undertakings: risk identification and risk control:

  - Risk identification is the process of examining and documenting the security posture of an organization's information technology and the risks it faces.

  - Risk control is the process of applying controls to reduce the risks to an organization's data and information systems.

- Risk management is an expected responsibility for managers in all organizations, and information security managers are usually tasked with many of the risk management responsibilities.

- Contingency planning is usually considered to be part of the risk management program within organizations.

- There are four basic strategies to control each of the risks that have been identified:

  - Eliminate or reduce the remaining uncontrolled risks (avoidance).

  - Transfer the risk to other areas or to outside entities (transference).

  - Reduce the impact should the vulnerability be exploited (mitigation).

  - Understand the consequences and accept the risk without control or mitigation (acceptance).

- A contingency plan (CP) is prepared by the organization to anticipate, react to, and recover from events that threaten the security of information and information assets in the organization, and, subsequently, to restore the organization to normal modes of business operations. Contingency planning involves four subordinate functions:
  - Business impact assessment
  - Incident response planning
  - Disaster recovery planning
  - Business continuity planning
- The business impact analysis is an investigation and assessment of the impact that various attacks can have on the organization.
- The actions an organization can and perhaps should take while the incident is in progress should be defined in a document referred to as the *incident response plan*.
- A disaster recovery (DR) plan deals with the preparation for and recovery from a disaster, whether natural or man-made.
- A business continuity (BC) plan ensures that critical business functions continue if a catastrophic incident or disaster occurs.
- Quality security programs begin and end with policy.
- Shaping policy is difficult because it must do the following:
  - Never conflict with laws.
  - Stand up in court, if challenged.
  - Be properly administered through dissemination and documented acceptance.
- Policies are organizational laws in that they dictate acceptable and unacceptable behavior within the context of the organization's culture.
- Standards are more detailed statements of what must be done to comply with policy.
- Practices, procedures, and guidelines effectively explain how to comply with policy.
- An enterprise information security policy, or EISP, is based on and directly supports the mission, vision, and direction of the organization and sets the strategic direction, scope, and tone for all security efforts.
- The issue-specific security policy, or ISSP, addresses specific areas of technology, requires frequent updates, and contains a statement on the organization's position on a specific issue.
- Systems-specific security policies are codified standards and procedures to be used when configuring or maintaining systems.

Review Questions

1. What is information security?
2. What is the CNSS, and how is the CNSS model of information security organized?
3. What three principles are used to define the C.I.A. triangle? Define each in the context in which it is used in information security.
4. What is a threat in the context of information security?

5. What is an asset in the context of information security?

6. What is a vulnerability in the context of information security?

7. What is risk management?

8. What are the component parts of risk management?

9. Who is expected to be engaged in risk management activities in most organizations?

10. What are the four basic strategies used to control risk? Define each.

11. What is a contingency plan?

12. List and describe the four subordinate functions of a contingency plan.

13. What is policy in general terms?

14. What is the enterprise information security policy and how is it used?

15. Why is shaping policy considered difficult?

16. What are standards? What are procedures? How are they each different from policy?

17. What is an issue-specific security policy?

18. List three example subjects that may be used as a basis for an issue-specific security policy.

19. What is a systems-specific security policy?

20. When is a systems-specific security policy used?

Exercises

1. Using a Web browser, search for any information security policies for your institution. Compare them to the example structures in this chapter. Are there sections missing? If so, which ones?

2. Using a Web browser, go to *http://www.gocsi.com* and download the latest CSI/FBI Cyber-crime Study. What threats are currently the most dangerous? Which threats represent problems for your home computer? Institution lab computers?

3. Using a Web browser, go to *http://cve.mitre.org*. What type of site is this and what information can it provide? Change the URL to *http://cve.mitre.org/cve* and enter the term *IP Validation Vulnerability* in the Keyword search field and click Search. What information are you provided? How would this be useful? Go to the Microsoft reference URL. What additional information are you provided? How would this be useful?

4. Using a Web browser, go to *http://www.securityfocus.com*. What information is provided under the BugTraq tab? Under the Vulnerabilities tab? On the Vulnerabilities tab, select Microsoft as the Vendor and Windows Messenger as the title. Look for a PNG Buffer Over-flow vulnerability. What information is provided under the Exploit tab? What does it mean? How could an attacker use this information? How could a security manager?

5. Using a Web browser, go to *http://csrc.nist.gov*. Click the Security Guidelines (800 Series) link. Find SP 800-12. Review the HTML version. What critical information could a security administrator or manager gain from this document? What other documents would be of value to the security manager or technician?

Further Discussion

The discussion questions from the opening scenario are going to be difficult to answer without more information. See the section that follows for more information about how HAL performs its IT functions and how HAL has organized its security functions.

HAL's organization charts are shown in the Figures 1-9 through 1-12.

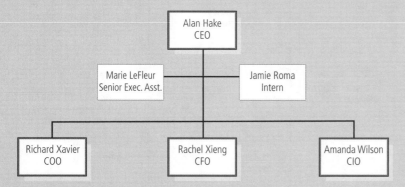

FIGURE 1-9   HAL high-level organization chart

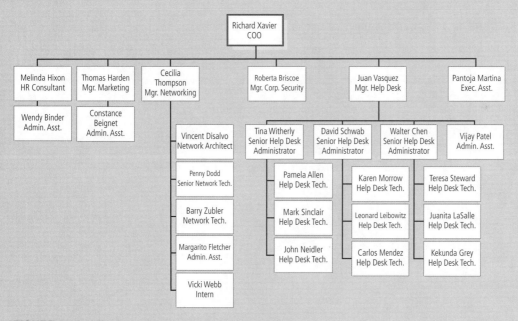

FIGURE 1-10   HAL operations unit organization chart

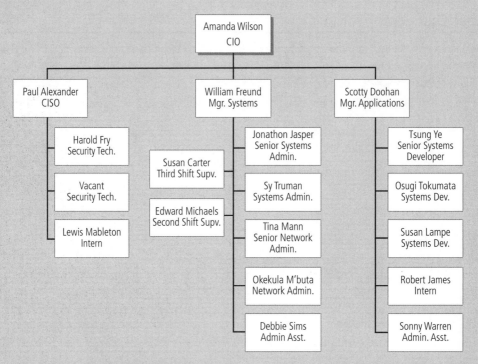

FIGURE 1-11 HAL IT unit organization chart

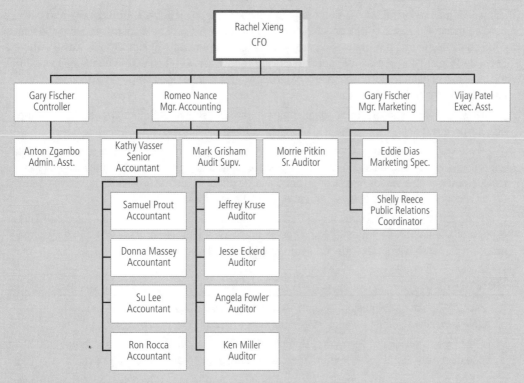

FIGURE 1-12   HAL financial unit organization chart

Established in June 1999, Hierarchical Access LTD (HAL) is an Internet service provider operating out of Marietta, Georgia, serving the northwest metropolitan Atlanta region. HAL provides basic Internet access, fast Internet access, and Web registration and hosting alternatives for small office/home office (SOHO) individuals and organizations. HAL is a privately owned company managed by the founder and CEO Alan Hake.

The CIO, Amanda Wilson, has over 15 years of technical experience and 10 years of experience as a senior IT manager. Shortly after taking the position as CIO at HAL, she hired Mike Alexander as manager of information security. A reorganization in 2003 resulted in an elevated recognition of the role of information security at HAL, and the assignment of the title of chief information security officer to Mike. Along with this increased recognition came the assignment of dedicated personnel and a budget of approximately $500,000 for equipment, personnel, and training. As shown in the preceding organization charts, currently Mike has two full-time security technician positions (one of which is unfilled) and an intern.

Two years ago, HAL began a major organization-wide effort to implement contingency planning. While Amanda is primarily responsible for the incident response plan development, she has appointed William Freund, manager of systems as the lead for the IR team. Mike was tasked with serving as a consultant for all three teams (incident response, disaster recovery, and business continuity) to assist in their development and implementation. The disaster recovery and business continuity teams are the responsibility of the chief operations officer, Robert Xavier, who appointed Cecil Thomson as lead for the disaster recovery team, and Juan Vasquez as lead for the business continuity team. The teams have been formed under their leadership and their planning documents have been created.

Now, back to some recommendations about how you should structure your solution for the discussion questions:

First, who should Paul call for this meeting? Look for those members of the organization that are responsible for operational matters in the systems and network areas. You may also need to include one or more senior managers who would be affected by these events and/or who can act as a conduit to the upper levels of the organizational hierarchy.

Finally, what other information can Paul and his team use to track down this incident? This is more of a brainstorming question, and you should think about resources and methods you may have encountered in your experience as an employee and/or as a student.

References

[1] ClickZ, "Population Explosion!" March 16, 2005, accessed April 25, 2005, from http://www.clickz.com/stats/sectors/geographics/article.php/5911_151151.

[2] BBC News, "Lessons of First WTC Bombing," *BBC News World Edition*, February 26, 2003, accessed April 20, 2005, from http://news.bbc.co.uk/2/hi/americas/2800297.stm.

[3] U. S. Karmarkar and V. Mangal, "Business Continuity and Technology in the Retail Sector," Business and Information Technologies Research Project, February 2, 2004, accessed April 20, 2005, from http://www.anderson.ucla.edu/documents/areas/ctr/bit/Retail%20ATT.pdf.

[4] Onrec.com, "SME Recruitment Agencies Invited by AXA to Star in Business Oscars," September 3, 2005, accessed April 20, 2005, from http://www.onrec.com/content2/news.asp?ID=6843.

[5] Michael E. Whitman, "Enemy at the Gates: Threats to Information Security," *Communications of the ACM* 46 (2003): 91–95.

[6] FOLDOC, "Intellectual Property," *FOLDOC Online*, March 27, 1997, accessed February 15, 2004, from http://foldoc.doc.ic.ac.uk/foldoc/foldoc.cgi?query=intellectual+property.

[7] Merriam-Webster, "hackers," *Merriam-Webster Online*, accessed February 15, 2004, from http://www.m-w.com.

[8] Robert Richardson, "2003 CSI/FBI Computer Crime and Security Survey," accessed June 15, 2004, from http:\\www.gosci.com.

[9] Sun Tzu, *The Art of War*, trans. Samuel B. Griffith (Oxford: Oxford University Press, 1988), 84.

[10] National Institute of Standards and Technology (NIST), *Risk Management Guide for Information Technology Systems (SP 800-30)*, (Gaithersburg, MD: NIST, January 2002).

[11] Carnegie Mellon University, "Detecting Signs of Intrusion," (2000), accessed February 17, 2005, from http://www.cert.org/security-improvement/modules/m09.html.

[12] Carnegie Mellon University, "Responding to Intrusions," (2000), accessed February 17, 2005, from http://www.cert.org/security-improvement/modules/m06.html.

[13] Charles Cresson Wood, "Integrated Approach Includes Information Security," *Security* 37 (February 2000): 43–44.

[14] National Institute of Standards and Technology (NIST), *An Introduction to Computer Security: The NIST Handbook (SP 800-12),* (Gaithersburg, MD: NIST, 2002).

[15] See note 14 above.

[16] Robert J. Aalberts, Anthony M. Townsend, and Michael E. Whitman, "Considerations for an Effective Telecommunications-Use Policy," *Communications of the ACM* 42 (June 1999): 101–109.

CHAPTER 2

PLANNING FOR ORGANIZATIONAL READINESS

In preparing for battle I have always found that plans are useless, but planning is indispensable.

—Dwight D. Eisenhower

OPENING SCENARIO

It was Friday night. All the employees were long gone for the day except for a select group of senior staff who were crowded around the conference table with binders open and index cards in hand. Paul, who was facilitating the meeting, turned to JJ, who was the acting incident manager for this meeting, and said, "It's your turn."

JJ looked at the next index card in his deck. He read two words that made him grimace: "Power out."

JJ looked to Paul and asked, "How widespread and for how long?"

"Beats me," Paul replied. "That's all I know."

JJ flipped through his now-tattered copy of the disaster recovery plan, finally settling on a page. He looked up and searched for the communications coordinator, Susan Lampe. Susan, a more experienced systems developer, was assigned as the person responsible for all communications during this disaster recovery practice session.

"Okay, Susan." He said. "Please call the power company and ask how widespread the outage is."

Susan, who was reading along on the same page as JJ, looked up. "Okay, I'll let you know as soon as I have an answer. Anything else?"

"Uh, yes. Just a minute." As JJ searched for his next step in the binder, Ed Michaels, the second shift supervisor, read aloud from his binder, "We've got about 45 minutes of battery time, but the generators need to be manually started. I'm going to need power to the servers to keep Web and network operations up."

continued

"Right! " JJ said. He turned to Fred, who represented the building management company that leases space to HAL. "Can you get a team to the generator and get it going?"

Looking up from his binder, Fred responded, "Okay. I'm on it. We already turned on the heaters. It takes 10 to 15 minutes to bring up from a cold start, and in this weather it's a very cold start. We need five to seven more minutes before we can crank the motor, and three to four minutes after that we can generate power."

Everyone at the table laughed. Even though the weather outside was 92 degrees and humid, the disaster scenario they were rehearsing was focused on a massive snowstorm impacting operations.

"How long will the generators run?" JJ asked.

Fred flipped a page in his binder and replied, "Days. If we have to, we can siphon gas from your new truck! With the reserve tank, and supplementing it with gas from employee vehicles, we have plenty of fuel, provided the generator doesn't break down."

"Whew! That's a relief" JJ smiled as he leaned back in his seat. "Okay, what's our next step?" He glanced over at Paul.

Paul said, "Good job everybody. Now, JJ, flip the next card."

Questions for Discussion:

- In the scenario, the group was practicing for a snow emergency. Other than power outages, what other incident cards would you expect to see? For each of the incident cards you listed, what would be the proper response of the organization?
- How often should an organization rehearse its contingency plans? Why is that frequency best for that organization?

LEARNING OBJECTIVES

Upon completion of this material, you should be able to:

- Identify an individual or group to create a contingency policy and plan
- Understand the elements needed to begin the contingency planning process
- Create an effective contingency planning policy
- Become familiar with the business impact analysis and each of the component parts of this important process
- Know the steps needed to create and maintain a budget for enabling the contingency planning process

INTRODUCTION

Planning for contingencies is a complex and demanding process. Like any such undertaking, it is improved by approaching it with a methodology that systematically addresses each challenge an organization might face during an incident, disaster, or other crisis. To develop a **contingency plan (CP)** like the one demonstrated in the opening scenario of this chapter, an organization must seriously consider the lengthy and complex effort it takes to organize the planning process, prepare the detailed and complete plans, commit to maintaining those plans at a high state of readiness at all times, rehearse the use of the plans with a rigor and diligence usually seen only in military organizations, and then maintain the processes necessary to keep a high state of readiness at all times. All this must happen amid the pressures of day-to-day operational demands and the give-and-take of resource allocations common to all organizations. Note that in the opening scenario, the rehearsal occurred after normal working hours; an organization and its employees should expect to make such a commitment to contingency planning. Unfortunately, few organizations can maintain a proper degree of readiness over an extended period of time. This chapter explores some of the preparatory and foundational steps to assure that the contingency planning process gets off to a solid start.

BEGINNING THE CONTINGENCY PLANNING PROCESS

To begin the process of planning for contingencies, an organization must first establish an entity to be responsible for the policy and plans that will eventually emerge from the process. This may be an individual or a team of employees, consultant, or contractors. Prior to any meaningful planning, those assigned must define the scope of the planning project and identify the resources to be used. Many times, a **contingency planning management team (CPMT)** is assembled for that purpose. The CPMT is also responsible for additional functions, including the following:

- Obtaining commitment and support from senior management
- Writing the contingency plan document
- Conducting the business impact analysis (BIA), which includes:
  - Assisting in identifying and prioritizing threats and attacks
  - Assisting in identifying and prioritizing business functions
- Organizing the subordinate teams, such as:
  - Incident response
  - Disaster recovery
  - Business continuity
  - Crisis management

A typical roster for the CPMT may include the following positions:

- A champion: As with any strategic function, the CP project should have a **champion**. This should be a high-level manager with influence and resources that can be used to support the project team, promote the objectives of the CP project, and endorse the results that come from the combined effort. In a CP project, this could be the CIO, or ideally the CEO.

- A project manager: A champion provides the strategic vision and the linkage to the power structure of the organization, but someone has to manage the project. A project manager, possibly a midlevel manager or even the CISO, must lead the project and make sure a sound project planning process is used, a complete and useful project plan is developed, and project resources are prudently managed to reach the goals of the project.
- Team members: The team members for this project should be the managers or their representatives from the various communities of interest: business, information technology, and information security.
- Representatives from other business units: Other areas of the business, such as human resources, public relations, finance, legal, and/or physical plant operations should also be represented. The team may also add representatives, for example:
  - Representative business managers who are familiar with the operations of their respective functional areas should supply details on their activities and provide insight into the criticality of their functions to the overall sustainability of the business.
  - Information technology managers familiar with the systems that could be at risk and with the Incident Response (IR) plans, Disaster Recovery (DR) plans, and Business Continuity (BC) plans that are needed to provide technical content within the planning process.
  - Information security managers to oversee the security planning of the project and provide information on the threats, vulnerabilities, attacks, and recovery requirements needed in the planning process.
- Representatives from subordinate teams: Team leaders from the subordinate teams, including the IR, DR, and BC teams, should also be included in the CPMT. In addition, if the organization has a crisis management (CM) team, it should also be represented. Teams other than the core members of the CPMT have key functions that are components of the overall contingency planning effort. These teams should be distinct entities, yet have one or more representatives on the CPMT—usually the team leaders. These teams are distinct because their individual functions are very different and may be activated at different times, or they may be activated concurrently. The subordinate teams may include the following teams:
  - The incident response team manages and executes the incident response plan by detecting, evaluating, and responding to incidents.
  - The disaster recovery team manages and executes the disaster recovery plan by detecting, evaluating, and responding to disasters, and by reestablishing operations at the primary business site.
  - The business continuity team manages and executes the business continuity plan by setting up and starting off-site operations in the event of an incident or disaster.
  - The crisis management team manages and mitigates the impact of personal loss and distress on the organization by attempting to minimize the loss of life, the quick and accurate accountability of personnel, and the quick and accurate notification of key personnel through alert rosters.

The relationship between the leaders of subordinate teams and the CPMT is shown in Figure 2-1.

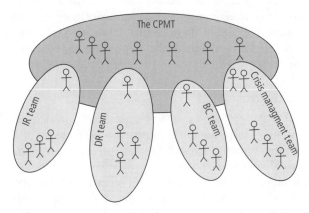

FIGURE 2-1   Teams engaged in contingency planning activities

Among the most critical start-up tasks of the CPMT is aligning support. This is explored in greater detail in the following paragraphs.

Commitment and Support of Senior Management

Just as with any major project or process within an organization, without a clear and formal commitment of senior executive management, the CP process will fail. Only when the executive leadership emphasizes the importance of this process, preferably through personal involvement by the top executive (CEO or president), or by using the leadership of a champion, will subordinate managers and employees provide the necessary time and resources to make the process happen. Support should then be gained from the *communities of interest* already noted in the preceding section.

For our purpose, a community of interest is generally thought of as a group of individuals united by shared interests or values within an organization and who share a common goal of making the organization function to meet its objectives. An organization then develops and maintains its own values, and that leads to the evolution of a unique culture. Within the context of this discussion, there are three identified communities of interest that have roles and responsibilities in information security. The roles that are fulfilled by each community of interest are as follows:

- Managers and practitioners in the field of information security
- Managers and practitioners in the field of information technology
- Managers and professionals from the general management of the organizations

In theory, each role (and the members of the communities of interest fulfilling that role) must complement the other; in practice, this is often not the case.

Information Security Management and Professionals

These job functions and organizational roles focus on protecting the organization's information systems and stored information from attacks. In fulfilling this role, these individuals are often tightly focused on protecting the integrity and confidentiality of systems, and sometimes lose sight of the equally important objective of availability. It is important for this community to remember that ultimately all the members of the organization are focused on meeting their strategic and operational objectives.

Information Technology Management and Professionals

Others in the organization are oriented to deliver value to the organization by designing, building, or operating information systems. This community of interest is made up of IT managers and various groups of skilled professionals in systems design, programming, networks, and other related disciplines usually categorized as IT, or information technology. This community has many of the same objectives as the information security community. They focus, however, more on costs of system creation and operation, ease of use for system users, and timeliness of system creation, as well as transaction response time. The goals of the IT community and the information security community do not always completely align, and depending on the organizational structure, this may cause conflict.

Organizational Management and Professionals

The organization's general management team and the rest of the resources in the organization make up the other major community of interest. This large group is almost always made up of other subsets of interest as well, including executive management, production management, human resources, accounting, and legal, to name a few. The IT community often categorizes these groups as users of information technology systems, while the information security community categorizes them as security subjects. The reality is that they are much more than this categorization implies. It is important for you to focus on the fact that all IT systems and information security objectives are created to implement the objectives of the broader organizational community and safeguard their effective use and operation. The most efficient IT systems operated in the most secure fashion ever devised are of no worth if they do not bring value to the broad objectives of the organization as a whole.

ELEMENTS TO BEGIN CONTINGENCY PLANNING

The elements required to begin the CP process are a planning methodology; a policy environment to enable the planning process; an understanding of the cause and effects of core precursor activities, known as the business impact analysis; and access to financial and other resources, as articulated and outlined by the planning budget. Each of these is explained in the sections that follow. Once formed, the CPMT begins the development of a CP document.

"The [CP] document expands the four elements noted earlier into a 7-step contingency process that an organization may apply to develop and maintain a viable contingency planning program for their IT systems. The CP document serves as the focus and collection point for the deliverables that come from the subsequent steps. These seven progressive steps are designed to be integrated into each stage of the system development life cycle:

1. Develop the contingency planning policy statement: A formal department or agency policy provides the authority and guidance necessary to develop an effective contingency plan.
2. Conduct the BIA: The BIA helps to identify and prioritize critical IT systems and components. A template for developing the BIA is also provided to assist the user.
3. Identify preventive controls: Measures taken to reduce the effects of system disruptions can increase system availability and reduce contingency life cycle costs.
4. Develop recovery strategies: Thorough recovery strategies ensure that the system may be recovered quickly and effectively following a disruption.
5. Develop an IT contingency plan: The contingency plan should contain detailed guidance and procedures for restoring a damaged system.
6. Plan testing, training, and exercises: Testing the plan identifies planning gaps, whereas training prepares recovery personnel for plan activation; both activities improve plan effectiveness and overall agency preparedness.
7. Plan maintenance: The plan should be a living document that is updated regularly to remain current with system enhancements."[1]

The discussion of the contingency planning policy and the business impact analysis occupies the balance of this chapter. The other five steps are referred to throughout the remainder of the book.

CONTINGENCY PLANNING POLICY

Effective contingency planning begins with effective policy. Before the CPMT can fully develop the planning document, the team must first receive guidance from the executive management, as described earlier, through formal contingency planning policy. The reason for policy is to define the scope of the CP operations and establish managerial intent with regard to timetables for response to incidents, recovery from disasters, and reestablishment of operations for continuity. This policy also establishes responsibility for the development and operations of the CPMT in general, and may also provide specifics on the constituencies of all CP-related teams.

Some managers recommend that the CP policy should, at a minimum, contain the following sections:[2]

- An introductory statement of philosophical perspective by senior management as to the importance of contingency planning to the strategic, long-term operations of the organization

- A statement of the scope and purpose of the CP operations, specifically stating the requirement to cover all critical business functions and activities
- A call for periodic (for example, yearly) risk assessment and business impact analysis by the CPMT, to include identification and prioritization of critical business functions (While this is intuitive to the CPMT, the formal inclusion in policy reinforces the need for such studies to the remainder of the organization.)
- A specification of the major components of the CP to be designed by the CPMT, as described earlier
- A call for, and guidance in, the selection of recovery options and business continuity strategies
- A requirement to test the various plans on a regular basis (for example, semi-annually, annually, or more often as needed)
- Identification of key regulations and standards that impact CP planning, and a brief overview of their relevancy
- Identification of key individuals responsible for CP operations, for example, establishment of the COO as CPMT lead, CISO as IR team lead, manager of business operations as DR team lead, manager of marketing and services as BC team lead, and legal council as crisis management team lead
- A challenge to the individual members of the organization, asking for their support, and reinforcing their importance as part of the overall CP process
- Additional administrative information, including the date of the document's original authoring, revisions, and a schedule for periodic review and maintenance

A high-level policy, as just described, is presented in the following example:

A Sample Generic Policy and High-Level Procedures for Contingency Plans[3]

Issue Statement

XX Agency Automated Information Systems Security Program (AISSP) Hand book, the Office of Management and Budget Circular A-130, Management of Federal Information Resources, Appendix III, Security of Federal Automated Information Resources requires a contingency plan be developed and tested for each major Automated Information System (AIS) facility and application. All systems that contain, use, or process Large Service Applications (LSA) data must have a documented plan on how the organization would continue its mission and provide continuity of data processing if service, use, or access were disrupted for an extended period of time.

Organization's Position

XX Agency has been entrusted with sensitive, private data to accomplish its goals. For the success of XX Agency programs, LSA data must be available in the event of disruptions. A contingency plan includes preparatory measures, response actions, and restoration activities planned or taken to ensure continuation of the mission-critical functions.

Applicability

These procedures apply to data contained in the LSA system.

Roles and Responsibility

Director, Federal Systems shall
publish and maintain policy guidelines for preparing and testing the LSA contingency plan, and assist in identifying the mission-critical applications.

Information Systems Security Officer (ISSO) shall
prepare policy guidelines for developing the LSA contingency plan, review the contingency plan, and ensure the LSA contingency plan is updated and tested annually.

Supervisors shall
assist in the development, review, and testing of the LSA contingency plan, determine which applications can revert to manual processing, determine which applications are mission critical and need priority automated processing, and provide the personnel needed for scheduled testing of the procedures.

LSA Security Officer shall
work with security personnel to develop the LSA contingency plan, and coordinate LSA contingency plan development, updating, and testing with XX Agency personnel.

Contingency Plan Policy

- A contingency planning committee composed of the LSA Security Officer and XX Organization personnel will develop, test, and maintain the LSA Contingency Plan. The plan should contain the following:
    - All mission-critical applications shall be identified and ranked according to priority and the maximum permissible outage for each critical application.
    - An inventory of all equipment and supplies and floor plan of the current operating facility shall be maintained.
    - Specify how frequently applications, data, software, and databases are backed up and where the backups are stored off site.
    - List the location of the alternate backup site.
    - Prepare alternate site operating procedures.
    - List the arrangement for delivery of backup data and software.
    - Identify the personnel designated to run the applications at the backup site; travel arrangements, lodging, and per diem should be addressed if the backup site is not local.
- Prepare recovery procedures.
- Prepare testing procedures for the contingency plan.
- Contingency plan shall be marked, handled, and controlled as sensitive unclassified information.
- Each page of the plan shall be dated.
- The plan shall be tested annually or when a significant change occurs to the application.

Compliance

The requirement for each facility that processes applications critical to the performance of the organizational mission is contained in the XX Agency AISSP Handbook, and in the Office of Management and Budget Circular A-130, Management of Federal Information Resources, Appendix III, Security of Federal Automated Information Resources.

Supplementary Information

XX Agency AISSP Handbook, May 1994
NIST Special Publication 800-12, *An Introduction to Computer Security: The NIST Handbook*, Chapter 11, "Preparing for Contingencies and Disasters." January 1999.

Points of Contact

Information Systems Security Officer   LSA Security Officer – XX Agency Site

(This document was written for a large application. It can be modified to serve as a chapter in an organization's information security manual by replacing any reference to one application with the words "all systems.")

Once the CPMT has the policy from the responsible senior executive, the CPMT lead calls a meeting to begin the planning process in earnest. Each CP meeting should be documented to provide guidance for future meetings, and to track progress and deliverables set by the committee. The next major step is to conduct a business impact analysis.

BUSINESS IMPACT ANALYSIS

The **business impact analysis (BIA)** is an investigation and assessment of the impact that various attacks can have on the organization. The BIA is a crucial component of the initial planning stages, because it provides detailed scenarios of the effects that each potential attack could have on the organization.

The BIA therefore adds insight into what the organization must do to respond to an attack, minimize the damage from the attack, recover from the effects, and return to normal operations. One of the fundamental differences between a BIA and the risk management processes discussed in Chapter 1 is that the risk management approach identifies the threats, vulnerabilities, and attacks to determine what controls can protect the information. The BIA assumes that these controls have been bypassed, have failed, or are otherwise ineffective in stopping the attack, and that the attack is successful. BIA takes up where the risk assessment process leaves off. It begins with the prioritized list of threats and vulnerabilities identified in the risk management process from Chapter 1, and enhances the list by adding some critical information. At this point, the question asked is: if the attack succeeds, what do you do then? Obviously, the organization's security team does everything in its power to stop these attacks, but as you have seen, some attacks, such as natural disasters, deviations from service providers, acts of human failure or error, and deliberate acts of sabotage and vandalism, may be unstoppable.

When undertaking the BIA, Zawada and Evans recommend the following five keys to BIA success:

1. "Scope the BIA appropriately, and take into account all categories of risk to the organization, as well as all categories of impact.
2. Develop a data-gathering plan that addresses the analytic needs of executive management. Collecting the right information is critical.
3. Use objective data to draw conclusions whenever possible, but recognize that subjective data from knowledgeable and experienced personnel can be equally important.
4. Seek executive management's requirements in advance of the study, and deliver the risk assessment and BIA results in a manner that meets those requirements.
5. Obtain validation from business process owners and executives to ensure committment."[4]

The CPMT conducts the BIA in five stages, as shown in Figure 2-2, and described in the sections that follow:

1. Threat attack identification and prioritization
2. Business unit analysis
3. Attack success scenario development
4. Potential damage assessment
5. Subordinate plan classification

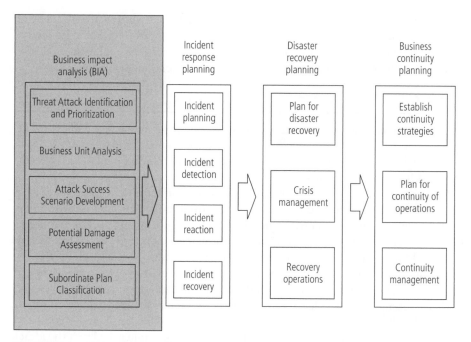

FIGURE 2-2 Major stages of CP: BIA

Note that large quantities of information are generated during the BIA data collection process. This data must be collected and organized so that meaningful and useful information is available for use in the overall CP development process. A discussion of data collection considerations is included later in this chapter after each of the five BIA investigation stages have been discussed.

Threat or Attack Identification and Prioritization

An organization that has followed the risk management process described in Chapter 1 will have already identified and prioritized threats facing it. In the business impact assessment, the lists of threats may be overly general, and as a result the organization may want to convert their list of threats to a list of attacks. Note that the examples listed here are predominantly threats related to information security. The focus of the CPMT in developing the BIA should also include non-information security threats such as work stoppages, serious illnesses (pandemics), and other critical threats.

List of Attacks

Again examining the Sun Tzu quote "Know your enemy," you begin by converting the list of threats from Chapter 1 to a list of attacks that can be used to create attack profiles.

This process begins by looking at each category of threats, and, based on additional information from available sources including trade press, professional experiences, targeted Web resources and academic reports, it is possible to generate a list of likely attacks within each category of threat. For example, in the category of deliberate software attacks it is possible to come up with attacks such as:

- E-mail viruses and worms
- E-mail-based social engineering
- Web-based malicious scripts
- Denial-of-service attacks on servers
- Spyware and malicious adware

The list of specific attacks is usually quite large, and thus some degree of categorization and perhaps summarization is often necessary.

It is possible that these categories may overlap multiple attacks, and vice versa. For example, a hacker who accesses an e-mail server, steals a number of credit card numbers, and then tries to blackmail the organization, may require multiple entries for attacks. The first attack was the exploitation of the network or server to gain access as a deliberate act of espionage or trespass. The hacker then conducted a deliberate act of theft by stealing the credit card numbers, and finally the hacker committed a deliberate act of information extortion when the blackmail attempt was made. Each of these components requires a separate entry in the list of attacks, because each one has different attack scenarios, as described in the next section.

Table 2-1 reviews some example attacks corresponding to specific threats from within the categories presented earlier.

TABLE 2-1 Threats and corresponding attacks

Threat	Attacks
Act of human error or failure	Accidental deletion of user desktop data or files by member of organization (accidental user data deletion)
	Accidental deletion of server data or files by member of organization (accidental server data deletion)
	Accidental release of critical information by member of organization, including due to social engineering efforts (accidental leak)
	Accidental error or failure to follow procedure in creating software or hardware vulnerabilities
	Accidental modification or deletion of data due to failure to follow policies or procedures
	Installation of unauthorized software
	Improper configuration of software or hardware
Compromises to intellectual property	Unauthorized installation of software in violation of its licensing (piracy)
	Release of organizational information performed outside the bounds of policy, sometimes classified as a "leak"
	Violation of fair use of copyrighted material (plagiarism)

TABLE 2-1 Threats and corresponding attacks (continued)

Threat	Attacks
Deliberate acts of trespass	Unauthorized logical access to organizational information or systems (hacker probe) Unauthorized physical access to organizational facilities (trespasser)
Deliberate acts of information extortion	Blackmail of organization for information assets (electronic extortionist)
Deliberate acts of sabotage or vandalism	Intentional and unauthorized modification or destruction of organizational information assets (electronic vandal) Physical damage or destruction of organizational assets (physical vandal)
Deliberate acts of theft	Illegal "taking" of organizational assets
Deliberate software attacks	E-mail viruses and worms, other viruses and worms E-mail-based social engineering (phishing) Web-based malicious script Denial-of-service attacks on organizational information assets Distributed denial-of-service attacks on organizational information assets
Forces of nature	Fire Flood Earthquake Lightning Landslide or mudslide Tornado or severe windstorm Hurricane or typhoon Tsunami Electrostatic discharge (ESD) Dust contamination Solar flare Electromagnetic radiation Humidity
Quality of service deviations from service providers	Network connection outage due to cable severance (phone or ISP) Network connection outage due to service faults (phone or ISP) Power blackout Power brownout Power surge Power spike Power fault Power sag Other issues (for example, water, sewage, garbage, and other utilities)
Technical hardware failures or errors	Equipment failure due to manufacturer or designer faults or defects (for example, HD crash)
Technical software failures or errors	Software failure due to manufacturer or designer faults or defects (for example, bugs or code problems) Unknown software access bypasses (loopholes and trapdoors)

TABLE 2-1 Threats and corresponding attacks (continued)

Threat	Attacks
Technological obsolescence	Use of antiquated or outdated technologies Failure to maintain or update antiquated or outdated equipment-based data storage

Threat or Attack Prioritization

Just as is performed in risk identification with threats, the attacks facing the organization must be prioritized based on criteria selected by the CP committee. Again, the use of a weighted analysis table is helpful in compiling this information. Input from the IT Department and the CISO office are crucial in crafting the categories and weights for traditional electronic attacks, but input from other agencies like finance and insurance companies may be needed to accurately calculate probabilities and damages from traditional forces of nature. Insurance companies in particular have extensive experience in determining the probability and likely damage from tornados, floods, earthquakes, and so on as the basis for insurance premiums.

Note that in this assessment and prioritization, organizations frequently use a scale to place values both for weights and for attack values. This provides a common, relative comparison between items, and prevents over-focusing on financial values. Some of the weights to consider in creating the weighted analysis that an organization might select include the following:

- Probability of occurrence: Obviously, attacks with a remote chance of occurrence receive less attention than those that occur frequently. Depending on the region in which the organization is located, lightening strikes may be much more frequent than earthquakes. Attacks such as hacker probes (unauthorized logical access to organizational information or systems) may similarly occur much more frequently than physical thefts (unauthorized logical access to organizational information or systems).
- Probability of success: Even if an attack occurs frequently, if it has a very low probability of success, then it will be taken less seriously than those with a high probability of success. The organization's level of preparedness directly influences the probability of a successful attack. An attack by a hacker on a Web server in an effort to steal credit card information may be highly unsuccessful if the organization has proxied the real Web server database from an intranet on the inside of a firewall.
- Extent of damage: If successful, how damaging to the organization would the attack be? This category has subcategories that may require consideration. *Damage* can be a relative term, depending on whether you look exclusively at financial damage, physical damage, damage to the organization's image, damage to the organization's market share, and so on. As a result, the organization may have to use this category as a basis for multiple entries into the weighted table.

- Cost to restore: Related to the previous category is the cost to the organization to restore to normal operations after an attack. This category provides a peek into the final attack scenario end case, in which the organization has to determine the total costs of a best-case, worst-case, and most-likely case attack. In this analysis, the tables use a ranking, rather than real numbers, to assess the costs in terms of finances, time, and the human resources needed to restore business operations. Some organizations may choose to separate time resources from financial resources, because they may have the budget to restore operations quickly, but the acquisition of replacement technologies or facilities may require an extensive amount of time.
- Impact of success on public image: Even though costs to restore might be low for a credit card theft, for example, the impact on the public image might be devastating, especially if it is not handled well.

Table 2-2 provides a sample, weighted analysis showing a few of these categories used to assess a select group of attacks. In this example, the organization determined that four criteria were of significance to this evaluation. Prior to the evaluation of each attack, the relative weights for the four criteria were established such that they add up to a value of 1.0. Each attack should then be evaluated for each of the four criteria using a relative response of 1–10. For example, software piracy is evaluated as being 8 out of 10 for probability of occurrence, 7 out of 10 for probability of success, 4 out of 10 for extent of damage, and so on. As is evident in this example, the attacks of accidental deletion of user desktop data, and the theft of customer information rate high as attacks, but data loss due to electrical failure and accidental server data loss rank low (most likely due to existing controls like conditioned power with Uninterruptable Power Supplies (UPS) and Redundant Arrays of Independent Disks (RAID) server arrays with redundant tape backups).

TABLE 2-2 Weighted analysis table of attacks

CRITERIA					
Attacks	Probability of Occurrence	Probability of Success	Extent of Damage	Cost to Restore	Total
(Criterion weight)	0.2	0.3	0.2	0.3	1
Software piracy	8	7	4	3	5.4
Accidental user data deletion	8	6	8	4	6.2
Accidental server data deletion	6	4	4	3	4.1
Data loss due to electrical failure	5	3	3	3	3.4
Data loss due to lightning strike	1	4	6	8	5
Web defacement (electronic vandalism)	8	1	2	1	2.6

TABLE 2-2 Weighted analysis table of attacks (continued)

	CRITERIA				
Attacks	Probability of Occurrence	Probability of Success	Extent of Damage	Cost to Restore	Total
Hacker probe	9	3	4	3	4.4
Theft of customer information	9	2	9	7	6.3

Business Unit Analysis

The second major BIA task is the analysis and prioritization of business functions within the organization. Each business department, unit, or division must be independently evaluated to determine how important its functions are to the organization as a whole. For example, recovery operations would probably focus on the IT Department and network operation before turning to the Personnel Department's hiring activities. Likewise, recovering a manufacturing company's assembly line is more urgent than recovering its maintenance tracking system. This is not to say that personnel functions and assembly line maintenance are not important to the business, but unless the organization's main revenue-producing operations can be restored quickly, other functions are irrelevant.

It is important to collect critical information about each business unit before beginning the process of prioritizing the business units (see the BIA Data Collection section later in the chapter). The important thing to remember is that the focus of this stage is to avoid "turf wars" and instead focus on the selection of those business functions that must be sustained to continue business operations. While one manager or executive might feel that their function is the most crucial to the organization, that particular function might prove to be less critical in the event of a major incident or disaster.

A weighted analysis table can be useful in resolving the issue of what business function is the most critical. The CPMT can use this tool by first identifying the categories that matter most to the organization. Using the example based on the case organization Hierarchical Access Ltd, typical external functions could include:

- Enroll new customers
- Manage customer accounts
- Provide Internet access
- Provide Internet services
- Provide help desk support
- Advertise services
- Support public relations

The team should then assign weights to each of these categories. Typically, weights are assigned that total up to a value of 1. Each criterion is assessed on its influence toward overall importance in the decision-making process—representing a 100 percent contribution to the solution. In the example shown in Table 2-3, the Impact on Profitability criterion is assessed as being 40% of the importance value to the organization, while each other criteria is assessed a percentage based on its importance. All of the criteria added together equal 100% of the importance. Once the categories to be used as criteria have been identified and weighted, the various business functions are listed. For each business function, an importance value is assessed using a scale of 1 to 10 for each of the criteria identified. Once this activity has been accomplished, the weights can be multiplied against the scores in each category and then summed to obtain the overall value of the function to the organization. In the example shown in Table 2-3, the business function Provide Internet access is determined to have a 10 out of 10 impact on profitability, while it has a 4 out of 10 impact on internal operations. Overall, that function is calculated as having a numerical score of 8.2. While the number 8.2 as an absolute does not mean anything specific, because it is the highest total weight calculated for any business function, this can be said to be the most important business function to the organization, based on the assumptions and evaluations made in this weighted factor analysis.

TABLE 2-3 Function-weighted prioritization

Business Functions	Impact on Profitability	Contribution to Strategic Objectives	Impact on Internal Operations	Impact on Public Image	Calculated Weight
	.4	.3	.2	.1	
Enroll new customers	8	8	3	6	6.8
Manage customer accounts	8	7	6	7	7.2
Provide Internet access	10	8	4	8	8
Provide Internet services	9	10	4	8	8.2
Provide help desk support	5	6	6	8	5.8
Advertise services	6	9	4	9	6.8
Support public relations	4	6	2	10	4.8

(*Note*: This is a partial table of functions and as such is only presented as an example.)

In this example, the core business functions have been confirmed as the most important to the organization, and will eventually result in being identified as those that must be reconstituted first and fastest. One useful tool in identifying and collecting information about the functions is the BIA questionnaire, discussed later in this chapter. The BIA questionnaire can be used to allow functional managers to directly enter information about their functions, the impacts the functions have on the business and other functions, and the dependencies that exist for the function from specific resources and outside service providers.

Attack Success Scenario Development

After the threat attack profiles have been developed and the business functions prioritized, the BIA team must create a series of scenarios depicting the effects of an occurrence of each threat on each prioritized functional area. This step can be a long and detailed process, because such occurrences may have implications for many functions. **Attack scenarios** or **attack profiles** should include scenarios depicting a typical attack, including its methodology, indicators of an attack, and broad consequences. After the attack profiles are completed, the business function details can be integrated with the attack profiles. Two examples of attack scenarios are presented here. The two examples are described using different methods of organizing the pertinent information.

Example of A Malicious Code Attack Scenario

Date of analysis:	June 23, 2009
Attack name/description:	Malicious code via e-mail
Threat/probable threat agents:	• Vandalism/script kiddies • Theft/experienced hacker
Known or possible vulnerabilities:	• Emergent weaknesses in e-mail clients • Inappropriate actions by employees, contractors, and visitors using e-mail clients • Emergent weakness in e-mail servers or gateways
Likely precursor activities or indicators:	Announcements from vendors and bulletins
Likely attack activities or indicators of attack in progress:	• E-mail volume measurements may show variances • Unusual system failures among clients • Unusual system failures among servers • Notification from e-mail recipients who may be ahead of us in attack life cycle
Information assets at risk from this attack:	All connected systems due to blended attack model now prevalent
Damage or loss to information assets likely from this attack:	• Denial of service for some clients almost certain • Denial of service for servers possible • Possible losses of data depending on nature of attack
Other assets at risk from this attack:	None likely
Damage or loss to other assets likely from this attack:	None likely
Immediate actions indicated when this attack is under way:	• *Disconnect e-mail gateway(s)* • *Update e-mail gateway-filtering patterns and apply* • *Update and distribute client-filtering patterns* • *Isolate all infected servers* • *Isolate all infected clients* • *Begin server recovery actions for infected servers* • *Begin client recovery actions for infected clients*
Follow-up actions after this attack was successfully executed:	*Review pattern update timing and procedure to assure adequacy*
Comments:	*None at this time*

DNS Attack Scenario (February 1996) [5]

Scenario

The victim has two machines, stooge.victim.org (IP address 10.10.10.1) and target.victim.org (IP address 10.10.10.2). The attacker has a machine www.attacker.org (IP address 172.16.16.16).

The victim has a firewall that prevents machines outside the victim's organization from making unauthorized network connections to any of the victim's machines. This prevents the attacker from launching a direct attack on the victim's machines. The victim's security depends on the firewall.

What the attacker does

The attacker creates a bogus machine name "bogus.attacker.org" and creates a DNS mapping from bogus.attacker.org to the pair of IP addresses (10.10.10.2, 172.16.16.16).

The attacker also writes an innocent-looking Java applet and attaches it to a Web page installed on www.attacker.org.

Triggering the attack

The victim, running his Web browser on stooge.victim.org, innocently visits a Web page on www.attacker.org. This causes the attacker's applet to be loaded into the victim's browser and to start running.

The applet performs some innocent function that is visible to the victim. It also silently attacks the victim's computer.

First, the applet asks to create a network connection to bogus.attacker.org. The Java system looks up the address "bogus.attacker.org," getting the IP address pair (10.10.10.2, 172.16.16.16). The Java system compares this address pair to the address of the machine that the applet came from (172.16.16.16). Since the two have the address 172.16.16.16 in common, Java allows the connection. However, the Java system actually connects to the first address on the list, namely 10.10.10.2 (target.victim.org).

The attacker's applet now has a network connection to target.victim.org. It can proceed to attack the defenses of target.victim.org, using any one of several common network security weaknesses.

A more sophisticated version of the attack allows the attacker's applet to systematically attack all of the machines in the victim's organization. The attacking applet can tell the attacker's DNS server which IP addresses to return, by encoding the IP addresses into the DNS name that is looked up. For example, the applet could look up boguss-10.10.10.2—172.16.16.16attacker.org if it wanted the DNS server to return the address pair given above.

Why the attack works

The key to the success of the attack is that the victim's firewall is helpless to prevent it. The firewall is supposed to protect the victim by preventing machines outside the firewall from opening arbitrary network connections to the victim's machines inside the firewall. In this attack, however, the dangerous network connections come from one of the victim's own machines, so the firewall is useless.

In effect, the attacker causes the victim's Web browser to attack the victim's own machines.

Using SATAN

Since the attacking applet can make network connections back to attacker.org, the applet can operate under the direction of a "real attacker" that is running back in attacker.org. For instance, a variant of the notorious security-probing program Satan could be used to direct the attack.

Third-party attacks

If the attacker can compromise a machine at third-party.org, it can still carry out the attack on victim.org. The attacker plants his applet on a Web server on www.third-party.org. When the victim loads a Web page from www.third-party.org, the attacking applet is loaded into the victim's machine. The applet can still use the DNS server at attacker.org to fool Java into allowing arbitrary connections. As above, the applet can connect to any desired machine on the Internet, so it can attack the victim's machines, and it can operate under the direction of a program or person somewhere in attacker.org.

A Web virus

The third-party version of the attack can be used to create a virus. The virus would be attached to an innocent-looking Web applet. When the applet was run by some person, the applet would attack machines in that person's organization. If it penetrated one of those machines, it would append the attacking code to any Web pages it found on the penetrated machines. The virus could spread from Web-server to Web-server in this manner.

Note: All of the machine names and IP addresses used in the example are fictitious. As far as we can tell, there are no real machines with these addresses connected to the Internet.

Potential Damage Assessment

From the detailed scenarios generated in the process just completed, the BIA planning team must estimate the cost of the best, worst, and most likely outcomes by preparing an **attack scenario end case**. This allows the organization to identify what must be done to recover from each possible case. At this time, the team does not attempt to determine how much to spend on the protection of business units—this issue is analyzed during risk management. The costs determined at that time include the actions of the response team members (described in the following sections) as they act to quickly and effectively recover from any incident or disaster. These cost estimates can persuade management representatives throughout an organization of the importance of planning and recovery efforts. Some of the base information used to complete the attack scenario end cases comes from the attack profiles described earlier. Here the attack profile to create potential damage assessments has been used. When added to the attack scenarios, a complete picture of the realistic threat caused by the attacks is possible.

The example that follows shows the type of additional information that can be added to one of the previous attack scenarios to compose an attack scenario end case. Note in each scenario, that while simplistic, a wealth of information is provided that can be used during the evaluation of future incidents to support the determination of the seriousness of any ongoing attack.

Malicious Code Attack Scenario Addendum

Date of analysis:	*June 23, 2009*
Attack name/description:	*Malicious code via e-mail*
Comments:	*None at this time*

Best case scenario for this attack:

As a best case scenario for this attack, the end user receiving the malicious code via e-mail recognizes the attack based on the training and awareness information provided quarterly. Virtually all e-mail-based attacks are via attached file. The current e-mail client allows the user to view the attachment name, without opening the file. Users trained to recognize unauthorized file attachements (.pif, .scr, .com, .exe, etc.) immediately delete the file and empty it from their e-mail trash folder.

Scenario risk: Moderate; only through continued training and awareness programs can we ensure the best case scenario prevails.

Scenario cost to organization: Very low; the only real cost is the time and effort employees must dedicate to filtering their e-mail. It is estimated however, that somewhere between 40—50 hours organization-wide are wasted processing e-mail with potentially malicious content.

Scenario probability of attack continuing and spreading: Very low

Worst case scenario for this attack:

As a worst case scenario for this attack, the end user receiving the malicious code via e-mail has disabled their antivirus and antispyware software (or disabled the automatic signature updates), and then opened an e-mail attachment containing malicious code. The code could then potentially subjugate the end user s e-mail address book and copy itself to other employees or to individuals and organizations outside the company, potentially opening the organization up to litigation for failure to protect its own systems. In addition, the local user could lose all local data and work effort. In the worst case, the user has not backed up local data for an extensive amount of time and loses key organizational files, which must either be reconstituted or replaced with new effort.

Scenario risk: Moderate; only through continued training, awareness programs, and enforcement of local user file backups can we ensure that this scenario does not occur.

Scenario cost to organization: Moderate; while the overall organization can be protected through the methods described in the other scenarios, there is a loss of local user data and work effort if this scenario prevails. The affected user is forced to restore key files, as described. Potential cost to the organization could be severe if those files were critical to organizational planning and operations. However, with the implementation of the centralized key file repository, which has daily backups, the organization can minimize the effects of this activity. Real costs to the organization could be in the thousands of dollars in lost man-hours, and potentially lost customer revenue, if customer service or public image suffers because of the lack of information or exposure.

Scenario probability of attack continuing and spreading: Low

Most likely case scenario for this attack:

As a most likely case scenario for this attack, the end user receiving the malicious code via e-mail may inadvertently open the attachment under the impression that it is an important file and potentially release the attached malicious code. With the current level of antivirus and antispyware software installed, there is a high probability that the protection software will activate, contain, and quarantine the malicious code before any real damage occurs.

Scenario risk: Moderate; only through continued maintenance and update of antivirus and antispyware programs can we ensure the most likely case scenario prevails.

Scenario cost to organization: Low. The only real cost is the time and effort employees must dedicate to ensuring their antivirus and antispyware software signatures are up to date. With the current managed signatures program, this is handled automatically, as are scheduled scans of 100 desktop systems each night. The challenge arises in educating employees not to abort these scans by shutting down their systems at night, as the scans will then be diverted to morning activation, rather than the 2 a.m. scans currently scheduled.

Scenario probability of attack continuing and spreading: Very low

Subordinate Plan Classification

After the potential damage has been assessed, and each scenario and attack scenario end case has been evaluated, a subordinate plan to deal with the aftermath of the attack must be developed or identified from among existing plans already in place. Some of these related plans may already be part of standard operating procedures, such as file recovery from backup. Other plans may be in place as part of an existing or prior disaster recovery planning (DRP) project or business continuity planning (BCP) project. Most attacks are not disastrous and fall into the category of incident response. Therefore, the BIA team likely has a number of new subordinate plans that are meant to be exclusively used at the incident level. Those scenarios that do qualify as disastrous are likely addressed in the DR plan or BC plan.

Each attack scenario end case is categorized as disastrous or not. The difference between the two classifications reflects whether the organization is able to take effective action during the event to combat the attack's effects. Attack end cases that are disastrous find members of the organization waiting out the attack and planning to recover from it after the attack ends. In a typical disaster recovery operation, the lives and welfare of the employee are the highest priority, as most disasters involve fires, floods, hurricanes, tornadoes, and the like.

For each end case, an addendum can be used to finalize this phase of the BIA. The example that follows provides an overview of the subordinate plan classification component of the end case.

Subordinate Plan Classification Addendum to End Case

Date of analysis:	*June 23, 2009*
Attack name/description:	*Malicious code via e-mail*
Threat/probable threat agents:	• *Vandalism/script kiddies* • *Theft/experienced hacker*
Known or possible vulnerabilities:	• *Emergent weaknesses in e-mail clients* • *Inappropriate actions by employees, contractors, and visitors using e-mail clients* • *Emergent weakness in e-mail servers or gateways*

Subordinate plan classification
This end case is relegated to the incident response planning committee for use in developing incident response capabilities for this type of attack. Once these response capabilities are developed, they, along with this document, are forwarded to the disaster recovery planning committee for use in developing sequential plans should the attack go unchecked during the initial incident response and a disastrous condition arises. At both the IR and DR levels, specific remedial actions are specified, including a review of current AV/AS software and implementation, user training and awareness programs, and end user data backup and restoration strategies.

BIA DATA COLLECTION

While the BIA data collection process is not a discrete step in the BIA process, it should have been used along the way to document the efforts accomplished in earlier steps. To effectively perform the BIA, a large quantity of information specific to various business areas and functions is needed. There are a number of methods for collecting this information.

Thus, a data collection plan should be established early on to make the overall process more effective. Some methods to collect this information include the following[6]:

- Online questionnaires
- Facilitated data-gathering sessions
- Process flows and interdependency studies
- Risk assessment research
- IT application or system logs
- Financial reports and departmental budgets
- BCP/DRP audit documentation
- Production schedules

Online Questionnaires

An online BIA questionnaire can provide a structured method to collect the information directly from those who know the most about the business areas and its functions. Using an online questionnaire on the organizational intranet can facilitate data collection and analysis. As an aid in collecting the information necessary to identify and classify the business functions and the impact they have on other areas of the organization, a BIA questionnaire can collect and provide useful information to answer these and other critical questions.

In general, the BIA questionnaire should contain questions about the following areas, as they apply to a business:

- "Function description: A brief description of the function being performed
- Dependencies: A brief description of the dependencies of the function. What has to happen or needs to be available before the function can be performed?
- Impact profile: Is there a specific time of day, day of the week, week of the month, or month of the year that the function is more vulnerable to risk/exposure or when the impact to the business would be greater if the function is not performed?
- Operational impacts: When would the operational impact to the business be realized if the function were not performed? Describe the operational impact.
- Financial impacts: When would the financial impact to the business be realized if the function were not performed? Describe the financial impact.
- Work backlog: At what point does the backlog of work start to impact the business?
- Recovery resources: What kind of resources are needed to support the function, how many are needed, and how soon are they needed after a disruption (for example, phones, desks, and PCs)?
- Technology resources: What software and/or applications are needed to support the function?
- Stand-alone PCs or workstations: Does the function require a stand-alone PC or workstation?
- Local area networks: Does the function require access to the LAN?
- Work-around procedures: Are there currently in place manual work-around

procedures that enable the function to be performed in the event that IT is unavailable? If so, how long can these work-arounds be used to continue the function?

- Work at home: Can the function be performed from home?
- Workload shifting: Is it possible to shift workloads to another part of the business that might not be impacted by the disruption?
- Business records: Are certain business records needed to perform the function? If so, are they backed up? How? With what frequency?
- Regulatory reporting: Are regulatory documents created as a result of the function?
- Work inflows: What input is received, either internally or externally, that is needed to perform the function?
- Work outflows: Where does the output go after it leaves the functional area, or, who would be impacted if the function were not performed?
- Business disruption experience: Has there ever been a disruption of the function? If so, give a brief description.
- Competitive analysis: Is there a competitive impact if the function is not performed? When would the impact occur? When would the company potentially start losing customers?
- Other issues and concerns: Are there any other issues relevant to the success of performing the function?"[7]

Other key issues that should be identified in the completion of the BIA include:

- **Recovery point objective (RPO):** "The point in time by which systems and data must be recovered after an outage as determined by the business unit"[8] or in other words, 'how much data can I afford to lose'.
- **Recovery time objective (RTO):** "The period of time within which systems, applications, or functions must be recovered after an outage (for example, one business day). RTOs are often used as the basis for the development of recovery strategies and as a determinant as to whether or not to implement the recovery strategies during a disaster situation. A similar term is *maximum allowable downtime*."[9] This might also be considered as 'how fast can I recover'.
- Dependencies between this function and other areas

The following BIA questionnaire, which is derived from a number of sources,[10] is organized into two major parts (Tables 2-4 and 2-5). Part I (Table 2-4) is designed to evaluate the entire business area and identify the critical functions contained within that area. Part II (Table 2-5) is designed to evaluate each specific function for impact, dependencies, and other critical information necessary for the BIA process, and eventually the CP plan.

TABLE 2-4   Business impact questionnaire, Part I

Part I: Business Area Impact **This questionnaire must be filled out for each business area within ABC Co.** **(Note: Excess form blanks compressed to save space)**

Function:

Business area:

Departments contained within this area:

Area manager:

Overall functional priority: (to be added
by CPMT)

Date of BIA questionnaire:

Questionnaire completed by:

Area Description (Describe the corporate mission of this area):

What functions are conducted within this area?

What changes have occurred within this area since the last BIA review?

What changes are expected within this area before the next BIA review?

Impact Assessment:

Select the statement that best describes the effect on this business area should there be an
unplanned interruption of normal operations:
ABC Co. will feel an impact within:

[ ]   8 hours of an interruption
[ ]   24 hours of an interruption
[ ]   3 days of an interruption
[ ]   5 days of an interruption
[ ]   10 days of an interruption
[ ]   30 days of an interruption

What is the estimated recovery time objective (RTO) for this area? (time after interruption before
operations are critically impacted)

[ ] Tier 1 (0–12 hours)	This business area is vital.
[ ] Tier 2 (12–24 hours)	This business area is critical.
[ ] Tier 3 (24–48 hours)	This business area is essential.
[ ] Tier 4 (48–72 hours)	This business area is important.

TABLE 2-4   Business impact questionnaire, Part I (continued)

Part I: Business Area Impact **This questionnaire must be filled out for each business area within ABC Co.** **(Note: Excess form blanks compressed to save space)**	
[ ] Tier 5 (72–96 hours)	This business area is noncritical.
[ ] Tier 6 (more than 96 hours)	This business unit/cost center is deferrable.

What is the estimated recovery point objective (RPO) for this function? (point in time by which function must be recovered to support operations)

[ ] Point 1 (less than 6 hours)	[ ] Point 2 (less than 24 hours)
[ ] Point 3 (less than 48 hours)	[ ] Point 4 (less than 72 hours)
[ ] Point 5 (more than 72 hours)	

Identify the extent of exposure that would be incurred by the business area and/or ABC Co. should an unplanned interruption occur:

Additional expense

Assets

Customer service

Revenue loss per day

Productivity loss per day

Financial exposure

Goodwill

Regulatory/legal

What is the estimated dollar loss for the company from this business area should an interruption occur for a period of more than:

	<$20,000	<$50,000	<$100,000	<$250,000	>$250,000
1 business day					
2 business days					
3 business days					
4 business days					
5 business days					
2 weeks					
3 weeks					
4 weeks					

TABLE 2-4   Business impact questionnaire, Part I (continued)

Part I: Business Area Impact
This questionnaire must be filled out for each business area within ABC Co.
(Note: Excess form blanks compressed to save space)

2 months
3 months
Dependencies
Describe below the key action steps/tasks that define the functionality of this business unit/cost center.

Frequency (X):	H Hourly	W Weekly	Q Quarterly	D Daily	M Monthly	A Annually
Function	Input	Source	X	Manipulated	Output	Recipient	X

Identify any networks (LAN, intranet, or Internet) or network-based applications or data sources the business areas depends on:

Network	Application/data source

Identify any service bureaus or external vendors the business areas depends on:

SB/vendor	Purpose

TABLE 2-5   Business impact questionnaire, Part II

Part II: Functional Impact
This questionnaire must be filled out for each major function within ABC Co.
Function:
Business area:
Department:
Senior manager:
Functional manager:
Overall functional priority: (to be added by CPMT)
Date of BIA questionnaire:
Questionnaire completed by:

TABLE 2-5   Business impact questionnaire, Part II (continued)

Part II: Functional Impact **This questionnaire must be filled out for each major function within ABC Co.**

Function description: (describe the processes necessary to support the function)

Function deliverables: (describe the output of this function as it supports the organization)

Dependencies

Input:
From what process does this function receive input to initiate its process? Include source name, location, and method of receipt.

What effect is there on this function if the input is not available?

What work-around is required to continue this function if the input is not available?

Output:
What process receives the deliverable from this function? Include client name, location, and method of receipt.

What effect is there on the client if this function is not available?

What work-around is required to provide the deliverable if this function is not available?

Resources:
What personnel resources are required to support this function?

What internal information is needed to support this function?

What external information is needed to support this function?

What application(s) is/are used by this function, and who provides support?

TABLE 2-5 Business impact questionnaire, Part II (continued)

Part II: Functional Impact
This questionnaire must be filled out for each major function within ABC Co.

What hardware is used by this function, and who provides support?

What network resource(s) is/are used by this function, and who provides support?

Impact:

For each of the following items, rate the function's impact on the corresponding criteria:

Activity	1 (no impact)	2 (low)	3 (moderate)	4 (high)	5 (very high)
Additional expense					
Assets					
Revenue loss per day					
Productivity loss per day					
Customer service					
Goodwill					
Regulatory/legal					

For each of the following activities, identify the extent to which the corresponding procedure or plan is implemented for this function:

Activity	None exist	Present but not implemented	Implemented but not rehearsed	Rehearsed but not tested	Fully implemented, rehearsed, and tested
Manual procedures					

Briefly describe the manual procedures for this function:

Risk mitigation plans

Briefly describe the risk mitigation plans for this function:

Incident response plans

Briefly describe the incident response plans for this function:

Disaster recovery plans

Briefly describe the disaster recovery plans for this function:

Business continuity plans

Briefly describe the business continuity plans for this function:

TABLE 2-5 Business impact questionnaire, Part II (continued)

| **Part II: Functional Impact** |
| **This questionnaire must be filled out for each major function within ABC Co.** |

What is the estimated recovery time objective (RTO) for this function? (time after interruption before operations are critically impacted)

[ ] Tier 1 (0–24 hours)	[ ] Tier 2 (24–48 hours)
[ ] Tier 3 (48–72 hours)	[ ] Tier 4 (72–96 hours)

What is the estimated recovery point objective (RPO) for this function? (point in time by which function must be recovered to support operations)

[ ] Point 1 (less than 6 hours)	[ ] Point 2 (less than 1 business day)
[ ] Point 3 (less than 2 business days)	[ ] Point 4 (less than 3 business days)
[ ] Point 5 (3 or more business days)	

Interdependencies

What is the relative importance of the following support functions to maintain this function in the event of a disaster?

Support Function	Not important	Somewhat important	Important	Very important	Extremely important
Telephones					
Cell phones					
Fax					
Radio					
Data network					
Other network					
Wireless data					
Internet					
Intranet					
Other: _____					
Other: _____					

What interdependencies exist between this function and other functions?

Supply chain
Environmental health & safety
Human resources
Major vendors & suppliers

TABLE 2-5   Business impact questionnaire, Part II (continued)

Part II: Functional Impact This questionnaire must be filled out for each major function within ABC Co.
Other:
Do your current IR/DR/BC plans have recovery strategies that meet your RTO for this function?
Does this function include an emergency response plan?
Date of last BIA assessment:
Have there been any changes to the business function since your last BIA assessment? If so, describe:

This questionnaire, while not as comprehensive as may be needed by some organizations, provides the core of the information needed to complete the BIA. This type of questionnaire could be administered as an HTML document on the company intranet, allowing ease of access and data collection and evaluation.

Facilitated Data-Gathering Sessions

The **focus group** or **facilitated data-gathering session** is another commonly used technique. Such techniques can be used to collect information directly from the end users and business managers. Time permitting, individuals from throughout a particular business area, along with their managerial team, are gathered to brainstorm the answers to the questions posed to complete the BIA process. Unless steps are taken to ensure a relaxed, productive session, these meetings may not yield the quantity or quality of information desired. Providing a clear structure to the sessions, while encouraging dialog, but restricting the managers' ability to take control of the sessions, is important to make sure that the end user representatives have an opportunity to contribute to the process.

Process Flows and Interdependency Studies

Systems diagramming is a common approach used in the discipline of systems analysis and design. It can be used to understand the operation of systems, and to chart process flows and interdependency studies both for manual and for automated systems. Common diagramming techniques, such as a use case diagram and supporting use cases, are specifically designed to understand the interactions between entities and business functions. The example of the interactions between Web commerce functions and customers are shown graphically in Figure 2-3, and the explanation of the usage of the business functions is explained in Table 2-6.

Use case diagram

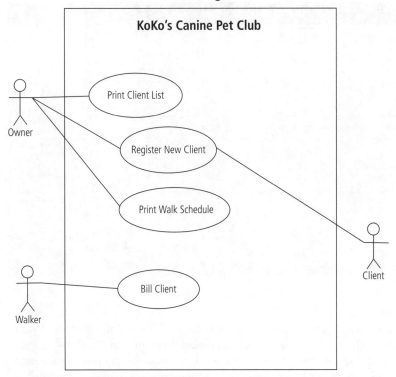

FIGURE 2-3 Sample use case diagram

TABLE 2-6 Example use case

Use Case Description		
Project Name: KoKo's Canine Pet Club		Date prepared: 11/21/08
Use case name: Register New Client	ID: 1	Importance level: High
Primary actor: Client	Use case type: Detail, Essential	
Stakeholder and interest: Client: Wants to get registered so they can use the dog-walking service Employees: Want more business so they can keep their job Owner: Wants as many customers as she can get to increase profit		
Brief description: This use case describes the process by which a new client and pet is registered with the pet club.		
Trigger: A new client comes into the store to register Trigger type: External		

TABLE 2-6   Example use case (continued)

Use Case Description

Relationships:
   Association: Client
   Include:
   Extend:
   Generalization:

Normal flow of events:
   1. A client comes into the store and requests to register with the service.
   2. Owner sits down with the client to discuss the service.
   3. Basic information is collected and entered directly into the system.
   4. Fees are negotiated and agreed on.
   5. Preferred walk time and walker are entered into the system.
   6. Client and pet are issued a customer number to uniquely identify them.

Subflows: None documented
Alternatives/exceptional flows: None documented

Other modeling techniques drawn from systems analysis skills include Uniform Modeling Language models such as class diagrams, sequence diagrams, and collaboration diagrams. Other types of documentation, such as traditional systems analysis and design modeling approaches, including workflow, functional decomposition, and dataflow diagrams, may also be useful. Many of these are quite complex, and their creation with the requisite level of detail may be beyond the abilities or resources available to the BIA team. However, if the organization already prepares these types of models as a function of ongoing systems development activities, then these modeling approaches may provide an excellent way to illustrate how the business functions. The examples here, showing a relatively simple process, have been greatly simplified. Figure 2-4 shows a simple class diagram drawn from the object classes used to support the use case documented earlier.

Figure 2-5 illustrates a collaboration diagram used to document the ways that the actors and object classes shown in Figure 2-4 interact.

Class diagram

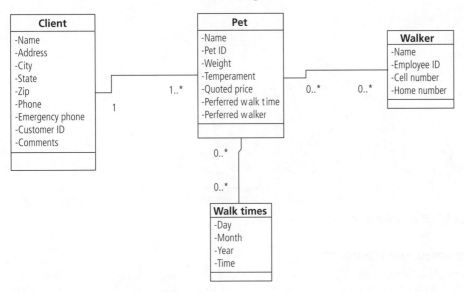

FIGURE 2-4   Example of a class diagram

Sequence Diagram

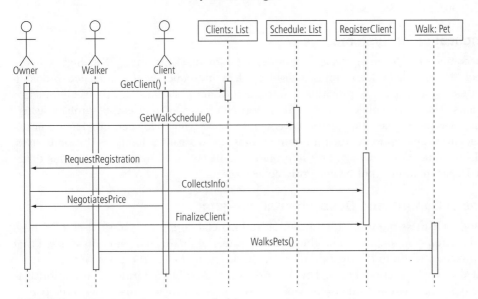

FIGURE 2-5   Example of a sequence diagram

Figure 2-6 documents the way in which object classes as described in Figure 2-4 interact as the system operates.

Collaboration diagram

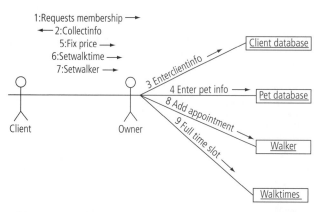

FIGURE 2-6   Example of a collaboration diagram

Risk Assessment Research

As described earlier, the organization's risk assessment and risk management efforts can provide a wealth of information that can be used in BIA efforts. While some modification may be necessary, as shown in previous sections, the risk management process is in fact the primary starting point for the BIA. If the organization has not performed this activity, some redundant efforts are required. In addition, the teams may collect information from outside sources on risk assessment.

IT Application or System Logs

When completing the many weighted tables used in the BIA, an IT staff may prove particularly valuable in determining categorical data on frequency of occurrence, probability of success, and so on by providing information from the various logs their equipment maintains. These logs collect and provide reports on failed login attempts, probes, scans, denial-of-service attacks, and viruses detected, to name a few. This can provide a much more accurate description of the attack environment the organization faces. In some cases, the BIA team may be able to ask for information to be collected from these systems that the IT Department may not be currently collecting.

Financial Reports and Departmental Budgets

Running a business requires great attention to financial detail. As a normal part of the administration of an organization, there are a number of financial documents created that can provide insight into the operations of the business, including the costs and revenues provided by each functional area. This information is useful in determining the prioritization of business areas and functions within those areas. It provides insight into the contribution of each to the organization's profitability and revenues.

The most common method of calculating business impact is to review financial reports and budgets. Lost sales, idle personnel costs, and other opportunity costs are easily obtained using these documents.

Audit Documentation

As is often the case in larger organizations, especially publicly traded firms, the organization has paid external consultants to audit their functions for compliance with federal and state regulations, with national or international standards, or as part of a proactive ongoing improvement program. These audit reports can provide additional information for the BIA process.

Production Schedules

Finally, information gained from production schedules, marketing forecasts, productivity reports, and a host of other business documents can also prove valuable in the completion of the BIA.

Although the organization may neither have all of these sources available, nor desire to include all of these recommended sources of information, it is obviously advantageous to include information collected from other sources rather than redundantly collecting it for this process. The important thing to remember is to make sure the information you use, if it is not collected directly by the BIA team, is current and accurate. Old, outdated information is often worse than no information at all, if it is used to make decisions that affect the organization's ability to react and recover from attacks.

BUDGETING FOR CONTINGENCY OPERATIONS

As a final component to the initial planning process for the CPMT, some financial consideration must be made to prepare to deal with the inevitable expenses associated with contingency operations. Although some areas such as incident response may not require dedicated budgeting, other areas, such as disaster recovery and business continuity, do require ongoing expenditures, investment, and service contracts to support their implementation. The ugly reality is that many organizations are "self-insured" against some types of losses, such as theft of technology, equipment, or other resources. Ideally, this means that in lieu of payments to an outside insurance organization, the organization invests a set amount each fiscal cycle into an account it can then draw upon should replacements be required. With tight budgets and drops in revenues, however, some organizations forego these investments, instead betting on the probability that such losses, if they occur, will be minimal and can be funded out of normal budgets. Should a disastrous expense occur, however, the organization is at risk of complete failure and possible closure. Some of the budgeting requirements of the individual components of CP planning are presented in the sections that follow.

Incident Response Budgeting

Incident response capabilities to a large extent are part of a normal IT budget. It is customary for the CIO to have his or her managers ensure that data backup and recovery schemes, described in later chapters, are part of the normal operations. In addition, uninterruptible power supplies (UPSs) are also part of the normal equipment expenditures of the IT operations. Other items frequently purchased that have an incident response role are antivirus software, antispyware software, redundant arrays of independent drives (RAID), and network attached storage (NAS) or storage area networks (SANs) for storing critical user files in a common area that can be included in the backup and recovery schemes. Overall, the inclusion of these items as part of normal controls or safeguards for IT operations fall within the normal information security function for the IT Department. Additional expenses might arise in the protection of user data outside the common storage areas. If end users want to back up their individual data, additional equipment, such as tape drives, or writeable DVD-ROM systems, is needed. With the inevitable death of the floppy disk, and the increase in popularity of its successor, the USB flash drive, the burden of protection of removable media has simply shifted. Now that modern systems are capable of booting from USB drives, the protection burden is now focused on these tools.

The only real area that additional budgeting is required is the maintenance of redundant equipment should equipment failures result from incident attacks. A "rule of three" is quite useful in preparing for this inevitability. An organization should keep three levels of computer system environments available for essential redundancy: an online production system, an online or very nearly online backup system and a quality assurance system to serve as a ready reserve for the production systems, and an offline testing and development system used to stage software nearing the end of the change management process. In most organizations, critical equipment has redundancy incorporated into the systems. Online "hot" servers like domain controllers, Web servers, database servers, and e-mail servers frequently have a backup or "warm" server providing redundant functions that are standing by in a near-online state. Should the hot server go down, the warm server steps up to become the hot server and provides the functions needed to the clients. In case the hot server goes down and the warm server goes up, the rule of three requires the organization to maintain a cold server or other equipment to allow the timely creation of a new warm server to continue to provide needed redundancy. The hot server can be taken offline and repaired as needed, while redundancy is still present in the system. Some common components such as network cards, small hubs, and the like may only require a few "shelved" items to provide redundancy for a larger number of in-use items. The key is to make sure that any offline cold server is equipped and configured exactly like the hot and warm versions. In fact, many organizations use the cold server as a test server to ensure that any added patches or upgrades do not negatively affect other applications or services.

Disaster Recovery Budgeting

The number-one budgetary expense for disaster recovery is insurance. Insurance policies provide for the capabilities to rebuild and reestablish operations at the primary site. Should fire, flood, earthquake, or other natural disaster strike, the insurance carrier oversees the funding of replacement structures and services until the primary site is restored. It is essential, therefore, that the insurance policies be carefully scrutinized to ensure that effective coverage is provided, with the understanding that the more comprehensive the policy, the more expensive the policy. Most insurance policies have deductibles, and larger deductibles provide lower monthly premiums. Setting aside a fund specifically dedicated to cover these deductibles ensures they do not cause financial problems while the organization is getting reestablished.

However, one problem with insurance is that much of the damage from electronic attacks is not covered in policies. Although forward-thinking insurance companies are slowly rolling out data loss insurance policies, most organizations are not able to afford them just yet. While natural disasters resulting in physical damage are quite common for insurance adjustors, they are just not prepared to handle loss of organizational revenue due to a disastrous distributed denial-of-service attack. If you think a DDoS would simply be an incident, consider the attacks on Amazon, eBay, E*TRADE, Dell, Yahoo, and a host of other companies in 2000 that resulted in lost revenues of over $1.7 billion over a four-hour period.[11]

While this type of disaster did not require relocation of the employees and equipment, it did require extensive reconfiguration of network connections, activation of backup carrier services and circuits, and a host of other disaster recovery procedures. Insurance was not available at the time to provide relief from lost revenue. Now it is, and it is interesting that it discriminates based on what a company is using to host its information.

"Okemos, Mich.-based J.S. Wurzler Underwriting Managers, one of the earliest agencies to offer hacker insurance, has begun charging its clients anywhere from 5 to 15 percent more if they use Microsoft Windows NT software instead of UNIX or Linux for their Internet operations...Other insurance brokers—including Marsh & McLennon, Aon, and Arthur J. Gallagher & Company—also provide hacker, or e-business security, insurance."[12] How do you decide if hacker insurance is needed?

> *First, does your company have annual sales or potential liability sufficient to warrant the expense of a "hacker insurance" policy?*
>
> *Second, does your company's online operations constitute a significant part of your business?*
>
> *Third, does your company maintain a database of confidential proprietary information about its customers or operations that can be accessed through the Net?*
>
> *Last, using realistic estimates, will your company lose a significant amount of money per hour if a hacker blocks access to your Web site?*[13]

There are a host of other expenses that are not covered by insurance, such as loss of other services (water, electricity, data) and others too numerous to note here. It is therefore important to look at the items the organization needs to support operations as part of the BIA, determine which are covered by insurance and which are not, and plan accordingly.

Business Continuity Budgeting

The area that requires the most budgeting and expenditures in the contingency planning operations is business continuity processes. As will be described in later chapters, the requirements to maintain service contracts to cover the contingencies facing the organization can be quite expensive. The service level agreements (SLAs) for hot sites, for example, require a dedicated duplicate facility complete with servers, networking devices, telephony devices, and essentially everything except data and personnel. The cost to maintain such a high level of redundancy can be staggering. Any level of continuity plan includes expenses, even contingency operations such as mobile services, which are capable of rolling out specially configured tractor-trailers equipped like offices that the organization can inhabit until they are ready to move operations back to the primary site. Unless the organization budgets and contracts for these services well in advance, it may find itself in a financial bind if it needs them and is is not prepared.

In addition, the organization should have a "war chest" of funds set aside to purchase items as they are needed during the continuity operations. An organization may consider establishing safety deposit boxes at a local bank with corporate credit cards, purchase orders, and even cash that can be easily accessed to pay for the resulting expenses of setting up everyone at an alternate site should the primary site be uninhabitable. Just the expenses associated with replacing office supplies from scratch can be quite staggering if the organization has to purchase sufficient stock to maintain operations for an extended time.

Another expense not normally budgeted is employee overtime. Having to reestablish operations at another location inevitably includes extensive overtime for non-salaried employees. Unless a reserve fund is prepared in advance, the expenses associated with late nights and early mornings can quickly mount, unbalancing the organization's precarious finances at such a hectic time.

Crisis Management Budgeting

The last item in the budget plan is crisis management. Although the details of crisis management are covered in later chapters, it is important to know that the fundamentals of crisis management are focused on the potential for physical and psychological losses associated with catastrophic disasters, like the World Trade Center attacks of September 11, 2001. The primary budgeting items here are employee salaries, should they be unable to come to work due to such a disastrous level of loss. The organization may want to establish a minimum, such as a 30-day budget for paid leave, as employees wait at home to determine if they in fact have a job to come back to.

Forward-thinking companies also want to consider budgeting for contributions to employee loss expenses such as funerals and burial expenses, as well as counseling services for employees and loved ones, if these are not specifically covered in the current benefits packages.

Chapter Summary

- Begin the process of planning for contingencies by establishing an individual or a team to be responsible for:
  - Obtaining commitment and support from senior management
  - Writing the CP planning document
  - Conducting the business impact analysis which includes:
    1. Assisting in identifying and prioritizing threats and attacks
    2. Assisting in identifying and prioritizing business functions
    3. Organizing the subordinate teams of incident response, disaster recovery, business continuity, and crisis management
- Beginning the CP process requires a planning methodology, the policy environment to enable the planning process, an understanding of the core precursor activity—known as the business impact analysis (BIA)—and the key enabling resource stream, which is articulated and outlined by the planning budget.
- The seven steps of the planning cycle are:
  1. Develop the contingency planning policy statement.
  2. Conduct the business impact analysis.
  3. Identify preventive controls.
  4. Develop recovery strategies.
  5. Develop an IT contingency plan.
  6. Plan testing, training, and exercises.
  7. Plan maintenance.
- CP policy should contain the following sections:

  Introduction

  A statement of the scope and purpose of the CP operations

  A call for periodic risk assessment and business impact analysis

  A specification of the major components of the CP to be designed by the CPMT

  A call for, and guidance in the selection of, recovery options and business continuity strategies

  A requirement to test the various plans on a regular basis

  Identification of key regulations and standards that impact CP planning, and a brief overview of their relevancy

  Identification of key individuals responsible for CP operations

  A challenge to the individual members of the organizations, asking for their support, and reinforcing their importance as part of the overall CP process
- The BIA provides information about systems and the threats they face.
- The BIA is made up of stages:
  1. Threat attack identification and prioritization

2. Business unit analysis
3. Attack success scenario development
4. Potential damage assessment
5. Subordinate plan classification

- Financial planning consideration must be made to prepare to deal with the inevitable expenses associated with contingency operations. The budgeting requirements of the individual components of CP planning are:
    - Incident response budgeting
    - Disaster recovery budgeting
    - Business continuity budgeting
    - Crisis management budgeting

Review Questions

1. What is the first step in beginning the contingency planning process?
2. What are the primary responsibilities of the CP planning team?
3. What four teams may be subordinate to the CPMT in a typical organization?
4. The CP process will fail without what critical element?
5. What are the three communities of interest, and why are they important to CP?
6. What are the seven steps in the CP process?
7. What are the major sections in the CP planning policy document?
8. What is a business impact analysis, and why is it important?
9. What are the five stages in the business impact analysis?
10. How does the Sun Tzu quote "Know yourself and know your enemy" relate to threat/attack analysis?
11. What are the 12 categories of threats to information security?
12. How do threats differ from attacks?
13. How is a weighted table useful in threat and attack prioritization?
14. What is the business unit analysis, and why is it important in CP? Who performs the BUA?
15. What is an attack success scenario, and who develops it?
16. What is a potential damage assessment, and what information does it contain?
17. Where can information be obtained to assist in the completion of the BIA?
18. What is a recovery point objective, and how does it differ from a recovery time objective?
19. How can system diagramming methods assist in a BIA?
20. How does budgeting differ in the various CP components (IR, DR, and BC)?

Exercises

1. Using a Web browser, look for examples of each of the 12 categories of threats to information security as reported in current news and trade press articles.

2. Using a Web browser, go to *http://gocsi.com* and download the most recent CSI/FBI survey (this may require registration), or receive a copy from your instructor. Map the threats identified in the most recent survey to the 12 categories, and identify threats not covered in each study.

3. Using the Threats and Corresponding Attacks from Table 2-2, create a list of the threats and attacks that (a) the computers in your school's laboratory are susceptible to, and (b) that computers in your home are susceptible to.

4. Using the information from Exercise 3, create a weighted analysis table of attacks for each environment (school and home) based on criteria and weights you identify.

5. Using a Web browser, search on the following terms: *business impact analysis*, *recovery point objective*, and *recovery time objective*. What information do you identify that can assist an organization in preparing their own BIA? Your instructor may ask you to bring this material to class for discussion.

Further Discussion

Some additional questions that you and your instructor might discuss are:

- Who should coordinate rehearsal of the contingency plans? Why would that be the appropriate person?

- What degree of cross-training between the various roles in the plans is most effective? Identify the advantages and disadvantages of such a cross-training plan. What trade-offs do you think exist between extensive and minimal cross-training?

- Notice that Amanda Wilson was not at this rehearsal. Do you think it is important that the CIO, or even the CEO, participate in this kind of readiness exercise? Why or why not?

- How can you make progress in contingency planning in the face of resistance from upper management?

References

[1] M. Swanson, A. Wohl, L. Pope, T. Grance, J. Hash, R. Thomas., "Contingency Planning Guide for Information Technology Systems," NIST Special Publication 800-34, accessed June 13, 2005, from http://csrc.nist.gov/publications/nistpubs/800-34/sp800-34.pdf.

[2] D. Bledsoe, "Formulating a Continuity Planning Policy," accessed May 11, 2005, from http://www.mcqsoft.com/formulate.htm.

[3] FASP. "Sample Generic Policy and High-Level Procedures for Contingency Plans," Federal Agency Security Practices—NIST, accessed May 11, 2005, from http://csrc.nist.gov/fasp/.

[4] B. Zawada and L. Evans, "Creating a More Rigorous BIA," CPM Group, November/December, accessed May 12, 2005, from http://www.contingencyplanning.com/archives/2002/novdec/4.aspx.

[5] SIPS. "DNS Attack Scenario," Computer Science Department, Princeton University, accessed May 11, 2005, from http://www.cs.princeton.edu/sip/news/dns-scenario.html.

[6] See note 4.

[7] SORM, "Business Continuity Impact Analysis," Texas State Office of Risk Management, accessed April 10, 2005, from http://www.sorm.state.tx.us/Risk_Management/Business_Continuity/bus_impact.php.

[8] DRJ, Business Continuity Glossary, *Disaster Recovery Journal* and DRI International. accessed April 20, 2005, from http://www.drj.com/glossary/drjglossary.html#r.

[9] See note 8.

[10] The material presented in the text was drawn from the following sources and was reorganized and rewritten. The authors would like to thank the following: G. Mohr "Canadian Center for Emergency Preparedness Business Impact Analysis Questionnaire." Tibbett & Britten Group WWW Document, viewed 6/22/05, http://www.ccep.ca/ccepbcp3.html; J. Rychalski, "Business Impact Analysis Questionnaire" AuditNet, November 2002. WWW Document viewed 6/22/05, http://www.auditnet.org/docs/BIAQuestionnaire.doc; M. Krause, & H. Tipton, "BIA Questionnaire Construction" CCCure Handbook of Information Security Management. WWW Document, viewed 6/22/05, http://www.cccure.org/Documents/HISM/290-291.html; SORM, State Office of Risk Management "Business Continuity Impact Analysis" WWW Document, viewed 6/22/05, http://www.sorm.state.tx.us/Risk_Management/Business_Continuity/bus_impact.php; DRJ. "Generally Accepted Practices For Business Continuity Practitioners," Disaster Recovery Journal and DRI International WWW Document, viewed 6/22/05, http://www.drj.com/GAP/gap.pdf.

[11] BBC, "'Mafiaboy' hacker jailed," BBC News, accessed May 5, 2004, from http://news.bbc.co.uk/1/hi/sci/tech/1541252.stm.

[12] E. Luening, "Windows users pay for hacker insurance," CNETNews.com, accessed May 12, 2005, from http://news.com.com/2100-1001-258392.html?legacy=cnet.

[13] D. Wood, "Does Your Company Need Hacker Insurance?" Doug Isenberg's GigaLaw.com, accessed May 14, 2005, from http://www.gigalaw.com/articles/2001-all/wood-2001-06-all.html.

CHAPTER **3**

INCIDENT RESPONSE: PREPARATION, ORGANIZATION, AND PREVENTION

If you can keep your head when all about you are losing theirs and blaming it on you, if you can trust yourself when all men doubt you, [...] yours is the Earth and everything that's in it.

—Rudyard Kipling

OPENING SCENARIO

It was two o'clock in the morning when his cell phone began to buzz. Paul turned in his bed once, then twice, before finally grabbing for the phone. Seeing that it was the Network Operations Center's number lit up on the display, he answered.

"Sorry to wake you, Paul." It was Susan Carter, the third shift supervisor. Now that everything was back to normal operations after the fire, she was working her usual hours again.

"What's up, Susan?" he replied groggily.

"We're getting slammed again by a DoS." She sounded worried.

"Just filter the traffic," Paul said. "If you have to, reconfigure the outside firewall."

"I did that already," Susan said. "Now it's coming in on a different port. This is the third one in about an hour."

"Uh oh. It's a live attack then." Wide awake now, Paul began to go over in his mind what he recalled about DoS attacks. Whenever a scripted attack came in, filtering out the port or network address on which the attack was coming in usually stopped it cold, at least for a while. If it changed, it meant only one thing. The attack was being orchestrated live.

"Okay," Paul replied while reaching for the laptop computer on his nightstand. "Give me a minute to get logged in."

For the next few minutes, he carefully scanned the logs on the firewall and border gateway over his VPN connection. He saw that all the attacks seemed to be within a certain range. "Susan, try adding a rule to filter ports 1400 through 2200."

As she clicked away on her end, something nagged Paul in the back of his mind. What was it? It had something to do with a new vulnerability he read about in the last few days.

"*Yes!*" Susan exclaimed. "I think that did it!"

continued

"Okay, pull all the logs and print them out, and we'll go over them when I come in." He leaned over to look at the clock. "In just under an hour."

"Okay, I'll have the coffee ready!" Susan laughed.

Paul leaned back in bed. "Maybe just a few more minutes of shut-eye," he thought. Then his cell phone rang again.

Questions for Discussion:

- Why would the presence of a live attacker cause more concern than a scripted attack?
- What circumstances would have led to this sequence of events becoming an incident instead of an annoyance?

LEARNING OBJECTIVES

Upon completion of this material, you should be able to:

- Know the process used to organize the incident response process
- Understand how policy affects the incident response planning process and how policy can be implemented to support incident response practices
- Know the techniques that can be employed when forming a security incident response team (SIRT)
- Learn the skills and components required to devise an incident response plan
- Know some of the concerns and trade-offs to be managed when assembling the final IR plan

INTRODUCTION

The umbrella of contingency planning addresses everything done by an organization to prepare for the unexpected. The incident response (IR) process is one element of contingency planning that focuses its efforts on detecting or attempting to detect and evaluate the level of severity of unexpected events. Whenever possible, the IR process should contain and resolve those incidents based on the IR plan. When incidents arise that cannot be contained or resolved, other elements of the contingency planning process are activated, using the documented escalation processes as noted throughout the plan. The incident response process is made up of several phases: preparation, detection and analysis, containment, eradication and recovery, and postincident activity.[1] Because of the complexity of the IR process, this chapter will address the initial preparation phase, Chapter 4 will cover the early components of the IR operations, and Chapter 5 will cover the remaining phases of the IR process. The following information is targeted specifically to creating an IR plan that an organization can use to effectively respond to incidents.

PREPARING FOR INCIDENT RESPONSE

When the contingency planning management committee (CPMT) completes each component of the business impact analysis, it begins to transfer the information gleaned from the organization to the various subordinate committees. To assist in their subordinate planning, the incident response committee, disaster recovery committee, and business continuity committee each get overlapping information on the attacks they could face, the prioritization of those attacks, and the attack scenario end cases. In fact, each committee gets as much of the overall contingency plan as that prepared by CPMT. After committee members have this information, they begin their subordinate plans. In the case of incident planning, the group follows these general stages:

- Form the IR planning committee.
- Develop the IR policy.
- Organize the SIRT.
- Develop the IR plan.
- Develop IR procedures.

To gain an overview of the ways IR planning is performed at other organizations, two examples of the IR planning life cycle are shown in Figures 3-1 and 3-2. Figure 3-1 shows how the U.S. National Institute of Standards and Technology (NIST) defines the IR planning process. As can be seen from the figure, this book follows the NIST approach very closely. Figure 3-2 provides a slightly broader perspective, showing how the Computer Emergency Response Team Coordinating Center (CERT/CC) approach to IR planning fits into its overall IR model. For a more thorough discussion of the handling of security incidents, including policy and planning, refer to the excerpt from RFC 2196 – Site Security Handbook, at the end of this chapter.

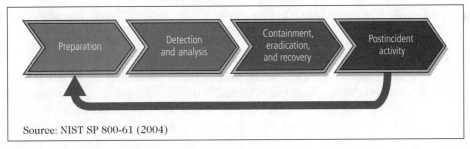

Source: NIST SP 800-61 (2004)

FIGURE 3-1   The NIST Incident Response Life Cycle[2]

Organizing the incident response planning process begins with staffing the IR planning committee. Much of the preliminary organizing effort was done by the CP team, but the IR team needs to be organized as a separate entity, and that process begins by identifying and engaging a collection of stakeholders, meaning a representative collection of individuals with a stake in the successful and uninterrupted operation of the organization

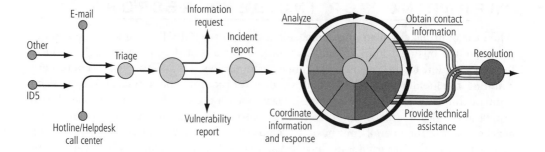

Source: CSIRT 77. Retrieved February 17, 2005 from http://www.cert.org/archive/pdf/csirt-handbook.pdf

FIGURE 3-2 The CERT Incident Handling Life Cycle[3]

information infrastructure. These stakeholders are used to collect vital information on the roles and responsibilities of the SIRT team. Typical stakeholders often include:

- Communities of interest, such as:
  - General management: This group needs to understand what the SIRT is and what it does. This group also needs to preauthorize interaction between SIRT and key business functions, should certain actions be necessary to arrest the spread and impact of an incident.
  - IT management: This group needs to understand the specific demands the SIRT will place on IT, and what resources and access they will require to successfully respond to an incident. This group similarly needs to pre-approve certain SIRT actions when those actions impact existing systems, networking functions, and connections.
  - InfoSec management: This group needs to understand the resource requirements the SIRT needs on hand or at easy access should they be needed at short notice.
- Organizational departments, such as:
  - The Legal Department needs to review the procedures of the SIRT and understand the steps the SIRT will perform to ensure they are within legal and ethical guidelines for your municipal, state, and federal jurisdictions. The Legal Department can provide guidance on developing contracts and service-level agreements for auxiliary and redundant services, nondisclosure agreements for business partners and other non-employee associations, and in reviewing policy and plan documents for liability issues.
  - The Human Resources Department helps InfoSec staff acquire personnel not already on hand to complete the SIRT team. Individuals with incident response experience may not currently be employed by the organization. The development of job descriptions and the interviewing and eventual hiring of candidates will benefit from close coordination with HR.

- The Public Relations Department needs to be briefed on what information can be and should be disclosed to the public if and when an incident occurs. Predefined public notices can be drafted and reviewed by PR to ensure the proper amount of information is provided to the appropriate agencies, law enforcement, and the media when the need arises.
- Depending on the organization of the company, some groups with an information security overlap will also need to be consulted, including:
  - Physical security
  - Auditing and risk management
  - Insurance
- Other interest groups, such as:
  - General end users need to know what transpires when the SIRT swings into action and how to respond to best assist in the development and testing of procedures and policies. These stakeholders are also most familiar with the functions of the business and can provide additional insight into these areas.
  - Others stakeholders, including key business partners, contractors, temporary employee agencies, and in some cases consultants[4]

INCIDENT RESPONSE POLICY

One of the first deliverables to be undertaken by the IR planning committee should be the incident response policy. As the planning committee forms a security incident response team (SIRT), key SIRT representatives join the IR planning committee in the development of policy to define the operations of the team and articulate the organizational response to various types of incidents, as well as advise end users how to contribute to the effective response of the organization, rather than contributing to the problem.

The incident response policy is similar in structure to other policies used by the organization. Just as the enterprise information security policy defines the roles and responsibilities for information security for the entire enterprise, the incident response policy defines the roles and responsibilities for incident response for the SIRT and others who will be mobilized in the activation of the plan. Table 3-1 provides an overview of the structure of a typical IR policy.

TABLE 3-1 Incident response policy elements

Statement of Management Commitment
Purpose and objectives of the policy
Scope of the policy (to whom and to what it applies and under what circumstances)
Definition of information security incidents and their consequences within the context of the organization
Organizational structure and delineation of roles, responsibilities, and levels of authority; should include the authority of the incident response team to confiscate or disconnect equipment and to monitor suspicious activity, and the requirements for reporting certain types of incidents
Prioritization or severity ratings of incidents

TABLE 3-1 Incident response policy elements (continued)

Statement of Management Commitment
Performance measures (as discussed in later chapters)
Reporting and contact forms

(Source: NIST SP 800-61)[5]

IR policy, like all well-written policies, must gain the full support of top management and be clearly understood by all affected parties. It is especially important to gain the support of those communities of interest that will be required to alter business practices or make changes to their information technology infrastructures. For example, if the SIRT determines the only way to stop a massive denial-of-service attack is to sever the organization's connection to the Internet, they should have a signed document locked in an appropriate filing cabinet preauthorizing such action. This prevents any perception of the SIRT team performing actions outside their level of authorization and protects both the SIRT team members and the organization from misunderstanding and potential liability.

Table 3-2 provides additional elements of the policy, beyond its content.

TABLE 3-2 Basic IR policy elements

Attribute	Description
Endorsed by management	Like the mission statement, a policy cannot be enforced unless it is endorsed by senior management.
Clear	Any team member, whether technical, management, or administrative, should be able to easily understand a given policy. Avoid unnecessary jargon, don't be ambiguous, and use very short sentences. If possible (according to your disclosure restrictions), ask someone who is not in security or IT to read your policies. If he or she cannot understand them, rewrite the policies!
Concise	A good policy is a short policy. A long policy is either a bad policy (or uses too many words) or one that may actually include a lot of procedures. Unfortunately, security policies in practice often tend not to be concise, and confusingly mix the management aspect (the policy) with the operational aspect (the procedures). This results in a mixture that nobody really cares for. Strive to avoid this condition!
Necessary and sufficient	A policy should include all that is needed to dictate appropriate behavior in some topic area (for example, security policy), but no more than that—no redundancy, no resiliency. That can be built into the corresponding procedures and quality control.
Usable	Avoid statements that sound nice but are meaningless because they are open to interpretation, for example, "state-of-the-art security will be provided." Common sense statements such as "treat your customers with respect" could be appropriate inside a policy; they are usable, because people share a common understanding about them.
Implementable	A policy must also be written in ways that lead to successful implementation. In the "treat your customers with respect" example, this may mean the addition of a statement essentially saying that the staff must be provided regular training to help them understand how to deal with customers.

TABLE 3-2 Basic IR policy elements (continued)

Attribute	Description
Enforceable	Policies must be enforceable; otherwise, they are of little or no value. Usually when a policy is implementable, it is also enforceable unless it contradicts itself. Concrete measures are needed to assess the usage of the policy. An example of a contradictory policy is the security policy that ranks internal information security as priority number 1, but at the same time ensures absolute privacy for its staff; the latter makes it hard or even impossible to enforce security in case of an insider threat.

(Source: Carnegie Mellon University)[6]

Just as in developing other policies, the involvement of those who will actually use the policies is critical in its development. In addition, interaction and review by the other CP teams, disaster recovery, and business continuity, will also aid in the development of clear, consistent, and uniform policy elements and structure. It is also useful to look at published policies from other agencies and organizations in developing the policy.[7] Other sources of information for the policies include:

- Organization charts for the enterprise and specific business functions
- Topologies for organizational or constituency systems and networks
- Critical system and asset inventories
- Existing disaster recovery or business continuity plans
- Existing guidelines for notifying the organization of a physical security breach
- Any existing incident response plans
- Any parental or institutional regulations
- Any existing security policies and procedures[8]

BUILDING THE SECURITY INCIDENT RESPONSE TEAM

In some organizations, the SIRT might simply be a loose or informal association of IT and InfoSec staffers who would be called up if an attack was detected on the organization's information assets. In other, more formal implementations, the SIRT (also referred to as a computer SIRT or CSIRT) is a set of policies, procedures, technologies, people, and data necessary to prevent, detect, react, and recover from an incident that could potentially damage the organization's information. At some level, every member of an organization is a member of the SIRT team, because every action they take could potentially cause or avert an incident.

Development of the SIRT involves the following stages:

- Collecting information from stakeholders
- Defining the IR team structure
- Determining the IR team services

Information Collection from Stakeholders

In forming the SIRT, the IR planning team needs to collect as much information as possible on the incident response and service needs of the organization. This information is used to craft the SIRT team and ensure the necessary skills and abilities are brought to bear on any situation the team might encounter. Even the definition of the organization and responsibilities of the SIRT may differ between the various communities of interest. Establishing the scope and responsibilities of the SIRT is one of the first tasks to be performed by the IR planning committee when forming the SIRT. The definitions of the SIRT and their functional areas, and the overall strategic focus of the SIRT, are two other important tasks.

After these are drafted, the team constituency and abilities should be determined. Again, conversations with stakeholders help identify the skills and abilities of the team, as well as the specific needs of the end users.

Some typical skills a SIRT team needs include experience in the following areas:

- Virus scanning, elimination, and recovery
- System administration
- Network administration (switches, routers, and gateways)
- Firewall administration
- Intrusion detection systems
- Cryptography
- Data storage and recovery (for example, RAID and/or Storage Area Networks)
- Documentation creation and maintenance

In addition to the technical skill listed, managerial experience associated with creating and following policy and plans is also highly desirable. Additional details on the skills and abilities needed for specific task assignments within incident response specialty areas are provided in subsequent sections of this chapter.

These experiences should be commensurate with the systems used by the organization. After this team is assembled, they can meet and begin reviewing the attack scenario end cases to determine if they warrant inclusion in the IR plan.

> *The following sections are adapted from NIST Special Publication 800-61 Computer Security Incident Handling Guide*[9] *and materials from CERT/CC*[10, 11]

Incident Response Team Structure

An incident response team should be available for contact by anyone who discovers or suspects that an incident involving the organization has occurred. One or more team members, depending on the magnitude of the incident and availability of personnel, then handle the incident. The incident handlers analyze the incident data, determine the impact of the incident, and act appropriately to limit the damage to the organization and restore normal services. Although the incident response team may have only a few members, the team's success depends on the participation and cooperation of individuals throughout the organization. This section identifies such individuals, discusses incident response team models, and provides guidance for selecting an appropriate model.

Team Models

Models used to develop incident response teams tend to fall into one of three structural categories:

1. Central incident response team: A single incident response team handles incidents throughout the organization. This model is effective for small organizations and for large organizations with minimal geographic diversity in terms of computing resources.

2. Distributed incident response teams: The organization has multiple incident response teams, each responsible for handling incidents for a particular logical or physical segment of the organization. This model is effective for large organizations (for example, one team per division) and for organizations with major computing resources at distant locations (for example, one team per geographic region or one team per major facility). However, the teams should be part of a single centralized entity so that the incident response process is consistent across the organization and information is shared among teams. This is particularly important because multiple teams may see components of the same incident or may handle similar incidents. Strong communication among teams and consistent practices should make incident handling more effective and efficient.

3. Coordinating team: An incident response team provides guidance and advice to other teams without having authority over those teams—for example, a department-wide team may assist individual agency teams. This model can be thought of as a SIRT for SIRTs. Because the focus of this document is central and distributed SIRTs, the coordinating team model is not addressed in detail in this chapter.

Incident response teams are often developed along one of these three staffing models:

1. Employees: The organization performs all of its incident response work, with limited technical and administrative support from contractors.

2. Partially outsourced: The organization outsources portions of its incident response work. Later sections discuss the major factors that should be considered with outsourcing. Although incident response duties can be divided among the organization and one or more outsourcers in many ways, a few arrangements have become commonplace:

   - The most prevalent arrangement is for the organization to outsource 24-hour-a-day, 7-day-a-week (24/7) monitoring of intrusion detection sensors, firewalls, and other security devices to an offsite-managed security services provider (MSSP). The MSSP identifies and analyzes suspicious activity and reports each detected incident to the organization's incident response team. Because the MSSP employees can monitor activity for multiple customers simultaneously, this model may provide a 24/7 monitoring and response capability at a skill and cost level that is superior to a comparable internal team.

- Some organizations perform basic incident response work in-house and call on contractors to assist with handling incidents, particularly those that are more serious or widespread. The services most often performed by the contractors are computer forensics, advanced incident analysis, incident containment and eradication, and vulnerability mitigation.

3. Fully outsourced: The organization completely outsources its incident response work, typically to an onsite contractor. This model is most likely to be used when the organization needs a full-time, onsite incident response team but does not have enough available, qualified employees.

Team Model Selection

When selecting appropriate structure and staffing models for an incident response team, organizations should consider the factors outlined in the following sections:

The Need for 24/7 Availability Larger organizations, as well as smaller ones that support critical infrastructures, usually need incident response staff to be available 24/7. This typically means that incident handlers can be contacted at any time by phone or pager, but it can also mean that an onsite presence is required at all times. Real-time availability is the best for incident response because the longer an incident lasts, the more potential there is for damage and loss. Real-time contact is often needed when working with other agencies and organizations—for example, tracing spoofed traffic back to its source through router hops. An incident response team that can quickly react to investigate, contain, and mitigate incidents should be genuinely useful to the organization.

Full-Time Versus Part-Time Team Members Organizations with limited funding, staffing, or incident response needs may have only part-time incident response team members. In this case, the incident response team can be thought of as a volunteer fire department. When an emergency occurs, the team members are contacted rapidly, and those who can assist do so. An existing group such as the IT help desk can act as a first point of contact for incident reporting. The help desk members can be trained to perform the initial investigation and data gathering and then alert the incident response team if it appears that a serious incident has occurred. Organizations with part-time team members should ensure that they maintain their incident response skills and knowledge.

Employee Morale Incident response work is very stressful, as are the on-call responsibilities of most team members. This combination makes it easy for incident response team members to become overly stressed. Many organizations also struggle to find willing, available, experienced, and properly skilled people to participate, particularly in 24-hour support.

Cost Cost is a major factor, especially if employees are required to be onsite 24/7. Organizations may fail to include incident-response-specific costs in budgets. For example, most organizations do not allocate sufficient funding for training and maintaining skills. Because the incident response team works with so many facets of IT, its members need much broader knowledge than most IT staff members. They must also understand how to use the tools of incident response, such as computer forensics software. The organization should also provide funding for regular team exercises so the team can gain practical experience and improve its performance. Other costs that may be overlooked are physical security for the team's work areas and communications mechanisms.

Staff Expertise Incident handling requires specialized knowledge and experience in several technical areas; the breadth and depth of knowledge required varies based on the severity of the organization's risks. Service providers may possess deeper knowledge of intrusion detection, vulnerabilities, exploits, and other aspects of security than employees of the organization. Also, managed security service providers may be able to correlate events among customers so that they can identify new threats more quickly than any individual customer could. However, technical staff members within the organization usually have much better knowledge of the organization's environment than an outsider, which can be beneficial in identifying false positives associated with organization-specific behavior and the criticality of targets.

Organizational Structures If an organization has three departments that function independently, incident response may be more effective if each department has its own incident response team. The main organization can host a centralized incident response entity that facilitates standard practices and communications among the teams.

Outsourcing Incident Response

With the increase in popularity of managed security services, many organizations are considering outsourcing at least part of their incident response capacity. Companies specializing in this area frequently install such equipment as firewalls and IDSs in the organization and then remotely monitor it from a centralized facility, much like a home security company does with fire and burglary monitoring. There are several advantages and disadvantages to this approach, as shown in Table 3-3.

TABLE 3-3 Advantages and disadvantages of outsourcing the incident response process

Advantages	Disadvantages
• Services provided by professionals trained in IR	• Potential loss of control of response to incidents
• 24/7 monitoring	• Possible exposure of classified organizational data to service providers
• Early notification of potential problems in region	• Locked in to proprietary equipment and services
• Formal reports and briefings on attacks and response	• Loss of services when contract expires, unless renewed
• Equipment specified and installed by well-trained professionals	• Loss of customization to the needs of each organization

TABLE 3-3 Advantages and disadvantages of outsourcing the incident response process (continued)

Advantages	Disadvantages
• No additional personnel costs or training requirements	• Organization's needs subjugated to service provider's needs
	• More important/prestigious companies given preference in response over smaller less prestigious ones

When considering the viability of outsourcing incident response services, organizations should carefully consider the following issues:[12]

Current and Future Quality of Work The quality of the service provider's work remains a very important consideration. Organizations should not only consider the current quality of work, but also the service provider's efforts to ensure the quality of future work, such as minimizing turnover and burnout and providing a solid training program for new employees. Organizations should think about how they could audit or otherwise objectively assess the quality of the service provided.

Division of Responsibilities Organizations are usually unwilling to give an outside resource authority to make operational decisions for the environment, such as disconnecting a Web server. It is important to decide the point at which the service provider hands off the incident response to the organization. One partially outsourced model addresses this issue by having the service provider deliver an incident report to the organization's internal team, along with recommendations for further handling of the incident. The internal team ultimately makes the operational decisions.

Sensitive Information Revealed to the Contractor Dividing incident response responsibilities and restricting access to sensitive information can limit the release of sensitive information. For example, a contractor can determine what user ID was used in an incident but not know what person is associated with the user ID. The contractor can report to the organization that user ID 123456 is apparently being used to download pirated software, yet the contractor won't know who 123456 is. Trusted employees within the organization can then take over the investigation.

Lack of Organization-Specific Knowledge Accurate analysis and prioritization of incidents are dependent on specific knowledge of the organization's environment. The organization should provide the service provider regularly updated documents that define what incidents the organization is concerned about, which resources are critical, and what the level of response should be under various sets of circumstances. The organization should also report all changes and updates made to its IT infrastructure, network configuration, and systems. Otherwise, the contractor has to make a best guess as to how each incident should be handled, inevitably leading to mishandled incidents and frustration on both sides. Lack of organization-specific knowledge can also be a problem when incident response is not outsourced if communications are weak among teams or if the organization simply does not collect the necessary information.

Lack of Correlation   Correlation among multiple data sources is very important. If the intrusion detection system records an attempted attack against a Web server, but the service provider has no access to the Web logs, it may be unable to determine whether the attack was successful. To be efficient, the contractor requires administrative privileges to critical systems and security device logs with remote access over a secure channel. This increases administration costs, introduces additional access entry points, and increases the risk of unauthorized disclosure of sensitive information.

Handling Incidents at Multiple Locations   Effective incident response work often requires a physical presence at the organization's facilities. If the service provider is off site, consider how quickly it can have an incident response team at any facility, and how much this will cost. Consider on-site visits; perhaps there are certain facilities or areas where the service provider should not be permitted to work.

Maintaining Incident Response Skills In-House   Organizations that completely outsource incident response should strive to maintain basic incident response skills in-house. Situations may arise in which the outsourcer is unavailable (for example, a new worm attacks thousands of organizations simultaneously or a natural disaster or national flight stoppage occurs). The organization should be prepared to perform its own incident handling if the service provider is unable to act. The organization's technical staff must also be able to understand the significance, technical implications, and impact of the service provider's recommendations.

Incident Response Personnel

Regardless of which incident response model an organization chooses, a single employee should be in charge of incident response. In a fully outsourced model, this person is responsible for overseeing and evaluating the service provided. In all other models, this responsibility is generally achieved by having a team manager and a deputy team manager, who assumes authority in the absence of the team manager. The manager typically performs a variety of tasks, including acting as a liaison with upper management and other teams and organizations, defusing crisis situations, and ensuring that the team has the necessary personnel, resources, and skills. Managers should also be technically adept and have excellent communication skills, particularly an ability to communicate to a range of audiences. They should also be able to maintain positive working relationships with other groups, even under times of high pressure.

Technical Skills   In addition to the team manager and deputy team manager, some teams also have a technical lead—a person with strong technical skills and incident response experience who assumes oversight of and final responsibility for the quality of the technical work that the entire incident response team undertakes. The position of technical lead should not be confused with the position of incident lead. Larger teams often assign an incident lead as the primary point of contact for handling a specific incident. Depending on the size of the incident response team and the magnitude of the incident, the incident lead may not actually perform any actual incident handling, such as data analysis or evidence acquisition. Instead, the incident lead may be coordinating the handlers' activities, gathering information from the handlers, providing updates regarding the incident to other groups, and ensuring that the team's needs are met, such as by arranging for food and lodging for the team during extended incidents.

Members of the incident response team should have excellent technical skills because they are critical to the team's success. Unless the team members command a high level of technical respect across the organization, people will not turn to them for assistance. Technical inaccuracy in functions such as issuing advisories can undermine the team's credibility, and poor technical judgment can cause incidents to worsen. Critical technical skills include system administration, network administration, programming, technical support, and intrusion detection. Every team member should have good problem-solving skills; there is no substitute for real-world troubleshooting experience, such as dealing with operational outages. It is not necessary for every team member to be a technical expert—to a large degree, practical and funding considerations will dictate this—but having at least one highly proficient person in each major area of technology (for example, particular operating systems, Web servers, and e-mail servers) is a necessity.

It is important to counteract staff burnout by providing opportunities for learning and growth. Suggestions for building and maintaining skills follow:

- Budget enough funding to maintain, enhance, and expand proficiency in technical areas and security disciplines, as well as less technical topics such as the legal aspects of incident response. Consider sending each full-time team member to at least two technical conferences per year and each part-time team member to at least one.
- Ensure the availability of books, magazines, and other technical references that promote deeper technical knowledge.
- Give team members opportunities to perform other tasks, such as creating educational materials, conducting security awareness workshops, writing software tools to assist system administrators in detecting incidents, and conducting research.
- Consider rotating staff members in and out of the incident response team.
- Maintain sufficient staffing so that team members can have uninterrupted time off work (for example, vacations).
- Create a mentoring program to enable senior technical staff to help less experienced staff learn incident handling.
- Participate in exchanges in which team members temporarily trade places with others (for example, network administrators) to gain new technical skills.
- Occasionally bring in outside experts (for example, contractors) with deep technical knowledge in needed areas, as funding permits.
- Develop incident-handling scenarios, and have the team members discuss how they would handle them.
- Conduct simulated incident-handling exercises for the team. Exercises are particularly important because they not only improve the performance of the incident handlers, but they also identify issues with policies and procedures and with communication.

Nontechnical Skills   Incident response team members should have other skills in addition to technical expertise. Teamwork skills are of fundamental importance because cooperation and coordination are necessary for successful incident response. Every team member should also have good communication skills. Speaking skills are particularly important because the team interacts with a wide variety of people, including incident victims, managers, system administrators, human resources, public affairs, and law enforcement. Writing skills are important when team members are preparing advisories and procedures. Although not everyone within a team needs to have strong writing and speaking skills, at least a few people within every team should possess them so the team can represent itself well in front of senior management, users, and the public.

Dependencies Within Organizations

It is important to identify other groups within the organization that may be needed to participate in incident handling so that their cooperation can be solicited before it is needed. Every incident response team relies on the expertise, judgment, and abilities of others, including the stakeholders specified in the previous sections.

Incident Response Team Services

The main focus of an incident response team is performing incident response; however, it is rare for a team to perform incident response only. In most organizations, the IR team work like volunteer firefighters, going about their primary responsibilities until an incident arises. When it does, through word of mouth or electronic notification, the team receives its orders and shifts gears to deal with the threat. In some organizations, the IR team is organized to provide IR services, which may significantly overlap with other traditional information security tasks, but have an IR focus. By constantly working with IR-based tools and technologies, the IR team stays trained and focused on incidents and can better deal with intrusions.

According to CERT CC, "CSIRT services can be grouped into three categories:

- Reactive services: These services are triggered by an event or request, such as a report of a compromised host, wide-spreading malicious code, software vulnerability, or something that was identified by an intrusion detection or logging system. Reactive services are the core component of CSIRT work.
- Proactive services: These services provide assistance and information to help prepare, protect, and secure constituent systems in anticipation of attacks, problems, or events. Performance of these services directly reduces the number of incidents in the future.
- Security quality management services: These services augment existing and well-established services that are independent of incident handling and traditionally performed by other areas of an organization such as the IT, Audit, or Training departments. If the SIRT performs or assists with these services, the SIRT's point of view and expertise can provide insight to help improve the overall security of the organization and identify risks, threats, and system weaknesses. These services are generally proactive, but contribute indirectly to reducing the number of incidents."[13]

Figure 3-3 shows specific services corresponding with these categories:

Examples of additional services that an incident response team might offer (according to NIST) are provided in the following sections.

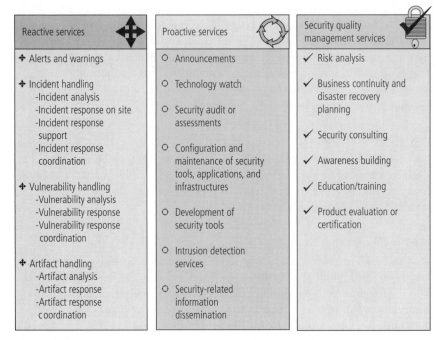

Reactive services	Proactive services	Security quality management services
✦ Alerts and warnings	○ Announcements	✓ Risk analysis

✦ Incident handling
  -Incident analysis
  -Incident response on site
  -Incident response
   support
  -Incident response
   coordination
	○ Technology watch
	
	○ Security audit or
	  assessments
	
	○ Configuration and
	  maintenance of security
	  tools, applications, and
	  infrastructures
		✓ Business continuity and
		  disaster recovery
		  planning
		
		✓ Security consulting
		
		✓ Awareness building

✦ Vulnerability handling
  -Vulnerability analysis
  -Vulnerability response
  -Vulnerability response
   coordination
	○ Development of
	  security tools
	
	○ Intrusion detection
	  services
		✓ Education/training
		
		✓ Product evaluation or
		  certification

✦ Artifact handling
  -Artifact analysis
  -Artifact response
  -Artifact response
   coordination
	○ Security-related
	  information
	  dissemination	

FIGURE 3-3 SIRT services[14]

Advisory Distribution

A team may issue advisories that describe new vulnerabilities in operating systems and applications and provide information on mitigating the vulnerabilities. Promptly releasing such information is a high priority because of the direct link between vulnerabilities and incidents. Distributing information about current incidents also can be useful in helping others identify signs of such incidents. It is recommended that only a single team within the organization distribute computer security advisories to avoid duplication of effort and the spread of conflicting information.

Vulnerability Assessment

An incident response team can examine networks, systems, and applications for security-related vulnerabilities, determine how they can be exploited and what the risks are, and recommend how the risks can be mitigated. These responsibilities can be extended so that the team performs auditing or penetration testing, perhaps making unannounced visits to sites to perform on-the-spot assessments. Incident handlers are well suited to performing vulnerability assessments because they routinely see all kinds of incidents and have firsthand knowledge of vulnerabilities and how they are exploited. However, because the availability of incident handlers is unpredictable, organizations should typically give primary responsibility for vulnerability assessments to another team and use incident handlers as a supplemental resource.

Intrusion Detection

An incident response team may assume responsibility for intrusion detection because others within the organization do not have sufficient time, resources, or expertise. The team generally benefits because it should be poised to analyze incidents more quickly and accurately, based on its knowledge of intrusion detection technologies. Ideally, however, primary responsibility for intrusion detection should be assigned to another team, with members of the incident response team participating in intrusion detection as their availability permits.

Education and Awareness

Education and awareness are resource multipliers—the more the users and technical staff know about detecting, reporting, and responding to incidents, the less drain there should be on the incident response team. This information can be communicated through many means: workshops and seminars, Web sites, newsletters, posters, and even stickers on monitors.

Technology Watch

A team can perform a technology watch function, which means that it looks for new trends in information security threats. Examples of this are monitoring security-related mailing lists, analyzing intrusion detection data to identify an increase in worm activity, researching new rootkits that are publicly available, and monitoring honeypots. The team should then make recommendations for improving security controls based on the trends that they identify. A team that performs a technology watch function should also be better prepared to handle new types of incidents.

Patch Management

Giving the incident response team the responsibility for patch management (for example, acquiring, testing, and distributing patches to the appropriate administrators and users throughout the organization) is generally not recommended. Patch management is a time-intensive, challenging task that cannot be delayed every time an incident needs to be handled. In fact, patch management services are often needed most when attempting to contain, eradicate, and recover from large-scale incidents. Effective communication channels between the patch management staff and the incident response team are likely to improve the success of a patch management program.

Additional Recommendations

Additional recommendations are summarized in the following sections.

Establish Capability

Organizations should be prepared to respond quickly and effectively when computer security defenses are breached. The Federal Information Security Management Act of 2002 (FISMA) requires federal agencies to establish incident response capabilities.

Create Policy

The incident response policy is the foundation of the incident response program. It defines which events are considered incidents, establishes the organizational structure for incident response, defines roles and responsibilities, and lists the requirements for reporting incidents, among other items.

Establish Policies and Procedures for Information Sharing

The organization will want or be required to communicate incident details with outside parties, such as the media, law enforcement agencies, and incident-reporting organizations. The incident response team should discuss this requirement at length with the organization's public affairs office, Legal Department, and management to establish policies and procedures regarding information sharing. The team should comply with existing organization policy on interacting with the media and other outside parties.

Provide Information

Federal civilian agencies are required to report incidents to FedCIRC; other organizations can contact other incident-reporting organizations. Reporting is beneficial because the incident-reporting organizations use the reported data to provide information to the reporting parties regarding new threats and incident trends.

Selecting an Incident Response Team Model

Organizations should carefully weigh the advantages and disadvantages of each possible team structure model and staffing model in the context of the organization's needs and available resources.

Select the Incident Response Team

The credibility and proficiency of the team depend to a large extent on the technical skills of its members. Poor technical judgment can undermine the team's credibility and cause incidents to worsen. Critical technical skills include system administration, network administration, programming, technical support, and intrusion detection. Teamwork and communications skills are also needed for effective incident handling. Because every incident response team relies on the expertise, judgment, and abilities of its team members, consider adding members from other teams, including management, information security, IT support, legal, public affairs, and facilities management.

Determine Which Services the Team Should Offer

Although the main focus of the team is incident response, most teams perform additional functions. Examples include distributing security advisories, performing vulnerability assessments, educating users on security, and monitoring intrusion detection sensors.

This concludes the material is adapted from NIST Special Publication 800-61 Computer Security Incident Handling Guide[15] and materials from CERT/CC.

INCIDENT RESPONSE PLANNING

An **incident response (IR) plan** is a detailed set of processes and procedures that anticipate, detect, and mitigate the effects of an unexpected event that might compromise information resources and assets. In an organization, unexpected activities occur periodically;
these are referred to as **events**. In CP, an event that threatens the security of the organization's information is called an **incident**. An incident occurs when an attack (natural or
human made) affects information resources and/or assets, causing actual damage or
other disruptions. **IR**, then, is a set of procedures that commence when an incident is
detected. IR must be carefully planned and coordinated, because organizations heavily
depend on the quick and efficient containment and resolution of incidents. The IR plan
is usually activated when an incident causes minimal damage—according to criteria set in
advance by the organization—with little or no disruption to business operations.

When one of the threats identified in Chapter 1 turns into a valid attack, it is classified as an information security incident, but only if it has all of the following characteristics:

- It is directed against information assets owned or operated by the organization.
- It has a realistic chance of success.
- It threatens the confidentiality, integrity, or availability of information
  resources and assets.

The prevention of threats and attacks has been intentionally omitted from this discussion because guarding against such possibilities is entirely the responsibility of the Information Security Department. It is important to understand that IR procedures are *reactive
measures* and, excluding the efforts taken to prepare for such actions, are *not considered a preventive control*.

The responsibility for creating an organization's IR plan usually falls to the chief information security officer (CISO). With the aid of other managers and systems administrators on the IR team, the CISO should select members from each community of interest to
form an independent IR team that executes the IR plan. The roles and responsibilities of
the members of the IR team should be clearly documented and communicated throughout the organization. The IR plan also includes an alert roster that lists certain critical
agencies to be contacted during the course of an incident. Planning for an incident and the
responses to it requires a detailed understanding of the information systems and the
threats they face. The IR planning team and SIRT seek to develop a series of predefined
responses that will guide the team and information security staff through the incident
response steps. Predefining incident responses enables the organization to react to a
detected incident quickly and effectively, without confusion or wasted time and effort.

As part of the six-step CP process discussed in detail in Chapter 2, the IR team creates the IR plan, and from there the IR procedures that are integral to the plan can begin to take shape. For every attack scenario end case, the IR team creates the incident plan made up of three sets of incident-handling procedures:

- During the incident: The planners develop and document the procedures that must be performed during the incident. These procedures are grouped and assigned to individuals. Systems administrators' tasks differ from managerial tasks, so members of the planning committee must draft a set of function-specific procedures.

- After the incident: Once the procedures for handling an incident are drafted, the planners develop and document the procedures that must be performed immediately after the incident has ceased. Again, separate functional areas may develop different procedures.

- Before the incident: The planners draft a third set of procedures, which are those tasks that must be performed to prepare for the incident. These procedures include the details of the data backup schedules, disaster recovery preparation, training schedules, testing plans, copies of service agreements, and business continuity plans, if any. At this level, the business continuity plan could consist of just additional material on a service bureau that stores data off-site via electronic vaulting, with an agreement to provide office space and to lease equipment as needed.

Although it may not seem logical to prepare the documentation of the IR plan in the order just described, this is a practical consideration. When the members of the IR team reach for the documentation, the primary concern is what must be done now, during the incident. This is followed by the need to access documented procedures on the follow-up activities. The final section on the procedures used for IR readiness and the steps needed to maintain the plan are included in the final section. That section of the IR plan is used only when an incident response is not underway. Each of these is discussed in detail in the following sections.

For each incident plan, the IR planning team will also begin to add other additional information as identified in the example shown following this paragraph. This information (to be discussed in detail later in this chapter) includes the trigger, the notification method, and response time. The notification method describes the manner in which the team receives its notification that an incident has occurred and the plan is to be executed. This could be by phone, pager, e-mail, loudspeaker, or word of mouth. The response time represents the time limit in which the team should optimally respond, and typically ranges from 30 minutes to 48 hours depending on the incident. Virus attacks, for example, would require a very quick response (in the 30 minutes to 1-hour range), while e-mail-spoofing attacks may be deferred for 24–48 hours, depending on the actions of the attacker.

Attack type:	
Trigger:	
Reaction force and lead:	
Notification method:	
Response time:	

Actions to be taken during this response:
1.
.
n.
Incident is ended and actions cease when:
Actions to be taken after incident response is ended:
1.
n.
Incident follow-up is ended and actions after the incident are complete when:
Preparation actions to be integrated into IR plans before incident response plan is needed:
1.
.
n.

Planning for the Response During the Incident

Beginning with the end in mind is useful in most planning activities. However, in the specific case of IR, you begin with the middle in mind, the actual incident response. The most important phase of the IR plan is the reaction to the incident, depicted here as "during the incident." When an event escalates to an incident, the team needs quick and easy access to the specific procedures necessary to identify, contain, and terminate the incident. Although the specifics of these actions are covered in Chapter 4, an overview here can assist in understanding the mechanics for use in developing this phase of the IR plan.

Triggering the IR plan

Each viable attack scenario end case is examined in turn by the IR team. As indicated earlier, representatives from the SIRT assist as part of this team, once the SIRT has been formed. The IR team discusses the end cases and begins to understand the actions that must be taken to react to the incident. The discussion begins with the **trigger**, the circumstances that cause the IR team to be activated and the IR plan to be initiated. This trigger could be a number of situations or circumstances, including the following:

- A phone call from a user to the help desk about unusual computer or network behavior
- Notification from a systems administrator about unusual server or network behavior
- Notification from an intrusion detection device
- Review of system log files indicating an unusual pattern of entries
- Loss of system connectivity
- Device malfunctions
- Other specific identifiable situations that result in the invocation of the IR plan

There are many indicators that an intrusion may be occurring, as is discussed in Chapter 4. Once an indicator has been reported, the IR team lead, or IR duty officer, makes the determination that the IR plan must be activated. An **IR duty officer** is a SIRT team member, other than the team leader, who is currently performing the responsibilities of the team leader in scanning the organization's information infrastructure for signs of an incident (again, as defined in Chapter 4). Once this individual detects a potential incident, he or she notifies the necessary team members and moves forward with the IR plan.

The Reaction Force

A specific set of skills are needed for each type of incident. Therefore, each attached scenario end case requires the IR planning team to determine what individuals are needed to respond to each particular end case. For example, different skills are probably needed to respond to a physical security threat as compared to a denial-of-service attack or an internal virus infestation. Each unique combination of skills can then be added to the IR plan section dedicated to this particular attack. In addition, the IR plan should specify the team leader for that particular incident. Should the incident begin to escalate, the IR team leader continues to add resources and skill sets as necessary to continue to attempt to contain and terminate the incident. In addition to specifying the leader, the IR plan should also specify the scribe, archivist, or historian for the incident. This individual is responsible for developing and maintaining a log of events for use in reviewing actions during the after-action review (which is described in a later section). The resulting team represents the Incident Response **reaction force** for that particular incident.

REACTION!

The Second Armored Cavalry Regiment (ACR) was the oldest cavalry regiment on continuous active duty until it was decommissioned in 1994. The 2nd ACR served as the vanguard of the 1st Armored Division in the sweep of Iraqi forces during the 1991 Gulf War. Before Desert Shield, the 2nd ACR was for many years responsible for the patrol and

continued

protection of the West Germany/East Germany/Czechoslovakian border. The regiment[14] consisted of three cavalry squadrons, a tank company, a howitzer battalion, and an air-cavalry squadron. This mission was carried out by placing one troop (a company-sized element) from each of the three front-line squadrons (a battalion-sized element) in various border patrol camps along the border for a 30–45 day rotation. Each of these border troops conducted constant surveillance of the border, ready to give early warning of potential border violations, political incidents, and even hostile invasions. Within the border camp, the border troop consisted of either a cavalry troop with 12 M3A1 Bradley Fighting Vehicles (BFVs) and 9 M1A1 Abrams Main Battle tanks, or a tank company with 14 M1A1s. Occasionally, units from outside the regiment took a shift on the border, but it was ultimately the 2nd ACR's responsibility to guard this stretch of territory.

The unit occupying the border camp was required to organize a series of elements capable of deploying in reaction to an incident on the border—be it a border crossing by a political defector or an invasion by a military force. The smallest such element was the "reaction force" made up of eight to ten soldiers manning two armored vehicles (M3A1s or M1A1s). It was required to be ready to deploy to an area outside the base within 15 minutes to combat a foe or report on the incident. While the routine patrols were conducted in HMMWVs (Hummers), the reaction elements had to deploy in battle vehicles. The next larger element was the "reaction platoon," the remainder of the reaction force's platoon (two additional Abrams, or four additional BFVs, and eight to twenty additional troops) that had to be ready to deploy within 30 minutes. Had the incident warranted it, the entire troop had to be prepared to depart the base within one hour. This deployment was rehearsed daily by the reaction force, weekly by the reaction platoon, and at least twice during border camp by the entire troop.

What does this scenario illustrate? An incident is an incident. The employees in an organization responding to a security incident are of course not expected to deploy fully armed to engage in combat against a physical threat. But the preparation and planning required to respond to an information security incident are not entirely different from that required to respond to a military incident, because in both cases, the same careful attention to detail must be paid, each potential threat scenario must be examined, and a number of responses commensurate with the level of the incident must be developed.

Actions Taken During the Incident

The next planning component is the determination of what must be done to react to this particular end case. In the event of a virus infestation, for example, the first action is to verify the presence of the virus by examining the antivirus software, system logs, and other monitoring systems. The help desk also queries users to determine if others have reported strange or unusual system or network behavior. Once it is determined that there is in fact a virus (or worm) infestation, the next step is performed—determining the extent of exposure. Is the infestation limited to one workstation or has it already spread?

Once the extent is determined, the team begins to attempt to quarantine the infestation, in this example, by first disconnecting infected systems from the network, and then by looking for evidence of continued spread, in case the virus has already jumped quarantine. Should isolating infected machines not contain the spread, then additional measures may be necessary, such as isolating network segments, terminating server sessions, disconnecting the Internet connection, and even shutting down the network servers. Once the infection is contained, the team continues to look for "flare-ups," which are small pockets of infestation that arise or activate once the primarily infected systems have been isolated. Only after all infected machines or systems have been isolated can the team begin the next phase—decontamination.

In the last phase of *actions during* for this example incident, the team begins disinfecting systems by running antivirus software, searching for spyware, and so on. Should antivirus software be functional and up to date, the presence of a new virus should be documented. Once all signs of contamination are eliminated, the *actions during* phase is complete.

Planning for After the Incident

Once the incident has been contained, and all signs of the incident removed, the *actions after* phase begins. During this phase, lost or damaged data is restored, systems scrubbed of infection, and essentially everything is restored to its previous state. The IR plan thus must describe the stages necessary to recovery from the most likely events of the incident. It should also detail other events needed for the *actions after* phase, like the protection from follow-on incidents, forensics analysis, and the after-action review.

Follow-on incidents are highly probable when infected machines are brought back online, or other infected computers, which may have been offline at the time of the attack, are brought back up. They are also likely in the event of a hacker attack, when the attacker retreats to a chat room and describes in specific detail to his or her associates the method and results of their latest conquest. Therefore, the identification of potential follow-on attacks should be of great concern. By identifying and resolving the avenues of attacks from the forensics analysis, the organization can prevent these incidents from recurring.

Forensics analysis is the process of systematically examining information assets for evidentiary material that can provide insight into how the incident transpired. Information on which machine was infected first or how a particular attacker gained access to the network provides information about unknown vulnerabilities or exploits. Care must be made to use an individual trained in forensic analysis, because the information found during the analysis may be potential evidence in civil or criminal proceedings. Forensic analysis is covered in detail in Chapter 5.

Before returning to routine duties, the IR team must also conduct an **after-action review (AAR)**. An AAR is a detailed examination of the events that occurred from first detection to final recovery. All key players review their notes and verify that the IR documentation is accurate and precise. All team members review their actions during the incident and identify areas where the IR plan worked, didn't work, or should be improved. This allows the team to update the IR plan. The AAR can serve as a training case for future staff. It also brings to a close the actions of the IR team.

Planning for Before the Incident

Planning for "before the incident" or *before actions* calls on the planners to implement good information technology and information security practices. However, specific incidents may have unique requirements to prevent. *Before actions* include both the preventative measures to manage the risks associated with a particular attack and the preparedness of the IR team. As described earlier in the "Reaction!" sidebar, it is only through routine rehearsal that the team can maintain a state of readiness to response to attacks. This process includes training the SIRT, testing the IR plan, selecting and maintaining the tools used by the SIRT, and training users of the systems and procedures controlled by the organization. The subject of risk management in general was covered in Chapter 1.

Training the SIRT

The primary responsibility of the IR team is to ensure the SIRT is prepared to respond to each incident they may face. This requires a host of ongoing training and rehearsal activities.

Training of incident response personnel can be conducted in a number of ways. There are several national training programs that focus on incident response tools and techniques. SANS offers a number of national conferences specifically designed to train the information security professional (see *www.sans.org*), and includes incident response topics. SANS even has a dedicated set of conferences—SANSFIRE (Forensics and Incident Response Education) specifically focused on incident response. Unlike other conferences, SANS is not designed for the hacker first, and everyone else second. Vendors such as Microsoft, Cisco, and Sun also provide incident response training for IT professionals. For government employees, the Department of Homeland Security (DHS) and the US CERT co-host a conference for incident response training (*www.us-cert.gov/events/2005/event/profiles/20050404gfirst.html*).

In addition to formal external training, the organization can set up its own training program, where senior, more experienced staff members share their knowledge with newer, less experienced employees. An ongoing training program should include this mentoring-type training to prevent specific organizational knowledge from leaving when already-trained employees depart.

Other training methods include a professional reading program. There are a host of high-quality information security journals and magazines that have articles and columns on incident response topics, including:

- The *SANS Reading Room* (*www.sans.org/rr*). Individuals seeking advanced SANS certification are required to write a practicum paper. Several of these papers include CP topics.
- *Computer Security Officer* (*www.csoonline.com*)
- *SC Magazine* (*www.scmagazine.com*)
- *Information Security Magazine* (*http://informationsecurity.techtarget.com*)

Unfortunately (at the time of this writing), there are no dedicated incident response journals or magazines. However, many of the disaster recovery journals identified in later chapters also have occasional articles on incident response. There are a number of online resources for incident response, including:

- Forum of Incident Response and Security Teams (FIRST): *www.first.org*
- U.S. Computer Emergency Readiness Team (US CERT): *www.us-cert.gov*
- CERT Coordination Center (CERT CC) at Carnegie Mellon University: *www.cert.org*
- NIST Computer Security Resource Center (CSRC): *http://csrc.nist.gov*
- Honeypots.net: *www.honeypots.net*

IR Plan Testing   A key part of training the SIRT is testing the IR plan. An untested plan is no plan at all. Very few plans are executable as initially written; they must be tested to identify vulnerabilities, faults, and inefficient processes. Once problems are identified during the testing process, improvements can be made, and the resulting plan will be reliable in times of need. Six strategies that can be used to test contingency plans are:[15]

- Desk check
- Structured walk-through
- Simulation
- Parallel testing
- Full interruption
- War gaming

Desk Check   The simplest kind of validation involves distributing copies of the IR plan to each individual that will be assigned a role during an actual incident. Each individual performs a desk check by reviewing the plan and creating a list of correct and incorrect components. While not a true test, it is a good way to review the perceived feasibility and effectiveness of the plan.

Structured Walk-Through   In a structured walk-through, all involved individuals walk through the steps they would take during an actual event. This can consist of an on-site walk-through, in which everyone discusses their actions at each particular location and juncture, or it may be more of a "chalk talk," in which all involved individuals sit around a conference table and discuss, in turn, their responsibilities as the incident would unfold.

Simulation   In a simulation, each involved individual works individually, rather than in a conference, simulating the performance of each task. The simulation stops short of the actual physical tasks required, such as installing the backup, or disconnecting a communications circuit. The major difference between a walk-through and a simulation is that individuals work on their own tasks, and are responsible for identifying the faults in their own procedures.

Parallel Testing   In the parallel test, individuals act as if an actual incident occurred, performing their required tasks and executing the necessary procedures without interfering with the normal operations of the business. Great care must be taken to ensure that the procedures performed do not halt the operations of the business functions, thus creating an actual incident.

Full Interruption   In full-interruption testing, the individuals follow each and every procedure, including the interruption of service, restoration of data from backups, and notification of appropriate individuals. This is often performed after normal business hours in organizations that cannot afford to disrupt or simulate the disruption of business functions. Although full-interruption testing is the most rigorous, unfortunately it is too risky for most businesses.

War Gaming   A favorite pastime of information security professionals is **war gaming**, which is realistic, head-to-head attack and defend information, security attacks, and incident response methods. This valid, effective training technique is so popular, there are national competitions at conferences like Black Hat (*http://blackhat.com*) and DEFCON (*www.defcon.org*).[16] War gaming competition at the collegiate level is appropriately held at the West Point Military Training Academy (*www.cs.ucsb.edu/~vigna/CTF*). There are a number of methods that the incident response team can use in training the SIRT as well as testing the IR plan. These are only valid if the SIRT team acts as defenders, using their own equipment or a duplicate environment, and follows the IR plan in the performance of the training. There is little to be gained from simply "going at it."

Common war gaming strategies include the following:

- Capture the flag: In this strategy, a "flag" or token file is placed on each team's system. The teams are given a predetermined amount of time to protect the systems, short of encrypting the flag, and then both defend their flag, and attempt to capture the opponent team's or teams' flag(s). This can be executed one-on-one or in a larger scope with multiple teams in a free-for-all.
- King of the hill: In this variation on capture the flag, one team is designated as king of the hill (KOTH), and has a flag planted in its systems. One or more other teams work independently to breach the KOTH security and obtain the file. This method may be better suited for SIRT training and testing, because it allows the KOTH team to focus exclusively on defensive tactics and IR plan implementation, rather than splitting the team between offensive and defensive operations.
- Computer simulations: In this type of war game, individual users or teams of users work to defend their systems and networks from simulated attacks. While there are not many of these types of computer simulations currently available, some organizations develop their own as a training technique, customizing them to their own systems and configurations.
- Defend the flag: In this combination of KOTH and computer simulations, a number of systems are set up to continually attack or simulate attacks on the target system. The defensive team must react to an escalating level of attacks to successfully defend their systems. The software to create the attacking

systems is easily found by searching the Web, and reputable companies such as Cisco use these tools in their training to teach their students how to properly configure firewalls, IDSs, and routers.

- Online programming-level war games: For technically advanced programmers, there are also online information security education and training war games like those at *www.pulltheplug.org*. At this site, four war games provide both an education in recognizing code-type attacks, and in defending against them:
  - "*Vortex*: By touring through the most common exploitable bugs, users of this war game are expected to have gained mastery in the basic fundamentals of system exploitation.
  - *Catalyst*: Binary analysis skills are integral to a comprehensive knowledge of security and security systems. This war game challenges players with various levels requiring binary object analysis.
  - *Semtex*: Offers network-based challenges, builds skills used in creating server/client applications, and challenges the user to figure out problems with various network protocols.
  - *Blackhole*: This war game was created to increase its players' ability for remote (and blind) exploitation."[17]

Even the CIA and the U.S. military use war games to train and test their troops in information security and information warfare tactics.[18] Unfortunately, hackers also have their own war games (*http://roothack.org*) that allow them to practice prior to conducting their own attacks.

At a minimum, organizations should conduct a periodic walk-through (or chalk talks) of each of the CP component plans. A failure to update each of these plans as the business and its information resources change can erode the team's ability to respond to an incident, or possibly cause greater damage than the incident itself.

NOTE

These testing methods will be referred to in other sections because they can be applied to all CP training and testing efforts. If this sounds like a military training effort, note that author Richard Marcinko, a former Navy SEAL, provides the following recommendations:

The more you sweat in training, the less you bleed in combat.
Training and preparation hurts.
Lead from the front, not the rear.
You don't have to like it, just do it.
Keep it simple.
Never assume.
You are paid for your results, not your methods.[21]

Tools for the SIRT

Table 3-4 shows the tools recommended by NIST for use by incident handlers.

TABLE 3-4 Tools and resources for incident handlers

119

Incident Handler Communications and Facilities

Contact information for team members and others within and outside the organization (primary and backup contacts), such as law enforcement and other incident response teams; information may include phone numbers, e-mail addresses, public encryption keys (in accordance with the encryption software described in the following), and instructions for verifying the contact's identity

On-call information for other teams within the organization, including escalation information

Incident reporting mechanisms, such as phone numbers, e-mail addresses, and online forms that users can use to report suspected incidents; at least one mechanism should permit people to report incidents anonymously

Pagers or cell phones to be carried by team members for off-hour support and on-site communications

Encryption software to be used for communications among team members, within the organization, and with external parties; software must use a Federal Information Processing Standards (FIPS) 140-2 validated encryption algorithm

War room for central communication and coordination; if a permanent war room is not necessary, the team should create a procedure for procuring a temporary war room when needed

Secure storage facility for securing evidence and other sensitive materials

Incident Analysis Hardware and Software

Computer forensic workstations and/or backup devices to create disk images, preserve log files, and save other relevant incident data

Laptops, which provide easily portable workstations for activities such as analyzing data, sniffing packets, and writing reports

Spare workstations, servers, and networking equipment, which may be used for many purposes, such as restoring backups and trying out malicious code; if the team cannot justify the expense of additional equipment, perhaps equipment in an existing test lab could be used, or a virtual lab could be established using operating system (OS) emulation software

Blank media, such as floppy disks, CD-Rs, and DVD-Rs

Easily portable printer to print copies of log files and other evidence from nonnetworked systems

Packet sniffers and protocol analyzers to capture and analyze network traffic that may contain evidence of an incident

Computer forensic software to analyze disk images for evidence of an incident

Floppies and CDs with trusted versions of programs to be used to gather evidence from systems

Evidence-gathering accessories, including hardbound notebooks, digital cameras, audio recorders, and chain-of-custody forms; plus evidence-storage bags, tags, and evidence tape are needed to preserve evidence for possible legal actions

Incident Response: Preparation, Organization, and Prevention

TABLE 3-4 Tools and resources for incident handlers (continued)

Incident Analysis Resources
Port lists, including commonly used ports and Trojan horse ports
Documentation for OSs, applications, protocols, and intrusion detection and antivirus signatures
Network diagrams and lists of critical assets, such as Web, e-mail, and File Transfer Protocol (FTP) servers
Baselines of expected network, system, and application activity
Cryptographic hashes of critical files to speed the analysis, verification, and eradication of incidents

(Source: NIST SP 800-61)[22]

Training the Users

Training the end user to assist in the process of incident response is primarily the responsibility of those individuals who provide security education training and awareness (SETA) for the organization. As part of the ongoing employee-training program, SETA trainers should instruct end users on the following tasks:

- What is expected of them as members of the organization's security team
- How to recognize an attack: Broken down by category, each user should be instructed on what to look for in an attack, including the key indicators.
- How to report a suspected incident, and to whom to report it: By e-mail or phone to the help desk, information security hotline, abuse@myorganization. com, or other designated mechanism
- How to mitigate the damage of attacks on the desktop: By disconnecting the system from the network if they suspect an attack in progress and reporting incidents promptly
- Good information security practices: Tasks that prevent attacks on the desktop, such as:
  - Keeping your antivirus software up to date
  - Using spyware detection software
  - Working with system administrators to keep operating system and applications up to date with patches and updates
  - Not opening suspect e-mail attachments
  - Avoiding social engineering attacks by not providing critical information over the phone or e-mail
  - Not downloading and installing unauthorized software or software from untrusted sources
  - Protecting passwords and classified information

While the specifics of developing a training program are beyond the scope of this book, you want to develop training that focuses on the audience and includes the following key elements:

Training for General Users   One method of ensuring that incident response is understood by general users is to provide training on the plan. This allows users to ask questions and receive specific guidance, and also allows the organization to emphasize key points. These general users also require training on the technical details of how to do their jobs securely, including good security practices, password management, specialized access controls, and violation reporting.

A convenient time to conduct this type of training is during employee orientation. During this critical time, employees are educated on a wide variety of organizational policies and procedures and on the organization's expectations of its employees. Because employees haven't established preconceived notions or methods of behavior, they are more likely to be receptive to this instruction. This is balanced against the issue that they are not yet familiar with the systems or their jobs, and, therefore, any particular issues about which they might have questions won't have arisen.

Training for Managerial Users   Management may have the same training requirements as the general user; however, managers expect a more personal form of training, with smaller groups, and more interaction and discussion. In fact, managers often resist organized training of any kind. This is another area in which a champion can exert influence; support at the executive level can convince managers to attend training events, which in turn reinforces the entire training program.

Training for Technical Users   Technical training for IT staff, security staff, and technically competent general users is more detailed than general user or managerial training, and may therefore require the use of consultants or outside training organizations, as described earlier.

Training Techniques and Delivery Methods

Good training techniques are as essential to successful training as thorough knowledge of the subject area. As explained by Charles Trepper in his article "Training Developers More Efficiently":

> Using the wrong method can actually hinder the transfer of knowledge and lead to unnecessary expense and frustrated, poorly trained employees. Good training programs, regardless of delivery method, take advantage of the latest learning technologies and best practices. Recent developments include less use of centralized public courses and more on-site training. Training is often needed for one or a few individuals, not necessarily for a large group. Waiting until there is a large-enough group for a class can cost companies lost productivity. Other best practices include the increased use of short, task-oriented modules and training sessions, available during the normal work week, that are immediate and consistent. Newer concepts in training also provide students with the training they need when they need it—a practice often called just-in-time training.[23]

Selection of the training delivery method is not always based on the best outcome for the trainee. Often other factors come first, like budget, time frame, and needs of the organization. The most common delivery methods are shown in Table 3-5.

TABLE 3-5 Training delivery methods

Method	Advantages	Disadvantages
One-on-one A dedicated trainer works with each trainee on the areas specified	• Informal • Personal • Customized to the needs of the trainee • Can be scheduled to fit the needs of the trainee	Resource intensive, to the point of being inefficient
Formal class A single trainer works with multiple trainees in a formal setting	• Formal training plan, efficient • Trainees can learn from each other • Interaction with trainer is possible • Usually considered cost effective	• Relatively inflexible • May not be sufficiently responsive to the needs of all trainees • Difficult to schedule, especially if more than one session is needed
Computer-based training (CBT) Prepackaged software that provides training at the trainee's workstation	• Flexible, no special scheduling requirements • Self-paced, can go as fast or as slow as trainee needs • Can be very cost effective	• Software can be very expensive • Content may not customize to needs of the organization
Distance learning and Web seminars Trainees receive a seminar presentation at their computers. Some models allow teleconferencing for voice feedback; others have text questions and feedback	• Can be live, or archived and viewed at trainee's convenience • Can be low or no cost	• If archived, can be very inflexible, with no mechanism for trainee feedback • If live, can be difficult to schedule
User support group When support is available from a community of users, it is commonly facilitated by a particular vendor as a mechanism to augment the support for products or software	• Allows users to learn from each other • Usually conducted in an informal social setting	• Does not use a formal training model • Centered around a specific topic or product
On-the-job training Trainees learn the specifics of their jobs, while working, using the software, hardware, and procedures they will continue to use	• Very applicable to the task at hand • Inexpensive	• A sink-or-swim approach where the trainee usually experiences no formal training program • Can result in substandard work performance until trainee gets up to speed

TABLE 3-5 Training delivery methods (continued)

Method	Advantages	Disadvantages
Self-study (noncomputerized) Trainees study materials on their own, usually when not actively performing their jobs	• Lowest cost to the organization • Places materials in hands of the trainee • Trainees can select material they need to focus on the most • Self-paced	• Shifts responsibility for training onto the trainee, with little formal support

(Source: NIST SP 800-12) [24]

ASSEMBLING AND MAINTAINING THE FINAL INCIDENT RESPONSE PLAN

Draft plans can be used for training staff and for the testing steps used to validate the effectiveness of the plan. Any errors or difficulties discovered during training or testing can then be remedied as the draft plans mature. Once the desired level of plan maturity is achieved and the drafts have been suitably reviewed and tested, the final assembly can commence.

Note that the testing process does not stop once the final plan is created. As indicated earlier, each scenario of the IR plan should be tested at least semiannually by performing at least a structured walk-through test and a more realistic type of test when possible. Obviously, if the IR plan was executed in response to an actual incident, then those sections that have seen actual use may not require the same degree of periodic retesting, assuming of course that no changes were made to the plan in the after-action review. Any plans that are modified should be scheduled for additional testing at the earliest opportunity.

Once all the individual components of the IR plan have been drafted and tested, the final IR plan document can be created. Every organization has its own preferences for the format and content for the IR plan. The most important thing is that the IR plan is developed, tested, and placed in an easy-to-access location. The following list of recommended practices describes the design and implementation of the physical IR plan to be deployed in such a manner to make it easy to locate and use in an emergency:

1. Select a uniquely colored binder. Red or yellow is recommended, because organizations are inundated with white binders.
2. On the spine of the binder, place red and yellow or red and white reflective tape. Why? Some incidents involve a loss of power. In a low-level light environment, whether by emergency exit light or flashlight, this binder will shine like a lighthouse, making it easy to identify and use.
3. Under the front slipcover place a classified document cover sheet. This identifies the book as a classified document. If the document were to fall into the wrong hands, knowing how an organization responds to a particular attack could reveal procedural vulnerabilities.
4. Place an index on the first page inside, preferably one with a color-coded bar corresponding to a set of tabs.

5. For each category of attacks, place the corresponding IR plan documents under a common tab, and label the index.

6. Organize the contents so that the first page contains the "during attack" actions, followed by the "after attack" actions, and finally the "before attack" actions. In an emergency, you want to be able to see the information most important to you first.

7. Attach copies of any relevant documents in the back under a separate tab, for example, copies of service agreements for the ISP, telephone, water, power, gas, and so on.

8. Add additional documents as needed.

9. Store in a secure but easily accessed location.

Figure 3-4 presents an example of pages from an IR plan.

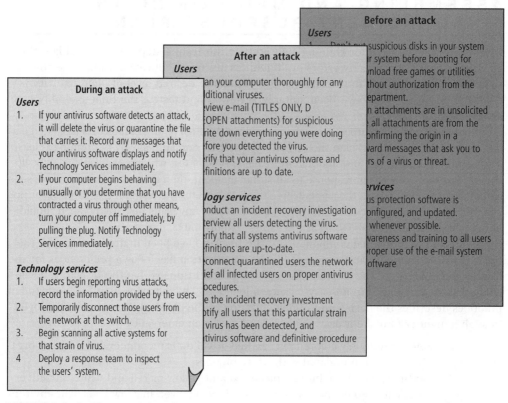

FIGURE 3-4 Incident response plan

Chapter Summary

- The incident response process has several phases, from initial preparation through postincident analysis.

  - During preparation, the organization also attempts to limit the number of incidents that might occur by selecting and implementing a set of controls based on the results of risk assessments.
  - Detection of security breaches is thus necessary to alert the organization whenever incidents occur.
  - The organization can act to mitigate the impact of the incident by containing it and ultimately recovering from it.
  - After the incident is adequately handled, the organization issues a report that details the cause and cost of the incident and the steps the organization should take to prevent future incidents.
- The incident response committee follows these general stages:
  - Form the IR planning committee.
  - Develop the IR policy.
  - Organize the SIRT.
  - Develop the IR plan.
  - Develop IR procedures.
- The process of organizing the incident response planning process begins with staffing the IR planning committee by identifying and engaging a collection of stakeholders. Typical stakeholders often include:
  - General management
  - IT management
  - InfoSec management
  - Legal Department
  - Human resources
  - Public relations
  - Physical security
  - Auditing and risk management
  - Insurance
  - General end users
  - Others stakeholders, including key business partners, contractors, temporary employee agencies, and in some cases consultants
- One of the first deliverables to be created by the IR planning committee should be the incident response policy, which is similar in structure to other policies used by the organization.

- The security incident response team (SIRT) is a set of policies, procedures, technologies, people, and data necessary to prevent, detect, react, and recover from anything that could potentially damage the organization's information. Development of the SIRT involves the following stages:
  - Collecting information from stakeholders
  - Defining the IR team structure
  - Determining the IR team services
- Models used to develop incident response teams tend to fall into one of three structural categories:
  - Central incident response team
  - Distributed incident response teams
  - Coordinating team
- Incident response teams are often developed along one of these three staffing models:
  - Employees
  - Partially outsourced
  - Fully outsourced
- SIRT services can include:
  - Reactive services
  - Proactive services
  - Security quality management services
  - Advisory distribution
  - Vulnerability assessment
  - Intrusion detection
  - Education and awareness
  - Technology watch
  - Patch management
- The incident response (IR) plan comprises a detailed set of processes and procedures that anticipate, detect, and mitigate the effects of an unexpected event that might compromise information resources and assets.
- For every case, the IR team creates the incident plan made up of three sets of incident-handling procedures:
  - During the incident
  - Before the incident
  - After the incident

Review Questions

1. What are the phases of the incident response development process?
2. What are the critical elements of each of the phases in the previous question?
3. What are the general stages followed by the incident response committee?
4. Who are the typical stakeholders of the incident response process?
5. What is recommended to be among the earliest deliverables to be created by the IR planning committee?
6. What is the security incident response team (SIRT)?
7. What stages are recommended to be used in the development of the SIRT?
8. What are the recommended structural categories of models that might be used to develop incident response teams?
9. What staffing models are commonly used for the incident response team?
10. What are the commonly provided SIRT services provisioned in large organizations?
11. What are the components of an incident response plan?
12. What are the sets of incident-handling procedures?

Exercises

1. Using a Web browser, identify at least five references you would want to use when training a SIRT team.
2. Using a Web browser, visit *www.mitre.org*. What information is provided there, and how would it be useful?
3. Using a Web browser, visit *www.securityfocus.com*. What is bugtraq, and how would it be useful? What additional information is provided under the Vulnerabilities tab?
4. Using a Web browser, visit *www.cert.org*. What information is provided there, and how would it be useful? Look for the tab for CSIRTs, and identify valuable information there.
5. Using a Web browser, search for other methods employed by industry or government to share information on possible incidents.

References

[1] Tim Grance, Karen Kent, and Brian Kim, *Computer Security Incident Handling Guide,* Special Publication SP 800-61 (National Institute of Standards and Technology, 2004), 3–1.

[2] See note 1.

[3] Carnegie Mellon University, *Handbook for Computer Security Incident Response Teams (CSIRT),* 77 (2003), http://www.cert.org/archive/pdf/csirt-handbook.pdf.

[4] Carnegie Mellon University, "Creating a Computer Security Incident Response Team: A Process for Getting Started" (2002), http://www.cert.org/csirts/Creating-A-CSIRT.html.

[5] See note 1.

[6] Carnegie Mellon University, *Handbook for Computer Security Incident Response Teams (CSIRT),* 40 (2003), http://www.cert.org/archive/pdf/csirt-handbook.pdf.

[7] Mary Hall, "Implementing a Computer Incident Response Team in a Smaller, Limited Resource Organizational Setting" (2003), http://www.sans.org/rr/paper.php?id=1065.

[8] See note 4.

[9] See note 1.

[10] See note 4.

[11] Moira J. West-Brown, Don Stikvoort, Klaus Peter Kossakowski, Georgia Killcrece, Robin Ruefle, Mark Zajicek, *Handbook for Computer Security Incident Response Teams (CSIRTs)* (April 2003), http://www.cert.org/archive/pdf/csirt-handbook.pdf.

[12] National Institute of Standards and Technology, *Guide to Information Technology Security Services,* Special Publication (SP) 800-35, http://csrc.nist.gov/publications/nistpubs/800-35/NIST-SP800-35.pdf. Also, CERT/CC, "Outsourcing Managed Security Services," http://www.cert.org/security-improvement/modules/omss/.

[13] Moira J. West-Brown, Don Stikvoort, Klaus Peter Kossakowski, Georgia Killcrece, Robin Ruefle, Mark Zajicek, *Handbook for Computer Security Incident Response Teams (CSIRTs)*, http://www.sei.cmu.edu/pub/documents/03.reports/pdf/03hb002.pdf.

[14] See note 13.

[15] See note 1.

[16] A company or troop is a unit consisting of approximately 100 soldiers; a battalion or squadron consists of five or six companies or troops, totaling approximately 500–600 soldiers. A regiment or brigade consists of five or six battalions or squadrons, totaling approximately 2500–3000 soldiers.

[17] Ronald L. Krutz and Russell Dean Vines, *The CISSP Prep Guide: Mastering the Ten Domains of Computer Security* (New York: John Wiley and Sons, 2001), 288.

[18] While the authors emphatically denounce the actions of hackers and the criminal acts associated with hacking, these conferences typically are attended not only by hackers, but also by information security professionals and representatives of law enforcement and the military. In keeping with our philosophy of "know your enemy," one cannot pass up the opportunity to visit the enemy's camp and observe them preparing for battle, learning their strategies and tactics firsthand.

[19] Pull The Plug, "Wargames," http://www.pulltheplug.org/wargames/index.html.

[20] *Reuters. "CIA Plays Cyberwar Games,"* ZDNet News: May 26, 26, 2005,http://news.zdnet.com/2100-1009_22-5722279.html

[21] Richard Marcinko and John Weisman, *Designation Gold* (New York: Pocket Books, 1998), preface.

[22] See note 1.

[23] Charles Trepper, "Training Developers More Efficiently," *InformationWeekOnline*, http://www.informationweek.com/738/38addev.htm.

[24] National Institute of Standards and Technology (NIST), *An Introduction to Computer Security: The NIST Handbook (SP 800-12)*, (Gaithersburg, MD: NIST, 2002).

CHAPTER 4

INCIDENT RESPONSE: DETECTION AND DECISION MAKING

A little fire is quickly trodden out; which, being suffered, rivers cannot quench.

—William Shakespeare, King Henry VI. Part III. Act iv. Sc. 8

OPENING SCENARIO

JJ had become quite bored with the discussion that was taking place in the conference room and had let his mind wander as he stared out the window.

Paul frowned at him as he repeated the question JJ had not heard. "Which sensor placement strategy do you think will get us the best network performance? For the IDS—you know—the project we're working on in this meeting?"

"Well," said JJ, "truth be told, I wonder if the network approach is the right way to go. I think we should move toward a host-based model, and limit the network intrusion system to a few critical subnetworks."

Paul thought a second. "Good point." He paused and then said, "Funny, I thought you were daydreaming, but that's a good point. I would like you to work up a new rough design based on a host-centric approach. We can review it tomorrow when we continue this meeting."

"OK, Paul," said JJ.

Later that day, JJ came into Paul's office. "I've got a couple of ideas I'd like your opinion on."

"Shoot," said Paul.

"I just attended a presentation where a CIO discussed ways to cut information security spending," JJ said. "He had some, well... radical ideas that paid off for him and his company."

"I'm all ears," Paul replied. The idea of going into this process with a cost-effective strategy had his undivided attention.

"Well this CIO indicated that he had invested quite a large amount of money into proprietary security technologies. Everything from firewalls, to scanners, to intrusion detectors. He then discovered that his maintenance and upgrade packages were costing him more than the original cost of the equipment."

continued

"I know that feeling," said Paul.

"Well, he discovered that there is a lot of open source software out there, you know the Linux and UNIX stuff," JJ continued.

"Uh, oh." Paul uttered, stopping JJ. "I see a potential problem there. We don't have any UNIX or Linux people on staff."

"That was his point." JJ leaned forward tapping Paul's desk for emphasis. "With the money he could save from ending the service contracts he was able to hire three good systems people and still save about half of his six-million-dollar budget."

"And if I don't have a million-dollar budget?"

"Then we just hire one or two guys, or hire one, and send one of our current network admins off to training. I found several local places that offer open source software training. At the top of the list is Snort training right here in town."

" I think you're onto something." Paul leaned forward, obviously intrigued by JJ's suggestion. "Tell you what, I want you to write a business case by reviewing the current expenditures, add the projected additions from the meeting earlier today, and then balance those against the cost of a plan for an open source approach, including a new hire, and training for one to two of our staff. Be brutally honest. We don't want to chase vaporware on this one. We need solid, tested stuff, and the skills to support it."

"Can do, Paul" JJ grinned. He liked it when Paul got behind his ideas.

"And have it to me by end of business tomorrow." Paul added.

The grin disappeared from JJ's face.

Questions for Discussion:

- What technologies can JJ recommend to Paul?
- Where can JJ go for more information and training on open source software?

LEARNING OBJECTIVES

Upon completion of this material, you should be able to:

- Understand the elements necessary to detect incidents that pose risk to the organization
- Know the components of an intrusion detection system
- Become familiar with the processes used in making decisions surrounding incident detection and escalation

INTRODUCTION

Among the earliest challenges incident response process planners must face is to determine how an organization classifies events as they occur. Some events are the product of routine system activities while others are critical indicators of situations needing an urgent response. **Incident classification** is the process of evaluating circumstances around organizational events, determining which events are possible incidents, or **incident candidates,** and then determining whether or not the event constitutes an actual incident. Where the design of the process used to make this judgment is the role of the incident response (IR) design team, the everyday process of classifying an incident is the responsibility of the IR team.

Initial reports from a variety of sources, including end users, intrusion detection systems, virus management software, and systems administrators, are all ways to track and detect incident candidates. Careful training in the reporting of an incident candidate allows end users, the help desk staff, and all security personnel to relay vital information to the IR team. After an actual incident is properly identified, the members of the IR team can effectively execute the corresponding procedures from the IR plan, including the notification of key response resources.

DETECTING INCIDENTS

Several different events occurring in and around an organization signal the presence of an incident candidate. Unfortunately, these same events may occur when a network becomes overloaded, a computer or server encounters an error, or some normal operation of an information asset mimics the appearance of an identified incident candidate. To help make the detection of actual incidents more reliable, D. L. Pipkin has identified three broad categories of incident indicators: *possible*, *probable*, and *definite*.[1] This categorization enables an organization to expedite the decision-making process of incident classification and ensure the proper IR plan is activated as early as possible. The categories are explored in the following sections.

Possible Indicators of an Incident

Using the criteria established by Pipkin, there are four types of incident candidates considered to be *possible* actual incidents:

1. Presence of unfamiliar files: Users might discover unfamiliar files in their home directories or on their office computers. Administrators might also find unexplained files that do not seem to be in a logical location or owned by an authorized user. See the Technical Details on rootkits for examples of unfamiliar files.
2. Presence or execution of unknown programs or processes: Users or administrators might detect unfamiliar programs running, or processes executing, on office machines or network servers. For more information on processes and services, see the Technical Details on processes and services.
3. Unusual consumption of computing resources: Consumption of memory or hard disk space might suddenly spike or fall. Many computer operating systems, including Windows 2000, Windows XP, and many UNIX variants, allow

users and administrators to monitor CPU and memory consumption. Most computers also have the ability to monitor hard drive space. In addition, servers maintain logs of file creation and storage.

4. Unusual system crashes: Computer systems can crash. Older operating systems running newer programs are notorious for locking up or spontaneously rebooting whenever the operating system is unable to execute a requested process or service. You are probably familiar with systems error messages such as "Unrecoverable Application Error," "General Protection Fault," and the infamous Windows NT Blue Screen of Death. However, if a computer system seems to be crashing, hanging, rebooting, or freezing more frequently than usual, the cause could be an incident candidate.

TECHNICAL DETAILS: ROOTKITS

"A rootkit is a set of tools used by an intruder after cracking a computer system. These tools can help the attacker maintain his or her access to the system and use it for malicious purposes. Rootkits exist for a variety of operating systems such as Linux, Solaris, and versions of Microsoft Windows."[2] The term *rootkit* is derived from the use of the set of software tools contained in the *kit* that is used to compromise the systems and then to obtain "root-" or administrator-level access to a system. But rootkits do more than gain system administrator level access, they hide their presence and provide the attacker with the ability to revisit the site and conduct additional attacks.

The Sysinternals organization defines four categories of rootkits:

- *Persistent rootkits: Associated with malware that activates each time the system boots and thus must store code in a persistent store (for example, Registry or file system), and configure a method by which the code executes without user intervention*
- *Memory-based rootkits: Malware that has no persistent code and therefore does not survive a reboot*
- *User-mode rootkits: Might intercept all calls to Windows APIs used by file system utilities to enumerate the contents of file system directories. When an application performs a directory listing, the rootkit intercepts and modifies the output to remove its own entries.*
- *Kernel-mode rootkits: Not only can it intercept the native API in kernel mode, but it also directly manipulates kernel-mode data structures. A common technique for hiding the presence of a malware process is to remove the process from the kernel's list of active processes. Thus effectively hiding the rootkit from the system itself.*[3]

continued

To install a rootkit, the attacker must first gain access by attacking through a port or exploiting a vulnerability. Once the attacker gains access, he or she installs the rootkit and gains administrative privileges. Unfortunately, these tools are freely available on the Web for all types of platforms. These tools, such as Hacker Defender, NT Rootkit, WinlogonHijack, to name a few of the Windows varieties, also have the ability to collect and store user login and password information; some even contain keystroke loggers. The mere presence of these tools indicates that either the system was compromised sometime in the past, or the system administrator is playing with fire. It may be possible for one attacker to piggyback onto another attacker's rootkit, so even using them on one's own system is potentially dangerous.

How do you detect rootkits? There are utilities to find these attacker tools. Microsoft Research (*http://research.microsoft.com*) has its own version titled Strider GhostBuster Rootkit Detection. It is designed to detect API-hiding rootkits. Sysinternals has a similar version titled RootkitRevealer (*www.sysinternals.com/Utilities/RootkitRevealer.html*) that also can detect hidden rootkits. As shown in Figure 4-1, the tool not only detects rootkits, but also detects mismatches between the Registry and the scan, and other native Windows file differences between APIs, the Registry, and the master file table. Thus some degree of expertise is needed to ascertain whether a rootkit is present. The presence of files titled hxdef100.exe, hxdef100.ini, and hxdefdrv.sys, among others, would be a strong indicator that the Hacker Defender Rootkit is present.

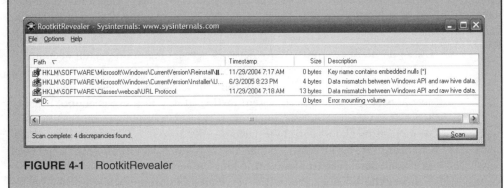

FIGURE 4-1   RootkitRevealer

Probable Indicators of an Incident

Pipkin further identifies four types of incident candidates that are *probable* indicators of actual incidents:

1. Activities at unexpected times: If traffic levels on an organization's network exceed the measured baseline values, an incident candidate is probably present. If this activity surge occurs when few members of the organization are at work, the probability becomes much higher. Similarly, if systems are accessing drives, such as floppy and CD-ROM drives, when the end user is not using them, an incident may also be occurring.

2. Presence of new accounts:. Periodic review of user accounts can reveal an account (or accounts) that the administrator does not remember creating or that are not logged in the administrator's journal. Even one unlogged new account is an incident candidate. An unlogged new account with root or other special privileges has an even higher probability of being an actual incident.

3. Reported attacks: If users of the system report a suspected attack, there is a high probability that an attack has occurred, which constitutes an incident. The technical sophistication of the person making the report should be considered.

4. Notification from IDS: If the organization has installed and correctly configured a host- or network-based intrusion detection system (IDS), then notification from the IDS indicates that an incident might be in progress. However, IDSs are seldom configured optimally and, even when they are, tend to issue many false positives or false alarms. The administrator must then determine whether the notification is real or if it is the result of a routine operation by a user or other administrator.

Definite Indicators

Pipkin's categories continue with a list of five types of incident candidates that are *definite* indicators of an actual incident. That is, they clearly and specifically signal that an incident is in progress or has occurred. In these cases, the corresponding IR plan must be activated immediately.

1. Use of dormant accounts: Many network servers maintain default accounts, and there often exist accounts from former employees, employees on a leave of absence or sabbatical without remote access privileges, or dummy accounts set up to support system testing. If any of these accounts begins accessing system resources, querying servers, or engaging in other activities, an incident is almost certain to have occurred.

2. Changes to logs: The smart systems administrator backs up system logs as well as system data. As part of a routine incident scan, systems administrators can compare these logs to the online versions to determine whether they have been modified. If they have, and the systems administrator cannot determine explicitly that an authorized individual modified them, an incident has occurred.

3. Presence of hacker tools: Network administrators sometimes use system vulnerability and network evaluation tools to scan internal computers and networks to determine what a hacker can see. These tools are also used to support research into attack profiles. Too often, the tools are used by employees, contractors, or outsiders with local network access to hack into systems. To combat this problem, many organizations explicitly prohibit the use of these tools without written permission from the CISO, making any unauthorized installation a policy violation. Most organizations that engage in penetration-testing operations require that all tools in this category be confined to specific systems, and that they not be used on the general network unless active penetration testing is under way.

4. Notifications by partner or peer: If a business partner or another connected organization reports an attack from your computing systems, then an incident has occurred.

5. Notification by hacker: Some hackers enjoy taunting their victims. If an organization's Web pages are defaced, it is an incident. If an organization receives an extortion request for money in exchange for its customers' credit card files, an incident is in progress.

Another way to describe the definite indicators from the Pipkin approach is the following list of the general types of events that, when they are confirmed to have occurred, indicate that an actual incident is underway, and the corresponding IR plan must be immediately activated. The general list of events encompasses:

- Loss of availability: Information or information systems become unavailable.
- Loss of integrity: Users report corrupt data files, garbage where data should be, or data that just looks wrong.
- Loss of confidentiality: You are notified of sensitive information leaks, or information you thought was protected has been disclosed.
- Violation of policy: If organizational policies addressing information or information security have been violated, an incident has occurred.
- Violation of law: If the law has been broken and the organization's information assets are involved, an incident has occurred.

Identifying Real Incidents

As was noted earlier, one of the first challenges facing IR plan designers is creating a process to collect and evaluate incident candidates to determine whether they are actual incidents (or circumstances likely to become incidents) or nonevents, also called false positive incident candidates. This is very important because most organizations can find themselves awash in many incident candidates, and the vast majority will be false positives.

Each organization must create its own processes that can be used to collect and evaluate incident candidates. Some may choose to have a single incident center where all incident candidates are sent from the earliest moment of recognition. Others may choose to have geographically separate review locations, perhaps based on time zones, where preliminary determinations about the status of an incident candidate can be assessed. Still other organizations may choose to isolate incident candidate evaluation based on business units, product lines, or some other criterion.[4]

Many organizations struggle with the relationship of the false positive incident candidate to the concept of noise. In a properly designed system (whether human or machine based) those candidates that are legitimate activities wrongly reported as incident candidates are noise and should be suppressed by the data collection procedures or programs. Most data collection systems are implemented with little or no formal training for the users of the process. When done properly, the training needs for incident candidate data collection should be extensive at first and then continue at a less intensive effort for the life of the system. The quality and quantity of the training, and the resulting skills of the staff involved in the data collection, will result in the removal of noise from the data collection process. Even the best-tuned incident candidate collection system generates false positives; usually, they are considered to be inherent in the nature of such systems. But, the ratio of false positive events to actual events needs to be kept to a manageable level with ongoing improvements to the collection processes.

Noise or false positives that may have been tuned from the collection system often result from several causes:

- Placement: The source of the incident candidate is a significant factor. If an automated intrusion detection system is placed outside the trusted subnetwork of the organization, it is likely to see a vast number of attempted attacks, which may be interpreted as incident candidates. Moving the sensor to be the first device inside the trusted subnetwork perimeter can reduce the number of events reported, allowing the control devices (firewall rules in this case) to have the desired effect before sending in the alarm.
- Policy: In some situations, organization policy may allow certain activities by employees that are later detected as incident candidates. For instance, if company policy allows network administrators within the company to use certain tools whose network signatures are classified by automated tools as network attacks (for instance, nmap, netbus, or any one of many widely available hacker tools) this will be a significant source of noise. Aligning data collection practices to align with policy parameters minimizes this kind of event.
- Awareness: In some cases, users are not aware of policy limitations on certain activities. For example, in the previous situation, if nmap is disallowed for use within the organization by policy, many system administrators may not be aware of the policy, and may use the tool for routine activities. An awareness program can help minimize the noise generated by this kind of activity.

Many organizations do not deal well with the effort to minimize noise and the false positives they generate. There must be a procedure defined for the data collection tuning process that results in a careful analysis of the effect each change has on the data collection rules. Left to their own devices, many automated intrusion detection system administrators simply turn off the reporting of some classes of events rather than perform an analysis of the events and determine if a change in the position of the data collector, an adjustment to policy, or increased awareness might be a better solution.

While the false positive issue gets a lot of attention, it is also important to avoid the occurrence of false negative reports. A **false negative** occurs when an incident that deserves attention is not reported. One example of a false negative comes from the character of Sherlock Holmes in Sir Arthur Conan Doyle's mystery "Silver Blaze." In the story, an expensive racehorse is stolen from its stable. Inspector Gregory of Scotland Yard asked Holmes if there were any particular aspect of the crime calling for additional study. Holmes replied, "Yes," and mentioned "the curious incident of the dog in the nighttime." Inspector Gregory replied, "The dog did nothing in the nighttime." Holmes said, "That was the curious incident." In this case, the failure of the dog to bark when Silver Blaze was stolen was a false negative report. If a data collection process such as an intrusion detection system fails to warn of a valid network attack, it becomes "the dog that did nothing in the nighttime."

Another factor to add to the tuning process is routine change. When new or modified systems are placed in service, the result may be a need for additional tuning of the data collection process. Newer technologies often change the way network traffic appears to both human and automated sensors. For example, some load-balancing appliances may generate significant traffic that probes the availability of the services it is attempting to balance. This traffic, if unanticipated, may be perceived as an incident candidate, when in fact it is merely noise.[5]

The objective of the tuning process is a mechanism whereby valid incident candidates are generated while controlling the generation of alerts based on legitimate network activities.

TECHNICAL DETAILS: PROCESSES AND SERVICES

In the domain of information processing, a process is a task being performed by a computing system. This is often done at the same time that the computer system is processing other tasks. Therefore, many processes may be underway at the same time, each of them being handled by the systems processor in turn.

Processes are often called *tasks* in embedded operating systems. The sense of *process* is *something that takes up time*, as opposed to *memory*, which is *something that takes up space*.

In general, an operating system process consists of:

- Memory: Contains executable code or task-specific data
- Operating system resources: These are allocated to the process, such as file descriptors or handles (Windows).
- Security attributes: Such as the process owner and the process's set of permissions
- Processor state: Such as the content of registers, physical memory addresses, and so on[6]

To view available processes provided on a Windows-based PC, use the Windows Task Manager (described in the exercise found in the appendix) as illustrated in Figure 4-2.

continued

Incident Response: Detection and Decision Making

FIGURE 4-2 Windows processes

Unfortunately, the task manager doesn't reveal all processes. Apparently Microsoft hid certain critical OS processes. However, another utility included in most versions of Windows is the System Information Utility (msinfo32.exe), located in the C:\program files\common files\microsoft shared\msinfo folder, which can detect all processes running on a particular system. Your instructor may provide an exercise for the use of this tool.

*To use **msinfo32** to hunt for Trojans, look down the task listings for running tasks and services for any which you don't recognize. Check the paths and filenames. Check the file properties, and run the executable or .dll through your virus scanner. If you find nothing, but still aren't sure, use the Startup Programs editor in the tools menu to disable the process, then restart your machine (make a backup of your system files first!). If nothing complains, leave the process disabled for now and carry on looking at the others. Eventually, you'll have only those processes you really need running on your machine. This will have the benefit of not only killing off any Trojans but also making your PC seem more responsive and generally quicker to start up.[7]*

Table 4-1 provides a partial list of system processes often found in a system running Windows 2000 Professional.

continued

TABLE 4-1 Some Windows 2000 processes[8, 9]

Process	Description
Csrss.exe	Client/server run-time subsystem and responsible for console windows, creating and/or deleting threads, and some parts of the 16-bit virtual MS-DOS environment
Dfssvc.exe	Provides server-side support for NetDfsxxx APIs that configure and maintain the Distributed File System topology
Dwwin.exe	The operating system client service that can report errors in user mode or kernel mode, and that reports unplanned shutdown events
Explorer.exe	The user shell, which includes the taskbar, desktop, and so on
Internat.exe	Runs at start-up; it loads the different input locales that are specified by the user. The locales to be loaded for the current user are taken from the registry key HKEY_CURRENT_USER\Keyboard Layout\Preload.
Llssrv.exe	The Licensing logging service client originally designed to help customers manage licenses for Microsoft server products that are licensed in the Server Client Access License (CAL) model
Lsass.exe	The local security authentication server; it generates the process responsible for authenticating users for the Winlogon service. This process is performed by using authentication packages such as the default Msgina.dll.
Msdtc.exe	ODBC applications can also use the Microsoft Distributed Transaction Coordinator to include multiple Microsoft SQL Server connections in a single transaction, even when the connections are to separate servers.
Mstask.exe	The task scheduler service, responsible for running tasks at a time predetermined by the user
Smss.exe	The session manager subsystem, which is responsible for starting the user session. This process is initiated by the system thread and is responsible for various activities, including starting the Winlogon and Win32 (Csrss.exe) processes and setting system variables.
Services.exe	Services Control Manager, which is responsible for starting, stopping, and interacting with system services
Spoolsv.exe	Spooler service is responsible for managing spooled print/fax jobs
Svchost	A generic process that acts as a host for other processes running from DLLs; therefore, don't be surprised to see more than one entry for this process
System.exe	Most system kernel-mode threads run as the System process.

continued

TABLE 4-1 Some Windows 2000 processes (continued)

Process	Description
System Idle Process	A single thread running on each processor, which has the sole task of accounting for processor time when the system isn't processing other threads
Taskmgr.exe	The process for Task Manager itself
Winlogon.exe	The process responsible for managing user logon and logoff; moreover, Winlogon is active only when the user presses CTRL+ALT+DEL, at which point it shows the security dialog box
Winmgmt.exe	A core component of client management in Windows 2000; this process initializes when the first client application connects, or it can be made to respond each time management applications request its services
Wmiprvse.exe	Windows Management Instrument resides in a shared service host with several other services. To avoid stopping all the services when a provider fails, providers are loaded into a separate host process named Wmiprvse.exe. More than one process with this name can be running. Each can run under a different account with varying security.
Wsrm.exe	The Windows System Resource Manager service, designed to manage multiple applications on a single computer or multiple users on a computer on which Terminal Services is in use. This supports a variety of scenarios, including consolidation, and can increase the efficiency with which physical hardware on a server is used by running applications.
Wsrmc.exe	Provides administrative control of the Windows System Resource Manager (WSRM) service using the command-line interface; the command-line interface provides equivalent administrative control to the WSRM snap-in

To view available services provided on a Windows-based PC or server, one can access the services function through the Administrative Tools menu in Control Panel, as illustrated in Figure 4-3.

continued

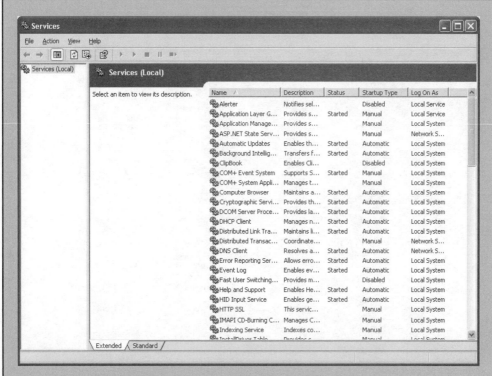

FIGURE 4-3 Windows services

More information about the services common to a Windows XP Professional installation are presented in Table 4-2. Note the Startup Type differs depending on individual configuration, and can be changed by the user.

TABLE 4-2 Some Windows XP Professional services

Service	Startup Type	Log On As
Alerter	Manual	Local Service
Application Layer Gateway	Manual	Local Service
Application Management	Manual	Local System
Automatic Updates	Automatic	Local System
Background Intelligent Transfer Service	Manual	Network Service

continued

TABLE 4-2 Some Windows XP Professional services (continued)

Service	Startup Type	Log On As
ClipBook	Manual	Local System
COM+ Event System	Manual	Local System
COM+ System Application	Manual	Local System
Computer Browser	Automatic	Local System
Cryptographic Services	Automatic	Local System
DHCP Client	Automatic	Local System
Distributed Link Tracking Client	Automatic	Local System
Distributed Transaction Coordinator	Manual	Network Service
DNS Client	Automatic	Network Service
Error Reporting	Automatic	Local System
Event Log	Automatic	Local System
Fast User Switching Compatibility	Manual	Local System
Help and Support	Automatic	Local System
Human Interface Device Access	Disabled	Local System
IMAPI CD-Burning COM	Manual	Local System
Indexing Service	Manual	Local System
Internet Connection Sharing	Manual	Local System
IPSec Services	Automatic	Local System
Logical Disk Manager	Automatic	Local System
Logical Disk Manager Administrative Service	Manual	Local System
Messenger	Automatic	Local Service
MS Software Shadow Copy Provider	Manual	Local System
Net Logon	Automatic	Local System
NetMeeting Remote Desktop Sharing	Manual	Local System
Network Connections	Manual	Local System

continued

TABLE 4-2 Some Windows XP Professional services (continued)

Service	Startup Type	Log On As
Network DDE	Manual	Local System
Network DDE DSDM	Manual	Local System
Network Location Awareness (NLA)	Manual	Local System
NT LM Security Support Provider	Manual	Local System
Performance Logs and Alerts	Manual	Network Service
Plug and Play	Automatic	Local System
Portable media serial number	Automatic	Local System
Print Spooler	Automatic	Local System
Protected Storage	Automatic	Local System
QoS RSVP	Manual	Local System
Remote Access Auto Connection Manager	Manual	Local System
Remote Access Connection Manager	Manual	Local System
Remote Desktop Help Session Manager	Manual	Local System
Remote Procedure Call (RPC)	Automatic	Local System
Remote Procedure Call (RPC) Locator	Manual	Network Service
Remote Registry	Automatic	Local Service
Removable Storage	Manual	Local System
Routing and Remote Access	Manual	Local System
Secondary Logon	Automatic	Local System
Security Accounts Manager	Automatic	Local System
Server	Automatic	Local System
Shell Hardware Detection	Automatic	Local System
Smart Card	Manual	Local Service
Service	Startup Type	Log On As
Smart Card Helper	Manual	Local Service

continued

TABLE 4-2 Some Windows XP Professional services (continued)

SSDP Discovery	Manual	Local Service
System Event Notification	Automatic	Local System
System Restore Service	Automatic	Local System
Task Scheduler	Automatic	Local System
TCP/IP NetBIOS Helper	Automatic	Local Service
Telephony	Manual	Local System
Telnet	Manual	Local System
Terminal Services	Manual	Local System
Themes	Automatic	Local System
Uninterruptible Power Supply	Manual	Local Service
UPnP Device Host	Manual	Local System
Upload Manager	Automatic	Local System
Utility Manager	Manual	Local System
Volume Shadow Copy	Manual	Local System
WebClient	Automatic	Local Service
Windows Audio	Automatic	Local System
Windows Firewall/Internet Connection Sharing	Automatic	Local System
Windows Image Acquisition (WIA)	Manual	Local System
Windows Installer	Manual	Local System
Windows Management Instrumentation	Automatic	Local System
Windows Time	Automatic	Local System
Wireless Zero Configuration Service	Automatic	Local System
WMI Performance Adapter	Manual	Local System
Workstation	Automatic	Local System

The presence of unexpected processes and services could indicate an intrusion or other incident. It is therefore imperative that incident response and information security personnel become familiar with the services and processes that *should* be present to simplify the task of identifying those services and process that *should not*.

INTRUSION DETECTION SYSTEMS

An **intrusion detection system (IDS)** is a network burglar alarm. It is designed to be placed in a network to determine whether or not the network is being used in ways that are out of compliance with the policy of the organization. To understand the technologies associated with IDS you must first understand the nature of the events it is attempting to detect.

An intrusion is a type of attack on information assets in which the instigator attempts to gain unauthorized entry into a system or network or disrupt the normal operations of a system or network. Whether or not this is done with the intent to steal or do harm, it remains outside the intended use of the system or network. Even when such attacks are automated or self-propagating, as in the case of viruses and distributed denial of services, they are almost always instigated by an individual whose purpose was to harm an organization.

Information security IDSs were first commercially available in the late 1990s. An IDS works like a burglar alarm inasmuch as it detects violations of the intended use of a network as defined by its configuration. This is analogous to a residential burglar alarm in that an opened window or door activates an alarm. The alarm from an IDS can be audible and/or visual (producing noise and lights), or it can be silent, taking the form of an e-mail message, pager alert, log entry, or network message to another system. With almost all IDSs, system administrators can choose the configuration of the various alerts and the associated alarm levels for each type of alert. Many IDSs enable administrators to configure the systems to notify them directly of trouble via e-mail or pagers. The systems can also be configured—again like a burglar alarm—to notify an external security service organization of the event. The configurations that enable IDSs to provide such customized levels of detection and response can become quite complex.

NOTE

A valuable source of information for more detailed study about IDSs is National Institute of Standards and Technology (NIST) Special Publication 800-31 "Intrusion Detection Systems," written by Rebecca Bace and Peter Mell and available through the NIST's Computer Security Resource Center at *http://csrc.nist.gov.*

IDS Terminology

To understand IDS operational behavior, you must first become familiar with some terminology that is unique to the field of IDSs. The following is a compilation of relevant IDS-related terms and definitions that were drawn from the marketing literature of a well-known information security company, TruSecure, but these terms are representative across the industry:

- **Alert or alarm:** An indication that a system has just been attacked or continues to be under attack. IDSs create alerts or alarms to notify administrators that an attack is or was occurring and may have been successful. Alerts and alarms may take the form of audible signals, e-mail messages, pager notifications, pop-up windows, or log entries written without taking any action.

- **False attack stimulus:** An event that triggers alarms and causes a false positive when no actual attacks are in progress. Testing scenarios that evaluate the configuration of IDSs may use false attack stimuli to determine if the IDSs can distinguish between these stimuli and real attacks.

- **False negative**: The failure of an IDS system to react to an actual attack event. Of all failures, this is the most grievous, for the very purpose of an IDS is to detect attacks.

- **False positive:** An alarm or alert that indicates that an attack is in progress or that an attack has successfully occurred when in fact there was no such attack. A false positive alert can sometimes be produced when an IDS mistakes normal system operations or activity for an attack. False positives tend to make users insensitive to alarms, which in turn can make them less inclined, and therefore slow, to react when an actual intrusion occurs.

- **Noise:** The ongoing activity from alarm events that are accurate and noteworthy but not necessarily significant as potentially successful attacks. Unsuccessful attacks are the most common source of noise in IDSs, and some of these may not even be attacks at all, but rather employees or other users of the local network simply experimenting with scanning and enumeration tools without any intent to do harm. The issue faced regarding noise is that most of the intrusion events detected are not malicious and have no significant chance of causing a loss.

- **Site policy:** The rules and configuration guidelines governing the implementation and operation of IDSs within the organization.

- **Site policy awareness:** An IDS's ability to dynamically modify its site policies in reaction or response to environmental activity. A *smart IDS* can adapt its reaction activities based on both guidance learned over time from the administrator as well as circumstances present in the local environment. Using a device of this nature, the IDS administrator acquires logs of events that fit a specific profile instead of being alerted for minor changes, such as when a file is changed or a user login fails. Another example of using a smart IDS is when the IDS knows it does not need to alert the administrator when an attack using a known and documented exploit is made against systems that the IDS knows to be patched against that specific kind of attack. When the IDS can accept multiple response profiles based on changing attack scenarios and environmental values, it makes the IDS that much more useful.

- **True Attack Stimulus:** An event that triggers alarms and causes an IDS to react as if a real attack is in progress. The attack may be actual when an attacker is at work on a system compromise attempt or it may be a drill, one of many ongoing tests of a network segment by security personnel using real hacker tools.

- **Confidence Value:** A value associated with an IDS' ability to detect and identify an attack correctly. The confidence value an organization places in the IDS is based on experience and past performance measurements. The confidence value, a type of *fuzzy logic,* provides an additional piece of information to assist the administrator in determining whether an attack alert is indicating that an actual attack in progress, or that the IDS is reacting to false attack stimuli and creating a false positive. For example, if a system deemed capable of reporting a denial-of-service attack with 90% confidence sends an alert, there is a high probability that an actual attack is occurring.

- **Alarm Filtering:** The is the process of classifying the attack alerts that an IDS detects in order to distinguish or sort false positives from actual attacks more efficiently. Once an IDS has been installed and configured, the administrator can set up alarm filtering by first running the system for a while to track what types of false positives it generates and then by adjusting the classification of certain alarms. For example, the administrator may set the IDS to discard certain alarms that he or she knows are produced by false attack stimuli or normal network operations. Alarm filters are similar to packet filters in that they can filter items by their source or destination IP addresses, but they have the additional capability of being able to filter by operating systems, confidence values, alarm type, or alarm severity.

- **Alarm Clustering:** A consolidation of almost identical alarms into a single higher-level alarm. This reduces the total number of alarms generated, reducing the administrative overhead. It also indicates if a relationship exists between the individual alarm elements.

- **Alarm Compaction:** Alarm clustering that is based on frequency, similarity in attack signature, similarity in attack target, or other similarities. Like the previous form of alarm clustering, this reduces the total number of alarms generated, reducing the administrative overhead. Alarm clustering can also indicate if a relationship exists between the individual alarm elements when they have specific similar attributes.

Why Use an IDS?

According to documentation of industry best practices from NIST, there are several compelling reasons to acquire and use an IDS:

- To prevent problem behaviors by increasing the perceived risk of discovery and punishment for those who would attack or otherwise abuse the system
- To detect attacks and other security violations that are not prevented by other security measures
- To detect and deal with the preambles to attacks (commonly experienced as network probes and other *doorknob-rattling* activities)
- To document the existing threat to an organization
- To act as quality control for security design and administration, especially of large and complex enterprises
- To provide useful information about intrusions that do take place, allowing improved diagnosis, recovery, and correction of causative factors[10]

In addition, drawn from the list above, one of the most often used justifications as to why organizations should install an IDS is that these systems can serve as straightforward deterrent measures. This is explained as increasing the fear of detection and discovery among would-be attackers or internal system abusers. If internal and external users know that an organization has an intrusion detection system, they are less likely to probe or attempt to compromise it, just as criminals are much less likely to break into a house that has been clearly marked as having a burglar alarm.

Another reason for installing an IDS is to cover the organization when its network fails to protect itself against known vulnerabilities or is unable to respond to a rapidly changing threat environment.

Forces Working Against an IDS

There are many factors that can delay or undermine an organization's ability to make its systems safe from attack and subsequent loss. For example, even though popular information security technologies such as scanning tools (to be discussed later in this chapter) allow security administrators to evaluate the readiness of their systems, they may still fail to detect or correct a known deficiency, or the administrators may perform the vulnerability-detection process too infrequently. And, even when a vulnerability is detected in a timely manner, it is not always corrected quickly. Also, because such corrective measures usually involve the administrator installing patches and upgrades, they are subject to delays caused by fluctuation in the administrator's workload.

To further complicate the matter, sometimes there are services that are known to be vulnerable, but they are so essential to ongoing operations that they cannot be disabled or otherwise protected in the short term. When there is a known vulnerability or deficiency in the system, an IDS can be particularly effective because it can be set up to detect attacks or attempts to exploit existing weaknesses. By, in effect, guarding these vulnerabilities, an IDS can become an important part of the strategy of Defense in Depth.

Most attacks against information systems begin with an organized and thorough probing of the organization's network environment and its defenses. This initial estimation of the defensive state of an organization's networks and systems is called *doorknob rattling* and is conducted first through activities collectively known as *footprinting* (which involves gathering information about the organization and its network activities and the subsequent process of identifying network assets), and then through another set of activities collectively known as *fingerprinting* (in which network locales are scanned for active systems, and then the network services offered by the host systems on that network are identified).

When a system is capable of detecting the early warning signs of footprinting and fingerprinting, much as neighborhood watch volunteers might be capable of detecting potential burglars casing their neighborhoods by skulking through and testing doors and windows, then the administrators may have time to prepare for a potential attack or to take actions to minimize potential losses from an attack.

Justifying the Cost

To justify the expenses associated with implementing security technology, such as an IDS (and other controls such as firewalls), security professionals are frequently required to prepare and defend a business case to justify the investment. Because deploying these technologies is often very expensive, almost all organizations require that project proponents document the threat from which the organization must be protected. The most frequently used method for doing this is to collect data on the attacks that are currently occurring in the organization and other similar organizations. While such data can be found in published reports or journal articles, firsthand measurements and analysis of the organization's own local network data are likely to be the most persuasive. As it happens, one means of collecting such data is by using IDS. Thus, IDSs are self-justifying systems—they can serve to document the scope of the threat(s) an organization faces and thus produce data that can help administrators persuade management that additional expenditures in information security technologies (for example, IDSs) are not only warranted but critical for the ongoing protection of information assets. Measuring attack information with freeware IDS tools (such as Snort) may be a method to start this process.

The concepts of quality assurance and continuous improvement are well known to most senior managers. IDS systems are often implemented at a step along the way to improved network security by adding an additional layer between the firewall and the server layers of defense. This means that an IDS can be justified using the concept of Defense in Depth. This is because an IDS can consistently pick up successful attacks that have compromised the outer layers of information security controls such as a firewall, but have not yet reached the valuable servers residing on the organization's trusted networks. When continuous improvement methodologies are applied to the results from the IDS, emergent or residual flaws in the security and network architectures can be identified and repaired. Such efforts expedite the incident response process as well.

Finally, even if an IDS fails to prevent an intrusion, it can still assist in the post attack review by helping a system administrator collect information on how the attack occurred, what the intruder accomplished, and which methods the attacker employed. This information can be used, as discussed in the preceding paragraph, to remedy any deficiency, as well as trigger the improvement process to prepare the organization's network environment for future attacks. The IDS may also provide forensic information that may be useful as evidence, should the attacker be caught and criminal or civil legal proceedings pursued. In the case of handling forensic information, an organization should follow the legally mandated procedures for handling evidence. Foremost among these is that information collected should be stored in a location and manner that precludes its subsequent modification. Other legal requirements and plans the organization has for the use of the data may warrant additional storage and handling constraints. As such, it may be useful for an organization to consult with legal counsel when determining policy governing this situation.[11]

IDSs operate as network-based, host-based, or application-based systems. A network-based IDS is focused on protecting network information assets. A host-based version is focused on protecting the server or host's information assets. Figure 4-4, shows an example that monitors both network connection activity and current information states on host servers. The application-based model works on one or more host systems that support a single application and is oriented to defend that specific application from special forms of attack. Regardless of whether they operate at the network host or application level, all IDSs use one of two detection methods: signature based or statistical anomaly based. Each of these approaches to intrusion detection is examined in detail in the following sections.

Classification of IDS by Network Placement

The placement of the sensor and detection devices or software programs has a significant affect on how the IDS operates. There are three widely used placement options: network-based, host-based, and application-based IDS.

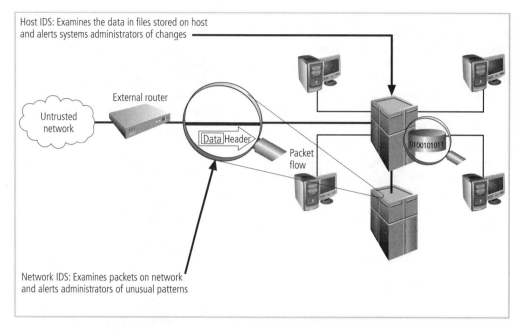

Host IDS: Examines the data in files stored on host and alerts systems administrators of changes

External router

Untrusted network

Data Header

Packet flow

0100101011

Network IDS: Examines packets on network and alerts administrators of unusual patterns

FIGURE 4-4   Intrusion detection systems

Network-Based IDS

A **network-based IDS (NIDS)** monitors traffic on a segment of an organization's network. A NIDS looks for indications of ongoing or successful attacks and resides on a computer or appliance connected to that network segment. When a situation occurs in which the NIDS is programmed to recognize as an attack, the NIDS responds. A NIDS examines the packets transmitted through an organization's networks. Its purpose is to look for patterns within network traffic that indicate an intrusion event is underway or about to begin. An example of this would be the observation of a number of network packets of a certain type that could indicate a denial-of-service attack is underway. Or, if someone notes the exchange of a series of packets in a certain pattern that could indicate that a port scan is in progress (as described in the Technical Details sidebar).

A network IDS can, therefore, detect many more types of attacks than a host-based IDS, but to do so requires a much more complex configuration and maintenance program. NIDSs are installed at a specific place in the network (such as on the inside of an edge router) so the traffic going in and out of a particular network segment can be watched. The NIDS can be deployed to watch a specific grouping of host computers on a specific network segment, or it may be installed to monitor all traffic between the systems that make up an entire network.

When placed next to a hub, switch, or other key networking device, the NIDS may use that device's monitoring port, also known as a **switched port analysis (SPAN)** port or mirror port. The monitoring port is a specially configured connection on a network device that is capable of viewing all of the traffic that moves through the entire device. Hubs were used in the early 1990s before switches became the popular choice for connecting networks in a shared-collision domain. Hubs received traffic from one node and retransmitted the traffic to all other nodes. This configuration allowed any device connected to the hub to monitor all traffic passing through the hub. Unfortunately, it also represented a security risk, because anyone connected to the hub could monitor all traffic that moved through that network segment. More recently, switches have been deployed on most networks, which, unlike hubs, create dedicated point-to-point links between their ports. This creates a higher level of transmission security and privacy and effectively eliminates the ability to eavesdrop on all traffic. Unfortunately, this ability to capture the traffic is necessary for the use of an IDS. Monitoring ports allow network administrators to collect traffic from across the network for analysis by the IDS as well as for occasional use in diagnosing network faults and measuring network performance.

The use of IDS sensors and analysis systems can be quite complex. One very common approach is to use an open source software program called Snort running on an open source Unix or Linux system. This can be managed and queried from a desktop computer using a client interface, as shown in Figure 4-5. This example shows a sample screen from Demarc Sentarus Enterprise (see *www.demarc.com*) displaying events generated by a Snort network IDS engine. For more information about how this approach might work in a variety of organizations, see *www.snort.org*.

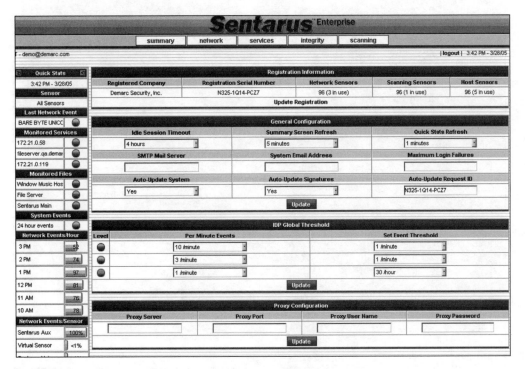

FIGURE 4-5 Demarc Sentarus Enterprise intrusion detection

TECHNICAL DETAILS: PORTS AND PORT SCANNING

*A **network port** is an interface for communicating with a computer program over a network. Network ports are usually numbered, and a network implementation such as TCP or UDP attaches a port number to data it sends; the receiving implementation uses the attached port number to figure out which computer program to send the data to. In TCP and UDP the combination of a port and a network address (IP number) is called a socket.*[12]

As described in RFC 793 and the IANA Port Numbers document, well-known port numbers range from 0 through 1023, registered port numbers from 1024 through 49151, and dynamic and/or private port numbers from 49152 through 65535.[13]

TCP/IP ports are the mechanism used by that protocol to enable access to a system. Table 4-3 shows the well-known TCP/IP ports that are commonly used by commercial applications. In addition, Table 4-4 lists ports that are known to have been frequently used by attackers.

TABLE 4-3 Well-known ports[14]

Port Number	Description	Port Number	Description
1	TCP Port Service Multiplexer (TCPMUX)	42	Host name server (Nameserv)
5	Remote Job Entry (RJE)	43	WhoIs
7	ECHO	49	Login Host Protocol (Login)
18	Message Send Protocol (MSP)	53	Domain Name System (DNS)
20	FTP—Data	69	Trivial File Transfer Protocol (TFTP)
21	FTP—Control	70	Gopher services
22	SSH Remote Login Protocol	79	Finger
23	Telnet	80	HTTP
25	Simple Mail Transfer Protocol (SMTP)	103	X.400 standard
29	MSG ICP	108	SNA gateway access server
37	Time	109	POP2

continued

TABLE 4-3 Well-known ports[14] (continued)

Port Number	Description	Port Number	Description
110	POP3	197	Directory Location Service (DLS)
115	Simple File Transfer Protocol (SFTP)	389	Lightweight Directory Access Protocol (LDAP)
118	SQL services	396	Novell Netware over IP
119	Newsgroup (NNTP)	443	HTTPS
137	NetBIOS Name Service	444	Simple Network Paging Protocol (SNPP)
139	NetBIOS Datagram Service	445	Microsoft-DS
143	Interim Mail Access Protocol (IMAP)	458	Apple QuickTime
150	NetBIOS Session Service	546	DHCP client
156	SQL Server	547	DHCP server
161	SNMP	563	SNEWS
179	Border Gateway Protocol (BGP)	569	MSN
190	Gateway Access Control Protocol (GACP)	1080	Socks
194	Internet Relay Chat (IRC)		

TABLE 4-4 Ports commonly used by hackers[15]

Port Number	Hacker Programs	Port Number	Hacker Programs
5	Midnight Commander	137	NetBios exploits
21	Doly Trojan	555	phAse zero, Stealth Spy
25	AntiGen, Email Password Attacks	1001	SK Silencer
80	Executer	1011	Doly Trojan
109	Sekure SDI, b00ger	1234	Ultor's Trojan

continued

TABLE 4-4 Ports commonly used by hackers[15] (continued)

Port Number	Hacker Programs	Port Number	Hacker Programs
1243	Sub-7	10167 U	Portal of Doom
1245	VooDoo Doll	10529	Acid Shivers
1807	SpySender	10666 U	Ambush
1981	ShockRave	12345	GirlFriend
1999	BackDoor	19932	DropChute
2001	The Trojan Cow	21544	NetBus
2023	Ripper Pro, HackCity	23456	EvilFtp, UglyFtp
2140	Deep Throat, The Invasor	26274	Delta Source
2801	Phineas Phucker	27374	Sub-7
3024	WinCrash	30100	NetSphere
3129	Master Paradise	31789	Hack'a'Tack
3150	DeepThroat, The Invaser	31337 U	BackOrifice
4092	WinCrash	31338	NetSpy
4950	ICQ Trojan	31339	NetSpy
5321	BackDoorz, Firehotchker	34324	Big Gluck, TN
5568	Robo-Hack	40412	The Spy
5714	WinCrash	47262	Delta Source
5741	WinCrash	50505	Sockets de Troie
5742	WinCrash	50766	Fore
6006	Bad Blood	53001	Remote Windows Shutdown
6670	DeepThroat	60000	DeepThroat
6711	Sub-7, DeepThroat	61466	TeleCommando
6969	GateCrasher	65000	Devil
9989	Ini-Killer	65535	RC1 Trojan

continued

When a review of log files, network scans, or just plain luck turns up one of these ports in use, the next step is to examine who or what is using this port to determine if the traffic is legitimate. As illustrated in Figure 4-6, many attacks come in through ports and then attack legitimate processes to allow themselves access or to conduct subsequent attacks.

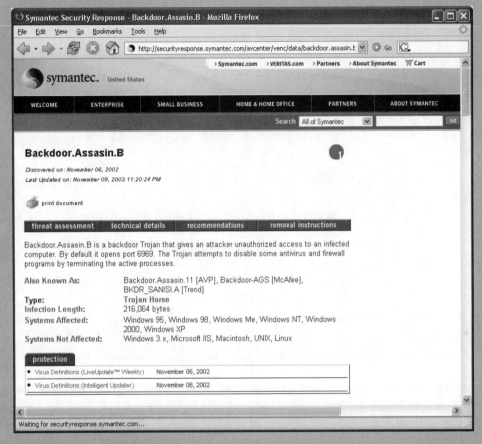

FIGURE 4-6   Backdoor.Assassin.B Trojan horse

Scanning and Enumeration   As noted earlier in the text, fingerprinting using scanning is the process of collecting information about computers. **Passive scanning** does this by listening to network traffic. **Active scanning** is accomplished by sending traffic and observing what traffic returns as a result. Once a target has been identified, **enumeration** is the process of identifying what resources are publicly available for exploit. Both methods must be used in conjunction with each other. You first scan the network to determine

continued

what assets or targets are on the network, and then you enumerate each target by determining which of its resources are available. Without knowing which computers and resources are vulnerable, it is impossible to protect these resources from attack. Chapter 12 contains several exercises that will show you how to determine exactly which computers are making resources available on the network and what vulnerabilities exist.

Scanning utilities are tools used to identify which computers are active on a network, as well as which ports and services are active on the computers, what function or role the machines may be fulfilling, and so on. These tools can be very specific as to what sort of computer, protocol, or resource they are scanning for, or they can be very generic. It is helpful to understand what sort of environment exists within your network so you can use the best tool for the job. The more specific the scanner is, the more likely it will give you detailed information that is useful later. However, it is also recommended that you make use of one or more very generic, broad-based scanners as well. This may help locate and identify nodes on the network of which you, as the administrator of the system, might not be aware. In addition, there are specific utilities that can be used as countersurveillance tools. Some of these tools may be able to help detect packet sniffers that are operating on the network. Many of the scanning tools available today are capable of providing both simple/generic and detailed/advanced functionality.

Some commonly used scanning tools (by both information security professionals and hackers) include the following:

- Nmap, a widely used port scanner (*http://insecure.org*)
- Nessus, a widely used, server-based vulnerability scanner (*www.nessus.org*)
- NEWT, a client-based vulnerability scanner (*www.tenablesecurity.com/ products/newt.shtml*)
- SuperScan, a client-based vulnerability scanner (*www.foundstone.com*)
- LANGuard, a client-based vulnerability scanner (*www.gfi.com*)

Use of these tools by an information security professional is essential in determining what ports are open and thus subject to attack by the hacker. Again—know your enemy!

Signature Matching   Using a process known as **signature matching**, Network IDSs must look for attack patterns by comparing measured activity to known signatures in their knowledge base to determine whether or not an attack has occurred or may be underway. This is accomplished by the comparison of captured network traffic using a special implementation of the TCP/IP stack that reassembles the packets and applies protocol stack verification, application protocol verification, and/or other verification and comparison techniques.

In the process of protocol stack verification, the NIDSs looks for invalid data packets, packets that are malformed under the rules of the TCP/IP protocol. A data packet is defined as invalid when its configuration does not match what is defined as valid by the various Internet protocols (TCP, UDP, IP). The elements of the protocols in use (IP, TCP, UDP, and application layers such as HTTP) are combined in a complete set called the protocol stack when the software is implemented in an operating system or application. Many types of intrusions, especially DoS and DDoS attacks, rely on the creation of improperly formed packets to take advantage of weaknesses in the protocol stack in certain operating systems or applications.

In application protocol verification, the higher-order protocols (HTTP, FTP, and Telnet) are examined for unexpected packet behavior or improper use. Sometimes an intrusion involves the arrival of valid protocol packets, but in excessive quantities. (In the case of the Tiny Fragment Packet attack, the packets are also excessively fragmented.) While the protocol stack verification looks for violations in the protocol packet structure, the application protocol verification looks for violations in the protocol packet use. One example of this kind of attack is **DNS cache poisoning**, when valid packets exploit poorly configured DNS servers to inject false information to corrupt the servers' answers to routine DNS queries from other systems on that network. Unfortunately, however, this higher-order examination of traffic can have the same effect on an IDS as it can on a firewall—it slows the throughput of the system. As such, it may be necessary to have more than one NIDS installed, with one of them performing protocol stack verification and one performing application protocol verification.

Advantages and Disadvantages of NIDS   Each organization must approach the justification, acquisition, and use of a NIDS with its own strategic objectives in mind. The advantages and disadvantages of NIDS are shown in Table 4-5.[16]

TABLE 4-5   Advantages and disadvantages of NIDS

Advantages	Disadvantages
Good network design and placement of NIDS devices can enable an organization to use a few devices to monitor a large network.	A NIDS can become overwhelmed by network volume and fail to recognize attacks it might otherwise have detected. Some IDS vendors are accommodating the need for ever-faster network performance by improving the processing of detection algorithms in dedicated hardware circuits to gain a performance advantage. Additional efforts to optimize rule set processing may also reduce overall effectiveness in detecting attacks.
NIDS are usually passive devices and can be deployed into existing networks with little or no disruption to normal network operations.	A NIDS requires access to all traffic to be monitored. The broad use of switched Ethernet networks has replaced the ubiquity of shared collision domain hubs. Because many switches have limited or no monitoring port capability, some networks are not capable of providing aggregate data for analysis by a NIDS. Even when switches do provide monitoring ports, they may not be able to mirror all activity within a consistent and reliable time sequence.
NIDS are not usually susceptible to direct attack and, in fact, may not be detectable by attackers.	NIDS cannot analyze encrypted packets, making some of the network traffic invisible to the process. The increasing use of encryption by some network services (such as SSL, SSH, and VPN) limits the effectiveness of NIDS.
	NIDS cannot reliably ascertain if an attack was successful or not; this causes the network administrator to perform an ongoing evaluation of the results of the logs of suspicious network activity.
	Some forms of attack are not easily discerned by NIDS, specifically those involving fragmented packets. In fact, some NIDS are particularly susceptible to malformed packets and may become unstable and stop functioning.

Host-Based IDS

A **host-based IDS (HIDS)** works differently from a network-based version of IDS. While a NIDS resides on a network segment and monitors activities across that segment, a host-based IDS resides on a particular computer or server, known as the host, and monitors activity only on that system. HIDSs are also known as *system integrity verifiers*,[17] because they benchmark and monitor the status of key system files and detect when an intruder creates, modifies, or deletes monitored files.

A HIDS is also capable of monitoring system configuration databases, such as the Windows Registry, in addition to stored configuration files like .ini, .cfg, and .dat files. Most HIDS work on the principle of configuration or change management, which means they record the sizes, locations, and other attributes of system files. The HIDS triggers an alert or alarm when one of the following changes occurs: file attributes change, new files are created, or existing files are deleted. A HIDS can also monitor system logs for predefined events.

The HIDS examines these files and logs to determine if an attack is underway or has occurred, and if the attack is succeeding or was successful. The HIDS maintains its own log file so that even when hackers successfully modify files on the target system to cover their tracks, the HIDS can provide an independent audit trail of the attack. Once properly configured, a HIDS is very reliable. The only time a HIDS produces a false positive alert is when an authorized change occurs for a monitored file. This action can be quickly reviewed by an administrator and dismissed as acceptable. The administrator may choose then to disregard subsequent changes to the same set of files. If properly configured, a HIDS can also detect when an individual user attempts to modify or exceed his or her access authorization and give himself or herself higher privileges.

A HIDS has an advantage over NIDS in that it can usually be installed in such a way that it can access encrypted information as it travels through the network. In this way, a HIDS is able to use the content of otherwise encrypted communications to make decisions about possible or successful attacks. Likewise, because the HIDS is designed to detect intrusion activity on only one computer system, all of the information the HIDS needs to determine whether any specific traffic is legitimate will be present for analysis. The nature of the network packet delivery, whether switched or in a shared collision domain, or whether or not packets are fragmented in transit is not material.

HIDS Configuration A HIDS relies on the classification of files into various categories. It then applies various notification actions, depending on the rules in the HIDS configuration. Most HIDS provide only a few general levels of alert notification. For example, an administrator can configure a HIDS to treat the following types of changes as reportable security events: changes in a system folder (for example, in C:\Windows or C:\WINNT) and changes within a security-related application (such as C:\Tripwire). In other words, administrators can configure the system to trigger an alert on any changes within a critical data folder.

The configuration rules may classify changes to a specific application folder (for example, C:\Program Files\Office) as being normal, and thus such changes are not reported. Administrators can configure the system to not only log all activity but also instantly page or e-mail any administrator if a reportable security event occurs. Although this change-based system seems simple, it seems to suit most administrators who are primarily concerned if unauthorized changes occur in specific and sensitive areas of the host file system.

Applications frequently modify their internal files, such as dictionaries and configuration templates, and users are constantly updating their data files. Unless a HIDS is very specifically configured, these actions can generate a large volume of false alarms.

Managed HIDS can monitor multiple computers simultaneously. They do this by creating a configuration file on each monitored host and by making each HIDS report to a master console system, which is usually located on the system administrator's computer. This master console monitors the information provided from the managed hosts and notifies the administrator when it senses recognizable attack conditions. Figure 4-7 provides a sample screen from Tripwire, a popular host-based IDS (see *www.tripwire.com*).

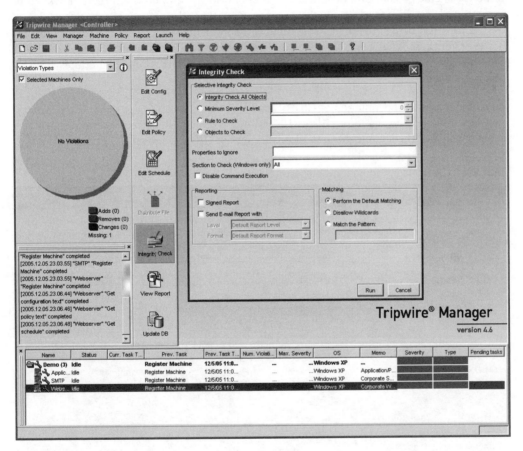

FIGURE 4-7 Tripwire HIDS

In configuring a HIDS, the system administrator must begin by identifying and categorizing folders and files. One of the most common methods is to designate folders using a pattern of red, yellow, and green categories. Critical systems components are coded red, and usually include the system Registry, any folders containing the key elements of the operating system, and application software. Critically important data should also be included in the red category. Support components, such as device drivers and other relatively important files, are generally coded yellow; and user data is usually coded green.

This is not to suggest that user data is unimportant, but in practical and strategic terms, monitoring changes to user data does have a lower priority. One reason for this is that users are often assigned storage space that they are expected to use routinely to maintain and back up their documents, files, and images. Another reason is that user data files are expected to change frequently—as users make modifications. System kernel files, on the other hand, should change only during upgrades or installations. Categorizing critical system components at a higher level than less important files ensures that the level of response to change is in proportion to the level of priority. Should the three-tier system be overly simple for an organization, there are systems that allow for an alternative scale of 0–100, with 100 being most mission critical and zero being unimportant. It is not unusual, however, for these types of scales to be overly refined and result in confusion regarding, for example, the prioritization of responses to level 67 and 68 intrusions. Sometimes simpler is better.

Advantages and Disadvantages of HIDS   Each organization must approach the justification, acquisition, and use of a HIDS with its own strategic objectives in mind. A summary of some of the advantages and disadvantages of HIDS is shown in Table 4-6.[18]

TABLE 4-6   Advantages and disadvantages of HIDS

Advantages	Disadvantages
A HIDS can detect local events on host systems, and it can also detect attacks that may elude a NIDS.	A HIDS poses more management issues because HIDS are configured and managed on each monitored host; this means that it requires more management effort to install, configure, and operate several HIDS than a comparably sized NIDS solution.
A HIDS functions on the host system, where encrypted traffic is decrypted and available for processing.	A HIDS is vulnerable to both direct attacks and to attacks against the host operating system. Either circumstance can result in the compromise and/or loss of HIDS functionality.
The use of switched network protocols does not affect a HIDS.	A HIDS is not optimized to detect multihost scanning, nor is it able to detect the scanning of nonhost network devices, such as routers or switches. Unless complex correlation analysis is provided, the HIDS is not aware of attacks that span multiple devices in the network.
A HIDS can detect inconsistencies in how applications and systems programs were used by examining records stored in audit logs. This can be used to detect some types of attacks, including Trojan horse programs.	A HIDS is susceptible to some denial-of-service attacks.
	A HIDS can use large amounts of disk space to retain the host OS audit logs, and may require the addition of disk capacity to the system to function properly.

TABLE 4-6 Advantages and disadvantages of HIDS (continued)

Advantages	Disadvantages
	A HIDS can inflict a performance overhead on its host systems, and in some cases may reduce system performance below acceptable levels.

Application-Based IDS

A refinement of the host-based IDS is the application-based IDS (AppIDS). Whereas the HIDS examines a single system for file modification, the application IDS examines an application for abnormal events. It usually does this by looking at the files created by the application and looking for anomalous occurrences such as users exceeding their authorization, invalid file executions, or other activities that would indicate that there is a problem in the normal interaction between the users, the application, and the data. By tracking the interaction between users and applications, the AppIDS is able to trace specific activity to individual users. One unique advantage of the AppIDS is its ability to view encrypted data. Because the AppIDS interfaces with data as it is processed by an application, and any encrypted data that enters an application is decrypted by the application itself, an AppIDS does not need to become involved in the decryption process. This allows an AppIDS to examine the encryption/decryption process and identify any potential anomalies in data handling or user access.

According to the Missouri State Information Infrastructure Protection Agency:

> application-Based IDS may be configured to intercept the following types of requests and use them in combinations and sequences to constitute an application's normal behavior:
>
> - *File system: File read or write*
> - *Network: Packet events at the driver (NDIS) or transport (TDI) level*
> - *Configuration: Read or write to the Registry on Windows*
> - *Execution space: Write to memory not owned by the requesting application, for example, attempts to inject a shared library DLL into another process.*[19]

As each organization determines its own needs for intrusion detection, some in the industry suggest a blended approach, using elements from NIDS, HIDS, and AppIDS approaches. A common practice is to implement HIDS/AppIDS on high-value servers and other critical systems, with the use of a robust NIDS for global infrastructure protection.

Advantages and Disadvantages of AppIDS　　Each organization must approach the justification, acquisition, and use of a AppIDS with its own strategic objectives in mind. The advantages and disadvantages of AppIDS are shown in Table 4-7.[20]

TABLE 4-7 Advantages and disadvantages of AppIDS

Advantages	Disadvantages
An AppIDS is aware of specific users and can observe the interaction between the application and the user; this allows the AppIDS to attribute unauthorized activities to specific and known users.	AppIDSs may be more susceptible to attack than other IDS approaches because applications are often less well protected than network and host OS components.
An AppIDS is able to operate even when incoming data is encrypted because it can operate at the point in the process when the data has been decrypted by applications and has not been reencrypted for storage.	AppIDSs are less capable of detecting software tampering and may be taken in by Trojan horse code or some other form of spoofing. It is usually recommended that AppIDSs be used in combination with HIDS and NIDS.

Classification of IDS by Detection Approach

The approach used to detect events also has a significant effect on how an IDS operates. There are two widely used detection options: *signature* and *statistical anomaly based*.

Signature-Based IDS

A **signature-based IDS** or **knowledge-based IDS** examines data traffic in search of patterns that match known signatures—that is, preconfigured, predetermined attack patterns. Signature-based IDS technology is widely used because many attacks have clear and distinct signatures.

For example:

- Footprinting and fingerprinting activities, which have an attack pattern that includes the use of ICMP, DNS querying, and e-mail routing analysis
- Exploits involving a specific attack sequence designed to take advantage of a vulnerability to gain access to a system
- Denial-of-service (DoS) and distributed denial-of service (DDoS) attacks, during which the attacker tries to prevent the normal usage of a system by overloading the system with requests so that its ability to efficiently process them is compromised and disrupted, and it begins denying services to authorized users[21]

The problem with this approach is that as new attack strategies are identified, the IDS's database of signatures must be continually updated. Failure to keep this database current can allow attacks that use new strategies to succeed. An IDS that uses signature-based methods works in ways much like most antivirus software. In fact, antivirus software is often classified as a form of signature-based IDS. This is why experts tell users that if they don't plan on keeping their antivirus software updated it will not work as effectively as it would with current updates.

Another weakness of the signature-based method is the time frame over which attacks occur. If attackers are purposefully slow and methodical, they may slip undetected through this type of IDS because their actions do not match the signatures that often include the time allowed between steps in the attack. The only way for a signature-based IDS to resolve this vulnerability is for it to collect and analyze data over longer periods of time, a process which requires substantially larger data storage capability and additional processing capacity.

Statistical Anomaly-Based IDS

Another approach for detecting intrusions is based on the frequency with which certain network activities take place. The **statistical anomaly-based IDS (stat IDS)**, or **behavior-based IDS**, collects statistical summaries by observing traffic that is known to be normal. This normal period of evaluation establishes a performance baseline. Once the baseline is established, the stat IDS periodically samples network activity, and using statistical methods, compares the sampled network activity to this baseline. When the measured activity is outside the baseline parameters it is said to exceed the **clipping level** (the level at which the IDS triggers an alert to notify the administrator). The data that is measured from the normal traffic and is used to prepare the baseline can include host memory or CPU usage, network packet types, and packet quantities. Later comparisons of measured traffic might reveal anomalies when compared to the baseline, thus triggering the alert.

The advantage of the statistical anomaly-based approach is that the IDS can detect new types of attacks, because it is looking for abnormal activity of any type. Unfortunately, these systems require much more overhead and processing capacity than signature-based ones, because they must constantly compare patterns of activity against the baseline. Another drawback is that these systems may not detect minor changes to system variables and may generate many false positives. If the actions of the users or systems on a network vary widely, with periods of low activity interspersed with periods of frantic packet exchange, this type of IDS may not be suitable, because the dramatic swings from one level to another will almost certainly generate false alarms. Due to the complexity of the configuration, the depth of commitment needed for ongoing operations, need for intensive computing capabilities to support real-time analysis, and the large number of false positive results usually generated, this type of IDS is less commonly used than the signature-based type.

Log File Monitors

A log file monitor (LFM), a type of IDS that is similar to the NIDS, reviews the log files generated by servers, network devices, and even other IDSs. These systems look for patterns in the log files that may indicate that an attack or intrusion is in process or has already succeeded. While an individual host IDS is only able to look at the activity in one system, the LFM is able to look at multiple log files from several different systems. The patterns that signify an attack can be subtle and hard to distinguish when one system is examined in isolation, but they may be much easier to identify when the entire network and its systems are viewed holistically. Of course this holistic approach requires the allocation of considerable resources it involves the collection, movement, storage, and analysis of very large quantities of log data.

Intrusion Prevention Systems

Recent development in the field of intrusion management has seen the advent of new terminology for an approach called intrusion prevention systems. The emergence of intrusion prevention systems (IPS) signaled a shift in approach away from passive detection of incidents. IPS is promised by its creators to be a more reactive approach built on both an ability to respond to known methods of attack and an ability to create adaptive responses to previously unknown attacks. This technology is closely aligned with so-called application defenses that make use of an understanding of what and how an application functions to make informed defensive decisions.

Inasmuch as it is an extension of past approaches to technological controls (making use of the existing capabilities of NIDS, HIDS, proxy-based firewalls, AppIDS, and multiprotocol firewall technologies), IPS is seen by many industry observers as an evolutionary approach to provide enhanced capabilities for layered defenses. Where some vendors may hype IPS as a revolutionary approach, some established IDS vendors use IPS's reactive capability to illustrate a maturity of the Defense in Depth model and the integration of multiple countermeasure technologies.

The biggest challenge with IPS is the tuning of the automated responses. While an IDS simply identifies an intrusion, the IPS is designed to prevent or react to one. To do so, one mechanism the IPS may have at its disposal is the severance of the communications circuit. This extreme measure may be justified when the organization is hit with a massive DDoS or malware-laden attack. The more likely problem may be the false positive detection of legitimate traffic, to which the IPS terminates the organization's connection, possibly creating a bigger problem than it attempts to resolve. As a result, care should be taken when selecting, implementing, and tuning an IPS to ensure that such a situation does not occur.

Automated Response

New technologies and capabilities are emerging in the field of incident response beyond the intent of IDS and IPS control models. Some of these build on traditional strategies and extend their capabilities and functions. Traditionally, systems were configured to detect incidents and then notify the human administrator. Now, new systems can respond to the incident threat autonomously, based on preconfigured options to go beyond simple defensive actions usually associated with IDS and IPS systems.

These systems, referred to as **trap and trace**, use a combination of resources to detect an intrusion and then to trace the intrusion back to its source. On the surface, this seems like an ideal solution. Security is no longer limited to defense. Now the security administrators can take the offense. They can track down the perpetrators and turn them over to the appropriate authorities. Under the guise of justice, some less scrupulous administrators might even be tempted to back hack, or hack into a hacker's system to find out as much as possible about the hacker. *Vigilante justice* would be a more appropriate term, and activities in this vein are deemed unethical by most codes of professional conduct. In tracking the hacker, administrators may wander through other organizations' systems. The wily hacker may use IP spoofing, compromised systems, or a myriad of other techniques to throw trackers off the trail. The result is that the administrator becomes a hacker himself, and therefore defeats the purpose of catching hackers.

Honeypots and Honeynets

There are more than legal drawbacks to trap and trace. The trap portion frequently involves the use of honeypots or honeynets. A **honeypot** is a computer server configured to resemble a production system, containing rich information just begging to be hacked. If a hacker stumbles into the system, alarms are set off, and the administrator notified.

> *Honeypots are closely monitored network decoys serving several purposes: they can distract adversaries from more valuable machines on a network; they can provide early warning about new attack and exploitation trends; and they allow in-depth examination of adversaries during and after exploitation of a honeypot. There are two general types of honeypots:*
>
> - *Production honeypots are easy to use, capture only limited information, and are used primarily by companies or corporations.*
> - *Research honeypots are complex to deploy and maintain, capture extensive information, and are used primarily by research, military, or government organizations.*
>
> *An example of a honeypot is a system used to simulate one or more network services. This honeypot could log access attempts to those ports including an attacker's keystrokes, and could give advanced warning of a more concerted attack.* [22]

Even smaller than the honeypot is the honeytoken. "The term *honeytoken* was first coined by Augusto Paes de Barros in 2003 on the honeypots mailing list... A **honeytoken** is just like a honeypot, you put it out there and no one should interact with it. Any interaction with a honeytoken most likely represents unauthorized or malicious activity."[23] An example would be a bogus file placed into a database, and monitored by the system. If the file is accessed, it is an indicator of unwanted activity.

Honeynets operate similarly, except that they consist of networks or subnets of systems, representing a much richer target. The Honeynet Project (*www.honeynet.org*) describes a **honeynet** (also known as a **honeypot farm**) in this manner:

> *(A honeypot Farm) Is a high-interaction honeypot designed to capture extensive information on threats. High-interaction means a honeynet provides real systems, applications, and services for attackers to interact with.... What makes a honeynet different from most honeypots is that it is an entire network of systems. Instead of a single computer, a honeynet is a network of systems designed for attackers to interact with. These victim systems (honeypots within the honeynet) can be any type of system, service, or information you want to provide... any interaction with a honeynet implies malicious or unauthorized activity. Any connections initiated inbound to your honeynet are most likely a probe, scan, or attack. Almost any outbound connections from your honeynet imply that someone has compromised a system and has initiated outbound activity.* [24]

Legal Issues with Honeypots and Honeynets

When using honeypots and honeynets, administrators should be careful not to run afoul of any legal issues. The first to be concerned with is the line between enticement and entrapment. Enticement is the process of attracting attention to a system by placing tantalizing bits of information in key locations. Entrapment is the action of luring an individual into committing a crime to get a conviction. Enticement is legal and ethical, whereas entrapment is not. It is difficult to gauge the effect such a system can have on the average user, especially if the individual has been nudged into looking at the information.

The next issue involves problems with the Fourth Amendment to the U.S. Constitution. The Fourth Amendment protects those persons residing in the United States against unwarranted search and seizure. Therefore, those organizations that operate in the United States or those who do business with those residing in the United States should exercise care to ensure that anyone connecting to the honeypot or honeynet does not inadvertently place information into that environment. This is discussed in detail in Chapter 5.

Other issues arise when dealing with the Electronic Communications Protection Act,[25] which prohibits recording of wire- or cable-based communications unless an exception applies. These exceptions include:

- Interception required as part of the course of normal work operations—as by a systems administrator for an ISP, or employee for a telephone company
- A court order authorizes it.
- It is performed by one of the parties involved, or with the permission of one of the parties involved.
- If the transmission is readily accessible to the general public
- Is radio-based and designed for the use of the general public, including amateur or citizens band radios
- Other reasons as defined in the act

Another federal law which specifically deals with the use of devices to collect information from a network user is the Pen Register, Trap and Trace Devices statute (pen/trap statute), which governs the real-time collection of noncontent traffic information associated with communications, such as the phone numbers dialed by a particular telephone or the destination or source IP address of a computer network user (data the statute refers to as "dialing, routing, addressing, or signaling information").[26] "Like the Wiretap Act's prohibition on interception of the contents of communications, the pen/trap statute creates a general prohibition on the real-time monitoring of traffic data relating to communications."[27]

There is also the *wasp trap syndrome*. For example, if a concerned homeowner installs a wasp trap in the backyard to trap the few insects he sees flying about, the scented bait used in the trap may attract far more wasps than were originally present. Just as in the use of the wasp trap, security administrators may choose to keep honeypots and honeynets off of their production networks to avoid drawing in potential attackers.

The downside of current enhanced automated response systems may outweigh their benefits. Legal issues associated with tracking individuals through the systems of others have yet to be resolved. What if the hacker that is backtracked is actually a compromised system running an automated attack? What are the legal liabilities of a counterattack? How can security administrators condemn a hacker, when they themselves may have illegally hacked systems to track the hacker? These issues are complex, but must be resolved to give the security professionals better tools to combat incidents.

INCIDENT DECISION MAKING

As mentioned earlier in the chapter, incident candidates are evaluated to determine which are truly incidents and which are false positives. This step in the process is the first point in time when an incident is known to be underway. According to US-CERT, the general approach to narrowing the list of incident candidates and thereby detecting incidents includes:

1. Collect incident candidates using well-documented procedures.
2. Investigate the candidates using systems and methods at your disposal.
3. If a candidate is determined to be other than an authorized activity, immediately initiate your intrusion response procedures.[28]

The evaluation procedure implemented in any organization should consider the practices recommended in Table 4-8.

TABLE 4-8 Summary of recommended practices[29]

Area	Recommended Practice
Preparation	• Establish a policy and procedures that prepare your organization to detect signs of intrusion. • Identify data that characterize systems and aid in detecting signs of suspicious behavior. • Manage logging and other data collection mechanisms.
Integrity of intrusion detection software	• Ensure that the software used to examine systems has not been compromised.
Behavior of networks and systems	• Monitor and inspect network activities for unexpected behavior. • Monitor and inspect system activities for unexpected behavior. • Inspect files and directories for unexpected changes.
Physical forms of intrusion	• Investigate unauthorized hardware attached to your organization's network. • Inspect physical resources for signs of unauthorized access.
Follow through	• Review reports by users and external contacts about suspicious and unexpected behavior. • Take appropriate actions upon discovering unauthorized, unexpected, or suspicious activity.

As Table 4-8 shows, there are some practices that each organization faced with structuring an incident decision classification process should adopt. The pages that follow discuss many of these practices and offer more details about how they should be incorporated into the overall process.

Collection of Data to Aid in Detecting Incidents

The routine collection and analysis of data is required to assist in the detection and declaration of incidents. Even if an incident is not detected in real time, the data collected by automatic recording systems can assist the teams in better understanding what are normal and routine operations for the systems that process, transmit, and store information for the organization. As part of *knowing yourself*, understanding the norm assists in the detection of the abnormal. Some of the information desirable for these teams to collect is presented in Table 4-9.[30]

TABLE 4-9 Data categories and types of data to collect

Data Category	Types of Data to Collect
Network performance	• Total traffic load in and out over time (packet, byte, and connection counts) and by event (such as new product or service release) • Traffic load (percentage of packets, bytes, connections) in and out over time sorted by protocol, source address, destination address, and other packet header data • Error counts on all network interfaces
Other network data	• Service initiation requests • Name of the user/host requesting the service • Network traffic (packet headers) • Successful connections and connection attempts (protocol, port, source, destination, time) • Connection duration • Connection flow (sequence of packets from initiation to termination) • States associated with network interfaces (up, down) • Network sockets currently open • Whether or not network interface card is in promiscuous mode • Network probes and scans • Results of administrator probes
System performance	• Total resource use over time (CPU, memory [used, free], disk [used, free]) • Status and errors reported by systems and hardware devices • Changes in system status, including shutdowns and restarts • File system status (where mounted, free space by partition, open files, biggest file) over time and at specific times • File system warnings (low free space, too many open files, file exceeding allocated size) • Disk counters (input/output, queue lengths) over time and at specific times • Hardware availability (modems, network interface cards, memory)
Other system data	• Actions requiring special privileges • Successful and failed logins • Modem activities • Presence of new services and devices • Configuration of resources and devices

TABLE 4-9 Data categories and types of data to collect (continued)

Data Category	Types of Data to Collect
Process performance	• Amount of resources used (CPU, memory, disk, time) by specific processes over time; top resource-consuming processes • System and user processes and services executing at any given time
Other process data	• User executing the process • Process start-up time, arguments, filenames • Process exit status, time, duration, resources consumed • The means by which each process is normally initiated (administrator, other users, other programs or processes), with what authorization and privileges • Devices used by specific processes • Files currently open by specific processes
Files and directories	• List of files, directories, attributes • Cryptographic checksums for all files and directories • Accesses (open, create, modify, execute, delete), time, date • Changes to sizes, contents, protections, types, locations • Changes to access control lists on system tools • Additions and deletions of files and directories • Results of virus scanners
Users	• Login/logout information (location, time): successful attempts, failed attempts, attempted logins to privileged accounts • Login/logout information on remote access servers that appears in modem logs • Changes in user identity • Changes in authentication status, such as enabling privileges • Failed attempts to access restricted information (such as password files) • Keystroke monitoring logs • Violations of user quotas

Applications	• Application- and service-specific information such as network traffic (packet content), mail logs, FTP logs, Web server logs, modem logs, firewall logs, SNMP logs, DNS logs, intrusion detection system logs, database management system logs
	• Services-specific information could be:
	  • For FTP requests: Files transferred and connection statistics
	  • For Web requests: Pages accessed, credentials of the requestor, connection statistics, user requests over time, which pages are most requested, and who is requesting them
	  • For mail requests: Sender, receiver, size, and tracing information; for a mail server, number of messages over time, number of queued messages
	  • For DNS requests: Questions, answers, and zone transfers
	  • For a file system server: File transfers over time
	  • For a database server: Transactions over time

Log files	• Results of scanning, filtering, and reducing log file contents • Checks for log file consistency (increasing file size over time, use of consecutive, increasing time stamps with no gaps)

TABLE 4-9 Data categories and types of data to collect (continued)

Data Category	Types of Data to Collect
Vulnerabilities	• Results of vulnerability scanners (presence of known vulnerabilities) • Vulnerability patch logging

Manage Logging and Other Data Collection Mechanisms

When one of the data sources used for incident decision making is coming from individual or aggregated log files, the management of those sources becomes more critical. The aggregated log files from network devices, servers, and even critical workstations can contain both indicators and documentation of the intrusion events. To be effective, logs must first be enabled. (Some systems do this by default; others must specifically be activated.) Then, protect your logs through the hardening of servers that create and store logs. Finally, manage your logs. Managing logs involves the following:

- Be prepared to handle the amount of data generated by logging. Some systems may result in literally gigabytes of data that must be stored or otherwise managed.
- Rotate logs on a schedule. As indicated, some systems overwrite older log entries with newer entries to comply with the space limitations of the system. Ensure the rotation of log entries is acceptable, rather than accepting system defaults.
- Archive logs. Log systems can copy logs periodically to remote storage locations. There is a debate among security administrators as to how long log files should be maintained. Some argue that log files may be subpoenaed during legal proceedings and thus should be routinely destroyed to prevent unwanted disclosure during this process. Others argue that the information to be gained from analyzing legacy and archival logs outweighs the risk. Still others take the middle ground and aggregate the log information, then destroy the individual entries. Regardless of the method employed, some plan must be in place to handle these files or risk loss.
- Encrypt logs. If the organization does decide to archive logs, they should be encrypted in storage. Should the log file system be compromised, this prevents unwanted disclosure.
- Dispose of logs. Once log files have outlived their usefulness, they should be routinely and securely disposed.[31]

Detecting Compromised Software

Who watches the watchers? (*Sed quis custodiet ipsos custudios?*) If the systems that monitor the network, servers, or other components are compromised, then the organization's incident detection is compromised. This can be accomplished through verification. One can have a separate HIDS sensor or agent monitor the HIDS itself. If you suspect the detection systems have been compromised, you can quarantine them and examine the installation, by comparing them to either the original installation files or to an insulated installation.

Watching the Network for Unexpected Behavior

Whether using manual intrusion detection or intrusion detection systems, it is imperative to constantly monitor networks for signs of intrusion. One accomplishes this in the following manner:

- *Notify users that network monitoring is being done.*
- *Review and investigate notifications from network-specific alert mechanisms (such as e-mail, voice mail, or pager messages).*
- *Review and investigate network error reports.*
- *Review network performance statistics and investigate anything that appears anomalous.*
- *Identify any unexpected, unusual, or suspicious network traffic and its possible implications.*
- *If you are reviewing network traffic on a system other than the one being monitored, ensure that the connection between them is secure.*[32]

Watching Systems for Unexpected Behavior

Similarly, systems used to store, process, and transmit critical data should be reviewed if displaying unusual or abnormal behavior. This includes the following:

- *Notify users that monitoring of process and user activities is being done.*
- *Review and investigate notifications from system-specific alert mechanisms (such as e-mail, voice mail, or pager messages).*
- *Review and investigate system error reports.*
- *Review system performance statistics and investigate anything that appears anomalous.*
- *Continuously monitor process activity (to the extent that you can).*
- *Identify any unexpected, unusual, or suspicious process behavior and its possible implications.*
- *Identify any unexpected, unusual, or suspicious user behavior and its possible implications.*
- *Identify other unexpected, unusual, or suspicious behavior and its possible implications.*
- *Periodically execute network mapping and scanning tools to understand what intruders who use such tools can learn about your networks and systems.*
- *Periodically execute vulnerability scanning tools on all systems to check for the presence of known vulnerabilities.*
- *If you are reviewing system activities on a host other than the one being monitored, ensure that the connection between them is secure.*[33]

Watch Files and Directories for Unexpected Changes

The task of monitoring file systems for unauthorized change is best performed by using a HIDS. This can be augmented by having a reporting process in place to allow users to alert the monitoring team of suspicious file activity. If a user claims unusual file activity, whether it be modification in size, content, or date, this may be an indicator of an incident. A HIDS may be configured to perform a scheduled scan of systems to compare the current version of files against an archive equivalent or hash value. Hash values are extremely useful in performing file verification. However, problems with false positives can occur if the file is routinely used by a user or the system. Choosing what files to monitor is as critical as the actual monitoring.

Investigate Unauthorized Hardware Attached to Your Organization's Network

There is existing software that is capable of scanning a network and identifying the type, configuration, and location of any device attached to the network. Unless the networking team, in cooperation with the information security team and the SIRT, periodically checks the network, both electronically and visually, an unauthorized piece of equipment may tap into the system and redirect or record traffic without authorization. Modem sweeps are another method of detecting unauthorized equipment. Visual inspections, while tedious, are the best way to detect an unknown device tapped into the network, such as a wireless access port rebroadcasting to an external receiver.

Inspect Physical Resources for Signs of Unauthorized Access

Physical access trumps electronic security. This saying, all too true, indicates that if an intruder can physically access a device, then no electronic protection can deter the loss of information, save that of a burglar alarm. Periodically, perhaps in conjunction with the networking inspection, the information security team should examine all doors, windows, locks, ceilings, and gates physically protecting the information resources contained within. Signs of tampering, attempted or successful breaching, or other malfeasance, should be documented and reported to the appropriate authorities.

An example of physical access trumping logical security comes from an incident in which a thief broke into a Visa International data processing center in California and stole a personal computer containing information on about 314,000 credit card accounts, including Visa, MasterCard, American Express, Discover, and Diners Club. Those who have worked with servers know that if a person has access to the computer systems, can remove and restore power, and can control the booting devices (floppy, hard disk, or optical media drives), they can circumvent all logical security controls added to the system. In this case, authorities speculate that the perpetrator stole the device for the resale value of the hardware, rather than the information it contained, but the fact remains the data was stolen as well and could easily have been misused.[34]

Review Reports About Suspicious and Unexpected Behavior

Users can be the front line in intrusion detection. By promptly reviewing all reports to the help desk, anonymous reporting hotlines and e-mail boxes, the SIRT and information security teams can detect a problem early enough to prevent it from spreading.

Take Appropriate Actions

Responding to an intrusion appropriately is a must. This topic is the basis of the next chapter, where it will be discussed in detail.

Challenges in Intrusion Detection

It should be painfully obvious by this point that the detection of intrusions can be a tedious and technically demanding process. Only those with advanced technical skills within a certain set of hardware and software can manually detect signs of an intrusion through reviews of logs, system performance, user feedback, and system processes and tasks. This underscores the value of two key facets of incident detection: (1) effective use of technology to assist in detection, and (2) the necessity of cooperation between incident response and information security professionals and the entire information technology department. The former is discussed in sufficient detail in the sections on IDS and IPS. With regard to the latter, the IT staff is best prepared to understand the day-to-day operations of the hardware, software, and networking components that support organizational operations on an ongoing basis. They can then work with the SIRT and information security teams to identify anomalies in the system performance and administration. This should underscore the necessity to integrate IT systems and network administrators as part of SIRT operations, if not SIRT team building.

Chapter Summary

- Incident candidates come from a number of different events occurring in and around the organization.
- There are three broad categories of incident indicators:
  - Possible indicators of an incident:
    - Presence of unfamiliar files
    - Presence or execution of unknown programs or processes
    - Unusual consumption of computing resources
    - Unusual system crashes
  - Probable indicators of an incident:
    - Activities at unexpected times
    - Presence of new accounts
    - Reported attacks
  - Definite indicators:
    - Use of dormant accounts
    - Changes to logs
    - Presence of hacker tools
    - Notifications by partner or peer
    - Notification by hacker
- When the following events are confirmed to have occurred, an actual incident is underway:
  - Loss of availability
  - Loss of integrity
  - Loss of confidentiality
  - Violation of policy
  - Violation of law
- IR plan designers must create a process to collect and evaluate incident candidates to determine whether they are actual incidents or nonevents, also called false positive incident candidates.
- Noise, or false positive that may have been tuned from the collection system, often results from several causes:
  - Placement
  - Policy
  - Awareness
- An intrusion detection system is designed to be placed in a network to determine if it is being used in ways that are out of compliance with the policy of the organization.
- Compelling reasons to acquire and use an IDS include:

- To prevent problem behaviors
- To detect attacks
- To detect the preambles to attacks
- To document the existing threat to an organization
- To act as quality control for security design and administration
- To provide useful information about intrusions that do take place

- Three widely used placement options are used: network-based, host-based, and application-based IDS.
  - A network-based IDS (NIDS) monitors network traffic on a segment of an organization's network looking for indications of ongoing or successful attacks.
  - A host-based IDS (HIDS) resides on a particular computer or server, known as the host, and monitors activity only on that site.
  - A refinement of the host-based IDS is the application-based IDS (AppIDS) that examines an application for abnormal events.
- Two approaches are used to detect IDS events, signature based and statistical anomaly based:
  - A signature-based IDS or knowledge-based IDS examines data traffic in search of patterns that match known signatures.
  - The statistical anomaly-based IDS compares stored baselines of normal activity against measures of current activity looking for significant differences.
- Intrusion prevention systems (IPS) signal a shift in approach away from passive detection of incidents and toward a more active approach.
- Incident candidates are evaluated to determine which are truly incidents and which are false positives.

Review Questions

1. What is an incident candidate?
2. What are the three broad categories of incident indicators?
3. What are the types of events that are considered possible indicators of actual incidents?
4. What are the types of events that are considered probable indicators of actual incidents?
5. What are the types of events that are considered definite indicators of actual incidents?
6. What are the types of events that, having occurred, indicate an event is occurring?
7. What is a false positive?
8. What is noise? Is noise different from a false positive event?
9. What are the causes of noise as described in the chapter?
10. What is an IDS?
11. What is a false positive?
12. What are the compelling reasons to acquire and use an IDS?

13. What are the three dominant placements for IDSs? Give one advantage and one disadvantage to each approach.

14. What are the dominant approaches used to detect intrusions in IDSs? Give one advantage and one disadvantage to each approach.

15. What is a log file monitor? What is it used to accomplish?

16. What is an IPS? In what ways it is different from an IDS?

17. What does the term *trap and trace* mean?

18. What is a honeypot? What is a honeynet? How are they different?

19. What activities go into a complete log management approach?

20. What are the two key facets needed to design, develop, and operate a comprehensive IDS?

Exercises

1. Using a Web browser, look for the open source and freeware intrusion detection tools listed in the chapter. Next, identify two to three commercial equivalents. What would the estimated cost savings be for an organization to use the open source or freeware versions? What other expenses would the organization need to incur to implement this solution?

2. Using a Web browser, search on the term *intrusion prevention systems.* What are the characteristics of an IPS? Compare the costs of a typical IPS to an IDS. Do they differ? What characteristics justify the difference in cost, if any?

3. Using a Web browser, visit the site *www.honeynet.org.* What is this Web site, and what does it offer the information security professional? Visit the *Know your Enemy* whitepaper series, and select a paper based on the recommendation of your professor. Read it and prepare a short overview for your class.

4. Using Table 4-4 and a Web browser, search on a few of the port numbers known to be used by hacker programs, such as Sub-7, Midnight Commander, and WinCrash. What significant information did you find in your search? Why should the information security manager be concerned about these hacker programs? What can he or she do to protect against them?

5. Using the list of possible, probable, and definite indicators of an incident, draft a recommendation to assist a typical end user in identifying these indicators. Alternatively, using a graphics package such as PowerPoint, create a poster to make the user aware of the key indicators.

References

1. Donald L. Pipkin, *Information Security: Protecting the Global Enterprise* (Upper Saddle River, NJ: Prentice Hall PTR, 2000), 256.

2. Wikipedia, "Rootkit (computing)," accessed June 3, 2005, from http://en.wikipedia.org/wiki/Rootkit.

3. SysInternals, "Rootkit Revealer," accessed June 3, 2005, from http://www.sysinternals.com/Utilities/RootkitRevealer.html.

4. V. Masurkar, "Responding to a Customer's Security Incidents—Part 2: Executing a Policy," Sun Microsystems Web site, March 2003, accessed July 3, 2004, from http://www.sun.com/blueprints/0403/817-1796.pdf.

5. M. Ranum, "False positives: A user's guide to making sense of IDS alarms," February 2003, accessed December 5, 2005, from http://www.secureworks.com/techResourceCenter/icsaFalsePositivesWhitePaper.pdf.

6. Wikipedia, "Process (computing)," accessed June 3, 2005, from http://en.wikipedia.org/wiki/Process_%28computing%29.

7. NoHack.Net, "Detecting & Removing Trojan Horses," accessed June 3, 2005, from http://www.nohack.net/detection.htm.

8. Microsoft, "Default Processes in Windows 2000," accessed June 3, 2005, from http://support.microsoft.com/default.aspx?scid=kb;en-us;263201.

9. Microsoft, "How Windows Resource Manager Works," accessed June 3, 2005, from http://www.microsoft.com/technet/prodtechnol/windowsserver2003/library/TechRef/c3541e6e-342d-45d2-a211-44c556306e91.mspx.

10. Rebecca Bace and Peter Mell, *Intrusion Detection Systems*, NIST Special Publication 800-31, November 2001, accessed February 15, 2004, from http://csrc.nist.gov/publications/nistpubs/800-31/sp800-31.pdf.

11. See note 10.

12. Wikipedia, "Port (computing)," accessed June 2, 2005, from http://en.wikipedia.org/wiki/Computer_port.

13. IANA, "Port numbers," accessed June 2, 2005, from http://www.iana.org/assignments/port-numbers.

14. Webopedia, "Well-known TCP port numbers," accessed September 26, 2005, from http://www.webopedia.com/quick_ref/portnumbers.asp.

15 Relevant Technologies, "Hacker Ports," accessed June 3, 2005, from http://www.relevanttechnologies.com/src_hacker_ports.asp.

16 See note 10.

17 Internet Security Systems, Inc. "Integrity Verifiers," 2005, accessed October 15, 2005, from http://www.iss.net/security_center/advice/Countermeasures/Intrusion_Detection/Integrity_Verifiers/.

18 See note 10.

19 Application-Based IDS, Compliance Component, accessed March 21, 2004, at http://siipc.mo.gov/PortalVB/uploads/CC%20-%20Application%20Based%20IDS%2004-03-03.doc.

20 See note 10.

21 Robert Graham, "FAQ: Intrusion Detection Systems," March 2000, accessed December 5, 2005, from http://www.ticm.com/kb/faq/idsfaq.html.

22 Honeypots.net, "Intrusion Detection, Honeypots and Incident Handling Resources," accessed September 22, 2005, from http://www.honeypots.org.

23 L. Spitzner, "Honeytokens: The Other Honeypot," July 2003, accessed September 25, 2005, from http://www.securityfocus.com/infocus/1713.

24 Honeynet Project, "Know Your Enemy: Honeynets," 2005, accessed September 21, 2005, from http://www.honeynet.org/papers/honeynet/.

25 18 U.S.C. § 2511.

26 18 U.S.C. §§ 3121–3127.

27 R. Salgado, "Legal Issues," in *Knowing the Enemy: Learning About Security Threats, The Honeynet Project*, accessed September 20, 2005, from http://www.honeynet.org/book/Chp8.pdf.

28 CERT, "Detecting Signs of Intrusions," CERT Security Improvement Modules, accessed May 25, 2005, from http://www.cert.org/security-improvement/modules/m09.html#1.

29 See note 28.

30 CERT, "Identify Data that Characterize Systems and Aid in Detecting Signs of Suspicious Behavior," CERT Security Improvement Modules, accessed May 25, 2005, from http://www.cert.org/security-improvement/practices/p091.html.

31 CERT, "Managing Logging and Other Data Collection Mechanisms," CERT Security Improvement Modules, accessed May 29, 2005, from http://www.cert.org/security-improvement/practices/p092.html.

[32] CERT, "Monitor and Inspect Network Activities for Unexpected Behavior," CERT Security Improvement Modules, accessed December 5, 2005, from http://www.cert.org/security-improvement/practices/p094.html.

[33] CERT, "Monitor and Inspect System Activities for Unexpected Behavior," CERT Security Improvement Modules, accessed May 29, 2005, from http://www.cert.org/security-improvement/practices/p095.html.

[34] "Computer's Theft May Cost Visa More Than $6 Million"; *Wall Street Journal*, Tuesday, Nov 19, 1996.

CHAPTER 5

INCIDENT RESPONSE: REACTION, RECOVERY, AND MAINTENANCE

The most extreme conditions require the most extreme response.

—Diana Nyad (b. 1949), U.S. long-distance swimmer

OPENING SCENARIO

It was late when Osbert Rimorr finished his programming assignment. He was taking a class that taught students at his university how to write worm programs and how to defend against them. Now, he was about to set into motion events that would affect the lives of numerous people all over the planet, even though he was working in a small computer lab at a relatively unknown campus.

His assignment was to create a multivector, self-replicating module that could take a payload across a network. While there were legitimate uses for a program such as this, perhaps to deploy patched versions of programs or perform unscheduled version upgrades for distributed applications, many IT professional frowned on this type of programming. It was far too easy to lose control and the consequences could be devastating.

Osbert was a conscientious student. He took great care to make sure the test payload was harmless. It was a little bigger than it needed to be, because he wanted to be able to trace it around the test lab easily. Well, in reality it was a lot bigger than it needed to be. After all, he really liked the fun parts he had written into his program and he couldn't bring himself to streamline the test payload. He had also varied the timing parameters from those suggested by his professor, making the program replicate itself much more quickly than the recipe had called for. After all, he did not want to wait around the lab for a long time to see the results of his test run.

continued

Osbert was using an impressive network in the small laboratory his professor had built for this project. Several racks of server computers were running many virtual systems, representing a large number of computers of almost every possible type. Variations in capabilities were built in to test the virulence of Osbert's efforts. To keep the project under control, the whole test network was isolated from the campus network. Osbert could reset each virtual system to its initial state with a simple command. A single status display showed all of the virtual systems in the lab using a small colored dot to represent each system. Osbert noticed that all of the dots were a steady green, reporting that each was in its original state.

As he prepared to click the Start icon on his screen, Osbert carefully checked all of the lab network's software settings one last time. Everything seemed in order, and he started the test. Almost too fast to see, the individual indicator dots on the master display turned red. A red light meant that a virtual computer had become compromised by his worm.

"Amazing," he said aloud. The display showed him that the entire lab had been compromised in under 600 milliseconds. No one in his class had even approached that level. Being able to get half of the widely varied systems to accept a worm had been the best record so far. Getting 100 percent so quickly meant that the results of his effort were quite impressive.

Feeling almost euphoric with his efforts, Osbert scooted his chair to the administrator's console and clicked the button to reset all the virtual machines to their initial state. The command had no effect.

"No matter," thought Osbert with a shrug. "I'll come back early tomorrow and restart all the servers."

Unfortunately for him, another student had made a slight but unauthorized change to the test network a few hours before Osbert began his test. The student had forgotten to disconnect a network cable that was running from the test network to a wall plate that connected to the general campus network. Osbert did not know it yet, but he had just unleashed his potent new worm on the Internet.

Roughly 90 seconds later, the first attempt to compromise a computer on the HAL company network was made. Just as in the lab, Osbert's worm took over the HAL mail server and had quickly infected every system in the company. As the worm copied itself madly over and over again, the servers at HAL quickly stopped doing their assigned tasks and spent all of their resources copying the worm to every computer they could reach.

Questions for discussion:

- Was Osbert acting ethically when he wrote his worm program? On what do you base your position?
- Was Osbert's professor acting ethically by assigning him the worm program? On what do you base your position?
- Who is responsible for this catastrophe? Osbert? His professor? The university? On what do you base your position?

INTRODUCTION

The best plans are the ones that improve results before they are needed. An organization may have spent great effort in developing an incident response (IR) plan yet still be unprepared when an incident occurs. It is not enough to simply prepare plans; it is necessary to alter the culture of the organization in ways to make the organization more responsive and resilient when incidents occur. The best plans may not always be the most thorough or the most elaborate; rather, the best plans are those that make a difference in the outcome when an incident occurs. An effective **Incident Response (IR)** plan guides an organization's response when an incident occurs, enables the prompt recovery of normal operations, and assists in the smooth transition to disaster recovery or business continuity plans when needed. Whether the incident is a worm outbreak like the one launched from Osbert's lab, a cleaning fluid spill on the loading dock, or rising floodwaters, IR plans should make organizations better able to overcome adverse incidents.

The most effective organizations have made maintenance of their IR plans an integral part of the regular business processes of the organization. When things go badly, it is very easy to lose sight of the long-term goals of an organization. The first sections of this chapter discuss selecting the proper strategy to direct an organization's response to an incident and to ensure that the necessary data is collected throughout the response. The collection of forensic data pertaining to an incident is necessary to guide the follow-up evaluation of the IR plan. Such data is also helpful when law enforcement becomes involved. The final section of this chapter will discuss the forensic data-collection process and how it is used in the context of incident response.

REACTION

How and when IR plans are activated is determined by the IR strategy the organization chooses to pursue. Whether a one-size-fits-all IR strategy or a more complex and responsive multipart approach is chosen, the organization must make sure the outcome from the planned response meets the organization's strategic and tactical needs.

Selecting an IR Strategy

Once an actual incident has been confirmed and properly classified, the IR team moves from the detection phase (which was the final phase discussed in the previous chapter) to the reaction phase. At this point, an organization must know how it should react and respond to the incident. Once activated, the IR plan is designed to stop the incident, mitigate its effects, and provide information that facilitates recovering from the incident. Determining what an organization should do in any given incident requires that the organization have in place one or more IR strategies. Some organizations may choose to have a single IR strategy in place for all incidents. Others may choose to have several optional plans to handle different circumstances. The range of options that can be included in these strategies is discussed shortly.

In formulating an incident response strategy there are several factors that influence the organization's decision process:

- "Are the affected systems impacting profitable operations?
- If information was stolen, what was the level of sensitivity or classification?
- Which business functions are being impacted and at what level?
- Has the incident been contained or is it continuing?
- What is the origin of the emergency? Is it internal or external to the organization?
- Is the incident public knowledge?
- What are the legal reporting requirements? Does the law require this matter to be reported immediately to authorities? Who are those authorities? Should this matter be handled as a human resources function? Should this matter be handled as a civil suit?
- What, if any, steps should be immediately taken to discover the identity of an outside-agency attacker?
- As of the moment the incident is contained, what are the financial losses?"[1]

IR Approaches

There are two general approaches or philosophies that are at either extreme in the range of options available to an organization as it responds to an incident. At one extreme in the direction of simplicity is a strategy of *protect and forget*. At the other extreme is a more complex strategy that involves more effort, more complex planning and response, more training and rehearsal, and that can be categorized as *apprehend and prosecute*.[2] With either approach, an organization's responses to an incident are fundamentally the same, but the data collection tasks differ dramatically.

In the first approach, the focus is on the defense of the data and the systems that house, use, and transmit it. Tasks performed when pursuing this strategy therefore focus on the detection, logging, and analysis of events for the purpose of determining how they happened and to prevent recurrence. Once the current incident is over, who caused it or why is almost immaterial. The other approach focuses on the identification and apprehension of the intruder (if a human threat-agent is involved), with additional attention given to the collection and preservation of potential evidentiary materials that might support administrative or criminal prosecution.

The key steps that are used in the *protect and forget* and in the *apprehend and prosecute* philosophies are shown in Table 5-1.

TABLE 5-1   Key steps in reaction strategies[3, 4]

Key Steps in *Protect and Forget*	Key Steps in *Apprehend and Prosecute*
1. Determine if the event is a real incident. 2. If the event is indeed an incident, terminate the current intrusion. 3. Discover how access was obtained and how many systems were compromised. 4. Restore the compromised systems to their preincident configuration. 5. Secure the method of unauthorized access by the intruder on all systems. 6. Document steps taken to deal with the incident. 7. Develop lessons learned. 8. Upper management performs a brief evaluation in the incident aftermath.	1. Determine if the event is a real incident. 2. If the event is an incident, and the circumstances warrant doing so, contact law enforcement. 3. Document each action taken, including the date and time, as well as who was present when the action was taken. 4. Isolate the compromised systems from the network. 5. If the organization has the capability, it should entice the intruder into a safe system that seemingly contains valuable data. 6. Discover the identity of the intruder while documenting his or her activity. 7. Discover how the intruder gained access to the compromised systems, and secure these access points on all uncompromised systems. 8. As soon as sufficient evidence has been collected, or when vital information or vital systems are endangered, terminate the current intrusion. 9. Document the current state of compromised systems. 10. Restore the compromised systems to their pre-incident configuration. 11. Secure the method of unauthorized access by the intruder on all compromised systems. 12. Document in detail the time in man-hours, as well as the cost of handling the incident. 13. Secure all logs, audits, notes, documentation, and any other evidence gathered during the incident and appropriately identify it to secure the "chain of custody" for future prosecution. 14. Develop lessons learned. 15. Upper management performs a brief evaluation in the incident's aftermath.

(Source: "Establishing a Computer Incident Response Plan" by D. Adler and K. Grossman)

It is hoped that one or more strategies for the reaction and recovery phases of an organization's IR have been completed prior to the actual declaration of an incident. When there is some flexibility involved in crafting the reaction and recovery response to an incident, the contingency planners should have provided some guidance to the IR team.

In the incident response phase, a number of actions taken by the IR team and others must occur quickly and may take place concurrently. An effective IR plan prioritizes and documents these steps to allow for efficient reference in the midst of an incident. These steps include notification of key personnel, assignment of tasks, interviewing individuals involved, and documentation of the incident.

ONGOING CASE: DETECTING THE WORM ATTACK

The worm that Osbert wrote began its life in a small laboratory somewhere in Eastern Europe. Within seconds, it had infected tens of thousands of Internet host computers as it fulfilled its design objective of spreading itself to every computer system it could reach. When it attacked a new network location, it spread to every other computer connected to that local network.

Osbert made a small mistake when he wrote his worm code. He overlooked the step of skipping the infection of an already infected computer. This meant that the Osbert worm (it quickly was called that because he left his name in the comments section of the program) was infecting the same computer hundreds and even thousands of times. As each infection took its toll on the processor and memory of a computer, the computer slowed down. In a matter of minutes, the first computers that had been infected slowed to a crawl. Only the most recently infected computers could still infect others, but that was enough to let the worm spread across the entire planet in just a few minutes. If a computer was connected to the Internet, it was infected. The only exception, ironically, was that Osbert's worm left network switches and routers unaffected; thereby assuring that every nook and cranny of the Internet was quickly infected.

What happened to HAL's impeccably prepared antivirus programs running on all desktop and server computers? Because it was a new worm, the pattern files did not recognize it. And, because Osbert had, in fact, discovered a completely new way to pass infections between computers, the infection spread to even those servers that were running newer software that was intended to intercept infections based on known behaviors instead of software patterns.

Because HAL had a significant number of systems connected to the Internet, they were infected in a matter of moments. It was as if all the computers in the data center hit a patch of molasses at the same time. The local time at the HAL data center was 5:17 a.m. when the phone rang at the help desk as HAL's customers noticed a slowing response time.

Kekunda Grey was working the third shift and had just taken a call from a customer reporting slow response time on the HAL network. She tried to connect to the server in question only to find the server was not responding.

Kekunda dialed the shift supervisor's phone number.

"Hello, Walter Chen speaking," he said.

Kekunda began, "Walter, we have a problem. Something is very wrong here."

CERT Intrusion Response Strategies

CERT provides nine best practices in responding to an intrusion. Note that these strategies are not for responding to nonintrusion incidents or denial-of-service attacks. The CERT strategies are the following:

- Establish policies and procedures for responding to intrusions: As part of the IR plan, intrusion response is a subcategory of incident response and focuses on those incidents specifically invading the organization's information infrastructure. Frequently, intrusion response is a direct result of an individual hacking effort. Effective development of the IR plan covers intrusions, as discussed in Chapter 3.
- Prepare to respond to intrusions: Also part of the IR plan is the preparation and training to respond to intrusions, as described in Chapters 3 and 4.
- Analyze all available information to characterize an intrusion: As discussed earlier in this chapter, the collection and analysis of information, including system logs, IDS reports and alerts, and user notifications can provide insight into the intrusion at hand.
- Communicate with all parties that need to be aware of an intrusion and its progress: As part of the IR plan, notification of key personnel who are specifically trained to respond to intrusion-type incidents is crucial.
- Collect and protect information associated with an intrusion: What information is important to collect at this time? Everything associated with the incident. This is the *who*, *what*, *where*, *why*, and *how* of the intrusion. This includes specific information on the systems that were compromised, the network paths used by the intruder, and files and directories that are suspected to be compromised. During this process, you should follow standard computer forensics procedures in the collection, protection, and preservation of information that could be of evidentiary value.
- Apply short-term solutions to contain an intrusion: As indicated earlier, this could include the following:
    - Temporarily shut down the compromised system.
    - Disconnect the compromised system (or network) from the local network (or the Internet).
    - Disable access to compromised file systems that are shared with other computers.
    - Disable system services, if possible.
    - Change passwords or disable accounts.
    - Monitor system and network activities.
    - Verify that redundant systems and data have not been compromised.
- Eliminate all means of intruder access: One key problem with a successful intrusion is the high probability that the attacker will immediately inform his or her peers about the successful intrusion, through posting in hacker discussion lists, chat rooms, e-mail, and so on. Not only do they want to gloat over

their victory, but they also want to allow others to benefit from their wisdom and success. Unless the problem that resulted in the intrusion is remedied, expect another wave of attacks by other intruders. However, as described earlier, the determination of the cause of the attack may take some time.

- Return systems to normal operation: The subject of this chapter, this task represents the true purpose of incident response—to make things as they were before the attack, but more secure.
- Identify and implement security lessons learned: The after-action review, described in Chapter 3, provides the opportunity to review actions and improve the process and plan. It can also provide training for future generations of SIRT professionals.[5]

Figure 5-1 provides an overview of the CERT intrusion response process.

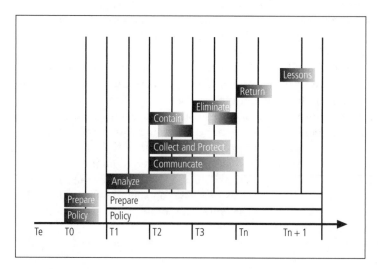

FIGURE 5-1 CERT intrusion response process[6]

Notification

As soon as the IR team determines that an incident is in progress, the right people must be immediately notified in the right order. Most response organizations, such as firefighters or the military, maintain an alert roster for all emergencies. An **alert roster** is a document containing contact information for the individuals that need to be notified in the event of an actual incident.

There are two ways to activate an alert roster: sequentially and hierarchically. A **sequential roster** requires that a contact person call each and every person on the roster. A **hierarchical roster** has the first person call certain other people on the roster, who in turn call other people, and so on. Each approach has advantages and disadvantages. The hierarchical system is quicker, because more people are calling at the same time, but the message can become distorted as it is passed from person to person. The sequential system is more accurate, but slower because a single contact person provides each responder with the message.

The **alert message** is a scripted description of the incident and consists of just enough information so that each responder knows what portion of the IR plan to implement without impeding the notification process. It is important to recognize that not everyone is on the alert roster—only those individuals who must respond to a specific actual incident. As with any part of the IR plan, the alert roster must be regularly maintained, tested, and rehearsed if it is to remain effective.

During this phase, other key personnel not on the alert roster, such as general management, must be notified of the incident as well. This notification should occur only after the incident has been confirmed, but before media or other external sources learn of it. In addition, some incidents are disclosed to the employees in general, as a lesson in security, and some are not, as a measure of security. Furthermore, other organizations may need to be notified, if it is determined that the incident is not confined to internal information resources, or if the incident is part of a larger-scale assault. For example, during Mafiaboy's distributed denial-of-service attack on multiple high-visibility Web-based vendors in late 1999, many of the target organizations reached out for help. In general, the IR planners should determine in advance whom to notify and when, and should offer guidance about additional notification steps to take as needed.

ONGOING CASE: NOTIFYING THE IR TEAM

Susan Carter hung up the phone. She had just taken a call from Walter Chen.

She quickly tried to connect her computer to several servers around the HAL network. She soon realized her desktop computer was no longer responding. It appeared to be hung or stuck, or something like that. At her next keystroke, the thing started to beep as she hit each key. She quickly rebooted it and found it would not come back up to a useable state.

She didn't waste much time. Instead, she reached for her IR plan notebook. She flipped it open to the first tabbed divider that was labeled *Activating the Incident Response Team*. She pulled out a sheet of paper and quickly wrote out the following:

At the present time all computing devices at HAL are inoperative. At 5:31 a.m. today Susan Carter declared a class 1 incident for HAL and all of its customers. All incident response team members are instructed to commence reaction and recovery activities at once.

She made a few copies of the note on the copier and then walked to the help desk room. She called out to the now-idled third-shift help desk operators, "Everyone! Since I am the senior manager on site, I am declaring an incident. I need three people to make phone calls please."

She handed the copied alert message to the first three people she could reach and they each pulled out the alert roster folders from their desk drawers and started calling the sections Susan assigned them.

continued

Documenting an Incident

As indicated in the previous chapter, as soon as an incident has been confirmed and the notification process is underway, the team should begin to document it. The documentation should record the *who, what, when, where, why,* and *how* of each action taken while the incident is occurring. This documentation serves as a case study after the fact to determine whether the right actions were taken and if they were effective. It also proves, should it become necessary, that the organization did everything possible to prevent the spread of the incident. Legally, the standards of due care protect the organization should an incident adversely affect individuals inside and outside the organization or other organizations that use the target organization's systems. Incident documentation can also be used as a simulation in future training sessions on future versions of the IR plan.

ONGOING CASE: STARTING THE PAPER TRAIL

It was 6:05 a.m., and Susan Carter was still the incident manager. She would stay with this incident as its manager until it was resolved, escalated to a disaster, or until she had been up for 20 hours. Unless things got better soon, she would have to declare this a disaster and then ride the tiger for another 10 hours unless one of the day-shift managers relieved her sooner.

She pulled a blank composition book from the file drawer. She wrote on the cover "INCIDENT LOG" along with the date. She flipped open the cover and wrote the date and time at the top of the first page. She saw that each page had been numbered already by one of her summer interns. She quickly jotted down the morning's activities and all the times and other details she could remember.

Incident Containment Strategies

One of the most critical components of IR is stopping the incident or containing its scope or impact. Incident containment strategies vary depending on the incident and on the amount of damage caused. Before an incident can be stopped or contained, however, the affected areas must be identified. During an incident is not the time to conduct a detailed analysis of the affected areas; those tasks are typically performed after the fact, in the forensics process. Instead, simple identification of what information and systems are involved determines the containment actions to be taken. Incident containment strategies focus on two tasks: stopping the incident and recovering control of the affected systems.

The IR team can attempt to stop the incident and attempt to recover control by means of several strategies. If the incident originates outside the organization, the simplest and most straightforward approach is to disconnect the affected communication circuits. Of course, if the organization's lifeblood runs through that circuit, this step may be too drastic. If the incident does not threaten critical functional areas, it may be more feasible to monitor the incident and contain it another way. One approach used by some organizations is to dynamically apply filtering rules to limit certain types of network access. For example, if a threat agent is attacking a network by exploiting a vulnerability in the Simple Network Management Protocol (SNMP), then applying a blocking filter for the commonly used IP ports for that vulnerability stops the attack without compromising other services on the network. Depending on the nature of the attack and the organization's technical capabilities, ad hoc controls can sometimes gain valuable time to devise a more permanent control strategy. Other containment strategies include the following:

- Disabling compromised user accounts
- Reconfiguring a firewall to block the problem traffic
- Temporarily disabling the compromised process or service
- Taking down the conduit application or server—for example, the e-mail server
- Stopping all computers and network devices

Obviously, the final strategy is used only when all system control has been lost, and the only hope is to preserve the data stored on the computers so that operations can resume normally once the incident is resolved. The IR team, following the procedures outlined in the IR plan, determines the length of the interruption.

Applying Containment Options

Consider the chapter case. What if, instead of a worm outbreak, the event had been a fire? And what if the key incident response personnel had been home sick, on vacation, or somehow unavailable? Think about how many people in your class or office aren't there on a regular basis. Many organizations require employees to travel periodically, with employees going off-site to meetings, seminars, training, or other diverse requirements. In considering these possibilities, the importance of preparedness becomes clear. Everyone should know how to handle an incident, not just the CISO and systems administrators.

ONGOING CASE: CONTAINING THE WORM AT HAL

Susan sighed. Every computer in the company had slowed to a stop. Not one single system connected to the network was functional. The only good news was that Juanita had reached the antivirus vendor's support line. Juanita was not able to download a patch, but she was able to listen to the recorded message about this new worm from the vendor's support line. This offered a technical work-around to recover from the worm. The light could be seen at the end of the tunnel.

The worm was benign and was only slowing down systems until they seemed to stop. Simply restarting a system, entering a few short command-line instructions, and restarting again should put any HAL system back in action. Unfortunately, if any one computer stayed up and running, it would reinfect any cleaned-up computers. It looked like a full stop was going to be needed, and each computer would have to be brought back onto the network one at a time. Once they had a computer running, the vendor had provided the pattern file to halt Osbert's worm in its tracks, but the system had to be restarted first.

Paul Alexander and Amanda Wilson walked into Susan's office together. She quickly briefed them, and they agreed to the planned full stop. Susan turned to her laptop. She had used it as a prototype to test the clean-up procedures from the vendor. They worked as advertised. She had already typed up the recovery procedure and her printer was spitting out copies as fast as it could. It was time for the tide to turn.

Interviewing Individuals Involved in the Incident

Part of determining the scale, scope, and impact of an incident is the collection of information from those reporting the incident and responsible for the systems impacted by the incident. This can be potentially dangerous when you consider that one of the individuals interviewed during incident response may in fact be the cause, in the case of an internal incident. Interviews involve three groups of stakeholders: end users, help desk personnel, and systems administrators. Each group can provide a different perspective of the incident as well as clues to its origin, cause, and impact. Interviews with end users require the SIRT to collect information in a manner that does not intimidate or overwhelm the end user with technical jargon and questions. The interview should make the user feel that he or she is contributing to the incident response capacity. Interviews with the help desk tend to be more technical, intense, and often seek information beyond that gained from the one or two individual users that initially contacted the help desk. Interviewers frequently ask the help desk staff to review previous trouble tickets looking for signs of similar attacks that could indicate a previous incident or attempted incident by the same attacker. Interviews with systems administrators similarly seek additional information, specifically logs from the affected systems, and possibly online or offline forensic images, to be analyzed in a lab. Computer forensics, although beyond the scope of this text, are a vital part of the incident response capacity. As such, a brief overview of the topic is presented later in this chapter.

Incident Escalation

An incident may increase in scope or severity to the point that the IR plan cannot adequately handle it. As important as knowing how to handle an incident is knowing at what point to hit the panic button and escalate the incident to a disaster, or to transfer the incident to an outside authority such as law enforcement or other public response unit. Each organization has to determine, during the business impact analysis, the point at which an incident is deemed a disaster. The criteria for making this determination must be included in the incident response plan. The organization must also document when to involve outside responders, as discussed in other sections. Escalation is one of those things that once done cannot be undone, so it is important to know when and where it should be used.

ONGOING CASE: ESCALATION

Susan seems to have avoided the need to escalate this incident to a disaster. Since HAL's IR team was able to get good information from the vendor and devise a containment and recovery plan in short order, it seemed that HAL would only lose about 90 minutes of production on its network—assuming, of course, the containment and recovery process worked as planned.

Susan plans to use the disaster recovery plan elements for system recovery to implement the recovery steps needed to wrap up this incident response.

The necessity of escalation, by activating the disaster plan, was not going to be needed... this time.

RECOVERY FROM INCIDENTS

Once an incident has been contained, and system control has been regained, incident recovery can begin. As in the incident response phase, the first task is to inform the appropriate human resources. Almost simultaneously, the IR team must assess the full extent of the damage to determine what must be done to restore the systems. Each individual involved should begin recovery operations based on the appropriate incident recovery section of the IR plan.

The immediate determination of the scope of the breach of confidentiality, integrity, and availability of information and information assets is called *incident damage assessment*. Incident damage assessment can take days or weeks, depending on the extent of the damage. The damage can range from minor (a curious hacker snooped around) to severe (the infection of hundreds of computer systems by a worm or virus). System logs, intrusion detection logs, and configuration logs, as well as the documentation from the incident response, provide information on the type, scope, and extent of damage. Using this information, the IR team assesses the current state of the information and systems and compares it to a known state. Individuals who document the damage from actual incidents must be trained to collect and preserve evidence in case the incident is part of a crime or results in a civil action.

The following sections detail the appropriate steps to be taken in the recovery process.[7]

Identify and Resolve Vulnerabilities

Although it may appear simple, identifying and resolving vulnerabilities could prove to be a major challenge in reestablishing operations. It is at this point that many discussions, books, and primers on intrusion detection are used to delve into the files of forensics data. Used both as a tool for intrusion analysis and as evidence collection and analysis, in this situation, forensics can also be used to best assess how the incident occurred and what vulnerabilities were exploited to cause the damage assessed. In some cases, as with natural disasters, computer forensics may not be necessary, but in those cases that involve hackers, worms, and other systems violations, it would be extremely beneficial to better understand exactly what went on.

If, during the process of determining what went wrong, evidentiary material is discovered that could be used in legal proceedings, it is imperative that the individuals performing the analysis be trained to recognize and handle the material in such a way that does not violate its value as evidence in civil or criminal proceedings. The section later in this chapter on *Computer Forensics* provides an overview of this field and some insight into what must be done to prevent doing more harm than good.

After any incident, address the safeguards that failed to stop or limit the incident, or were missing from the system in the first place, and install, replace, or upgrade them. Whether due to a faulty, malfunctioning, or misconfigured network security device, such as a firewall, router, or VPN connection, or whether due to a breach in policy or data protection procedures, whatever safeguards that were already in place must be examined to determine if they were part of the incident. If the incident was due to a missing safeguard, an assessment as to why the safeguard was not in place should be conducted. It may be determined that the incident occurred because a planned safeguard had not been procured yet, or it may be determined that a safeguard that could have prevented or limited the incident was previously assessed as being unnecessary. Whatever the findings, they should be clearly documented as to which safeguards and controls were not present or performing as specified in order to rectify the situation by repairing, reconfiguring, replacing, or procuring those safeguards.

Evaluate monitoring capabilities, if present. Improve detection and reporting methods, or install new monitoring capabilities. Many organizations do not have automated intrusion detection systems. Some feel that the performance does not justify the cost, especially when perceptions of "it can't happen to me" cloud the judgment of those responsible for the recommendation. It is interesting that individuals who sell residential burglar alarms and monitoring services know that the best time to sell consumers new products and services is when an incident occurs in their neighborhood. Small warning signs stating that a premises is being monitored pop up rapidly in neighborhoods where recently someone's home was broken into, valuables were stolen, or dwellings were vandalized. The sad part is that some decision makers must witness firsthand or secondhand the damage, destruction, or loss caused by an incident before they are willing to commit to the expenses of intrusion monitoring. The really sad part is that in some cases, open source software can provide many of the capabilities needed with little or no additional hardware or software expense to the organization (such as Snort, found at *www.snort.org*). Although each set of circumstances needs to be carefully analyzed, in many cases the increased expense to train staff and provide support for open source solutions costs much less than replacing existing proprietary solutions.

If you don't have monitoring capabilities, get them. If you have them, review their implementation and configuration to determine if they failed to detect the incident. Network IDSs won't detect all incidents, especially attacks that are not network based. Burglar and fire alarm systems are also needed to detect physical forms of incidents.

Restore Data

Unfortunately, many organizations associate the entire incident response process with simple data backup and recovery schemes. Although important at this phase of the recovery plan, it is hoped that you have a much deeper appreciation for the need for more than data backup plans in the IR plan. The IR team must understand the backup strategy used by the organization, restore the data contained in backups, and then use the appropriate recovery processes from incremental backups or database journals to re-create any data that was created or modified since the last backup. The Technical Details material in Chapter 6 will provide additional insight into the use of these techniques to facilitate data recovery.

Restore Services and Processes

Compromised services and processes must be examined, verified, and then restored. If services or processes were interrupted in the course of regaining control of the systems, they need to be brought back online.

Continuously monitor the system. If an incident happened once, it could easily happen again. Hackers frequently boast of their exploits in chat rooms and dare their peers to match their efforts. If word gets out, others may be tempted to try the same or different attacks on your systems. It is therefore important to maintain vigilance during the entire IR process.

Restore Confidence Across the Organization

The IR team may wish to issue a short memorandum outlining the incident and assuring all that the incident was handled and the damage was controlled. If the incident was minor, say so. If the incident was major or severely damaged systems or data, reassure the users that they can expect operations to return to normal as soon as possible. The objective of this communication is to prevent panic or confusion from causing additional disruption to the operations of the organization.

ONGOING CASE: RECOVERY AT HAL

It was almost too easy. Recovery operations began at 6:40 a.m. Fortunately, there was already a plan in place for a complete system power down and restart. Susan had pulled up the correct subordinate plan dealing with a full-system power cycle and had revised it to exclude recycling the battery backups and power distribution systems. These steps were not needed in this case. She also had briefed all of the first-, second-, and third-shift systems and network support team who had been able to make it in to the offices during the steps involved in restarting the systems in the company.

Now, it was just a matter of a lot of work by lots of people.

MAINTENANCE

The ongoing maintenance of the IR plan is not a trivial commitment for an organization to fulfill. It includes procedures to complete effective after-action review meetings, plan review and maintenance, ongoing training of staff that will be involved in incident response, and the rehearsal process that maintains readiness for all aspects of the incident plan.

The After-Action Review

Before returning to its routine duties, the IR team must conduct an **after-action review** (**AAR**). The after-action review entails a detailed examination of the events that occurred from first detection to final recovery. All key players review their notes and verify that the IR documentation is accurate and precise. All team members review their actions during the incident and identify areas where the IR plan worked, didn't work, or should improve. This exercise allows the team to update the IR plan. AARs are conducted with all participants in attendance. The SIRT team leader presents a timeline of events and highlights who was involved at each stage, with a summary of their actions.

Ideally, that individual relates what they discovered or did, and any discrepancies between documentation and the verbal case are noted. The entire AAR is recorded for use as a training case for future staff. All parties should treat the AAR not as an inquisition, but as a discussion group to relate their piece of the experience, and to learn how others dealt with it. If properly structured and conducted, the AAR can have a positive effect on the organization's IR capacity and employee confidence in responding to incidents. If poorly handled, the AAR can actually reduce the organization's ability to react because individuals, especially users, may prefer to sweep potential incidents under the rug rather than risk improperly responding and having to face "the firing squad." The AAR brings the IR team's actions to a close.

AAR to Document Lessons Learned and Generate IR Plan Improvements

At the end of the incident review, the AAR serves as a review tool, allowing the team to examine how the team responded to the incident. Examining the documentation of the incident should reveal the point at which the incident was first detected, the point in time the IR plan was enacted, and how the first responders and SIRT reacted. This is not to cast blame on an individual or group for substandard performance, but to ensure that the best methods of reacting were employed, and that any mistakes made during the process, whether from a failure to follow the IR plan or from errors in the IR plan, are not made again. The IR plan is continually reexamined during AARs to ensure the procedures included are in fact the best method of responding to the particular incident. Should the AAR reveal that the incident represents a new type or variation of incident, additional material can be added to the IR plan to better prepare the team for future interactions.

AAR as Historical Record of Events

An additional use of the AAR is a historical record of events. This use may or may not be a requirement for legal proceedings, depending on the laws that apply to your area. In any case, it is useful to be able to establish a timeline of events, drawn from a number of different sources, to show the evolution of the incident, from first identification to final resolution. This timeline then serves other purpose as described in the following sections. Important information can be gained from the examination of the amount of time it took to respond to an incident.

AAR as Case Training Tool

One of the more positive aspects of an incident is: "That which does not kill us, makes us stronger."[8] By examining the events of past attacks, students of information security and incident response can learn from others' actions, whether correct or incorrect. You can learn as much from mistakes as from successes. As Thomas Edison is credited with saying, "I have not failed. I've just found 1000 ways that won't work."

Honest effort in the pursuit of one's goals is not failure. By studying the AAR reports from an organization's past incidents, not only do the new information security professionals and incident response team members become familiar with the system, plans, and responses of the organization, but they also get a lesson in how to deal with the challenges of incident response in general. Part of "knowing yourself" is knowing how you and your team handle victories as well as defeats. But even in defeat, as in the case of a successful and painful attack, the organization must continue forth, recovering from its battles, rebuilding its defenses, to fight another day.

AAR as Closure

One final quote on the AAR and its reports is offered, this one from Yogi Berra: "It ain't over, til it's over." People require closure to events, especially traumatic ones. The AAR serves as closure to the incident. Even though there may be a great deal of work left to recover data and systems and to train and retrain users and SIRT members, for the most part, once the AAR report is filed, the incident has come to a close. The team goes back to their normal routine and responsibilities associated with protecting information and preparing for the next incident.

ONGOING CASE: THE HAL WORM AAR

Everything was back to normal. Susan was preparing for the after-action report. She pulled out the HAL standard AAR outline. As she reviewed each agenda item, she realized that this would be a textbook instance of the AAR and she could use the standard meeting agenda.

She mused to herself, "Well, if you have to be the incident manager, at least be thankful it was all routine." She looked at her watch. It was 1:20 in the afternoon. She should be home by 4:00 and was then due back at her desk for normal third-shift work at 11:30 that night. She wouldn't even miss much sleep.

Plan Review and Maintenance

The specific processes used by organizations to maintain the IR vary from one organization to another, but some commonly used maintenance techniques can be noted. When plan shortcomings are noted, the plan should be reviewed and revised to accommodate the specific details of the deficiency. Deficiencies may come to light based on after-action reviews when the plans are used for actual incidents, during rehearsals when the plan is used in simulated incidents, or by review during periodic maintenance. It is also recommended that at periodic intervals, such as one year or less, an assigned member of management should undertake some degree of review of the incident response plan. Some questions that might be useful in this review include the following:

- Has there been any use of this plan in the past review period?
- Were any AAR meetings held, and have the minutes of any such meetings been reviewed to note deficiencies that may need attention?
- Have any other notices of deficiency been submitted to the plan owner, and have they been addressed yet?

Depending on the answer to the questions above, the plan may need to be reviewed and amended by the CPMT. All changes proposed to the IR plan must be coordinated with the CPMT so that changes to the IR plan stay aligned with the use of other contingency planning documents used in the company.

Training

A systematic approach to training is needed to support the incident response plan. Because the nature of the IR plan dictates that any number of people may be called upon to fill the roles identified in the plan, the organization must undertake training programs to assure itself that a sufficient pool of qualified staff members are available to meet the needs of the plan when it is activated.

The training plan should also include references to the provisioning of actual or contingent credentials needed to execute the containment and recovery steps in the plan. It does little good to have trained and qualified staff on hand to restart servers under the auspices of the IR plan if the staff do not have the proper credentials to authorize those actions.

Cross-training is also needed to make assurances that enough staff with the proper skills are available for all reasonably realistic scenarios. Remember that in some cases, the IR plan, the DR plan, and the BC plan may all be functioning concurrently. Staff should be sufficiently cross-trained and authorization provisioning should be in place to allow a sufficient employee response to all likely scenarios.

Rehearsal

This ongoing and systematic approach to planning requires that plans be rehearsed until those responding are prepared for the actions they are expected to perform. When structured properly, rehearsals can also function to supplement training events by pairing some staff as understudies to more experienced staff members. Where possible, major planning elements should be rehearsed. Rehearsal adds value by exercising the procedures, identifying any shortcomings, and providing the opportunity to improve the plan before it is needed. In addition, rehearsals make people more effective when an actual event occurs.

Rehearsals that closely match reality are called **war games**. A war game or simulation uses a subset of plans that are in place to create a realistic test environment. This adds to the value of the rehearsal and can enhance training. Some organizations hold significant rehearsal events with high degrees of realism. Other make due with less realistic conference room rehearsals.

INTRUSION FORENSICS

As a critical component of the recovery phase of incident response, it is important to understand how computer and network forensics can be used to assist in the determination of **root cause analysis** and incident effect. Root cause analysis is the determination of the initial flaw or vulnerability that allowed the incident to occur by examining the systems, networks, and procedures that were involved.

Forensics is "the coherent application of methodical investigatory techniques to solve crime cases, while **computer forensics** involves the preservation, identification, extraction, documentation, and interpretation of computer media for evidentiary and/or root cause analysis."[9] Like information security in general, computer forensics involves as much art as science. However, the use of established methodologies can facilitate the collection of *legally defensible* evidentiary material. Why the emphasis on legally defensible? Even through the process may be initiated as a response to an incident, or as part of a routine outprocessing of an employee, you never know when you might stumble across evidentiary material that requires reporting to law enforcement. Therefore, treat each investigation as if it will end in legal proceedings. **Evidentiary material** is information, graphics, images, or any other physical or electronic item that could have value as evidence of guilt (or innocence) in a legal proceeding, whether criminal or civil. Computer forensics is still in its infancy, as computer-based evidence has only been admissible in legal proceedings for the past few decades.

The field of computer forensics combines skills from a number of disciplines, yet has its roots in two— computer science and criminal justice. While the latter provides detailed knowledge in the handling and presentation of evidentiary material, the former is required to successfully obtain it, because within a computer system are a myriad of nooks and crannies to hide information. Even the deletion of information and the reformatting of data storage units will not hinder the acquisition of evidence by a skilled forensic analyst. Such an expert in computer forensics can gain employment either as a corporate forensics analyst, an employee or agent of a law enforcement agency, or as a freelance investigator and expert witness.

Computer Forensics Methodology

At its heart, computer forensics follows a simple three-step methodology:

1. Collect the evidentiary material.
2. Analyze the evidentiary material.
3. Report on the evidentiary material.

However, the implementation of this methodology proves to be somewhat more complex. Throughout the entire process, the most crucial components include the strict following of established procedures and the rigorous documentation of process and findings.

Collecting Evidentiary Material

The first and most important part of computer forensics is the identification and collection of evidentiary material without damage or modification of its content. This is a rather straightforward process in the world of fingerprints, blood evidence, and paper trails, but in the world of computer forensics, you find that the process of collecting evidence can result in its modification unless strict care is rendered. If the evidence is modified or damaged in any way, it becomes substantially more difficult to have it accepted in a legal proceeding. Unfortunately for the computer forensics expert, the layman jury and judges frequently do not have the technical background to differentiate between normal systems updates and modifications and the deceitful efforts of one attempting to manipulate the indications of the evidence. As a result, unless one can prove "beyond a reasonable doubt" that the evidence is unmodified and contains its original content, it frequently will be thrown out as tainted.

Motivations and Circumstances for a Search

Another consideration for the collection of evidentiary material is the purpose or motivation behind its collection. The laws governing search and seizure for the private sector are much more straightforward than for those in the public sector. However, there are certain conditions that must be met to ensure that any evidentiary material found is admissible in any legal proceedings that follow, whether administrative or judicial. These are covered in more detail in the *Computer Forensics: Search and Seizure* sidebar. In general, law enforcement agents must either have a search warrant or the employer's consent to search for evidentiary materials. For a private organization to search an employee's computer, the following sequence of events usually occurs:

1. The employee has been notified in policy that such a search may occur. This policy must be treated as all others by having the employee read, understand, and agree to it, with the policy also receiving equitable implementation. It is also useful to include notifications in network and system banners reminding users that such searches may occur.
2. The search must be "justified at its inception." This means that there was a legitimate business reason for the search, such as the search was specifically to locate legitimate work product or to investigate work-related misconduct involving organizational resources that is based on reliable information. In the first case, if the organization routinely searched every employee's computer, or conducted truly random searches and uncovered potential evidentiary material, then the findings are admissible. If the employee was working on a product for the organization, and an authorized individual, that is, supervisor,

manager, or assistant were looking for that product, and discovered evidence of misconduct, then such evidence is equally admissible. In the latter case, if the InfoSec Department received information that someone was conducting unauthorized activities using organizational resources the search may be justified.

3. The search must also be "permissible in its scope," meaning the search had a specific focus and that the search was constrained to that focus. One cannot look for Word documents on a system e-mail server unless there is a clear link between the two, such as the employee reported e-mailing the document. This requirement does not prohibit the use of materials found during a normal business search, but prevents a total inventory search when the search should have been constrained to one or two folders or directories.

4. The organization had clear ownership over the container in which the material was discovered. This precludes searches of the employee's person, personal belongings, and personal technologies, but does not exclude those containers provided by the organization for the employee's use, such as a PDA, cell phone, laptop, and so on. One gray area is the use of employee-purchased briefcases, satchels, and backpacks used to transport work. One area that has not yet been challenged in court is the requirement to search a personal computer used by a telecommuter. However, it is feasible that this may transpire in the near future, with the increase in telecommuting and remote computing.

5. The search must be authorized by the responsible manager or administrator. For systems, the senior system administrator must allow the search, unless of course this individual is a suspect in an internal investigation. For most organizational equipment, a designated manager must provide authorization. Forward-thinking organizations are designating a senior executive officer such as the chief information officer as a magistrate to authorize organizational searches. Even then, the search itself should be conducted by a designated, disinterested individual such as the CISO or other individual recommended by legal council.

Once these conditions are met, an organization should have a reasonable degree of confidence in their ability to look for and collect potentially evidentiary material. This does not mean that any administrative or judicial actions will go unchallenged. However, it does mean that the organization has a much stronger case to refute any allegations of impropriety.

COMPUTER FORENSICS: SEARCH AND SEIZURE AND THE PUBLIC SECTOR

The field of computer forensics is evolving rapidly. Organizations are increasingly able to evaluate the technologies used by their employees and former employees to determine if criminal activities or work-related misconduct have occurred. Even in the face of new storage devices and technologies, the trained forensic analyst is capable of performing the mission of acquiring, authenticating, analyzing, and reporting the presence or absence of evidentiary material stored on computer media. But the underlying question facing this discipline is not technological; it is legal, ethical, and managerial. It is not, *can* the investigator seize and examine computer media, but rather *should* they? The decision to search for and seize potential evidentiary material has proven to be a legal quagmire. While there are some straightforward guidelines in the corporate and private sectors, when examining this decision in the public sector, it rapidly becomes evident that it is not a simple, straightforward decision. This discussion seeks to examine the controversial influences on the decision to search for and seize computer media in the public sector. This discussion presents the relevant case law and makes recommendations for institutions and the faculty, staff, and students who make up these institutions.

The Fourth Amendment and Workplace Searches

At the heart of the discussion is the examination of personal privacy, as alluded to in the Fourth Amendment of the U.S. Constitution, which states:

> *The right of the people to be secure in their persons, houses, papers, and effects, against unreasonable searches and seizures, shall not be violated, and no Warrants shall issue, but upon probable cause, supported by Oath or affirmation, and particularly describing the place to be searched, and the persons or things to be seized.*[10]

It is interesting that when the founding fathers drafted this document, it was intended not as a direct protection of privacy per se, but more as a set of controls to prevent misuse of power by law enforcement. The Fourth Amendment basically states that citizens have a right against searches of their person and property without authorization by an appropriate entity. This expectation of privacy has been stretched by case law to include the workplace. While it may appear to be contradictory that an employee has an expectation of privacy in the workplace, as one begins to examine the overlap between work and personal property, the confusion emerges.

Warrantless Searches and the Public Sector

The legal link establishing the starting point for "warrantless" workplace searches is the Supreme Court's complex decision in *O'Connor v. Ortega*.[11] This case delineated the workplace into two sectors, public and private. Within the private sector, the Supreme Court stated: "Every warrantless workplace search must be evaluated carefully on its facts.

continued

In general, however, law enforcement officers can conduct a warrantless search of private (i.e., nongovernment) workplaces only if the officers obtain the consent of either the employer or another employee with common authority over the area searched."[12] As established in the O'Conner case and as illustrated in the Department of Justice's *Manual for Computer Search & Seizure*:

> *In public (i.e., government) workplaces, officers cannot rely on an employer's consent, but can conduct searches if written employment policies or office practices establish that the government employees targeted by the search cannot reasonably expect privacy in their workspace. Further, government employers and supervisors can conduct reasonable work-related searches of employee workspaces without a warrant even if the searches violate employees' reasonable expectation of privacy.*[13]

While this clarification makes it more difficult for law enforcement to search without warrants, mainly due to the lack of clear *employer* identification, it also establishes a clear precedence for the public sector employer to conduct "work-related searches." The employer or supervisor has the right to enter the employee's office: (1) if the organization has established policy permitting such searches by employers, supervisors, coworkers, or even the public; (2) to obtain work-related material such as reports of files needed to support the ongoing function of the organization; and (3) to investigate work-related misconduct. While the employer or supervisor doesn't need a warrant, they do need the equivalent of "probable cause;" that is, the search must be "justified at its inception and permissible in its scope."[14] The former requires that there must be a reasonable expectation that the search will provide evidence of work-related misconduct, or is part of a normal search, meaning not "fishing" for evidence. This process does allow the employer or supervisor to make use of those items discovered when searching for other specific items. A search is permissible in its scope when the search was a reasonable search and did not exceed the supervisor's or employer's scope of authority. This means the employer cannot look in areas that would not be part of a normal or routine search, such as the personal belongings of an employee.

This probable cause may be challenged if the employee chooses to contest the search, whether or not evidentiary material was found. If the employer or supervisor cannot produce some fact or corroborating evidence that suggested work-related misconduct, the search can be declared unconstitutional, any evidentiary material found during the search ruled inadmissible, and damages awarded the employee. Simply finding evidence of misconduct does not justify the search.[15]

continued

203

The Expectation of Privacy

As the courts ruled in *Katz v. United States*,[16] "A search is constitutional if it does not violate a person's *reasonable* or *legitimate* expectation of privacy. This inquiry embraces two discrete questions: first, whether the individual's conduct reflects *an actual (subjective) expectation of privacy*, and second, whether the individual's subjective expectation of privacy is *one that society is prepared to recognize as reasonable.*"[17] This argument hinges on the establishment of an "expectation of privacy." In both the public and private sectors, privacy essentially boils down to the level of expectation provided to the employee by policy. When the organization has clear policy stating that employees have no expectation of privacy (outside certain legal areas, including the restroom), then warrantless searches can occur almost at will. Just as with any organizational policy, the policy must be distributed, read, understood, and agreed to for it to be legally enforceable. While ignorance of the law is no excuse (*ignorantia legis neminem excusat*), ignorance of policy is. Simply having a policy permitting employers or law enforcement to search an employee's office without a warrant is not enough.[18] The reasonable expectation of privacy test formulated by the *O'Connor* decision asks whether a government employee's work space is "so open to fellow employees or to the public that no expectation of privacy is reasonable."[19] Questions of whether the employee has exclusive access to the work space, as in a private office, or whether other employees are routinely allowed into the space, influence this decision. The level of access an employee has over their workspace can change their expectation of privacy. Allowing free access versus providing personal keys to offices with locking doors or providing locking cabinets within the offices impacts this interpretation. When conducting investigations, law enforcement officials specifically look for indicators of "no privacy" in the workplace, as in written policies, posted notices, and electronic banners. This comment from a United States Federal Court case in 2002 illustrates the issue:

> In general, government employees who are notified that their employer has retained rights to access or inspect information stored on the employer's computers can have no reasonable expectation of privacy in the information stored there (See [7])...Other courts have agreed with the approach articulated in Simons and have held that banners and policies generally eliminate a reasonable expectation of privacy in contents stored in a government employee's network account.[20]

Another perspective on this issue comes from one of this text's reviewers:

> The Simons decision basically allows a company wide leeway in searching computers in adherence of their policies in efforts to protect their systems—in this case, in a governmental organization. While Simons had a private office, and thus an expectation of privacy, he had also visited porn sites in violation of a policy stating that this was a no-no and that network activity was being monitored so that policies could be enforced. His IP address was found in the network logs showing him visiting porn sites, and his computer was

continued

remotely searched by network administrators. They subsequently found child porn and called law enforcement authorities, who then obtained a search warrant. His defense was not that he hadn't downloaded child porn but that the initial search was illegal. (The courts disagreed)."[21]

However, simple presence of a warning, whether warning banner, or employee handbook, or manual, may not be enough.[22] In the absence of policy or warning banners, courts almost assuredly infer an expectation of privacy in the use of a computer.[23] The challenge comes in the application of Fourth Amendment protection to computer media and the electronic information contained within. As per the Department of Justice's *Manual For Search and Seizure*:

To determine whether an individual has a reasonable expectation of privacy in information stored in a computer, it helps to treat the computer like a closed container such as a briefcase or file cabinet. The Fourth Amendment generally prohibits law enforcement from accessing and viewing information stored in a computer without a warrant if it would be prohibited from opening a closed container and examining its contents in the same situation.[24]

Exceptions to the Fourth Amendment

There are a number of exceptions to the requirement for warrants specified by the Fourth Amendment, as the courts have continually struggled with balancing reasonable expectations of privacy by the individual with the needs of law enforcement and organizations in conducting searches. With rapidly changing information technology, how these exceptions are handled will be an ongoing challenge for the courts, organizations, and individuals. These exceptions include: 1) Consent, 2) Plain View, 3) Exigent Circumstances, 4) Search Incident to a Lawful Arrest, 5) Inventory Searches, 6) Border Searches, and 7) International Issues. The two most relevant exceptions are discussed here:

If the individual or a "person with authority" *consents* to the search, then no warrant is needed. The challenge is whether the consent is implicit or explicit or whether it was voluntarily given.[25, 26] Fortunately for the individual, the burden of proof is the government's. The problem arises under two issues: The first is the scope of consent—if an individual consents to the search of part of a system, does this infer consent to search the entire system? Second, who is authorized to provide this consent? Can family, friends, or roommates provide this consent? With regard to *who* can provide consent, if the technology is used or owned by more than one individual, any one of those individuals can consent to the search. As such, there is no reasonable expectation of privacy.[27]

The next area of exemption for the Fourth Amendment is the concept of *plain view*. An item is in plain view if it is readily observable by the investigator without manipulation of the environment in which the information resides.[28] This also means that if an investigator is conducting a lawful search of a computer hard drive and discovers evidence of another crime, the supplemental evidence is considered in plain view. However, if the investigator is authorized to search specific folders, and opens folders outside of the authorized search area, the discovered information may not be considered "in plain view."[29] Note

continued

that most of these exceptions really only apply to law enforcement officials, because investigators who are not members of a law enforcement agency are not bound by the Fourth Amendment, unless they are acting as an "agent of the law"—meaning that they are working on behalf of or at the request of a law enforcement agency.

Complications Associated with Other Laws and Policy

It would appear from the preceding discussion that public academic institutions' employees would only enjoy Fourth Amendment protection to the extent provided to all public-sector employees. When just considering the Fourth Amendment, this may be the case. This would indicate that law enforcement needs a warrant, while the employer or employer's representative (a department chair or dean) need only probable cause associated with work misconduct or suspicion of criminal conduct. However, there is another issue that complicates the Fourth Amendment interpretation. As stated in the Department of Justice *Manual for Search and Seizure*:

> *In many cases, workplace searches will implicate federal privacy statutes in addition to the Fourth Amendment. For example, efforts to obtain an employee's files and e-mail from the employer's network server raise issues under the Electronic Communications Privacy Act, 18 U.S.C. §§ 2701–2712, and workplace monitoring of an employee's Internet use implicates Title III, 18 U.S.C. §§ 2510–2522.*[30]

One such statute is the 1976 Copyright Act (Title 17, U.S. Code), which extends protection to the owners of intellectual property. While this act in and of itself does not prevent an institution from seizing and searching computer systems in the public sector, its use in conjunction with organizational policy can. For example, if an employee at Kennesaw State creates intellectual property without substantial investment by the university other than those resources normally available to the individual, then the individual owns the intellectual property and is entitled to 100% of any royalties derived from that intellectual property. Using this policy, it is a logical assumption that works leading to the development of intellectual property, works resulting from the development of intellectual property, and works in progress are all the personal property of the individual, and the institution permits the individual to store their information (personal property) on equipment issued to them, then they are forfeiting their rights to search and seize that property at will. There is a special case in the creation of intellectual property that falls under the concept of "work for hire"—a situation where an employee creates intellectual property at the behest or requirement of an employer. In this case, the employer is considered to be the author and thus the owner of the intellectual property.[31]

Other relevant statues include the Electronic Communications Protection Act (ECPA), and the Privacy Protection Act (PPA). The Electronic Communications Privacy Act of 1986 is a collection of statues that regulates the interception of wire, electronic, and oral communications. These statues are frequently referred to as the Federal Wiretapping Acts. They address the following areas:[32]

- Interception and disclosure of wire, oral, or electronic communications

continued

- Manufacture, distribution, possession, and advertising of wire, oral, or electronic communication-intercepting devices
- Confiscation of wire, oral, or electronic communication-intercepting devices
- Evidentiary use of intercepted wire or oral communications
- Authorization for interception of wire, oral, or electronic communications
- Authorization for disclosure and use of intercepted wire, oral, or electronic communications
- Procedure for interception of wire, oral, or electronic communications
- Reports concerning intercepted wire, oral, or electronic communications
- Injunction against illegal interception

These statutes work in cooperation with the Fourth Amendment of the U.S. Constitution, which prohibits search and seizure without a warrant. Among other things, "Under the ECPA, a warrant is required to search e-mail on a public system that is stored for less than 180 days. If the mail is stored for more than 180 days, law enforcement agents can obtain it either by using a subpoena (if they inform the target beforehand) or by using a warrant without notice."[33]

The Privacy Protection Act of 1980 (PPA), codified as 42 U.S.C. § 2000aa et seq., protects journalists from being required to turn over to law enforcement any work product and documentary materials, including sources, before it is disseminated to the public. Journalists who most need the protection of the PPA are those that are working on stories that are highly controversial or about criminal acts because the information gathered may also be useful for law enforcement. For instance, a criminal suspect may talk openly to a journalist who promises not to print her name, but will not go to law enforcement for fear of arrest. While law enforcement would like to obtain this type of information from a journalist, the PPA protects the journalist's freedom to publish such information under the First Amendment without government intrusion."[34]

(Source: An earlier version of this article was presented at the Southern Association for Information Systems Conference, February 2005 and was published in that conference's Proceedings.)

Acquiring Computer Evidence

The first step in acquiring computer evidence is the establishment of search and seizure procedures. Based on the Department of Justice's *Searching and Seizing Computers and Related Electronic Evidence Issues*,[35] the investigator should perform the following:

1. Prepare the evidence collection kit: A good investigator should have at his or her disposal a collection of tools to assist in the collection of evidence. For the computer investigator, this means backup computer equipment (floppy drives, CD drives, CD writers, DVD writers) and a host of special equipment designed to obtain data without modification (such as write blockers and bit stream copy devices such as the ImageMASSter). In addition, the investigator should have several large blank hard drives, storage containers, evidence collection bags, inventory logs, a digital camera, and other supplies.

2. Acquire a permission (search warrant) by submitting a statement of intent (affidavit) to an authorized individual (magistrate): As described earlier, one must first have permission to execute a search. This permission may be verbal, but is preferred in writing. In the legal community, this means submitting an affidavit or sworn statement to a magistrate or judge in order to obtain a search warrant. In the private sector, this may simply mean submitting a letter to the CIO to obtain a signature authorizing the search.

3. Secure the scene: Even though the private sector searches may not involve law enforcement officers, it may help to have physical security employees or at least a few InfoSec Department members present to separate the suspect from the crime scene and thus prevent the destruction of evidentiary material. For the least confrontation, the search should be conducted after normal business hours to prevent interference from the suspect or fellow workers and minimize the impact on business operations.

4. Photograph and sketch the scene: To prove the evidence was obtained from the suspect's office or area, it is helpful to photograph and sketch the entire room. This also facilitates a **black bag operation (op)** or search in which the suspect never knows a search occurred, because the scene is restored to its original state.

5. Identify any potentially evidentiary material: Employees can be sneaky when it comes to hiding information. For best results, secure all computer storage media and log files and examine them in the laboratory. Some material may not be digital, such as printouts, notes, photocopies, books, journals, and manuals. Although it may not be feasible to go through an entire office's filing system, a quick search of desk drawers, the desktop, and "at-hand" locations should reveal any relevant materials. For most businesses, evidence must be extracted from the source (as in a hard drive) or extracted electronically. An organization may not be able to afford taking a key electronic commerce server offline to look for evidentiary material.

6. Tag, inventory, and secure the material: Every item found should be placed in a secure evidence bag, inventoried and logged. Legally, law enforcement must return business property back to its owner, and if the property is lost, the agency could be sued, or worse, any resulting legal proceedings overturned. Once all materials have been collected or 'bagged and tagged' they must be secured for transportation.

7. Transport the material to a secure location with limited access, maintaining the chain of custody (also known as chain of evidence): The **chain of custody** or **chain of evidence** is a log of everyone who has had access to or possession of evidentiary material from its collection to its presentation during legal proceedings. This log includes who collected the evidence, how and where, who had possession when not in storage, and when was it in storage. To refute any claims that the material is not the material collected, or that it has been modified by unauthorized individuals, the chain serves as proof that the material has not left the possession of the authorized individuals. When not in use, the material must be secured. Even private businesses should have a

secure locker or safe with very restricted access that can be used to store this type of material.

Figure 5–2 shows an example of a chain-of-custody document.

EVIDENCE/PROPERTY CUSTODY DOCUMENT			TRACKING NUMBER:	
			CASE NUMBER	
RECEIVING ACTIVITY		LOCATION		
NAME, GRADE AND TITLE OF PERSON FROM WHOM RECEIVED ☐ OWNER ☐ OTHER		ADDRESS *(Including Zip Code)*		
LOCATION FROM WHERE OBTAINED		REASON OBTAINED	DATE/TIME OBTAINED	

ITEM NO.	QUANTITY	DESCRIPTION OF ARTICLES *(Include model, serial number, condition and unusual marks or scratches)*

CHAIN OF CUSTODY

ITEM NO.	DATE	RELEASED BY	RECEIVED BY	PURPOSE OF CHANGE OF CUSTODY
		SIGNATURE	SIGNATURE	
		NAME, GRADE OR TITLE	NAME, GRADE OR TITLE	
		SIGNATURE	SIGNATURE	
		NAME, GRADE OR TITLE	NAME, GRADE OR TITLE	
		SIGNATURE	SIGNATURE	
		NAME, GRADE OR TITLE	NAME, GRADE OR TITLE	
		SIGNATURE	SIGNATURE	
		NAME, GRADE OR TITLE	NAME, GRADE OR TITLE	
		SIGNATURE	SIGNATURE	
		NAME, GRADE OR TITLE	NAME, GRADE OR TITLE	

FIGURE 5-2 Evidence Log or Chain of Custody

ITEM NO.	DATE	CHAIN OF CUSTODY (CONTINUED)		PURPOSE OF CHANGE OF CUSTODY
		RELEASED BY	RECEIVED BY	
		SIGNATURE	SIGNATURE	
		NAME, GRADE OR TITLE	NAME, GRADE OR TITLE	
		SIGNATURE	SIGNATURE	
		NAME, GRADE OR TITLE	NAME, GRADE OR TITLE	
		SIGNATURE	SIGNATURE	
		NAME, GRADE OR TITLE	NAME, GRADE OR TITLE	
		SIGNATURE	SIGNATURE	
		NAME, GRADE OR TITLE	NAME, GRADE OR TITLE	
		SIGNATURE	SIGNATURE	
		NAME, GRADE OR TITLE	NAME, GRADE OR TITLE	
		SIGNATURE	SIGNATURE	
		NAME, GRADE OR TITLE	NAME, GRADE OR TITLE	

FINAL DISPOSAL AUTHORITY

RELEASE TO OWNER OR OTHER (Name/Organization)

DESTROY

OTHER (Specify)

FINAL DISPOSAL AUTHORITY

ITEM(S)_____ON THIS DOCUMENT, PERTAINING TO THE INQUIRY/INVESTIGATION INVOLVING:

_____(IS)(

ARE) NO LONGER
(Grade)   (Name)   (Organization)

REQUIRED AS EVIDENCE AND MAY BE DISPOSED OF AS INDICATED ABOVE. *(If articles must be retained do not sign, but explain in separate correspondence.)*

(Typed/Printed Name, Grade, Title)   (Signature)
(Date)

WITNESS TO DESTRUCTION OF EVIDENCE

FIGURE 5-2 Evidence Log or Chain of Custody (continued)

8. Document everything: One investigator should document the process, whether with a camcorder or with copious notes. This record can serve as proof that the investigation was professional, legitimate, and did not exceed its authority.

Analyzing the Evidentiary Material

The technical aspects of analyzing evidence are so advanced as to preclude a detailed discussion here. However, the overall process involves the following:

1. Imaging the data: Data on digital media is almost never directly examined on the media. Investigators create a copy or image of the data or device and then examine the copy. This is performed by using a read-only data collection device to extract the information without the possibility of accidentally writing to the media. If you write to the media, it modifies the body of information stored there. In the case of an image, a device pulls all the bits off the

storage device and copies them into a single file, similar to "zipping" or archiving. Some investigators make an identical copy of a suspect's hard drive, and then create the image from the copy. Caution should be exercised when using this approach because the receiving hard drive must be scrubbed with special software to prevent any information stored there by a previous investigation or the manufacturer from contaminating the evidence.

2. Creating a hash of the evidence to provide authentication: One method of ensuring that the image analyzed is the same as that originally collected from the evidentiary material is the hash. Hashing is a process by which a mathematical algorithm turns a variable-length input into a fixed-length output. Until recently, MD5 was the industry standard for hashing, creating a 128-bit, hexadecimal output from a file or image. However the NIST Secure Hash Algorithm (SHA) has gained in popularity, especially since problems have been found with the MD5 algorithm. Two researchers have been able to create two different documents with the same MD5 hash value, both of which have meaningful content, rather than being collections of random bits.[36] It is useful to hash the entire evidence image and the individual files. It is possible to identify a graphical image from the hash value without having to look at the file itself. In the case of child pornography, this is the preferred method. Law enforcement agencies have a database of documented images, with hashes, that they use to verify file content without having to visually review the material.

Figure 5-3 shows the hashing tool HashCalc (available from *www.slavasoft.com/hashcalc*) creating multiple hash values for a file.

3. Creating working backups of the image: One of the guiding principles in forensics research is to avoid contamination of the evidence by working with copies whenever possible. After hashing the evidence drive image, you create several working copies, one of which may have to be shared with a defense attorney. You then use these working images for your forensics analysis. In any case, there must be at least one witness to the creation of the original image and the duplication of that image. It is also advantageous to store at least one copy in a safe, offsite location, perhaps with a legal council, to refute any accusations of tampering. The original evidence drive should be returned to the storage facility and continue to be protected and tracked through the chain of custody.

4. Using an investigative tool to look for evidentiary material in the image: There are two dominant tools that can be used to examine computer evidence. Although there are a host of others that support the process, most organizations use either Encase (*www.guidancesoftware.com*) or ForensicsToolKit (*www.accessdata.com*). Both have their strengths and weaknesses, and both are generally accepted as tools to examine evidentiary material without possibility of contamination. While Encase is more robust and contains tried-and-true utilities for both image acquisition and analysis, FTK is generally easier to use for the less experienced analyst, and thus easier for corporate programs to get established, but has a much less robust image acquisition utility. Neither tool is inexpensive, and both

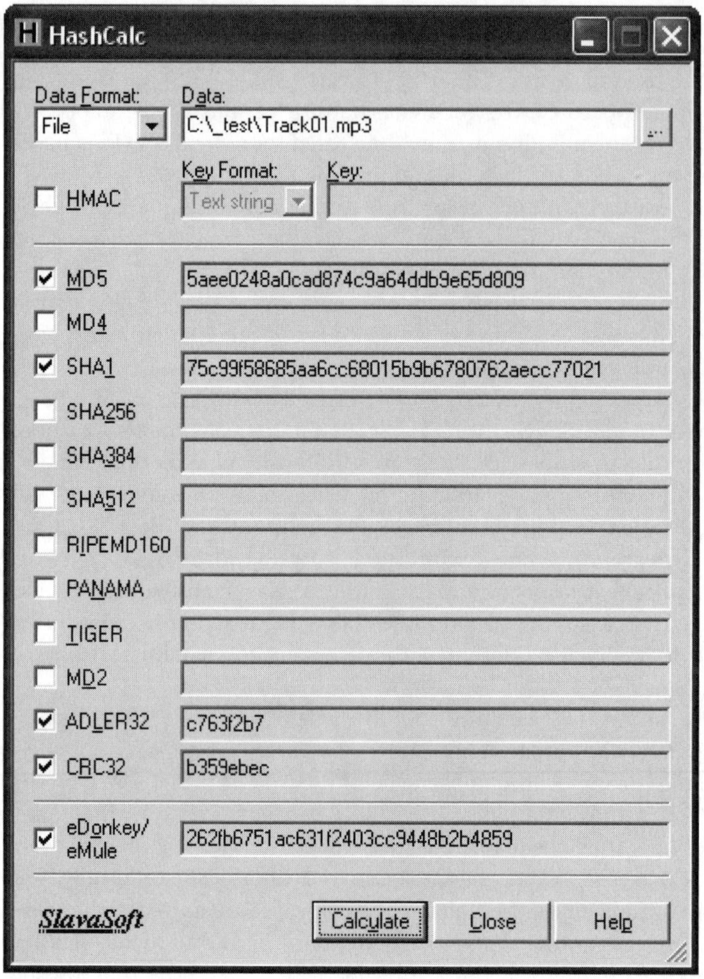

FIGURE 5-3 Hash Tool Example

require formal training for a user to become proficient. Figures 5-4 and 5-5 show these tools. When using the tools, both begin with an index of all terms found in the evidentiary material. This index substantially speeds up the searching for key terms relative to the investigation. However, the indexing itself can be quite time consuming, and on a large drive (say, greater than 40 GB) could take several hours if not days. Once complete, the index can be searched for key terms. Images are also cataloged, and the researcher can look for evidence of malfeasance. Any found evidence can be added to an electronic case file, and then reports generated. Should the investigation reveal encrypted or password-protected materials, there are tools (or modules for existing utilities) available to assist in the recovery of information.

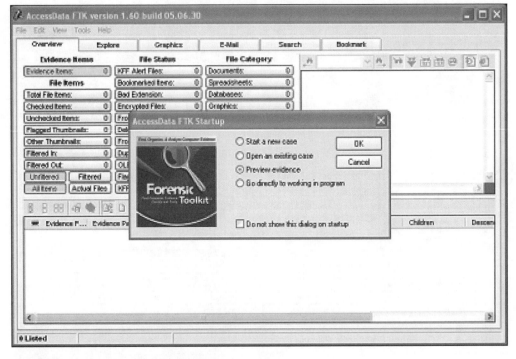

FIGURE 5-4 Access Data's Forensic Toolkit

5. Documenting everything, including the findings: The investigator should record the *who*, *what*, and *where* of all evidentiary material discovered. Specifically, the documentation should include the analysis techniques, what was found, and where it was located. Sample excerpts should be included in the documentation. This information is included in the final report. The investigator should also document the discovery of other material that may be pertinent to other investigations. For example, if an employee is being investigated for participating in online gambling during work hours, and you discover that the employee was also using the organization's assets to support a personal business, then that information can be reported as part of the investigation. As an aside, be cautious in the use of checklists in collecting evidence and preparing documentation and reports, because any notes made by the investigator can be called into evidence during proceedings. Should it be determined that the investigator failed to follow all checklists equally, it could cast doubt on the validity of the evidence.

All of this must be accomplished without modifying the evidence. Although there are legitimate instances where data must be collected "live" or online, for the most part, an investigator should never attempt to directly access information from a computer keyboard. As mentioned earlier, even normal system modifications, such as file access times, can be used to support a defense argument of evidence tampering.

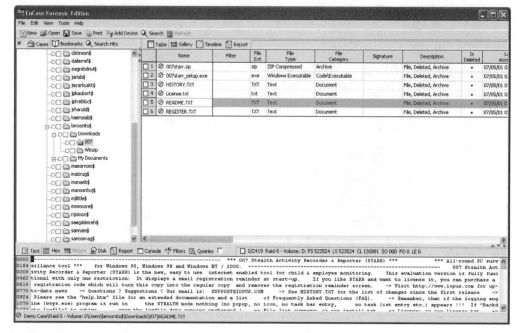

FIGURE 5-5 Guidance Software's Encase

Reporting on the Evidentiary Material

Once evidence has been located, a complete report should be filed with the responsible individual, either an executive in the corporate world or the district attorney in the legal world. The documentation should include everything from the material supporting the affidavit, the signed affidavit itself, a description of the search, any materials uncovered during the search, and the results of the computer forensics examination. It then is up to the responsible official to determine if there is enough evidence to warrant administrative or legal proceedings. Administrative proceedings could result in dismissal, either temporary or permanent, reprimand, or could negatively affect performance evaluations. Legal proceedings depend on the judge and/or jury for potential punishment, depending on the crimes involved. Be aware that the investigator will most likely be called into proceedings to testify on his or her efforts, beginning from the events leading up to the search through the analysis of computer media. The key is to be prepared, answer only the question asked, and be honest—lawyers don't ask questions they don't already know the answers to.

MANAGING EVIDENTIARY DATA IN AN ELECTRONIC ENVIRONMENT

Once the forensics and other incident data have been collected, the organization should have plans for how to make use of the information during and immediately after the incident. This includes the question of whether or when to involve law enforcement, how to keep upper management informed of emerging events, and how to perform loss analysis.

Law Enforcement Involvement

When an incident violates civil or criminal law, it is the organization's responsibility to notify the proper authorities. Selecting the appropriate law enforcement agency depends on the type of crime committed. The Federal Bureau of Investigation (FBI), for example, handles computer crimes that are categorized as felonies. The U.S. Secret Service investigates crimes involving U.S. currency, counterfeiting, and certain cases involving credit card fraud and identity theft. The U.S. Treasury Department has a bank fraud investigation unit, and the Securities and Exchange Commission has investigation and fraud control units as well. However, the heavy caseloads of these agencies mean that they typically prioritize those incidents that affect the national critical infrastructure or that have significant economic impact. The FBI Web site, for example, states that the FBI Computer Intrusion Squad:

> *Pursues the investigation of cyber-based attacks, primarily unauthorized access (intrusion) and denial-of-service, directed at the major components of this country's critical information, military, and economic infrastructures. Critical infrastructure includes the nation's power grids and power-supply systems, transportation control systems, money transfer and accounting systems, defense-related systems, and telecommunications networks. Additionally, the Squad investigates cyber attacks directed at private industry and public institutions that maintain information vital to national security and/or the economic success of the nation.*[37]

In other words, if the crime is not directed at or doesn't affect the national infrastructure, the FBI may not be able to assist the organization as effectively as state or local agencies can. However, in general, if a crime crosses state lines, it becomes a federal matter. The FBI may also become involved at the request of a state agency, if it has the resources to spare.

Each state, county, and city in the United States has its own law enforcement agencies. These agencies enforce all local and state laws, handle suspects, and secure crime scenes for state and federal cases. Local law enforcement agencies rarely have computer crimes task forces, but the investigative (detective) units are quite capable of processing crime scenes and handling most common criminal violations, such as physical theft, trespassing, damage to property, and the apprehension and processing of suspects in computer-related crimes.

Involving law enforcement agencies has both advantages and disadvantages. Such agencies are usually much better equipped at processing evidence than a business organization. Unless the security forces in the organization have been trained in processing evidence and computer forensics, they may do more harm than good when attempting to extract information that can lead to the legal conviction of a suspected criminal. Law enforcement agencies are also prepared to handle the warrants and subpoenas necessary when documenting a case. They are adept at obtaining statements from witnesses, affidavits, and other required documents. For all these reasons, law enforcement personnel can be a security administrator's greatest allies in prosecuting a computer crime. It is therefore important to become familiar with the appropriate local and state agencies before you have to make a call announcing a suspected crime. Most state and federal agencies offer awareness programs, provide guest speakers at conferences, and offer programs such as the InfraGard program of the FBI (*www.infragard.net*). These agents clearly understand the challenges facing security administrators.

The disadvantages of law enforcement involvement include possible loss of control of the chain of events following an incident, including the collection of information and evidence and the prosecution of suspects. An organization that wants to simply reprimand or dismiss an employee should not involve a law enforcement agency in the resolution of an incident. In addition, the organization may not hear about the case for weeks or even months because of heavy caseloads or resource shortages. A very real issue for commercial organizations when involving law enforcement agencies is the tagging of equipment vital to the organization's business as evidence. This means that assets can be removed, stored, and preserved to prepare the criminal case. Despite these difficulties, if the organization detects a criminal act, it has the legal obligation to notify the appropriate law enforcement officials. Failure to do so can subject the organization and its officers to prosecution as accessories to the crimes or for impeding the course of an investigation. It is up to the security administrator to ask questions of law enforcement agencies to determine when each agency needs to be involved and specifically which crimes are addressed by each agency.

Reporting to Upper Management

Once the SIRT has conducted a preliminary assessment of the incident, its impact on the organization, the organization's success or failure in responding to the incident, and the progress of the recovery, the SIRT leader should make a report to upper management, typically the CISO and CIO. As mentioned earlier, the first notification that an incident was in progress should have occurred only after the incident has been confirmed, but before media or other external sources learn of it. At this point, executive management above the CIO level will most likely be pressing for details because at some point they will be approached by the media for information. Upper management usually request assistance in drafting a press release to notify the general public and a specific notification to any stakeholders impacted by the event.

Loss Analysis

One of the first questions that upper management has for the investigative team is: "How much was lost, and how much will it cost us to recover?" The first question may take some time to accurately answer. Fortunately, in most cases, an incident only results in the costs associated with internal recovery. In determining the costs associated with an incident, consider the following:

- Cost associated with the number of person-hours diverted from normal operations to react to the incident
- Cost associated with the number of person-hours to recover data
- Opportunity costs associated with the number of person-hours that individuals could have been working on a more productive task
- Cost associated with reproducing lost data (if possible)
- Legal costs associated with prosecuting offenders (if possible)

- Costs associated with loss of market advantage or share due to disclosure of proprietary information
- Costs associated with acquisition of additional security mechanisms ahead of budget cycle

If the incidents were acts of nature, then additional costs associated with the repair or replacement of facilities may also be a consideration. If the incidents involved power problems, additional costs associated with replacing computers or other electrical equipment should be considered.

In the short term, management needs an immediate impact assessment. This impact assessment is a quick determination of the extent of damage or loss and the associated cost or value. In the event of a minor or moderate incident, the report may be short, such as that shown in this example:

SAMPLE IMPACT ASSESSMENT

Impact of virus infestation in ABC Corp was minor, with two infected user systems and no infected servers. Infestation was contained at 2300 June 20, with no loss of data. Estimated cost was 12 person-hours used to identify and contain the outbreak, and 10 person-hours of lost productivity as these two individuals were denied access to their systems as a result of the virus. It was determined that the outbreak occurred when a user downloaded and opened an e-mail attachment from a spoofed managerial account, infecting her system and that of one of her workmates, whose e-mail was CC'd on the original infected e-mail. Recommend additional awareness training for users on e-mail viruses. Total cost/loss to organization is under $500 (in personnel costs).

In more complex situations, the analysis of an incident may be much more extensive and include how the intruder gained access to a system, how the intruder established or elevated access privileges until he or she was able to gain control of the system, and whether the intruder compromised databases, deleted or destroyed files, or modified log entries. These types of assessments may find real damages in the hundreds of thousands of dollars, especially if intellectual property is compromised or customer data is stolen.

Chapter Summary

- An IR plan requires significant effort to enable the organization to react when an incident occurs, begin the prompt recovery of normal operations, and/or make the smooth transition to disaster recovery or business continuity plans when needed.
- An organization may choose to have a single Incident Response (IR) strategy in place for all incidents, or they may have additional strategic options planned.
- Two approaches mark either extreme on the range of options: a strategy of *protect and forget* or *apprehend and prosecute*.
- CERT provides best practices in responding to an intrusion.
- When an incident is in progress, the right people must be immediately notified using either a sequential or hierarchical roster.
- An alert message is a scripted description of the incident and consists of minimal information.
- As soon as an incident has been confirmed and the notification process is under way, the team should begin to document it.
- A critical element of the IR is stopping the incident or containing its scope or impact.
- Incident containment strategies can include the following:
    - Disabling compromised user accounts
    - Reconfiguring a firewall to block the problem traffic
    - Temporarily disabling the compromised process or service
    - Taking down the conduit application or server—for example, the e-mail server
    - Stopping all computers and network devices
- Each organization must determine the point at which an incident is deemed a disaster.
- Once the incident has been contained and the extent of the damage has been determined, incident recovery can begin and involves the following steps:
    - Identify the vulnerabilities that allowed the incident to occur and spread, and resolve them.
    - Address the safeguards that failed to stop or limit the incident, or were missing from the system in the first place, and install, replace, or upgrade them.
    - Evaluate monitoring capabilities (if present).
    - Restore the data from backups.
    - Restore the services and processes in use.
    - Continuously monitor the system.
    - Restore the confidence of the members of the organization's communities of interest.
- Ongoing maintenance of the IR plan requires effective after-action review meetings, periodic plan review and maintenance, and ongoing training of staff that will be involved in incident response as well as a rehearsal process.

Review Questions

1. Would you say that IR requires a lot or a little organizational commitment? What are the major commitments an effective IR requires?

2. What are the key factors that influence the selection of an IR strategy for an organization?

3. What labels are assigned to the two extremes of strategy options often used to frame the debate about IT strategies?

4. What are the key steps included in the *protect and forget* IR strategy?

5. What are the key steps included in the *apprehend and prosecute* IR strategy?

6. What best practice steps are recommended by CERT to include in IR strategies?

7. What are the types of alert rosters used to support an incident plan?

8. What is an alert message, and what does it accomplish?

9. What purposes does the ongoing preparation of an incident log accomplish?

10. What precursor activities must be accomplished before meaningful containment decisions can be made?

11. What are the primary options from which to select when making containment choices?

12. What is *escalation* in the context of an incident response? What are the primary escalation options?

13. What is the primary objective of recovery operations during an incident response?

14. What are the key steps used to accomplish recovery?

15. Why is the restoration of user confidence an important step in the recovery process?

16. What is an after-action review? What are the primary reasons for undertaking an after-action review?

17. What are the primary techniques used for plan review and maintenance?

18. What is the difference between training and cross-training? Why are both necessary?

19. What purpose does rehearsal serve? Why should organizations continue to rehearse once a plan is known to work?

20. What is computer forensics? Why is this important in the context of incident response?

Exercises

1. Using a Web browser, go to *www.cert.org/security-improvement*. Review the module on Detecting Signs of Intrusions. What information would be important to include in a training program for: (a) information security technicians; (b) systems administrators; and (c) business personnel?

2. Using a Web browser, go to *www.cert.org/security-improvement*. Review the module on Responding to Intrusions. What information would be important to include in a training program for: (a) information security technicians; (b) systems administrators; and (c) business personnel?

3. Using a Web browser, go to *www.us-cert.gov/current*. Identify the top current incident threats. Categorize the incidents as either technical or behavioral (such as phishing). What is the largest group?

4. Using a Web browser, go to *www.first.org*. What is this organization, and what is its purpose? What are the advantages of membership? Disadvantages?

5. Using a Web browser, go to *www.sans.org/rr*, the SANS reading room. What headings are available that would benefit someone preparing to organize and train an incident response team? Select one of these headings and then select a paper from within it. Summarize the paper and bring your summary to class to discuss.

Further Discussion

1. What additional safeguards could have been added to Osbert's lab to make it less likely to cause the events described?

2. Susan seems to have been able to take control of the incident from an early point in its development. If she had taken control later in the process, would any aspects of the response have been different?

3. It seems that HAL has a policy of sticking with an incident manager once an incident is under-way and then until some predefined escalation occurs or some amount of elapsed time has passed. Is this a good practice? What are some alternative approaches to consider in this regard?

4. When Paul and Amanda arrived on the scene, would you have expected them to respond in a way different from what was depicted in the chapter? What would you have expected them to do?

References

[1] A.Sterneckert, *Critical Incident Management*. (Boca Raton, FL: Auerbach/CRC Press LLC, 2004).

[2] D. Adler and K. Grossman, "Establishing a Computer Incident Response Plan," Accessed July 17, 2004, from http://www.fedcirc.gov/library.documents/82-02-70.pdf.

[3] See note 2.

[4] See note 2.

[5] CERT, "Apply Short-Term Solutions to Contain An Intrusion," CERT Security Improvement Modules. Accessed May 31, 2005, from http://www.cert.org/security-improvement/practices/p049.html.

[6] CERT, "Responding to Intrusions," CERT Security Improvement Modules. Accessed May 31, 2005, from http://www.cert.org/security-improvement/modules/m06.html.

[7] Donald L. Pipkin. *Information Security: Protecting the Global Enterprise*, (Upper Saddle River, NJ: Prentice Hall PTR, 2000), 285.

[8] Friedrich Nietzsche, "Friedrich Nietzsche Quotes," Accessed May 20, 2005 from http://www.brainyquote.com/quotes/quotes/f/friedrichn101616.html.

[9] W. G. Kruse and J. G. Heiser, *Computer Forensics. Incident Response Essentials* (Boston: Addison-Wesley, 2001).

[10] Fourth Amendment, U.S. Constitution, accessed October 10, 2004, from http://caselaw.lp. findlaw.com/data/constitution/amendments.html.

[11] O'Connor v. Ortega, 480 U.S. 709 (1987), accessed October 10, 2004, from http://caselaw.lp. findlaw.com/scripts/getcase.pl?court=US&vol=480&invol=709.

[12] See note 12.

[13] Searching and Seizing Computers and Obtaining Electronic Evidence in Criminal Investigations, accessed September 10, 2004, from http://www.cybercrime.gov/searching.html.

[14] See note 14.

[15] United States v. Hagarty, 388 F.2d 713, 717 (7th Cir. 1968).

[16] Katz v. United States, (389 U.S. 347, 362 (1967).

[17] See note 14.

[18] M. Whitman and H. Mattord, *Principles of Information Security* (Boston: Course Technology, 2004).

[19] See note 12.

[20] United States v. Angevine, 281 F.3d 1130, 1134-35 (10th Cir. 2002).

[21] Anonymous textbook reviewer.

[22] See note 21.

[23] United States v. Slanina, 283 F.3d 670, 676-77 (5th Cir. 2002).

[24] See note 14.

[25] Schneckloth v. Bustamonte, 412 U.S. 218, 219 (1973).

[26] United States v. Milian-Rodriguez, 759 F.2d 1558, 1563-64 (11th Cir. 1985).

[27] United States v. Matlock, 415 U.S. 164 (1974).

[28] Horton v. California, 496 U.S. 128 (1990).

[29] United States v. Maxwell, 45 M.J. 406, 422 (C.A.A.F. 1996).

[30] See note 14.

[31] U.S. Copyright Office, "What is Copyright?" accessed October 12, 2004, from http://www. copyright.gov/circs/circ1.html#wci.

[32] LII. "Chapter 119—Wire and Electronic Communications Interception and Interception of Oral Communications," accessed May 10, 2005, from http://www4.law.cornell.edu/uscode18/usc_ sup_01_18.html.

[33] EPIC, "Analysis of New Justice Department Guidelines on Searching and Seizing Computers," accessed May 10, 2005, from http://www.epic.org/security/epic_guidelines_ analysis.html.

[34] EPIC, "The Privacy Protection Act of 1980," accessed May 10, 2005, from http://www.epic.org/ privacy/ppa.

[35] "Guide to First Responders and the [3] Searching and Seizing Computers and Obtaining Electronic Evidence in Criminal Investigations," accessed September 10, 2004, from http://www. cybercrime.gov/searching.html.

[36] M. Daum and S. Lucks, "Attacking Hash Functions by Poisoned Messages: The Story of Alice and her Boss," accessed June 19, 2005, from http://www.cits.rub.de/MD5Collisions.

[37] Federal Bureau of Investigation, "Technology Crimes (San Francisco)," accessed from http://www.fbi.gov/contact/fo/sanfran/sfcomputer.htm.

222

CHAPTER **6**

CONTINGENCY STRATEGIES FOR BUSINESS RESUMPTION PLANNING

Men at some time are masters of their fates. The fault, dear Brutus, is not in our stars, but in ourselves.

—William Shakespeare (1564–1616), Julius Caesar (Act I, Scene ii)

OPENING SCENARIO

Bobby was not having a good day. He started the morning by oversleeping and had clocked in 15 minutes late. Rushing through the mailroom doors, Bobby splashed coffee from his cup into a full cart of mail someone had left standing close to the door. Only heroic blotting kept him from ruining a couple hundred incoming envelopes. It looked like important stuff, too. As he hurriedly gathered and scooped the mail out of the cart, one of the thick yellow envelopes slipped from his hand and fell to the floor exploding into a cloud of white powder over the mail cart.

"Ooof" was the noise Bobby made when he puffed all the air out of his lungs, mouth, and nose as he backed quickly away from the cart and out the mailroom door. After all, they had just had the refresher training for emergency procedures in the mailroom, and so he knew to exhale quickly, and get out as rapidly as possible. Everyone else in the mailroom did the same; this was the exact maneuver the team had rehearsed just a week ago. Exhale, exit, and hit the big red button that turned off the ventilators to the room and set off the emergency alarm. Bobby stopped with his back to the mailroom door. He and the mailroom team waited for the turmoil he knew would follow.

An hour later, Alan Hake, CEO of HAL, sat with his incident team at the coffee shop across the street, reviewing their planned response to this crisis. The team, as outlined in the incident response plan, was made up of COO Richard Xavier, CFO Rachel Xieng, CIO Amanda Wilson, plus Roberta Briscoe, manager of corporate security, and Pantoja Martina, supervisor of the administrative staff and the mailroom.

As they were reviewing the response plan in place for contaminated mail, along with the supporting DR and BC plans, a man in a fireman's dress uniform walked up to their table and said, "Hi. I am Deputy Fire Chief Corbett. Are you the folks from HAL?"

continued

"Yes," said Alan. "Please, sit with us." He gestured to an empty chair at their impromptu conference table.

Deputy Chief Corbett sat and then said, "The field test showed the white powder in the mailroom is not a pathogen nor a contaminant within its limited test range. We sent a sample to the forensics lab, and they are expediting processing. We should have an answer back by 2:00 p.m."

Alan and the team had watched him carefully as he spoke. They seemed to relax a little. Alan asked, "What about the mailroom staff? What's their status?"

The deputy chief answered, "They seem none the worse for wear. We isolated them and ran them through the standard biochemical decontamination protocol. Not very pleasant, nor a very modest activity, but the team is clean and dry and standing by in isolation suits waiting for the final lab results. If they were contaminated, we can't do any more until we know what the contaminant is." He smiled and said, "I suggest a long lunch for you to make your contingency plans. If the test comes back with a contaminant, it is our experience your office space will be off-limits for three to four weeks—maybe longer." He stood up and returned to the command vehicle parked in the street outside the office building.

Alan flipped open his master contingency planning binder. "At least we don't have to make up a plan. Let's review our next steps in case our offices are closed for the next month," he said.

Questions for discussion:

1. What other crises or catastrophes can happen in a mailroom that could prompt an emergency procedure like the one illustrated here?

2. What goals should be included when planning for the resumption of critical business functions at an alternate site for four weeks? What would be different if the planning horizon were 30 weeks instead?

3. When the organization makes a plan like the one described here, what parts of the plan should be from the contingency planning management team (CPMT), and what parts should come from the subject area experts?

LEARNING OBJECTIVES

Upon completion of this material, you should be able to:

- Know and understand the relationships between the overall use of contingency planning and the subordinate elements of incident response, business resumption, disaster recovery, and business continuity planning

- Become familiar with the techniques used for data and application backup and recovery

- Know the strategies employed for resumption of critical business processes at alternate and recovered sites

INTRODUCTION

As introduced in Chapter 2 and discussed further in the introduction to Chapter 3, the umbrella of contingency planning addresses everything done by an organization to prepare for the unexpected. This includes something as trivial as evaluating an alarm from an intrusion detection system, to responding to the never-ending stream of new viruses and worms in e-mail systems, to a catastrophe like the one that might befall a company, as illustrated in this chapter's opening scenario. However, the incident response (IR) process focuses its efforts on detecting, evaluating, and reacting to an incident; the later phases of the process are focused on keeping the business functioning, even if the physical plant is destroyed or unavailable. When the IR process cannot contain and resolve an incident, it falls to the business resumption plan to resume normal operations quickly or else expedite continuity plans to quickly initiate operations at an alternate site until normal operations can resume at the primary site. The relationships between the elements of the continuity plan were illustrated earlier in Figure 3-3 of Chapter 3.

A **business resumption (BR) plan** is usually considered to have two major elements: the disaster recovery (DR) plan, which lists and describes the efforts to resume normal operations at the primary places of business; and the business continuity (BC) plan, which contains the steps for implementing critical business functions using alternate mechanisms until normal operations can be resumed at the primary site or elsewhere on a permanent basis. The **primary site** is the location or group of locations at which the organization executes its functions. The BC plan operates concurrently with the DR plan when the damage is major or long term. The example illustrated in Figure 6-1 shows that a large-scale distributed denial-of-service (DDoS) attack may require both the activation of the DR plan to restore the primary site, and the activation of a BC plan to enable critical functions to be undertaken elsewhere until normal operations can resume. Because of the complexity of the business resumption planning process, the remaining chapters of this book are devoted to the topic.

Throughout the remainder of this book, you may notice clear parallels to the material discussed in earlier chapters regarding incident response plans. This is intentional, because the performance of these tasks is similar, whether for an incident or a disaster. This chapter introduces the elements of business resumption planning (BRP). It addresses some facets of BRP that are common throughout disaster recovery and business continuity plans, as well as having had some applicability to incident recovery plans covered previously. Chapter 7 will cover DR preparation and implementation, Chapter 8 will cover DR operations and maintenance, Chapter 9 will cover BC preparation and implementation, Chapter 10 will cover BC operations and maintenance, and Chapter 11 will cover the expanded needs of crisis management.

Some experts may argue that the two elements of business resumption planning (being disaster recovery and business continuity) are so closely linked that they are indistinguishable. However, each has a distinct place, role, and planning requirement. A quick review of Figure 1-6 from Chapter 1 will reinforce this interpretation of the relationship among the parts of the overall contingency planning process. Figure 6-2 shows how the elements of business resumption fit together.

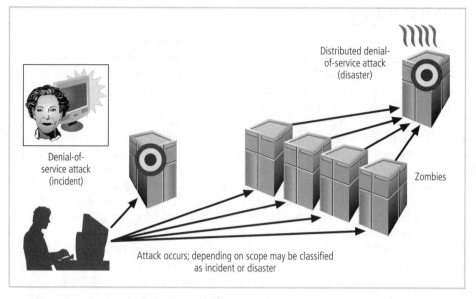

FIGURE 6-1   Incident response and disaster recovery

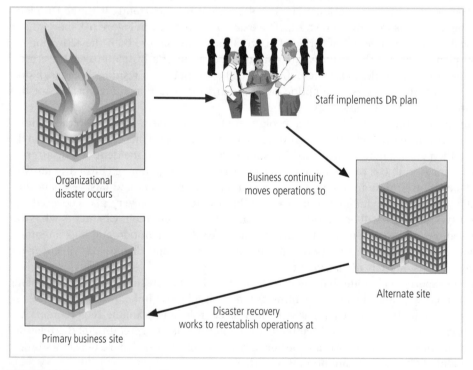

FIGURE 6-2   Business resumption

Further, each of the components of CP (IRP, DRP, and BCP) comes into play at a specific time in the life of an event. In Chapter 1, Figure 1-5 illustrates this sequence and shows the overlap that may occur. How the plans interact and the ways in which they are brought into action are discussed in many locations in this chapter and in the chapters that follow.

Regardless of the type of response needed (IR, DR, or BC), organizations require a reliable method of restoring information and reestablishing all operations, both IT operations and other business functions. Whether the objective is a simple file recovery from a backup of a file that has been accidentally deleted, or whether it involves the transfer of an entire application's database to an alternate facility, there are certain commonalities found in the backup and restoration of computerized data. There are five key procedural mechanisms that facilitate the restoration of critical information and the continuation of business operations. They are:

1. Delayed protection
2. Real-time protection
3. Server recovery
4. Application recovery
5. Site recovery[1]

The first four of these mechanisms are included in the following section, "Data and Application Resumption," and the fifth item is discussed in the later section, "Site Resumption Strategies."

DATA AND APPLICATION RESUMPTION

There are a number of methods for data backup and management. The most commonly used varieties include disk backup and tape backup and are presented here. The important point is to use backup methods based on an established policy. In general, data files and critical system files should be backed up daily, with nonessential files backed up weekly.

Equally important is the determination of how long data should be stored. Some data may have legal requirements for retention and require that specific information be stored for years. Other data may not be covered by law or regulation, and it may be in the organization's best interest to destroy it quickly. Management should create a formal plan that includes the recommendations from legal counsel that conform to the applicable laws, regulations, and standards to provide direction for data retention. For routine data backups of critical data, the organization only needs to retain the one or two most recent copies (daily backups) and at least one off-site copy. For full backups of entire systems, at least one copy should be stored in a secure location, such as a bank vault, security deposit box, or remote branch office.

Disk-to-Disk-to-Tape: Delayed Protection

With the decrease in the costs of storage media, including hard drives and tape backups, more and more organizations are creating massive arrays of independent but large-capacity disk drives to store information at least temporarily. In fact, many home users are using similar methods, adding external USB-mounted ATA drives, in the 200–300 GB range, and simply copying critical files to these external and portable devices as routine backup. The availability of these devices not only precludes the time-consuming nature of tape backup, but also avoids the costs and implementation challenges of tape at the individual user level. It also allows quick and easy recovery of individual files and directories, avoiding the tedious method of extracting the same from tape.

Individuals and organization alike can then build libraries of these devices, or massively connected storage area networks, to support larger-scale data backup and recovery. The problem with this technology is the lack of redundancy should both the online and backup versions fail, due to a virus or hacker intrusion. This is why periodically the secondary data disk series should be backed up to tape, thus the disk-to-disk-to-tape heading for this section. The use of the secondary disk series prevents the need to take the primary set offline for duplication, and also reduces the resource usage on the primary systems. The disk-to-disk initial copies can be made efficiently and simultaneously with other system processes.

The following sections overview the use of complex disk drive storage media using various levels of redundancy. To better understand what goes on during incident response or disaster recovery data restoration, you should understand how system backups are created. Data backup is a complex operation and involves selecting the backup type, establishing backup schedules, and even duplicating data automatically using a variety of redundant array of independent drives (RAID) structures.

Types of Backup

There are three basic types of backups: full, differential, and incremental. A **full backup** is just that, a full and complete backup of the entire system, including all applications, operating systems components, and data. The advantage of a full backup is that it takes a comprehensive snapshot of the organization's system. The primary disadvantages are that it requires large media to store such a large file, and the backup can be time consuming. A **differential backup** is the storage of all files that have changed or been added since the last full backup. The differential backup works faster and uses less storage space than the full backup, but each daily differential backup is larger and slower than that of the day before. For example, if you conduct a full backup on Sunday, then Monday's backup contains all the files that have changed since Sunday, and Tuesday's backup contains all the files that have changed since Sunday as well, including Monday. By Friday, the file size has grown substantially. If one backup is corrupt, the previous day's backup contains almost all of the same information. An **incremental backup** only archives the files that have been modified that day, and thus requires less space and time than the differential to create. The downside to incremental backups is that if the need to restore the data arises, multiple backups would need to be restored to restore the full system. In general, incremental backups are designed to complete the backup in the shortest amount of elapsed time. An incremental backup will also be economical in the amount of room needed to store the backup data. Differential backups yield the shortest elapsed time needed to restore files when they must be re-created from the backup media.

Regardless of the strategy employed, some fundamental advice must be heeded: first, all on-site and off-site storage must be secured. It is common practice to use fireproof safes or filing cabinets to store tapes. The off-site storage in particular must be in a safe location, such as a safety deposit box in a bank or with a professional backup and recovery service. The trunk of the administrator's car is not considered secure off-site storage. It is also important to provide an air-conditioned environment for the tapes, preferably in an airtight, humidity-free, static-free storage container. Each tape must be clearly labeled, and write protected. Because tapes frequently wear out, it is important to retire them periodically and introduce new media.

Tape Backups and Recovery: General Strategies

There is still value in tape backups as a cost-effective method for organizations to maintain large quantities of data. Traditionally, tape has been able to store larger quantities of data in smaller containers. The most common types of tape media include digital audio tape (DAT), quarter-inch cartridge (QIC) tapes, 8 mm tape, and digital linear tape (DLT) for small organizations and individual users. Each type of tape has its restrictions and advantages.

The first component of a backup and recovery system is the scheduling of the backups, coupled with the storage of these backups. The most common schedule is a daily on-site, incremental or differential backup, with a weekly off-site full backup. Most backups are conducted during twilight hours, when systems activity is lowest, and the probability of user interruption is limited. There are also some popular methods for selecting the files to back up. These include the six-tape rotation method, Grandfather-Father-Son, and the Towers of Hanoi.

Six-Tape Rotation

The **six-tape rotation** method of backup uses a rotation of six sets of media and is perhaps the most simple and well known. It uses five media sets per week and offers roughly two weeks of recovery capability. Shown here, is its five-step process:

1. Use six tape or media sets labeled Monday, Tuesday, Wednesday, Thursday, Friday1, and Friday2.
2. Beginning on Friday, use Friday1 for a full backup. If more than one unit of media is needed for a set, label the unit Friday1a, Friday1b, and so on. Take this media set off-site, and store it in a secure location.
3. The following week, each day use the Monday through Thursday media sets for differential or incremental backups. As shown in Table 6-1, incremental may be most appropriate for this method, because it uses the fewest tapes.
4. On the second Friday, use the Friday2 media set (Friday2a, Friday2b, and so on). Take these Friday2 full backup media sets off-site to the secure storage location, and retrieve the Friday1 full backup set to use the following week. Some organizations may choose to store the week's worth of differential or incremental backups along with the weekly full backups. Other organizations prefer to keep the midweek partial backups in the data center for more convenient access.
5. On the following week, reuse the Monday through Thursday media sets.

In the event a recovery is needed, the organization first attempts to recover the file(s) using the Monday through Thursday tapes if they are on hand. If the file that needs to be restored is not contained within the backups that are on hand, the last full backup that was stored off-site is retrieved, and the file(s) recovered from that media. For additional ease of use and redundancy, an organization may choose to make a copy of each full backup so that an on-site version can be kept in the data center and an off-site set of full backup (Friday) tapes can be sent to the secure storage location. This will prevent the need to retrieve the off-site set should the needed file(s) not be in the backup media that is kept onsite.

Grandfather-Father-Son

The Grandfather-Father-Son (GFS) method of backup uses five media sets *per week* and allows recovery of data for the previous three weeks. This method is a six-step process that uses 15 media sets when properly implemented.

1. The first week uses the first five media sets (group A).
2. The second week uses the second five media sets (group B).
3. The third week uses the third set of five media sets (group C).
4. In the fourth week, the group A media sets are reused.
5. In the fifth week, the group B media sets are reused.
6. In the sixth week, the group C media sets are reused.

Every second or third month, a group of media sets are taken out of the cycle for permanent storage and a new set is brought in. This method equalizes the wear and tear on the tapes and helps to prevent tape failure.

The Towers of Hanoi

The Towers of Hanoi is more complex approach than the previous two methods and is based on statistical principles to optimize media wear. This 16-step strategy assumes that five media sets are used per week, with a backup each night.

1. The first night media set A is used.
2. The second night media set B is used.
3. The third night media set A is reused.
4. The fourth night media set C is used.
5. The fifth night media set A is reused.
6. The sixth night media set B is reused.
7. The seventh night media set A is reused.
8. The eighth night media set D is used.
9. The ninth night media set A is reused.
10. The 10th night media set B is reused.
11. The 11th night media set A is reused.
12. The 12th night media set C is reused.
13. The 13th night media set A is reused.
14. The 14th night media set B is reused.
15. The 15th night media set A is reused.
16. The 16th night media set E is used.

Tape A is used for incremental backups after its first use and must be monitored closely as it tends to wear out faster than the other tapes.

Which rotation method is best? Table 6-1 lists the advantages and disadvantages of each method.

TABLE 6-1 Selecting the best rotation method[2]

Rotation Method	Advantages	Disadvantages
Six-tape rotation	Requires only a few tapes, which provides an easy and cheap rotation method; it is ideal for small data volumes (as much capacity as one tape can hold)	Keeps only a week's worth of data, unless you regularly archive the full backup tapes
Grandfather-Father-Son (GFS)	Provides the most secure data protection and implements monthly archival of tapes; it is also a simple method, which most software supports	Requires more tapes, which can become expensive
The Towers of Hanoi	Allows for easy full-system restores (no shuffling through tapes with partial backups on them). This is ideal for small businesses that are concerned with being able to do full restores. Also, it is more cost effective than GFS (uses fewer tapes).	Requires a difficult rotation strategy, which is not as straightforward to implement as the other rotation methods.Unless your backup software supports it, this method is too complex to track tape rotation manually. Also requires a time-consuming full backup every session.

Backup and Recovery Elapsed Time

One of the drawbacks of tape backups is the time required to store and retrieve information. As Tables 6-2 and 6-3 show, even differential or incremental backups to tape can take some time to complete.

TABLE 6-2 Tape backup times[3]

DIFFERENTIAL BACKUP: TIME AND TAPES REQUIRED				
Day	Type of Backup	Size	Time	No. of Tapes
Friday	Full	160 GB	4 hours	3 tapes
Monday	Differential	45 GB	1.1 hours	1 tape
Tuesday	Differential	56 GB	1.4 hours	1 tape
Wednesday	Differential	67 GB	1.7 hours	2 tapes
Thursday	Differential	83 GB	2.1 hours	2 tapes
	Total	411 GB	10.3 hours	9 tapes
INCREMENTAL BACKUP: TIME AND TAPES REQUIRED				
Day	Type of Backup	Size	Time	No. of Tapes
Friday	Full	160 GB	4 hours	3 tapes
Monday	Incremental	45 GB	1.1 hours	1 tape
Tuesday	Incremental	11 GB	.3 hours	1 tape

TABLE 6-2 Tape backup times (continued)

INCREMENTAL BACKUP: TIME AND TAPES REQUIRED				
Day	Type of Backup	Size	Time	No. of Tapes
Wednesday	Incremental	11 GB	.3 hours	1 tape
Thursday	Incremental	16 GB	4 hours	1 tape
	Total	243 GB	6.1 hours	7 tapes

Note: These examples are based on a weekly backup cycle with a tape drive that can transfer data at 40 GB/hour on a 60 GB capacity tape.

TABLE 6-3 Tape restoration times[4]

DIFFERENTIAL RESTORATION: TAPES REQUIRED FOR RESTORE PROCESS		
Day	Type of Backup	Tapes Used
Friday	Full	Tape 1, 2, 3
Monday	Differential	Tape 4
Tuesday	Differential	Tape 5
Wednesday	Differential	Tape 6, 7
Thursday	Differential	Tape 8, 9
Tapes required for complete system restore		**Tapes 1, 2, 3, 8, 9**
INCREMENTAL RESTORATION: TAPES REQUIRED FOR RESTORE PROCESS		
Day	Type of Backup	Tapes Used
Friday	Full	Tape 1, 2, 3
Monday	Incremental	Tape 4
Tuesday	Incremental	Tape 5
Wednesday	Incremental	Tape 6
Thursday	Incremental	Tape 7
Tapes required for complete system restore		**All 7 tapes**

Note: These examples are based on a weekly backup cycle with a tape drive that can transfer data at 40 GB/hour on a 60 GB capacity tape.

Redundancy-Based Backup and Recovery Using RAID

Another form of data backup is that of online disk drives used for redundancy. The usage of **redundant array of independent disks (RAID)** systems can overcome some of the limits of magnetic tape backup systems, and, as seen later in the section titled "Real-Time Protection, Server Recovery, and Application Recovery," RAID systems provide enhanced capabilities. Unlike tape backups, RAID uses a number of hard drives to store information across multiple drive units. For operational redundancy, this can spread out data and, when coupled with checksums, can eliminate or reduce the impact of a hard drive failure. There are nine established RAID configurations described in the following paragraphs, and even though some of these offer capabilities covered later in the chapter, all are presented together in the next section. Some approaches can offer more than simple data redundancy, such as the capabilities to procide complete application-level redundancy by using a process that mirrors entire servers, or by using a form of server fault tolerance, such as SFTIII by Novell. Although RAID does not address the need for off-site storage because it is answered by the magnetic tape solution, RAID does deal with the most common need for restore requests, which is recovery from hard drive failure.

RAID Level 0

This is not a form of redundant storage. RAID 0 creates one larger logical volume across several available hard disk drives and stores the data in segments, called stripes, across all the disk drives in the array. This is also often called **disk striping** without parity and is frequently used to combine smaller drive volumes into fewer, larger volumes to gain the advantages that larger volumes offer. Unfortunately, failure of one drive may make all data inaccessible. In fact, this level of RAID does not improve the risk situation when using disk drives, but rather increases the risk of losing data from a single drive failure.

RAID Level 1

Commonly called **disk mirroring**, RAID level 1 uses twin drives in a computer system. The computer records all data to both drives simultaneously, providing a backup if the primary drive fails. It is a rather expensive and inefficient use of media. A variation of mirroring is called **disk duplexing**. With mirroring, the same drive controller manages both drives, but with disk duplexing, each drive has its own controller. Mirroring is often used to create duplicate copies of operating system volumes for high-availability systems. Using this technique, a plan can be developed that mirrors and then splits disk pairs to create highly available copies of critical system drives. This can make multiple copies of critical data or programs readily available when needed for high-availability computing environments.

RAID Level 2

This is a specialized form of disk striping with parity, and is not widely used. It uses a specialized parity coding mechanism known as the Hamming code to store stripes of data on multiple data drives and corresponding redundant error correction on separate error-correcting drives. This approach allows the reconstruction of data in the event some of the data or redundant parity information is lost. There are no commercial implementations of RAID level 2.

RAID Levels 3 and 4

RAID 3 uses byte-level striping of data, and RAID 4 uses block-level striping of data. These approaches use a process in which the data is stored in segments on dedicated data drives, and parity information is stored on a separate drive. Similar to RAID 0, one large volume is used for the data, but the parity drive operates independently to provide error recovery.

RAID Level 5

This form of RAID is most commonly used in organizations that balance safety and redundancy against the costs of acquiring and operating the systems. It is similar to RAID 3 and RAID 4 in that it stripes the data across multiple drives, but there is no dedicated parity drive. Instead, segments of data are interleaved with parity data and are written across all of the drives in the set. RAID 5 drives can also be **hot swapped**, meaning they can be replaced without taking the entire system down.

RAID Level 6

This is a combination of RAID 1 and RAID 5 in that it "performs two different parity computations or the same computation on overlapping subsets of the data."[5]

RAID Level 7

This is a proprietary variation on RAID 5 in which the array works as a single virtual drive. RAID level 7 is sometimes performed by running special software over RAID 5 hardware.

RAID Level 10

RAID 10 is a combination of RAID 1 and RAID 0. Raid 0 is used for its performance, and RAID 1 is used for its fault tolerance.

Some of the more common implementations of RAID are illustrated in Figure 6-3.

Database Backups

When systems make use of databases, whether hierarchical, relational, or object-oriented, they require special considerations when planning backup and recovery procedures. Depending on the type of database and the software vendor, the database may or may not be able to be backed up with the utilities that are provided with the operating systems of the servers on which the database is run. A further consideration is whether or not system backup procedures can be used without interrupting the use of the database. In the case of some relational databases, a system backup can work correctly only if all user access to the database is stopped. For these databases to be used while they are being backed up, additional backup tools are often needed. Some other considerations for a database being properly safeguarded are to make sure the system administrators understand if there are special journal file requirements used by the database management software, such as run-unit journals or after-image journals that enable database concurrency functions. If these file systems and the files they use are not backed up properly, the backup tapes or disk images may be unusable when they are used to restore the prior state of the system.

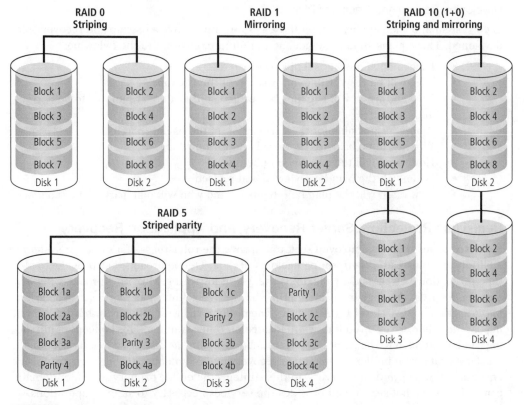

FIGURE 6-3 Popular RAID implementations

Application Backups

Some applications use file systems and databases in ways that invalidate the customary way of doing backup and recovery. In some cases, applications write large binary objects as files and manage pointers, and they handle internal data structures in ways that make routine backups unable to handle the concurrency or complexity of the application. Make sure that members of the application support and development teams are part of the planning process when these system backup plans are made and that these team members are included in training, testing, and rehearsal activities.

Backup and Recovery Plans

Even the best backups are inadequate unless they can be used to successfully restore systems to an operational state. Each backup and recovery setting should be provided with complete recovery plans. The plans need to be developed, tested, and rehearsed periodically.

Developing Backup and Recovery Plans

Each system and each application on those systems must have a backup and recovery plan developed. These plans should include, at a minimum, answers to the following:

- How and when will backups be created?
- Who will be responsible for creation of the backups?
- How and when will backups be verified so that they are known to be correct and reliable?
- Who is responsible for the verification of the backup?
- Where will be backups be stored and for how long?
- How often will the backup plan be tested?
- When will the plan be reviewed and revised?
- How often will the plan be rehearsed, and who will take part in the rehearsal?

Real-Time Protection, Server Recovery, and Application Recovery

Some strategies that are employed seek to improve the robustness of a server or system in addition to or instead of performing backups of data. One approach that provides real-time protection as well as data backup is the use of mirroring. Mirroring provides duplication of server data storage by using multiple hard drive volumes, as was described earlier in the section on RAID level 1. RAID level 1 can be achieved with software or hardware, writing data to other drives, even if they are located on other systems. This concept of mirroring can be extended to the point of vaulting and journaling, as discussed in later sections.

One strategy for implementing server recovery and redundancy through mirroring servers uses hot, warm, and cold servers. In this strategy, the online primary server, or domain controller, is the hot server, and provides the services necessary to support operations. The warm server serves as an ancillary or secondary server or domain controller, and it services requests when the primary is busy or down. The cold server is the administrator's test platform, and it should be identically configured to the hot and warm servers. Before a patch, upgrade, or new application is applied to the hot and warm servers, it is first tested on the cold server. Should the hot server go down, the warm server automatically takes over as the hot server, and the cold server can be added as the new warm server while the hot server is taken offline for repair. Recent advances in server recovery have developed **bare metal recovery** technologies designed to replace operating systems and services when they fail. These applications allow you to reboot the affected system from a CD-ROM or other remote drive, and quickly restore your operating system by providing images backed up from a known stable state. Although Linux and UNIX versions abound, the Windows versions are more difficult to come by, because Linux and UNIX kernels run easily from small storage locations (such as Knoppix and Helix), but Windows is only just developing a stand-alone bootable CD platform. Use of bare metal recovery applications, in conjunction with routine backups, allows the recovery of entire servers quickly and easily.

The next level of recovery is application recovery or clustering plus replication. The use of software replication can provide increased protection again data loss. Clustering services and application recovery work similarly to the hot, warm, and cold redundant server model described earlier. It is common practice for system administrators to install applications on multiple servers so that if one fails to provide the service, a secondary system steps up and takes over the roll. Application recovery expands on this premise for applications:

rather than simple services providing fail-over capabilities for critical applications, application recovery uses software to detect the failure of the primary application server and to then activate the secondary application server to begin accepting and servicing requests.

As noted earlier, mirroring of data, whether through the use of RAID level 1 or alternative technologies, can increase the reliability of primary systems and also enhance the effectiveness of business resumption strategies. The techniques of vaulting and journaling combined dramatically increase the level of protection, and are discussed in the sections that follow.

Electronic Vaulting

The bulk transfer of data in batches to an off-site facility is called **electronic vaulting** and is illustrated in Figure 6-4. This transfer is usually conducted via leased lines or data communications services provided for a fee. The receiving server archives the data as it is received. Some disaster recovery companies specialize in electronic vaulting services. The primary criteria for selecting an electronic vaulting (or e-vaulting) solution are the cost of the service and the required and available bandwidth. Because e-vaulting means transferring data off site, one must guarantee the organization has the capability to do so without impacting other operations. If the organization does not currently have enough bandwidth to support e-vaulting, they must select a vendor to obtain the additional bandwidth needed. With the continual decrease in pricing structures, it may be advantageous to get the extra bandwidth, whether or not your organization feels it is necessary.[6]

Electronic vaulting can be more expensive than tape backup and slower than data mirroring, so one should consider the use of e-vaulting only for data that warrants the additional expense, such as critical transactional data and customer databases. If the organization already has a data classification or prioritization scheme, the organization may already know what data is most critical. These means of categorizing data assets may have been put in place during the business impact analysis or in the development of a risk assessment processes. While e-vaulting can be performed over public infrastructure using VPNs, the data must be encrypted while in transition, which can slow the data transfer rate.

For managed solutions from vendors, typically a software agent is installed on all servers to be included into the e-vaulting process. Once installed, the software initiates a full backup of data to the remote vault and then prepares to continuously copy data as it is created or modified. The vendor is then responsible for the maintenance and protection of the data. Access to the data can then be obtained through a Web interface or by using installed software to facilitate restoration or validation of transferred data. If the organization desires to transfer data to its own vault, different applications can facilitate the transfer between organization-owned equipment over public or private communications links. In either case, the routine transfer of data should not impact the organization's networks; however, those organizations with network connections below T-1 (1.544 Mbps) should consider upgrading to T-1, DSL, or cable modem speeds.[7]

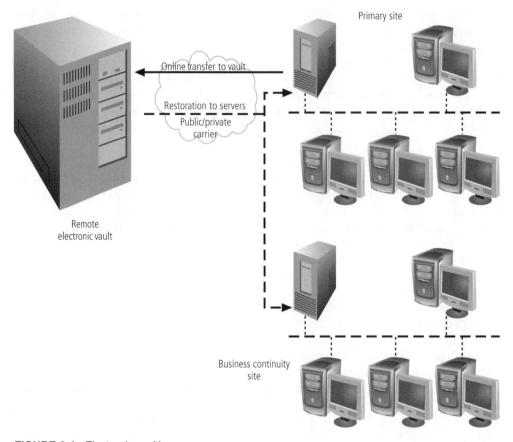

FIGURE 6-4 Electronic vaulting

Remote Journaling

Remote journaling (RJ) is the transfer of live transactions to an off-site facility. RJ was first developed by IBM in 1999 for its OS 400 – V4R2 operating system. RJ differs from electronic vaulting in that only transactions are transferred, not archived data, and the transfer is performed online and much closer to real time. Although electronic vaulting is much like a traditional backup with a dump of data to the off-site storage, remote journaling involves online activities on a systems level, much like server fault tolerance, where data is written to two locations simultaneously. However, this can be performed asynchronously if preferred. RJ facilitates the recovery of key transactions in near real-time. Figure 6-5 shows an overview of the remote journaling process.

When journaling is enabled for a given object, the operating system initiates a process that creates a record of the object's behavior. All changes are recorded by the journal into a journal entry, which is stored in a journal receiver, similar to storing a record in a database file. Once the journal receiver is full, or reaches a preset level, a new journal receiver is linked to the journal, and the full receiver is available for storage to tape, for example. For recovery, the stored receivers can be pulled from tape and applied to the data

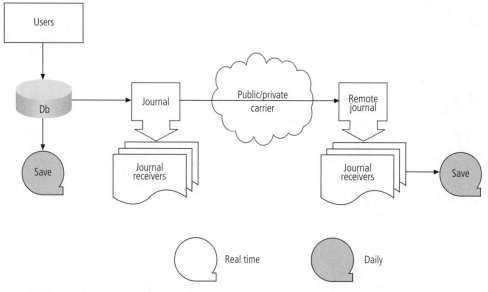

FIGURE 6-5 Remote journaling[8]

in the production database, restoring the data to a known stable point. Remote journaling involves the transference of journal entries to a remote journal, which in turn stores them to a remote journal receiver. This remote journal receiver then is transferred to remote tape or other storage when full, creating a virtual real-time backup of the entries.[9]

Database Shadowing

Database shadowing, also known as **databank shadowing**, is the storage of duplicate online transaction data, along with the duplication of the databases at the remote site to a redundant server. It combines electronic vaulting with remote journaling, writing multiple copies of the database simultaneously in two separate locations. This technology can be used simply, with multiple databases on a single drive in a single system or using databases in remote locations, across a public or private carrier, as shown in Figure 6-6. Shadowing techniques are generally used for organizations needing immediate data recovery after an incident or disaster. The "shadowed" database is available for reading as well as writing, and thus serves as a dynamic off-site backup. Database shadowing also works well for read-only functions, such as the following:

- Data warehousing and mining
- Batch reporting cycles (quarterly and year-end reports, and so on)
- Complex SQL queries
- Local online access at the shadow site
- Load balancing[10]

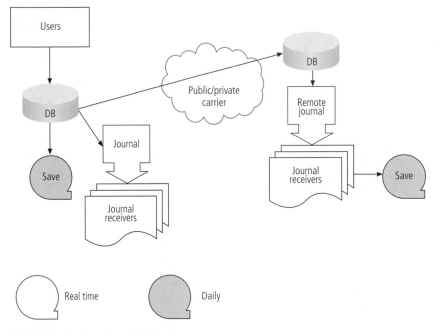

FIGURE 6-6   Database shadowing

Database shadowing is performed by having each transactional event written simultaneously to multiple databases. In its original incarnation, database shadowing was only possible to a secondary partition or database on the original drive, or to a secondary drive in the same machine (disk mirroring or duplexing). However, with the introduction of third-party software, these same transactions can be buffered, transmitted across a network, and stored in a shadow database on a remote server.

As each transaction occurs, the primary database and shadowed database both receive the transaction entry, update, or deletion request. Only the primary database responds to the transaction application, but both databases make the requested entry, modification, or deletion. Once a problem occurs with the primary database, the secondary database can be accessed to serve as a redundant copy. If the redundant copy is on the same system, the transactions can continue without interruption. If the copies are on a remote system, the copy must be read back to the original system, restoring the data to provide a local copy, in order to prevent latency in the transaction process.

Network-Attached Storage and Storage Area Networks

Two other advances in data storage and recovery are **Network-Attached Storage (NAS)** and **Storage Area Networks (SANs)**. Although similar in name, the two have unique implementations and configurations. NAS, as opposed to direct-attached storage, is commonly a single device or server that attaches to a network, and uses common communications methods, such as Windows file sharing, NFS, CIFS, HTTP directories, or FTP, to provide an online storage environment. Commonly implemented as additional storage space, NAS is configured to allow users or groups of users to access data storage. NAS does not work well with real-time applications because of the latency of the communication methods.

SANs are similar in concept but differ in implementation. NAS uses TCP/IP-based protocols and communications methods, but SANs use fiber-channel direct connections between the systems needing the additional storage and the storage devices themselves. This difference is illustrated in Figure 6-7 and described in Table 6-4.[11]

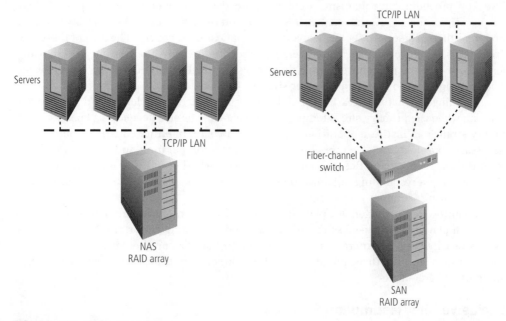

FIGURE 6-7 NAS versus SANs

TABLE 6-4 NAS versus SANs

	NAS	SAN
Connectivity	Any machine that can connect to a LAN and use standard protocols (such as NSF, CIFS, or HTTP)	Only server-class devices with SCSI fiber channel; has a topology limit of 10 km
Addressing, identification, and file transfer	By filename with NAS handling security, including permissions, authentication, and file locking	By disk block number, with no individual security control
OS support	Greater sharing, especially between differing OSs	OS dependent and not compatible with all OSs
File system backups and mirrors	Managed by NAS head unit; done on files to save time and bandwidth	Managed by servers; done on blocks, requiring destination to be greater than source volumes

For general file sharing or data backup use, NAS tends to provide a more compatible solution. For high-speed and higher-security solutions, SANs may be preferable. With SANs, only those devices connected to the SAN can access it. With NAS, anyone who can snoop the IP address can access, or attempt to access, it.

SITE RESUMPTION STRATEGIES

Five key procedural mechanisms were introduced in the opening paragraphs of this chapter. Up to this point, the chapter has focused on the first four of these: Delayed protection, real-time protection, server recovery, and application recovery. The fifth of these key procedures, site recovery, is covered next. This section presents the steps needed to plan for and execute the procedure to quickly establish critical capabilities at an alternate site when the organization's primary site or sites are not available.

Providing alternate processing capability may be needed to implement a disaster recovery plan when the primary site is temporarily unavailable or else needed as a business continuity strategy to institute operations at an alternate site. In either case, it is sometimes necessary to quickly put a computing environment into operation and make sure it can meet the expected needs. Resumption of IT services, whether at a site under the exclusive control of a responding organization or at a site using shared resources, is discussed in the following sections.

A contingency management planning team (CPMT) can choose from several strategies when planning for business resumption. The determining factor of which strategy is used is usually cost. In general, the exclusive control options are hot sites, warm sites, and cold sites, and the three popular shared-use options are timeshare, service bureaus, and mutual agreements.

Exclusive Site Resumption Strategies

When an organization wants its operations to resume at a location over which it has exclusive control, it can select from the options shown in Table 6-5, which provides an overview comparison of these options.

TABLE 6-5 Exclusive-use site criteria selection[12]

Site	Cost	Hardware Equipment	Telecomm-unications	Setup Time	Location
Cold site	Low	None	None	Long	Fixed
Warm site	Medium	Partial	Partial/full	Medium	Fixed
Hot site	Medium/high	Full	Full	Short	Fixed
Mobile site	High	Dependent	Dependent	Dependent	Not fixed
Mirrored site	High	Full	Full	None	Fixed

Hot Sites

A **hot site** is a fully configured computer facility with all services, communications links, and physical plant operations that is capable of establishing operations at a moment's notice. Hot sites duplicate computing resources (servers, appliances, and support computers), peripherals, phone systems, applications, and workstations. Essentially, it is a duplicate facility that needs only the latest data backups and the personnel to function. Some versions can even be staffed around the clock to transfer control of the data processing almost instantaneously. To do so, the organization must use electronic vaulting, remote journaling, or data shadowing. This creates a virtual mirroring of the core IT functions. It is also the most expensive alternative available. Other disadvantages include the need to provide maintenance for all the systems and equipment at the hot site, as well as physical and information security. However, if the organization requires a round-the-clock capability for near real-time recovery, the hot site is the optimum strategy.

Prices for hot sites are based on a number of included options, such as personnel costs, and can total more than $10,000 per month, depending on the speed of changeover needed. The ultimate in hot sites is a **mirrored site**, which is identical to the primary site, and includes live or periodic data transfers. As such, it is capable of immediate operations. Some organizations may choose to build essential redundancy into the functional specifications of their plant and equipment. This ensures that their environment includes redundant capabilities in locations that are sufficiently isolated to avoid coincidental loss, and with sufficient capacity to meet all critical needs even if one facility is removed from service.

Figure 6-8 provides a conceptual representation of a hot site.

Site includes floor space, HVAC, office furniture, servers (with applications), client workstations, network and telecom connections, office equipment, and possibly onsite staff

FIGURE 6-8 Hot site

Warm Sites

A **warm site** provides some of the same services and options of the hot site, but typically software applications are either not included, not installed, or not configured. It frequently includes computing equipment and peripherals with servers but not client workstations. The warm site also has connections or access to data backups or off-site storage to facilitate quick data recovery. A warm site has some of the advantages of a hot site, but at a lower cost. The downside is that it may require several hours, perhaps days, to make a warm site fully functional. Prices for warm sites are customized to the needs of the customer, but typically range upward of $5000 per month. It is possible for an organization to make contractual arrangements with an equipment provider that maintains stocks of critical equipment in a central facility to reprovision an entire data center with as few as 12 hours, notice.

Figure 6-9 provides a conceptual representation of a warm site.

Site includes floor space, HVAC, some office furniture, and servers (w/o applications)

FIGURE 6-9 Warm site

Cold Sites

A **cold site** provides only rudimentary services and facilities. No computer hardware or peripherals are provided. All communications services must be installed after the site is occupied, and frequently there are no quick recovery or data duplication functions to the site. A cold site is an empty room with standard heating, air conditioning, and electrical service. Everything else is an added cost option. Despite these disadvantages, a cold site may be better than nothing. The primary advantage is cost. The most useful feature of this approach is to reduce competition for suitable floor space should a widespread disaster strike, but some organizations are prepared to struggle to lease new space rather than pay maintenance fees on a cold site. A cold site can typically cost upward of $2000 per month, and as such is not a trivial investment.

Figure 6-10 provides a conceptual representation of a cold site.

Site includes floor space, HVAC, and some office furniture

FIGURE 6-10   Cold site

Mobile Sites and Other Options

In addition to these basic strategies, there are also some specialized alternatives available, such as a rolling mobile site configured in the payload area of a tractor-trailer (Figure 6-11). Externally stored resources, like a rental storage area containing duplicate or second-generation equipment, also can be used. These alternatives are similar to the "Prepositioning of Overseas Materiel Configured to Unit Sets" (POM-CUS) sites of the Cold War era, in which caches of materials to be used in the event of an emergency or war were stored awaiting need. An organization might arrange with a prefabricated building contractor for immediate, temporary facilities (mobile offices) on site in the event of a disaster.

FIGURE 6-11   Mobile site[13]

Shared Site Resumption Strategies

When an organization needs to plan for resumption and cannot justify the expense of an exclusive-use strategy, there are shared-use options that can be used for planning.

Time-Share

The first of the three shared-use options is the time-share. A **time-share** operates like one of the three sites described earlier, but is leased in conjunction with a business partner or sister organization. The time-share allows the organization to provide a disaster recovery/business continuity option while reducing the overall cost. The primary disadvantage is the possibility that more than one organization involved in the time-share might need the facility simultaneously. Other disadvantages include the need to stock the facility with the equipment and data from all organizations involved, the complexity of negotiating the time-share with the sharing organizations, and the possibility that one or more parties might exit the agreement or sublease their options. It is much like agreeing to co-lease an apartment with a group of friends. One can only hope the organizations remain on amiable terms, because they all could potentially gain physical access to each other's data.

Service Bureaus

A **service bureau** is a service agency that provides a service for a fee. In the case of disaster recovery/continuity planning, the service is the provision of physical facilities in the event of a disaster. These agencies also frequently provide off-site data storage for a fee. Contracts with service bureaus can specify exactly what the organization needs under what circumstances. A service agreement usually guarantees space when needed, even if this means that the service bureau has to acquire additional space in the event of a widespread disaster. It is much like the rental car provision in your car insurance policy. The disadvantage is that service contracts must be renegotiated periodically and rates can change. This option can also be quite expensive.

Mutual Agreements

A **mutual agreement** is a contract between two organizations for each to assist the other in the event of a disaster. It stipulates that each organization is obligated to provide the necessary facilities, resources, and services until the receiving organization is able to recover from the disaster. This arrangement can be a lot like moving in with relatives or friends. It doesn't take long for an organization to wear out its welcome. Many organizations balk at the idea of having to fund (even in the short term) duplicate services and resources. Additional irritants can be the need to allow access to a partner's employees and contractors as well as the provisioning of office space.

Still, mutual agreements between divisions of the same parent company, between subordinate and senior organizations, or between business partners, may be a cost-effective solution when both parties to the agreement have a mutual interest in each other's continued operations and they both have similar capabilities and capacities. When an organization finds itself relying on a mutual agreement for its alternate processing needs, they should use a memorandum of understanding (MOU) to make sure that as many issues as possible are resolved before the need materializes.

"An MOU, memorandum of agreement (MOA), or a service-level agreement (SLA) for an alternate site should be developed specific to the organization's needs and the partner organization's capabilities. The legal department of each party must review and approve the agreement. In general, the agreement should address at a minimum, each of the following elements:

- Contract/agreement duration
- Cost/fee structure for disaster declaration and occupancy (daily usage), administration, maintenance, testing, annual cost/fee increases, transportation support cost (receipt and return of off-site data/supplies, as applicable), cost/expense allocation (as applicable), and billing and payment schedules
- Disaster declaration (such as circumstances constituting a disaster and notification procedures)
- Site/facility priority access or use
- Site availability
- Site guarantee
- Other clients subscribing to same resources and site, and the total number of site subscribers, as applicable
- Contract/agreement change or modification process
- Contract/agreement termination conditions
- Process to negotiate extension of service
- Guarantee of compatibility
- IT system requirements (including data and telecommunication requirements) for hardware, software, and any special system needs (hardware and software)
- Change management and notification requirements, including hardware, software, and infrastructure
- Security requirements, including special security needs
- Staff support provided or not provided
- Facility services provided or not provided (use of on-site office equipment, cafeteria, and so on)

- Testing, including scheduling, availability, test time duration, and additional testing, if required
- Records management (on-site and off-site), including electronic media and hardcopy
- Service-level management (performance measures and management of quality of IT services provided)
- Workspace requirements (chairs, desks, telephone, PCs)
- Supplies provided or not provided (office supplies)
- Additional costs not covered elsewhere
- Other contractual issues, as applicable
- Other technical requirements, as applicable"[14]

Service Agreements

Whether an organization is making arrangements for an exclusive-use location or a shared-use location, the terms and conditions of that site should be known to all parties by negotiating and executing a service agreement. **Service agreements** are the contractual documents guaranteeing certain minimum levels of service provided by vendors. It is imperative that service agreements be reviewed and in some cases mandated to support incident, disaster, and continuity planning. If a service provider makes no legal assurances as to level of performance, the organization will be unable to require replacement, redundant, or alternative forms of services should the primary be compromised by the contingency.

An effective service agreement should contain the following sections, as illustrated in the Sample Service Agreement that appears at the end of the chapter:

- Definition of applicable parties
- Services to be provide by the vendor
- Fees and payments for these services
- Statements of indemnification
- Nondisclosure agreements and intellectual property assurances
- Noncompetitive agreements (covenant not to compete)

Definition of Applicable Parties

The introductory paragraph in any legal document serves to identify to whom the document applies. Service agreements, as contractual legal documents, are no different. Note that in many documents the long formal names of the two parties are substituted with an abbreviated name, as in "the Client," "the Vendor," or "the Service Provider."

Services Provided by the Vendor

In this section, the vendor or service provider must specify exactly what the client is to receive in exchange for the payments identified in the following section. Because this service agreement is a legal document, if a service is not explicitly identified in this section, it will not be required for the vendor to provide. Any verbal agreements, compromises, or special arrangements must be fully documented. The critical elements of this section should include the specifications of the services expected from the vendor for the protection of, and restoration of, services if an incident or disaster occurs. Some organizations also include contingency operations, such as "for a nominal fee the Vendor agrees to provide additional services to an alternate location within X amount of time following an incident or disaster requiring relocation of the Client's primary business." However, this type of arrangement typically requires a separate agreement, usually called a Business Continuity Service Agreement or Contract.

In the boxed example at the end of this chapter, titled "Sample Service Agreement," there are statements specifically indicating that the vendor agrees to: (a) protect the content of the client, (b) back up the client's content, and (c) indicate as to restoration of services after internal (system or software failure) or external events. This information is important in determining whether a separate agreement is needed to assure compliance with the special needs of the organization for data backup and recovery agreements. Without these specific statements, there is no warrantee that the vendor will protect anything but its own software and hardware, and the client is required to conduct its own data backup and restoration.

Fees and Payments for These Services

This section indicates what the vendor receives in exchange for the services rendered. While the most common exchange is financial, it is not unusual to see an exchange of services, goods, or other securities. The terms of contract and any special fees, such as late fees, returned check fees, or discounts for early payment, could be specified here. A common inclusion is 2/10 net 30, indicating a 2% discount if paid within 10 days, with the net payment due in 30 days, usually for shipped goods paid by invoice, unlike the annual contract indicated here.

Statements of Indemnification

Frequently found in legal documents of this type are statements that the vendor is not liable for actions taken by the client. If the vendor incurs any financial liability based on the use of the vendor's services (in other words, the vendor gets sued because of the use of the services) then the client is responsible for the liability. So, if a client were to put up an insulting Web site that got the client and the vendor sued, the client would be responsible for any fees or expenses incurred by the vendor. Failure to do so inevitably results in additional legal fees from both parties, as the vendor sues to recoup its losses.

Nondisclosure Agreements and Intellectual Property Assurances

It is important for both parties to understand the level of agreement as to the protection and disclosure of the intellectual property of the client. The nondisclosure agreement covers the confidentiality of information from everyone except authorized law enforcement officials or served legal papers directing the vendor to provide certain information. The vendor is expected to certify the validity of these documents, and then provide the information as required. They are prohibited, however, from providing information based on the personal or professional requests of individuals, including law enforcement, without warrant or subpoena, regardless of how Hollywood depicts the process.

If the client does not want the vendor to view the contents of its directory, it can ask for that agreement. If the vendor wants to restrict the type of business performed on its systems, it can ask for that agreement. The two parties must formalize the expectations on both sides with regard to the protection of confidentiality of the services and business information to be shared. Even in a breach of contract, the clause stipulating that a breach of one clause (such as the fees paid, as in a late or missing payment) does not negate the legality of another clause (the disclosure of information); this prevents the vendor from selling off information to recoup financial losses.

Also in the area of monitoring, most state laws and certainly federal law permit a service provider to view the contents of their systems in the routine conduct of business and maintenance on those systems. This means that the vendor can review the contents of the directory, but does not mean they can review the contents of the files within the directory. These same laws permit network administrators to review the headers of packets but not the packet data contents. Just because one has access to information does not give authorization to review the contents. Any expectation or requirement of monitoring should be stipulated in the agreements as well.

Noncompetitive Agreements (Covenant Not to Compete)

While not essential to service agreements, it is nice to see an agreement for the client not to use the vendor's services to compete directly with the vendor, and for the client not to use vendor information to gain a better deal with another vendor. In the early days of MCI and Sprint, federal regulation required (and still requires) a common carrier to offer services even to companies that will in turn use those services to compete. MCI and Sprint leased services from AT&T to establish their start-ups and then moved to their own networks. Outside of the telecommunications and cable television industries, where court orders can mandate specific arrangements between competitive organizations, there is no requirement that an organization allow subleases that can create an advantage for a competitor. For example, a company such as HAL (the company mentioned in the opening chapter scenario) could lease a large amount of space from a Web services company ostensibly as a contingency for business resumption needs. It is possible that HAL might enter the Web services business and turn around and further sublease the space in competition with the original lessor. This would create a competitive arrangement that works against the original lessor and they are likely to want an agreement in place that prohibits HAL from doing business in this way. The following example of an agreement between HAL and its web hosting company shows how a service agreement might be structured.

SAMPLE SERVICE AGREEMENT
CONTRACT FOR SERVICES[15]
BETWEEN

SEQUENTIAL LABEL AND SUPPLY, hereafter referred to as the "Client," and HIERARCHICAL ACCESS LTD, hereafter referred to as the "Vendor."

The Client and the Vendor hereby agree to the following terms and conditions regarding Web hosting and related services, hereafter referred to as the "services."

1. VENDOR'S RESPONSIBILITIES

The Vendor will arrange and manage a Web site and Web domain hosting for the Client. The Vendor will lease the agreed amount of up to 2 GB of Web storage space on its servers and, on the Client's behalf, register a domain name of "SequentialLabel.com" and host this domain name on its primary and secondary name servers. The Vendor will support ongoing maintenance and support of the hardware hosting the virtual presence of the Client, and warrantee the following:

• 24/7 availability with less than one hour per month downtime due to maintenance, to be performed with advanced warning and at a time suited to the needs of the Client (for example, between 2 a.m. and 4 a.m. on Sundays)
• 24/7 access to the directory for the purposes of populating and modifying the contents of the Web directory
• 24/7 technical support for equipment and Web hosting issues to the Client
• A dedicated account manager who will guarantee return of communications (phone, fax, or e-mail) within one hour during normal business hours or within one hour of start of business day for after-hours communications
• Weekly backup of all Client content, with 24/7 access to archived copies, and with Vendor agreeing to retain two newest versions for Client access
• Restoration of Web presence due to down equipment caused by equipment or software failure within two hours
• Restoration of Web presence due to natural disasters, power failure, or other incidents or disasters as quickly as possible, depending on the extent and damages of these acts

The Vendor will not be responsible for the contents of the Web directory, including the creation, modification, or technical support of the Web documents, except as they pertain to the operation of the underlying hardware and software. The Vendor reserves the right to inspect said contents for technical support of the systems housing the content, and to warrantee that no illegal or illicit activities or commerce are transpiring. The Vendor does not permit the use of its facilities for adult-oriented commerce or recreations, or for illegal activities.

2. COSTS AND TERMS

a. Basic Service: The Client agrees to compensate the Vendor for providing those services expressed in this agreement for the price of $10,000.00.

b. Term: The initial term of this agreement will be 12 months and will commence from the date of this agreement. Unless terminated as provided by this agreement, the agreement shall thereafter automatically renew for successive 12-month terms.

c. Taxes: The Vendor will pay for any and all sales and use taxes, duties, or levies imposed by any authority, government, or government agency in connection with the Web services, including property taxes and the Vendor's income taxes.

3. INDEMNIFICATION

The Client hereby agrees to protect, hold free and harmless, defend, and indemnify the Vendor from any and all claims or demands of any kind and from all liability, penalties, costs, losses, damages, expenses, claims, or judgments (including attorney's fees) resulting from legal issues arising from the conduct of electronic commerce or the display of the Client's Web content. Any and all fees associated with legal proceedings against the Vendor as a direct consequence of the display or hosting of the Client's material will be covered totally and in full by the Client. Liability for any services or fees incurred by the Vendor as a result of this contract will be paid for by the Client, including but not limited to notary public, arbitration, mediation, legal, and court fees.

4. GENERAL

a. The Vendor shall not assign or transfer any rights or obligations under this agreement without the Client's prior written approval.

b. Breach of any contract provision by the Vendor can only be waived in writing.

c. Waiver of any breach by the Vendor shall not be deemed to be a waiver of any other breach.

d. This agreement constitutes the entire agreement between the parties with respect to Web services and cannot be modified without the express written consent of all parties.

e. Neither the Client nor the Vendor has made any promise, representation, or warranty, explicit or implied, not set forth in this contract.

f. If any portion of this agreement is held by a court of competent jurisdiction or mutually agreed on authority, to be invalid, void, or unenforceable, the remainder will nevertheless continue in full force without impairment or invalidation.

g. This agreement shall be governed and interpreted by the laws of this state applicable to such contracts entirely made and performed in said jurisdiction and venue.

5. NONDISCLOSURE AND INTELLECTUAL PROPERTY

The Vendor hereby acknowledges and agrees that all information disclosed to the Vendor by the Client, whether written or oral, relating to the Client's business activities; its customer names and addresses; all operating plans; information relating to its existing services, new or envisioned; the Client's products or services and the development thereof; scientific, engineering, or technical information; the Client's marketing or product promotional material, including brochures, product literature, plan sheets, and any and all reports generated to customers or to the Vendor with regard to customers; unpublished lists of names; and all information relating to the Client's order processing, pricing, cost, and quotations; and any and all information relating to the Client's relationship with customers and the Vendor, is considered confidential information and is proprietary to, and is considered the invaluable trade secret of the Client (collectively "Confidential Information").

The Vendor retains the right to review the contents of its directories in the normal course of business and as part of the ongoing maintenance of the systems and software supporting the Client's intellectual property.

The Vendor understands that the Client desires to keep such Confidential Information in the strictest confidence, and that the Vendor's agreement to do so is a continuing condition of the receipt and possession of Confidential Information, and a material provision of this agreement, and a condition that shall survive the termination of this agreement. Consequently, the Vendor shall use Confidential Information for the sole purpose of performing its obligations as provided herein. The Vendor agrees:

i) Not to disclose Confidential Information to future or existing competitors

ii) To limit dissemination of Confidential Information to only those of the Vendor employees who have a need to know such Confidential Information in order to perform their duties as set forth herein

iii) To return Confidential Information, including all copies and records thereof, to the Client upon receipt of a request from the Client, or termination of the agreement as provided herein, whichever occurs first

6. NONCOMPETITION

a. The Vendor covenants and agrees that the Vendor will not directly or indirectly, own, manage, operate, join, control, work for, or permit the use of its name by, or be connected in any manner with, any business activity which is directly competitive with any aspect of the business of the Client, (as set forth in the business plan delivered to the Vendor herewith), which is the same business of the Client, as previously conducted, and as said business may evolve in the ordinary course between the date of this agreement and its termination whether said business is conducted by the Client or any successor or assign.

b. The Client covenants and agrees that the Client will not directly or indirectly, own, manage, operate, join, control, work for, or permit the use of its name by, or be connected in any manner with, any business activity which is directly competitive with any aspect of the business of the Vendor (as set forth in the business plan delivered to the Client herewith), which is the same business of the Vendor, as previously conducted, and as said business may evolve in the ordinary course between the date of this agreement and its termination whether said business is conducted by the Vendor or any successor or assign.

c. The parties hereto agree that the provisions of this agreement extend to the employees and officers of their respective companies/businesses. Said principals further agree to provide the requisite internal security of the subject data within their respective organizations and with respect to any and all additional sources who may be parties to the transactions or proposed transactions.

IN WITNESS WHEREOF, the parties hereto, agreeing to be bound hereby, execute this agreement on this _____ day of _____.

_____   _____
President & CEO,   President & CEO
Sequential Label and Supply, Inc.   Hierarchical Access Limited
on behalf of the Client   on behalf of the Vendor

Chapter Summary

- The umbrella of contingency planning addresses everything done by an organization to prepare for the unexpected, and later, parts of the process are focused on keeping the business alive.

- A BR plan has two major elements; the DR plan for resuming normal operations at the primary sites and the BC plan that activates critical business functions using an alternate site.

- Each of the components of BRP (DRP and BCP) comes into play at a specific time in the life of an incident and overlap may occur.

- There are five key procedural mechanisms that facilitate the restoration of critical information and the continuation of business operations:
  1. Delayed protection
  2. Real-time protection
  3. Server recovery
  4. Application recovery
  5. Site recovery

- A backup plan is essential; data files and critical system files must be backed up frequently, and nonessential files can be backed up less frequently.

- Equally important is the determination of how long data should be stored.

- Many organizations are creating massive arrays of independent but large-capacity disk drives to store information and copy critical files to these devices as routine backup.

- There are three basic types of backups: full, differential, and incremental.
  - A full backup is a full and complete backup of the entire system, including all applications, operating systems components, and data.
  - A differential backup is the storage of all files that have changed or been added since the last full backup.
  - An incremental backup archives only the files that have been modified that day, and thus requires less space and time than the differential.

- Another form of data backup is that of online disk drives used for redundancy. The usage of RAID systems can overcome some of the limits of magnetic tape backup systems and provide enhanced capabilities.

- When systems make use of databases, whether hierarchical, relational, or object-oriented, they require special considerations when planning backup and recovery procedures.

- Some applications use file systems and databases in ways that invalidate the customary way of doing backup and recovery. In some cases, applications write large binary objects as files, manage pointers, and create internal data structures in ways that make routine backups unable to handle the concurrency or complexity of the application.

- Even the best backups are inadequate unless they can be used to successfully restore systems to an operational state. Each backup and recovery setting should be provided with complete recovery plans, including testing and rehearsal.

- To provide real-time protection, also known as replication, a popular feature used in server support is the use of mirroring and duplication of server data storage with RAID techniques.

- The bulk transfer of data in batches to an off-site facility is called electronic vaulting and is usually conducted with the receiving server archiving the data as it is received.

- Remote journaling is the transfer of live transactions to an off-site facility so that all changes are recorded.

- Database shadowing, also known as databank shadowing, is the storage of duplicate online transaction data, along with the duplication of the databases at the remote site to a redundant server.

- Several strategies are possible when planning for business resumption, including: hot sites, warm sites, cold sites, time-share, service bureaus, and mutual agreements.

  - A hot site is a fully configured computer facility, with all services, communications links, and physical plant operations capable of establishing operations at a moment's notice.

  - A warm site provides some of the same services and options of the hot site, but typically software applications are either not included, or not installed and configured.

  - A cold site provides only rudimentary services and facilities, and no computer hardware or peripherals are provided.

  - A time-share operates like one of the three sites described above, but is leased in conjunction with a business partner or sister organization.

  - A service bureau is a service agency that provides a service for a fee, such as the provision of physical facilities in the event of a disaster.

  - A mutual agreement is a contract between two organizations for each to assist the other in the event of a disaster.

- Service agreements are the contractual documents guaranteeing certain minimum levels of service provided by vendors.

- An effective service agreement should contain a definition of applicable parties, a list of services to be provided by the vendor, fees and payments for those services, a statement of indemnification, nondisclosure agreements and intellectual property assurances, and noncompetitive agreements.

Review Questions

1. What purpose does business resumption planning serve?
2. What are the latter parts of the contingency plans focused on?
3. What are the major elements of a business resumption plan?
4. What does a disaster recovery plan strive to do?
5. What does a business continuity plan strive to do?

Contingency Strategies for Business Resumption Planning

6. When does each element of a contingency plan come into play?

7. How does an organization deal with the overlap present in the elements of a contingency plan?

8. What are the key procedures common to all of the ways that are used in the restoration of critical information and the continuation of business operations?

9. What are the relative recommended backup frequencies for various types of information found in organizations?

10. What are the major types of backups?

11. What is encompassed in a full backup?

12. What is encompassed in a differential backup?

13. What is encompassed in an incremental backup?

14. What is a redundant array of independent disks (RAID), and what are its primary uses? How can it be used in a backup strategy?

15. In what way are the backup needs of systems that use databases different from the back-ups ordinarily used to safeguard non-database systems?

16. Other than simply identifying what to back up, when to back it up, and how to restore it, a complete backup recovery plan should include what other elements?

17. What is electronic vaulting, and how is it used in a backup strategy?

18. What is remote journaling, and how is it used in a backup strategy?

19. What is a hot site? A warm site? A cold site? How are they different?

20. What is a time-share? A service bureau? A mutual agreement? What is each used for in a contingency planning sense?

Exercises

1. The introduction scenario represents a unique type of incident/disaster. Using a Web browser, search for information related to preparing an organization against such terrorist attacks as: (a) anthrax, (b) sarin or other toxic gas, or (c) a suspected biological attack (like smallpox).

2. Using a Web browser, search for available commercial applications using various forms of RAID technologies, such as RAID 0 through RAID 5. What is the most common implementation? What is the most expensive?

3. Not too long ago, tape backup was the industry standard. Is it still? Using a Web browser or your local library electronic journal search tool, review the popular trade press journals to determine if tape, disk, or drive backups seem to be more prevalent now, or what is predicted to be the new standard for the near future.

4. Using a Web browser, search for vendors providing alternate site strategies such as hot sites, warm sites, and cold sites. How prevalent are they? What about mobile sites?

5. This chapter provides one example of a service agreement. Using a Web browser, search for other examples. How do they differ? What areas are common to all?

References

1. Ian Garland, Servo Plc, "Business Continuity in a Windows Environment," December 14, 2004, accessed June 24, 2005, from http://www.servo.co.uk/enews/letter/asp/art_bus.asp?art=38&uid.

2. Exabyte, "The Basic Backup Guide," accessed July 6, 2005, from http://www.exabyte.com/support/online/documentation/whitepapers/basicbackup.pdf.

3. See note 2.

4. See note 2.

5. Answers.com, "RAID," accessed October 12, 2005, from http://www.answers.com/RAID.

6. Rick Cook, "Deciding on Electronic Vaulting," January 22, 2002, accessed July 7, 2005, from http://searchstorage.techtarget.com/tip/1,289483,sid5_gci797551,00.html?bucket=ETA.

7. LiveVault Online Backup Service, "How Electronic Vaulting Works," accessed July 7, 2005, from http://www.usdatatrust.com/service/how_it_works.asp.

8. Based in part on graphics from Chris Hird and Shield, "Remote Journaling and Data Recovery," accessed July 8, 2005, from http://www.shield.on.ca/download/Remote%20Journaling%20and%20Data%20Recovery.pdf.

9. iTera, "The Benefits of Remote Journaling in iSeries High-Availability Solutions," accessed July 8, 2005, from http://advgroup.com/NEWpdfs/Benefits%20of%20Remote%20Journaling%20-%20whitepaper.pdf.

10. ENet, "Data Recovery Without Data Loss," accessed July 11, 2005, from http://www.enet.com/enet.com.nsf/PAGES_RRDF_Recov.html?OpenPage&charset=iso-8859-1.

11. NAS vs SAN, "Technology Overview," accessed July 11, 2005, from http://www.nas-san.com/differ.html.

12. M. Swanson, A. Wohl, L. Pope, T. Grance, J.Hash, R. Thomas, "Contingency Planning Guide for Information Technology Systems [NIST Special publication 800-34], accessed July 13, 2005, from http://csrc.nist.gov/publications/nistpubs/800-34/sp800-34.pdf.

13. SunGard Web site, http://www.availability.sungard.com/Resources/Virtual+Tours/Mobile/NA-Mobile+Recovery-Slideout.htm.

14. See note 12.

15. Based on Onecle's "AGREEMENT BETWEEN 649.COM, INC. AND MILLMEDIA, S.A.," accessed July 11, 2005, from http://contracts.onecle.com/649/millmedia.svc.1999.11.01.shtml, which is in turn based on public documents filed in compliance with SEC regulations.

CHAPTER 7

DISASTER RECOVERY: PREPARATION AND IMPLEMENTATION

There's a special providence in the fall of a sparrow. If it be now, 't is not to come; if it be not to come, it will be now; if it be not now, yet it will come: the readiness is all.

—William Shakespeare, Hamlet (Act V, Scene ii)

OPENING SCENARIO

"It's just horrendous," Paul said as he looked across the HAL company parking lot at the neighboring college campus. From where he stood, Paul had a clear view of the recreation building he had entered hundreds of times during his college years. Now the building was a wreck of ashes, mud, and snow. If it hadn't been for the heavy snowstorm the night before, the fire probably would have burned the structure to the ground. Firefighters, weary from the long night's battle with the blaze, stood around the building, ever-watchful for flare-ups or other signs that their work wasn't over.

A familiar voice called out, "Paul, is everyone okay?" Paul turned and saw JJ walking across the lot.

"Yes, thank goodness," Paul replied. "There was no one in the building."

"What an awful mess. Do they know what started it?" JJ asked.

"They suspect a lightning strike on the roof. That roof was at least a hundred years old." Paul sighed. "I guess they'll have to rebuild."

"I hope so," JJ said. "The basketball team was finally starting to pull it together. A few more wins and they could have been contenders." JJ looked back at the ruined building. "I guess they'll have to find another building for the college to hold home games." JJ turned back from the view of the college. "Sorry about the alma mater, dude. Let me buy you a cup of coffee."

"Sure, JJ." As Paul turned away, he looked up at the glass and steel of HAL's modern office building, aware that it could burn almost as quickly as the ancient gymnasium. Paul thought for a moment.

"Say, JJ, when was the last time we went over our disaster recovery plan?"

continued

Questions for discussion:

- Are any organizations exempt from the need for a disaster recovery plan?
- Do you think the college faces a disaster with the loss of the gymnasium? What factors can make the loss of an entire building merely an incident and not a disaster?

LEARNING OBJECTIVES

Upon completion of this material, you should be able to:

- Understand the ways to classify disasters, both by speed of onset and source
- Know who should form the membership of the disaster recovery team
- Understand the key functions of the disaster plan
- Explain the key concepts included in the NIST approach to technical contingency planning
- Describe the elements of a sample disaster recovery plan
- Understand the need for simultaneous wide access to the planning documents as well as the need for securing the sensitive content of the DR plans

INTRODUCTION

The disaster recovery elements of the contingency planning process are often taken for granted in many organizations. Often, the information technology (IT) community of interest, under the leadership of the CIO, is given responsibility for disaster recovery planning because they are keenly interested in keeping IT systems available during and immediately following disasters. Unfortunately, some organizations abdicate the overall responsibility for disaster readiness to the IT Department, including aspects that are not necessarily related to information technology. In a perfectly balanced approach, the IT Department focuses on IT system disaster preparations, and all other business units prepare in a similar fashion.

Disaster recovery planning is the preparation for and recovery from a disaster, whether natural or man-made. In some cases, actual incidents detected by the Incident Response (IR) team escalate to the disaster level, and the IR plan is no longer adequate to handle the effective and efficient recovery from the loss. For example, if a malicious program evades containment actions and infects and disables all of an organization's systems and its ability to function, the disaster recovery (DR) plan is activated. Sometimes events are by their nature immediately classified as disasters, such as fire, flood, storm damage, or earthquake.

As was discussed in earlier chapters, the continuity planning team creates the disaster recovery team, then assists in the development of the disaster recovery plan. In general, an incident is categorized as a disaster when the organization is unable to contain or control the impact of an incident, or when the level of damage or destruction from an incident is so severe the organization is unable to quickly recover. The distinction between an actual incident and an immediate disaster may be subtle. The CP team must document in the DR plan whether an event is classified as an incident or a disaster. This determination is critical because it determines which plan is activated. The key role of a DR plan is defining how to reestablish operations where the organization is usually located.

DISASTER CLASSIFICATIONS

A DR plan can classify disasters in a number of ways. The most common method is to separate natural disasters, such as those described in Table 7-1, from man-made disasters. *Acts of terrorism*, including cyberterrorism or activism, *acts of war*, and those *acts of man* that may begin as incidents and escalate into disasters are all examples of man-made disasters. Another way of classifying disasters is by speed of development. **Rapid onset disasters** are those that occur suddenly, with little warning, taking the lives of people and destroying the means of production. Rapid onset disasters may be caused by earthquakes, floods, storm winds, tornadoes, or mud flows. **Slow onset disasters** occur over time and slowly deteriorate the capacity of an organization to withstand their effects. Hazards causing these disaster conditions typically include droughts, famines, environmental degradation, desertification, deforestation, and pest infestation.[1]

TABLE 7-1 Natural disasters and their impact on information systems

Disaster Type	Description
Fire	Damages the building housing the computing equipment that comprises all or part of the information system. Also encompasses smoke damage from the fire and water damage from sprinkler systems or firefighters. Can usually be mitigated with fire casualty insurance or business interruption insurance.
Flood	Can cause direct damage to all or part of the information system or to the building that houses all or part of the information system. May also disrupt operations through interruptions in access to the buildings that house all or part of the information system. Can sometimes be mitigated with flood insurance or business interruption insurance.
Earthquake	Can cause direct damage to all or part of the information system or, more often, to the building that houses it. May also disrupt operations by interrupting access to the buildings that house all or part of the information system. Can sometimes be mitigated with specific casualty insurance or business interruption insurance, but is usually a specific and separate policy.
Lightning	Can directly damage all or part of the information system or its power distribution components. It can also cause fires or other damage to the building that houses all or part of the information system. May also disrupt operations by interrupting access to the buildings that house all or part of the information system as well as the routine delivery of electrical power. Can usually be mitigated with multipurpose casualty insurance or business interruption insurance.
Landslide or mudslide	Can damage all or part of the information system or, more likely, the buildings that house it. May also disrupt operations by interrupting access to the buildings that house all or part of the information system as well as the routine delivery of electrical power. Can sometimes be mitigated with casualty insurance or business interruption insurance.
Tornado or severe windstorm	Tornadoes or windstorms can directly damage all or part of the information system or, more likely, the buildings that house it. May also disrupt operations by interrupting access to the buildings that house all or part of the information system as well as the routine delivery of electrical power. Can sometimes be mitigated with casualty insurance or business interruption insurance.
Hurricane or typhoon	Can directly damage all or part of the information system or, more likely, the buildings that house it. Organizations located in coastal or low-lying areas may experience flooding (see Flood entry). May also disrupt operations by interrupting access to the buildings that house all or part of the information system as well as the routine delivery of electrical power. Can sometimes be mitigated with casualty insurance or business interruption insurance.

Disaster Type	Description
Tsunami	A very large ocean wave caused by an underwater earthquake or volcanic eruption. Can directly damage all or part of the information system or, more likely, the buildings that house it. Organizations located in coastal areas may experience tsunamis. Tsunamis may also cause disruption to operations by interrupting access or electrical power to the buildings that house all or part of the information system. Can sometimes be mitigated with casualty insurance or business interruption insurance.
Electrostatic discharge (ESD)	Can be costly or dangerous when it ignites flammable mixtures and damages costly electronic components. Static electricity can draw dust into clean-room environments or cause products to stick together. The cost of ESD-damaged electronic devices and interruptions to service can range from a few cents to millions of dollars for critical systems. Loss of production time in information processing due to ESD impact is significant. Although not usually viewed as a threat, ESD can disrupt information systems and is not usually an insurable loss unless covered by business interruption insurance.
Dust contamination	Can shorten the life of information systems or cause unplanned downtime.
Excessive precipitation	Even when it is not encountered in conjunction with one of the listed types of disasters, too much precipitation can lead to disasters in their own right. Rain, freezing rain, sleet, snow, hail, and fog can all cause situations that cause losses, such as through property damage when a roof collapses under the weight of excessive snow. Sometimes excessive precipitation leads to another listed type of disaster such as flood or mudslide. Still other circumstances can lead to losses that are not as obvious, such as intense fog causing roadways to be closed or public transportation systems to be shut down.

265

FORMING THE DISASTER RECOVERY TEAM

The contingency planning management team (CPMT) assembles a disaster recovery team. Although the IT and Information Security (InfoSec) departments contribute representatives to this team, it must also include members from outside these two groups. Because much of the work of the DR team is about the reestablishment of business operations at the primary site, the team leader and many of the members should be drawn from the organization's functional areas. Not only is this team responsible for the planning for DR, it also leads the DR process when the disaster is declared. Key considerations in developing the DR team include its organization, as well as the need to identify and collect needed documentation and equipment.

Organization

The DR team consists of a team leader, who is also a member of the CPMT, and representatives from every major organizational unit. Specific members may be selected either for their unique skills, an ability to provide liaison between organizational elements, or for other specialized needs. The membership of the DR team should be distinctly separate from that of any other contingency-related team, because each team has differing responsibilities when activated in a real disaster, and it is very possible that more than one team will be active at the same time. Therefore, it is important that DR team members do not serve with either the IR team or the business continuity (BC) team, because the duties of each team may overlap if an incident escalates into a disaster that requires the implementation of the business continuity plan. The primary DR team includes representatives from some or all of the following, depending on the organization and industry:

- Senior management
- Corporate support units (specifically including human resources, legal, and accounting)
- Facilities
- Fire and safety
- Maintenance staff
- IT technical staff (specifically including database, systems, and networking)
- IT managers
- InfoSec technicians
- InfoSec managers

As previously noted, the organization and membership of the DR team should be distinctly separate from that of the BC team, because each team has differing responsibilities when activated in a real disaster. Depending on the size of the organization, there may be many subteams within the disaster recovery team responsible for separate sequences of activities. Note that in some organizations the IT teams may be much more concentrated, such as only having a hardware, software, and networking team, rather than be further dividing as described here:

- Disaster management team: The command and control group responsible for all planning and coordination activities. The management team consists of the previously described representatives working together to design the disaster recovery plan. During a disaster, this group coordinates all efforts and receives reports from and assigns work to the other teams.
- Communications team: This team contains representatives from the public relations and legal departments, if such exist. This team serves as the voice of the management of the organization, providing feedback to anyone desiring additional information about the organization's efforts in recovering from the disaster. Members of this team interface with upper management, the disaster management team, law enforcement, the press, employees and their families, and the general public. All communications are directed from and to this team.
- Computer recovery (hardware) team: This team works to recover any physical computing assets that might be useable after the disaster. In smaller organizations this team may be combined with other IT-related teams. The findings of this team are incorporated into any insurance claims, or postdisaster recovery purchases for restoration of operations.
- Systems recovery (OS) team: The OS team works to recover operating systems and may contain one or more specialists on each OS the organization employs. This group works closely with the hardware and applications teams to reestablish systems functions during recovery. The OS team also works to reestablish user accounts and remote connectivity in conjunction with the network team.

- Network recovery team: The network team works to determine the extent of damage to the network wiring and hardware (hubs, switches, and routers) as well as Internet and intranet connectivity. The network team works to reestablish functions by repairing or replacing damaged or destroyed components. This group works closely with the Internet service provider to reestablish connectivity.
- Storage recovery team: Should the organization have storage area networks or network attached storage, this group works with the others to recover information and reestablish operations. In some cases, this group may have to wait to begin their efforts until the hardware, systems, and applications teams have completed their operations. This group may also interface with the data management group to restore data from backups to their storage areas.
- Applications recovery team: Just as the hardware and OS teams operate to reestablish operations, so does the applications team. Once the previous groups have systems back up and running, the applications team recovers applications and reintegrates users back into the systems.
- Data management team: Working with all of the other teams, the data management team is primarily responsible for data restoration and recovery. Whether from on-site, off-site, or online transactional data, this group is expected to quickly assess the recoverability of data from systems on site and then make recommendations to the management team as to whether off-site data recovery is needed.
- Vendor contact team: This team works with suppliers and vendors to replace damaged or destroyed materials, equipment, or services, as determined by the other teams. Based on recommendations by the management team, this group can work from preauthorized purchase orders to quickly order replacement equipment, applications, and services, as the individual teams work to restore recoverable systems.
- Damage assessment and salvage team: This group of specialized individuals provides the initial assessments of the extent of damage to materials, inventory, equipment, and systems on site. They are responsible for physically recovering salvageable items to be transported to a location where the other teams can evaluate them. Items that are obviously beyond recovery are identified by the salvage team and reported to the management team. This group is also responsible for coordinating physical security with law enforcement and any private security service through the communications and vendor teams.
- Business interface team: This group works with the remainder of the organization to assist in the recovery of nontechnology functions. Careful coordination of effort is required to comply with the findings of the business impact analysis in determining the priority of reestablishment of business functional areas, so that the most critical functions are reconstituted first. As the liaison between business and IT, this group ensures that each group can work on their own recovery efforts, without interfering with the other.

- Logistics team: This group consists of the individuals responsible for providing any needed supplies, space, materials, food, services, or facilities needed at the primary site. While the vendor contact team may order needed services and supplies, this group serves as the go-to team to physically acquire and transport the needed resources to the appropriate location. This group also serves as the providers of the minute tasks that make the operations move smoothly.[2]
- Other teams as needed: The other business functions may require specialized teams to assist in the recovery of their operations. As such, these teams would focus on the reestablishment of key business functions as determined by the BIA.

Special Documentation and Equipment

All members of the team should have multiple copies of the DR (and BC) plans in their homes, vehicles, and offices, because they cannot predict when they will receive an emergency call and be required to activate the plans. It is also important for the responsible team members to have access to certain disaster recovery materials should the need arise. The equipment an individual needs differs based on their role and responsibilities. In general, some of the equipment needed may include:

- Data recovery software to recover information from damaged systems
- Redundant hardware and components to rebuild damaged systems
- Copies of building blueprints to direct recovery efforts. On these prints, the following locations should be indicated:
  - Key server cabinets or closets
  - Data communications cabinets or closets
  - Power distribution and UPSs
  - Important document storage (paper copies)
  - Data backup storage
  - Keys and access cards to secure undamaged areas after the disaster has passed
  - Communications lines
  - Fire suppression systems and access points
  - Water lines
  - Gas lines
  - Flammables and combustibles
- Key phone numbers (or complete phone books or directories) of:
  - Fire, police, and rescue (other than 911)
  - Insurance contacts
  - Building inspectors
  - Service providers:
    - Water
    - Gas
    - Power
    - Data communications
    - Telecommunications
    - Sewer

- Alert roster first contacts: The individuals who will initiate the contact of all employees to inform them of the disaster and advise them whether or not they should report for work.
- Fire and water damage specialists
- Emergency supplies:
  - Flashlight and extra batteries
  - Emergency communications (2-way radios, not cellular phones, because they are infrastructure dependent)
  - Poncho
  - First-aid kit
  - Toilet paper
  - Snacks
  - Drinking water
  - Toolkits

Many of these items seem frivolous, but when these teams spend 12- to 24-hour shifts for days on end working at a disaster site, with inoperable facilities and services, these items may prove invaluable.

DISASTER PLANNING FUNCTIONS

DR planning is an important part of the contingency planning process as was described in detail in the introduction to Chapter 6. All of the various pieces of contingency planning an organization should be guided by are included in the approach used in this book, which is drawn from the National Institute of Standards and Technology's (NIST's) Special Publication 800-34.[3] This document, the *Contingency Planning Guide for Information Technology Systems*, includes elements designed to implement *incident*, *disaster*, and *continuity* recovery efforts as part of a comprehensive planning function. The specifics of developing plans and policies for each of these three components are similar. In this chapter, the NIST strategy is focused on disaster recovery.

NOTE

Those aspects of the NIST approach that apply to incident response planning have been discussed in earlier chapters, and those topics that belong exclusively to business continuity will be discussed in Chapters 8 and 9.

Although policies may differ from company to company, the approach taken here is that the first step in the effort to craft any contingency plan is the development of enabling policy or policies. The focus then shifts to developing the requisite plans. Both of these elements are part of the broader contingency planning process.

Recall that Chapter 1 introduced a planning process recommended by NIST that showed the use of seven discreet steps. In the broader context of organizational contingency planning, these steps form the overall CP process. These process steps are to be used again here within the narrower context of the DRP process. The following steps are discussed in the next several sections, each of which contains a DRP-based discussion:

1. Develop the DR planning policy statement: A formal department or agency policy provides the authority and guidance necessary to develop an effective contingency plan.
2. Review the business impact analysis (BIA): The BIA was prepared to help to identify and prioritize critical IT systems and components. Reviewing what was discovered is an important step in the process.
3. Identify preventive controls: Measures taken to reduce the effects of system disruptions can increase system availability and reduce contingency life cycle costs.
4. Develop recovery strategies: Thorough recovery strategies ensure that the system can be recovered quickly and effectively following a disruption.
5. Develop the disaster recovery plan document: The plan should contain detailed guidance and procedures for restoring a damaged system.
6. Plan testing, training, and exercises: Testing the plan identifies planning gaps, whereas training prepares recovery personnel for plan activation; both activities improve plan effectiveness and overall agency preparedness.
7. Plan maintenance: The plan should be a living document that is updated regularly to remain current with system enhancements.

Develop the DR Planning Policy Statement

The DR team, led by the business manager designated as the DR team leader, begins with the development of the DR policy. The policy provides an overview of an organization's philosophy on the conduct of disaster recovery operations and serves as the guide for the development of the DR plan. The DR policy itself may have been created by the organization's CPMT and handed down to the DR team leader. Alternatively, the DR team may be assigned the role of developing the DR policy. In either case, the disaster recovery policy contains the following key elements, which are described in the subsequent sections. An actual example is provided at the end of each section to further illustrate the point.

- Purpose
- Scope
- Roles and responsibilities
- Resource requirements
- Training requirements
- Exercise and testing schedules
- Plan maintenance schedule
- Special considerations (such as information storage and maintenance)

Purpose

The purpose of the disaster recovery program is to provide for the direction and guidance of any and all disaster recovery operations. In addition, the program provides for the development and support for the disaster recovery plan. In everyday practice those responsible for the program must also work to emphasize the importance of creating and maintaining effective disaster recovery functions at the organization. As with any major enterprise-wide policy effort, it is important for the disaster recovery program to begin with a clear statement of executive vision. Once the vision is articulated, it should be included in the organization's policies. The primary vehicle for this is the **business disaster recovery policy**, which applies to the entire organization. Unfortunately, it is typical to see DR policies appear only in IT Departments. A preferred solution is for an organization-wide, business-focused DR policy to be established at the highest level of the organization and then passed down through subordinate units of the organization so that each unit may prepare its own complementary disaster recovery process and plan. The organization's DR group may require a universal planning approach, but this can only occur after the business DR policy is completed, thus creating the context to assure all planning processes can interoperate.

The purpose of this policy is to ensure that business function and information resource investments made by the *organization* are protected against service interruptions, including large-scale disasters, by the development, implementation, and testing of disaster recovery (DR) plans.

For purposes of this policy, disaster recovery planning includes, but is not limited to, the documentation, plans, policies, and procedures that are required to restore normal operation to a division impacted by man-made or natural outages or disasters at *the organization's* primary or permanent alternate site.

The policy assists *the organization* to:
- Identify business resources that are at risk.
- Implement useful plans to protect against identified threats and mitigate risk.
- Implement tested emergency procedures when a service outage occurs.
- Implement and test procedures that enable reestablishment of services at the primary site or permanent alternate site following a disaster.
- Develop a plan that enables full recovery and the resumption of normal operations.[4]

Scope

This section of the policy identifies the organizational units and groups of employees to which the policy applies. This clarification is important in case the organization is geographically disbursed or is creating different policies for different organizational units.

> This policy applies to all *the organization's* divisions and departments within *the organization*, and to the individuals employed therein.

Roles and Responsibilities

This section identifies the roles and responsibilities of the key players in the disaster recovery operation. This list can range from the responsibilities of the executive management, down to the individual employee. Note in the following examples that some sections may be duplicated from the organization's contingency planning policy. For smaller organizations, this redundancy can be eliminated, because many of the functions are performed by the same group. Some policy examples are as follows:

The chief operation officer, as *the organization's* contingency planning officer, appoints a disaster recovery planning officer from his or her office.

The chief financial officer appoints an individual to assist the disaster recovery planning officer in securing service agreements necessary to reestablish operations at *the organization's* primary place of business, or at a permanent alternate site as dictated by the situation.

The appointed disaster recovery planning officer oversees all phases and functions of the disaster recovery planning process and reports divisional readiness directly to the contingency planning officer.

Each division must have a disaster recovery plan that identifies and mitigates risks to critical functions and sensitive information in the event of a disaster.

The plan shall provide for contingencies to restore operations and information if a disaster occurs. The disaster recovery plan for each division may be a subset of *the organization's* comprehensive disaster recovery plan. The concept of a disaster recovery focuses on business resumption at the primary place of business.[5]

Each division shall:
- Develop disaster recovery plans.
- Maintain and update disaster recovery plans annually.
- Test disaster recovery plans annually.
- Train their employees to execute the recovery plans.[6]

Division heads are responsible for the oversight of their respective division's management and use of IT resources. An annual disaster recovery/business continuity plan confirmation letter must be submitted to the CIO by August 31 of each year. By way of this letter, the head of each division confirms to the executive management that a disaster recovery/business continuity plan has been reviewed, updated, and tested.

The auditor may audit division disaster recovery/business resumption plans and tests for

Resource Requirements

Should the organization desire, it can allocate specific resources to be dedicated for the development of disaster recovery plans. While this may include directives for individuals, it can be separated from the previous section for emphasis and clarity.

> The chief financial officer provides the necessary contractual agreements and funds to warrant availability of resources should they be required to rebuild *the organization's* primary business site or to select a suitable permanent alternative. The CFO also ensures suitable funds to support the development and annual testing of the DR plan.

Training Requirements

In this section of the policy, the training requirements for the various parts of the organization and the various types of employee categories are defined and highlighted.

> Training for the DR plan consists of:
>
> - Making employees aware of the need for a disaster recovery plan
> - Informing all employees of the existence of the plan and providing procedures to follow in the event of an emergency
> - Training all personnel with responsibilities identified in the plan to perform the disaster recovery procedures
> - Providing the opportunity for recovery teams to practice disaster recovery skills[7]

Exercise and Testing Schedules

Stipulation for the frequency of testing of the DR plan can include both the type of exercise or testing and the individuals involved.

> A quarterly walk-through of all DR plans is conducted with all key DR team representatives.
>
> Annually, the DR officer, in coordination with the CP officer, conducts an unannounced disaster recovery exercise. Each key individual is provided with a specific type of disaster and asked to function as if the disaster were genuine. Results are discussed in an after-action review with the executive management team.

Plan Maintenance Schedule

All good plans include a schedule and instructions for the review and update of the plan. This section should address the frequency of such a review, along with who is involved in the review. It is not necessary for the entire DR team to be involved, but the review can be combined with a periodic test of the DR (as in a talk-through) as long as the resulting discussion includes areas for improvement for the plan.

> The disaster recovery policy must be reviewed at least annually to assure its relevance.
>
> Just as in the development of such a policy, a planning team that consists of upper management and personnel from information security, information technology, human resources, or other operations should be assembled to review the disaster policy.[8]

Special Considerations

One or more additional sections may be included. For example, a policy section to direct organizational efforts on the topic of information storage and retrieval plans of the organization may be included. This may be referred to as *Data Storage and Recovery* or *Data Backup and Recovery* and would be where the general on-site and off-site backup schemes are highlighted. The use of off-site but online data storage may also be specified. Although the specifics do not have to be covered, the individuals responsible, identified in earlier sections, should be able to implement the strategy based on this guidance.

> The CIO, in conjunction with the CISO, ensures a generally accepted data storage and recovery scheme is implemented, with weekly off-site data storage using a secure transportation method.
>
> The CIO evaluates and implements appropriate off-site but online data storage to record transactional data providing a recovery time objective of no longer than 24 hours, once hardware has been recovered.

Review the Business Impact Analysis

Fortunately, the need for BIA within the DR context requires only a review of the version developed by the CPMT to ensure compatibility with DR specific plans and operations. Because much of the work done by the CP includes business managers as well as IT and InfoSec representatives, the document is usually acceptable as it was prepared and released by the CPMT.

Identify Preventive Controls

Once again this function is performed as part of ongoing information security posture. Effective preventive controls implemented to safeguard online and physical information storage also facilitate its recovery. At a minimum, the DP team should review and verify that the generally accepted data storage and recovery techniques discussed in Chapter 6 are implemented, tested, and maintained. The team should also ensure that sufficient and secure off-site data storage is implemented, tested, and maintained, including any remote transactional or journaling functions.

Develop Recovery Strategies

Thorough recovery strategies ensure that the system may be recovered quickly and effectively following a disruption.

Although it may be virtually impossible to prepare for all diverse contingencies, ranging from floods to fires to tornadoes or even man-made disasters, it is important to have the recovery strategies in place for the most expected disasters. Based on the BIA conducted early in the process, the *after the action* actions must be thoroughly developed and tested.

Contrary to popular belief, the DR strategies go substantially beyond the *recovery* portion of *data backup and recovery* and must include the steps necessary to fully restore the organization to its operational status. This includes personnel, equipment, applications, data, communications, and support services (like power and water). Only through close coordination with these services can the organization quickly reestablish operations at its principle location, the primary objective of the DR plan.

One key aspect of the DR strategy is the enlistment and retention of qualified general contractors capable of quickly assessing any physical damage the organization may have sustained and pulling in the necessary subcontractors to rebuild the facility. As such, the contracting of such options is a key aspect of the recovery strategy and plan. It is thus useful to include this general contractor in disaster recovery training and rehearsals, allowing the contractor the opportunity to determine what resources he or she needs to rebuild part or all of the organizational structure. If the facilities the organization occupies are leased, the leasing agency may also need to play a role in acting as intermediary between the DR team and any contractors needed.

Develop the DR Plan Document

The DR planning document should contain the specific and detailed guidance and procedures for restoring lost or damaged capability. Any procedures that have already been prepared must be aggregated, then reviewed for completeness, tested for accuracy, and then formally published. The responsibility for creating the DR plan itself, unlike the IR plan, does not usually fall to the CISO. As a general business activity, the disaster team leader may be from upper management, such as the chief operations officer, or one of his or her senior managers. Earlier, this book discussed how the IR team develops three sets of incident-handling procedures for every attack scenario end case, based on the BIA. The disaster recovery team (or management team, as described previously) takes this same information and the information from the IR team and begins developing its own procedures for the DR plan. The DR team converts the incidents to disasters, adds any not used by the IR team, and creates disaster scenarios. The DR team also develops three sets of activities for each disaster scenario. Recall that the activities are presented in sections in the sequence in which they are most frequently used.

Because the activities used during a disaster are most urgently needed in the event of plan activation, they are placed in the binder first. The activities that are part of the follow-up plan, to be used once the disaster has been resolved, are placed second, and the planned activities that should be integrated into every daily procedure and activity, which are only occasional referenced for change management purposes, are placed third. Each of these is discussed in additional detail in the sections that follow.

1. During the disaster: The planners develop and document the procedures that must be performed during the disaster, if any. These procedures are grouped and assigned to individuals. Systems administrators' tasks differ from managerial tasks, so members of the planning committee must draft a set of function-specific procedures. Obviously, some disasters may preclude organizational response, unless the individuals are at work when the disaster strikes. For these types of disasters, evacuation plans, locations of shelters, fire suppression systems, and other emergency reaction items must be organized and placed into easy-to-read documents that can be referred to during the disaster.

2. After the disaster: Once the procedures for handling or reacting to a disaster are drafted, the planners develop and document the procedures that must be performed immediately after the disaster has ceased. Again, separate functional areas may develop different procedures. If the damage from the disaster is substantial enough, crisis management procedures may be needed, as described in Chapters 10 and 11.

3. Before the disaster: The planners draft a third set of procedures listing those tasks that must be performed to prepare for the disaster. These procedures include data backup information, disaster recovery preparation, training schedules, testing plans, copies of service agreements, and business continuity plans, if any.

Similar to the incident plan addendum created in the IR planning process, the DR team should create disaster response plan addendums (see Figure 7-1). For each disaster scenario to be included, these addendums are created by taking the information from the anticipated disaster (whether an escalated incident or original disaster scenario), and adding the informational items, as shown in the following example. This information includes the trigger, the notification method, and response time. The notification method describes the manner in which the team receives its notification that a disaster has occurred and the plan is to be executed. Again, this could be by phone, pager, e-mail, loudspeaker, or word of mouth.

The response time represents the time that the team should optimally respond by, and typically ranges from 30 minutes to 48 hours, depending on the disaster. Some natural disasters (fires, floods, earthquakes, or tornadoes) may strike with little or no warning, requiring an immediate response, while escalations from spam denial-of-service attacks may be deferred for 24 to 48 hours, depending on the actions of the attacker.

Disaster response plan addendums to disaster scenario end case	
Disaster type:	
Trigger:	
Team lead:	
Notification method:	
Response time:	
Actions during disaster:	
1.	
2.	
N.	
Actions during disaster are complete when:	
Actions after disaster:	
1.	
2.	
N.	
Actions after disaster are complete when:	
Actions before disaster:	
1.	
2.	
N.	
Actions after disaster are complete when:	
1.	
2.	
N.	

FIGURE 7-1   Sample disaster response plan addendum

Planning for Actions Taken During the Disaster

The disaster response, like incident response, usually begins with a trigger. In disaster recovery, the **trigger** is the point at which a management decision to react is made in reaction to a notice or other data such as a weather report or an activity report from IT indicating the escalation of an incident. In disaster recovery, most triggers are in response to one or another natural events. Some of these events have a long build-up, such as a tropical depression growing to a tropical storm and finally a hurricane. The hurricane may take days to reach full strength and then landfall. Some inland cities may have sufficient time to prepare for the actual disaster, while others may have very little time because they cannot accurately predict the exact landfall or impact of the storm. Similarly, a normal summer storm may suddenly spawn tornadoes, resulting in immediate damage. The best work in planning for actions during the disaster is the development of the disaster end cases, creating reaction scenarios that direct employees to safety, and then developing training programs for the *actions before* phase.

The next planning component is the determination of what must be done to react to this particular disaster scenario. The dominant reaction may be to either warn employees not to come to work that day or to direct employees to a shelter. This requires the identification of such a location as part of the planning process. For IT-based disasters, the IR team works closely with the disaster recovery team lead to determine what is required from both groups. In the event of a widespread, disastrous technology attack, the incident response group works primarily on restoring internal systems, while the disaster recovery group activates the groups responsible for data, applications, systems, networking, and communications to assist in handling the event and providing information to other organizational units and external parties. Once all signs of the disaster have ceased, the "actions during" phase is complete.

Planning for Events Occurring After the Disaster

Once the incident has been contained, and all signs of the incident removed, the *actions after* phase begins. During this phase, lost or damaged data is restored, systems scrubbed of infection, and essentially everything is restored to its previous state. The IR plan plan thus must describe the stages necessary to recover from the most likely events of the incident. It should also detail other events necessary to the *actions after* phase, such as the protection from follow-on incidents, forensics analysis, and the after-action review.

Follow-on incidents are highly probable when infected machines are brought back online or when other infected computers that may have been offline at the time of the attack are brought back up. Follow-on incidents are also likely in the event of a hacker attack, when the attacker retreats to a chat room and describes in specific detail to his or her associates the method and results of their latest conquest. Therefore, the identification of potential follow-on attacks should be of great concern. By identifying and resolving the avenues of attacks from the forensics analyses, the organization can prevent these incidents from recurring.

Forensics analysis is the process of systematically examining information assets for evidentiary material that can provide insight into how an incident transpired. Information on which machine was infected first or how a particular attacker gained access to the network provides information as to unknown vulnerabilities or exploits. Care must be made to use an individual trained in forensic analysis, because the information found during the analysis may be potential evidence in civil or criminal proceedings. Forensic analysis is covered in additional detail in later chapters.

Before returning to routine duties, the IR team must also conduct an **after-action review (AAR)**. The AAR is a detailed examination of the events that occurred from first detection to final recovery. All key players review their notes and verify that the IR documentation is accurate and precise. All team members review their actions during the incident and identify areas where the IR plan worked, didn't work, or should improve. This allows the team to update the IR plan. The AAR can serve as a training case for future staff. It also brings to a close the actions of the IR team.

Planning for Actions Taken Before the Disaster

Planning for actions before the disaster in general is the process of implementing all of the actions found in common information security practices. However, some specific incidents may have unique requirements for preparation that go beyond those normal actions. The actions taken before the disaster phase not only include preventive measures to manage the risks associated with a particular attack but also the actions taken to enhance the preparedness of the IR team. Because each disaster scenario identifies the specific preparatory actions needed to best prepare for that scenario, it is a challenge to predict what is required. However, DR planning usually includes actions in the areas of staffing, training, equipping, stocking of critical consumables, and execution of service and support contracts to enable rapid responses.

One important note for both DR and IR planning: when selecting an off-site storage location for data backups or stored equipment, extra care should be taken to minimize the risk at that storage location. In many instances, a large-scale disaster may destroy or damage both the primary location and the off-site storage location if the latter is not carefully selected.

Plan Testing, Training, and Exercises

Training management and staff in the proper performance of their roles described in the disaster recovery plan can be used to test the validity and effectiveness of the DR plan as well as prepare the various teams to use it. Any problems found in the plan identified during training can be incorporated into the draft document. Once the drafts have been reviewed and tested, the final assembly can commence. As with the IR plan, testing the DR plan is an ongoing activity with each scenario tested at least semiannually and at least at a walk-through level. Once all the individual components of the DR plan have been drafted and tested, the final DR plan document can be created, similarly in format and appearance to the IR plan, as described in Chapter 3. This format will be described in greater detail in Chapter 8.

Plan Maintenance

The plan should be a dynamic document that is updated regularly to remain current with system enhancements. The organization should plan to revisit the DR plan at least annually to update the plans, contracts, and agreements, and make the necessary personnel and equipment modifications, as dictated by the business operations. If the organization changes its size, location, or business focus, the DR management team, along with the other management teams, should begin anew with the CP plan, and reexamine the BIA. The maintenance process used for DR plans is discussed in greater detail in Chapter 8.

TECHNICAL CONTINGENCY PLANNING CONSIDERATIONS

This section, taken and adapted from NIST SP 800-34, discusses technical contingency planning (as business resumption planning integrating DR and BC) and considerations for specific types of IT systems.[9] The information presented in this section will assist the reader in selecting, developing, and implementing specific technical contingency strategies based on the type of IT system. Because each system is unique, information is provided at a level that may be used by the widest audience. All of the information presented may not apply to a specific IT system. Therefore, the contingency planning coordinator should draw on the information as appropriate and modify it to meet the system's particular contingency requirements. The following IT platforms are addressed in this section:

- Desktop computers and portable systems
- Servers
- Web sites
- Local area networks
- Wide area networks
- Distributed systems
- Mainframe systems

For each IT platform type, technical measures are considered from two perspectives. First, the document discusses technical requirements or factors that the contingency planning coordinator should consider when planning a system recovery strategy. Second, technology-based solutions are provided for each platform. The technical considerations and solutions addressed in this section include preventive measures and recovery measures. Several of these contingency measures are common to all IT systems. Common considerations include the following, all of which are mentioned in subsequent sections:

- Frequency of backup and off-site storage of data, applications, and the operating system
- Redundancy of critical system components or capabilities
- Documentation of system configurations and requirements
- Interoperability between system components and between primary and alternate site equipment to expedite system recovery
- Appropriately sized and configured power management systems and environmental controls

Desktop Computers and Portable Systems

Contingency considerations for desktop and portable systems should emphasize data availability, confidentiality, and integrity. To address these requirements, the systems manager should consider each of the following practices:

- Store backups off site.
- Encourage individuals to back up data.
- Provide guidance on saving data on personal computers.
- Standardize hardware, software, and peripherals.
- Document system configurations and vendor information.
- Coordinate with security policies and system security controls.
- Use results from the BIA.

Data from the BIA of major applications and general support systems should be used to determine the recovery requirements and priorities to implement.

Contingency Strategies

Among the strategies that should be considered for desktop computer and portable systems are:

- Document system and application configurations.
- Standardize hardware, software, and peripherals.
- Provide guidance on backing up data.
- Ensure interoperability among components.
- Coordinate with security policies and controls.
- Back up data and store off site.
- Back up applications and store off site.
- Use alternate hard drives.
- Image disks and standardize images.
- Implement redundancy in critical system components.
- Use uninterruptible power supplies.

Servers

Servers support file sharing and storage, data processing, central application hosting (such as e-mail or a central database), printing, access control, user authentication, remote access connectivity, and other shared network services. Local users log onto the server through networked PCs to access resources that the server provides. Because servers can support or host numerous critical applications, server loss could cause significant problems to business processes. To address server vulnerabilities, the following practices should be considered:

- Store backup media and software off site.
- Standardize hardware, software, and peripherals.
- Document system configurations and vendors.
- Coordinate with security policies and system security controls.
- Use results from the BIA.

The BIA of major applications and general support systems should provide information to assist in determining the recovery requirements and priorities. Server contingency planning should emphasize reliability and availability of the network services provided by the server.

Contingency Strategies

Among the strategies that should be considered for servers are:

- Document system and application configurations.
- Standardize hardware, software, and peripherals.
- Coordinate with security policies and controls.
- Ensure interoperability among components.
- Back up data and store off site.
- Back up applications and store off site.
- Use uninterruptible power supplies.
- Implement redundancy in critical system components.
- Implement fault tolerance in critical system components.

- Replicate data.
- Implement storage solutions.

Web Sites

Web sites present information to the public or authorized personnel via the Internet or a private intranet. An external Web site also may be an electronic commerce (e-commerce) portal, through which the organization may provide services over the Internet. A Web site may be used internally by an organization to provide information, such as corporate policies, human resources forms, or a phone directory to its employees.

In addition to the information presented in the section discussing servers, several factors should be considered when determining the Web site recovery strategy. Practices for Web site contingency planning include the following measures:

- Document Web site.
- Web site programming should use documented change management.
- Web site coding should be relative, not absolute—allowing quick reconfiguration if needed.
- Coordinate contingency solutions with appropriate security policies and security controls.
- Coordinate contingency solutions with incident response procedures.
- Use results from the BIA.

Web site contingency solutions should ensure the reliability and availability of the Web site and its resources. When choosing contingency solutions for a Web site, the Web site's supporting infrastructure must be considered carefully. In addition to servers, the supporting infrastructure could include the LAN hosting the Web site.

Contingency Strategies

Among the strategies that should be considered for Web sites are:

- Document Web site.
- Code, program, and document Web site properly.
- Coordinate with security policies and controls.
- Consider contingencies of supporting infrastructure.
- Implement load balancing.
- Coordinate with incident response procedures.

Local Area Networks

A local area network (LAN) is owned by a single organization; it can be as small as two PCs attached to a single hub or it may support hundreds of users and multiple servers.

When developing the LAN recovery strategy, the contingency planning coordinator should follow the information presented earlier in the sections regarding desktops, servers, and Web sites. In addition, the following practices should be considered:

- The physical and logical LAN should be well documented.
- System configuration and vendor information should be well documented.
- Coordinate with security policies and security controls.
- Use results from the BIA.

When developing the LAN contingency plan, the contingency planning coordinator should identify **single points of failure** that affect critical systems or processes outlined in the BIA. This analysis could include threats to the **cabling system**, such as cable cuts, electromagnetic and radio frequency interference, and damage resulting from fire, water, or other hazards.

Contingency Strategies

Among the strategies that should be considered for LANs are:

- Document the LAN.
- Coordinate with vendors.
- Coordinate with security policies and controls.
- Identify single points of failure.
- Implement redundancy in critical components.
- Monitor the LAN.
- Integrate remote access and wireless area network technology.

Wide Area Networks

In addition to connecting LANs, a wide area network (WAN) also can connect to another WAN, or it can connect a LAN to the Internet. WAN contingency considerations should enhance the ability of recovery personnel to restore WAN services after a disruption. The following practices complement WAN recovery strategies to create a more comprehensive WAN contingency capability:

- Document the WAN.
- Document systems configurations and vendors.
- Coordinate with security policies and security controls.
- Use results from the BIA.

WAN contingency solutions include all of the measures discussed for PCs, servers, Web sites, and LANs. In addition, WAN contingency planning must consider the communications links that connect the various LANs. WAN contingency strategies are influenced by the type of data traveling over the network. A WAN that hosts a mission-critical distributed system may require a more complete and robust recovery strategy than a WAN that connects multiple LANs for simple resource sharing purposes.

Contingency Strategies

Among the strategies that should be considered for WANs are:

- Document the WAN.
- Coordinate with vendors.
- Coordinate with security policies and controls.
- Identify single points of failure.
- Install redundancy in critical components.
- Institute service-level agreements.

Distributed Systems

Distributed systems are implemented in environments in which clients and users are widely dispersed. These systems rely on LAN and WAN resources to facilitate user access, and on the elements comprising the distributed system require synchronization and coordination to prevent disruptions and processing errors.

Contingency considerations for the distributed system draw on the concepts discussed for the previous platforms. Because the distributed system relies extensively on local and wide area network connectivity, distributed system contingency measures are similar to those discussed for LANs and WANs:

- Standardize hardware, software, and peripherals.
- Document systems configurations and vendors.
- Coordinate with security policies and security controls.
- Use results from the BIA.

Because a distributed system spans multiple locations, risks to the system and its supporting infrastructure should be analyzed thoroughly in the BIA process. As discussed earlier, distributed system contingency strategies typically reflect the system's reliance on LAN and WAN availability.

Contingency Strategies

Among the strategies that should be considered for distributed systems are:

- Standardize components.
- Document system.
- Coordinate with vendors.
- Coordinate with security policies and controls.
- Consider server contingency solutions.
- Consider the LAN contingency solution.
- Consider the WAN contingency solution.

Mainframe Systems

Unlike the client/server architecture, the mainframe architecture is centralized. The clients that access the mainframe are *dumb* terminals with no processing capabilities. The dumb terminals accept output only from the mainframe. However, PCs also can access a mainframe by using terminal emulation software.

Although the mainframe computer is larger and more powerful than the platforms discussed previously, it shares many of the same contingency requirements. Because a mainframe uses a centralized architecture, the mainframe does not have the inherent redundancy that a distributed system or network provides. As a result, mainframe availability and data backups are critical. The following measures should be considered when determining mainframe contingency requirements:

- Store backup media off site.
- Document system configurations and vendors.
- Coordinate with network security policy and system security controls.
- Utilize results from the BIA.

Mainframes require different contingency strategies from distributed systems because data is stored in a single location. Contingency strategies should emphasize the mainframe's data storage capabilities and underlying architecture. Redundant system components are critical to ensure that a failure of a system component, such as a power supply, does not cause a system failure.

Contingency Strategies

Among the strategies that should be considered for mainframe systems are:

- Back up data and store off site.
- Document system.
- Coordinate with vendors.
- Coordinate with security policies and controls.
- Implement redundancy and fault tolerance in critical system components.
- Consider hot site or reciprocal agreement.
- Institute vendor service-level agreements (SLAs).
- Replicate data.
- Implement storage solutions.
- Use uninterruptible power supplies.

Summary of Technical Contingency Planning Considerations

For IT contingency planning, the contingency planning coordinator should consider technical measures from the following two perspectives when planning a system recovery strategy:

- Contingency considerations discuss technical requirements or factors to complement the contingency solution.
- Contingency solutions are technically based and are used to implement the contingency strategy.

Table 7-2 summarizes all contingency considerations and solutions identified in the previous sections and the associated IT platforms. The contingency considerations and solutions are presented at the highest level and do not represent an all-inclusive list. Because each system is unique, the contingency planning coordinator must assess each IT system using the results of the BIA to determine not only which considerations and solutions presented are appropriate, but also whether considerations and solutions not presented, or presented for other IT platforms, are applicable.

TABLE 7-2 Technical contingency planning summaries[10]

Contingency Considerations*	Desktop Computer/Portable System	Server	Web Site	LAN	WAN	Distributed System	Mainframe System
Document system, configurations, and vendor information	X	X	X	X	X	X	X
Encourage individuals to back up data	X						
Code, program, and document properly			X				
Coordinate contingency solutions with security policy	X	X	X	X	X	X	X
Coordinate contingency solutions with system security controls	X	X	X	X	X	X	X
Consider contingencies of supporting infrastructure			X			X	
Consider hot site and reciprocal agreements							X
Coordinate with incident response procedures			X				
Coordinate with vendors				X	X	X	X
Institute vendor SLAs					X		X
Provide guidance on saving data on personal computers	X						
Standardize hardware, software, and peripherals	X	X				X	
Store backup media off site	X	X					X
Store software off site	X	X					
Contingency Solution*							
Back up system, applications, and/or data	X	X					
Ensure interoperability among components	X	X					
Identify single points of failure				X	X		

287

TABLE 7-2   Technical contingency planning summaries (continued)

	Desktop Computer/Portable System	Server	Web Site	LAN	WAN	Distributed System	Mainframe System
Image disks	X						
Implement fault tolerance in critical components		X					X
Implement load balancing		X	X				
Implement redundancy in critical components	X	X		X	X		X
Implement storage solutions		X					X
Integrate remote access and wireless technologies				X			
Monitor				X			
Replicate data		X					X
Use alternate hard drives	X						
Use uninterruptible power supplies	X	X					X

* Contingency considerations discuss technical requirements or factors to complement the contingency solution.

**Contingency solutions are technically based and are used to implement the contingency strategy.

SAMPLE DISASTER RECOVERY PLANS

An example of what may be found in a disaster recovery plan is shown in Figure 7-2 and discussed in Table 7-3. This has been adapted from a plan prepared by the Texas State Library and Archives, State and Local Records Management Division.[11]

EXAMPLE DISASTER RECOVERY PLAN

1. Name of agency_____

2. Date of completion or update of the plan_____

3. Agency staff to be called in the event of a disaster:

   Disaster Recovery Team:

   Name: Numbers: Position:

   _____
   _____
   _____

   Building Maintenance_____

   Building Security_____

   Legal Advisor_____

   Note below who is to call whom upon the discovery of a disaster (Telephone Tree):

   1

4. Emergency services to be called (if needed) in event of a disaster:

   Service: Contact Person: Number:

   Ambulance_____

   Carpenters_____

   Data Processing Backup_____

   Electrician_____

   Emergency Management Coordinator_____

   Exterminator_____

   Fire Department_____

   Food Services_____

   Locksmith_____

   Plumber_____

   Police_____

   Security Personnel (extra)_____

   Software Vendor_____

   Temporary Personnel_____

   Utility Companies:

   Electric_____

   Gas_____

   Water_____

   Others:

   2

FIGURE 7-2 Sample disaster recovery plan

5. Locations of in-house emergency equipment and supplies (attach map or floor plan with locations marked):

Batteries_____

Badges (employee identification)_____

Camera /Film_____

Cut-off Switches and Valves:

Electric_____

Gas_____

Water_____

Sprinkler System (if separate) _____

Extension Cords (heavy-duty) _____

Fire Extinguishers_____

Flashlights_____

Ladders_____

Mops/Sponges/Buckets/Brooms_____

Nylon Monofilament_____

Packing Tape/String/Sissors_____

Paper Towels (white)_____

Plastic Trash Bags_____

Rubber Gloves_____

Transistor Radio (battery powered)_____

3

---

6. Sources of off-site equipment and supplies (if maintained on-site, note location):

Item:	Contact/Company:	Number:

Cellular Phone_____

Dehumidifiers_____

Drying Space_____

Dust Masks_____

Fans_____

Fork Lift_____

Freezer/Wax Paper_____

Freezer Space/Refrigeration Truck_____

Fungicides_____

Generator (portable)_____

Hard Hats_____

Pallets_____

Plastic Milk Crates_____

Pumps (submersion)_____

Rubber Boots_____

Safety Glasses_____

Trash Can (all sizes)_____

Vacuum/Freeze Drying Facilities_____

Waterproof Clothing_____

Wet-Dry Vacuum_____

4

FIGURE 7-2 Sample disaster recovery plan (continued)

7. Salvage Priority List:

Attach a copy of the records retention schedule identifying all vital/essential records series. The location and record medium of the preservation duplicate for each vital records series should be noted.

It is also very helpful if other records series are reviewed to determine their priority for salvage should a disaster occur. The following questions can be helpful in determining priorities:

1. Can the records be replaced? At what cost?
2. Would the cost of replacement be less or more than restoration of the records?
3. How important are the records to the agency?
4. Are the records duplicated elsewhere?

To simplify this process, priorities may be assigned as follows:

1. Salvage at all costs.
(example, records that are historically valuable or non-vital records that are important to agency operations and very difficult to recreate)

2. Salvage if time and resources permit.
(example, records that are less important to the agency or somewhat easier to recreate)

3. Dispose of as part of general cleanup.
(example, records that do not need to be salvaged because they are convenience copies and the record copy is at another location)

8. Agency Disaster Recovery Procedures:

Attach a list of specific procedures to be followed in the event of a disaster in you agency, including responsibilities of in-house recovery team members.

9. Follow-up Assessment:

A written report, including photographs, should be prepared after recovery and attached to a copy of the disaster plan. The report should note the effectiveness of the plan, and should include an evaluation of the sources of supplies and equipment, and of any off-site facilities used.

(Adapted from *Basic Guidelines for Disaster Planning in Oklahoma*)

5

FIGURE 7-2 Sample disaster recovery plan (continued)

The plan has nine major sections, each of which is described in Table 7-3. Many organizations, particularly those with multiple locations and hundreds of employees, would find this plan too simple. However, the basic structure provides a solid starting point for any organization.

TABLE 7-3 Sample DR plan elements

Element	Description
Name of organization or department	This section of the plan identifies the department, division, or institution to which this particular plan applies; this is especially important in organizations that are large enough to require more than one plan.
Date of completion or update of the plan and test date	Self-explanatory

TABLE 7-3 Sample DR plan elements (continued)

Element	Description
Staff to be called in the event of a disaster	This roster should be kept current. It will not help the organization to have a roster of employees no longer with the company. This section should also identify key support personnel such as building maintenance supervisors, physical security directors, legal counsel, and the starting points on the alert roster. A copy of the alert roster (also known as the telephone tree) should be attached.
Emergency services to be called (if needed) in event of a disaster	While dialing 911 will most certainly bring police, firefighters, and an ambulance, the organization may have equally pressing needs for emergency teams from the gas, electric, and water companies. This section should also list electricians, plumbers, locksmiths, and software and hardware vendors.
Locations of in-house emergency equipment and supplies	This section should include maps and floor plans with directions to all critical in-house emergency materials, including shutoff switches and valves for gas, electric, and water. It should also provide directions to key supplies, including first-aid kits, fire extinguishers, flashlights, batteries, and a stash of office supplies. It is a good idea to place a disaster pack on every floor in an unlocked closet or readily accessible location. Again, these should be inventoried and updated as needed.
Sources of off-site equipment and supplies	These items include contact sources for mobile phones, dehumidifiers, industrial equipment such as forklifts and portable generators, and other safety and recovery components.

TABLE 7-3 Sample DR plan elements (continued)

Element	Description
Salvage priority list	Although the IT director may have just enough time to grab the last on-site backup before darting out the door in the event of a fire, most likely there are additional materials that can be salvaged if recovery efforts permit. In this event, recovery teams should know what has priority. This list should specify whether to recover hard copies or if the effort should be directed toward equipment. Similarly, it specifies whether the organization should focus on archival records or recent documents. The plan should include the locations and priorities of all items of value to the organization. When determining priorities, you should ask questions such as: Are these records archived elsewhere (off-site), or is this the only copy? Can these records be reproduced if lost, and if so, at what cost? Is the cost of replacement more or less than the cost of the value of the materials? It may be useful to create a simple rating scheme for materials. Data classification labels can be adapted to include disaster recovery information. For example, some records may be labeled: "Salvage at all costs," or "Salvage if time and resources permit," or "Do not salvage."
Agency disaster recovery procedures	This very important section outlines the specific assignments given to key personnel, including the disaster recovery team, to be performed in the event of a disaster. If these duties differ by type of disaster, it may be useful to create multiple scenarios, each listing the duties and responsibilities of the parties involved. It is equally important to make sure that everyone identified has a copy of the DR plan stored where they can easily access it, and that they are familiar with their responsibilities.
Follow-up assessment	The final section details what is to be accomplished after disaster strikes; specifically, what documentation is required for recovery efforts, including mandatory insurance reports, required photographs, and the after-action review format.

293

The Combined DR Plan/BC Plan

Because the DR plan and BC plan are closely related, many organizations prepare the two at the same time, and may combine them into a single planning document. Such a comprehensive plan—often referred to as a business resumption plan, or simply a contingency plan—must be able to support the reestablishment of operations at two different locations: one immediately at an alternate site and one eventually back at the primary site. Therefore, although a single planning team can develop the combined disaster and resumption plan, execution of the plan requires separate execution teams.

FINAL COMMENTS ON THE DR PLAN

The planning process for the DR plan/BC plan should be tied to, but distinct from, the planning process used to create the IR plan. As you learned earlier in the chapter, an incident may escalate into a disaster when it grows dramatically in scope and intensity. It is important that the three processes be so tightly integrated that the reaction teams can easily transition from incident response to disaster recovery and business continuity planning.

One useful resource is the business continuity plan template provided by the Federal Agency Security Practices section of the Computer Security Resource Center (CSRC) at the NIST (see *http://fasp.nist.gov*). Even though it is labeled a contingency plan, this Web page provides a template plan, complete with instructions designed for agencies working with the Department of Justice (DOJ). The instructions specifically describe the approach taken for the template, allowing easy conversion to suit many public and private organizations. This document is included at the end of this book as Appendix B. Other excellent examples and other supporting information can be found at the *Disaster Recovery Journal*'s download site (*www. drj.com/new2dr/samples.htm*).

Finally, when the plan is completed, it needs to be stored and kept available in as many locations and formats as are consistent with the needs for appropriate access by key staff, while maintaining positive control of the content. These plans can contain a wealth of sensitive data that would be a significant loss to the organization if the data fell into the wrong hands. Planners need to make arrangements for the ways that planning documents are copied and stored to accommodate the availability requirement while making sure the necessary confidentiality is maintained.

Chapter Summary

- Disaster recovery planning is the preparation for and recovery from a disaster.

- The disaster recovery team, working with the CPMT, develops the DR plan.

- The key role of a DR plan is defining how to reestablish operations where the organization is usually located.

- A DR plan can classify disasters as being either natural disasters or man-made disasters (acts of terrorism, acts of war, and so on). The DR plan can also classify disasters by assessing speed of development as either rapid onset or slow onset disasters.

- The CPMT assembles the disaster recovery team, which is tasked with the reestablishment of business operations at the primary site; this team is responsible for the planning for DR and leadership once a disaster is declared.

- The DR team consists of representatives from every major organizational unit, plus specialized members selected for their unique capabilities or perspective.

- Members of the DR team do not serve with either the IR team or the BC team because the duties of each team may overlap if an incident escalates into a disaster requiring implementation of the business continuity plan.

- The organization of the DR team should be distinctly separate from that of the business continuity team, because each team has differing responsibilities when activated in a real disaster.

- The DR team may have many subteams responsible for individual actions, including:
  - Disaster management team
  - Communications team
  - Computer recovery (hardware) team
  - Systems recovery (OS) team
  - Network recovery team
  - Storage recovery team
  - Applications recovery team
  - Data management team
  - Vendor contact team
  - Damage assessment and salvage team
  - Business interface team
  - Logistics team
  - Other teams as needed

- All members of the DR team should have multiple copies of the DR (and BC) plans in their homes, vehicles, and offices, because they cannot predict when they will receive a call and be required to activate the plans.

- It is also important for the responsible team members to have access to certain disaster recovery materials should the need arise.

- The first step in the effort to craft any contingency plan is the development of an enabling policy or policies. The focus then shifts to developing the requisite plans.
- The NIST planning process adapted for DR planning is:
  1. Develop the contingency planning policy statement.
  2. Conduct or review the business impact analysis.
  3. Identify preventive controls.
  4. Develop recovery strategies.
  5. Develop an IT contingency plan.
  6. Plan testing, training, and exercises.
  7. Plan maintenance.
- The DR team, led by the business manager designated as the DR team leader, begins with the development of the DR policy.
- The policy provides an overview of the organization's philosophy on conducting disaster recovery operations, and serves as the guide for the development of the DR plan.
- Effective preventive controls implemented to safeguard online and physical information storage also facilitate its recovery.
- Thorough recovery strategies ensure that the system may be recovered quickly and effectively following a disruption.
- The DR plan itself should contain detailed guidance and procedures for restoring lost or damaged information and is prepared in three groups:
  - During the disaster
  - After the disaster
  - Before the disaster
- Training in the use of the disaster recovery plan can be used to test the validity and effectiveness of the DR plan as well as prepare the various teams to use it.
- Testing the DR plan is an ongoing activity, with each scenario tested at least semiannually and at least at a walk-through level.

Review Questions

1. Why do some organizations abdicate all responsibility for DR planning to the IT Department?
2. What are the ways that a disaster may emerge and become an issue for an organization?
3. What entity is responsible for creating the DR team? What other preparatory contingency planning work will this entity have completed prior to the DR Plan development process in a well-planned contingency planning environment?
4. What are the ways that an organization might choose to classify disasters? What are the types of disasters possible within each classification method?
5. Who serves on the DR team? Are there limitations on the number and type of contingency planning teams to which any individual should be assigned?
6. What are the commonly used subteams of the DR team? What role does each play?

7. What are some examples of special documentation or equipment that may be needed for DR team members?

8. What are the steps that are generally followed in the DR development process?

9. What key elements should be included in the DR policy?

10. What are recovery strategies, and why are they important to the DR process?

11. What are the three general categories of DR activities?

12. Why would the DR activity groups be presented out of sequence (during, after, or before) instead of being ordered as before, during, or after?

13. What are the major activities planned to occur during the disaster?

14. What are the major activities planned to occur after the disaster?

15. What are the major activities planned to occur before the disaster?

16. What is a DR plan addendum, and why will one or more of them be prepared?

17. What is a DR after-action review, and what are the primary outcomes from it?

18. According to NIST SP 800-34, what two perspectives should be used to plan a system recovery strategy?

19. What are the major topic headings used in the sample DR plan offered by this chapter?

20. What are the advantages of combining the DR and BC plans? What are the disadvantages?

Exercises

1. Using a Web browser, search for the following terms: *business continuity planning*, *disaster recovery planning*, *business resumption planning*, and *contingency planning*. Review the examples and definitions you find. What do you notice about the terminology?

2. Using a Web browser, access an online disaster recovery journal, for example, *www.drj. com*. Review the articles in the latest issue (this may require some form of user registration). Identify articles from which Cecilia would benefit at this point in her process. Bring them to class to discuss.

3. Using a Web browser, search for the term *disaster recovery plan*. Identify three or four examples of what appear to be comprehensive plans, different from the samples presented in this chapter. What do these have in common? Create an outline for a DR plan using these examples. Bring them to class to discuss.

4. Using a Web browser, search for the terms *data backup*, *data recovery*, and *data storage strategies*. What are the available options for performing these tasks? How do they relate to disaster recovery?

5. Review the opening scenario. Does Paul's final comment lead you to believe that HAL has done some DR work already? Now consider your home. What disaster recovery tasks should you perform to prevent a disaster like a fire from being as catastrophic as it might? Make a list of these tasks and bring to class to discuss.

References

[1] Disaster Preparedness Training Programme, International Federation of Red Cross and Red Crescent Societies, accessed March 1, 2003, from http://www.ifrc.org/what/dp/manual/introdp.pdf.

[2] Evan Marcus and Hal Stern, "Beyond Storage: 12 Types of Critical Disaster Recovery Teams," December 30, 2003, accessed July 15, 2005, from http://searchstorage.techtarget.com/tip/1,289483,sid5_gci942811,00.html.

[3] M. Swanson, et al. Contingency Planning Guide for Information Technology Systems, NIST Special Publication 800-34, accessed July 13, 2005, from http://csrc.nist.gov/publications/nistpubs/800-34/sp800-34.pdf.

[4] Based on "Disaster Recovery Policy," accessed July 14, 2005, from http://www.isb.wa.gov/policies/portfolio/500P.doc.

[5] NITC, "Disaster Recovery Policy," accessed July 14, 2005, from http://www.nitc.state.ne.us/tp/workgroups/security/policies/sections_for_graph/sectionBandCfor_3.pdf.

[6] See note 4.

[7] See note 5.

[8] Disaster recovery policy template, Web page, accessed July 15, 2005, from http://templatezone.com/pdfs/DisasterRecoveryPolicy.pdf.

[9] See note 3.

[10] See note 3.

[11] Texas State Library and Archives, State and Local Records Management Division, "Example Disaster Recovery Plan," accessed May 21, 2003, from http://www.tsl.state.tx.us/slrm/disaster/recovery_plan.pdf.

CHAPTER **8**

DISASTER RECOVERY: OPERATION AND MAINTENANCE

Our disaster recovery plan goes something like this—Throw your hands up and shout "HELP! HELP!"

—*Dilbert* by Scott Adams

OPENING SCENARIO

Susan pulled into her usual parking place near the HAL offices and wondered what was going on. There were emergency vehicles all over the place; fire trucks and police cars were scattered all around the office building where HAL's offices were, and there was even an ambulance waiting.

Grabbing her briefcase and jacket, she walked quickly to the fire department command truck and asked, "What's going on?"

The fireman who seemed to be in charge asked, "Who might you be?"

"Susan Carter, I am the third-shift IT supervisor at HAL, on the third floor, in the data center."

"Not tonight," he said. "There's a major structural fire underway in this building. We have begun getting it under control, and everyone is out of the structure. No one was injured. There were only a few of your second-shift staff inside. But no one is going into the structure at this time. It will be at least noon before the inspectors are done and you can get started with your recovery."

"OK," she said. She walked to the ambulance where the paramedics were looking over the second shift from the HAL data center. She saw the second-shift supervisor breathing from an oxygen mask. Now that she had quickly appraised the situation, she turned back toward her car. Once she sat down in her car, she pulled out her company cell phone and hit the speed dial for her boss, Amanda Wilson.

"Hello," said a voice, clearly awakening from a deep sleep.

"Amanda? Susan Carter here. I am just getting to work, and there is a huge fire in the building. I think we have a disaster on our hands. Everyone is out safely and it seems no one took any lasting harm. But the offices are in a bad state."

continued

"Oh, no! Good that everyone is okay. Do you think the on-site backups are going to be usable?" asked Amanda.

"I wouldn't bet on it," said Susan.

"OK," said Amanda. She pondered just a moment, and then said to Susan, "Declare a disaster and activate recovery plan D and continuity plan A immediately. I will be there in 20 minutes."

Susan called the HAL automated phone system, knowing it was located off site at a secure service provider's location. When the HAL greeting started, she authenticated herself. She then recorded a brief message outlining the disaster that had befallen HAL, and which disaster and continuity plans were to be followed. When she finished the message, she confirmed that the alert roster was to be processed with the message she had just recorded. She knew that everyone who needed to know about this catastrophe would be called in the next few minutes. The system would keep trying each person at each of their possible phone numbers until they were reached.

Susan next pulled out her laptop and slid in the CD with all HAL incident, disaster, and continuity plans. She quickly pulled up her master planning document, selected the disaster recovery plan, clicked option D, and began to read. She reached for her phone to make the next call.

Questions for Discussion:

- Whom do you think Susan will call next according to her plan?
- What is the first priority for Susan in the next 30 minutes?

LEARNING OBJECTIVES

Upon completion of this material, you should be able to:

- Understand the key challenges an organization faces when engaged in disaster recovery operations
- Know what actions organizations take to prepare for the activation of the DR plan
- Recognize what critical elements compose the response phase of the DR plan
- Know what occurs in the recovery phase of the DR plan
- Understand how an organization uses the resumption phase of the DR plan
- Know how an organization resumes normal operations using the restoration phase of the DR plan

INTRODUCTION

An organization should operate on the premise that it is only a matter of time until a disaster strikes. Only through meticulous preparation and ongoing diligence can an organization properly respond when a disaster occurs. An organization that plans to succeed beyond its next disaster reacts quickly and decisively, to restore operations at its primary locations. When that is not possible, or in the event of a total loss, an organization must be prepared to promptly reestablish operations at a new permanent location.

NOTE

Because the plans and procedures used for disaster recovery are very similar to those undertaken for incident response as well as business continuity actions, many parts of the text in this chapter will seem very similar to the information found in Chapter 3. An organization can interchangeably use many of the approaches discussed across all of the areas within business resumption planning: incident response, disaster recovery, and business continuity planning.

FACING KEY CHALLENGES

Part of the challenge with disaster planning is that disasters are not confined to the IT Department, nor are they limited to the assets of an organization. Frequently, when a disaster occurs, it is widespread enough to affect departments and various levels of authority in an organization, affect the community that encompasses the organization, and perhaps affect vendors and suppliers. It is inconvenient when an organization loses its electrical power, but it can be even worse when an entire neighborhood or city goes dark, because lives and property may be at stake. It is important to realize that in the midst of reestablishing operations, there may be ongoing challenges associated with local emergency services, service providers, and nonbusiness issues. The following areas are likely to be affected:

- *Basic emergency and transportation services: Routine calls for service may not be answered, and the agencies' priorities can likely involve life-threatening or life-saving situations only.*
- *Food and survival supplies: Deliveries to food stores and hospitals may be interrupted or hijacked. Citizens may immediately begin stockpiling their own reserves (emptying stores).*
- *Water supplies and sanitation: Water and sewer pipes may break, crack, or clog, thus reducing or eliminating water flow.*
- *Electrical power: Power lines may be destroyed, overloaded, or collapse, rendering electricity-dependent devices unusable.*
- *Products and services delivered by vendors and service providers: The geographical area affected may be closed to outside traffic, or the vendors may be too busy answering other calls for service.*
- *Telecommunications services (both land line and cellular): Telephone trunks and switching stations can become overloaded by people trying to call into or out of the affected area.*
- *Transportation services: Freeways, highways, and surface streets can become gridlocked.*[1]

A seemingly routine event can quickly spin out of control, creating a *worst-case scenario*. This is when a situation results in service disruptions for weeks or months, requiring a government to declare a state of emergency. In dire circumstances, local or national government could declare martial law to prevent or combat social disorder. Even if people are not confined to their homes, only some of an organization's employees may be available for work.

Fortunately, most disasters are short lived, lasting only hours or a few days. Even the worst winter storms tend to clear up within a week. Whether employees are at work or home, a disaster recovery (DR) plan should be prepared to deal with whatever contingencies arise and for a range of duration.

Depending on the scope of the disaster, implementing the DR plan typically involves the following five phases, which may or may not overlap with the business continuity plan (discussed in Chapter 9):

- Preparation: The planning and rehearsal necessary to respond to a disaster
- Response: The identification of a disaster, notification of appropriate individuals, and immediate reaction to the natural disaster
- Recovery: The recovery of necessary business information and systems
- Resumption: The restoration of critical business functions
- Restoration: The reestablishment of operations at the primary site, as it was before the disaster

PREPARATION: TRAINING THE DR TEAM AND THE USERS

Aside from the planning requirements discussed in Chapter 7, there is a great deal of effort and work to be done in preparing for disasters. Note that in disaster recovery planning there is no prevention phase, unlike incident response planning. This is because the vast majority of disasters cannot be prevented. Organizations should take whatever steps possible to minimize losses by preparing for those events that cannot be prevented. No organization can reduce the probability of being in the zone of destruction from an earthquake, but they can be prepared to deal with the aftermath in the most expeditious and least disruptive ways possible. Consider the following examples:

- An organization that has an office in Los Angeles, California, should prepare for the probability of earthquakes.
- An organization that has an office in Tulsa, Oklahoma, should prepare for tornadoes.
- An organization that has an office in Miami, Florida, should prepare for hurricanes.
- Organizations that have offices in certain areas of Alaska, Hawaii, or Washington state should prepare for volcanoes.
- Organizations that have a substantial Internet presence should prepare for electronic disasters, such as massive denial-of-service attacks.

Preparation means making an organization ready for possible contingencies that escalate to disaster. Earlier, Chapter 2 described the development of the business impact analysis, one of the first steps in preparation. Chapter 7 described the organizing and staffing of the various teams necessary to assist in disaster recovery. In Chapter 7, the text described the development of the DR plan, which is the essential plan to focus disaster recovery efforts should a disaster strike. One of the last tasks necessary to prepare for a disaster is to train the various stakeholders and then practice the plan.

Throughout the rest of this chapter, the case of the HAL company will be used to illustrate how an organization might experience the unfolding of a disaster and use its DR plans. As you may remember from earlier chapters, HAL has been preparing for disasters such as the one depicted in the opening scenario. The examples that follow, set off from the text in a box, show how HAL copes with the disaster that began in the chapter's opening scenario.

ONGOING CASE: HAL PREPARATIONS FOR CONTINGENCY PLANNING

Juan reviewed his notes again. The first item on the list was checked off—designation of the appropriate Disaster Recovery Plan. The rest of the items on the list were still blank.

Two years ago, HAL began a major organization-wide effort to implement contingency planning. While Amanda is primarily responsible for the incident response plan development, she has appointed William Freund, manager of systems as the lead for the incident response team. Paul was tasked with serving as a consultant for all three teams (incident response, disaster recovery, and business continuity) to assist in their development and implementation. The disaster recovery and business continuity teams are the responsibility of the chief operations officer, Robert Xavier, who appointed Susan Carter as lead for the disaster recovery team and Juan Vasquez as lead for the business continuity team. The teams were formed under their leadership, and planning documents were created as described in earlier chapters.

The preparation phase is a continuous one. However, other phases are activated by triggers (described in previous chapters), which can originate from a number of sources, including the following:

- Management notification: If management has been keeping track of an imminent disaster, they may choose to implement the DR plan before the disaster actually occurs in order to move their employees out of harm's way or to move them to areas of increased safety and security. This is common when natural disasters, such as hurricanes, tornadoes, and wildfires, build and threaten large areas.
- Employee notification: As described in the opening scenario, an employee may come across the disaster, or the disaster may occur in the area in which an employee is working. If a fire were to break out during the work day, or if an employee came to work to find evidence of a disaster, this is the most likely source.
- Emergency management notification: Organizations such as the Federal Emergency Management Agency (FEMA) or state equivalents such as Georgia EMA (GEMA), the Centers for Disease Control and Prevention, or other state or federal agencies may notify individual organizations or entire areas of imminent or ongoing disaster.

- Local emergency services: Local fire departments, police departments, or medical personnel may provide information that allows the organization to react to imminent or ongoing disasters. With the ongoing emphasis from the Department of Homeland Security, even local communities are beginning to establish disaster management programs.
- Media outlets: Depending on the circumstances and the organization's policy on press and public relations, official statements should be carefully coordinated.

Disaster Recovery Planning as Preparation

Developing an effective DR plan is the cornerstone of preparation for the organization. A quick review of the objectives of DR plan reveals that the three primary goals are the following:

1. Eliminate or reduce the potential for injuries or the loss of human life, damage to facilities, and loss of assets and records. A comprehensive assessment of each department within the institution is required to ensure that appropriate steps have been taken to:
   - Minimize disruptions of services to the institution and its customers.
   - Minimize financial loss.
   - Provide for a timely resumption of operations in case of a disaster.
   - Reduce or limit exposure to potential liability claims filed against the institution and its directors, officers, and other personnel.
2. Immediately invoke the emergency provisions of the disaster recovery plan to stabilize the effects of the disaster, allowing for appropriate assessment and the beginning of recovery efforts. Staff and other resources then minimize the effects of the disaster and provide for the fastest possible recovery.
3. Implement the procedures contained in the disaster recovery plan according to the type and impact of the disaster. When implementing these procedures, all recovery efforts must be prioritized as follows:
   - Employees: Not only must we help to ensure their survival as a basic human concern, but also because of their anticipated performance in helping other persons on the organization's premises when the disaster strikes.
   - Customers: As is done with employees, the organization must help to ensure the survival of or care for customers affected by the disaster: physically, mentally, emotionally, and financially.
   - Facilities: After ensuring the safety of employees and customers, each facility is secured as shelter both for people and for assets.
   - Assets: Conducting a damage assessment determines which assets have been destroyed, which ones are at risk, and what resources are left.
   - Records: Documenting the disaster and the actions taken by the organization's personnel—when combined with comprehensive videotapes of facilities that are obtained during routine facility inspections—reduce the likelihood of legal actions, while helping to assess the responsibility for losses.

To plan for disaster, the CP team engages in scenario development and impact analysis, and thus categorizes the level of threat each potential disaster poses. When generating a disaster recovery scenario, an organization starts first with the most important asset—people. Are the human resources with the appropriate organizational knowledge available to restore business operations? Cross-training employees ensures that operations and a sense of normalcy can be restored as quickly as possible. In addition, the DR plan must be tested regularly so that the DR team can lead the recovery effort quickly and efficiently.

Key Features of the DR Plan

The key points the CP team must build into the DR plan include: the clear delegation of roles and responsibilities; the execution of the alert roster and notification of key personnel; the use of employee check-in systems; the clear establishment and communication of business resumption priorities; the complete and timely documentation of the disaster; and preparations for alternative implementations. Each of these is discussed in the sections that follow.

Everyone assigned to the DR team should be aware of his or her duties during a disaster. Some may be responsible for coordinating with local services, such as fire, police, and medical care. Some may be responsible for the evacuation of personnel, if required. Others may be tasked to simply pack up and leave.

Key personnel may include external groups such as the fire, police, or medical services mentioned earlier, as well as insurance agencies, disaster teams like the Red Cross, and other specialized management teams within the organization.

Organizations should make provisions for manual or automated procedures to verify the status of those employees, contractors, and consultants that are affected by a disaster.

During a disaster response, the first priority is always the preservation of human life. Data and systems protection is subordinate when the disaster threatens the lives, health, or welfare of the employees or members of the community. Only after all employees and neighbors have been safeguarded can the disaster recovery team attend to other protecting organizational assets.

Just as in an incident response, the disaster must be carefully recorded from the onset. The documentation is used later to determine how and why the disaster occurred.

Mitigation of impact is the inclusion of action steps to minimize the disaster-associated damage on the operations of the organization. The DR plan should specify the responsibilities of each DR team member, such as the evacuation of physical assets or making sure all systems are securely shut down to prevent further loss of data.

Plans should include alternative implementations for the various systems components should primary versions be unavailable. This includes standby equipment, either purchased, leased, or under contract with a disaster recovery service agency. Developing systems with excess capacity, fault tolerance, auto recovery, and fail-safe features facilitates a quick recovery. Something as simple as using Dynamic Host Control Protocol (DHCP) to assign network addresses instead of using static addresses allows systems to quickly and easily regain connectivity without technical support. Networks should support dynamic reconfiguration; restoration of network connectivity should be planned. Data recovery requires effective backup strategies and flexible hardware configurations. System management should be a top priority. All solutions should be tightly integrated and developed in a strategic plan to provide continuity. Piecemeal construction can result in another disaster if incompatible systems are thrust together.

Additional Preparations

As part of DR readiness, each employee should have two types of emergency information in his or her possession at all times. The first is personal emergency information—whom to notify in case of an emergency (next of kin), medical conditions, and a form of photo identification. The second is a set of instructions on what to do in the event of an emergency. This snapshot of the DR plan should contain a contact number or hotline for calling the organization during an emergency, emergency services numbers (fire, police, medical), evacuation and assembly locations (storm shelters, for example), the name and number of the disaster recovery coordinator, and any other needed information. This information is often encapsulated into a wallet-sized, laminated card for convenience and portability.

The DR plan must also include references to another process that many organizations plan for separately—crisis management. These are the action steps taken during and after a disaster. **Crisis management** is a set of focused steps that deal primarily with the safety and state of the people from the organization who are involved in the disaster. The DR team works closely with the crisis management team to assure complete and timely communication during a disaster. Crisis management is covered in additional detail in Chapter 11.

DR Training and Awareness

As described in Chapter 3, training all of the people who have an interest in the disaster planning process involves a number of different approaches, as presented in the following sections. Training focuses on the particular roles each individual is expected to execute during an actual disaster. For most employees, disaster preparation is limited to awareness training, conducted as part of an annual or semiannual security education, training, and awareness (SETA) program for all employees. During this session, employees are made aware of general procedures for responding to disasters, including the use of the alert roster, described in the following section.

General Training for All Teams

An important note to keep in mind is that for most teams, the best training is to be well prepared to do their normal jobs. It is unusual for the organization to assign someone to a team—like the networking team—who does not have a background or responsibilities in that area. It is possible, should the organization be shorthanded, but in general the IT staff is assigned to jobs within their normal job description. It is also important to note that these individual may be a bit rusty in certain tasks and technical skills. Some managers may not have installed or configured a server or networking device in some time and may require assistance. Therefore, the training and rehearsals should be able to identify those individuals with less-than-ideal technical skills and provide them with the opportunity to brush up on their responsibilities when a disaster occurs. Note that not all systems may be recovered during the disaster; the priorities are established during the business impact analysis (BIA).

Another normal business function that can assist disaster recovery efforts is job rotation. The routine cross-training of all employees for at least one other job, both vertically (as in prepare to do your boss's job) and horizontally (as in prepare to do your colleague's job) prepares the organization to handle normal personnel shortages or outages (maternity and paternity leave, sick days, injuries, vacations, conferences, training programs, and so on). If all positions have at least two employees prepared to perform them, preparing for a disaster is that much easier.

One area of operations not commonly covered in training in the civilian sector is the operations under adverse conditions, or **degraded mode**. Military personnel spend far more hours working in less-than-ideal circumstances than under optimal conditions. When training, periodically try this variation, including loss of power or lighting, loss of communications (phone or network), and so on to see how employees can adapt to these conditions. During a disaster, it is much more likely that some but not all utilities will be available. Training for each specialization team consists of tasks unique to their responsibilities, as described in the next 12 sections.

Disaster Management Team Training

This is the command and control group responsible for all planning and coordination activities. Training, rehearsal, and testing for the management team is predominantly communicative in nature. This team must be able to quickly and effectively communicate the resources they need for their subordinate teams to function. It must also be able to communicate the directions from the higher teams (the CP management team) and peer teams (the IR and BC management teams).

Communications Team Training

This is the information dissemination group responsible for interacting and communicating with the external environments. The communications team trains by preparing information notices, news releases, and internal memorandums and directives to provide information to all groups and teams as to what their current tasks and responsibilities are. Because the members of this group may also be responsible for the alert system, they should be involved in the routine rehearsal and testing of that system to better prepare them to handle information requests from employees during actual disasters.

Computer Recovery (Hardware) Team Training

This is the hardware recovery and reconstitution team. Ideally, this team practices and trains during normal operations. However, in normal business operations, if a computer sustains even minor damage, the organization may simply opt to replace it rather than rebuild. This team requires advanced training to rebuild systems by scavenging parts from a number of damaged systems to get as many systems as possible up and running as quickly as possible. Training should also include how to deal with systems damaged by water, heat, and dust. This team should work closely with the other technology teams (OS, applications, network, and data) in their preparation. If systems are not too badly damaged, a local repair facility like the one shown in Figure 8-1 may come into play.

FIGURE 8-1 Computer repair bench

Systems Recovery Team Training

This is the team responsible for recovering and reestablishing operating systems (OSs). Just as with the hardware team, the OS team may rehearse their disaster recovery duties during normal operations. Their disaster recovery training most likely consists of being able to quickly recover a system's operating system in preparation for reinstallation of applications and data. The responsibilities of this team may likely be combined with those of the other IT teams. However, if the organization stores its OS, applications, and data separately, each requires at least one individual responsible for acquiring the archived copy and reestablishing each information asset to a usable state.

Network Recovery Team Training

This is the team responsible for reestablishing connectivity between systems and to the Internet (if applicable). Network recovery teams may be used to replacing downed systems, but it is unlikely that they have experience in physically repairing damaged systems. Therefore, much of their disaster recovery operations training should focus on establishing ad hoc networks quickly but securely. The most convenient networking tools available today are wireless networks—encrypted, of course. This team then needs training on quickly converting recovered systems to wireless operations, installing and configuring wireless access points, and securely distributing connection information to all users who need to connect. The team leader for the networking team should have a "stash" of wireless networking components stored outside the organization that can be quickly relocated to the organization to assist in recovering internal connectivity. Internet connectivity may be much more difficult, and interaction with the vendor through the vendor team and/or the communications team may be necessary. With the increase in popularity in wireless Internet connectivity (that is, WiMAX) the organization may want to contract for any services that are available in the area as a contingency plan that can be scaled up when needed. This team also requires training in the use and implementation of this technology.

It may also fall to this team to establish voice communication networks during a disaster. Should some or all employees be issued mobile phones, a directory of the numbers can serve in this capacity should the need arise. In the event that local circuits are affected, short-range FM radios (walkie-talkies) or even satellite phones should be stored for distribution when needed. The teams need to provide training on the use and implementation of this technology as well.

Storage Recovery Team Training

This team is responsible for the recovery of information and the reestablishment of operations in storage area networks or network attached storage. This team, like the hardware team, may need training in rebuilding damaged systems. Their function may in fact be subsumed in that team's responsibilities or those of the networking team. This team needs training in recovering data from off site, along with the data management team. A photo of a fixed-media drive damaged by a head crash, as shown by the scarred disk surfaces, is shown in Figure 8-2.

FIGURE 8-2 Damaged hard drive

Applications Recovery Team Training

This is the team responsible for recovering and reestablishing operations of critical business applications. Like the others, it consists of skills performed during normal operations, but requires coordination and training in doing so under adverse circumstances. This team will almost certainly have user representation, and the effectiveness of the team is heavily influenced by the ability to create an effective liaison with the business units that use the application.

Data Management Team Training

This is the team primarily responsible for data restoration and recovery. Their training correspondingly focuses on quick and accurate restoration of data from backup. It should also include the recovery of data from damaged systems. It may be necessary to recover transactional information recorded on local systems since the last routing backup, and therefore it is useful to have the ability to extract information from systems with some damage. For severely damaged systems, there are organizations capable of extracting data from all but the most catastrophically damaged systems, but these services are not inexpensive. Even the relatively durable optical media formats are not invulnerable. An example of a CD damaged by excessive heat, as shown by the cracking of the silver data layer, is shown in Figure 8-3.

FIGURE 8-3 Damaged optical media

Vendor Contact Team Training

This team is responsible for working with suppliers and vendors to replace damaged or destroyed equipment or services, as determined by the other teams. Training is best obtained through normal work in equipment procurement, whether as an IT employee or as a professional purchasing agent. This team should contain representatives from both groups if possible. Training should focus on methods of obtaining resources as quickly as possible, as well as a familiarity of the preferred vendors for each piece of equipment and type of services. Should these be unavailable, the individual team members should be trained in methods of obtaining comparable products from other vendors. Vendor relationships are crucial during a disaster. A poor relationship, or a questionable supplier, may result in hardships such as expensive or unavailable replacements.

Damage Assessment and Salvage Team Training

This team is perhaps the most unique of all with regard to disaster recovery skills and training. This team is responsible for providing the initial assessments of the extent of damage to equipment and systems on site and/or for physically recovering equipment to be transported to a location where the other teams can evaluate it. The basic background for an individual responsible for this duty falls under the umbrella of hardware repair. Individuals who have worked repairing computers for the general public (that is, technical support in a large retail chain) most likely have seen many of the problems they will encounter in disaster recovery activities, such as water and physical damage. The average organization may not have damage assessment and salvage expertise on staff, and may thus have to outsource it. There are programs available to professionally trained individuals for conducting salvage and assessment of technology systems.

Business Interface Team Training

This team is responsible for working with the remainder of the organization to assist in the recovery of nontechnology functions. As another communications function, the training of this team could combine technical and nontechnical functions to ensure that the technology needs of the business groups are met. Training involves interfacing with the various business groups to determine their routine needs. Representatives from the help desk may be well suited for this team.

Logistics Team Training

This team is responsible for providing any needed supplies, space, materials, food, services, or facilities needed at the primary site—other than vendor-acquired technology and other materiel obtained by the vendor team. Individuals may simply need basic training in local purchasing to serve on this team, because they serve as health, welfare, and moral support for the other teams doing their jobs. Simply being ready to prepare and provide meals, a rest area, and someone to talk to may be the best qualifications.

The HAL DR team has been prepared for their role in any disaster with specific forms of training. The structure and preparation of the HAL teams is discussed in the following example.

ONGOING CASE: HAL PREPARATIONS IN TEAM ORGANIZATION

Due to the size of the organization, HAL has chosen to organize its DR teams based on the following structure:

Management and Communications Team

The management and communications team is responsible for the planning, implementation, and activation of the DR plan. During an actual emergency, this team, consisting of three managers (including the team lead), coordinates all recovery operations. This is done once the site has been released by any emergency personnel present (fire, police, medical, and so on). Part of this team includes two individuals responsible for handling all communications to subordinate teams, the media, management, and any stakeholders who need to be informed of the situation. In the disaster HAL is facing from the fire in the opening scenario, the disaster management team is William Freund, Susan Carter, and Edward Michaels. At HAL, this happened to be the first-, second-, and third-shift data center supervisors. William will act as the primary disaster manager once he reports to the scene to relieve Susan.

Damage Assessment and Salvage Team

This team consists of two individuals from the hardware group at HAL who will quickly determine whether any equipment that remains after the disaster is salvageable. Their job is to, within four hours, identify what equipment needs immediate replacement and what equipment is still in working order. They are under standing orders to replace first, rebuild later, as some damage may not be detectable for some time.

Hardware and Networking Team

The hardware team is responsible for all devices and communications circuits within HAL. The team consists of three subgroups with two people in each group: one focused on servers, one on network devices, and one focused on cabling. HAL has service agreements with all vendors from which it leases its equipment that allow 24-hour replacement of all equipment that is stolen, damaged, or destroyed. Cabling, on the other hand, requires physical reinstallation. The cabling group will coordinate with a local installation company that has guaranteed 24–48 hour response. In the meantime, an off-site cache of wireless equipment will allow connectivity as soon as the Internet connection is reestablished. A partnership agreement with other businesses in the neighborhood allows temporary use of their connectivity for internal on-site operations, until the primary circuit is back up.

Software and Data Team

The software and data team assume the responsibilities of the operating systems, applications, and data management teams as described earlier. This team is responsible for recovering all software-based information assets as needed after a disaster. Based on HAL's data backup and recovery plans, the operating systems, applications, and data are all backed up weekly, with daily differential data backups. The transaction journals and change management documents are stored online in a secured account, allowing recovery of all information to within four hours of the disaster.

continued

DR Plan Testing and Rehearsal

In practice, the testing of DR plan elements, and the training and rehearsal of the plans can be overlapped. In the strictest sense, an organization rehearses when they simply practice the steps to be performed during a disaster—like a fire drill. Testing, on the other hand, involves assessment, whether internal or external. Internal testing can include employees conducting self-assessments after an exercise by completing feedback surveys indicating what they thought worked well and what didn't. Other methods include peer evaluations and formally appointing internal assessors, who evaluate performance by drafting formal reports for each department or division manager. External testing can come from standardization boards or consultants (for example, ISO 9000), certification or accreditation groups, or a group selected by the organization's management from a sister company. The U.S. Army conducts large-scale unit assessments called ARTEPs (Army Readiness Testing and Evaluation Program) to determine how ready the organization is to deal with various mission-critical tasks.

Ideally, employees should receive classroom-style, structured training before they are expected to perform in a large-scale exercise. Jumping straight into large-scale rehearsals or testing can cause more problems than it solves. Although it is beneficial for an employee to see what a large-scale disaster reaction looks like (based on the axiom that "sweating in training can prevent bleeding in combat"), it will only be confusing rather than educational if the employees are not prepared for it. Rehearsing the plan should start small and escalate to larger-scale exercises. Many organizations never test and rehearse beyond the desk check or structured walk-through, and though some rehearsal is better than none, the further along this scale of rehearsal and testing the organization can progress, the better off they are when an actual disaster occurs.

Because disaster recovery uses the same basic types of rehearsal and testing types as described for incident response, in some cases the following sections repeat information found in Chapter 3. An organization can interchangeably use these strategies in both disaster recovery and incident response:

- DR plan desk check: Involves providing copies of the DR plan to all teams and team members for review. Again, although the desk check is not a true test, it is a good way to review the perceived feasibility and effectiveness of the plan.
- DR plan structured walk-through: All involved individuals walk through the steps they would take during an actual disaster, either on site or as a conference room discussion.

- DR plan simulation: Each involved individual or team works independently, rather than in conference, simulating the performance of each task, stopping short of the actual physical tasks required, such as restoring the backup or rebuilding a particular server or communications device.
- DR plan parallel testing: Individuals or teams act as if an actual disaster occurred, performing their required tasks and executing the necessary procedures, without interfering with the normal operations of the business. Due to the catastrophic nature of disasters, this type of testing is not as popular in disaster recovery rehearsal and testing as it is in IR. If an individual is responding to an incident, they may be expected to handle the incident while continuing normal work. During a disaster, however, individuals will most likely suspend normal operations until their business function is reestablished or reconstituted either at the primary location or at an alternate site as part of the business continuity operations.
- DR plan full-interruption: The individuals follow each and every procedure, including the interruption of service, restoration of data from backups, and notification of appropriate individuals. It is not uncommon to see state and local agencies requesting the assistance of organizations to prepare their disaster teams for disasters such as chemical contamination, biological warfare, or nuclear emergencies. Even so, the probability that an organization is mature enough in their rehearsal and testing methodology to attempt full-interruption exercises is quite slim.
- DR plan War Gaming: Unlike the IT community's fascination with IR war gaming, as described in Chapter 3, there are few venues for disaster recovery war gaming. As such there is little work in this arena. Some state and federal agencies do host inter- and intra-agency exercises that allow representative and liaison officers to work together on state and national emergencies. However, there is little effort or interest with organizations in this area. The exception lies in the larger corporations that are part of the national infrastructure—power, gas, communications, and other vital service providers. Their war gaming falls under the realm of state- and federal-mandated emergency readiness to prepare for terrorists strikes, rather than a corporate effort to maintain business functions for continuity of the organization.

The following example describes how HAL has done a little work in preparing its staff for using the disaster plan.

Rehearsal and Testing of the Alert Roster

One last area of rehearsal and testing is the use of an alert roster. As described in Chapter 3, this is also used in the IR plan, BC plan, and during crisis management. Contact information on the individuals to be notified in the event of an actual incident or disaster is contained in an alert roster document. The alert roster must be tested more frequently than other components of the plans because it is the area subject to change due to employee turnover. In the active military, National Guard and reserves, and in many corporate settings, alert rosters are tested at least quarterly. The two activation methods discussed in Chapter 3, *sequential* and *hierarchical*, are selected based on the organization's preferences and organizational structure. For smaller, more informal organizations, the sequential roster, which requires that a contact person call each and every person on the roster, may be preferred. For larger, more formal organizations, the hierarchical roster, which requires that the first person call other designated people on the roster, who in turn call other designated people, and so on, may be more appropriate. For example, the CEO may call the members of the executive team, who then in turn each call their senior managers, who then contact their individual employees or subordinate managers. This would make the alert process closely follow the organization chart. In either, it is important to ensure that the alert message is properly formed and distributed. In this case, the **alert message** is a scripted description of the *disaster* and consists of just enough information so that each responder knows what portion of the *DR plan* to implement without impeding the notification process. Unlike the IR plan alert roster, the DR plan roster must have a mechanism to contact everyone in the organization, especially if part of the message is "don't report to work today, but call this number for more information."

Some organizations can make use of an **auxiliary phone alert and reporting system**. As was illustrated in the opening scenario of this chapter, this type of system can be used both to distribute information about the disaster and to collect information about the status of the employees. It can also greatly streamline the process and complete it in much shorter elapsed time than a manual alert system.

A related usage of telecommunications technology is the "I'm OK" automated emergency response line. This service allows employees, when notified of a disaster, either by the alert system or through the public media, to call a predetermined number. Some organizations have their employees put this information on a card in their wallet or purse. Employees report their status by entering their employee number into an automated system, and then obtain information as to whether or not they should show up for work and where. This system is also extremely useful for efforts, where critical individuals, who may not be at their home and thus out of reach through normal alert procedures, can be informed that they are needed at an alternate location.

Once all employees have been trained (or made aware), have rehearsed, and have been tested on their DR responsibilities, they should be ready for implementation during an actual disaster. Be cognizant of the fact that no matter how prepared you think you are for a particular disaster, you really aren't. The key skills to retain from the rehearsals are flexibility, decisive decision making, and professionalism.

In the following example, HAL's approach to notification is described.

ONGOING CASE: HAL PREPARATIONS IN NOTIFICATION SYSTEMS

Many organizations are turning to the new automated reporting and notification systems, as described in the opening scenario. These systems allow remote entry of notification messages, and automated notifications, eliminating the need for sequential or hierarchical manual notification. This does not eliminate the need to make sure that everyone is notified;, spot checks should be done to make sure everyone received the message.

Two hours later, JJ pulled into the HAL parking lot.

Susan was in the parking lot. She knocked on his window. "Didn't you get the message? No one is to show up for work until notified."

"Sorry," JJ replied as he got out of his car. "I wasn't home. I was visiting a... friend." JJ looked sheepish.

"I'll be glad when the new cell phones get in," Susan said. "Then we can add those numbers to the alert system. We've had about 75% success with the automated notification, but with vacations, visits to relatives, and... friends, we're just not catching everyone. The new phones should allow us to do that."

"If everyone keeps them turned on and charged," JJ said, grinning.

"Okay, okay, so I let the battery die once—once!" Susan grinned back.

DISASTER RESPONSE PHASE

Once a source has indicated the presence or threat of a disaster, the organization initiates the DR plan and begins the next phase, the response phase. The **response phase** is the phase associated with implementing the reaction to a disaster facing the organization and is focused on those actions designed to control or stabilize the situation, if that is possible. The response phase is designed to:

- Protect human life and well-being (physical safety)
- Attempt to limit and contain the damage to the organization's facilities and equipment
- Manage communications with employees and other stakeholders.

The response phase involves activating the disaster recovery plan and following the steps outlined therein. Organizations without such a plan will find themselves attempting to perform these steps ad hoc, in the midst of the disaster. The diversity of possible disasters, and, thus, plans reacting to them, can result in disparate responses, so preparation for one type of disaster alone, such as fire, proves a less-than-sufficient reaction to other disasters, such as hurricanes or tornados.

HAL's initial response to the disaster declaration is described in the following example.

ONGOING CASE: HAL DISASTER RESPONSE

As described in the opening scenario, HAL's management has chosen to implement a pre-defined response, Plan D. In HAL's disaster recovery plan, disasters are prioritized according to a value based on probability of occurrence and potential damage. Given HAL's geographic location and industry, the top five disasters and the corresponding DR plans are as follows:

A. Regional service outage (power or Internet)
B. Massive malware attack
C. Massive denial-of-service attack
D. Fire
E. Storm (hurricane, tornado, and associated flooding)

Although the local electrical service provider does an admirable job, power outages do occur, and given HAL's electronic revenue stream, extended outages could be serious. The same goes for HAL's Internet connection, because a good piece of HAL's revenue comes from hosted Web presences. Recent upgrades in redundant backbones throughout Georgia made such a loss of service less probable, but still the most costly disasters can come from long-term outages.

Susan quickly reread the checklist. Even though she knew it by heart, she knew she could not afford to make a mistake. She quickly called the four DR team leaders and asked them to meet her in the coffee shop across the street from HAL. The coffee shop occupied the first floor of a building, but the second floor was vacant. The owner had agreed to allow HAL to use the empty space as a command center, should such a need arise. A conference table and chairs were all that occupied the vacant loft. Susan connected her laptop to the coffee shop's wireless network, another perk of the coffee house, confident in her system's VPN, firewall, and antivirus protection. As she sipped one of many cups of coffee to follow, she quickly laid out a plan of attack for the teams, based on Plan D. They, like she, were very familiar with the scenario, one of Paul's favorites during the simulations. She breathed a quiet thank you for the time and effort Paul had put into those drills. The plan was very straightforward.

continued

Once the fire department released the building, and provided the structure was still sound, the damage control team would swing into action and determine the extent of the damage to the data center. Offices would have to wait. The second-floor data center was build to handle moderate fires, as well as floods, but you never knew how bad the damage was until you surveyed it. And judging from the flames that came out of the third-floor offices, it could be very bad.

As the team leaders came in, Susan briefed them on their duties. Everyone except the damage and salvage team would have to wait. Tim Wilcox had his team ready to go downstairs. He compared Susan's checklist with his own, and nodded.

"The fire inspector was just here. He said there's no major structural damage, but there's plenty of fire, water, and smoke damage on the first and third floors," Susan reported. "Apparently some bad wiring on the first floor caused the fire, and it ran up the wall to the second and third floor. He also stated it appeared the fire-suppression system on the second floor helped contain the damage there, but there was some water damage from the third-floor sprinklers and fire department hoses."

Over the next two hours, Tim and his team crawled through the muck and soot that used to be HAL's offices. The report on the data center was promising—minor water damage to exposed systems. Apparently at least two of the open racks—legacies from early budget cycles—allowed the water to saturate active servers. Those in closed cabinets appeared fine. At least one networking closet was also soaked, because the sprinkler head had not been disconnected when the closet was converted from storage, in spite of the clear specification to the general contractor.

Tim reported his findings to Susan. She nodded with each item. "So it is bad, but not catastrophic," she stated.

"Correct," Tim said. "The data center needs a good 24-hour cleanup, and then it can go online again, but the third-floor executive offices are toasted. The floor needs to be gutted and rebuilt. First floor has one damaged office, but apparently the fire ran up the wiring and didn't spread much on the floor."

Next, the hardware teams went in. They pulled all questionable systems from the open racks and networking closet. Across the street, the logistics/vendor team placed orders with the key vendors. The vendor assured them that they would have their replacement equipment overnight.

RECOVERY PHASE

The third phase of disaster recovery, or rather the second phase of the implemented disaster plan, is the recovery phase. During the **recovery phase**, the organization begins the recovery of the most time-critical business functions—those necessary to reestablish business operations and prevent further economic and image loss to the organization. The focus of this phase is to get back up and running as quickly as possible, even if the operations are limited to some degree. As part of the recovery phase, the organization determines whether or not to activate the Business Continuity Plan, unless this decision has been already been made, as described in the opening scenario. In most circumstances, an organization needs to perform an assessment of the situation before deciding to relocate key functions.

Once in a while, everyone gets a little luck. In the following example, the HAL company finds out that even good planning for disasters can be assisted with good fortune.

ONGOING CASE: HAL'S RECOVERY PART I

"That's right, sir. The data center will not require relocation, just the administrative offices on the third floor," Susan said, as she reported the damage to Robert. Although concerned over the losses to the administrative offices, he was very pleased to hear that the damage to the data center, the heart of HAL's operations, was minimal.

"I expect we need between four and six servers, three 24-port switches, and several thousand feet of wiring to get the data center back up and running," she continued. "We also need to replace all open racks with enclosed cabinets, something we should have done months ago."

"I agree," said Robert. "You have the emergency P-Card, authorize the purchases, and let's get back up and running. Let me know if you have any, and I mean *any* problems."

"Will do," Susan said. She held up the P-Card, a special credit card with virtually no purchasing limit. She remembered chartering an airplane in previous years, so generous was its limit.

Although in this case, it may not be needed. Every vendor contacted had offered to bill them as usual, net 30, or due in 30 days. That should be more than enough time to handle the administrative paperwork. Right now the only thing being charged was a rather large coffee bill. She wondered how Juan was doing setting up the new temporary offices down the street. Since Juan activated his BC plan, she hadn't seen him or his team.

In the recovery phase, the organization begins to recover the most critical business operations; the less-critical operations wait until the resumption phase. In most organizations, the production or service functions that generate revenue for the organization are most crucial. The primary goals associated with the recovery phase include:

- Recover critical business functions.
- Coordinate recovery efforts.
- Acquire resources to replace damaged or destroyed materials and equipment.
- Evaluate the need to implement the business continuity plan.

The steps involved in business resumption, even when the technical infrastructure is restored, can be complex and challenging. This example from HAL shows a part of that complexity.

ONGOING CASE: HAL'S RECOVERY PART II

As described, the critical functions come first.

"So the data center's operational?" Susan seemed doubtful. After all, it had only been one day since the fire ravaged the building.

continued

"Yes ma'am," JJ smiled. "Damage was less than anticipated. The new gas suppression systems worked as expected, and everyone had ample warning so no one was exposed to the control agent. The estimates Tim gave you were right on, but I think we can rebuild about half of the servers. The networking team indicates that the closet is a total loss, though. They plan to pull a cabinet from across town and have it back up by close of business tomorrow. It's not critical to the data center though; it was primarily for internal communications."

"So the Internet circuit's unharmed?" Susan knew what questions her bosses would be asking shortly, and she wanted to have all the answers. Her bosses were currently at the temporary offices a few blocks away getting set up. Juan seemed as good at business continuity as he was at his "day job."

"That's correct," JJ said. "Both redundant links were imbedded in fire-resistant material in steel conduit on opposite walls. One got a bit scorched, but the fiber optics are still transmitting. We're a go as of 3 p.m.!"

"What about other business functions?" Susan asked.

"You'll have to ask the other teams," JJ replied. "I think we're starting to transition to secondary functions about now, and the help desk should be operational on the first floor pretty soon. But all the primaries are complete—data center and Internet circuit. The secondaries—help desk, internal support, and administration—are split between the two sites, so I really don't know."

"OK, I'll make some calls," Susan noted.

RESUMPTION PHASE

Although the recovery phase focuses on critical business operations, resumption focuses on functions that are not as critical. The goals and purpose of the two phases are similar, and in most instances, the transition from one to the other is not noticeable. Organizations simply go from one task to the next on the list of operations to get back up and running. The BIA should be the guiding document in creating the list of primary, or critical, functions and secondary ones. This differs dramatically between organizations. The goals therefore are:

- Initiate implementation of secondary functions.
- Finalize implementation of primary functions.
- Identify additional needed resources.
- Continue planning for restoration.

Some of these goals are implemented according to the business continuity plan and thus are postponed until the restoration phase ends and the physical facilities have been restored at the primary site and the organization is ready to return.

The interface between DR plan and BC plan is one of the more complex and difficult to execute. The following example shows how HAL works through this topic.

"What's the status on the help desk?" Susan asked. She was speaking to Tina Witherly, the help desk manager, who eagerly awaited permission to move back in the building.

"We're still waiting on the phone company," Tina replied. "Networking is up."

All morning the phone company had been double-checking the telephone connections to the first and second floors. The third floor would have to wait until a general contractor rebuilt the internal structures.

About that time, a young man in a Telco uniform came into the coffee shop. Since things were running so smoothly, Susan had been taking her breaks in a booth of the coffee shop, rather than the conference room upstairs. It allowed her to watch the workers going in and out of the building.

"Susan Carter?" The Telco worker asked.

"Right here," Susan replied.

"First floor is completely up, and I've got most of the second floor talking, too. But there's a bad trunk running up the north wall that needs replacing, and it'll take another four to six hours to get to it. That's the wall the fire ran up, and it fried all the lines to the third floor."

"OK, but are at least some of the phones on the second floor working?" Susan asked.

"Almost all. There are about three or four boxes on the north wall that need replacing," he said.

"Great! Thanks!" Susan turned to Tina, "Go to it, and let me know how it goes."

A few hours later, Tina called Susan's cell phone. "When you get a chance, you should swing by. We're up and running, and believe it or not, our voice mail is not exploding!"

One of the worst fears after the disaster was that HAL might experience an enraged customer base with customers losing connectivity and having personal and small business Web sites offline. But apparently the news of the fire had spread. With few exceptions, customers were sympathetic and could tolerate the inconvenience, especially when the local news reported the progress of the recovery. It seemed that HAL would be able to reestablish most connections by the weekend, when most of their residential customers would need them most.

Susan was wondering how the other secondary functions were progressing, when Robert came into the coffee shop. He smiled. "Good sign," thought Susan.

"We're getting along well," Robert said, anticipating Susan's question. "What's your progress?"

"We're still in business here," she said. Over the next hour she briefed Robert on the progress in the data center and help desk. He seemed very pleased that the most critical business functions were spared the brunt of the fire. They were lucky, this time.

321

RESTORATION PHASE

In what is considered the final phase of the disaster recovery plan implementation, the organization conducts the operations necessary to rebuild the facilities and reestablish operations at "home base." Should the disaster cause more damage than is repairable at the primary site, then this phase involves the selection of a new permanent home for the organization. One must also consider that this phase may also represent the end of a business too damaged by the disaster to recover, as even "the best schemes of mice and men oft go awry." Organizations don't like to think about it, but it is a possibility.

The restoration phase formally begins once all assessments of the damage have been accomplished and the rebuilding of the primary site commences. As stated earlier, the change from the previous phases to this phase may be subtle and overlapped.

The primary goals for the restoration phase are to:

- Repair all damage to the primary site *or* select or build a replacement facility.
- Replace the damaged or destroyed contents of the primary site to include supplies, equipment, and material.
- Coordinate the relocation from temporary offices to the primary site or to a suitable new replacement facility.
- Restore normal operations at the primary site, beginning with critical functions and continuing with secondary operations.
- Stand down the DR teams and conduct the after-action review.

Repair or Replacement

There are two possibilities for organization in the restoration phase: reestablish operations at the primary site or establish operations at a new permanent site. The actions taken are obviously very different. Each option is examined in turn, in the context of HAL.

Reestablish the Primary Site

For this situation, the organization is able to rebuild the damaged facilities at the primary site. Given the probability that a disaster will not completely destroy a facility, the organization can, as the running HAL scenario has shown, continue at least partial operations at the primary site while repairs are being made. In the ongoing HAL case featured throughout the chapter, the administrative offices were the most damaged. Administrative offices are the easiest to relocate, considering the complexities of data centers, manufacturing facilities, and customer service offices. Whether or not they are damaged, it is in an organization's best interest to temporarily relocate the administrative function and provide the space to the operational functions.

Move to a New Permanent Site

- There is the distinct possibility that the disaster is so severe that the primary site becomes uninhabitable. At that point the organization is faced with two choices: bulldoze and rebuild or select a new location. If the organization has purchased the land the building is (was) on, then the first option may be the best option. The downside is that it may be months before the organization can relocate. The business continuity solution may not be feasible for such a long-term stay, and intermediate locations may be required. In this case, the organization may have to lease temporary facilities until the new building is constructed.

- In the other option, the organization may choose to select a new location. This may be necessary when the organization cannot relocate for an extended stay at temporary locations while the primary site is reconstructed, or in situations where the organization does not own the primary structure. As has been the experience of some organizations located in the South, especially around New Orleans after Hurricane Katrina, some disasters may force an organization to first temporarily, then permanently, move operations. The owning agency may not elect to rebuild in a timely manner, leaving the organization stuck in temporary facilities. It may be easier to just find a new suitable location. The downside is that if the organization has customers that visit the primary site, they will require redirection, through mailing or other means of communication. The selection of a new permanent site is a complex decision and requires a management team to identify candidate sites, coordinate on-site visits, and review the facilities before selecting a suitable replacement. Due to the scope of a disaster, permanent and temporary staff may not be available due to them having to relocate their families. One solution, using an outside contractor, is shown in the following example drawn from HAL's experience.

ONGOING CASE: HAL'S RESTORATION

Susan shook the contractor's hand. The general contractor, on agreement with HAL, had just completed his walk-through of the offices. He stated, "We can have a cleanup crew here tomorrow. It'll take about two days to gut the third floor. I'll have a framing crew in the next day, with electricians and networking by the end of the week. I can have a drywall team in first of next week. We should be able to carpet the week after, and then you're ready for furniture and moving in."

"That's great!" Susan exclaimed. "I really expected this to take months!"

"Normally it would have, but you got lucky on two counts," he grinned shyly. "First, my crews have just finished a major job, and the next won't start for three weeks, so I have to be done by then."

"And second?" Susan asked.

"And second, my daughter works in your help center."

It only took 48 hours to completely restore the data center. Most of the damage was to wiring in the walls and ceilings of the second and third floor. The Internet connection was up and running within 12 hours, thanks in no small part to a very dedicated support team.

Restoration of the Primary Site

Once the physical facilities are rebuilt, next the contents must be replaced. Office furniture, desktop computers, photocopy equipment, filing systems, office supplies, and a host of other materials must be acquired. Most offices just don't realize exactly how much "stuff" they need to run their operations.

Office supplies aside, the organization may need substantial reinvestment in office equipment. Care should be taken to determine what insurance will and will not cover, as well as examining the service contracts to determine if damage or destruction to leased equipment is covered by the provider. This atmosphere of returning to work is shown in the following example.

Relocation from Temporary Offices

As indicated earlier, the organization may have relocated to an alternate site or to temporary facilities at the primary site. The movement back to the primary site signals the beginning of the end for most members of the organization. Before the staff settles back into their offices and their normal routines, their transition must be carefully coordinated. If the organization has been operating out of the temporary facilities for an extended period of time, this may not be a simple operation. Even in short-term functions, an administrative office generates an inordinate amount of paperwork, the relocation of which inevitably gets scrambled. If data functions were relocated, the restoration of computing equipment is even more difficult, because damage to systems and components can occur in transit.

Data-management practices are even more crucial before and after moves. In some instances, it may be advantageous to have a movement coordinator to plan and coordinate the relocation of personnel, equipment, materials, and data from the alternate to the primary location. This is discussed in more detail in Chapters 9 and 10, and is described briefly in the following example.

325

Resumption at the Primary Site

As indicated earlier, the organization may not be able to reestablish critical functions on site, hence the need for a business continuity plan. If the company had been unable to reestablish on site functions, or if it had relocated the critical functions, the previous step (relocation from temporary offices) moves them back to their offices. The next challenging step is to reestablish normal operations. There may have been a number of tertiary operations and functions that were suspended while the organization worked to keep afloat at the temporary location. These day-to-day operations help to stabilize the organization and keep it running efficiently. Some of these functions could include:

- Managing employee benefit packages
- Employee training and awareness programs
- Organizational planning retreats and meetings
- Routine progress meetings and reports
- Long-term planning activities
- Research and development activities

This is not to infer that these activities are unimportant, but that in the overall scope of a disaster, these things can wait until normal operations have been reestablished.

At this point, the business itself has been reconstituted, and it is functioning as before the disaster. The only task remaining is to review what happened during the disaster and to determine how the organization handled it.

The return to normal activates is a great relief to all of the members of the organization, and HAL's staff is no exception, as shown in the following example.

Standing Down and the After-Action Review

Standing down represents the deactivation of the disaster recovery teams, releasing the individuals back to their normal duties. In an ideal situation, these individuals would have focused exclusively on their disaster recovery roles until they were released. Consider it the National Guard or Reserves model. The reality is that these employees more likely worked double duty, handling both their disaster recovery jobs and keeping an eye on their normal duties to make sure nothing suffered from their absence.

Perhaps the last formal activity the organization performs before declaring the disaster officially over is the after-action review (AAR). As described in previous chapters, the purpose of the after-action review is to provide a method for management to obtain the input and feedback from representatives from each group. Each team and subteam leader should first obtain this feedback from their team members, concerning both the specifics of this disaster and the suitability of the disaster recovery plan. This information is then compiled and combined with the official disaster log, maintained by a designated representative during the event. This official log serves both as a legal and planning record of the event and as a training tool for future team members. One of the ongoing challenges of organizational training is turnover. Eventually employees get promoted, relocated, move to different organizations, or released outright. The team that gained valuable experience during the event may not be the same team that faces the next. Thus it is important to capture as much organizational knowledge as possible about the disaster to help train the next generation.

The last step is the creation and archiving of the official report. Outcomes from the after-action review (AAR), combined with the reports of the individual teams, are combined into one document and archived for future use—as stated previously—to train current and future team members. This report may also be a legal requirement when the insurance company, Legal Department, or parent organization requires a record of what happened to ensure there was no negligence. If by chance, an individual was injured or killed during the disaster or events that followed, the legal proceedings that inevitably ensue require as much documentation as possible to determine if liability exists.

When all is said and done, the members of the teams go back to their normal jobs and, save for periodic training, put the disaster behind them as shown in the example that follows.

ONGOING CASE: HAL'S AAR

The individual team leaders shuffled into the newly rebuilt, and substantially larger, conference room. For many of them, it had been a long, hard month of work. Susan and Robert hadn't given each subordinate team much time to settle into their routine before calling this meeting, wanting to capture everything while it was fresh in their minds. Nancy Haskell, Susan's assistant and designated disaster scribe, read through the official disaster report:

"The disaster was officially called at 5:00 a.m., when Susan Carter arrived on site. She initially noted the presence of fire and rescue on site. Upon conversation with Captain Rick Marcella of the City Fire Department, it was determined that substantial damage had occurred to the third floor of HAL's primary office and that minor damage had occurred to both the first and second floor. She immediately notified Amanda Wilson, who declared the event a disaster and directed Susan Carter to activate the disaster recovery."

Nancy's voice continued for almost an hour, while each team member listened intently, making occasional notes. When she finished, Robert asked for comments and clarifications. Each team leader in turn made notes where they found minor inaccuracies or provided additional information. Once each team had made its comments and Nancy typed the corrections, Robert stood. "As of 4 p.m. today, four weeks and two days after declaring a disaster, I recommend we stand down. Official copies of your individual reports are due in my office in one week, along with recommended changes to the DR plan. We will reconvene at the next scheduled DR training session in six weeks." Robert nodded toward Paul, who sat to his left. "At that time we will make recommended changes, and rehearse the updates. This meeting is adjourned. Great work everyone, it was greatly appreciated." With that, the disaster was officially over.

Chapter Summary

- An organization should operate on the premise that it is only a matter time until a disaster strikes.

- Only through meticulous preparation and ongoing diligence can an organization properly respond when a disaster occurs.

- A worst-case scenario is when a situation results in service disruptions for weeks or months, requiring a government to declare a state of emergency.

- Implementing the disaster recovery plan typically involves five phases:

  - Preparation: The planning and rehearsal necessary to respond to a disaster

  - Response: The identification of a disaster, notification of appropriate individuals, and immediate response to the natural disaster

  - Recovery: The recovery of necessary business information and systems

  - Resumption: The restoration of critical business functions

  - Restoration: The reestablishment of operations at the primary site as it was before the disaster

- The goals of disaster recovery and business resumption planning are to: (1) eliminate or reduce the potential for injuries or the loss of human life, damage to facilities, and loss of assets and records; (2) stabilize the effects of the disaster; and (3) implement the procedures contained in the disaster recovery and business resumption plan according to the type and impact of the disaster to resume operations.

- During the recovery phase, the organization begins the recovery of the most critical business functions as quickly as possible.

- Resumption focuses on the remaining unrestored functions.

- The restoration phase seeks to: repair all damage to the primary site or arrange for a replacement facility; replace the damaged or destroyed contents of the primary site; coordinate the relocation from temporary offices to the primary site or to a suitable new replacement facility; restore normal operations at the primary site, beginning with critical functions and continuing with secondary operations; and stand down the DR teams and conduct the after-action review.

Review Questions

1. List and describe the ongoing challenges that organizations face when confronted with a disaster.

2. What is a worst-case scenario? What role does it play in an organization's planning process?

3. What are the primary goals of business resumption planning?

4. What are the key features of the disaster recovery plan?

5. What is crisis management, and how is it different from disaster recovery?

6. List and describe the phases in a DR plan. How might some of these phases overlap with the BC plan?

7. Give some examples of how geographic location can influence which disasters an organization can expect.

8. What is job rotation? Why is it a useful practice from a DR plan perspective?

9. What is meant by operations in degraded mode? Should organizations engage in training that prepares for operations in this mode?

10. What should be the primary focus of the training provided to the network recovery team?

11. What are the primary duties of the business interface team? How should their training proceed?

12. List and describe the various rehearsal and testing strategies an organization can employ.

13. Why must the alert roster and the notification procedures that use it be tested more frequently than other components of the DR plan?

14. What functions can an auxiliary phone alert and reporting systems perform for an organization in a DR plan situation?

15. Describe the use of an "I'm okay" line. When and how might an organization make use of this technology?

16. List and describe the triggers of the DR plan.

17. What are the primary objectives of the response phase of the DR plan?

18. What are the primary objectives of the recovery phase of the DR plan?

19. What are the primary objectives of the resumption phase of the DR plan?

20. What are the primary objectives of the restoration phase of the DR plan?

Exercises

1. Imagine that a disaster, like a fire, has befallen your home, damaging your belongings and some of the interior walls. What would your priorities be in assessing the damage and working to reoccupy your home? Create a prioritized list and timetable to accomplish this task.

2. This chapter listed several natural disasters that routinely occur in various parts of the United States. Using a Web browser or library research tool, identify the disasters that occur regularly in your area. Prioritize this list based on probability of occurrence and potential damage. What should organizations in your area do to prepare for these disasters?

3. Using a Web browser, search for organizations in your area (and nearby areas) that offer disaster recovery training. What topics do they cover in their training? Create a list of each and look for commonalities.

4. Using a presentation tool such as PowerPoint, create a short disaster recovery training presentation overviewing the key points found in Exercise 3. Bring it to class to share with your peers.

5. Using a Web browser, or local directory, search for organizations that provide disaster recovery services. Make a list, and then scratch out those that provide only data backup services or provide only alternate site services (BC services). How many are left? Why is this list so much shorter than the first? What services do the remaining organizations offer?

References

[1] D. Turner, "Disaster Recovery & Business Resumption Planning" (n.d.), BankersOnline.com, accessed April 23, 2005, from http://www.bankersonline.com/security/sec_disasterrecovery.html.

330

CHAPTER 9

BUSINESS CONTINUITY PREPARATION AND IMPLEMENTATION

Human history becomes more and more a race between education and catastrophe.

—H. G. Wells

The group walked through the area before one member exclaimed, "That's my name." Each desk had the name of a member of the organization, derived from the reservation form that Juan Vasquez had submitted before setting up the on-site tour. The group quickly realized the room had been laid out exactly like HAL's administrative offices. The interesting part was that all power, data, and telephone cabling dangled from the room's 20-foot-high, exposed rafter ceilings.

"The secret is in the floor plan." Amy continued. "We lay out a scaled replica of your floor plan on the bay floor with tape. We then drop in cabling using a lift, and then move in walls and desks. Our crews did this in about two hours. Obviously, you wouldn't be the only ones reserving space in the building, but this grand old mill can house about four companies of this size. And if it's full, we have another building we've converted about 10 miles away. If for some reason this building wasn't available, we would provide you with space in that facility at a 10 percent discount to compensate you for the drive."

Juan ran through his checklist one last time. The building had everything he expected in a cold site, at a substantially lower price than he anticipated. If he contracted with this organization, then worked with the vendors that supplied HAL's hardware, he could guarantee his boss, Robert Xavier, a four-hour recovery point objective (RPO) for administration, a six-hour RPO for the help-desk, and a 12- to 24-hour RPO for the entire data center with critical functions established in four to six hours. This was significantly better than he had hoped, and he knew Robert would be pleased.

"We'll take it," he said, extending his hand.

Questions for discussion:

- Why is it important for an organization such as HAL to have a site like this set up?
- What features would HAL be looking for in a cold site like this?
- What major items should be on Juan's checklist?

LEARNING OBJECTIVES

Upon completion of this material, you should be able to:

- Understand the elements of business continuity
- Recognize who should be included in the business continuity team
- Know the methodology used to construct the business continuity policy and plan, and be able to participate in such a planning process when required
- Become familiar with several tips useful for creating effective business continuity plans
- Recognize and be able to reference two sample business continuity plans

INTRODUCTION

Business continuity (BC) planning represents the final response of the organization when faced with any interruption of its critical operations. Due to a lack of high-quality planning, over half of all of the organizations that close their doors for more than a week never open them again. In general, BC is the rapid relocation of an organization's critical business functions to another location. BC is specifically designed to get the organization's most critical services up and running as quickly as possible in order to enable the continued operation of the organization and thereby assure its existence and minimize the financial losses from the disruption.

The reader of this chapter will find a clear parallel with Chapter 7, which covered the preparation for and the implementation of the DR planning process. Because the processes of DR and BC, both of which play a part in the business resumption (BR) plan, are similar in many regards, it follows that there will be repetition in the underlying preparations and planning. However, where the two may look very similar in structure, and perhaps even in content, the two have very different objectives. DR focuses on resuming operations at the primary site, but BC concentrates on resuming critical functions at an alternate site.

Just as in DR planning, the identification of critical business functions and the resources to support them are the cornerstone of the process used to create the business continuity (BC) plan. The processes performed during the business impact analysis (BIA) are the source of this information. When a disaster strikes and makes functioning at the primary site impossible, these critical functions are the first to be reestablished at the alternate site. The CP team needs to appoint a group to evaluate and compare the various alternatives and recommend which strategy should be selected and implemented. The strategy selected often uses some form of off-site facility, which must be inspected, configured, secured, and tested on a periodic basis. The selection should be reviewed periodically to determine if a better alternative has emerged or whether the organization needs a different solution.

Many organizations with operations in New York had their business continuity efforts (or lack thereof) tested critically on September 11, 2001. Similarly, other organizations located in the Gulf Coast region of the United States had their BCP effectiveness tested as a result of the 2005 hurricane season. When these organizations considered how much business continuity they wanted to have, they were faced with establishing two design parameters for their BC planning process: the recovery time objective (RTO) and the recovery point objective (RPO). The **recovery time objective (RTO)** is the amount of time that passes before an infrastructure is available once the need for BC is declared. Reducing RTO requires mechanisms to shorten start-up time or provisions to make data available online at a failover site. The **recovery point objective (RPO)** is the point in the past to which the recovered applications and data at the alternate infrastructure will be restored. In database terms, this is the amount of data loss that will be experienced as a result of the resumption at the alternate site. Reducing RPO requires mechanisms to increase the synchronicity of data replication between production systems and the backup implementations for those systems.

Commenting on the impacts of the September 11, 2001 attacks, Tucker and Hunter have observed that:

> Many aspects of business continuity plans worked as well, or better, than expected, but all organizations faced unforeseen obstacles and complications—the plane crashes, loss of key people, communication failures and overloads, transportation lockdowns, bomb threats, building evacuations, [etc]. This lingering recovery is far from the neat, precise hours and days called for in the RTO and RPO that many specify in their planning process.
>
> [The following are recommended lessons learned]:
>
> - Revise your business continuity plans based on the new realities. Change the assumptions and scenarios, include Plan B options, provide coverage for key roles, and extend planned time to recover. Then rehearse frequently and realistically.
> - Build a resilient IT infrastructure that can better withstand damage to networks and distributed systems.
> - Arrange for alternate workspace that include workstations, e-mail, and network connectivity.
> - Understand how to manage crises using central coordination and consistent and accurate internal and external communications.[1]

Not everything works as planned, however. As Gartner Group observed,

> A new awareness of enterprise vulnerability—brought into sharper focus by 9/11, but driven by larger, more permanent forces—is driving an accelerated hype cycle in BCP. [This] trend will resonate through every industry sector, causing a reassessment of many basic business needs. For this reason, it is also likely to draw unprecedented amounts of high-level attention from executives anxious to secure their top lines against customer and confidence erosion.
>
> One likely consequence is that BCP and DR staff will find themselves faced with unexpected, often nontechnical questions. More seriously, they may find that their rock-solid hardware and software recovery plans are fatally compromised by staffing shortages or a failure of executive-level sponsorship and follow-through. Business managers, too, may be presented with almost unprecedented planning demands, to the extent that they might believe that their ability to conduct normal operations has been seriously derailed by "yet another management fad."[2]

ELEMENTS OF BUSINESS CONTINUITY REVISITED

Much of the material from this section was previously discussed in Chapter 6 when the overall topic of business resumption was introduced. Due to its essential nature and high degree of importance, it is summarized here as a refresher. Refer to that chapter for details when necessary.

Continuity Strategies Revisited

When the CP team is developing the organization's contingency approach, the team can choose one or several strategies to continue disrupted functions. The determining factor as to which strategy or strategies will be employed is usually limited by the consideration of cost. In general, there are three strategic options that make provisions for exclusive use and three strategic options that make provisions for shared use. The exclusive-use options are: hot sites, warm sites, and cold sites. The three shared-use options are: time-share, service bureaus, and mutual agreements.

Hot Sites

A hot site is a fully configured computer facility, with all services, communications links, and physical plant operations. Hot sites duplicate computing resources, peripherals, phone systems, applications, and workstations. Essentially, it is a duplicate facility that only needs the latest data backups and the personnel to function. If the organization uses one of the data services listed in the following sections, a hot site can be fully functional within minutes. It is, therefore, the most expensive alternative available. Other disadvantages include the need to provide maintenance for all the systems and equipment at the hot site, as well as physical and information security. However, if the organization requires a round-the-clock capability for near real-time recovery, the hot site is the optimum strategy.

Warm Sites

A warm site provides many of the same services and options of the hot site, but typically software applications are either not included, or not installed and configured. It frequently includes computing equipment and peripherals with servers but not client workstations. A warm site has many of the advantages of a hot site, but at a lower cost. The down side is that it requires several hours, perhaps days, to make a warm site fully functional.

Cold Sites

A cold site provides only rudimentary services and facilities. No computer hardware or peripherals are provided. All communications services must be installed after the site is occupied. A cold site is an empty room with standard heating, air conditioning, and electrical service. Everything else is an added cost option. Despite these disadvantages, a cold site may be better than nothing. The primary advantage is cost. The most useful feature of this approach is to reduce contention for suitable floor space should a widespread disaster strike, but some organizations are prepared to struggle to lease new space rather than pay maintenance fees on a cold site.

Time-Shares

A time-share operates like one of the three sites just described, but is leased in conjunction with a business partner or sister organization. The time-share allows the organization to provide a disaster recovery/business continuity option while reducing the overall cost. The primary disadvantage is the possibility that more than one organization involved in the time-share might need the facility simultaneously. Other disadvantages include the need to stock the facility with the equipment and data from all organizations involved; the complexity of negotiating the time-share with the sharing organizations; and the possibility that one or more parties might exit the agreement or sublease their options. It is much like agreeing to co-lease an apartment with a group of friends. One can only hope the organizations remain on amiable terms, because they all could potentially gain physical access to each other's data.

Service Bureaus

A service bureau is a service agency that provides a service for a fee. In the case of disaster recovery/continuity planning, the service is the provision of physical facilities in the event of a disaster. These agencies also frequently provide off-site data storage for a fee. Contracts with service bureaus can specify exactly what the organization needs under what circumstances. A service agreement usually guarantees space when needed, even if this means that the service bureau has to acquire additional space in the event of a widespread disaster. It is much like the rental car provision in your car insurance policy. The disadvantage is that service contracts must be renegotiated periodically and rates can change. This option can also be quite expensive.

Mutual Agreements

A mutual agreement is a contract between two organizations for each to assist the other in the event of a disaster. It stipulates that each organization is obligated to provide the necessary facilities, resources, and services until the receiving organization is able to recover from the disaster. This arrangement can be a lot like moving in with relatives or friends. It doesn't take long for an organization to wear out its welcome. Many organizations balk at the idea of having to fund (even in the short term) duplicate services and resources. Still, mutual agreements between divisions of the same parent company, between subordinate and senior organizations, or between business partners, may be a cost-effective solution when both parties to the agreement have a mutual interest in each other's continued operations and both have similar capabilities and capacities.

Alternative Strategies

In addition to these six basic strategies, there are also some specialized alternatives available, such as a rolling mobile site configured in the payload area of a tractor-trailer or a rental storage area containing duplicate or second-generation equipment. These alternatives are similar to the "pre-positioning of overseas material configured to unit sets" (POM-CUS) sites of the Cold War era, in which caches of materials to be used in the event of an emergency or war were stored awaiting need. An organization might arrange with a prefabricated building contractor for immediate, temporary facilities (mobile offices) on-site in the event of a disaster.

Off-Site Data Recovery Revisited

Regardless of the continuity strategy employed, once the hardware environment is functional and the application and network software infrastructure is replicated, data must be put in place to enable critical business functions. The organization must be able to move data into the recovery site's systems. There are a number of options available that go beyond the elements found in traditional backup methods. These approaches can minimize the time needed to resume operation.

Electronic vaulting involves the batch transfer of data to an off-site facility. This transfer is usually conducted via leased lines or data communications services provided for a fee. The receiving server archives the data as it is received. Some disaster recovery companies specialize in electronic vaulting services.

Remote journaling involves the transfer of live transactions to an off-site facility. It differs from electronic vaulting in that only transactions are transferred, not archived data, and the transfer is online and occurs much closer to real-time. While electronic vaulting is much like a traditional backup with a dump of data to the off-site storage, remote journaling involves online activities on a systems level, much like server fault tolerance where data is written to two locations simultaneously.

Database shadowing involves the storage of duplicate online transaction data, along with the duplication of the databases at the remote site to a redundant server. It combines electronic vaulting mentioned earlier with remote journaling—writing multiple copies of the database simultaneously in two separate locations.

The combination of a relocation strategy with an off-site data storage recovery strategy allows the organization to plan to quickly reestablish critical business functions at a remote location. Even if the organization need only relocate part of their function, or relocate functions internally as was presented in the earlier chapter scenarios, having the strategy and plan laid out greatly simplifies and improves the organization's chances of resuming operations quickly enough to prevent catastrophic loss to the organization's future viability.

BUSINESS CONTINUITY TEAM

As is the case in the development of a DR plan, a BC plan is created by a team of specialists. Under the overall direction of the contingency planning management team (CPMT), the business continuity (BC) team leader begins by assembling the BC team. Just as was performed with the DR team, the Information Technology and Information Security departments contribute representatives to the BC team to provide technical services when the organization begins relocation to an alternate site. The real advantage provided by a properly assembled BC team is in the breadth and depth of the nontechnical members drawn from business units in the organization. The following section provides an overview of the organization of a properly diverse BC team.

BC Team Organization

Just like the DR team, the BC team itself should consist of representatives from every major organizational unit. Unlike the DR team, the need for specialized technology-focused members is significantly reduced, and the emphasis should be placed in generalized business and technology skills instead of highly specialized technical skills. Members of the BC team need to be able to set up preliminary facilities to support the relocation of critical business functions, as specified in the business impact analysis. Therefore, the team should include representatives from the following:

- Senior management
- Corporate functional units (specifically including the Human Resources, Legal, and Accounting departments)
- IT managers, plus a few technical specialists with broad technical skill sets
- Information security managers, with a few technical specialists

As was reinforced in Chapter 7, the BC team should contain different individuals than the DR team, because the BC team will be required to immediately relocate off-site to begin the transition to the alternate location, while the DR team will need to remain behind and work at the primary site to determine what is salvageable, what is not, and what needs to be done to reestablish operations at the primary site.

Depending on the size of the organization, within the BC team there may be many sub-teams responsible for individual actions.

- Business continuity management team: This is the command and control group responsible for all planning and coordination activities. The management team consists of organization representatives as described above, working together to facilitate the transfer to the alternate site. During relocation, this group coordinates all efforts and receives reports from and assigns work to the other teams. With the BC version of this group, the team handles the functions performed by the communications, business interface, and vendor contact teams under the DR model.
- Operations team: This group works to establish the core business functions needed to sustain critical business operations. The specific responsibilities of this team vary dramatically between organizations, because their operations differ. In HAL's case, this team would work to establish the help desk function and coordinate with the other teams to establish the temporary data center.
- Computer setup (hardware) team: This team works to quickly set up the hardware needed to establish operations in the alternate site. This team typically is responsible for both desktop PCs and rack-mounted servers. In smaller organizations, this team may be combined with other IT-related teams.
- Systems recovery (OS) team: The OS team works to install operating systems on the hardware installed by the hardware team. This group works closely with the hardware, apps, and data teams to establish system functions during relocation. The OS team also works to set up user accounts and remote connectivity in conjunction with the network team.
- Network recovery team: The network team works to establish short- and long-term networks, including the network hardware (hubs, switches, and routers), wiring, and Internet and intranet connectivity. The network team typically

installs wireless networks in the short term to provide immediate connectivity, unless wired services can be brought online quickly. Companies providing services, as in the opening scenario, already have the cabling ready and connected to a central rack or cabinet, only requiring installation of firewall, router, server, and Internet connections to bring the company online securely.

- Applications recovery team: The application team works with the Hardware and OS teams to get internal and external services up and running to begin supporting business functions.
- Data management team: Just as with the DR equivalent, the data management team works with other teams for data restoration and recovery. Whether from on-site, off-site, or online transactional data, this group is expected to work to recover data to support the relocated business functions.
- Logistics team: The final group consists of the individuals responsible for providing any needed supplies, materials, food, services, or facilities needed at the alternate site. This group serves as the go-to team to physically acquire and transport the needed resources to the appropriate location. This group also serves as the providers of the smaller tasks that make the operations move smoothly.[3]

Just as with the disaster recovery teams, some organizations may consolidate these functions into smaller teams, or even into a single team. At a minimum, the organization needs the ability to set up hardware, software, and data; handle the purchasing of needed supplies; and then coordinate with the organization's executive management team at the primary site to determine which functions should be relocated to the BC site. This information, coupled with the BC plan, allows the BC team(s) to prepare for operations with all business and IT-based pieces in place.

Special Documentation and Equipment

All members of the team should have multiple copies of the BC plans readily available in all locations from which they may be asked to respond in the event of mobilization. This might include ready access to copies stored securely in their homes, vehicles, and offices, because team members cannot predict when they will receive a call and be required to activate the plans. It is also important for the responsible team members to have access to certain prepositioned business continuity materials should the need arise. Equipment needed by individuals will differ based on their roles and responsibilities. A broad list of some of the equipment needed includes all of those items listed in Chapter 7 in the section titled "Special Documentation and Equipment," as well as the modifications suggested here:

- The specifics of the hardware elements on the list depend on the type and degree of coverage provided by the BC alternate site strategy and enabling contracts. In a fully designed strategy, only portable computers, software media, licenses, and backup copies of data to be restored need be ready for deployment.
- Replacement or redundant computing and network, power, and telecommunications hardware and spares are not usually staged for BC deployment, but rather are specified for provisioning by the BC site provider.

339

- Utilities infrastructure arrangements are likewise usually included in the provision specification for the BC site provider.
- BC versions of contact information need to be carefully planned and created because the location from which they will be used may prove to be a complicating factor; for instance, the local policy contact number may be different at the BC site.
- Emergency supplies are still required, but the nature and quantity may be adjusted to take into account the need for the high degree of portability required.

Many of these items may seem frivolous, but when you have to reconstitute a functioning enterprise far from your home base of operations, the materials you bring with you may make the difference in the degree of success experienced in the relocation effort. Many of the things listed are not suitable for pre-positioning or transportation to the BC site and may need to be acquired as needed and where needed. As a result, one key requirement for BC operations are purchasing cards (sometimes called *P-cards*)—essentially credit cards owned by the organization that can be used to purchase needed office supplies and various elements of equipment.

Unless the organization contracts for the hot site equivalent, office equipment such as desktop computers, phones, faxes, and so on are not provided. As a result, these either need to be purchased or leases need to be pre-signed allowing for on-demand delivery. Some BC organizations provide this equipment as an option, while some organizations prefer to simply contract with their current service providers to get extra equipment shipped on short notice.

One technique an organization can employ to simplify the equipment needed at a remote BC site is to provide all managers with a laptop computer for remote work and require that they securely store their essential files on this laptop. By requiring that the manager take the laptop to and from work each day, and update it before returning home, should the organization need to relocate to an alternate site, fewer systems would be needed, because the employees could then work off their laptops, simply requiring Internet connections. With the rapid spread of enhanced broadband and wireless networking technologies, organizations can be even more flexible and prepared.

One organization that came to this model of BC readiness was the City of New York Police Department. In the aftermath of the September 11 terrorist attack, the New York High Tech crimes unit found itself in a real bind. Not only were valued officers lost in the attack, but most of their active case files and critical evidence were lost. To provide some measure of business continuity in the event of future disasters, the agency issued laptops to all agents, and required them to take all active case files home on these securely encrypted systems.

BUSINESS CONTINUITY POLICY AND PLAN FUNCTIONS

BC is an element of contingency planning, and it is best accomplished using a repeatable process or methodology. As you will recall from Chapter 1, NIST Special Publication 800-34, the *Contingency Planning Guide for Information Technology Systems*,[4] includes guidance for planning for incidents, disasters, and situations calling for business continuity. The approach used in that document has been adapted for BC use in the section that follows.

The first step in all contingency efforts is the development of policy; then the effort moves to plans. In some organizations these are considered co-requisite operations, while some organizations argue that policy must precede planning. Other organizations argue that the development of policy is a function of planning. In this book, the approach used is to develop the BC policy prior to developing the BC plan, both of which are part of BC planning. As you will also recall from Chapter 1, the NIST approach used in SP 800-34 defines a seven-step process used to develop and maintain a viable contingency planning program. The steps from the NIST approach have been adapted here for the specifics of the BC planning process:

1. Develop the BC planning policy statement: A formal organizational policy provides the authority and guidance necessary to develop an effective continuity plan.
2. Review the business impact analysis: The BIA helps to identify and prioritize critical IT systems and components.
3. Identify preventive controls: Measures taken to reduce the effects of system disruptions can increase system availability and reduce continuity life cycle costs.
4. Develop relocation strategies: Thorough relocation strategies ensure that critical system functions may be recovered quickly and effectively following a disruption.
5. Develop the continuity plan: The continuity plan should contain detailed guidance and procedures for restoring a damaged system.
6. Plan testing, training, and exercises: Testing the plan identifies planning gaps, whereas training prepares recovery personnel for plan activation; both activities improve plan effectiveness and overall agency preparedness.
7. Plan maintenance: The plan should be a living document that is updated regularly to remain current with system enhancements.

The steps of this methodology as they are applied to the specifics of the BC planning process are further discussed in the following sections.

Develop the BC Planning Policy Statement

Much like the process employed in DR planning, the BC team, led by the business manager designated as the BC team leader, begins with the development of the BC policy, which overviews the organization's philosophy on the conduct of business continuity operations and serves as the guiding document for the development of the BC planning. The BC policy itself may be a function of the CP team, handed down to the BC team lead, or actually developed with his or her assistance, to guide in subsequent operations. In either case, the business continuity policy contains eight key elements, all of which are described in the following sections:

- Purpose
- Scope (as it applies to the organizational units' functions subject to business continuity planning)
- Roles and responsibilities
- Resource requirements
- Training requirements
- Exercise and testing schedules
- Plan maintenance schedule
- Special considerations (for example, information storage and maintenance)

You may have noticed that this process is virtually identical in structure to that of the disaster recovery policy and plans as laid out in Chapter 7. This is intentional because the processes are generally the same, with minor differences in implementation.

Purpose

What is the purpose of the business continuity program at the organization? It is to provide the necessary planning and coordination to facilitate the relocation of critical business functions should a disaster be of such magnitude as to prohibit continued operations at the primary site.

As uncommon as DR plans are in the organization, BC plans are even more so.

With any major enterprise-wide policy document, it is important to begin with the executive vision as it pertains to the topic at hand. DR is no different. The primary policy is the BC policy that applies to the entire organization.

The following example shows a sample purpose statement.

The purpose of this policy is to ensure that business function and information resource investments made by ABC Company are protected against service interruptions, including large-scale disasters, by the development, implementation, and testing of business continuity (BC) plans.

For purposes of this policy "business continuity planning" includes, but is not limited to, the documentation, plans, policies, and procedures that are required to establish critical business functions to a division impacted by man-made or natural outages or disasters, at the organization's temporary alternate site.

The policy will assist the organization to:
- Identify business resources that are at risk.
- Implement and test plans and procedures that enable reestablishment of critical services at the alternate site following a disaster.[5]

Scope

This section identifies the organizational units and groups of employees to which the policy applies. This clarification is important in case the organization is geographically disbursed, or is creating different policies for different organizational units.

The following example shows a sample scope statement.

> This policy applies to all organizational divisions and departments within ABC Company, and to the individuals employed therein.

Roles and Responsibilities

This section identifies the roles and responsibilities of the key players in the business continuity operation. This listing can range from the responsibilities of the executive management down to the individual employee. Note in the following examples that some sections may be duplicated from the organization's contingency planning policy. For smaller organizations, this redundancy can be eliminated because many of the functions are performed by the same group of individuals. The following example shows a roles and responsibilities statement.

The Chief Operation Officer, as ABC Company's contingency planning officer, will appoint a business continuity planning officer from his or her office.

The chief financial officer will appoint an individual to assist the business continuity planning officer in securing service agreements necessary to establish operations at an alternate site as dictated by the situation.

The appointed business continuity planning officer will oversee all phases and functions of business continuity planning process and will report divisional readiness directly to the contingency planning officer.

Each division must have a business continuity plan that identifies critical functions. The plan shall provide for contingencies to restore operations and information if a disaster occurs and relocation to the alternate site is deemed necessary. The business continuity plan for each division may be a subset of the organization's comprehensive disaster recovery plan. The concept of a disaster recovery focuses on business resumption at the primary place of business.[6]

Each organization shall:
- Develop business continuity plans.
- Maintain and update business continuity plans annually.
- Test business continuity plans annually.
- Train their employees to execute the continuity plans.[7]

Division heads are responsible for the oversight of their respective division's management and use of IT resources. An annual disaster recovery/business continuity plan confirmation letter must be submitted to the CIO by August 31 of each year. By way of this letter, the head of each division confirms to the executive management that a disaster recovery/business continuity plan has been reviewed, updated, and tested.

The auditor may audit organization disaster recovery/business continuity plans and tests for compliance with policy and standards.

Resource Requirements

Should the organization desire, it can allocate specific resources to be dedicated for the development of business continuity plans in the Resource Requirements statement. Although this may include directives for individuals, it can be separated from the previous section for emphasis and clarity.

The following example shows a sample resource requirements statement.

> The chief financial officer will provide the necessary contractual agreements and funds to warranty availability of resources should they be required to reestablish operations at a suitable alternative site. The CFO will also ensure suitable funds to support the development and annual testing of the BC plan.

Training Requirements

In this section, the training requirements for the various employee groups are defined and highlighted. The following example shows a sample training requirements statement.

> Training for the BC plan will consist of:
> - Making employees aware of the need for a business continuity plan
> - Informing all employees of the existence of the plan and providing procedures to follow in the event of an emergency
> - Training all personnel with responsibilities identified in the plan to perform the business continuity procedures
> - Providing the opportunity for recovery teams to practice business continuity skills[8]

Exercise and Testing Schedules

Stipulation for the frequency of testing the BC plan can include both the type of exercise or testing and the individuals involved. The following example shows a sample exercise and testing schedule statement.

> A walk-through of all BC plans will be conducted with all key BC team representatives, annually.
>
> Annually, the BC officer, in coordination with the CP officer, will conduct an unannounced business continuity exercise. Each key individual is provided with a specific type of relocation request and asked to function as if the relocation were genuine. Results are discussed in an after-action review with the executive management team.

Plan Maintenance Schedule

All good plans include a schedule and instructions for the review and update of the plan. This section should address the frequency of such a review, along with who will be involved in the review. It is not necessary for the entire BC team to be involved, but the review can be combined with a periodic test of the BC (as in a talk-through) as long as the resulting discussion includes areas for improvement for the plan.

The following example shows a sample plan maintenance statement.

> The business continuity policy must be reviewed at least annually to assure its relevance. Just as in the development of such a policy, a planning team that consists of upper management and personnel from information security, information technology, human resources, or other operations should be assembled to review the BC policy.[9]

Special Considerations

As described in Chapter 7, in extreme situations, the DR and BC plans overlap. Thus, this section provides an overview of the information storage and retrieval plans of the organization. The use of off-site but online data storage is also specified. While the specifics do not have to be covered, the individuals responsible, identified in earlier sections, should be able to implement the strategy based on this guidance.

The following example shows a sample special considerations statement.

> The CIO in conjunction with the CISO will ensure that a generally accepted data storage and recovery scheme is implemented, with weekly off-site data storage, using a secure transportation method.
>
> The CIO will evaluate and implement appropriate off-site but online data storage to record transactional data providing a recovery time objective of no longer than six hours, once hardware has been installed.

Review the BIA

Again, the BIA simply requires a review of the version developed by the CP to ensure compatibility with BC specific plans and operations. Because much of the work done by the CP included business managers as well as IT and information security representatives, the document will usually be acceptable as is.

Identify Preventive Controls

Once again, this function is performed as part of the ongoing information security posture. Effective preventive controls implemented to safeguard online and physical information storage also facilitate the information's recovery. At a minimum, the BC team should review and verify that the generally accepted data storage and recovery techniques discussed in Chapter 6 are implemented, tested, and maintained. The BC team should also ensure that sufficient and secure off-site data storage is implemented, tested, and maintained, including any remote transactional or journaling functions.

Develop Relocation Strategies

Thorough recovery strategies ensure that the system may be recovered quickly and effectively following a disruption. Although it may be virtually impossible to prepare for all diverse contingencies, ranging from floods to fires to tornadoes or even man-made disasters, it is important to have the continuity strategies in place for the most widely expected events. Based on the BIA conducted early in the process, the "after the action" actions must be thoroughly developed and tested.

Develop the Continuity Plan

The BC plan includes detailed guidance and procedures for moving into the contracted alternate site. The procedures developed and tested previously are documented and formalized in the plan. Just as with the DR plan, the responsibility for creating the BC plan does not usually fall to the CISO. The BC team leader is most likely a general manager from the operations or production division, appointed by the chief operations officer, chief finance officer, or chief executive officer. This officer guides the management team in the development of specific plans to execute once the CEO declares such a move to be necessary. In most cases, the trigger for such a decision is the evaluation of the damage to the primary site, conducted by the DR team, and reported to the CP team, who in turn advises the organization's executive management group.

Once the trigger has been tripped, the extent of the BC move depends on the extent of damage to the organization. This is why subordinate BC plans are so important. An organization may sustain sufficient damage to move some, but not all of its functions. Each subordinate group must then be prepared to pack whatever they can salvage and then relocate to the alternate site. The BC team should have already arrived and begun designating the locations for each function.

The BC plan consists of three distinct phases of operation, the first of which must be done prior to any disaster requiring relocation. These phases are preparation for BC actions, relocation to the alternate site, and return to the primary site.

Preparation for BC Actions

The developers of the BC plan must first specify what must be done before the relocation occurs. Unlike the DR plan, the extent of the disaster affects the method of relocation, not the type of disaster or the selection of services. The more devastating the disaster (or the more damage caused by it), the more of an organization must be relocated to the alternate site.

In this phase of the BC plan, the organization specifies what type of relocation services are desired and what type of data management strategies are deployed to support relocation.

From the variety of relocation services available—hot, warm, or cold sites, as well as the three time-share and the mobile site options—the plan specifies what type of resources are needed and desired to support ongoing operations.

Relocation to the Alternate Site

This phase of the BC plan is the official beginning of actual BC operations. The plan should specify under what conditions and how the organization relocates from the primary site to the alternate. Some of the items to be covered include the following:

- Identification of advance party and departure point: At a minimum, the BC plan should specify the BC team serving as the **advance party** (the group responsible for initiating the occupation of the alternate facility) to initiate the preparation of the location. It should also include information as to what trigger signals the relocation of the advance party to the BC site. This is usually done by verbal directive of the CP team leader, as directed by the CEO.

- Notification of service providers: One of the first tasks of the advance party is to notify a number of individuals, including all necessary service providers (power, water, gas, telephone, Internet) as well as the BC site owner so that they can begin activating the necessary resources to get the BC site up and running. The plan should contain this critical information as well as designate who should notify the service providers and when. As the BC advance party arrives at the BC site, they should meet with the site manager and conduct a detailed walk-through to assess the status of the facility and identify any problems. This is the same type of inspection performed when leasing an apartment or home. If the organization does not identify any preexisting problems, they may be charged for the repairs when they leave. Of course, the contract stipulates whether this is necessary.

- Notification of BC team to move to BC site: The next group to relocate to the BC site is the main body of the BC team. While the two or three individuals that make up the BC advance party move to the site first, the remainder of the team follows as soon as the BC team lead directs them to do so. The BC plan should reflect this information.

- Acquisition of supplies, materials, and equipment: Before the BC team arrives at the site, some members may have preliminary tasks, such as purchasing supplies, materials, and equipment or acquiring them from off-site storage. The BC plan should contain information on what materials should be purchased or obtained from off-site storage, and who is responsible for acquiring what. Some of this material may need to be ordered from a vendor, such as replacement computing equipment. The BC plan should also contain this information, and ensure that preapproved purchasing orders or purchasing cards are available to the BC team.

  Some organizations may want to have all BC team members meet at the BC site prior to beginning their procurement activities. This method allows the BC team leader to conduct a face-to-face coordination to ensure everyone knows their responsibilities and to issue the purchasing orders or cards. If this is the case, the BC plan should contain this information. In any case, to prevent the misuse of this emergency procurement operation, it may be best to have all BC team members working in two-person teams, one with acquisition authority and the other with approval authority.

- Notification of employees to relocate to BC site: At some point during the BC, the rest of the organization's employees report to the BC site. These individuals receive this notification through a predetermined mechanism at a predetermined time, both of which must be specified in the BC plan. It is also useful to have issued each employee a summary document or card containing the location of the BC site along with directions to the site and the phone numbers of a few of the individuals who will be already on site, in case additional information is needed.

- Organization of incoming employees: Medium and large organizations will typically not move all employees at one time. Larger organizations may need a schedule indicating what groups are to move in what sequence so too many employees don't try to get into the BC site at one time. As a result, any scheduling of employee movement is contained in the BC plan. This information varies depending on whether the organization experiences a disaster requiring relocation during the business day or after business hours.

Some organizations prefer to simply send employees home until such time that they determine that the BC site is ready to be occupied. At that time, they begin notifying employees to arrive at a specific date and time, based on the criticality of business functions those employees fill.

As employees arrive at the new site, it is helpful to have a reception area established where each employee is provided information on where their new work area is located, and to provide them with any other needed information. To facilitate this, it is useful to have an in-processing packet prepared, or stored electronically off-site. This way the organization can quickly draft the needed instructions to the individual employees. Because not all employees may know the extent of the damage to the organization's facilities, an inclusion of a disaster summary and the assessed damage should be provided to employees as soon as possible, perhaps in this document set. Supplementary information, including what organizational elements have been relocated, and what their contact numbers are, should also be either directly distributed or placed in the new work areas. Preprinted signage can be used to direct incoming employees as they wander into the new site.

Each new employee, in addition to their in-processing package, should receive a briefing to answer any questions not covered in the document set. This briefing should, at a minimum, include safety issues, including emergency relocation from the BC site, parking recommendations, locations of facilities, and regional food or scheduled food services for the new work area. It should conclude with a positive message about the ability of the organization to survive due to the proactive BC planning, and a hearty admonition to "get to work."

The BC plan should overview which of these options are adopted by the organization and who is responsible for overseeing and implementing them.

Return to the Primary Site

At some point, the organization is notified that the primary site has been restored to working order. At that time, the organization prepares to relocate individuals to the primary site. To accomplish this in a orderly fashion, the BC plan should have procedures documented for "clearing" the BC site and redirecting employees to their normal work offices. Overall, the operations that must be specified in the BC plan to support return to the primary site include the following:

- Scheduling of employee move: Note that not all business functions may return at the same time, just as not all will relocate to the BC site in the same order or time. The organization may have the most critical functions continue to work out of the BC site until all support personnel are relocated and support services are functional at the primary site. The organization may also want to wait for a natural break in the business week, like the weekend. In any case, the BC plan should contain information on who will begin directing the move back to the primary site, and generally in what order the business functions and associated personnel will move.

- Vanguard clearing responsibilities: The term **clearing** is used in the military and government sectors to represent the process of moving out of temporary facilities and returning them to the owners or managers. The concept is the same here. The BC team, as temporary stewards of the facilities, are responsible for coordinating the shutdown of services, packing and moving the temporary equipment and supplies, and the return of the facilities to the BC site owner. The BC plan should contain these critical details. The subordinate activities include the following:

    - Disconnecting services: Each of the service providers contacted during the move-in need to be notified of the date the organization will no longer need the services. Again, these include power, water, gas, telephone, and Internet, as needed. Not all services may be needed, depending on the arrangements with the BC site owners.

    - Breakdown of equipment: All of the equipment used by the organization while at the BC site must be made ready for transportation to the primary site or to storage locations. The timing on this shutdown is critical, because the organization most likely requires a backup to off-site storage before shutting down the equipment. Then the DR team at the primary site can bring their equipment online and download the most recent backups, thus preventing loss of information in transition.

    - Packing and placing in storage or transporting to primary: All of the supplies, materials, and equipment purchased or obtained while at the BC site need to be packed up and shipped back to the primary site or to storage in anticipation for the next relocation. Unless the BC plan includes details on who is responsible for what, valuable materials may be lost in the shuffle. Prior to packing, a detailed inventory must also be taken to prevent pilferage and to assess any damage that may occur in transit.

        An important item to consider is whether individuals will be permitted to relocate their own supplies and materials. Although it may be easier to allow individual employees to clean out their own offices and take their supplies back to the primary site using their personal vehicles, the damage, loss, and liability issues associated with such an action may make it prohibitive. If an individual were injured loading or unloading equipment from personal vehicles, or equipment were damaged, destroyed, or stolen from a personal vehicle, complications may arise. The organization may prefer to hire professional movers or at least lease moving vehicles. This, too, must be specified in the BC plan.

- Transfer of building to BC service provider and clearing: The final activity at the BC site is the walk-through with the site manager to identify any damage to the facility caused by the organization. The BC team then documents their findings, compares them with the list made during the move-in, and coordinates any needed expenses with the manager. Once all parties are satisfied with the clearing, the keys are returned to the manager and the BC team moves back to the primary site.

BC After-Action Review

Just as was performed by the IR and DR teams, before returning to routine duties, the BC team must also conduct an after-action review, or AAR. All key players review their notes and verify that the BC documentation is accurate and precise. All team members review their actions during the incident and identify areas where the BC plan worked, didn't work, or should improve. This allows the team to update the BC plan. The BC plan AAR is then stored to serve as a training case for future staff. This formally ends the BC team's responsibilities for this business continuity event.

BC Plan Testing, Training, and Exercises

Training employees and management to use the business continuity plan also tests the validity and effectiveness of the BC plan as well as prepares the various teams to use it. Any problems in the plan that are identified during training can be incorporated into the draft document. Once the drafts have been reviewed and tested, the final assembly of the plan can commence. As with the IR plan and the DR plan, testing the BC plan is an ongoing activity, with each scenario tested at least semiannually and at least at a walk-through level. Once all the individual components of the BC plan have been drafted and tested, the final BC plan document can be created, similar in format and appearance to the IR plan, as described in Chapter 3, and the DR plan as described in Chapter 7. This format will be described in greater detail in Chapter 10.

BC Plan Maintenance

The plan should be a dynamic document that is updated regularly to remain current with system enhancements. The organization should plan to revisit the BC plan at least annually to update the plans, contracts, and agreements and to make the necessary personnel and equipment modifications, as dictated by the business operations. If the organization changes its size, location, or business focus, the BC management team, along with the other management teams, should begin anew with the CP plan, and reexamine the BIA. The maintenance process used for BC plans is discussed in greater detail in Chapter 10.

TIPS FOR CREATING EFFECTIVE BCPS

To assist in creating more effective BC plans, some suggestions from practitioners in the field have been collected and placed here for your review.

Tips from Progress Software

Progress Software, a company that provides both the software tools for developing systems and the services to help organizations develop systems, offers the following tips for effective BC planning:

- Always keep at least one phone line separate from any other phone system you have.
- Try to locate communications equipment in more than one location.
- Utilize "remote call forwarding."
- Use uninterruptible power supplies (UPS) to provide emergency power to phone systems and network components.
- At the very least, designate an emergency meeting place where all staff are to convene, particularly if the offices must be evacuated.
- Obtain employee cell phones from at least two different service providers.
- Ensure employees with home PCs have e-mail and Internet access so they can perform some of their duties at home, if needed.
- Print wallet-sized cards for employees with emergency phone numbers, emergency procedures, and other important instructions to follow in the aftermath of a crisis.[10]

Tips from Doug Kavanagh at Continuity Central

Doug Kavanagh is an experienced business continuity professional with over 20 years of experience in the field. He is employed as a Senior Consultant with Strohl Systems, a firm that specializes in BCP software and services. The article from which the following list is drawn was published by him at Continuity Central, a Web portal that concentrates on the discipline of contingency planning. These tips emphasize the use of Recovery Timeframe Objectives (RTO) to support BC Plan development.

To determine which plans should be written and in what order, the following prioritization steps should be followed:

1. Determine the critical processes for each business unit (from the BIA).
2. Input these processes (complete with RTOs and priorities) to BCP software.
3. Associate each process with the appropriate business unit crisis management plan.
4. Align critical processes within each RTO tier.
5. Within each tier, assign a criticality rating (1–10); one tier should be reserved for processes or systems that are needed to support at least 25 percent of the revenue or critical services.
6. Identify known dependencies between processes, and add those dependencies to the BCP software.
7. Identify owners of processes or systems in the shortest timeframe (zero days) and owners of processes and systems upon which these processes depend.

8. Identify what plan developer resources are available to support plan development for the zero day and dependent processes.

9. Coordinate and support the development of plans while using resources available.

10. If insufficient resources are available to support creation of multiple plans at once, then prioritize plan development by its criticality rating.

11. If some departments or business units do not have any plans that need to be developed supporting the zero-day timeframe, identify the shortest RTO processes for those business units.

12. Support the development of plans for those processes, provided resources are available.

13. Continue to develop plans for processes where RTOs are the shortest until all critical processes and systems have procedures for recovery.[11]

SAMPLE BUSINESS CONTINUITY PLANS

The contingency plan provided at the end of Chapter 7 also incorporated aspects of business continuity planning. The combined approach to integrate BCP and DRP is commonplace in industry, and you may most likely see this in your professional endeavors. However, it is important to understand the unique aspects of each before dealing with a combined approach.

The U.S. Department of Homeland Security (*ready.gov*) has developed a combined DR/BC document (also known as a Business Resumption Plan, Emergency Plan, or Preparedness Plan). It is intended to provide small and medium-sized businesses with a starting point to assist them in developing a plan both for disaster recovery and for business continuity. The following form is based on that document:[12]

READY.GOV
U.S. Department of Homeland Security

Sample Emergency Plan

Sample Business Continuity and Disaster Preparedness Plan

☐ PLAN TO STAY IN BUSINESS

If this location is not accessible we will operate from location below:

_____
Business Name

_____
Address

_____
City, State

_____
Telephone Number

_____
Business Name

_____
Address

_____
City, State

_____
Telephone Number

The following person is our primary crisis manager and will serve as the company spokesperson in an emergency.

If the person is unable to manage the crisis, the person below will succeed in management:

_____
Primary Emergency Contact

_____
Telephone Number

_____
Alternative Number

_____
E-mail

_____
Secondary Emergency Contact

_____
Telephone Number

_____
Alternative Number

_____
E-mail

☐ EMERGENCY CONTACT INFORMATION

Dial 9-1-1 in an Emergency

_____
Non-Emergency Police/Fire

_____
Insurance Provider

Sample Business Continuity and Disaster Preparedness Plan (cont'd)

☐ BE INFORMED

The following natural and man-made disasters could impact our business.

- o _____
- o _____
- o _____
- o _____

☐ EMERGENCY PLANNING TEAM

The following people will participate in emergency planning and crisis management.

- o _____
- o _____
- o _____
- o _____
- o _____

☐ WE PLAN TO COORDINATE WITH OTHERS

The following people from neighboring businesses and our building management will participate on our emergency planning team.

- o _____
- o _____
- o _____
- o _____
- o _____

☐ OUR CRITICAL OPERATIONS

The following is a prioritized list of our critical operations, staff and procedures we need to recover from a disaster.

Operation	Staff in Charge	Action Plan
_____	_____	_____
_____	_____	_____
_____	_____	_____
_____	_____	_____
_____	_____	_____

355

READY.GOV
U.S. Department of Homeland Security

Sample Emergency Plan

Sample Business Continuity and Disaster Preparedness Plan (cont'd)

☐ **SUPPLIERS AND CONTRACTORS**

Company Name: _____

Street Address: _____

City: _____ State: _____ Zip Code: _____

Phone: _____ Fax: _____ E-Mail: _____

Contact Name: _____ Account Number: _____

Materials/Service Provided: _____

If this company experiences a disaster, we will obtain supplies/materials from the following:

Company Name: _____

Street Address: _____

City: _____ State: _____ Zip Code: _____

Phone: _____ Fax: _____ E-Mail: _____

Contact Name: _____ Account Number: _____

Materials/Service Provided: _____

If this company experiences a disaster, we will obtain supplies/materials from the following:

Company Name: _____

Street Address: _____

City: _____ State: _____ Zip Code: _____

Phone: _____ Fax: _____ E-Mail: _____

Contact Name: _____ Account Number: _____

Materials/Service Provided: _____

Sample Business Continuity and Disaster Preparedness Plan (cont'd)

☐ **EVACUATION PLAN FOR** _____ **LOCATION**
(Insert address)

 o We have developed these plans in collaboration with neighboring businesses
  and building owners to avoid confusion or gridlock.
 o We have located, copied and posted building and site maps.
 o Exits are clearly marked.
 o We will practice evacuation procedures ____ times a year.

If we must leave the workplace quickly:
_____
_____

1. Warning System: _____

 We will test the warning system and record results ____ times a year.

2. Assembly Site: _____

3. Assembly Site Manager & Alternate: _____

 a. Responsibilities Include:
 _____
 _____
 _____

4. Shut Down Manager & Alternate: _____

 a. Responsibilities Include:
 _____
 _____
 _____

5. _____ is responsible for issuing all clear.

357

READY.GOV
U.S. Department of Homeland Security

Sample Emergency Plan

358

Sample Business Continuity and Disaster Preparedness Plan (cont'd)

☐ **SHELTER-IN-PLACE PLAN FOR** _____ **LOCATION**

(Insert address)

    o We have talked to co-workers about which emergency supplies, if any, the company
        will provide in the shelter location and which supplies individuals might consider
        keeping in a portable kit personalized for individual needs.
    o We will practice shelter procedures _____ times a year.

If we must take shelter quickly

_____

_____

1. Warning System:_____

   We will test the warning system and record results _____ times a year.

2. Storm Shelter Location: _____

3. "Seal the Room" Shelter Location:_____

4. Shelter Manager & Alternate:

      a. Responsibilities Include:

      _____

      _____

      _____

5. Shut Down Manager & Alternate:

      a. Responsibilities Include:

      _____

      _____

      _____

6. _____is responsible for issuing all clear.

Sample Business Continuity and Disaster Preparedness Plan (cont'd)

☐ **COMMUNICATIONS**

We will communicate our emergency plans with co-workers in the following way:

_____
_____

In the event of a disaster we will communicate with employees in the following way:

_____
_____

☐ **CYBER SECURITY**

To protect our computer hardware, we will:

_____

To protect our computer software, we will:

_____

If our computers are destroyed, we will use back-up computers at the following location:

_____

☐ **RECORDS BACK-UP**

_____ is responsible for backing up our critical records including payroll and accounting systems.

Back-up records including a copy of this plan, site maps, insurance policies, bank account records and computer back ups are stored onsite _____.

Another set of back-up records is stored at the following off-site location:

_____

If our accounting and payroll records are destroyed, we will provide for continuity in the following ways:

_____

Sample Business Continuity and Disaster Preparedness Plan (cont'd)

☐ **EMPLOYEE EMERGENCY CONTACT INFORMATION**
The following is a list of our co-workers and their individual emergency contact information:

_____	_____	_____
_____	_____	_____
_____	_____	_____
_____	_____	_____

☐ **ANNUAL REVIEW**
We will review and update this business continuity and disaster plan in _____.

360

Sample BC Plan for ABC Company

The following plan represents a good overview plan for BC operations. It was developed based on numerous sources and includes the minimum information needed to function in a BC relocation operation. It is not complete, because there is limited space to include such an example in this text. In many cases, annotations have been made inside braces such as these: {Additional Details}. The braces indicate that additional information would be included by the planners for the use of the BC team members.

Business Continuity Plan for ABC Company

Overview:

To ensure that ABC Co. continues to function in its competitive arena, minimum functional requirements have been established to sustain critical operations if the primary facilities are damaged or destroyed. Should the extent of such damage preclude continued operations within the facility itself, some or all of the organization's functions will be relocated to an alternate site as planned.

Objectives

The objectives of this plan are twofold:

1. To ensure that critical business functions are maintained, while the organization reestablishes operations at the primary facility or at a new permanent alternate facility
2. To minimize the impact of interruptions on the services provided to our customers

Note that the plan presented here cannot possibly account for every possible event, thus the management team must use its discretion in reacting to each unique scenario.

Disastrous Events:

The following events have been evaluated and determined to be realistic threats to the continued operations of ABC Co. They are listed here along with probabilities of occurrence and are ranked on a scale of 1 to 10, with 1 being highly unlikely and 10 being highly probable. This information was extracted from the business impact analysis for ABC Corp. For additional details see that document.

{Additional examples should be provided}

	Ranking
Category 1: Building Loss or Unavailability	
Building loss due to fire:	7
Loss of main HQ building	
Worst case: Catastrophic loss	
Implement BC Option A	
Best case: Loss of 1 or more offices	
Implement BC Option C	
Most likely: Loss of 40–50% of offices	
Implement BC Option B	
Loss of production facility	
Loss of data center	
Building loss due to tornado:	5
Building loss due to flooding:	3
Building loss due to other circumstances:	1

{Note: For each category and subcategory this document would contain a brief overview of the threats and potential attack scenarios from the BIA, along with the corresponding BC plan options to be implemented if this particular version occurs}

Category 2: Data Loss or Unavailability
Data loss due to natural disaster (fire, flood, tornado, and so on):	3
Data loss due to external attacker—hacker:	5
Data loss due to external attacker—malware:	7
Data unavailability due to massive DoS attack:	4
Data loss due to other circumstances:	2

Category 3: Personnel Loss or Unavailability
Personnel loss due to natural disaster:	4
Personnel loss due to mass illness:	2
Personnel loss due to other circumstances:	2

Category 4: Services Loss or Unavailability
Power loss:	7
Internet loss:	7
Telephony loss:	6
Other service loss (water, gas, sewage, and so on):	3

Category 5: Other Potential Loss or Unavailability
Rioting:	2
Terrorist attack:	4
Hostage situation:	5
Animal or insect infestation:	1
Other potential loss or unavailability	2

Data Protection Strategies:

Director of IT will continue standard data backup strategies from the on-site RAID array. Specifically: Monday through Thursday onsite differential backups. Friday full backups are stored off-site at a fire- and theft-proof location to be determined by the director. The organization will also engage in remote journaling for critical transations.

{Additional details as needed}

Business Continuity Strategies:

Option A:
Relocate operations to alternate site 1—downtown disaster sanctuary facilities.
Under this option all designated operations (as per BIA) are relocated according to the deployment plan below. This facility provides an open production bay, organized with portable cubicle walls, desks, power, available Internet and telephone services (not activated), parking, and restroom facilities. This facility can support temporary data center functions, but no dedicated HVAC, power, or Internet access services are pre-designated. Contact information is available in Appendix A-1.

{Additional details as needed describing the facility, services, location, and so on.}

Option B: Relocate operations to alternate site 2—space-available offices.
Under this option, up to 15 offices and up to 45 personnel can be located to temporary offices provided by a contractor specializing in small-office continuity strategies. The contractor, also a commercial real estate office, will provide available office space in the general area to accommodate displaced offices. This facility does not have the capability to relocate data center functions. Contact information is available in Appendix A-2.

{Additional details as needed describing the facility, services, location, and so on.}

Option C: Relocate operations to internal offices.
Under this option, noncritical business functions are suspended, and critical functions in affected areas relocated to:

{Additional details as needed describing the facility, services, location, and so on.}

Option D: Relocate operations to alternate site 3—Dixie's Data Center.
Under this option the data center requires total relocation, and a designated facility has been contracted to provide critical data center functions using leased equipment. This electronic storage and access facility leases available data space and bandwidth, providing secure VPN connections from any site with Internet access. Critical data and applications can be ported from on-site or off-site backups and operations reestablished within 12–24 hours. Contact information is available in Appendix A-3.

{Additional details as needed describing the facility, services, location, and so on.}

Option E: **Mobile facilities from Trailers-R-US come to primary site and set up in employee lot 1.**

Under this option, a mobile business continuity service relocates between one and five mobile office and data center facilities to the organization's site and connects to available on-site services. Designed primarily for fire- and flood-damaged facilities, this option provides the organization with the ability to set up operations on-site and continue operations while supervising clean-up and other disaster recovery operations. Contact information is available in Appendix A-4.

{Additional details as needed describing the facility, services, location, and so on.}

Option F: **Termination of primary services and activation of alternates**

Under this option, primary services that are failing or under direct attack are temporarily terminated and identified alternatives activated:

Power: Primary: Southern Power Co.—Special service contract providing on-site service within 4 hours, unless regional disaster affects all service. See Appendix B-1 for details.

        Alternate: On-site diesel generators—48-hour operations with on-site fuel, resupply guaranteed within 24 hours from local service stations. See Appendix B-2 for details.

Internet: Primary: Internet Direct—Special service contract providing on-site service and internal secondary circuits should primaries be affected by anything other than a regional disaster. See Appendix B-3 for details.

        Alternate: Global Communications—Alternate contract to provide service via cellular Internet access for administrative staff and redundant fiber-optic circuits for data center. See Appendix B-4 for details.

Telephony: Primary: SoTelCo—Special service contract providing on-site service within 12 hours, unless all circuits affected by a regional disaster. See Appendix B-5 for details.

        Alternate: HappyTalk—Cellular telephony via handsets already in use by management team. Extra phones in off-site storage to be activated in accordance with special contract with provider. See Appendix B-6 for details.

Redeployment Plans:

Plan A: Total Redeployment

Under this plan the entire organization requires relocation to an alternate site as specified earlier. All secondary functions are suspended and all critical functions sustained. The entire organization will return to their home of record or designated emergency shelter until such time as they are needed for redeployment.

Trigger: Decision by vice president of operations in response to an event representing total loss of primary facilities.

Advance party:

The vice president of operations as CP director and his designated BC team leader with select appropriate individuals will immediately relocate to the site as determined above and prepare for operations. The following individuals will have the corresponding responsibilities:

BC team leader: Update the automated notification system with instructions as to when individual employees should report, and to where. Manage overall operations and specify equipment and supplies needed. Coordinate in-processing of all employees, including the creation of in-processing packets, office layouts, and other needed functions.

Services team: These individual will immediately begin setting up operations at the primary site to continue critical business services. ABC Co. is a customer service organization, so this will involve establishing telephony, Internet access, and a call center. Once the critical functions are ready, the services team will coordinate incoming employee assignments.

Hardware team: The hardware team will initially work on two divergent tasks: reestablishment of a temporary call center in accordance with the earlier plan and retrieving equipment from off-site storage as needed. The hardware team will then pull emergency laptops from storage, noncritical functions, and other locations as needed, and set up individual workstations. The hardware team will then provide tech support for incoming employees as needed.

Data and software team: Once the hardware team has the temporary data center operational, the software team will restore the most current backup from on-site/off-site locations as available. The software team will then assist in establishment of individual workstations, and then provide technical support for incoming employees as needed.

Supplies and equipment (S&E) team: S&E team will first activate any contracts to have needed office equipment installed at the alternate site (networks, photocopy, fax, and printing), based on recommendations of the BC team leader. Next, using available organizational motor pool assets, acquire needed office supplies from local supply stores. Once supplies have been obtained, the S&E team will assist incoming employees in establishing workstations.

Main body:
Once notified by the automated system, the critical functions employees will relocate to the alternate site. Secondary function employees will also relocate to the alternate site and provide support, as needed, for critical function personnel. This includes replacing unavailable personnel, in accordance with ABC Co.'s emergency task training plan. All other personnel will be placed on paid leave unless needed to supplement critical functions or other operations (DR or B teams).

Plan B: Partial Redeployment
Under this plan portions of the organization's critical functions will be relocated or redeployed to an alternate site as per a selected BC option.
Trigger: Decision by vice president of operations in response to an event representing partial loss of primary facilities.

Team Responsibilities: …

Plan C: Internal Reorganization
Under this plan, displaced portions of the organization's critical functions will be relocated to a site within the organization. Less critical functions will be suspended and the personnel redeployed to support critical functions, reorganization, and general support.
Trigger: Decision by vice president of operations in response to an event representing partial loss of primary facilities, with internal capacity for reorganization.

Team Responsibilities: …

Appendices:
Appendix A: Business Continuity Alternate Site Agreements
Appendix B: Service Contracts
Appendix C: Automated Emergency Notification System Instructions
Appendix D: Offsite Equipment Stores
Appendix E: Emergency Phone Numbers, Including Service Providers
Appendix F: Chain of Command for BC Operations

Document Management:

Signatories:

Document developed and submitted: _____

Date: _____

Document Approved: _____

Date: _____

Document Version Control

Document Name:	Business Continuity Plan (BCP)
Document Status:	Draft
Version Number:	3.1
Date:	September 1, 2010
Author:	Mike Edwards
Authorized By:	Herbert James

Distribution: All CP committee and subcommittee members (IR, DR, BC), ABC Corp managerial team, all IT employees

Change History

Version	Issue Date	Author	Reason for Change
Draft 1.0	9/5/2009	M. Edwards	Initial draft
Draft 2.0	12/15/2009	M. Edwards	Revision of first draft
Draft 3.0	5/5/2010	M. Edwards	Second revision
Draft 3.1	9/1/2010	M. Edwards	Submitted for executive approval

Chapter Summary

- Business continuity planning represents the final response an organization can offer when faced with the interruption of critical operations.

- The BC process focuses on the critical services as identified in the business impact analysis, and is designed to get the organization's most critical services up and running as quickly as possible.

- The identification of critical business functions (from the BIA) and the resources to support them is the cornerstone of the process used to create the business continuity plan.

- A CP team can choose from exclusive-use options (hot sites, warm sites, and cold sites,) or shared-use options (time-share, service bureaus, and mutual agreements).

  - A hot site is a fully configured computer facility, with all services, communications links, and physical plant operations.

  - A warm site provides many of the same services and options of the hot site, but typically software applications are either not included or not installed and configured.

  - A cold site provides only rudimentary services and facilities.

  - A time-share operates like one of the three sites described earlier, but is leased in conjunction with a business partner or sister organization.

  - A service bureau is a service agency that provides a service for a fee.

  - A mutual agreement is a contract between two organizations for each to assist the other in the event of a disaster.

  - In addition to these six basic strategies, there are also some specialized alternatives such as mobile sites or externally stored resources.

- The organization must be able to move data into the recovery site's systems. Options include electronic vaulting, remote journaling, and/or database shadowing.

- The BC plan will be created by a team of specialists, drawn from the information technology and information security departments, plus a broad and deep selection of non-technical members drawn from business units across the organization.

- Depending on the size of the organization, within the BC team there may be many sub-teams responsible for individual actions:

  - Business continuity management team

  - Operations team

  - Computer setup (hardware) team

  - Systems recovery (OS) team

  - Network recovery team

  - Applications recovery team

  - Data management team

  - Logistics team

- Some organizations may consolidate these functions into smaller teams or even into a single team.

- All members of the team should have multiple copies of the BC plans readily available in all locations from which they may be asked to respond in the event of mobilization.

- BC is an element of contingency planning, and it is best accomplished using a repeatable process or methodology.

- The BC team develops the BC policy, which includes the following elements:

  - The purpose of the business continuity program, which is to provide the necessary planning and coordination to facilitate the relocation of critical business functions, should a disaster be of such magnitude as to prohibit continued operations at the primary site

  - The scope, which identifies the organizational units and groups of employees, to which the policy applies

  - The roles and responsibilities of the key players in the business continuity operation

  - Specific resources to be dedicated for the development of business continuity plans are identified

  - Training requirements for the various employee groups are defined and highlighted.

  - The frequency of testing for the BC plan is identified.

  - The schedule and instructions for the review and update of the plan are specified.

- The Balance of the CP development process methodology includes the following:

  - BIA review

  - Identification of preventive controls

  - Development of relocation strategies

  - Development of the continuity plan to include detailed guidance and procedures for moving into the contracted alternate site, including elements for preparation for BC actions

  - Relocation to the alternate site and return to primary site

  - Preparation for CP testing, training, and exercises

  - Development of a plan for CP maintenance

Review Questions

1. What is BC planning?

2. What percentage of businesses that close their doors for more than one week are able to resume business operations?

3. What is the difference between disaster recovery and business continuity?

4. What is the primary site in the context of contingency planning?

5. What is the alternate site in the context of contingency planning?

6. What is RTO, and why is it essential that this parameter be defined early in the BC planning process?

7. What is RPO, and why is it essential that this parameter be defined early in the BC planning process?

8. List and describe the exclusive-use options used in the CP process.

9. List and describe the shared-use options used in the CP process.

10. What are the specialized alternatives to the exclusive-use and shared-use options?

11. List and describe the approaches to off-site data recovery described in the text.

12. What organizational groups should be represented in the BC management team?

13. Why is overlap among individuals between the IR, DR, and BC teams not advisable?

14. List and describe the subteams that support the BC team.

15. What degree of similarity exists between the special documentation and equipment needs of the DR and BC planning processes?

16. What should be the first step in any given part of a contingency planning process? What NIST document is used to inform this process?

17. How is the BIA used in the DR and BC planning methodologies?

18. List and describe the component parts of the BC policy document.

19. List and describe the three phases of the BC plan.

20. What are the advantages of having an AAR process in the BC plan?

Exercises

1. Using a Web browser, visit SunGard's availability services at *www.availability.sungard.com*. Look for options that map to the alternatives in this chapter. Does the organization offer hot, warm, or cold services? Does it offer mobile services and so on?

2. Using your local telephone directory, look for companies in your region that offer business continuity services. Map them to the alternatives in this chapter as in Exercise 1.

3. Using a Web browser, visit Continuity Central's Web site at *www.continuitycentral.com*. Click the information link under "Select a category." What topic listings would be of interest to someone writing a BC plan? Select two or three articles from one of the listings and bring them to class for discussion.

4. Using a Web browser, visit Continuity Central's Web site at *www.continuitycentral.com*. Click the jobs link under "Select a category." What postings are available in business continuity? What skills and attributes are being sought in a candidate?

5. Using a Web browser or your library's article search tool, look for articles describing the impact of major events on businesses, such as Hurricane Katrina in New Orleans or the 9/11 attack in New York and Washington, D.C. Look for details on how the businesses dealt with the disaster through BC planning. Is there any discussion of companies that went out of business due to loss of facilities that did not have BC plans? That did have BC plans?

References

1 C. Tucker, C. and R. Hunter, "September 11: Business Continuity Lessons," accessed April 15, 2005, from http://www.conasis.org/may_2002premiersummary.pdf.

2 R. De Lotto and A. Earley, "Business Continuity Planning for FSPs," Letter From the Editor, February 28, 2002, accessed May 12, 2005, from http://www.gartner.com/pages/story.php.id.2407. s.8.jsp.

3 Evan Marcus and Hal Stern, "Beyond Storage: 12 Types of Critical Disaster Recovery Teams," December 30, 2003, accessed July 15, 2005, from http://searchstorage.techtarget.com/tip/ 1,289483,sid5_gci942811,00.html.

4 M. Swanson, et al. *Contingency Planning Guide for Information Technology Systems*, NIST Special Publication 800-34, accessed July 13, 2005, from http://csrc.nist.gov/publications/ nistpubs/800-34/sp800-34.pdf.

5 Disaster Recovery Policy, accessed July 14, 2005, from http://www.isb.wa.gov/policies/ portfolio/500P.doc.

6 NITC, "Disaster Recovery Policy," accessed July 14, 2005, from http://www.nitc.state.ne.us/tp/ workgroups/security/policies/sections_for_graph/sectionBandCfor_3.pdf.

7 See note 5.

8 See note 6.

9 Disaster Recovery Policy, WWW Document accessed 7/15/05 from http://templatezone.com/ pdfs/DisasterRecoveryPolicy.pdf.

10 Progress Software, "Business Continuity Planning: A Progress Guide to Survival," accessed May 3, 2005, from www.progress.com/progress_software/web/global/fathom_management/ docs/bcp_guide.pdf.

11 Doug Kavanagh, "How to Prioritize the BCP Effort with Recovery Timeframe Objectives," accessed December 18, 2005, from http://www.continuitycentral.com/feature090.htm.

12 U.S. Department of Homeland Security, "Sample Emergency Plan," accessed July 30, 2005, from http://www.ready.gov/business/downloads.html.

CHAPTER 10

BUSINESS CONTINUITY OPERATIONS AND MAINTENANCE

Learn from the past. Look to the future. Live in the present.

—Steve Henthorn

OPENING SCENARIO

"Wilco." And then the line went dead.

Cecilia smiled to herself. Juan could certainly be counted on in a crisis when his military background showed. That short, cryptic message meant that he had received her message and "will comply." A one-line message from Juan meant that he recognized the gravity of the situation and was moving decisively to execute his duties.

Cecilia had just called Juan to notify him of the fire at HAL's administrative offices. After a few short questions, mainly to determine if everyone was okay, Juan put on his business continuity team leader's hat and went to work.

Questions for discussion:

- What will Juan's first order of business be, and whom will he contact first?
- What additional tasks lie ahead for Juan and his team?

LEARNING OBJECTIVES

Upon completion of this material, you should be able to:

- Discuss the details of how a BC plan implementation unfolds
- Understand the methods used to continuously improve the BC process
- Describe the steps taken to maintain the BC plan

INTRODUCTION

This chapter is about putting the business continuity (BC) plan to work when an organization needs to get critical services back in action. This is done at an alternate location if the critical services cannot be quickly restored using the disaster recover (DR) plan at the primary site of operations. This assumes the creation of a workable plan, such as the plan described in Chapter 9. Another portion of this chapter is devoted to the process of continuous improvement of the existing plan and the ongoing maintenance of that plan.

The approach taken with this chapter, much like that used in Chapter 8, uses an extended case. As information is explained, it is further illustrated by using an ongoing case that expands the story of the HAL company's experiences with continuity planning and operations.

IMPLEMENTING THE BC PLAN

Implementation of the BC plan occurs when the organization experiences a circumstance in which it cannot reasonably expect to return to normal operations at the primary site. An organization may reach a predetermined state, known as a *trigger point* or *set point*. This was described in Chapter 9, where the responsible executive or senior manager indicates that the organization is to relocate to a preselected alternate site. This is not a decision to be taken lightly. In addition to the substantial expenses the organization incurs leasing the alternate site, there inevitably are additional expenses associated with establishing and using duplicate utilities and services, additional office supplies, and temporary equipment. Thus, the organization should ensure that the benefits of implementing the BC plan justify the expense. On the other hand, if the damage from the disaster is severe enough to disrupt business operations, the decision to implement the BC plan is straightforward.

Implementation of the BC plan involves the obvious preparations for the BC action: relocation to the alternate site—first the BC advanced team, then the main team, and subsequently the rest of the organization's affected employees; establishment of operations; and finally return to the primary site or new permanent alternate site. The outline of the business continuity plan developed in Chapter 9 is used here to illustrate the operations of HAL as they undertake a BC operation from final preparation through the relocation tasks and back to normal operations when they can return to their primary site.

Preparation for BC Actions

The same disaster recovery team preparation functions described in Chapters 7 and 8 are used by a business continuity team, as was described in detail in Chapter 9. Unlike the disaster recovery team, whose reactions are based on the nature of the disaster that has befallen their organizations, the BC team can expect that when they are activated, their functions will always be generally the same—to prepare to duplicate one or more of the organization's critical business functions at an alternate site. Which specific alternate site will be used and which critical business functions will be implemented depend on the details of the disaster that took the primary site out of service. Planning and training encompass the bulk of the preparation activities. From desk checks to walk-throughs to full-blown interruption testing, the entire organization should be prepared for their role in a BC operation.

Prepare Action Plans for Critical Functions

Preparation for all possible contingencies is usually not practical. However, preparing the organization with one or several general training programs focused on implementing critical business functions at an alternate site can ensure that everyone involved is ready for the implementation of the specifics of any particular BC operation that is needed. Preparations for these specific alternatives at an off-site facility can be made with minimum disruption to normal business functions.

In this chapter's ongoing case, the critical functions that are prepared for alternative deployment are designated as *command & control* (sometimes noted as C&C). These functions comprise the core administrative functions that are required to keep the company operational for 90 days. They are the customer service function (which is mainly focused on the delivery of help desk services to HAL's customers), the IT operation function (those infrastructure elements needed to support either or both of C&C and customer services), and a small but critical element called the customer installation function.

In light of this designation of critical functions, the BC team should rehearse setting up one or more of these functions at an alternate site. Due to the complexities of these individual functions, the size and scale of the operations, and the ways in which they interoperate depending on which of them are to be implemented, these functions may or may not be able to be co-located at the same BC alternate site. As a result, each may have its own designated BC site, separate from, but coordinated with the others.

The following example describes HAL's critical functions as identified for BC planning purposes.

ONGOING CASE: HAL'S CRITICAL FUNCTIONS

For HAL, customer services and C&C functions could both work within the same alternate site, because both require similar physical and logical infrastructure elements (offices, computers, networks, and systems). These two critical services result in the relocated staff needing access to the company network and information systems and access to telephone services in order to provide their intended services.

The IT operations function requires a substantially more specialized set of infrastructure elements in order to be deployed, but a preconfigured server farm, with several high-speed Internet connections, could be adapted to support the needs of the IT operations. The customer installation function works out of a small management office, coordinating the on-site installation of customer hardware and software, and as such could, if necessary, work out of the department manager's home or from a workstation at the C&C site.

Integrating Routine Operations to Improve BC Effectiveness

For general operational efficiency, and in order to improve resiliency in the event of disaster or the need for continuity operations, organizations may choose to make any number of changes in routine policies and procedures and to perform activities in ways to improve the effectives of the BC preparations. In the following example, HAL is shown to have done some things in everyday operations to make themselves more reliant in the face of the need for business continuity operations.

ONGOING CASE: RESILIENCY AT HAL

The management team at HAL made the decision early on to provide each mission-critical employee with a capable laptop computer and a cell phone. In addition, the service contracts in place from the vendors for these devices have guaranteed delivery of additional compatible equipment and services as needed. The administrative staff makes use if its assigned laptops for remote access. This allows them to work from home for occasional telecommuting and to maintain remote access when traveling. These laptops are configured with secure VPN capabilities that can operate over dial-up, DSL, cable-modem, and wireless network service providers. Although expensive in everyday use, this capability allows maximum flexibility when contingencies require implementation of the BC plan. HAL policy requires that the employees may not leave their laptops at the office, but must either leave them at their home or carry them to work each day. This strategy ensures that the organization has deployed a significant distributed computing capability should the workstations at the primary facility be damaged or destroyed. Effective backup strategies ensure that frequent synchronization of desktop and laptop systems are completed. When this is completed along with: 1) a validated server file system backup using off-site storage; 2) the completion of a verified backup of databases to offsite repositories; and 3) the remote journaling of all online transaction systems, it makes it more likely that the critical data needed by the organization remains available when it is needed to begin operations at an alternate site.

As an important note, when implementing any BC strategy at an alternate site, the IT staff involved must sustain the backup strategies and practices used at the primary site. This is because good backup practices can safeguard losses that occur while operating in the suboptimum conditions of the contingency deployment when errors or faults could cause additional disruptions and also because the organization needs to relocate to the primary site.

Other preparations an organization may undertake include the issuance of so-called P-cards (credit or debit cards used in structured purchasing programs) to designated BC team members. One model uses a small group of employees designated to be part of the BC advance team or deployment group who are issued P-cards so they are prepared to make emergency purchases of critical supplies. In the event critical functions are relocated, these designated employees coordinate the acquisition of a predefined list of materials from a local office supply store. Another preparation is the off-site storage of key forms used by the company. Even in the event the organization moves to an intranet—with electronic, rather than paper, forms—some hard copy documents allow the organization to function until the intranet is reestablished.

As the following example explains, HAL's staff is well prepared for the BC operation it is eventually going to perform.

ONGOING CASE: HAL'S PREPARATIONS FOR BC

Juan checked his notes, for the fifteenth time. Everything was going smoothly, too smoothly. During rehearsals something was always overlooked. He reflected on Paul's training exercises. Some of the upper managers scoffed at the continuous rehearsals, whether over a conference table or wandering around the office with clipboards. He recalled that even a few skipped the on-site walk-through, stating other pressing business. It wasn't until the CEO himself stepped in that they began to pay attention; even then some were reluctant. "I wonder what they're thinking now," Juan mused to himself.

Paul had insisted on at least one walk-through every quarter. They already had experience from three conference table walk-throughs, two office walk-throughs, and one on-site exercise since that time. Juan had been at this exact spot about four months earlier when they made the initial visit after suggesting HAL contract for the services. Contingencies, Inc. had been working steadily to upgrade the facility since then. The floor had a new vinyl surface, the lighting had been significantly upgraded, and the walls had been stripped of their industrial appearance and gleamed with a fresh coat of light blue paint. The building itself was shaped like a square doughnut; the central courtyard had been converted from a smoking patio to a small courtyard complete with trees, plants, and benches.

Juan reviewed his notes again. The first item on the list was checked off—designation of the appropriate business continuity plan. The rest of the items on the list were still blank.

The preparation undertaken by an organization inevitably pays off in efficiency of the operation once the business continuity plan is implemented. The hours spent walking through the rehearsals, discussing, and improving the plans result in much smoother functions under pressure. The worst time to develop the business continuity plan is while activating the critical business functions in response to a disaster.

Relocation to the Alternate Site

The decision to move specific critical functions sets into motion a series of carefully choreographed subordinate activities. An initial decision regarding whether or not essential functions are to be started at the alternate site is then followed by the decision of which services are to be activated. This is followed with a determination of when each service must be available. Should damage be severe enough, or if the disaster is ongoing, as in hurricanes, floods, or other severe circumstances, the decision to implement BC operations may have to be deferred until information is available or access to the primary site for a damage assessment is possible. Once the decision is made, the advance party is deployed to begin coordinating the move, key service providers are notified, the remainder of the BC team is directed to the site, and needed supplies and materials are acquired.

Next, the affected employees are relocated to the BC site, and as they arrive, are organized and then directed to begin work. The initial work is on remediation of any remaining issues with the site. This eventually gives way to the setup activities, a final review of the fitting-out of the alternate site, and eventual establishment of the routine execution of the critical service being resumed. These activities are described in the following sections.

The Advance Party

The identification of the advanced party is an important part of the BC plan. The advance party should include members or representatives of each of the major BC teams. Although each organization can choose to implement a unique set of BC teams, the most common include the following:

- Business continuity management team: The command and control group may consist of one or two individuals, including the team leader, responsible for coordinating all BC implementation functions. In HAL's case, the team leader, Juan, and the assistant team leader, Joey, handle all C&C functions for the continuity management team.
- Operations team: This group works to establish the core business functions needed to sustain critical business operations. For an administrative case, the office manager, vice president, or director of administrative services may handle this responsibility. In HAL's case, the office manager, Tracy Jackson, would assist in overseeing the configuration of the alternate site to establish the administrative offices. If the data center were affected, the director or assistant director of the data center would handle the task.
- Computer setup (hardware) team: This team works to quickly set up the hardware needed to establish operations in the alternate site. Because in HAL's example, the affected offices are administrative, only user systems need support. With the HAL policy on administrative laptops, the support focuses on peripherals and ancillary components.
- Systems recovery (OS) team: The OS team works to install operating systems on the hardware installed by the hardware team. If the equipment used for the alternate site is new, or the organization has a specialized configuration, then some time may be required to install and configure the workstations and servers to support the implementation at the alternate site. In HAL's case, only minor support is needed to get the laptops configured to access the new network connections. One or two people would be sufficient to configure the incoming employees as needed.
- Network recovery team: The network team works to establish short- and long-term networks, including the network hardware (hubs, switches, and routers) and wiring, and Internet and Intranet connectivity. Working with the hardware and OS teams, the network recovery team could have a major installation on their hands if the alternate site does not have premises wiring implemented. In this case, a wireless implementation would be the preferred solution. In HAL's case, the ceiling drops provide a connection to a local networking cabinet, with Internet access. Through this access, the staff can access the intranet once the primary site is reoccupied.
- Applications recovery team: The application team works with the hardware and OS teams to get internal and external services up and running to begin supporting business functions. If the primary applications were PC based, standardization allows the use of preconfigured images to be pushed to the workstations. If the applications are network based, then backups to off-site storage allow reestablishment with relatively little effort. In HAL's case,

office productivity software is installed on each desktop workstation. A few internal applications are housed within the intranet, but these will be unavailable until the primary site can be reoccupied by the data center staff. The applications staff can implement a temporary server and reinstall the needed applications if management feels the delay in reoccupying the primary site would be longer than acceptable.

- Data management team: Just as with the DR equivalent, the data management team works with other teams for data restoration and recovery. Because in HAL's case, the data center can be reoccupied with virtually no loss in data, there will be little need for the data management team. In a more severe case, however, this team would be working closely with other teams to get temporary services up and running, ready to support both internal staff and external customers.

- Logistics team: The final group consists of the individuals responsible for providing any supplies, materials, food, services, or facilities needed at the alternate site. As illustrated in following sections, some staff is dedicated to obtaining the needed supplies to make the offices functional. In extreme cases, these same staffers can handle other nonemergency services, such as food and sanitation needs. At HAL, Stacy Wilcox is coordinating the logistics team, and based on her checklist, has already begun procuring the needed supplies. Once this responsibility is complete, her task shifts to handling incoming personnel.

In the scenario that follows, the central nature of the advance party is illustrated.

ONGOING CASE: HAL'S ADVANCED PARTY

"Joey, this is Juan. Business continuity plan B is in effect. Round up the team and meet me at Contingency, Inc.'s site."

Joey Bishop was the assistant shift supervisor for the first shift and long-time friend of Juan. In fact, they served together in the Army. They were accustomed to dealing with stressful situations.

"Wilco," came the reply, and then the line went dead.

Juan looked at his checklist. He had routed his three most important team members to the alternate site. Each knew their responsibilities, but he had reviewed their tasks on the phone with them just the same. There was no room for mistakes. Each had a similar checklist, and knew what to do first. Next he needed to get the site prepared for its coming role.

Notifying Service Providers

It is often necessary to alert service providers to activate their services required to make an alternate site operational. Depending on the service, some or all of these may be notified by the BC vendor. If that notification is not managed by the contingency site's operator, the BC team lead should contact the necessary vendors (power, telephone, data, or possibly water service providers). When mobile contingency facilities are part of the plan, on-site coordination is often needed get these services connected to the mobile offices.

In the following example, detailed planning pays off as HAL gets ready to begin delivering services from its contingency site.

Activating the BC Site

Once a BC plan is activated, one of the first responsibilities of the BC team leader is to notify the human resources, who then implement it. The advance teams immediately begin working their checklists, preparing the site for the imminent arrival of the balance of the assigned staff.

The following scenario shows how the critical path to offering contingency services is often created by the members of the advance team preparing the contingency site.

Supplies and Equipment

Organizations need supplies to make work happen. Sometimes the lack of the most mundane supplies can substantially hinder operations. As a well-known proverb says, "For want of a nail the shoe was lost. For want of a shoe the horse was lost. For want of a horse the rider was lost. For want of a rider the battle was lost. For want of a battle the kingdom was lost. And, all for the want of a horseshoe nail."

It may not be easy to determine what supplies and equipment a particular function needs to conduct operations. However, it would be troublesome to find out after the organization has settled into the alternate site that someone needs to make a list of supplies and equipment and then begin procurement. The creation of a checklist for each function should be part of the planning process. This may result in either the pickup of prepurchased and prepositioned supplies or a shopping trip to a local supplier.

But, some equipment is either too expensive or too unique to allow prepurchasing, prepositioning, or purchasing locally. Computer equipment, whether servers, end-user systems, peripherals, or storage devices, can be predetermined, and then orders placed, with a rush request from a reliable vendor. If the need is dire enough, then local purchasing may be the only viable option. Some vendors offer services to quickly deliver a specific list of equipment selected to closely match the needs of each of the planned contingency options. One notification can have this order on its way to the alternate site. The catch is acquiring the necessary technical equipment on short notice. This is one reason organizations should consider the distribution of laptops and cell phones to minimize last-minute purchases and the inevitable delay and higher-than-necessary expense.

In the scenario that follows, HAL marshals its resources and executes its plans to get the needed supplies to the right place at the right time.

ONGOING CASE: HAL'S SUPPLIES

Stacy Wilcox walked into Office Supplies, a local office supply store, to meet the store manager, even though the store had been closed for hours. She came in from the loading dock and could see three stock clerks with shopping carts, completing the process of plucking items from the shelves. The store manager had organized this effort, just as it had been rehearsed. The contract with HAL had been in place for months, and this activity had been rehearsed twice. Even though two of the staff members working at the moment were too new to have been involved in the rehearsals, one of them was fully up to speed and the work was progressing nicely. Lists that each person carried were used to pick cases of paper, pens, paper clips, staplers and staples, sticky notes, highlighters, even coffee pots and coffee. The carts were quickly filled as the needed items were plucked from the store shelves. As each cart was filled, the clerks took it to the back of the store where the items were checked off another list and packed into cardboard cartons. Each carton was taped shut as it was filled and then stacked onto a pallet that was on the forks of a waiting forklift.

continued

"That's it, ready to go," said the senior clerk.

The forklift roared to life and rolled out to the loading dock and placed the pallet of supplies into the bed of Stacey's pickup. She signed the manifest the store manager held for her and then got into her truck for the short drive to the alternate site at Contingency, Inc.

At that moment, Joey walked up to Juan at the alternate site. He was pushing a cart filled with boxes branded with a Quick Copy logo. "Here are the staffing packets. Hot off the presses. Stacy should be here from Office Supplies shortly."

"Great," said Juan, checking the item off his list. "Go ahead and set up at the desk by the front door until Stacy gets in, then let her man the desk. Tell the others to start stocking the desks with supplies as soon as she gets here."

Less than 15 minutes later, Stacy arrived. Joey looked up from his desk where he was busy stacking and sorting the staffing packets. "Where's the stuff?"

Stacy nodded toward the loading dock where two workers were already unloading boxes from her truck.

"Juan wants you to staff the front desk to be ready for processing the incoming staff while I get the rest of the printing order from my car. Frank is bringing in the computer equipment as we speak."

Juan looked up from across the bay, then looked down and checked another item off his list.

Frank Rawles entered pushing a cart of printers. He had spent the last two hours unloading the technological supplies the offices would need. While the BC vendor provided an industrial-grade photocopier, all of the other technology used by HAL, the printers, monitors, keyboards, and mice were HAL's own responsibility. Now, when an employee brought in their assigned laptop and cell phone, they could use the monitors, keyboards, and mice to make a fully functional remote office.

Juan checked another item off his list.

Staff Relocation to the BC Site

The next step in implementing the BC plan is getting the employees that will be using the alternate site to that site when it is ready for occupancy. At the earliest point that a reliable prediction is possible, a notification of that time can be given to the affected staff members. The staffing packets prepared earlier are used to guide the employees once they show up. Some organizations may prefer to wait until the beginning of the next scheduled shift, or the start of the next business day to move the employees to the alternate site. Other organizations, with more time-critical missions, can't wait that long and may require employees to start at the alternate site in the middle of a scheduled shift.

In the following example, HAL's users get the word it is time to report for work at the alternate site.

Cecilia smiled. "Great work Juan, that's two hours ahead of schedule. I'll update the notification system."

Juan had just informed Cecilia that his team was ready to receive employees at the alternate site. Although upper management would probably stay at the primary site to assess the damage, the administrative staff and other managers would need to begin handling the inevitable flood of customer calls that would already be filling the call center systems. At the offices where the call center would normally handle these queries, the staff would not be allowed back because the fire department was still dealing with the after-fire analysis. It could be hours or days before they could resume normal business functions at that location. If repairs are needed, it may be weeks. In the meantime, the customer's needs for service must be met.

An automated call system dialed the numbers on record for each call center employee. The message was: "This is the HAL call center automated notification and employee check-in system. If you are assigned to the fourth floor at 123 West Main Street, you are directed to report to the Contingency, Inc. building at 233 North River Street at 1 p.m. today. Please park in lot B. We are currently occupying bay #1. A security officer will direct you to your lot and bay when you arrive. If you have any questions or are unable to report, please call your supervisor. All other employees are not expected to report to the West Main Street building until they are notified that the facility is safe to resume operations. Please follow your unit contingency plan for alternate work site arrangements. If you have misplaced your contingency operations packet, please contact your supervisor. The number for the HAL check-in service is 800-555-8765. Please call one to two hours before your scheduled work start time to receive the latest news about circumstances at HAL. At the tone, enter your employee number followed by the pound sign, to indicate that you have received this message. You will then be asked to verify your current status and availability to report."

Organization Relocated Staff

As the employees begin relocating to the alternate site, there will inevitably be confusion. Not every employee will have been able to participate in prior business continuity planning (BCP) events. As a result, the calming influence of a friendly face and well-planned check-in procedures can improve the employees' ability to quickly assimilate into the new environment and begin working productively. The staffing packets contain information on the location of assigned workspace, office support equipment and resources, new phone lists, locations of their colleagues and supervisors, and other information. The packets serve to expedite the transition and get the staff that is responding into the swing of the new arrangements as quickly as possible.

The following example shows how this process works at HAL as the call center staff reports for the first shift at the alternate site.

A short while later, the first employees showed up. Stacy smiled. "Hi, Pamela! Welcome to HAL's continuity annex. Here's your packet. Your office is right there." She pointed.

Pamela and Steve chatted nervously. They flipped through their packet. Copies of the floor plan looked strangely familiar. They were able to quickly find their offices, and settled in. The desks were equipped with the bare essentials. A desk lamp, two legal pads, pens, paper clips, a stapler, a power cord, and a data connection were provided in each office. Pamela set her laptop on the desk, connected the power and data cables, and turned it on. Inside her packet was a document summarizing each employee's responsibilities. Her job, even though her supervisor had not arrived yet, was to begin to answer the calls in HAL's voice mail system that were left in the customer support mailbox. For the next hour, as her colleagues trickled in, she reassured one customer after another that the network interruptions were temporary, and that they would be operational as soon as possible. A few customers were upset, fewer still were rude, but most were just glad to hear that the interruption was temporary and that HAL would be operational shortly.

By the end of the day, Pamela and her colleagues had answered every phone call and e-mail message received. She watched as supervisors congratulated each and every employee. Now she could turn her attention to her normal duties: answering new support calls as they came in over the rerouted telephone system.

Returning to a Primary Site

The last event that occurs at the BC alternate site is the preparation and relocation to the primary site once it is restored and ready for resumption of operations. This task involves the scheduling of the employee move and the clearing of the BC site. Finally, an after-action review is conducted, incorporating lessons learned into the plan and bringing closure to the process.

Scheduling the Move

The simplest way to handle the relocation to the primary site is to schedule the move to occur over a weekend, with some employees working extra hours to shut down the alternate site and others loading office materials and equipment for transportation back to the primary site. During the last few hours of the Friday afternoon, each employee can pack up their office and prepare to have their materials relocated to the primary site. Each office worker should carefully label a box containing their work papers and so on and leave it in a clearly marked area or on top of their desk before they leave the building. In large organizations, the collection and transportation of the work materials may take more time than a two-day weekend can provide. If the organization had to relocate production facilities or data centers, or basically anything other than administrative functions, then it may take weeks to relocate all the equipment and materials to the primary site. However, in the ideal scenario, employees stop work on Friday afternoon and resume work Monday morning back at their primary sites. Data center or other IT employees can then conduct backups on Friday afternoon, after close of business, and then reload the data and transactions at the primary site so that it is available Monday morning. From the perspective of most employees, they simply go home on Friday, and then show up to work on Monday with little break in their work regime.

As an aside, it is important for the organization to collect the extra office supplies purchased for the move. Expendable supplies should be relocated to the organization's supply closets, while some durable goods, such as staplers, scissors, extra phones, and typewriters, can be placed into storage in anticipation of the next disaster.

Clearing Activities

The final steps involve closing down the organization's presence at the alternate site. Among the activities that occur during this phase are disconnecting temporary services, equipment disassembly, packaging of recovered equipment and supplies, storage or transportation of recovered equipment and supplies, and clearing the control of the assigned space from the BC service provider. Most of these steps are spelled out in the contract with the provider of the alternate site floor space and/or in the BC plan.

Settling In Back at the Primary Site

Even in the ideal scenario, with employees leaving the BC site on Friday and reporting back to the primary site on Monday, there will inevitably be a resettling period at the primary site. If the employees have been relocated to the BC site for an extended period of time and it is not in the same area as their primary residence, they may or may not have had to live in temporary housing. In addition to the basic issues involved in moving to and from the alternate work site, some workers may have personal issues occupying their attention. If the root cause of the contingency operation is a widespread incident at the organization's primary location, it will likely affect some or all of the employees' personal lives as well. For instance, if a severe storm caused the relocation, not only was damage at work a factor, but employees may have experienced their own property damage and/or family distress from these events.

On top of that, alternate work conditions such as working for temporary supervisors, while their primary supervisor was working on the disaster recovery team to restore the primary site, may cause additional interpersonal issues during the emergency. It could also mean that the staff was ignoring routine tasks performed at the primary site, which were suspended while only critical functions were performed at the BC site. In any event, there is a transition period when employees reestablish their normal routines, including the reactivation of noncritical business functions and implementation of the original work processes.

There may even be the challenges associated with learning new business functions or operations. Some managers may take advantage of the transition to implement new procedures or policies, designed to streamline operations. If the managers found out that they were able to work effectively at the BC site without certain responsibilities, policies, or procedures, they may elect to eliminate them altogether. The organization may have suspended upgrades or updates to business functions or information storage and processing and may elect to integrate them as the primary facility is reestablished. Employees returning to the primary site will require a reindoctrination including any training or awareness activities the organization feels necessary to streamline the reintegration.

In the following example, HAL gets back to routine work.

ONGOING CASE: HAL'S SETTLING IN

"OK, ladies and gentlemen! I need your attention for a minute!" Robert Xavier shouted to be heard over the excited chattering of the new employees as they came back into work. It had been almost six weeks since the fire, and many employees were looking forward to getting back to work at HAL's corporate offices.

"I know it's been a while since most of you have been in the building, but we've implemented a few changes while you were gone!" Robert smiled as a few employees looked nervously about. "I assure you that these changes will make doing your job better! First, due to the fire and other considerations, the company that occupied the fifth floor has elected not to renew their lease, and we've purchased that space and expanded our operations. The new corporate offices are now on the fifth floor. The rest of the administrative offices are still on the fourth floor, but there is a new floor plan. Stacy and Juan will pass that out to you as you come in as part of your in-processing packets."

Stacy and Juan glanced at each other as they began handing out the packets to the employees crowding to enter the building. "Deja vu?" Stacy asked, grinning.

BC After-Action Review

Just as with the IR and DR events, once the BC activities have come to a close and the organization has reoccupied its primary facility or new permanent alternate facilities, the team should meet to discuss what worked and what didn't. Prior to this meeting, each team member should sit down and type up what happened from their perspective, and include their commentary on what worked well and what needs improvement. Each team member should have the opportunity to include information into a master report, which is compiled upon completion of the after-action review (AAR).

The AAR should come from the timeline captured by the team scribe, historian, archivist, or whatever the team decides to call the individual responsible for documenting the events. This detailed timeline provides a structure to the events, along with the ability to determine if actions were performed on, ahead of, or behind schedule. Everyone gets to speak at an AAR; no one should be restricted from voicing their unbiased opinion. The smallest detail can derail future efforts, if not corrected. The resulting additions should be incorporated into a final report, called "Summary of Events," and presented to the executive management and finally archived for posterity.

In the following example, HAL engages in the AAR.

CONTINUOUS IMPROVEMENT OF THE BC PROCESS

If there is one constant in business today, it is that change is inevitable. Even the best of BCP projects produce plans that leave room for improvement and that must be maintained. The best organizations make the ongoing process improvement a key factor in their repeatable BCP processes. Maintenance activities in the BC environment are discussed in the following major section of this chapter. This section looks at how the BCP processes can be improved.

Improving the BC Plan

The reliance that modern organizations place on their information systems goes far beyond what was common only a few years ago. Continuing convergence of business systems and the integration of networks and the Internet into everyday business activities have made business and e-business nearly synonymous. This reliance on technical infrastructure has most organizations concerned about business continuity planning. Circumstances have reached the point, however, when merely having prepared a plan is not adequate to the challenges.[1] Many times the process used to create a continuity planning process results in the following:[2]

- Reliance: Relying on a comfortable BCP process and the resulting BC plan can lead to a false sense of security and potential business failure if the plan is not updated regularly and fully tested. An untested plan is no plan at all, and a plan in which the organization does not have confidence will not survive a real continuity operation.
- Scope: Companies often limit the scope of their efforts to systems recovery. When structuring, funding, and reviewing its BCP approach, organizations should pay attention to both the needs of information systems recovery and the continuity of the critical business functions. Far too many organizations limit BC processes to IT systems recovery, assuming if the IT systems are working, they will find a way to make the business systems function around them.
- Prioritization: A formal process that prioritizes key business processes is a critical step that often does not get sufficient attention from senior management. As part of the BIA, identification and prioritization of critical business functions ensures they will be supported in the event of a disaster requiring implementation of the BC plan. The failure to properly prioritize may result in situations that appear absurd in retrospect, such as a data center with working computers but no functioning network circuits, or an e-commerce site that works without the ability to ship products from the warehouse.
- Plan update: Formal mechanisms are often not in place to force a plan update on a regular basis or when significant systems or business process change occurs. Periodical review and maintenance of the plan is essential in keeping the document current. Normal operations in all but the most somnolent organization mean that core business processes evolve over time and the continuity plan must be kept up to date if it is to serve any purpose when invoked.
- Ownership: Senior management often appoints the wrong person, and more often, not the best person to manage the BCP process. As stated in earlier chapters, a champion is needed: someone high enough in the organizational ranks to provide the needed leadership, management, influence, and resources to make the project succeed and who is sufficiently detail oriented and motivated to make sure the BCP process is in place and up to date.
- Communications: Communications issues are often overlooked or viewed as peripheral to the core issues. As outlined in the example BC plan in Chapter 9, it is important to establish planned communications with all stakeholders, including employees, service providers, and customers. Redundant communications procedures are often indicated because BC plans are almost always activated when conditions are less than optimal.
- Security: This is often not considered a key deliverable in BC processes. Information systems security controls are often disregarded or fall by the wayside during plan development, resulting in a greater risk exposure during recovery operations.

- Public relations: Practitioners often fail to plan for public relations and investor considerations, therefore missing the opportunity to control perceptions by the public and investors. The communications teams outlined in Chapter 9 have the specific responsibility to address public relations requirements. The public and the press can be valuable aids in recovering.
- Insurance: Many BCP processes fail to adequately plan to support the filing of insurance claims resulting in delayed or reduced settlements. Insurance is a critical part of both disaster recovery and business continuity. Involvement of the organization risk management team and a close coordination with the insurance agent is essential in expediting much-needed reimbursement from claims, rather than have the cost of recovery offset organizational earnings.
- Service evaluation: Many companies poorly evaluate recovery products (hot site, cold site and planning software), relying on vendor-supplied information. This often leads to a solution that may not adequately address a company's needs.

This list of shortcomings has occasioned many practitioners to observe shortcomings in the way BCP processes are performed. One such observation is made in the following comments from Kathleen Lucey, a Fellow of the Business Continuity Institute. She is a Managing Partner at Montague Technology Management, Inc. and was named by IBM Corporation as the 1998 Business Continuity Practitioner of the Year.

Just yesterday I said to a professional chef with 20+ years of high-level experience in his industry that I was beginning to feel like business continuity was becoming like cooking—everyone thinks that all they need is a "secret recipe" and they can turn out professional dishes, achieve their lifelong dream of opening a restaurant, and so on. Somehow business people have become universal "do-it-yourselfers," failing to understand that the deep and broad knowledge and the painfully honed skills gained from experience are far more important than the business continuity recipe.

Here are some important points to consider when developing a business continuity plan:

1. *A business continuity plan is not a single unified plan. It is a set of specialized team plans documenting the backup and continuity strategies decided upon, based on the company's needs collected through a BIA or other method, and the actions required to implement that strategy to re-create, restore, and relocate a business. There are several types of plans, each with some differences in content, but no team plan includes information about policy, history, and so forth. Each includes only that information necessary for that team to accomplish its functions. I am getting pretty discouraged with those who think that the plan is the strategy. I have found that companies tend to do rather well on IT recovery plans, less well on business unit plans, and abysmally on logistics, communication plans, and overall coordination. This makes sense because technical recovery is relatively simple, once you have got the bugs out through testing and your data is available; business unit recovery is more complex, but still not terribly difficult. Logistics and*

coordination processes are definitely not easy, particularly when you leave the military or emergency sectors. A very small percentage of private-sector organizations do logistics well.

2. *IDR—individual default response. Within each plan, the individual default response of each team member during work hours and outside work hours is listed by team member name. People pay attention to information associated with their names, not with roles, such as team member. The IDR can also be coded, along with other critical information, on individualized wallet cards that each person carries at all times.*

3. *Use an automated notification system that allows for preprogrammed messages, ad hoc messages, and voice-text translation. We all know that call trees are like passwords: they just don't work—and never have. Remember that you can use these systems to do regular notification tests painlessly—reports are automatically generated. Add up the time that you and everyone else spends on this, and the product starts to look very good, even as a testing tool. And obviously such a system can perform much better than any manual call tree during an emergency. So do not put the contact information of team members in the team plan. Put it in an ASP-based high-performing automated notification system. Sell this kind of system to your management based on higher business continuity program productivity and ROI, not just on superior performance during the catastrophic emergency that they suspect will never happen. One caveat: make sure that the service that you subscribe to has fully redundant sites far from each other and that it can be accessed through phone or the Internet. Make sure nothing goes on your site, because your emergency communication system will disappear when your site does! Sounds pretty obvious, but until the current generation of products, companies in fact put emergency communication boxes in their primary sites!*

4. *Keep your detailed reference information—electronic and nonelectronic—off-site and out of your plan. A good place for technical recovery information, past tests, command-level system re-creation scripts, and so on, is the site where you plan to re-create your systems. Coordination information and contractual information can be in your command center. If you have more than one command center, replicate the information in each and store a copy off-site as well, just in case. Just do not put it in the plans. Make your maintenance requirements minimal, and you will have a chance to have current information.*

5. *Don't forget that the best recovery is one that does not have to happen. Make sure that you identify all risks in mission-critical resources (not just IT) in a risk assessment. Then eliminate those risks where it is reasonable to do so, and lower their probability or occurrence where feasibility allows. No, you never get 100 percent, but the 80/20 rule applies here. Painful experience teaches that many interruptions are self-generated and fully avoidable. This is another topic entirely, but one that you need absolutely to address.*

6. *One more hint: More and more of us in the profession are understanding that recovery planning for the total catastrophic event (the so-called worst-case scenario) is not the best way to go. If you plan to deal with the interruptions that have a high probability of occurrence, you will get more immediate payback from your business continuity efforts. Work up to the worst case gradually—don't start with it. But again, this is a whole other subject.*

My advice to someone who is new to business continuity, but is nonetheless charged with doing a business continuity plan for regulatory or other purposes: Hire someone to advise you and take their advice. There is no reasonable justification for any enterprise to expect you to do something well that you have never done before and where you have no training or knowledge. Knowing the business and knowing IT is not equal to knowing business continuity. This is a complex professional skill that takes time and pain to acquire. And guess what? It is continually evolving. Sorry, there are no silver bullets here. If your organization is too small to pay someone to advise you, at least get some training. Just remember that you need a whole lot more than a recipe! And, that you will truly get nowhere if you are expecting to do this in your spare time.[3]

Improving the BC Staff

The most likely way to improve an organization's capabilities in the area of BC is to provide training and encourage professionalism among those assigned to the role. There are a number of organizations that provide professional training for BC team members. This training ranges from managerial to technical, depending on the provider. Although most organizations can train their own personnel, it helps if at least one team member, preferably the team leader or CISO, has attended formal BCP training.

BC Training

There are many choices in obtaining BC training. These options range from classes taught through continuing education programs to private professional training institutions to national conferences. There are many Web sites dedicated to sharing information in this area, such as the Institute of Internal Auditors, which has a page with over 40 references to business continuity vendors and trainers (*www.theiia.org/itaudit/?fuseaction=catref&catid=8*).

Additional BC institutions offering training opportunities are shown in Table 10-1.

TABLE 10-1 BC training institutions

Institution	URL
Association of Contingency Planners	http://www.acp-international.com/
Business Continuity Institute	http://www.thebci.org/
Business Continuity Planners Association	http://www.bcpa.org/
Disaster Recovery Institute International	http://www.drii.org/
Disaster Recovery Journal	http://www.drj.com/
Institute for Business Continuity Training	http://www.ibct.com/
Management Advisory Services & Publications	http://www.masp.com/
Sentryx	http://www.sentryx.com/
Survive	http://www.survive.com/

Note that some of the institutions listed in Table 10-1 are organizations that provide services only to their members at annual conferences and events. Several other organizations host annual conferences in which academic and practitioner presentations on BC are conducted. The authors themselves have presented papers on the subject at regional and national conferences, such as the Association for Information Systems (*www.ais.org*), the Colloquium for Information Systems Security Education (*www.ncisse.org*), and the Information Security Curriculum Development Conference (*http://infosec.kennesaw.edu/InfoSecCD2005/*). An organization should use care in selecting conferences to ensure that appropriate topics are part of the agenda.

When considering BC training, keep in mind that Continuity Central conducted an extensive satisfaction survey on BC training. With over 200 responses they found a general lack of approval for available options as described in this observation:

> *Just 1.2 percent of respondents say that current training opportunities are excellent, with a further 20.4 percent stating that they are adequate. A resounding 65.5 percent say that training opportunities are somewhat inadequate, and 13 percent think that they are totally inadequate.*

On the positive side, budgets for business continuity training are generally either increasing (37 percent) or remaining the same (49.3 percent). Only 13.7 percent of respondents report that their budgets have been cut since last year. However, only 37 percent of respondents actually have a formal business continuity training budget.

The survey also looked at the types of venue in which people would prefer to be trained. External but informal facilities, such as hotel seminar rooms, are the most popular choice (41.2 percent), followed by respondent's own in-house training rooms (18.9 percent). A formal academic institution is the next most popular choice (15.3 percent), and almost a quarter of respondents (24.1 percent) would like their training delivered online.[4]

BC Professional Certification

Many organizations and working professionals believe that professional associations and professional certification work together to improve the results of the BC processes in their organizations. It is not always necessary to achieve a professional certification in order to join an association. However, the acquisition of a widely recognized certification is one method to receive an independent acknowledgment of the knowledge, skills, and possible background of the individual who aspires to lead the BC processes in an organization.

There are two dominantly recognized professional institutions certifying business continuity professionals, the Business Continuity Institute (BCI, www.theBCI.org), headquartered in the United Kingdom, and DRI International (DRII, www.DR.org), headquartered in Falls Church, Virginia, in the United States. Both are member-owned, not-for-profit organizations. Both offer certification at different grade levels. Both agree on 10 specific disciplines—the Common Body of Knowledge—as the basis for certification. Both have an international presence: the BCI has approximately 1100 members in 31 countries, and the DRII has approximately 2500 members in 15 countries.

Although there are many similarities between the two organizations, there are significant differences in their certification philosophy and methodology:

- *The BCI bases its certification on the knowledge gained through professional experience. Applicants are required to complete a scored-assessment matrix, listing their applicable experience in each of the 10 disciplines. This information is validated by the applicant's references (two required).*
- *DRII also requires written references. The DRII bases its certification on the applicant's score on a multiple-choice test. Both require a specified length of time working in the profession to qualify for the various grades.[5]*

No endorsement of one certification or professional association over another is made here. However, some programs are more widely recognized as being leaders in the industry. These certification programs are presented in the following three sections.

Disaster Recovery Institute International (DRII)

For those interested in DRII certification with *less* than two year's experience, the Associate Business Continuity Professional (ABCP) certification is available. The requirements for the ABCP certification are:

- Take and pass the DRII qualifying examination with a score of at least 75 percent.
- Complete an online application for the certification.
- On approval, DRII will notify you of your status and the required recertification period, and send you your credentials.[6]

For those interested in DRII certification with *at least* two year's experience, the Certified Business Continuity Professional (CBCP) certification is available. The requirements for the CBCP certification are:

- Possess at least two years of significant practical experience in five of the subject areas of the professional practices for business continuity planners. Experience must have occurred within a 10-year period from your application date and must focus on your business continuity and disaster recovery planning responsibilities and accomplishments.
- At least two of the five selected subject areas must include: #3: Business Impact Analysis; #4: Developing Business Continuity Strategies; #6: Developing and Implementing Business Continuity Plans; or #8: Maintaining and Exercising Business Continuity Plans.
- Pass DRII's qualifying examination with a minimum score of 80%. If you achieved ABCP status within the last three years, you are not required to retake the exam.
- Complete the online application for professional certification.
- Tell your references about your application. Ask for their prompt assistance when DRII sends your subject area pages to them to substantiate your experience.[7]

The Business Continuity Institute

The Business Continuity Institute (BCI) offers one certification, the BCI Professional Recognition Program, which includes a professional and a nonprofessional membership.

Professional membership includes the grades: Fellow, Member, Specialist, and Associate. All who apply for any of these categories of membership need to complete a professional application form in addition to the general application form. The professional application form is scored and assessed by a panel of the BCI Membership Committee and a grade of membership is offered based on experience. Fellows, Members, and Specialists are

Statutory Members of the BCI, and have the right to vote in elections for Board Directors, at the AGM, and on those issues which the Board may wish to put to the membership.

Nonprofessional membership includes the grades Affiliate and Student. Affiliate membership is often taken by those very new to the profession who don't yet have the experience to apply for professional membership...Those applying for these nonprofessional categories of membership need to complete a general application form.[8]

International Knowledge Domains

It is interesting that DRII and BCI have co-published 10 subject areas for certification, resulting in a truly international body of knowledge necessary for certification. These 10 areas are listed in Table 10-2.

TABLE 10-2   DRII and BCI certifications[9]

Subject Area Description
Subject Area 1: Project Initiation and Management Establish the need for a business continuity management (BCM) process or function, including resilience strategies, recovery objectives, business continuity, and crisis management plans. Obtain management support and organize and manage the formulation of the function or process either in collaboration with, or as a key component of, an integrated risk management initiative.
Subject Area 2: Business Impact Analysis Identify the impacts resulting from disruptions and disaster scenarios that can affect the organization and techniques that can be used to quantify and qualify such impacts. Identify time-critical functions, their recovery priorities, and interdependencies so that recovery time objectives can be set.
Subject Area 3: Risk Evaluation and Control Determine the events and external surroundings that can adversely affect the organization and its resources (facilities, technologies, and so on) with disruption as well as disaster, the damage such events can cause, and the controls needed to prevent or minimize the effects of potential loss. Provide cost-benefit analysis to justify investment in controls to mitigate risks.
Subject Area 4: Developing Business Continuity Management Strategies Determine and guide the selection of possible business operating strategies for continuation of business within the recovery point objective and recovery time objective, while maintaining the organization's critical functions.
Subject Area 5: Emergency Response and Operations Develop and implement procedures for response and stabilizing the situation following an incident or event, including establishing and managing an emergency operations center to be used as a command center during the emergency.
Subject Area 6: Developing and Implementing Business Continuity and Crisis Management Plans Design, develop, and implement business continuity and crisis management plans that provide continuity within the recovery time and recovery point objectives.

TABLE 10-3 DRII and BCI certifications (continued)[10]

Subject Area Description
Subject Area 7: Awareness and Training Programs Prepare a program to create and maintain corporate awareness and enhance the skills required to develop and implement the business continuity management program or process and its supporting activities.
Subject Area 8: Maintaining and Exercising Business Continuity and Crisis Managements Plans Preplan and coordinate plan exercises, and evaluate and document plan exercise results. Develop processes to maintain the currency of continuity capabilities and the plan document in accordance with the organization's strategic direction. Verify that the plan will prove effective by comparison with a suitable standard, and report results in a clear and concise manner.
Subject Area 9: Crisis Communications Develop, coordinate, evaluate, and exercise plans to communicate with internal stakeholders (employees, corporate management, and so on), external stakeholders (customers, shareholders, vendors, suppliers, and so on), and the media (print, radio, television, Internet, and so on).
Subject Area 10: Coordination with External Agencies Establish applicable procedures and policies for coordinating continuity and restoration activities with external agencies (local, state, national, emergency responders defense, and so on), while ensuring compliance with applicable statutes or regulations.

MAINTAINING THE BC PLAN

As with the incident response and disaster recovery plan, the BC plan requires a formal maintenance and update strategy. When the organization rehearses the plan and follows the preparatory steps to ready the plan for deployment, they may discover suggestions for improvement. These ideas should be documented for later use in the maintenance process. The after-action reviews also provide valuable ideas for the improvement of the plan. The plan should be reviewed, formally, at least once each year. Note that in a very dynamic environment this review may need to occur more frequently.

The Periodic BC Review

The BC review, conducted by the planning team, with input from all necessary stakeholders, serves the following purposes:

- A refresher on the content of the plan
- An assessment of the suitability of the plan
- An opportunity to reconcile BC activities with other regulatory activities
- An opportunity to make needed minor changes that have been documented but not implemented since the last formal review

Just because an organization conducts an exercise and finds areas for improvement in the BC plan does not mean the document is hauled out and immediately revised. While this would be ideal, it would also mean the document is in a constant state of flux, with employees unsure as to which is the "official" version.

As a result, it is important to collect recommendations for improvement, through the events discussed previously, but it is also important to queue these for consideration at the next formal review. Each recommendation for change is not automatically implemented. Each recommendation must be carefully weighed to determine if the change represents true improvement in the overall plan. Sometimes a modification in one team's actions can have unforeseen consequences to other teams or even the overall organization.

If, for example, someone recommends that an organization postpone updating the automated notification system until the BC team has completed all preparation tasks at the alternate site, the organization may find that the organization is delayed hours if not days before it can resume operations. Therefore, it is as important to have all ideas evaluated as it is to have them heard before adding them to the plan.

BC Plan Archivist

One of the requirements of the BC plan is to have an individual responsible for the maintenance of the document. This individual either works with or is the BC team leader and works to schedule the meeting for the periodic review. Upon completion of the meeting, the responsible scribe, historian, or archivist (or whatever the organization chooses to term him or her) will similarly be responsible for updating the master document and redistributing copies for approval. Once the document is formally approved, the new master is distributed to the appropriate individuals.

An additional requirement for this individual is the collection of, and the secure destruction of, the old version of the document. As described in earlier chapters, as a classified document, the BC plan must be carefully managed. Outdated copies must be collected, accounted for, and shredded or otherwise securely disposed of. Once the new copies are in the proper hands, and the old copies properly handled, this individual then returns to the ongoing job of collecting and storing recommendations for change for the next iteration.

Chapter Summary

- Implementation of the BC plan occurs when an organization comes to the conclusion that it cannot reasonably expect to resume essential operations at the primary site of operations. Such a decision is not to be taken lightly because it almost always incurs a substantial expense.

- Implementation of the BC plan involves making preparations for the BC action, relocating to the alternate site (first the BC advanced team, then the main team, and subsequently the rest of the organization's affected employees), establishing operations, and finally returning to the primary site or new permanent alternate site.

- Preparation for all possible contingencies is not usually practical; however, preparing the organization with one or several general training programs focused on implementing the alternate versions of known critical business functions can make the organization ready to implement the specifics of any particular BC operation.

- The initial decision about which essential functions are to be instantiated at the alternate site is followed quickly by determination of when they must be available.

- Affected employees are relocated to the BC site, and as they arrive, are organized and then directed to begin work.

- The advance party should include members or representatives of each of the major BC teams and may include the business continuity management team, operations team, computer setup (hardware) team, systems recovery (OS) team, network recovery team, applications recovery team, data management team, and the logistics team.

- Organizations need supplies and equipment to make work happen, and sometimes the lack of the most mundane supplies can substantially hinder operations.

- As soon as a reliable prediction can be made about when the site can be occupied by the essential staff, notification of that time can be given to the affected staff members.

- The final event that occurs at the BC alternate site is the preparation for and relocation to the primary site once it is restored and ready for resumption of operations.

- Just as with the IR and DR events, once the BC activities have come to a close and the organization has reoccupied its primary facility or new permanent alternate facilities, the team should meet to discuss what worked and what didn't in an after-action review.

- All BC planning projects produce plans that leave room for improvement.

- The most likely way to gain capability in the staff that performs the BC processes is to provide training and encourage professionalism among those assigned to each role.

- Many organizations and working professionals believe that professional associations and professional certification work together to improve the results of the BC processes in their organizations.

- The BC review, conducted by the planning team with input from all necessary stakeholders, serves as an opportunity to make minor changes as needed.

Review Questions

1. When does an organization implement the BC plan?

2. What is the trigger point in the BC process?

3. What are the critical steps in the BC implementation process?

4. Is it practical to prepare for all possible contingencies? How can this best be handled?

5. Why must the staff at the alternate site continue to observe backup strategies that are in place at the primary site?

6. What is usually regarded as the worst time to prepare a BC plan?

7. When a decision to activate critical services at an alternate site is made, what is the next decision needed?

8. What is an advance party, and what do they accomplish?

9. List and describe the BC teams that are usually included in the advance team.

10. What are the reasons that can cause an alternate site vendor to omit prepositioning all needed equipment necessary for a successful deployment at the alternate site?

11. What reasons might cause confusion and disorder at the alternate site when workers begin reporting?

12. What steps should be followed in the process to return to the primary site?

13. What is continuous improvement, and why does it apply to BC processes?

14. List and describe the 10 factors that may require BC processes to need improvement.

15. What are two ways to add capability to the BC team?

16. Name and describe two BC-related training providers.

17. Name and describe three BC-related certifications.

18. List and describe the international knowledge domains of BC certification.

19. What is the recommended maximum interval for BC plan review?

20. What role does the BP plan archivist fill?

Exercises

1. Using a Web browser or your local phone directory, look for organizations that provide business continuity services. How many do you find? What services do they promote?

2. Using a Web browser, search on the terms *business continuity* and *alternate site.* What do you find? What services are promoted?

3. Using a Web browser or your library's electronic search tool, look for articles on organizations that had to relocate because of the 2005 hurricane season. Specifically look for organizations that had to set up operations at an alternate site. How many mention having a BC plan in place? Bring the articles to class to discuss.

4. Using a Web browser, search on the terms *business continuity* and *training exercises.* What do you find? What type of exercises are promoted for BC?

5. Using a Web browser, search on the terms *business continuity* and *certification*. What do you find? Can you find any certifications other than those listed in this chapter? What core skills do the certifications you find promote?

References

[1] KnowledgeLeader, "Business Continuity Planning: Ten Common Mistakes," accessed November 20, 2005, from http://www.knowledgeleader.com/iafreewebsite.nsf/content/BusinessContinuityManagementBCPTenCommonMistakes!OpenDocument.

[2] See note 1.

[3] K. Lucey, "Business Continuity Plan Development Explored," accessed October 1, 2005, from http://www.continuitycentral.com/feature0106.htm.

[4] Continuity Central, "Business Continuity Training Is Generally Inadequate," April 16, 2004, accessed October 5, 2005, from http://www.continuitycentral.com/news01136.htm.

[5] L. Kalmis, "The Case for Business Continuity Certification," 2003, accessed October 1, 2005, from http://www.rothstein.com/articles/contcert.html.

[6] DRII, "Associated Business Continuity Professional," accessed October 10, 2005, from http://www.drii.org/displaycommon.cfm?an=1&subarticlenbr=21.

[7] DRII, "Certificate Information," accessed October 10, 2005, from http://www.drii.org/displaycommon.cfm?an=1&subarticlenbr=1.

[8] BCI, "Membership Grades," accessed October 5, 2005, from http://www.thebci.org/membershipgrades.htm.

[9] BCI, "Certification Standards," 2004, accessed October 5, 2005, from http://www.thebci.org/certificationstandards.htm.

[10] See note 9.

400

CHAPTER 11

CRISIS MANAGEMENT AND HUMAN FACTORS

The easiest period in a crisis situation is actually the battle itself. The most difficult is the period of indecision—whether to fight or run away. And the most dangerous period is the aftermath. It is then, with all his resources spent and his guard down, that an individual must watch out for dulled reactions and faulty judgment.

—Richard M. Nixon

OPENING SCENARIO

When the phone rang and the caller ID showed Colorado, Marie LeFleur expected to hear the voice of Alan Hake. He was scheduled to meet with a key supplier of HAL's networking equipment later that day in Littleton. But, it wasn't Alan; it was the police.

After Marie identified herself as Alan's assistant, they informed her that the business jet HAL had rented for this trip crash-landed in poor weather at the small airstrip close to the supplier's offices. Regretfully, there were no survivors.

After this disastrous news, Marie began to mechanically answer the questions from the police investigator. She was told what would happen next and what to expect as the investigation into the accident proceeded with business-like efficiency. Marie hung up the phone feeling numb and disoriented from the news. She stared for a moment at the cup of coffee she had poured herself only moments ago. Suddenly, nothing seemed urgent or important, except thinking about her boss and those who had traveled with him to Colorado.

The meeting they had planned to attend had included five HAL employees: Alan Hake, CEO; Amanda Wilson, CIO; Bill Freund, the manager of systems; Tina Mann, senior network administrator; and the newest HAL employee, Janet Dasher, who was just hired last week as a network technician. Using the chartered jet had been a matter of economics; the whole group could get to the meeting and back to headquarters in a single day for the price of just two people flying commercial. It seemed like a good idea at the time.

Marie thrust her head into her hands, crying. What was she supposed to do now?

Questions for discussion:

- After you review the organization charts from the end of Chapter 1, who do you think will be in charge of the company at this moment? Why do you think that person will be in charge?
- Who decides who is in charge when senior managers are lost? Is that answer different in the short term as opposed to the long term?

INTRODUCTION

Organizations typically respond to a crisis by focusing on technical issues and economic priorities, and overlook the steps needed to preserve the most critical assets of the organization—its people. Whether employees, vendors, customers, or neighbors, the people in and near the threat to the organization often are addressed last. Where data and the preservation of financial stability are concerned, companies spend large amounts of their resources in planning for off-site backup, alternate sites, incident responses, and disaster recovery exercises. However, the events of September 11, 2001, taught most organizations one tragic lesson: people cannot be readily replaced. Many of the organizations ravaged by the 2001 attack were prepared to some extent for a crisis because of the previous events in the World Trade Center in 1993. Those organizations had contingency plans, off-site data backup, responses planned to the expected types of incidents, and all the disaster and contingency preparations that could be developed. The blind spot, because no such event in recent memory had seen it, was the massive loss of human life that resulted from the collapse of the twin towers of the World Trade Center. Such catastrophes set new benchmarks that re-address scope of devastation, intensity of damage, or severity of impact. Although disaster management plans are capable of dealing with the loss of property and data, and business continuity plans are capable of relocating the organization to sustain continuity of operations, neither one can truly prepare for the devastating impact the loss of people has on the organization.

CRISIS MANAGEMENT IN THE ORGANIZATION

Crises arrive at organizations whether expected or not and whether or not contingency plans and crisis management preparations are in place. Before moving on to the details of planning for crises and ideas on how to manage them, this section covers the terminology of crisis management and a few of the myths that surround the subject.

Crisis Terms and Definitions

If you ask any 10 people what a *crisis* is, odds are you will get 10 different answers. For this reason, organizations should develop a clearly defined idea of what constitutes a crisis and what must be done when a crisis occurs. The Institute for Crisis Management (ICM) has defined a **crisis** as the following:

> A significant business disruption that stimulates extensive news media coverage. The resulting public scrutiny can affect the organization's normal operations and also could have a political, legal, financial, and governmental impact on its business. Crises are typically caused by:
>
> 1. Acts of nature (storms, earthquakes, volcanic action, and so on)
> 2. Mechanical problems (ruptured pipes, metal fatigue, and so on)
> 3. Human errors (the wrong valve was opened, miscommunication about what to do, and so on)
> 4. Management decisions and indecision (the problem is not serious, nobody will find out, and so on)
>
> Most of the crises ICM has studied fall in the last category and are the result of management not taking action when they were informed about a problem that eventually would grow into a crisis.[1]

Based on the rate of occurrence and amount of time the organization has as a warning, crisis events can be categorized into two types: sudden crisis and smoldering crisis.

Sudden Crisis

A **sudden crisis** is defined by the ICM as the following:

> A disruption in the company's business that occurs without warning and is likely to generate news coverage and may adversely impact employees, investors, customers, suppliers, and other stakeholders. A sudden crisis may be:
>
> - A business-related accident resulting in significant property damage that disrupts normal business operations
> - The death or serious illness or injury of management, employees, contractors, customers, visitors, and so on as the result of a business-related accident
> - The sudden death or incapacitation of a key executive
> - Discharge of hazardous chemicals or other materials into the environment
> - Accidents that cause the disruption of telephone or utility service
> - Significant reduction in utilities or vital services needed to conduct business
> - Any natural disaster that disrupts operations or endangers employees
> - Unexpected job action or labor disruption
> - Workplace violence involving employees, family members, or customers.[2]

Smoldering Crisis

A **smoldering crisis** is defined by the ICM as follows:

Any serious business problem, which is not generally known within or without the company, that may generate negative news coverage if or when it goes "public" and could result in more than a predetermined amount in fines, penalties, legal damage awards, unbudgeted expenses, and other costs. Examples of the types of smoldering business crises, which would prompt a call to the crisis management team, could include:

- *Sting operation by a news organization or government agency*
- *OSHA or EPA violations which could result in fines or legal action*
- *Customer allegations of overcharging or other improper conduct*
- *Investigation by a federal, state, or local government agency*
- *Action by a disgruntled employee such as serious threats or whistleblowing*
- *Indications of significant legal, judicial, or regulatory action against the business*
- *Discovery of serious internal problems that will have to be disclosed to employees, investors, customers, vendors, and/or government officials.* [3]

Crisis management (CM) is defined as those actions taken by an organization in response to an emergency situation in an effort to minimize injury or loss of life. This emergency situation could be isolated, as in a traffic accident, or widespread, as in a natural disaster. Another group of professional crisis managers, Crisis Management International (CMI), has offered definitions for other key terms in the field of crisis management, including the following:

- ***Emergency response*** *consists of all activities related to safely managing the immediate physical, health, and environmental impacts of an incident. These include providing first aid and emergency medical services; containing any fire or hazardous materials that may have been released; securing sites; and evacuating people who are not actively part of the emergency response.*
- ***Crisis communications*** *typically refers to the public relations aspect of crisis management. It involves communicating both internally and externally about what happened and what the organization is doing to manage the crisis. The key audiences to be addressed are employees, shareholders, media, customers, suppliers, and the surrounding community.*
- ***Humanitarian assistance*** *consists of efforts designed to address the psychological and emotional impact on the workforce. In contrast to emergency response, which typically focuses on the immediate safety of the workforce, humanitarian assistance refers to the range of services necessary to get your employees back to original levels of productivity.* [4]

Crisis Misconceptions

There are a number of misconceptions about crises that should be dispelled. The first is that the majority of business crises are sudden crises such as industrial accidents or terrorist attacks. Some studies have indicated that there are significantly more smoldering crises than sudden crises. Another myth is that crises are most commonly the result of employee mistakes or acts of nature. Unfortunately, the most prevalent are the direct or indirect result of management actions, inactions, or decisions.[5]

As illustrated in Figure 11-1, most of the categories reported in the annual Institute of Crisis Management survey[6] are managerial in nature. As illustrated in Figure 11-2, if the categories are grouped by area, there is a clear dominance of management-based crises.

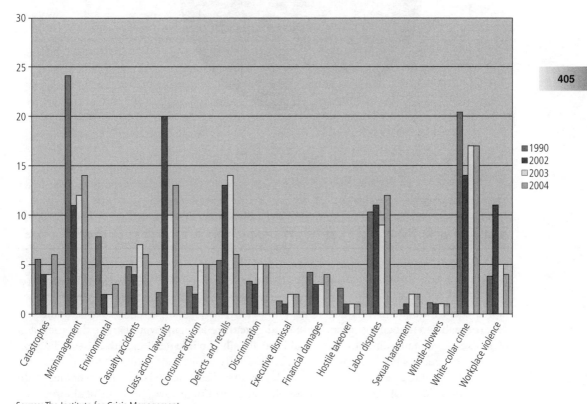

Source: The Institute for Crisis Management

11-1 Types of crises[7]

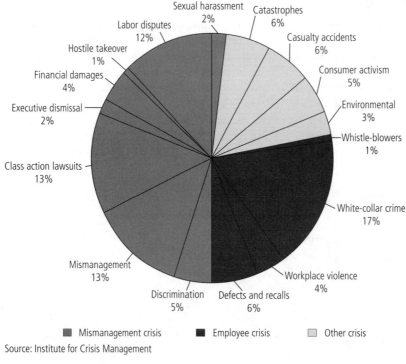

Sexual harassment 2%
Catastrophes 6%
Labor disputes 12%
Casualty accidents 6%
Hostile takeover 1%
Consumer activism 5%
Financial damages 4%
Environmental 3%
Executive dismissal 2%
Whistle-blowers 1%
Class action lawsuits 13%
White-collar crime 17%
Mismanagement 13%
Workplace violence 4%
Discrimination 5%
Defects and recalls 6%

■ Mismanagement crisis   ■ Employee crisis   ☐ Other crisis

Source: Institute for Crisis Management

11-2 Comparing managerial crises[8]

PREPARING FOR CRISIS MANAGEMENT

Organizations must prepare for the topic of crisis management just as they must for the critical topics of incident response (IR), disaster recovery (DR), and business continuity (BC). Unlike the topics in the broad area known as contingency planning (CP), which it is hoped occur infrequently, managers have to deal with crises on a regular basis. Some crises are small and innocuous, others large and catastrophic. Some would argue that the role of an executive management team should specifically include dealing with crises. The most effective executives have learned to deal successfully with crises. This is often the result of careful planning executed decisively to deal with issues quickly before harm comes to the organization. Keeping the various crises that arise well managed, and out of the media when possible, will serve to promote the strategic objectives of the organization.

General Preparation Guidelines

Some tips that can be useful as an organization prepares to improve its CM processes include the following offered by the Value Based Management Portal:

1. *Prepare contingency plans in advance (crisis management teams can be formed at very short notice, rehearsing of crises of various kinds).*
2. *Immediately and clearly announce internally that the only persons to speak about the crisis to the outside world are the crisis team members.*

3. *Move quickly (the hours after the crisis first breaks are extremely impor-*
   tant, because the media often build upon the information in the first hours).
4. *Use crisis management consultants.*
5. *Give accurate and correct information (trying to manipulate information*
   will seriously backfire if it is discovered, also internally).
6. *When deciding upon actions, consider not only the short-term losses, but*
   focus also on the long-term effects.[9]

The organization doesn't want to find itself in a position to make excuses for why it wasn't prepared for a crisis. Among the excuses frequently offered by companies in this situation are the following:

- Denial: "It can't happen to us."
- Deferral or low prioritization: "We've got more important issues to handle."
- Ignorance: "Risk? What risk?"
- Inattention to warning signs: "I didn't see it coming."
- Ineffective or insufficient planning: "I thought we were ready!" [10]

Preparation for crisis management can follow the same multistep process used for the IR, DR, and BC teams and plans. You are encouraged to review those sections as appropriate. Rather than reiterate the steps used for those functions, the following sections focus on the two most critical components, the CM teams and the CM plan.

Organizing the Crisis Management Team

According to Bruce Blythe at the CMI, the following is true of the crisis management planning committee:

> The **crisis management planning committee** is the group charged with analyzing vulnerabilities, evaluating existing plans, and developing and implementing the comprehensive crisis management program. Sometimes the crisis management planning committee ends up being the crisis management team, but often the members are different. This planning committee should include representatives of all appropriate departments and disciplines and champions committed to get the task accomplished, who have the support of senior leadership to shepherd the planning process through to completion. The planning committee is most effective if you have a mix of creative and analytical people. In addition, an outside consultant can offer objective advice and guidance.
>
> The crisis management team consists of individuals responsible for handling the response in an actual crisis situation. They should be trained and tested through simulations. The crisis management team exists to protect core assets—people, finances, and reputation—during times of risk. This team must be able to work well together under pressure and should have clearly delineated responsibilities and levels of authority.[11]

Unlike other teams, the CM team may only consist of a few individuals. It may also be relatively devoid of technically proficient individuals, because the primary focus of this group is the command and coordination of human resources in an emergency. Crisis management is focused on the physical, mental, and emotional health and well-being of the people in the organization. The CM team members may typically include the following:

- Team leader: The team leader is responsible for overseeing the actions of the crisis management team and for coordinating all crisis management efforts in cooperation with disaster recovery and/or business continuity planning, on an as-needed basis. A natural fit for the team leader would be a senior manager or executive in the human resources field.

- Communications coordinator: The communications coordinator is responsible for managing all communications between the CM team, management, employees, and the public, including the media and local and state governments. There may be several individuals working in this area with an intermediate supervisor. The larger the organization, the more communications there are to be coordinated. A manager or supervisor from the organization's internal communications department, if such exists, would be a natural fit for this position.

- Emergency services coordinator: The emergency services coordinator is responsible for contacting and managing all interaction between the organization's management and staff and any needed emergency services, including utility services. If an emergency is present and life or limb are at risk, someone skilled in interacting with emergency services is needed to serve as a liaison or contact person. These emergency services include not only the traditional police, fire, and ambulance services, but also the utilities and services the organization uses that in times of emergency are disrupted or represent a further danger to employees (that is, natural gas or propane). A manager or supervisor in corporate (physical) security would be prepared to handle this type of responsibility.

- Other members as needed: In certain organizations there may be a need to have representatives from different business areas assisting in the coordination of the employees, the CM team, and any external agencies or authorities. In some cases, each manager or supervisor may be a team member, responsible for conducting head counts, identifying possible missing or injured personnel, or generally distributing information on an as-needed basis.

Head Count   A **head count** is the physical accountability of all personnel and is essential in determining an individual's whereabouts during an emergency (whether they are still inside a building or not). Head counts are the responsibility of the first-line supervisor, who reports this information to his or her manager, who then aggregates the totals for reporting up the corporate chain of command. The old army adage *present or accounted for* describes the information that must be reported to prevent leaving an injured or unconscious employee inside a building during an emergency.

The planning team is also responsible for developing the CM plan, which will guide the team's actions during a crisis.

Crisis Management Team Planning Preparation

In preparing for the first crisis management team meeting, it is helpful to have a number of questions and, it is hoped, a number of answers to assist in the team's organization and initial strategies. A number of possible questions include the following:

1. What kind of notification system do we have or do we need? Is it automated or manual? Is it able to reach all employees or just management and the crisis team during business hours and after business hours? How long does it take?
2. Do we have an existing crisis management plan? If so, how old is it, and when was it last used or tested?
3. What internal operations must be kept confidential to prevent embarrassment or damage to the organization? How are we currently protecting that information?
4. Do we have an official spokesperson for the organization? Who is our alternate?
5. What information should we share with the media if we have a crisis? With our employees?
6. What crises have we faced in the past? What crises have other organizations in our region faced? In our industry? Have we changed how we operate as a result of these crises?

These questions, and others added by the planning team, should stimulate conversation. This information, along with the same business impact analysis information provided to other teams (IR, DR, BC) can provide the foundation for shaping the crisis management plan. The use of scenarios, complete with best-case, worst-case, and most likely outcomes, can provide insight into the preparation of the CMP.

Crisis Management Critical Success Factors

Academics define critical success factors as "those few things that must go well to ensure success for a manager or an organization, and, therefore, they represent those managerial or enterprise areas, that must be given special and continual attention to bring about high performance."[12] The CSF approach was first defined by John Rockart in 1982.[13] Since then, it has been applied to a number of diverse managerial challenges. In this case, those factors critical to the success of crisis management boil down to seven areas vital to CMP.[14] They are discussed in the following sections.

Leadership

There is a clear difference between management and leadership. The distinction between a leader and a manager arises in the execution of organizational tasks. The leader influences employees so that they are willing to accomplish objectives. A leader is expected to lead by example and demonstrate personal traits that instill a desire in others to follow. In other words, leadership provides purpose, direction, and motivation to those that follow. On the other hand, a manager administers the resources of the organization.

A manager creates budgets, authorizes expenditures, and hires employees. This distinction between a leader and a manager is important because leadership may not always be a function of a manager, and it is not unusual for non-managers to be assigned to leadership roles. Many times, however, managers fulfill both the role of management and leadership. During a crisis, however, one of two things happens: either the leadership rises to the challenge and provides effective leadership, or the opposite occurs, and the leadership is ineffective in providing guidance, decision making, and management of resources to resolve or at least ride out the crisis with minimal impact on the organization or its employees. Some of the skills important in a leader during crisis management include the following:

- Multitasking: Handles multiple tasks concurrently
- Rational under pressure: Even when things get hectic, the leader can remain calm, cool, and collected.
- Empathy: The leader listens and relates to those he or she is responsible for.
- Quick, effective, decision making: Makes the best possible decision quickly
- Delegation: Assigns appropriate tasks to others best suited to assist
- Communications: In communication with all parties involved
- Prioritization: Handles most critical tasks first

Speed of Response

In the medical profession, the first hour after injury is referred to as the *golden hour*. If a person is treated by medical personnel during this hour, they have the highest probability of recovery. The same can be said of crisis management. If as much as possible can be handled in the first hour—removal of personnel from harm, execution of CMP, notification of emergency services, and delegation of tasks—then the organization and its personnel will have the highest probability of coming out of the crisis with minimal impact.

A Robust Plan

The plan is the heart of the crisis management response. A good plan, clearly defined, rehearsed, and managed can provide the organization the best possible chance of surviving a crisis. This is the subject of the next major section.

Adequate Resources

When a crisis occurs, having the right resources available at the right place can mean the difference between success and catastrophe. Some of the more critical resources include the following:

- Access to funds, especially cash
- Communications management, for the flood of incoming information requests
- Transportation to and/or away from the crisis area
- Legal advice
- Insurance advice and service
- Moral and emotional support
- Media management
- An effective operations center

Funding

When a disaster strikes, it is not the time to be cheap. Spend what you need, when you need it, and financially you will be much better off than if you attempt to save money. The organization that cuts corners in a crisis may find itself spending substantially more in legal fees and punitive damages should an injured employee, or the family of a deceased employee, convince the courts that the organization didn't do everything it possibly could to prevent the injury or death. Some of the expenses that may arise during or after a crisis include:

1. Employee assistance programs, including counseling
2. Travel expenses, including lodging
3. Employee overtime for hourly staff
4. Replacement of lost, damaged, or destroyed property for employees
5. Compensation for those who were injured

Caring and Compassionate Response

While business is business, at some point it has to be people concerned about people. During a crisis, people need to know the organization cares about them. This means that the crisis team and management have the necessary people skills and are able to demonstrate that they understand the personal issues the employees are going through. Sometimes a hot cup of coffee and a kind ear are more valuable than overtime and a quick memo indicating that the company will survive. Having comfort items such as warm food, beverages, blankets, and so on may prove beneficial psychologically as well as physically.

Excellent Communications

Not knowing what is happening can be construed as a form of torture. Keeping the employees, the community, and the media informed of the events and the organization's efforts can alleviate anxiety and assure everyone that the organization is making strong positive steps toward making things right. Some items to consider when planning the communications portion of the CMP include the following:

- Have key personnel undergo media training to understand and learn how to work with the media.
- Know who your stakeholders are and keep them apprised.
- Tell it all, tell it fast, and tell the truth.
- Have information ready to distribute, either verbally or in writing.
- Express pity, praise, and promise.[15]

Developing the Crisis Management Plan

The CM team must put together a document, just like the other continuity planning teams, that specifies the roles and responsibilities of individuals during a crisis. This document, as illustrated in the example *Crisis Management Plan for Hierarchical Access Limited* later in this chapter, provides instruction not only for the CM team, but also for the individual employees. It can serve as both policy and plan, although some organizations may choose to have separate documents. Although the specifics of a good CM plan may vary, a typical document contains the sections described next.

Purpose

The introduction to the document should provide an overview of the purpose, as well as identify the individuals to whom the document applies.

Crisis Management Planning Committee

The identification of the CM planning committee is an important section in any CM document. This section not only identifies the individuals, but it also defines the difference between the planning committee and the operating team. Identification of CM personnel can be by name or by position. By indicating the individual by name, the organization could avoid any ambiguities in the assignment of responsibilities. However, this requires frequent updates and can be an extensive list in larger organizations. Identification by position requires clarification in the event of similar job titles, but ensures that whomever holds the position is responsible for the corresponding CM activities.

This section could also specify the frequency and location of the planning committee meetings.

Crisis Types

To avoid confusion, a definitions section identifying the types of crises that could result in implementation of this plan is helpful. A simplistic method of defining crises is to group them into three or four categories, each with a corresponding level of response required of the organization. One example could be the following:

- Category 1: Minor damage to physical facilities or minor injury to personnel addressable with on-site resources or limited off-site assistance. Category 1 crises may not require implementation of the plan but simply assistance in coordinating with emergency services.
- Category 2: Major damage to physical facilities or injury to personnel requiring considerable off-site assistance. Category 2 events last longer than category 1 events and may impact more than a few personnel.
- Category 3: Organization-wide crisis requiring evacuation of organizational facilities, if possible, and/or cessation of organizational functions pending resolution of the crisis. Category 3 crises represent the highest level of impact on the organization and may be in conjunction with local, state, or federal emergency relief efforts.

Individual organizations may prefer a more granular scheme with more levels to permit a more appropriate response. For small to medium-sized organizations, three levels may be sufficient.

Crisis Management Team Structure

The next section of the document should identify the CM team and their responsibilities. This is not the planning team, but rather the group of individuals who handle the crisis in the event the CM plan is activated. A CM team may be formed "to develop and maintain awareness of the crisis or emergency situation for [HAL] management and to coordinate support and assistance for crisis and emergency responders."[16]

Using the team structure described earlier, the three-person (or more) team is identified by names or titles and has their responsibilities outlined.

Responsibility and Control

This section may be included under the previous one. However, it is important to note the level of authority granted to the CM team leader or whether an executive-in-charge assumes overall responsibility. In some organizations, especially state and federal emergency management agencies, if an emergency is declared, the CM team leader may have authority over all public and private organizations until such time as the emergency is resolved. This is specifically designed to allow this individual to gather and use whatever resources are needed to deal with the problem. This individual would have a number of liaison officers from the various emergency services advising him or her, but would retain ultimate authority.

The concept of the executive-in-charge is similar to the military chain of command. A **chain of command** is a list of officials ranging from an individual's immediate supervisor through the top executive of the organization. "Running from the president to the secretary of defense to the commander of the combatant command, the chain of command for the United States military is spelled out by the Goldwater-Nichols Department of Defense Reorganization Act of 1986. The secretaries of the military departments assign all forces under their jurisdiction to the unified and specific combatant commands to perform missions assigned by those commands."[17]

The **executive-in-charge** is the ranking executive on-site when the crisis or emergency arises and is authorized to initiate the CM plan. Due to the travel-intensive positions of most senior executives, it is entirely feasible that one or more of the senior managers of an organization, the chief executive officer, president, or senior vice president, may not be available for consultation when a crisis arises. As a result, it is important for organizations to have a clearly defined executive-in-charge roster indicating the levels of seniority of the executives. The first few levels may be straightforward:

1. Chief executive officer/president
2. Senior vice president
3. Vice president for operations (or production or services, whichever is most critical to the organization's operations)

After that point, the list could get ambiguous. Should the chief information officer be next or should the vice president of human resources? Unless the organization has defined this ranking, the CM plan may not be implemented, or worse, people could be injured or killed. Organizations have traditionally maintained these lists, at least at the executive level. Formal inclusion in the CM plan allows the identification of an individual who can declare an emergency or crisis and begin the reaction process. This individual becomes the executive-in-charge.

The chief executive officer is primarily responsible for the implementation and control of the crisis management plan. In the event of his or her unavailability or incapacitation, the vice president of operations serves as the second in command. The remainder of the chain of command flows based on seniority with the organization from the vice president team. Should all vice presidents be unavailable or incapacitated, the crisis management team leader serves as the executive-in-charge.

413

Once the responsible individual has received notification of a crisis category event, he or she makes the determination as to whether or not to implement the crisis management plan, along with any other needed plans (for example, disaster recovery or business continuity). The crisis management team then begins work to minimize the threat to personnel safety and to identify any potential loss of life or health.

Implementation

The next section provides information on the implementation of the plan, including contingencies. The organization cannot assume the telephones or data communications networks will be functional. The real skill in developing CM plans is preparing for contingencies. A good plan provides alternatives for both optimal situations—as in functioning phones, electricity, and so on—and suboptimal situations with reduced services. Actions to be taken under each of the situations should be identified. Key tasks include communications to emergency services, management, and the employees. Initial responsibilities for the CM team are also identified.

Crisis Management Protocols

This section provides detailed notification protocols for individuals in the organization based on a number of common crisis or emergency events. As noted in the McMaster University crisis plan, these events could include the following:

- *Medical emergency: Epidemic or poisoning*
- *Violent crime or behavior: Robbery, murder, suicide, personal injury (existing or potential), and so on*
- *Political situations: Riots, demonstrations, and so on*
- *Off-campus incidents or accidents involving employees*
- *Environmental or natural disasters: Fires, earthquakes, floods, chemical spills or leaks, explosions, and so on*
- *Bomb threats*[18]

For each of these emergencies, initial notification instructions should be provided so that each employee knows whom to contact and when. These "initial response" protocols are the first step in the deployment of the complete CM plan.

Crisis Management Plan Priorities

The next section details the priorities of effort for the CM team and other responsible individuals in the event a crisis or emergency is declared. This requires the establishment of a number of general priorities, each of which has a number of subordinate priorities. This section also details the objectives for each priority level. First-level priority objectives must be accomplished as quickly as possible once the CM plan is implemented, followed by second- and third-level priorities.

Appendices

Attached to the CM plan could be a number of valuable appendices. Some of the more important are listed here:

- Critical phone numbers (communications roster) providing the office, home, and/or mobile numbers of key individuals, including management, the CM team, and emergency services and utilities.
- Building layouts or floor plans with emergency exits, fire-suppression systems, fire extinguishers, and other emergency equipment clearly marked. Assembly areas should also be designated. An **assembly area** (AA) is an area where individuals should gather in the event of a specific type of emergency to facilitate quick head count. For example, an AA would be outside in a parking lot in the event of a fire, in the basement in the event of a severe storm or tornado, or on the top floor or roof in the event of a flood. Why use assembly areas? AAs allow the organization to quickly account for all its staff in an area out of harm's way, minimizing the risk of additional injury. There may also be the chance that the crisis involves a criminal act, such as a terrorist attack, and the AA provides a mechanism to get everyone out of the crime scene and thus prevent contamination of possible evidentiary material. AAs also facilitate communication with staff and assessment of individual needs, as well as improve ease of access by emergency services.
- Planning checklists detailing who should prepare what are also beneficial to both planning and execution of CM plans. In planning, the organization knows who is responsible for what tasks, and during execution everyone knows who has the most current information.

Sample CM Plan

Appendix C of this book provides an example of a typical CM plan drafted for HAL (the fictitious company used in the book's opening scenarios and ongoing cases).

Crisis Management Training and Testing

Training in crisis management follows the same blueprints and procedures that IR, DR, and BC follow. Using desk check, talk-throughs, walk-throughs, simulation, and other exercises on a regular basis helps prepare the organization for crises, as well as helps keep the CMP up to date. Some training exercises unique to CM are described in the following sections.

Emergency Roster Test

Performed after hours, or on weekends, emergency roster tests, also known as notification tests or alert roster tests, seek to determine the ability of the employees to respond to a notification system, whether automated or manual. For tests to work properly, the organization should ask employees to let the company know if they are leaving town for the weekend for a predetermined period of time. This could be conducted in one of two fashions. In the first, employees are notified by phone that they are to call a predetermined number and report in. The exercise is concluded when all employees still in the area have called in. In the second, employees are notified by phone that they are to assemble at a predetermined place and time. On the following weekend, the alert roster is tested. To ensure that panic does not ensue, the organization may elect to include a code word or phrase to indicate that this is a test only. Once the employees show up, they may be given a quick overview of what the next logical step would be in a real crisis and summarily dismissed, or they may be rewarded with an impromptu tailgate barbeque (for example).

The example that follows describes a test of the alert roster at HAL.

ONGOING CASE: ALERT ROSTER TEST AT HAL

Version 1

Notice from the automated notification system: Attention HAL employees: This is a test of the emergency notification system. All HAL employees are directed to immediately report in their employee ID number at the following switchboard: (404) 555-3557. This is a test; however, all employees are required to report in, even if they are traveling.

Version 2

Notice from the automated notification system: Attention HAL employees: This is a test of the emergency notification system. All HAL employees are directed to assemble at the civic center parking lot at 11:00 a.m. today. This is a test; however, all employees are required to assemble unless they are traveling out of town with prior notification to their supervisors.

Tabletop Exercises

Another common CM rehearsal involves a scenario-driven talk-through, also known as a tabletop exercise, because most employees involved assemble around a conference table. In a technique like that presented in the opening scenario in Chapter 2, employees are given a general scenario, a sequence of several unfolding events or "injections" and asked to describe how they would respond. Messages can be passed around the table simulating coordination and communication, and the entire activity documented. An organization could go so far as to set up temporary e-mail accounts, and have all employees bring laptops and send their communications via e-mail, providing a record of the exercise. Unlike the emergency roster tests, tabletops exercises are usually scheduled, with employees planning to be out of their offices for the duration of the exercise. However, it is possible to schedule an emergency roster test with a tabletop exercise immediately following. It might smooth some stressed employee nerves, however, if the organization provided some notice, as in "Keep the first weekend of the month free for the next four months, in case we need an emergency budget meeting," or similar planning strategy.

Simulation

During Army Readiness Training and Evaluation Programs (ARTEPs), individual soldiers would periodically be "killed" or "wounded" by the issuing of "kill cards." Kill cards were simulation injections that informed a particular soldier that they were the victim of some injury or malady. That soldier would then drop, and simulate the injected condition. The soldier's squad would be expected to diagnose the situation, apply first aid, and handle the "injured" soldier appropriately. Organizations could conduct similar simulations by first notifying the employees that on one of a predetermined number of days, a crisis could occur. That crisis would affect one or more of the organization's staff, no notice would be given, and the remaining employees would be expected to respond accordingly, short of notifying emergency services. Some organizations may even go so far as to schedule a simulation in conjunction with a fire department training exercise, and notify their local emergency response unit to provide more realism to the simulation. In either event, an employee or group of employees would be notified that a crisis had occurred and that they had been affected in some manner. These employees would then simulate the situation, and other employees would respond.

These simulations work equally well with small-scale events, like an employee injury or illness, or larger scale events, like an unknown powder in someone's mail. The larger the event, the more coordination is needed and the more disruption will occur to the business. However, disruption during a simulation is good practice for disruption during a crisis.

First Aid Training

Although most organizations are not expected to provide emergency medical services, clinic services, or other on-site health care, many larger organizations have developed training and formal procedures to assist first responders in the event of medical emergencies. Although these services are most often activated to deal with individual health incidents and support local authorities and emergency medial services, they can also come into play during crisis responses activities.

First aid kits are a good idea to have available at any organization, but they do little good if the people present at the crisis or other event do not know how to properly use the contents of the kits. Whenever possible, some employees should be encouraged to have first aid and cardiopulmonary resuscitation (CPR) training. The contents of pre-positioned first aid kits need to be routinely checked to ensure that the contents are not outdated or missing. It is common for employees to use first aid kit consumables such as aspirin or bandages.

Beyond the ubiquitous and routine first aid kits, relatively inexpensive and easy-to-use heart defibrillators became available in recent years. These can be strategically located within a facility and should also be checked on a set schedule.

Other Crisis Management Preparations

In addition to the planning activities that the organization conducts during CM preparation, there are a number of other efforts that can benefit the organization should the CMP be needed. These include emergency kits, emergency identification cards, and medical condition notifications.

Emergency Kits

Ever have the lights go out in your home at night? Did you know where you store a working flashlight? What about matches and candles? Assembling or purchasing emergency kits is a positive proactive way to ensure that the organization is ready for a crisis. Similar to the disaster recovery kits discussed in Chapter 7, these kits provide some essential components that will probably be needed in the event of a disaster or crisis. Some common items found in emergency kits include the following:

- Copies of the DR, BC, and CM plan
- Laminated checklist of preliminary steps in CM plan for easy access during the crisis
- Laminated map with marked assembly areas and shelters to provide information on safe places to gather in the event of an emergency
- Laminated card with emergency numbers—gas, power, water, and so on—for quick reference
- Flashlight and spare batteries to assist in low light
- Reflective vests to allow personnel to work in low light or adverse weather conditions
- Warning triangle to mark off potential danger areas from traffic
- Caution tape to mark off areas from foot or automobile traffic
- First aid kit with disposable gloves to assist those injured in the crisis and protect those rendering assistance
- Clipboard, notepad, and pen for written notes and communications
- Permanent marker to mark anything that needs it—even people
- Spray paint or other high-visibility markers

A quick note on the many and varied uses of the permanent marker. It is a common practice among medical personnel in the military to mark the forehead or hands of an individual who is injured and who has received some type of first aid. Emergency services personnel arriving on the scene will know that some attention has been provided. In some cases, if the person has a medical condition, such as an allergy, diabetes, or the like, writing this on their body makes sure it is noticed should someone not be able to stay with the person or if the person is unconscious. Likewise, when the process of evacuation is underway, emergency personnel use spray paint to indicate which building has been searched or cleared and the status of any identified hazards.

ID Cards

A recent trend in corporate settings is to provide each employee with a crisis management identification card. This card serves two purposes. First, it serves as a quick reference for critical crisis management information by providing the automated information notification number, along with a few select emergency phone numbers. Second, it provides critical personal information to those assisting the individual should the individual be unable to communicate this information. A sample is provided in Figure 11-3. Some organizations have gone so far as to turn this document into a key fob, briefcase tag, or other easy-to-access item. Caution should be used to protect these cards, however, due to the sensitive personal information they contain.

Hierarchical Access, Ltd.
Emergency Information Personal Data Card

Name:________________ Blood Type:____
Work Loc:________________ Ph:________
Supervisor:________________ Ph:________
Medical Conditions:________________
____
Allergies:____________________
____
Next of Kin:________________ Ph:________
Children in Daycare (Y/N)
Where:________________ Ph:________
________________ Ph:________
Other Contact:________________ Ph:________

Hierarchical Access, Ltd.
Emergency Information Personal Data Card

In the unlikely event of an emergency, all HAL employees are instructed to contact the emergency notification system and register an "I'm OK" message: Ph. (800) 555-1234 or (404) 555-1234. Additional instructions will be provided at that time.

For Corp. HQ on Main Street:

- For a tornado, hurricane, or other severe storm: Go to the basement.
- For a flood: Go to the corporate conference room.
- For a building fire: Go to the parking lot.

Report to your supervisor immediately upon arriving at an assembly area.

In case of emergency, contact 911 immediately, and then notify the crisis management team leader at x5678 or notify the company switchboard.

FIGURE 11-3 Emergency ID card

Medical Alert Tags and Bracelets

Although the protection of personal privacy is of the utmost importance to most organizations, it may be necessary to ask employees if they have a medical condition and to provide detailed information to the organization so that the information can be relayed to medical assistance should the need arise. Although this is done in part with the emergency ID cards, another tool to assist emergency service personnel is the use of medical alert tags or bracelets. These medical notifications should be encouraged for all personnel with allergies, diabetes, or other special medical conditions. A crisis will inevitably be serious for some individuals; it is worse to receive assistance that compounds any injuries received during the event.

POST CRISIS TRAUMA

Soldiers aren't the only ones who suffer from post-traumatic stress disorder. As organizations found out immediately after 9/11, anyone can suffer the side effects of a severe traumatic episode. It is important for organizations that have just emerged after a crisis to realize that their work is not done. It is important to look out for the well-being of all individuals, not just those directly impacted by the crisis. It could take days before the health, welfare, and work of some to show the negative effects of a crisis.

Post-Traumatic Stress Disorder

Post-traumatic stress disorder (PTSD) is a condition that has been known in the past by different names—shellshock, battle fatigue, or battle neuroses. A current definition of PTSD comes from the National Center for PTSD, which states that "PTSD is a psychiatric disorder that can occur following the experience or witnessing of life-threatening events such as military combat, natural disasters, terrorist incidents, serious accidents, or violent personal assaults like rape. People who suffer from PTSD often relive the experience through nightmares and flashbacks, have difficulty sleeping, and feel detached or estranged, and these symptoms can be severe enough and last long enough to significantly impair the person's daily life."[19]

Because this is a widely recognized psychiatric disorder, dealing with PTSD is not a process to be undertaken by the typical organization. Your crisis management plan should make preparations for the fallout from PTSD either through a specific plan within the context of crisis management or using a program such as EAP, which is discussed in the following section.

Employee Assistance Programs

An important action an organization should take *before* a traumatic event is to ensure that the organization has at its disposal an employee assistance program (EAP). Some organizations carry EAPs as part of their health benefits, while others contract on an as-needed basis. EAPs can provide a variety of counseling services to assist employees in coping with the changes in life resulting from surviving a crisis. The organization should not simply shunt their responsibilities onto an EAP; the EAP can serve as a vital component of the recovery process.

EAPs fill the need to talk through issues that people are unable to deal with on their own. A humanitarian response team may be part of the crisis management team, staffed with counselors, legal aides, medical professionals, and even interpreters.

Immediately After the Crisis

As mentioned earlier, after a crisis, use assembly areas to gather employees, conduct head counts, and assess injuries and needs of the employees. In addition to the use of automated notification systems and supervisor head counts, the organization should consider using a buddy system for employee accountability. Pairing up employees can provide additional redundancy in identifying missing or injured staff. It also ensures that employees are not left alone and that they have at least one person to talk to.

Once the crisis has passed and employees are accounted for and treated, they can then be formally released by management. Organizations should resist the urge to move employees out of the organization's AAs as quickly as possible. The constant flow of employees through the AAs can result in some individuals "falling between the cracks." This occurs when a supervisor or manager thinks an employee has been accounted for by another supervisor or manager. By marshalling all employees in the AAs, a positive accountability can be obtained, ensuring no individual is left behind and that no one leaves without needed medical assistance. The stress of the crisis may also cause shock, which, if allowed to develop unchecked, can negatively affect the individual, as described in the section on PTSD. These individuals should not be allowed to drive themselves home and should be escorted either by a friend, buddy, or appropriate emergency services personnel.

Before allowing the employees to leave, it is helpful to hold one final information briefing to provide employees with an overview of what happened, who if anyone was affected, and what the organization's next course of business will be. If the crisis caused the implementation of the DR plan or BC plan, now is the time to advise the staff as to when and where they should next report for work. It is also beneficial to advise employees not to speak with the media. Although people may desire their "15 minutes of fame," the media has a tendency to report the worst of an incident, not the best, therefore, all communications should be routed through the CM communications officer through formal press releases.

Dealing with Families

A complete crisis management plan prepares organization management and staff to interact with family members, especially if serious injury or loss of life has occurred. These family members will be angry and frustrated at insufficient information. They may be looking to lash out at anyone they believe to be the cause of, or a contributing factor in, their loved one's situation. The intricacies of this interaction may be such that professional assistance may be needed from legal counsel, grief counselors, and employees formally trained to deal with these situation. Always try to follow up with those employees receiving medical care at clinics or hospitals. The "we care" attitude organizations want to portray can only be reinforced through personal interaction. Visiting injured employees or grieving families can reassure the affected that the organization is committed to seeing them through their situation.

GETTING PEOPLE BACK TO WORK

Once the organization has called employees back to work following a crisis, whether at the primary site or at an alternate site through the BC plan, it is helpful for the executive management to again conduct a briefing of all employees, either directly or through managers and supervisors. Employees will be starved for information, and without the facts, the rumor mill will run rampant. Providing employees with the facts, management's response, impact on the organization, and plans to recover will ease the employees' concerns about the security of their jobs, the welfare of their coworkers, and help provide closure to the crisis. The inclusion of timetables for recovery further alleviates anxiety.

A typical approach uses internal counseling sessions, both individual and group, to allow employees to vent their feeling about the crisis. In years past, concern expressed by industry came in the form of organizations holding "critical incident stress debriefing (CISD) sessions." In such sessions:

> *People recount what they experienced. Disturbing research now indicates that, although well-intentioned and often well-received, debriefings can in some cases exacerbate the distress people are feeling. Some research indicates diagnoses of post-traumatic stress disorder are more likely, while there is no objective evidence that debriefing actually accelerates people's recovery processes . . . Research and best practice standards indicate that it is vital to have only skilled crisis-management professionals monitor and follow up on your workforce as it recovers over the longer term, and to provide additional support services.*[20]

Dealing with Loss

One unfortunate consequence of crisis is the loss of coworkers, supervisors, and subordinates. Whether through death, serious injury, or an unwillingness to return to the workplace where a crisis occurred, employees may leave the organization. As a result, vital skills and organizational knowledge may be lost. If organizations are not prepared for the inevitable loss of these vital assets, they may find themselves suffering from additional effects of the crisis. How can organizations prepare for the loss of skills and knowledge? There are a number of techniques, including cross-training, job and task rotation, and redundancy. Beyond these concerns, discussed in the sections immediately following, when attrition in the chain of command occurs, succession planning can shorten the time it takes to return the organization to effective operation. This topic is discussed in the final section of this chapter.

Cross-Training

Cross-training is the process of ensuring that every employee is trained to perform at least part of the job of another employee. This can be done through many of the formal training techniques covered in earlier chapters, but it usually occurs through on-the-job training and one-on-one coaching. The challenge of preparing for cross-training is in ensuring that employees do not feel that they are being prepared for termination. This is best done by advising all employees ahead of time about the cross-training program and involving them in identifying their critical job functions. Lists of critical job functions within a department can then be crossed to another employee. It is not essential for the organization to cross-train all of an employee's work, only that portion that is critical to the continued operation of the company. Once a master list of critical functions is created, the supervisor can document all employees that are primarily trained to perform the function, because there may be more than one, as well as document those personnel qualified to perform the function should the primary be unavailable. This list should be reviewed periodically and updated as personnel change.

Job and Task Rotation

Job rotation is another approach to minimize the loss of personnel from an organization. **Job rotation** is the movement of employees from one position to another so they can develop additional skills and abilities. In many industries, there is a clear career progression from a lower-level position to a higher one. A software developer may be initially employed as a debugger, then promoted to code writing, then to software analysis, and finally to project management. This means that in an emergency this person could be called upon to perform the lower-level jobs.

This is an example of **vertical job rotation**. **Horizontal job rotation** is the movement of employees between positions at the same organizational level, rather than through progression and promotion. In this case, employees hired to assist in one area such as manning a help desk could be rotated to another area, such as assisting in the installation and configuration of client workstations. The key difference is whether the movement of the employee is representative of typical career progression or whether it is simply a change in position to prevent burnout and provide interest.

Task rotation is functionally similar to job rotation, but only involves the rotation of a portion of a job, rather than the entire position. Employees may rotate certain tasks, such as a software development team rotating the responsibilities to document the software development process, or systems administrators rotating the backup management responsibilities. Task rotation may be preferred for independent responsibilities, but may not cover all tasks performed by an individual.

Personnel Redundancy

Another method of providing assurance in the coverage of critical skills and knowledge is through personnel redundancy. Personnel costs are one of the largest expenses of a business, so the hiring of **redundant personnel**, individuals who are hired above and beyond the minimum number of personnel needed to perform a business function, may not be the best option for all businesses. However, if an organization can hire a few key personnel, and staff them to provide redundancy to two or more key staff positions, they may find themselves better suited to handle the loss of personnel in a crisis.

LAW ENFORCEMENT INVOLVEMENT

Organizations should not hesitate to contact law enforcement during a crisis. These professionals are trained in skills that are specifically geared to crisis management, including crowd control, search and rescue, first aid, and physical security. For the most part, the extent of involvement of law enforcement is the assistance rendered when the organization contacts emergency services, such as by dialing 911 in the United States. Typically, local law enforcement is involved, including a few patrol officers and perhaps a local detective. However, in some crises, the level of involvement may escalate quickly, through state investigative agencies to federal agents and officers.

Federal Agencies

There are a number of federal agencies that might be involved in a crisis, depending on the type and scope of the crisis. A few of the key agencies are discussed in the following sections.

Department of Homeland Security

The Department of Homeland Security (DHS at *www.dhs.gov*) is the single federal agency most specifically organized to handle crises, especially those involving threats to the safety of U.S. citizens and potential damage to the U.S. infrastructure. If it involves terrorist attacks, DHS is at the forefront. The following information is from the DHS Vision, Mission, and Strategic Goals:

> *Vision*
> *Preserving our freedoms, protecting America ...we secure our homeland.*
>
> *Mission*
> *We will lead the unified national effort to secure America. We will prevent and deter terrorist attacks and protect against and respond to threats and hazards to the nation. We will ensure safe and secure borders, welcome lawful immigrants and visitors, and promote the free flow of commerce.*

Strategic Goals

Awareness—Identify and understand threats, assess vulnerabilities, determine potential impacts, and disseminate timely information to our homeland security partners and the American public.

Prevention—Detect, deter, and mitigate threats to our homeland.

Protection—Safeguard our people and their freedoms, critical infrastructure, property, and the economy of our nation from acts of terrorism, natural disasters, or other emergencies.

Response—Lead, manage, and coordinate the national response to acts of terrorism, natural disasters, or other emergencies.

Recovery—Lead national, state, local, and private-sector efforts to restore services and rebuild communities after acts of terrorism, natural disasters, or other emergencies.

Service—Serve the public effectively by facilitating lawful trade, travel, and immigration.

Organizational excellence—Value our most important resource, our people. Create a culture that promotes a common identity, innovation, mutual respect, accountability, and teamwork to achieve efficiencies, effectiveness, and operational synergies.[21]

DHS has a six-point agenda for its mission to best address threats to the nation:

The six-point agenda will guide the department in the near term and result in changes that will:

1. *Increase overall preparedness, particularly for catastrophic events.*
2. *Create better transportation security systems to move people and cargo more securely and efficiently.*
3. *Strengthen border security and interior enforcement and reform immigration processes.*
4. *Enhance information sharing with our partners.*
5. *Improve DHS financial management, human resource development, procurement, and information technology.*
6. *Realign the DHS organization to maximize mission performance.[22]*

DHS also sponsors a public education site to provide information on preparing for crisis at *Ready.gov*.

> *Ready.gov is a common-sense framework designed to launch a process of learning about citizen preparedness. One of the primary mandates of the Department of Homeland Security is to educate the public, on a continuing basis, about how to be prepared in case of a national emergency—including a possible terrorist attack.*[23]

Federal Emergency Management Agency

Although the Federal Emergency Management Agency (FEMA) received some unfavorable reviews in the aftermath of Hurricane Katrina, their mission is a critical one:

> *Since its founding in 1979, the mission of FEMA has been clear: to prepare for, mitigate against, respond to, and help individuals and communities recover from natural and man-made disasters. FEMA was established through the consolidation of the emergency management functions formerly administered by five different federal agencies.*

> *The vision and mission will be achieved through a series of goals focused around FEMA's lines of business that build a strong internal foundation based on human capital development and performance-based management. FEMA is designed to meet customer needs as follows:*

> - *Goal 1: Reduce loss of life and property.*
> - *Goal 2: Minimize suffering and disruption caused by disasters.*
> - *Goal 3: Prepare the nation to address the consequences of terrorism.*
> - *Goal 4: Serve as the nation's portal for emergency management information and expertise.*
> - *Goal 5: Create a motivating and challenging work environment for employees.*
> - *Goal 6: Make FEMA a world-class enterprise.*[24]

Secret Service

The U.S. Secret Service has a dual mission. The most visible mission is to protect high-level politicians, but the Secret Service also investigates crimes related to financial securities:

> *The United States Secret Service is mandated by statute and executive order to carry out two significant missions: protection and criminal investigations. The Secret Service protects the president and vice president, their families, heads of state, and other designated individuals; investigates threats against these protectees; protects the White House, vice president's residence, foreign missions, and other buildings within Washington, D.C.; and plans and implements security designs for designated national special security events. The Secret Service also investigates violations of laws relating to counterfeiting of obligations and securities of the United States; financial crimes that include, but are not limited to, access device fraud, financial institution fraud, identity theft, computer fraud; and computer-based attacks on our nation's financial, banking, and telecommunications infrastructure.*[25]

Federal Bureau of Investigation

The Federal Bureau of Investigation (FBI) deals with many crimes that are potential crises. The FBI mission is "to protect and defend the United States against terrorist and foreign intelligence threats and to enforce the criminal laws of the United States."[26] The FBI currently has jurisdiction over violations of more than 200 categories of federal law, including counterterrorism, counterintelligence, cybercrime, public corruption, civil rights violations, organized crime, white-collar crime, and major thefts and violent crimes.

As described by Special Agents Sayers & Esposito, the FBI Computer Intrusion Squad has the following mission:

> *The investigation of cyber-based attacks, primarily unauthorized access (intrusion) and denial-of-service, directed at the major components of this country's critical information, military, and economic infrastructures. Critical infrastructure includes the nation's power grids and power-supply systems, transportation control systems, money transfer and accounting systems, defense-related systems, and telecommunications networks.*
>
> *Additionally, the squad investigates cyberattacks directed at private industry and public institutions that maintain information vital to national security and/or the economic success of the nation.*[27]

In other words, if the crime isn't directed at or doesn't affect the national infrastructure, the FBI may not be able to assist as effectively as state or local agencies. As a rule of thumb, however, if the crime crosses state lines, it becomes a federal matter. The FBI may also become involved at the request of a state agency, if it has the manpower available.

Federal Hazardous Materials Agencies

Hazardous material (HAZMAT) agencies are trained to deal with radiological, biological, or chemical threats. Whether terrorist in origin or as a result of an accident, as in a train derailment, these agencies must assist to contain the contamination and restrict exposure to the contaminant. When these incidents are the result of a transportation accident, most are handled by the Department of Transportation's Office of Hazardous Materials Safety. In the event of a criminal or terrorist act, the Department of Homeland Security (DHS), and/or the FBI, either leads or supports the response. However, in the event the materials are potentially radioactive, a special group from the U.S. Department of Energy's (DOE) Nuclear Incident Response Team is responsible for assessment and control.

State Agencies

Most likely your organization will interact with state agencies, more frequently than with federal agencies. State agencies are willing to work with trade associations, individual businesses, and local governments to assist both in emergency preparations and in actual crisis management. These agencies are discussed in the following sections.

State Emergency Management Agency

Most states have some form of state emergency management agency (SEMA) as the state's point of interaction with the federal DHS and FEMA agencies. As an example, in the state of Georgia, the SEMA's mission is: "To provide a comprehensive and aggressive all-hazards approach to homeland security initiatives, mitigation, preparedness, response, recovery, and special events. The purpose of our mission is to protect life and property and to prevent and/or reduce the negative impact of natural and man-made events in Georgia."[28]

State Investigative Services

Many states have their own version of the FBI, a state bureau of investigation (SBI). There is a great deal of variety in the names of the SBI agency. For example, in Texas, the primary state-level investigatory agency is the Texas Rangers, in Georgia it is the GBI, and in several states it is simply a function of the state police. These agencies may be associated with the state highway patrol, or they may be in a separate agency. In most states, an SBI arrests suspects, serves warrants, and enforces laws that regulate property owned by the state or any state agency. An SBI may also assist local law enforcement officials in pursuing criminals and enforcing state laws. The state investigative office may not have a special agency dedicated to computer crime. In most situations, an SBI becomes involved when requested by a local law enforcement office.

State Hazardous Materials Agency

Just like the DOE's HAZMAT groups, each state may in its transportation department have a team prepared to handle emergency spills from trucks, trains, and aircraft. Whether internal fuel or carried cargo, many substances carried on our roadways, railways, and airways would be hazardous to local residents and businesses if spilled, incinerated, or exploded.

Local Agencies

Some crises may only involve local entities or agencies. Even local agencies may have special training or preparation to assist with emergencies.

Local Law Enforcement

Each county and city has its own law enforcement agency. These agencies enforce all local and state laws and handle suspects and security crime scenes for state and federal cases. Local law enforcement agencies seldom have a computer crimes task force, but the investigative (detective) units are quite capable of processing crime scenes and handling most common criminal activities, such as physical theft or trespassing, damage to property, and the apprehension and processing of suspects of computer-related crimes.

Police Special Weapons

When dealing with terrorist or disgruntled employee activities, a police special weapons unit such as SWAT (special weapons action team) or SORT (special operations response team) may be called upon to handle the situation. These teams are elite police officers with extensive training in special weapons and tactics, prepared to handle hostage, sniper, terrorist, or other high-risk situations.

Bomb Detection and Removal

Another special police unit is the bomb detection and removal squad, also known as the bomb disposal unit or just the bomb squad. In some jurisdictions these individual may be part of the special weapons unit; in others they may have their own department. These individuals are trained to deal with incendiary, explosive, or contaminating devices, including to some extent radiological, biological, and chemical agents. Their job is straightforward: secure and remove any suspect item to a secure facility. With some explosive devices, a controlled detonation in place is used to remove the threat.

MANAGING CRISIS COMMUNICATIONS

An essential part of keeping the organization together and functioning during and after a crisis is managing the communications both internal and external to the organization. Some communications can be managed, as in the communications between the crisis team, management, and the employees. However, other communications may prove to be beyond the control of the organization altogether. This could include communications with law enforcement, emergency services, and especially the media.

Crisis Communications

Jonathan Bernstein of Bernstein Crisis Management, LLC offers 11 steps of crisis communications, reprinted here with permission.[29]

THE 11 STEPS OF CRISIS COMMUNICATIONS

By Jonathan Bernstein

Crisis: An unstable or crucial time or state of affairs whose outcome will make a decisive difference for better or worse (Webster's New Collegiate Dictionary).

Every organization is vulnerable to crises. The days of playing ostrich are gone. You can play, but your stakeholders will not be understanding or forgiving because they've watched what happened with Bridgestone-Firestone, Bill Clinton, Arthur Andersen, Enron, WorldCom, 9-11, the Asian tsunami disaster and—even as I write this—Hurricane Katrina.

If you don't prepare, you *will* take more damage. And when I look at existing "crisis management" plans when conducting a "crisis document audit," what I often find is a failure to address the many communications issues related to crisis and disaster response. Organizations do not understand that without adequate communications:

- Operational response will break down.
- Stakeholders (internal and external) will not know what is happening and quickly be confused, angry, and negatively reactive.
- The organization will be perceived as inept, at best, and criminally negligent, at worst.

The basic steps of effective crisis communications are not difficult, but they require advance work in order to minimize damage. The slower the response, the more damage is incurred. So if you are serious about crisis preparedness and response, read and implement these 11 steps of crisis communications, the first eight of which can and should be undertaken before any crisis occurs.

Step 1: Identify Your Crisis Communications Team

A small team of senior executives should be identified to serve as your company's crisis communications team. Ideally, the team is led by the company CEO, with the firm's top public relations executive and legal counsel as his or her chief advisers. If your in-house PR executive does not have sufficient crisis communications expertise, he or she may choose to retain an agency or independent consultant with that specialty. Other team members should be the heads of major company divisions, to include finance, personnel, and operations.

Let me say a word about legal counsel. Sometimes, during a crisis, a natural conflict arises between the recommendations of the company's legal counsel on the one hand, and those of the public relations counsel on the other. Although it may be legally prudent not to say anything, this kind of reaction can land the company in public relations "hot water" that is potentially as damaging, or even more damaging, than any financial or legal ramification. Fortunately, more and more legal advisors are becoming aware of this fact and are working in close cooperation with public relations counsel. The importance of this understanding cannot be underestimated. Arthur Andersen lost its case and went out of business due to the judgment rendered by the court of public opinion, not the judgment of a court of law.

continued

Step 2: Identify Spokespersons

Within each team, there should be individuals who are the only ones authorized to speak for the company in times of crisis. The CEO should be one of those spokespersons, but not necessarily the primary spokesperson. The fact is that some chief executives are brilliant business people but not very effective in-person communicators. The decision about who should speak is made after a crisis breaks, but the pool of potential spokespersons should be identified and trained in advance.

Not only are spokespersons needed for media communications, but for all types and forms of communications, internal and external, including on camera, at a public meeting, at employee meetings, and so on. You really don't want to be making decisions about so many different types of spokespersons while "under fire."

Step 3: Spokesperson training

Two typical quotes from well-intentioned company executives summarize the reason your spokespersons should receive professional training in how to speak to the media:

"I talked to that nice reporter for over an hour and he didn't use the most important news about my organization."

"I've done a lot of public speaking. I won't have any trouble at that public hearing."

Regarding the first example, there are a good number of segments from *60 Minutes* showing people who *thought* they knew how to talk to the press. In the second case, most executives who have attended a hostile public hearing have gone home wishing they had been [better prepared].

All stakeholders—internal and external—are just as capable of misunderstanding or misinterpreting information about your organization as the media, and it is your responsibility to minimize the chance of that happening.

In one example of such confusion, a completely healthy, well-managed $2 billion company's stock price dropped almost 25 percent in one day because Dow Jones reported that a prominent securities firm had made a "sell" recommendation which it later denied ever making. The damage, of course, was already done.

Spokesperson training teaches you to be prepared to respond in a way that optimizes the response of all stakeholders.

Step 4: Establish Communications Protocols

Initial crisis-related news can be received at any level of a company. A janitor may be the first to know there is a problem or maybe someone in the personnel department, or notification could be in the form of a midnight phone call from an out-of-town executive. Who should be notified, and where do you reach them?

An emergency communications tree should be established and distributed to all company employees, telling them precisely what to do and whom to call if there appears to be a potential for or an actual crisis. In addition to appropriate supervisors, at least one member of the crisis communications team, plus an alternate member, should include their cell phone, office, and home phone numbers on the emergency contact list.

continued

Some companies prefer not to use the term *crisis*, thinking this may cause panic. Frankly, using *potentially embarrassing situations* or similar phrases doesn't fool anyone. Particularly if you prepare in advance, your employees will learn that *crisis* doesn't even necessarily mean "bad news," but simply "very important to our company, act quickly."

Step 5: Identify and Know Your Stakeholders

Who are the stakeholders that matter to your organization? Most organizations care about their employees, customers, prospects, suppliers, and the media. Private investors may be involved. Publicly held companies have to comply with Securities and Exchange Commission and stock exchange information requirements. You may answer to local, state, or federal regulatory agencies.

Step 6: Decide on Communications Methods

For each stakeholder group, you need to have, in advance, complete e-mailing, postal mailing, fax, and phone number lists to accommodate rapid communication in time of crisis. And you need to know what type of information each stakeholder group is seeking, as well as the best way to reach each of your contacts.

Another thing to consider is whether you have an automated system established to ensure rapid communication with those stakeholders. You should also think about backup communications options such as toll-free numbers for emergency call-ins or special Web sites that can be activated in times of crisis to keep various stakeholders informed and/or to conduct online incident management.

Consider these factors in advance and rapid communication during crises will be relatively easy.

Step 7: Anticipate Crises

If you're being proactive and preparing for crises, gather your crisis communications team for long brainstorming sessions on all the potential crises that can occur at your organization. There are at least two immediate benefits to this exercise:

- You may realize that some of the situations are preventable by simply modifying existing methods of operation.
- You can begin to think about possible responses, about best-case and worst-case scenarios, and so on. Better now than when under the pressure of an actual crisis.

In some cases, of course, you know that a crisis is going to occur because you're planning to create it, such as laying off employees or making a major acquisition. Then, you can proceed with Steps 9 through 11, even before the crisis occurs.

There is a more formal method of gathering this information that I call a "vulnerability audit," about which more information is available at my Web site, *www.bernsteincrisismanagement.com*.

continued

Step 8: Develop Holding Statements

Although full message development must await the outbreak of an actual crisis, "holding statements"—messages designed for use immediately after a crisis breaks—can be developed in advance to be used for a wide variety of scenarios to which the organization is perceived to be vulnerable, based on the assessment you conducted in Step 7 of this process. An example of holding statements by a hotel chain with properties hit by a natural disaster—before the company headquarters has any hard factual information—might be:

- "We have implemented our crisis response plan, which places the highest priority on the health and safety of our guests and staff."
- "Our hearts and minds are with those who are in harm's way, and we hope that they are well."
- "We will be supplying additional information when it is available and posting it on our Web site."

The organization's crisis communications team should regularly review holding statements to determine if they require revision and/or whether statements for other scenarios should be developed.

Step 9: Assess the Crisis Situation

Reacting without adequate information is a classic "shoot first and ask questions afterward" situation in which you could be the primary victim. But, if you've done all of the above first, it is a "simple" matter of having the crisis communications team on the receiving end of information coming in from your communications tree, ensuring that the right type of information is being provided so that you can proceed with determining the appropriate response.

Assessing the crisis situation is, therefore, the first crisis communications step you can't take in advance. But if you haven't prepared in advance, your reaction will be delayed by the time it takes your in-house staff or quickly hired consultants to run through Steps 1 to 8. Furthermore, a hastily created crisis communications strategy and team are never as efficient as those planned and rehearsed in advance.

Step 10: Identify Key Messages

Holding statements available is a starting point, but the crisis communications team must continue developing the crisis-specific messages required for any given situation. The team already knows, categorically, what type of information its stakeholders are looking for. What should those stakeholders know about "this" crisis? Keep it simple—have no more than three main messages for all stakeholders and, as necessary, some audience-specific messages for individual groups of stakeholders.

continued

433

Avoiding Unnecessary Blame

An unfortunate consequence of any crisis is the human need to place blame. Whether a crisis comes from nature or is caused by human error or action, the media seeks to assign responsibility, especially if there were casualties. For example, some may say that the organization's management didn't do enough to prepare for the crisis, they reacted too slowly, they reacted inappropriately, or they just didn't react. Sometimes, accountability is entirely appropriate, especially if negligence was a factor. But, sometimes accidents happen and people get hurt or killed. The organization's challenge is to stay prepared to respond.

However, there is a significant difference between fault and blame. Fault occurs when management could have done something, in line with due diligence or due care, to better prepare or react to a crisis. Blame occurs as a human response to deal with the inexplicable travesty associated with loss—loss of life, of limb, or of property. If the organization does experience a disaster, in which they feel they were not at fault, there are steps they can proactively take to avoid being blamed.[30] They are discussed in the following sections.

Examine Your Vulnerabilities

Look for situations that could escalate to crises that could be interpreted as blameful. Start with the business impact analysis and move through the crisis management plan. Is there anything more you could reasonably be expected to do to prevent or better prepare for this event? Will your planned reaction create further risk to your employees or to others? If your CM plan goes as expected for each crisis, would you be proud to be on the news, or ashamed?

Manage Outrage to Defuse Blame

Be prepared to show off how prepared you were for an emergency. Whether the emergency is natural or a result of human error or action, your ability to demonstrate you were prepared can go a long way to holding off blame. If the crisis occurs on your company property and is in some way related to the functions of your organization, one method to defuse the outrage that will follow is to "seek and accept responsibility." Tylenol's actions in the 1980s not only saved their company, but also served as a case study for how to handle a crisis.

> In fall 1982, McNeil Consumer Products, a subsidiary of Johnson & Johnson, was confronted with a crisis when seven people on Chicago's West Side died after ingesting an Extra-Strength Tylenol capsule laced with cyanide. The news traveled quickly and was the cause of a massive, nationwide panic. Many marketing experts thought that Tylenol was doomed...
>
> As [their] public relations campaign plan was constructed, Johnson & Johnson's top management put customer safety first, before company profit and other financial concerns. They immediately alerted consumers across the nation, via the media, not to consume any type of Tylenol product. They told consumers not to resume using the product until the extent of the tampering could be determined... Along with stopping the production and advertising of Tylenol, they recalled all Tylenol capsules from the market, including approximately 31 million bottles of Tylenol, with a retail value of more than 100 million dollars.[31]

Johnson & Johnson went further, offering to swap Tylenol tablets for anyone who had Tylenol capsules in their homes. Their executives were seen visibly mourning at the funerals of the individuals poisoned in the event. After the first phase of the Johnson & Johnson plan was complete, less than six weeks after the poisonings, the company set out to recover from the crisis. They began by reintroducing Tylenol capsules in industry-leading, triple-seal, tamper-resistant packaging, becoming the first organization to comply with the Food and

Drug Administration's mandates. "The package has glued flaps on the outer box, which must be forcibly opened. Inside, a tight plastic seal surrounds the cap and an inner foil seal wraps over the mouth of the bottle... The label carries the warning: 'Do not use if safety seals are broken.' "[32] Johnson & Johnson continued by flooding the market with deep discount coupons and discount retail pricing. A new, bold advertising campaign was launched. The company heavily marketed professionals in the medical community, asking for testimonials to support the new packaging campaign. In the end, Johnson & Johnson returned to its trusted position, perhaps stronger than it was previously.

Questions to Help Avoid Blame

To further address the issues that could cause blame, and thus affect the organization after a disaster, the organization should finalize their planning by asking the following questions, even of the training scenarios they undertake:[33]

- Should you have foreseen the incident and taken precautions to prevent it?
- Were you unprepared to respond effectively to the incident after it occurred?
- Did management do anything intentionally that caused the incident to occur or that made it more severe?
- Were you unjustified in the actions you took leading up to and following the incident?
- Is there any type of scandal or cover-up related to your involvement in the incident?

The answers to these questions may reveal inadequacies in the planning or training process. Fortunately, if these inadequacies are discovered in sufficient time, before an actual emergency, the organization can avoid unnecessary blame and react more quickly to a crisis.

SUCCESSION PLANNING

When during a crisis a loss of life occurs, it is extremely difficult for individuals to function in the wake of such a catastrophe, particularly when the loss of life was witnessed by other members of the organization. When the organization's chain of command is broken and post-traumatic stress among the survivors hampers action, there are several key plans that an organization can use to help individuals continue to function and allow for the continued operation of the organization. This is also the case in the face of less catastrophic events. Whether a loss of an employee is caused by a fatal misadventure during a crisis or something as routine as leaving for another job, the performance of the organization will likely suffer. One such key plan is called **succession planning** (SP). It is the process that enables an organization to cope with any loss of personnel with a minimum degree of disruption to the functionality of the organization. The following material first explains the key elements of succession planning and then goes on to discuss the two ways that SP is typically used.

Elements of Succession Planning

Succession planning is widely recognized in corporate settings as an essential executive-level function. Assuring the orderly succession of promotions through the ranks over time does not happen smoothly unless carefully managed. The approach to SP included here draws heavily from the work of Dr. Michael Beitler, an academic researcher and industry consultant. Of great utility is his online article "Succession Planning" which was used as a basis for much of what is included in this section.[34] Dr. Beitler's approach is based on a six-step model that directs what senior management of an organization should do:

- Assure an alignment between the strategic plan of the organization and the intent of the SP process.
- Strive to identify the key positions in the organization's staffing plan that should be protected by SP processes.
- Seek out the current and future candidates for these critical positions from among the members of the organization.
- Develop training programs and development opportunities to make sure that potential successors to key positions are ready when needed.
- Integrate the SP process into the organizational culture to make sure that line management implements the intent of the SP process, and not merely the minimum requirements.
- Make sure that the SP process is complementary to the staff development programs throughout the HR functions of the organization.

Each of these management objectives is discussed in turn in the following paragraphs.

Alignment with Strategy

Every aspect of an organization's structure and operations should be aligned with the strategic planning needs as articulated by the organization's values statement and mission statement. The succession planning process and the contingency planning processes are no exception. The best SP process is created to meet the current and future needs of the organization's strategic plan as well as the needs indicated by the contingency planning process. The strategic plan of the modern organization is not a static one. Likewise, the SP and its components must also be dynamic in maintaining their alignment.

As noted by Beitler, "Changes in the strategic plan should automatically mandate a review of the succession plan."[35] One way of making this more likely to be successful is to make those responsible for the strategic plan also responsible for verifying the currency of the alignment with correlated plans, specifically the succession plan.

Like all well-formed planning tools, the succession plan must include its own mission statement or statement of purpose as well as be a uniquely customized approach for the needs of the specific organization for which it is developed.

Identifying Positions

After alignment with the overall strategic and contingency planning needs is assured, the SP process moves on to identify the key positions that should be included. The usual metric used to delineate the key positions is that each position included in the succession plan is one where the loss of an incumbent will cause great economic loss, result in significant disruption of operations, or create a significant risk to secure operations of critical systems. The thresholds for economic loss, degree of disruption, or increased risk must be established by the executives responsible for the SP process.

Once the key positions are identified, at minimum by title and preferably by some form of staffing identifier, each of these key positions must have the critical competencies and skills for that position identified. This should not simply be a restatement of the credentials of the incumbent, and it also should not be an elaborate upgrading to some desired degree of competence in future candidates. Rather, it needs to be a reasoned assessment of the needs stated in general terms to permit a reasonable degree of success in matching future candidates, while assuring successful deployment of the selected candidate into the key position.

Identifying Candidates

As a rule, managers tend to seek out and advance those who are similar to themselves. In itself, this is not a bad thing so long as it is not the sole criterion. Subjective assessment of individuals as suitable for the identified competencies of key positions should be based on objective evaluation of relevant criteria as interpreted using the judgment of experienced executives. Performance appraisals, especially those that include subordinates and peers, must be a significant part of the assessment process. Top-down evaluations of performance are not adequate to the task, because they leave a blind spot in the process where the self-perpetuating nature of the executive community comes to dominate the process.

When possible, validated psychological assessments of viable candidates should be collected and considered as part of the assessment process. A more complete picture of the candidates is revealed with a process that includes documenting the goals and objectives and reviewing a self-assessment of the candidates. When the candidates are assembled into a roster of possible candidates for the key positions, it will yield a very useful in-depth chart showing multiple candidates for each key position.

Developing Successors

Those members of the organization who are identified as having a role as a successor for one or more of the key positions in the SP process should have development objectives established. These objectives should not be separate from routine goal-setting and assessment activities undertaken for all members of the organization; rather, the SP objectives should be added to and then integrated with the routine objective setting and HR assessment processes. In addition to the expected training and development activities (skill training, seminars, and educational attainment), SP candidates should also have access to company-specific development activities including mentoring and other organizational real-time learning opportunities.

Integration with Routine Processes

To get the maximum value of the SP process, it must be operated by the line managers that form the core of the broad executive team of the organization. The key tasks of identifying positions and candidates and developing these candidates to be ready when needed cannot be delegated to the staff members of the HR department. Rather, line managers must be held accountable for these tasks.

Balancing SP and Operations

The SP process is part of the fabric of management execution in the company. As such it is but one of many accountabilities of the managers in the organization. It is important, but no more so than many of the planning, organizing, leading, and controlling activities common to managers everywhere. The challenge is to make sure that SP is considered no less important than any of these other activities and that each part of the SP process is integrated into this daily fabric of management decision making.

Succession Planning Approaches for Crisis Management

Most large and many medium-sized organizations already have SP programs in place. Those organizations that do not are cautioned that all CM plans must include provisions for dealing with losses in key positions as described in the earlier section on "Dealing With Loss." More complete CM plans should include a more thorough approach to SP such as that described in the previous section, "The Elements of SP." Regardless of the degree of SP being deployed, one decision that must be made and built in to the plan is the degree of visibility accompanying the SP process in the organization.

This concept of visibility or, as some call it, transparency regards the degree of information about the succession plan that is known to the members of the organization prior to their need to know about it. The two extremes of transparency discussed in the following sections illustrate the concepts involved. One extreme is an approach where all participants and many nonparticipant employees are aware of the process, know how they fit into it, and have a set of preconceived notions about how succession works in the organization. At the opposite extreme are organizations where the SP process is kept from the awareness of members of the organization until they need to know the details.

Operationally Integrated Succession Planning

The more visible approach is in place when the SP process is any one of the following:

- Fully developed as a supervisory process in the organization
- Fully integrated into the routine management processes of the organization
- Well known to the incumbents of key positions
- Well known to potential successors to those key positions

Organizations in this mode of operation do not need to make special provision for SP when integrating the SP process into the contingency processes. These organizations are well on their way to creating a resilient organization, capable of sustaining itself in the face of great adversity and even the most trying of crises.

Crisis-Activated Succession Planning

At the other end of the spectrum of transparency is the concealed version of SP. One of the issues facing organizations in this mode is the desire to conceal details about SP for critical business roles. Some organizations may choose not to reveal SP processes for a variety of valid reasons, including a desire to avoid alarming the members of the organization or to avoid revealing critical information to competitive intelligence gathering. These organizations must develop a contingent SP that is prepared using less open methods than an integrated plan would use. If a concealed SP process is used, the mechanisms used to backfill vacant key positions must become part of the crisis management operational plan, and the complexities this creates must be built into the plan.

439

Chapter Summary

- A crisis is a significant business disruption that stimulates extensive news media coverage and could have a political, legal, financial, and governmental impact on the business.

- Crises are typically caused by acts of nature, mechanical problems, human errors, or management decisions and indecisions.

- Crisis events can be categorized into two types based on the rate of occurrence and amount of time the organization has as a warning: sudden crisis and smoldering crisis.

  - A sudden crisis is a disruption in the company's business that occurs without warning.

  - A smoldering crisis is any serious business problem that is not generally known within or without the company.

- Crisis management is defined as those actions taken by an organization in response to an emergency situation in an effort to minimize injury or loss of life.

- There are a number of myths about crises that should be dispelled. Those myths are: there are more smoldering crises than sudden crises, and the most prevalent causes are the direct or indirect result of management actions, inactions, or decisions.

- The crisis planning committee should include representatives of all appropriate departments and disciplines who have the support of senior leadership.

- The planning committee is most effective if you have a mix of creative and analytical types. In addition, an outside consultant can offer objective advice and guidance.

- The crisis management team consists of individuals responsible for handling the response in an actual crisis situation and who are trained and tested through simulations.

- The crisis management team exists to protect core assets—people, finances, and reputation—during times of crisis.

- In preparing for the first crisis management team meeting, it is helpful to know the following:

  - What kind of notification system do we have or need?

  - Do we have an existing crisis management plan?

  - What internal operations must be kept confidential to prevent embarrassment or damage to the organization's reputation?

  - Do we have an official spokesperson for the organization?

  - What information should we share with the media if we have a crisis?

  - What crises have we faced in the past?

- The critical success factors for crisis management are: leadership, speed of response, a robust plan, adequate resources, funding, caring and compassionate response, and excellent communications.

- The CM team must put together a document that serves as both policy and plan and which should contain a purpose, a crisis management planning committee, a list of crisis types, crisis management team structure, responsibility and control, implementation, crisis management protocols, crisis management plan priorities, and appendices.

- Training in crisis management follows the same blueprints and procedures that IR, DR, and BC follow.
- Some training exercises unique to CM could include the following: emergency roster test, tabletop exercises, and simulation.
- In addition to the planning activities, other efforts can benefit the organization should the CMP be needed, including emergency kits, emergency identification cards, and medical condition notifications.
- Providing the employees the facts, management's response, impact on the organization, and plans to recover can ease the employees' concerns about the security of their jobs, the welfare of their coworkers, and assist in providing closure to the crisis.
- There are a number of techniques, including cross-training, job and task rotation, and redundancy that deal with the loss of critical staff.
- Organizations should not hesitate to contact law enforcement as needed during a crisis.
- Critical U.S. federal agencies include the Department of Homeland Security, Federal Emergency Management Agency, the Secret Service, the Federal Bureau of Investigation, and the federal hazardous materials agencies.
- An essential part of keeping the organization together and functioning during and after a crisis is managing communications that are both internal and external to the organization.
- Succession planning (SP) is the process used to enable an organization to cope with the loss of key personnel with a minimum of disruption.
- SP is based on a six-step model that directs an organization to assure alignment between the strategic plan of the organization and the SP process; identify the key positions; seek candidates for critical position; develop training programs and development opportunities; integrate the SP process into the organizational culture; and make sure that the SP process is complementary to development programs.

Review Questions

1. What is a crisis?
2. What is crisis management?
3. What are the generally accepted causes of a crisis?
4. What is a sudden crisis? How is it different from a smoldering crisis?
5. What is emergency response?
6. What is crisis communications?
7. What is humanitarian assistance?
8. List the general preparation guidelines. Which one of these seems to offer the most benefit with the least effort?
9. What is the crisis management planning committee, and how does it differ from the crisis management team?
10. Who should be on the crisis management planning committee? Who should be on the crisis management team?

11. What is a head count? How and when is it used in crisis management?

12. What are the critical success factors for crisis management planning?

13. What sections should be included in a crisis management plan?

14. What is the chain of command? What role is played by the executive-in-charge? Who might be named to this role?

15. What is an assembly area? When and how is it used in crisis management?

16. What is PTSD? Who should be involved in treating PTSD among members of an affected organization?

17. What is EAP? How is it used in crisis management?

18. When dealing with the loss of staff, what strategies can be employed?

19. What are the federal agencies that may be involved during a crisis? What role does each play?

20. What is succession planning? Why is it an important part of crisis management planning?

Exercises

1. Using a Web browser, go to the Web site *www.redcross.org* for the American Red Cross. What disaster services do they offer? Which would be beneficial for an organization experiencing a crisis?

2. Using a Web browser, go to the Web site *www.cmiatl.com*. Search for the title "Blindsided," or use a search tool to locate the text. Read the introduction describing the shootings that happened in Atlanta. What effect do you think this event had on the organization? Bring your comments to class for discussion.

3. Using a Web browser and a search tool or your library's electronic resources, look for stories on crises that have happened in the past six months in your region. What crisis management efforts, if any, served to mitigate the effect on the local businesses and residents?

4. Using a Web browser, go to the Department of Homeland Security's Web site at *www.dhs.gov*. Look under "Emergencies and Disasters." What services does the DHS have to offer organizations? Look for the link to the National Response Plan. Download it and read it. What information would be beneficial to organizations in their crisis management planning?

5. Using a Web browser and a search tool, search for the terms *school crisis management plan*. What information would be valuable to your institution in planning for a crisis? Does your institution have a crisis management plan? Find out.

References

[1] Institute for Crisis Management, "Crisis Definitions," accessed October 10, 2005, from http://www.crisisexperts.com/crisisdefinitions.htm.

[2] See note 1.

[3] See note 1.

[4] Crisis Management International, "Integrated Crisis Management Defined," Disaster Resource Guide, 2004, accessed October 10, 2005, from http://www.cmiatl.com/news_article61.html

5. Institute for Crisis Management, "Crisis Myths," accessed October 10, 2005, from http://www.crisisexperts.com/myths.htm.

6. See note 5.

7. See note 5.

8. See note 5.

9. Value Based Management.Net, "Some Help and Hints about Crisis Management," accessed October 10, 2005, from http://www.valuebasedmanagement.net/methods_crisis_management_advice.html.

10. B. Blythe, "The Human Side of Crisis Management," July 2004, accessed October 15, 2005, from http://www.cmiatl.com/news_article63.html.

11. See note 4.

12. A. Boynton and R. Zmud, "An Assessment of Critical Success Factors," *Sloan Management Review*, 25 (Summer 1984): 17–27.

13. J. Rockart, "The Changing Role of the Information Systems Executive: A Critical Success Factors Perspective," *Sloan Management Review*, 24 (Fall 1982): 3–13.

14. D. Perl, "Critical Success Factors for Effective Crisis Management," accessed October 11, 2005, from http://www.bernsteincrisismanagement.com/nl/crisismgr050815.html#cmu.

15. See note 14.

16. Lewis & Clark College, "Crisis Management Plan," Oct 15, 2003, accessed October 12, 2005, from http://www.lclark.edu/dept/hrpolicy/crisis_manage.html.

17. FOX News, "U.S. Military Chain of Command," February 24, 2003, accessed October 11, 2005, from http://www.foxnews.com/story/0,2933,74696,00.html.

18. McMaster University, "Crisis Management Plan," November 18, 1997, accessed October 11, 2005, from http://www.mcmaster.ca/policy/hlthsafe/crisis.htm#types.

19. The National Center for PTSD, accessed November 28, 2005, from http://www.ncptsd.va.gov/facts/general/fs_what_is_ptsd.html.

20. B. Blythe, "Blindsided: A Manager's Guide to Catastrophic Incidents in the Workplace," accessed October 10, 2005, from http://www.cmiatl.com/news_article51.html.

21. Dept. of Homeland Security, "The DHS Strategic Plan—Securing Our Homeland," accessed October 19, 2005, from http://www.dhs.gov/dhspublic/interapp/editorial/editorial_0413.xml

22. Dept. of Homeland Security, "Department Six-point Agenda," accessed October 19, 2005, from http://www.dhs.gov/dhspublic/interapp/editorial/editorial_0646.xml.

23. Dept. of Homeland Security, "Ready.gov," accessed October 19, 2005, from http://www.dhs.govhttp://www.dhs.gov/dhspublic/display?theme=36.

24. FEMA, "Mission and Organization," accessed October 19, 2005, from http://www.fema.gov/pdf/ofm/9mis_031103.pdf.

25. Secret Service, "Mission Statement," accessed October 19, 2005, from http://www.secretservice.gov/mission.shtml.

26. Federal Bureau of Investigation, "What We Investigate," accessed October 19, 2005, from http://www.fbi.gov/hq.htm.

27 The Center for Information Systems Security Studies and Research, *Lecturer Notes*, accessed January 26, 2006, from http://cisr.nps.navy.mil/guests/sayers04.html.

28 Georgia Office of Homeland Security and Emergency Management Agency, "Mission," accessed October 19, 2005, from http://rome.gema.state.ga.us/.

29 J. Bernstein, "11 Steps of Crisis Communications," September 1, 2005, accessed October 10, 2005, from http://www.bernsteincrisismanagement.com/nl/crisismgr050901.html. Reprinted with permission.

30 See note 22.

31 T. Kaplan, "The Tylenol Crisis: How Effective Public Relations Saved Johnson & Johnson," accessed October 10, 2005, from http://www.personal.psu.edu/users/w/x/wxk116/tylenol/crisis.html.

32 H. Goodman, "PR Effort Launches New Tylenol Package," *Kansas City Times*, November 12, 1982.

33 See note 22.

34 Michael Beitler, "Succession Planning," accessed November 28, 2005, from http://www.mikebeitler.com/freestuff/articles/Succession-Planning.pdf.

35 See note 34.

SECURITY INCIDENT HANDLING

Author's note: This appendix is reproduced verbatim from Chapter 5 of the RFC 2196 Site Security Handbook

(Source: http://www.faqs.org/rfcs/rfc2196.html)

SECURITY INCIDENT HANDLING

This chapter of the document supplies guidance to be used before, during, and after a computer security incident occurs on a host, network, site, or multisite environment. The operative philosophy in the event of a breach of computer security is to react according to a plan. This is true whether the breach is the result of an external intruder attack, unintentional damage, a student testing some new program to exploit a software vulnerability, or a disgruntled employee. Each of the possible types of events, such as those just listed, should be addressed in advance by adequate contingency plans.

Traditional computer security, while quite important in the overall site security plan, usually pays little attention to how to actually handle an attack once one occurs. The result is that when an attack is in progress, many decisions are made in haste and can be damaging to tracking down the source of the incident, collecting evidence to be used in prosecution efforts, preparing for the recovery of the system, and protecting the valuable data contained on the system.

One of the most important, but often overlooked, benefits for efficient incident handling is an economic one. Having both technical and managerial personnel respond to an incident requires considerable resources. If trained to handle incidents efficiently, less staff time is required when one occurs.

Due to the worldwide network, most incidents are not restricted to a single site. Operating systems vulnerabilities apply (in some cases) to several millions of systems, and many vulnerabilities are exploited within the network itself. Therefore, it is vital that all sites with involved parties be informed as soon as possible.

Another benefit is related to public relations. News about computer security incidents tends to be damaging to an organization's stature among current or potential clients. Efficient incident handling minimizes the potential for negative exposure.

A final benefit of efficient incident handling is related to legal issues. It is possible that in the near future organizations may be held responsible if one of their nodes is used to launch a network attack. In a similar vein, people who develop patches or work-arounds may be sued if the patches or work-arounds are ineffective, resulting in compromise of the systems, or if the patches or work-arounds themselves damage systems. Knowing about operating system vulnerabilities and patterns of attacks and then taking appropriate measures to counter these potential threats is critical to circumventing possible legal problems.

The sections in this chapter provide an outline and starting point for creating your site's policy for handling security incidents. The sections are as follows:

1. Preparing and planning: What are the goals and objectives in handling an incident?
2. Notification: Who should be contacted in case of an incident?

   - Local managers and personnel
   - Law enforcement and investigative agencies
   - Computer security incidents handling teams
   - Affected and involved sites
   - Internal communications
   - Public relations and press releases

3. Identifying an incident: Is it an incident, and how serious is it?
4. Handling: What should be done when an incident occurs?
   - Notification: Who should be notified about the incident?
   - Protecting evidence and activity logs: What records should be kept from before, during, and after the incident?
   - Containment: How can the damage be limited?
   - Eradication: How can the reasons for the incident be eliminated?
   - Recovery: How can service and systems be reestablished?
   - Follow-up: What actions should be taken after the incident?
5. Aftermath: What are the implications of past incidents?
6. Administrative response to incidents

The remainder of this chapter details the issues involved in each of the important topics listed above and provides some guidance as to what should be included in a site policy for handling incidents.

Preparing and Planning for Incident Handling

Part of handling an incident is being prepared to respond to an incident before the incident occurs in the first place. This includes establishing a suitable level of protection as explained in the preceding chapters. Doing this should help your site prevent incidents as well as limit potential damage resulting from them when they do occur. Protection also includes preparing incident handling guidelines as part of a contingency plan for your organization or site. Having written plans eliminates much of the ambiguity that occurs during an incident and leads to a more appropriate and thorough set of responses. It is vitally important to test the proposed plan before an incident occurs through "dry runs." A team might even consider hiring a tiger team to act in parallel with the dry run. (Note: A tiger team is a team of specialists that try to penetrate the security of a system.)

Learning to respond efficiently to an incident is important for a number of reasons:

1. Protecting the assets that could be compromised
2. Protecting resources that could be utilized more profitably if an incident did not require their services
3. Complying with (government or other) regulations
4. Preventing the use of your systems in attacks against other systems (which could cause you to incur legal liability)
5. Minimizing the potential for negative exposure

As in any set of planned procedures, attention must be paid to a set of goals for handling an incident. These goals are prioritized differently depending on the site. A specific set of objectives can be identified for dealing with incidents:

1. Figure out how it happened.
2. Find out how to avoid further exploitation of the same vulnerability.
3. Avoid escalation and further incidents.
4. Assess the impact and damage of the incident.
5. Recover from the incident.
6. Update policies and procedures as needed.
7. Find out who did it (if appropriate and possible).

Due to the nature of the incident, there might be a conflict between analyzing the original source of a problem and restoring systems and services. Overall goals (such as assuring the integrity of critical systems) might be the reason for not analyzing an incident. Of course, this is an important management decision, but all involved parties must be aware that without analysis the same incident may happen again.

It is also important to prioritize the actions to be taken during an incident well in advance of the time an incident occurs. Sometimes an incident may be so complex that it is impossible to do everything at once to respond to it; priorities are essential. Although priorities vary from institution to institution, the following suggested priorities may serve as a starting point for defining your organization's response:

- Priority 1:Protect human life and people's safety; human life always has precedence over all other considerations.
- Priority 2: Protect classified and/or sensitive data. Prevent exploitation of classified and/or sensitive systems, networks, or sites. Inform affected classified and/or sensitive systems, networks, or sites about already occurred penetrations. (Be aware of regulations by your site or by government.)
- Priority 3: Protect other data, including proprietary, scientific, managerial, and other data, because loss of data is costly in terms of resources. Prevent exploitations of other systems, networks, or sites and inform already affected systems, networks, or sites about successful penetrations.
- Priority 4: Prevent damage to systems (loss or alteration of system files, damage to disk drives, and so on). Damage to systems can result in costly down time and recovery.

- Priority 5: Minimize disruption of computing resources (including processes). It is better in many cases to shut down a system or disconnect it from a network than to risk damage to data or systems. Sites have to evaluate the trade-offs between shutting down, disconnecting, and staying up. There may be service agreements in place that may require keeping systems up even in light of further damage occurring. However, the damage and scope of an incident may be so extensive that service agreements may have to be overridden.

An important implication for defining priorities is that once human life and national security considerations have been addressed, it is generally more important to save data than system software and hardware. Although it is undesirable to have any damage or loss during an incident, systems can be replaced. However, the loss or compromise of data (especially classified or proprietary data) is usually not an acceptable outcome under any circumstances.

Another important concern is the effect on others, beyond the systems and networks where the incident occurs. Within the limits imposed by government regulations it is always important to inform affected parties as soon as possible. Due to the legal implications of this topic, it should be included in the planned procedures to avoid further delays and uncertainties for the administrators.

Any plan for responding to security incidents should be guided by local policies and regulations. Government and private sites that deal with classified material have specific rules that they must follow.

The policies chosen by your site on how it reacts to incidents shape your response. For example, it may make little sense to create mechanisms to monitor and trace intruders if your site does not plan to take action against the intruders if they are caught. Other organizations may have policies that affect your plans. Telephone companies often release information about telephone traces only to law enforcement agencies.

Handling incidents can be tedious and require any number of routine tasks that could be handled by support personnel. To free the technical staff it may be helpful to identify support staff who can help with such tasks as photocopying, faxing, and so on.

Notification and Points of Contact

It is important to establish contacts with various personnel before a real incident occurs. In many instances, incidents are not real emergencies. Indeed, often you can handle the activities internally. However, there may also be many times when others outside your immediate department need to be included in the incident handling. These additional contacts include local managers and system administrators, administrative contacts for other sites on the Internet, and various investigative organizations. Getting to know these contacts before incidents occur helps to make your incident handling process more efficient.

For each type of communication contact, specific points of contact (POC) should be defined. These may be technical or administrative in nature and may include legal or investigative agencies as well as service providers and vendors. When establishing these contacts, it is important to decide how much information is shared with each class of contact. It is especially important to define ahead of time what information is shared with the users at a site, with the public (including the press), and with other sites.

Settling these issues is especially important for the local person responsible for handling the incident, as that is the person responsible for the actual notification of others. A list of contacts in each of these categories is an important time-saver for this person during an incident. It can be quite difficult to find an appropriate person during an incident when many urgent events are ongoing. It is strongly recommended that all relevant telephone numbers (also electronic mail addresses and fax numbers) be included in the site security policy. The names and contact information of all individuals who will be directly involved in the handling of an incident should be placed at the top of this list.

Local Managers and Personnel

When an incident is under way, a major issue is deciding who is in charge of coordinating the activity of the multitude of players. A significant mistake is to have a number of people who are each working independently instead of working together. This only adds to the confusion of the event and can lead to wasted or ineffective effort.

The single POC may or may not be the person responsible for handling the incident. There are two distinct roles to fill when deciding who shall be the POC and who will be the person in charge of the incident. The person in charge of the incident makes decisions as to the interpretation of policy applied to the event. In contrast, the POC must coordinate the effort of all the parties involved with handling the event.

The POC must be a person with the technical expertise to successfully coordinate the efforts of the system managers and users involved in monitoring and reacting to the attack. Care should be taken when identifying who this person will be. It should not necessarily be the same person who has administrative responsibility for the compromised systems as such administrators often have knowledge sufficient only for the day-to-day use of the computers and lack in-depth technical expertise.

Another important function of the POC is to maintain contact with law enforcement and other external agencies to assure that multiagency involvement occurs. The level of involvement is determined by management decisions as well as legal constraints.

A single POC should also be the single person in charge of collecting evidence, because, as a rule of thumb, the more people that touch a potential piece of evidence, the greater the possibility that it will be inadmissible in court. To ensure that evidence will be acceptable to the legal community, collecting evidence should be done following predefined procedures in accordance with local laws and legal regulations.

One of the most critical tasks for the POC is the coordination of all relevant processes. Responsibilities may be distributed over the whole site, involving multiple independent departments or groups. This requires a well-coordinated effort in order to achieve overall success. The situation becomes even more complex if multiple sites are involved. When this happens, rarely can a single POC at one site be able to adequately coordinate the handling of the entire incident. Instead, appropriate incident response teams should be involved.

The incident handling process should provide some escalation mechanisms. To define such a mechanism, sites need to create an internal classification scheme for incidents. Associated with each level of incident are the appropriate POC and procedures. As an incident is escalated, there may be a change in the POC that will need to be communicated to all others involved in handling the incident. When a change in the POC occurs, the old POC should brief the new POC in all background information.

Lastly, users must know how to report suspected incidents. Sites should establish reporting procedures that work both during and outside normal working hours. Help desks are often used to receive these reports during normal working hours, while beepers and telephones can be used for out-of-hours reporting.

Law Enforcement and Investigative Agencies

In the event of an incident that has legal consequences, it is important to establish contact with investigative agencies such as the FBI and Secret Service in the United States, as soon as possible. Local law enforcement, local security offices, and campus police departments should also be informed as appropriate. This section describes many of the issues that are confronted, but it is acknowledged that each organization has its own local and governmental laws and regulations that impact how they interact with law enforcement and investigative agencies. The most important point to make is that each site needs to work through these issues.

A primary reason for determining these points of contact well in advance of an incident is that once a major attack is in progress, there is little time to call these agencies to determine exactly who the correct point of contact is. Another reason is that it is important to cooperate with these agencies in a manner that fosters a good working relationship and that is in accordance with the working procedures of these agencies. Knowing the working procedures in advance and the expectations of your point of contact is a big step in this direction. For example, it is important to gather evidence that is admissible in any subsequent legal proceedings, and this requires prior knowledge of how to gather such evidence. A final reason for establishing contacts as soon as possible is that it is impossible to know the particular agency that will assume jurisdiction in any given incident. Making contacts and finding the proper channels early on make responding to an incident go considerably more smoothly.

If your organization or site has a legal counsel, you need to notify this office soon after you learn that an incident is in progress. At a minimum, your legal counsel needs to be involved to protect the legal and financial interests of your site or organization. There are many legal and practical issues, a few of which are listed below:

- Whether your site or organization is willing to risk negative publicity or exposure to cooperate with legal prosecution efforts
- Downstream liability: If you leave a compromised system as-is so it can be monitored and another computer is damaged because the attack originated from your system, your site or organization may be liable for damages incurred.
- Distribution of information: If your site or organization distributes information about an attack in which another site or organization may be involved or the vulnerability in a product that may affect ability to market that product, your site or organization may be liable for any damages (including damage of reputation).
- Liabilities due to monitoring: Your site or organization may be sued if users at your site or elsewhere discover that your site is monitoring account activity without informing users.

Unfortunately, there are no clear precedents yet on the liabilities or responsibilities of organizations involved in a security incident or who might be involved in supporting an investigative effort. Investigators often encourage organizations to help trace and monitor intruders. Indeed, most investigators cannot pursue computer intrusions without extensive support from the organizations involved. However, investigators cannot provide protection from liability claims, and these kinds of efforts may drag out for months and may take a great deal of effort.

On the other hand, an organization's legal counsel may advise extreme caution and suggest that tracing activities be halted and an intruder shut out of the system. This, in itself, may not provide protection from liability and may prevent investigators from identifying the perpetrator.

The balance between supporting investigative activity and limiting liability is tricky. You need to consider the advice of your legal counsel and the damage the intruder is causing (if any) when making your decision about what to do during any particular incident.

Your legal counsel should also be involved in any decision to contact investigative agencies when an incident occurs at your site. The decision to coordinate efforts with investigative agencies is most properly that of your site or organization. Involving your legal counsel also fosters the multilevel coordination between your site and the particular investigative agency involved, which in turn results in an efficient division of labor. Another result is that you are likely to obtain guidance that can help you avoid future legal mistakes.

Finally, your legal counsel should evaluate your site's written procedures for responding to incidents. It is essential to obtain a "clean bill of health" from a legal perspective before you actually carry out these procedures.

It is vital when dealing with investigative agencies to verify that the person who calls asking for information is a legitimate representative from the agency in question. Unfortunately, many well-intentioned people have unknowingly leaked sensitive details about incidents, allowed unauthorized people into their systems, and so on, because a caller has masqueraded as a representative of a government agency. (Note: This word of caution actually applies to all external contacts.)

A similar consideration is using a secure means of communication. Because many network attackers can easily reroute electronic mail, avoid using electronic mail to communicate with other agencies (as well as others dealing with the incident at hand). Nonsecured phone lines (the phones normally used in the business world) are also frequent targets for tapping by network intruders, so be careful!

There is no one set of established rules for responding to an incident when the local government becomes involved. Normally (in the United States), except by legal order, no agency can force you to monitor, to disconnect from the network, to avoid telephone contact with the suspected attackers, and so on. Each organization has a set of local and national laws and regulations that must be adhered to when handling incidents. It is recommended that each site be familiar with those laws and regulations, as well as identify and get to know the contacts for agencies with jurisdiction well in advance of handling an incident.

Computer Security Incident Handling Teams

There are currently a number of computer security incident response teams (CSIRTs) such as the CERT Coordination Center, the German DFN-CERT, and other teams around the globe. Teams exist for many major government agencies and large corporations. If such a team is available, notifying it should be of primary consideration during the early stages of an incident. These teams are responsible for coordinating computer security incidents over a range of sites and larger entities. Even if the incident is believed to be contained within a single site, it is possible that the information available through a response team could help in fully resolving the incident.

If it is determined that the breach occurred due to a flaw in the system's hardware or software, the vendor (or supplier) and a computer security incident handling team should be notified as soon as possible. This is especially important because many other systems are vulnerable, and these vendor and response team organizations can help disseminate help to other affected sites.

In setting up a site policy for incident handling, it may be desirable to create a sub-group, much like those teams that already exist, that is responsible for handling computer security incidents for the site (or organization). If such a team is created, it is essential that communication lines be opened between this team and other teams. Once an incident is under way, it is difficult to open a trusted dialogue between other teams if none has existed before.

Affected and Involved Sites

If an incident has an impact on other sites, it is good practice to inform them. It may be obvious from the beginning that the incident is not limited to the local site, or it may emerge only after further analysis.

Each site may choose to contact other sites directly or they can pass the information to an appropriate incident response team. It is often very difficult to find the responsible POC at remote sites. and the incident response team can facilitate contact by making use of already established channels.

The legal and liability issues arising from a security incident differ from site to site. It is important to define a policy for the sharing and logging of information about other sites before an incident occurs.

Information about specific people is especially sensitive, and may be subject to privacy laws. To avoid problems in this area, irrelevant information should be deleted and a statement of how to handle the remaining information should be included. A clear statement of how this information is to be used is essential. No one who informs a site of a security incident wants to read about it in the public press. Incident response teams are valuable in this respect. When they pass information to responsible POCs, they are able to protect the anonymity of the original source. But, be aware that in many cases the analysis of logs and information at other sites will reveal addresses of your site.

All the problems discussed above should be not taken as reasons not to involve other sites. In fact, the experiences of existing teams reveal that most sites informed about security problems are not even aware that their site had been compromised. Without timely information, other sites are often unable to take action against intruders.

Internal Communications

It is crucial during a major incident to communicate why certain actions are being taken and how the users (or departments) are expected to behave. In particular, it should be made very clear to users what they are allowed to say (and not say) to the outside world (including other departments). For example, it wouldn't be good for an organization if users replied to customers with something like, "I'm sorry the systems are down. We've had an intruder and we are trying to clean things up." It would be much better if they were instructed to respond with a prepared statement like, "I'm sorry our systems are unavailable. They are being maintained for better service in the future."

Communications with customers and contract partners should be handled in a sensible but sensitive way. One can prepare for the main issues by preparing a checklist. When an incident occurs, the checklist can be used with the addition of a sentence or two for the specific circumstances of the incident.

Public relations departments can be very helpful during incidents. They should be involved in all planning and can provide well-constructed responses for use when contact with outside departments and organizations is necessary.

Public Relations—Press Releases

There has been a tremendous growth in the amount of media coverage dedicated to computer security incidents in the United States. Such press coverage is bound to extend to other countries as the Internet continues to grow and expand internationally. Readers from countries where such media attention has not yet occurred can learn from the experiences in the United States and be forewarned and prepared.

One of the most important issues to consider is when, who, and how much to release to the general public through the press. There are many issues to consider when deciding this particular issue. First and foremost, if a public relations office exists for the site, it is important to use this office as liaison to the press. The public relations office is trained in the type and wording of information released and can help to assure that the image of the site is protected during and after the incident (if possible). A public relations office has the advantage that you can communicate candidly with them; the PR office provides a buffer between the constant press attention and the need of the POC to maintain control over the incident.

If a public relations office is not available, the information released to the press must be carefully considered. If the information is sensitive, it may be advantageous to provide only minimal or overview information to the press. It is quite possible that any information provided to the press will be quickly reviewed by the perpetrator of the incident. Also note that misleading the press can often backfire and cause more damage than releasing sensitive information.

Although it is difficult to determine in advance what level of detail to provide to the press, here are some guidelines to keep in mind:

- Keep the technical level of detail low. Detailed information about the incident may provide enough information for others to launch similar attacks on other sites or even damage the site's ability to prosecute the guilty party once the event is over.

- Keep the speculation out of press statements. Speculation of who is causing the incident or the motives are very likely to be in error and may cause an inflamed view of the incident.
- Work with law enforcement professionals to assure that evidence is protected. If prosecution is involved, assure that the evidence collected is not divulged to the press.
- Try not to be forced into a press interview before you are prepared. The popular press is famous for the "2 a.m." interview, where the hope is to catch the interviewee off guard and obtain information otherwise not available.
- Do not allow the press attention to detract from the handling of the event. Always remember that the successful closure of an incident is of primary importance.

Identifying an Incident

Is It Real?

This stage involves determining if a problem really exists. Many, if not most, signs often associated with virus infection, system intrusions, malicious users, and so on are simply anomalies such as hardware failures or suspicious system or user behavior. To assist in identifying whether there really is an incident, it is usually helpful to obtain and use any detection software that may be available. Audit information is also extremely useful, especially in determining whether there is a network attack. It is extremely important to obtain a system snapshot as soon as one suspects that something is wrong. Many incidents cause a dynamic chain of events to occur, and an initial system snapshot may be the most valuable tool for identifying the problem and any source of attack. Finally, it is important to start a log book. Recording system events, telephone conversations, time stamps, and so on can lead to a more rapid and systematic identification of the problem and is the basis for subsequent stages of incident handling.

There are certain indications or "symptoms" of an incident that deserve special attention:

- System crashes
- New user accounts: The account RUMPLESTILTSKIN has been unexpectedly created, or high activity exists on a previously low-usage account.
- New files: Usually with novel or strange filenames, such as data.xx or k or .xx
- Accounting discrepancies: In a UNIX system you might notice the shrinking of an accounting file called /usr/admin/lastlog, something that should make you very suspicious that there may be an intruder.
- Changes in file lengths or dates: A user should be suspicious if .EXE files in an MS-DOS computer have unexplainably grown by over 1800 bytes.
- Attempts to write to system: A system manager notices that a privileged user in a VMS system is attempting to alter RIGHTSLIST.DAT.
- Data modification or deletion: Files start to disappear.
- Denial of service: A system manager and all other users become locked out of a UNIX system, now in single user mode.
- Unexplained poor system performance

- Anomalies: "GOTCHA" is displayed on the console or there are frequent unexplained "beeps."
- Suspicious probes: There are numerous unsuccessful login attempts from another node.
- Suspicious browsing: Someone becomes a root user on a UNIX system and accesses file after file on many user accounts.
- Inability of a user to log in due to modifications to his or her account.

By no means is this list comprehensive; listed here are only a number of common indicators. It is best to collaborate with other technical and computer security personnel to make a decision as a group about whether an incident is occurring.

Types and Scope of Incidents

Along with the identification of the incident is the evaluation of the scope and impact of the problem. It is important to correctly identify the boundaries of the incident in order to effectively deal with it and prioritize responses.

To identify the scope and impact, a set of criteria should be defined that is appropriate to the site and to the type of connections available. Some of the issues include the following:

- Is this a multisite incident?
- Are many computers at your site affected by this incident?
- Is sensitive information involved?
- What is the entry point of the incident (network, phone line, local terminal, and so on)?
- Is the press involved?
- What is the potential damage of the incident?
- What is the estimated time to close out the incident?
- What resources could be required to handle the incident?
- Is law enforcement involved?

Assessing the Damage and Extent

The analysis of the damage and extent of the incident can be quite time consuming, but it should lead to some insight into the nature of the incident and aid investigation and prosecution. As soon as the breach has occurred, the entire system and all of its components should be considered suspect. System software is the most probable target. Preparation is key to be able to detect all changes for a possibly tainted system. This includes using a checksum on all media from the vendor using an algorithm that is resistant to tampering. (See sections 4.3 of *RFC 2196 Site Security Handbook* at *http://www.faqs.org/rfcs/rfc2196.html.*)

Assuming original vendor distribution media are available, an analysis of all system files should commence, and any irregularities should be noted and referred to all parties involved in handling the incident. It can be very difficult, in some cases, to decide which backup media are showing a correct system status. Consider, for example, that the incident may have continued for months or years before discovery, and the suspect may be an employee of the site or otherwise have intimate knowledge or access to the systems. In all cases, the preincident preparation determines what recovery is possible.

If the system supports centralized logging (most do), go back over the logs and look for abnormalities. If process accounting and connect time accounting is enabled, look for patterns of system usage. To a lesser extent, disk usage may shed light on the incident. Accounting can provide much helpful information in an analysis of an incident and subsequent prosecution. Your ability to address all aspects of a specific incident strongly depends on the success of this analysis.

Handling an Incident

Certain steps are necessary to take during the handling of an incident. In all security-related activities, the most important point to be made is that all sites should have policies in place. Without defined policies and goals, activities undertaken remain without focus. The goals should be defined by management and legal counsel in advance.

One of the most fundamental objectives is to restore control of the affected systems and to limit the impact and damage. In the worst-case scenario, shutting down the system or disconnecting the system from the network may be the only practical solution.

As the activities involved are complex, try to get as much help as necessary. While trying to solve the problem alone real damage might occur because of delays or missing information. Most administrators take the discovery of an intruder as a personal challenge. By proceeding this way, other objectives as outlined in the local policies may not always be considered. Trying to catch intruders may be a very low priority compared to system integrity, for example. Monitoring a hacker's activity is useful, but it might not be considered worth the risk to allow the continued access.

Types of Notification and Exchange of Information

When you have confirmed that an incident is occurring, the appropriate personnel must be notified. How this notification is achieved is very important to keeping the event under control both from a technical and emotional standpoint. The circumstances should be described in as much detail as possible in order to aid prompt acknowledgment and understanding of the problem. Great care should be taken when determining to which groups detailed technical information is given during the notification. For example, it is helpful to pass this kind of information to an incident handling team as they can assist you by providing helpful hints for eradicating the vulnerabilities involved in an incident. On the other hand, putting the critical knowledge into the public domain (e.g., via USENET newsgroups or mailing lists) may potentially put a large number of systems at risk of intrusion. Do not assume that all administrators reading a particular newsgroup have access to operating system source code or can even understand an advisory well enough to take adequate steps.

First of all, any notification to either local or off-site personnel must be explicit. This requires that any statement (be it an e-mail message, phone call, fax, beeper, or semaphone) providing information about the incident be clear, concise, and fully qualified. When you are notifying others who will help you handle an event, a "smoke screen" only divides the effort and creates confusion. If a division of labor is suggested, it is helpful to provide information to each participant about what is being accomplished in other efforts. This not only reduces duplication of effort, but allows people working on different parts of the problem to know where to obtain information relevant to their part of the incident.

Another important consideration when communicating about the incident is to be factual. Attempting to hide aspects of the incident by providing false or incomplete information may not only prevent a successful resolution to the incident but may even worsen the situation.

The choice of language used when notifying people about the incident can have a profound effect on the way that information is received. When you use emotional or inflammatory terms, you raise the potential for damage and negative outcomes of the incident. It is important to remain calm both in written and spoken communications.

Another consideration is that not all people speak the same language, and misunderstandings and delays may arise, especially if it is a multinational incident. Other international concerns include differing legal implications of a security incident and cultural differences. However, cultural differences do not only exist between countries. They even exist within countries, between different social or user groups. For example, an administrator of a university system might be very relaxed about attempts to connect to the system via telnet, but the administrator of a military system is likely to consider the same action as a possible attack.

Another issue associated with the choice of language is the notification of nontechnical or off-site personnel. It is important to accurately describe the incident without generating undue alarm or confusion. Although it is more difficult to describe the incident to a nontechnical audience, it is often more important. A nontechnical description may be required for upper-level management, the press, or law enforcement liaisons. The importance of these communications cannot be underestimated and may make the difference between resolving the incident properly or escalating it to some higher level of damage.

If an incident response team becomes involved, it might be necessary to fill out a template for the information exchange. Although this may seem to be an additional burden and adds a certain delay, it helps the team to act on this minimum set of information. The response team may be able to respond to aspects of the incident of which the local administrator is unaware. If information is given out to someone else, the following minimum information should be provided:

- Time zone of logs: In GMT or local time
- Information about the remote system, including host names, IP addresses, and perhaps user IDs
- All log entries relevant for the remote site
- Type of incident (what happened, why should you care)

If local information such as local user IDs is included in the log entries, it is necessary to sanitize the entries beforehand to avoid privacy issues. In general, all information that might assist a remote site in resolving an incident should be given out, unless local policies prohibit this.

Protecting Evidence and Activity Logs

When you respond to an incident, document all details related to the incident. This can provide valuable information to yourself and others as you try to unravel the course of events. Documenting all details ultimately saves you time. If you don't document every relevant phone call, for example, you are likely to forget a significant portion of information you obtain, requiring you to contact the source of information again. At the same time, recording details provides evidence for prosecution efforts, providing the case moves in that direction. Documenting an incident also helps you perform a final assessment of damage (something your management, as well as law enforcement officers, will want), and provides the basis for later phases of the handling process: eradication, recovery, and follow-up of lessons learned.

During the initial stages of an incident, it is often not feasible to determine whether prosecution is viable, so you should document as if you are gathering evidence for a court case. At a minimum, you should record the following:

- All system events (audit records)
- All actions you take (time tagged)
- All external conversations, including the person with whom you talked, the date and time, and the content of the conversation

The most straightforward way to maintain documentation is keeping a logbook. This allows you to go to a centralized, chronological source of information when you need it, instead of requiring you to page through individual sheets of paper. Much of this information is potential evidence in a court of law. Thus, when a legal follow-up is a possibility, one should follow the prepared procedures and avoid jeopardizing the legal follow-up by improper handling of possible evidence. If appropriate, the following steps may be taken:

1. Regularly (every day, for example) turn in photocopied, signed copies of your logbook (as well as media you use to record system events) to a document custodian.
2. The custodian should store these copied pages in a secure place such as a safe.
3. When you submit information for storage, you should receive a signed, dated receipt from the document custodian.

Failure to observe these procedures can result in invalidation of any evidence you obtain in a court of law.

Containment

The purpose of containment is to limit the extent of an attack. An essential part of containment is decision making, such as determining whether to shut a system down, disconnect from a network, monitor system or network activity, set traps, or disable functions such as remote file transfer.

Sometimes this decision is trivial; shut the system down if the information is classified, sensitive, or proprietary. Bear in mind that removing all access while an incident is in progress obviously notifies all users, including the alleged problem users, that the administrators are aware of a problem; this may have a deleterious effect on an investigation. In some cases, it is prudent to remove all access or functionality as soon as possible, then restore normal operation in limited stages. In other cases, it is worthwhile to risk some damage to the system if keeping the system up might enable you to identify an intruder.

This stage should involve carrying out predetermined procedures. Your organization or site should, for example, define acceptable risks in dealing with an incident, and should prescribe specific actions and strategies accordingly. This is especially important when a quick decision is necessary and it is not possible to first contact all involved parties to discuss the decision. In the absence of predefined procedures, the person in charge of the incident often does not have the power to make difficult management decisions (such as losing the results of a costly experiment by shutting down a system). A final activity that should occur during this stage of incident handling is the notification of appropriate authorities.

Eradication

Once the incident has been contained, it is time to eradicate the cause. But before eradicating the cause, great care should be taken to collect all necessary information about the compromised systems and the cause of the incident, as they are likely to be lost when cleaning up the system.

Software may be available to help you in the eradication process, such as antivirus software. If any bogus files have been created, archive them before deleting them. In the case of virus infections, it is important to clean and reformat any media containing infected files. Finally, ensure that all backups are clean. Many systems infected with viruses become periodically reinfected simply because people do not systematically eradicate the virus from backups. After eradication, a new backup should be taken.

Removing all vulnerabilities once an incident has occurred is difficult. The key to removing vulnerabilities is knowledge and understanding of the breach.

It may be necessary to go back to the original distribution media and recustomize the system. To facilitate this worst-case scenario, a record of the original system setup and each customization change should be maintained. In the case of a network-based attack, it is important to install patches for each operating system vulnerability that was exploited.

As discussed in the section on protecting evidence and security logs, a security log can be most valuable during this phase of removing vulnerabilities. The logs showing how the incident was discovered and contained can be used later to help determine how extensive the damage was from a given incident. The steps taken can be used in the future to make sure the problem does not resurface. Ideally, one should automate and regularly apply the same test as was used to detect the security incident.

If a particular vulnerability is isolated as having been exploited, the next step is to find a mechanism to protect your system. The security mailing lists and bulletins is a good place to search for this information, and you can get advice from incident response teams.

Recovery

Once the cause of an incident has been eradicated, the recovery phase defines the next stage of action. The goal of recovery is to return the system to normal. In general, bringing up services in the order of demand to allow a minimum of user inconvenience is the best practice. Understand that the proper recovery procedures for the system are extremely important and should be specific to the site.

Follow-Up

Once you believe that a system has been restored to a "safe" state, it is still possible that holes, and even traps, could be lurking in the system. One of the most important stages of responding to incidents is also the most often omitted, the follow-up stage. In the follow-up stage, the system should be monitored for items that may have been missed during the cleanup stage. It would be prudent to utilize some of the tools mentioned in Chapter 7 of

RFC 2196 Site Security Handbook as a start. Remember, these tools don't replace continual system monitoring and good systems administration practices.

The most important element of the follow-up stage is performing a postmortem analysis. Exactly what happened, and at what times? How well did the staff involved with the incident perform? What kind of information did the staff need quickly, and how could they have gotten that information as soon as possible? What would the staff do differently next time?

After an incident, it is prudent to write a report describing the exact sequence of events: the method of discovery, correction procedure, monitoring procedure, and a summary of lesson learned. This aids in the clear understanding of the problem. Creating a formal chronology of events (including time stamps) is also important for legal reasons.

A follow-up report is valuable for many reasons. It provides a reference to be used in case of other similar incidents. It is also important to obtain a monetary estimate of the amount of damage the incident caused as quickly as possible. This estimate should include costs associated with any loss of software and files (especially the value of proprietary data that may have been disclosed), hardware damage, and manpower costs to restore altered files, reconfigure affected systems, and so forth. This estimate may become the basis for subsequent prosecution activity. The report can also help justify an organization's computer security effort to management.

Aftermath of an Incident

In the wake of an incident, several actions should take place. These actions can be summarized as follows:

1. An inventory should be taken of the systems' assets, including a careful examination that should determine how the system was affected by the incident.
2. The lessons learned as a result of the incident should be included in a revised security plan to prevent the incident from recurring.
3. A new risk analysis should be developed in light of the incident.
4. An investigation and prosecution of the individuals who caused the incident should commence, if it is deemed desirable.

If an incident is based on poor policy, and unless the policy is changed, then one is doomed to repeat the past. Once a site has recovered from an incident, site policy and procedures should be reviewed to encompass changes to prevent similar incidents. Even without an incident, it would be prudent to review policies and procedures on a regular basis. Reviews are imperative due to today's changing computing environments.

The whole purpose of this postmortem process is to improve all security measures to protect the site against future attacks. As a result of an incident, a site or organization should gain practical knowledge from the experience. A concrete goal of the postmortem is to develop new proactive methods. Another important facet of the aftermath may be end user and administrator education to prevent a recurrence of the security problem.

Responsibilities

Not Crossing the Line

It is one thing to protect one's own network, but quite another to assume that one should protect other networks. During the handling of an incident, certain system vulnerabilities of one's own systems and the systems of others become apparent. It is quite easy and may even be tempting to pursue the intruders in order to track them. Keep in mind that at a certain point it is possible to "cross the line," and with the best of intentions become no better than the intruder.

The best rule when it comes to propriety is to not use any facility of remote sites that is not public. This clearly excludes any entry onto a system (such as a remote shell or login session) that is not expressly permitted. This may be very tempting; after a breach of security is detected, a system administrator may have the means to "follow it up" to ascertain what damage is being done to the remote site. Don't do it! Instead, attempt to reach the appropriate point of contact for the affected site.

Good Internet Citizenship

During a security incident there are two choices to make. First, a site can choose to watch the intruder in the hopes of catching him, or the site can go about cleaning up after the incident and shut the intruder out of the systems. This is a decision that must be made very thoughtfully, as there may be legal liabilities if you choose to leave your site open, knowing that an intruder is using your site as a launching pad to reach out to other sites. Being a good Internet citizen means that you should try to alert other sites that may have been affected by the intruder. These affected sites may be readily apparent after a thorough review of your log files.

Administrative Response to Incidents

When a security incident involves a user, the site's security policy should describe what action is to be taken. The transgression should be taken seriously, but it is very important to be sure of the role the user played. Was the user naive? Could there be a mistake in attributing the security breach to the user? Applying administrative action that assumes the user intentionally caused the incident may not be appropriate for a user who simply made a mistake. It may be appropriate to include sanctions more suitable for such a situation in your policies (such as education or a reprimand to the user) in addition to more stern measures for intentional acts of intrusion and system misuse.

SAMPLE CONTINGENCY PLAN TEMPLATE

*This template can be found at: http://csrc.nist.gov/fasp/FASPDocs/
contingency-plan/contingencyplantemplate.doc.*

**<Facility/System>
Contingency Plan**

**Version <number>
<Date submitted>**

Submitted to:

Submitted by:

<Facility name>
<Facility address>
<Facility address>
<Facility address>

Table of Contents

Appendix B

1   Executive Summary

Written upon completion of document. Contains introductory descriptions from all sections.

2   Introduction

This document contains the contingency plan for the <Facility/System>. It is intended to serve as the centralized repository for the information, tasks, and procedures that are necessary to facilitate the <Facility/System> management's decision-making process and its timely response to any disruptive or extended interruption of the department's normal business operations and services. This is especially important if the cause of the interruption is such that a prompt resumption of operations cannot be accomplished by employing only normal daily operating procedures.

In terms of personnel and financial resources, the information tasks and procedures detailed in this plan represent the <Facility/System> management's demonstrated commitment to response, resumption, recovery, and restoration planning. Therefore, it is essential that the information and action plans in this plan remain viable and be maintained in a state of currency in order to ensure the accuracy of its contents. To that end, this introduction is intended to introduce and familiarize its readers with the organization of the plan.

It is incumbent upon every individual who is in receipt of the <Facility/System> contingency plan, or any parts thereof, or who has a role and/or responsibility for any information or materials contained in the document, to ensure that adequate and sufficient attention and resources are committed to the maintenance and security of the document and its contents.

Because the information contained in this document describes <Facility/System> management's planning assumptions and objectives, the plan should be considered a sensitive document. All of the information and material contents of this document should be labeled, "Limited Official Use."

The <Facility/System> management has recognized the potential financial and operational losses associated with service interruptions and the importance of maintaining viable emergency response, resumption, recovery, and restoration strategies.

The <Facility/System> contingency plan is intended to provide a framework for constructing plans to ensure the safety of employees and the resumption of time-sensitive operations and services in the event of an emergency (fire, power or communications blackout, tornado, hurricane, flood, earthquake, civil disturbance, and so on).

Although the <Facility/System> contingency plan provides guidance and documentation upon which to base emergency response, resumption, and recovery planning efforts, it is not intended as a substitute for informed decision making. Business process managers and accountable executives must identify services for which disruption will result in significant financial or operational losses. Plans should include detailed responsibilities and specific tasks for emergency response activities and business resumption operations based on predefined time frames.

Constructing a plan and presenting it to senior management may satisfy the immediate need of having a documented plan. However, this is not enough if the goal is to have a viable response, resumption, recovery, and restoration capability. To establish that capability, plans and the activities associated with their maintenance (such as training, revision, and exercising) must become an integral part of <Name> operations.

A contingency plan is not a one-time commitment and is not a project with an established start and end date. Instead, a contingency plan is an ongoing, funded business activity budgeted to provide resources required to do the following:

- Perform activities required to construct plans.

- Train and retrain employees.

- Develop and revise policies and standards as the department changes.

- Exercise strategies, procedures, team, and resources requirements.

- Re-exercise unattained exercise objectives.

- Report ongoing continuity planning to senior management.

- Research processes and technologies to improve resumption and recovery efficiency.

- Perform plan maintenance activities.

Developing a contingency plan that encompasses activities required to maintain a viable continuity capability ensures that a consistent planning methodology is applied to all of the <Facility or Systems>. Contingency plan elements necessary to create a viable, repeatable and verifiable continuity capability include the following:

- Implementing accurate and continuous vital records, data backup, and off-site storage

- Implementing capabilities for rapid switching of voice and data communication circuits to alternate site(s)

- Providing alternate sites for business operations

- Constructing a contingency organization

- Implementing contingency strategies

2.1 Purpose

The purpose of this plan is to enable the sustained execution of mission-critical processes and information technology systems for <Facility/System> in the event of an extraordinary event that causes these systems to fail minimum production requirements. The <Facility/System> contingency plan assesses the needs and requirements so that <Facility/System> may be prepared to respond to the event in order to efficiently regain operation of the systems that are made inoperable from the event.

2.2 Scope

[Insert information on the specific systems, locations, facility divisions, technical boundaries, and physical boundaries of the <Facility/System> contingency plan.]

2.3 Plan Information

The contingency plan contains information in two parts related to the frequency of updates required. The first part contains the plan's **static information**, the information that remains constant and is not subject to frequent revisions. The second part contains the plan's **dynamic information**, the information that must be maintained regularly to ensure that the plan remains viable and in a constant state of readiness. This dynamic information is viewed as the action plan. The action plan should be considered a living document and always requires continuing review and modification in order to keep up with the changing <facility/system> environment.

The static information part of the contingency plan is contained in a Microsoft Word file and printed as part of this document. This static information should be read and understood by all employees, users, and administrators of the <Facility/System>, or at least by those individuals who are involved in any phase of business response, resumption, recovery, or restoration.

The dynamic information resides in the database of the <System Name> and is printed as output for the appendixes of this document. By using the database, dynamic information that is vital to the survival of the <Facility/System> is easy to manage and update. The Web-enabled database is designed for maintenance of personnel contact lists, emergency procedures, and technical components. It is already in operation for <Name> agencies.

For ease of use and reference, the static and dynamic information is maintained separately. Although it is necessary to be familiar with the static information during resumption, it should not be necessary to read that information at the time of the event. The completed action plan of dynamic information provides all the necessary lists, tasks, and reports used for response, resumption, or recovery.

3 Contingency Plan Overview

3.1 Applicable Provisions and Directives

The development of the <Facility/System> contingency plan is required by executive decisions and to meet regulatory mandates. The <Facility/System> management must maintain an information assurance infrastructure that ensures that its information resources maintain availability, confidentiality, integrity, and nonrepudiation of its data. Furthermore, <Facility/System> management must ensure their strategic information resources management capabilities. Therefore, the <Facility/System> contingency plan is being developed in accordance with the following executive decisions, regulatory mandates, provisions, and directives:

- Office of Management and Budget Circular A–130, Revised (Transmittal Memorandum No. 4), Appendix III, Security of Federal Automated Information Resources, November 2000.

- Computer Security Act of 1987, Public Law 100-235, January 1988.

- Presidential Decision Directive 63, Critical Infrastructure Protection, May 1998.

- Presidential Decision Directive 67, Enduring Constitutional Government and Continuity of Government Operations, October 1998.

- Executive Order 12656, Assignment of Emergency Preparedness Responsibilities, November 1988.

- Federal Information Processing Standards (FIPS) Publication 87, Guidelines for ADP Contingency Planning, March 1981.

- DOJ Order 2640.2D, Information Technology Security, July 12, 2001.

The <Facility/System> contingency plan is designed to be in accordance with the strategic intent of the <Name> and the <Name>'s functional and operational mission.

3.2 Objectives

The <Facility> is dependent on the variety of systems classified as either general support systems (GSSs), which provide mission-critical functions of connectivity, Internet access, and e-mail, or that are classified as major applications (MAs), which are specific software programs written to produce output to fulfill the <Facility's> service to its customers or enable the <Facility/System> to operate. Although many threats and vulnerabilities can be mitigated, some of the threats cannot be prevented. Therefore, it is important that <Facility/System> develop contingency plans and disaster recovery plans to ensure the uninterrupted existence of its business functions and continued service to the <Name> and the public.

The primary focus of a contingency plan revolves around the protection of the two most important assets of any organization: personnel and data. All facets of a contingency plan should address the protection and safety of personnel and the protection and recovery of data. The primary objective of this plan is to establish policies and procedures to be used for information systems in the event of a contingency to protect and ensure functioning of those assets. This includes establishing an operational capability to process designated critical applications, recovering data from off-site backup data sets, and restoring the affected systems to normal operational status. The plan seeks to accomplish the following additional objectives:

- Minimize the number of decisions that must be made during a contingency.

- Identify the resources needed to execute the actions defined by this plan.

- Identify actions to be undertaken by designated teams.

- Identify critical data in conjunction with customers that will be recovered during the hot site phase of recovery operations.

- Define the process for testing and maintaining this plan and training for contingency teams.

3.3 Organization

In the event of a disaster or other circumstances that bring about the need for contingency operations, the normal organization of the <Facility> will shift into that of the contingency organization. The focus of the <Facility/System> will shift from the current structure and function of "business as usual" to the structure and function of an <Facility/System> working towards the resumption of time-sensitive business operations. In this plan, the <Facility/System's> contingency organization operates through phases of response, resumption, recovery, and restoration. Each phase involves exercising procedures of the <Facility/System> contingency plan and the teams executing those plans. The teams associated with the plan represent functions of a department or support functions developed to respond, resume, recover, or restore operations or facilities of the <Facility/System> and its affected systems. Each of the teams is composed of individuals with specific responsibilities or tasks that must be completed to fully execute the plan. Primary and alternate team leaders, who are responsible to the plan owner, lead each team.

Each team becomes a subunit of the <Facility's> contingency organization. Coordination teams may be singular for the <Facility>, whereas technical teams are likely system specific. Figure 3-1, shows the contingency planning organizational chart as the base organizational structure. The teams are structured to provide dedicated, focused support in the areas of their particular experience and expertise for specific response, resumption, and recovery tasks, responsibilities, and objectives. A high degree of interaction among all teams is required to execute the corporate plan. Each teamís eventual goal is the resumption of stable and normal business operations and technology environments. Status and progress updates are reported by each team leader to the plan owner. Close coordination must be maintained with <system> and <Name> management and each of the teams throughout the resumption and recovery operations.

The <Facility/System> contingency organizationís primary duties are as follows:

- To protect employees and information assets until normal business operations are resumed

- To ensure that a viable capability exists to respond to an incident

- To manage all response, resumption, recovery, and restoration activities

- To support and communicate with employees, system administrators, security officers, and managers

- To accomplish rapid and efficient resumption of time-sensitive business operations, technology, and functional support areas

- To ensure regulatory requirements are satisfied

- To exercise resumption and recovery expenditure decisions

- To streamline the reporting of resumption and recovery progress between the teams and management of each system

Appendix B

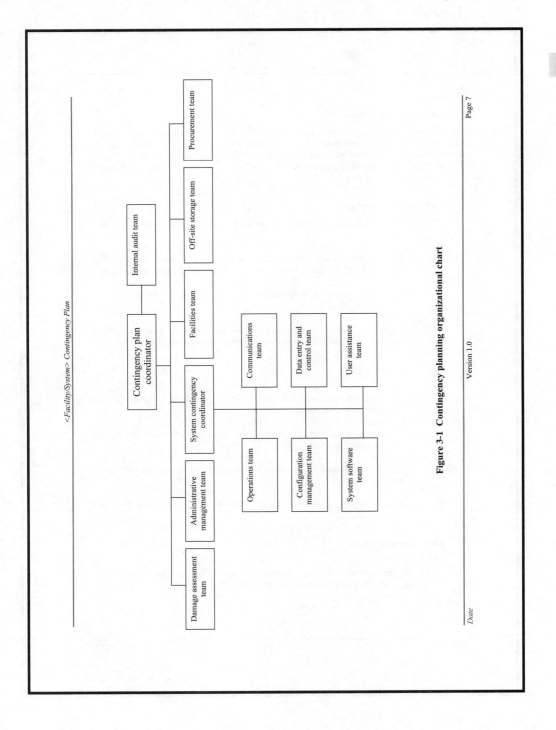

Figure 3-1 Contingency planning organizational chart

3.4 Contingency Phases

The <Facility/System> contingency plan coordinator, in conjunction with <Facility/System> and <Name> management determines which teams or team members are responsible for each function during each phase. As tasking is assigned, additional responsibilities, teams, and task lists need to be created to address specific functions during a specific phase.

3.4.1 Response Phase

- To establish an immediate and controlled <system> presence at the incident site

- To conduct a preliminary assessment of incident impact, known injuries, extent of damage, and disruption to the <system's> services and business operations

- To find and disseminate information on if or when access to the <system's> facility will be allowed

- To provide <system> management with the facts necessary to make informed decisions regarding subsequent resumption and recovery activity

3.4.2 Resumption Phase

- To establish and organize a management control center and headquarters for the resumption operations

- To mobilize and activate the support teams necessary to facilitate and support the resumption process

- To notify and apprise time-sensitive business operation resumption team leaders of the situation

- To alert employees, vendors, and other internal and external individuals and organizations

3.4.3 Recovery Phase

- To prepare and implement procedures necessary to facilitate and support the recovery of time-sensitive business operations

- To coordinate with higher headquarters to discern responsibilities that will fall upon <system> business operations recovery teams and technology recovery teams

- To coordinate with employees, vendors, and other internal and external individuals and organizations

3.4.4 Restoration Phase

- To prepare procedures necessary to facilitate the relocation and migration of business operations to the new or repaired facility

- Implement procedures necessary to mobilize operations, support, and technology department relocation or migration

- Manage the relocation/migration effort as well as perform employee, vendor, and customer notification before, during, and after relocation or migration

3.5 Assumptions

[Include any assumptions that the contingency plan hinges on. This could range from absolutely necessary conditions to helpful information in support of the contingency plan phases.]

- That all necessary memorandums of agreement (MOAs) and memorandums of understanding (MOUs) have been executed.

3.6 Critical Success Factors and Issues

This section addresses the factors and issues that specifically apply to the <Facility/System> contingency plan project that have been identified to be critical to the successful implementation of the contingency plan. These factors are as follows:

- Absolute commitment by senior management to contingency planning and disaster recovery

- Budgetary commitment to disaster recovery

- Modifications and improvements to the current scheduling procedures for the retention and transportation of backup files to the off-site storage facility

- Development and execution of the necessary memorandums of agreement (MOAs), memorandums of understanding (MOUs), and service-level agreements (SLAs)

- Completion of requirement assessment for, and then completion of, the procurement of a diesel-generated alternate power source

3.7 Mission-Critical Systems, Applications, and Services

The following essential mission-critical systems, applications, and services must be recovered at the time of disaster in the following order due to critical interdependencies.

<Facility/System> has identified the applications and services shown in Figure 3-2 as mission critical:

Systems acronym	System name
Exchange mail	Microsoft E-mail system
Internet connectivity	UUNet

Figure 3-2 Mission-critical systems

3.8 Threats

When developing strategies for a contingency plan, it is helpful to consider the entire range of probable and possible threats that present a risk to an organization. From that range of threats, likely scenarios can be developed and appropriate strategies applied. A disaster recovery plan should be designed to be flexible enough to respond to extended business interruptions, as well as major disasters.

The best way to achieve this goal is to design a contingency plan that can be used to address a major disaster, but is divided into sections that can be used to address extended business interruptions. Although each of the identified threats could result in a disaster by itself, in a major disaster several of the threats might be present concurrently or occur sequentially, depending on the circumstances.

As a result, it is advisable to develop several levels of strategies that can be applied as needed. For example, a localized fire in the computing center may render some of that space unusable. An appropriate strategy for that event may be temporary relocation of personnel to another office within <Name> headquarters or in other suitable local office space in another office building or hotel. An event that requires temporary evacuation of the computer center, such as a truck accident in the tunnel and a chemical spill that may require several days to resolve, may necessitate switchover capabilities and possible regional mirrored redundancy capabilities that are transparent to the users. An event of greater magnitude, such as an explosion, may render the <Name of headquarters or national office> unusable for an extended duration and might necessitate a strategy based on mirrored redundancy as well as a secondary strategy involving a commercial hot site. Time sensitivity and mission criticality in conjunction with budgetary limitations, level of threat, and degree of risk are major factors in the development of recommended strategies. (See Section 6 for recommended strategies.)

3.8.1 Probable Threats

The table below depicts the threats most likely to impact the <Facility> and components of <systems> and their management. The specific threats that are represented by (XX) are considered the most likely to occur within the <system> environment.

Probability of threats			
Probability of occurrence:	**High**	**Medium**	**Low**
Air conditioning failure		X	
Aircraft accident			X
Blackmail		X	
Bomb threats		X	
Chemical spills or HazMat	X		
Cold, Frost, or Snow			X
Communications loss		X	
Data destruction		X	
Earthquakes			X
Fire	XX		
Flooding or water damage			X
Nuclear mishaps			X
Power loss or outage	XX		
Sabotage or terrorism		X	
Storms or hurricanes			X
Vandalism or rioting		X	

Figure 3-3 <System>: risk analysis matrix

4   System Description

[In this section include information for each system under ownership or controlling authority of the <Facility/System>.]

Controlling authority assumes that a function or mission element of the <Facility/System> has been contracted to an outside entity that provides the facilities, hardware, software, and personnel required to perform that task. <Name> and the <Facility> retain the oversight of that operation and therefore are the controlling activity for that system.

4.1 Physical Environment

[Include the building location, internal facilities, entry security measures, alarms, and access control.]

4.2 Technical Environment

[Include accurate description of hardware (processors, memory, and media storage) and system software (operating system and applications). Include number of users, interconnected systems, and operational constraints.]

[Put specific software and hardware inventories, SLAs, vendor contacts in appendixes.]

5 Plan

5.1 Plan Management

5.1.1 Contingency Planning Workgroups

The development of recovery strategies and work-arounds require technical input, creativity, and pragmatism. The best way to create workable strategies and cohesive teams that leverage out-of-the-box thinking is to involve management and information resource management personnel in an ongoing informative dialogue. The <Facility/System Name> management has developed and is facilitating contingency planning workgroups to assist in the development and review of strategies, teams, and tasks.

5.1.2 Contingency Plan Coordinator

A coordinator and an alternate should be appointed by <Facility> management and system owners to monitor and coordinate the <Facility/System> contingency plan, training and awareness, exercises, and testing. Additionally, this person coordinates strategy development with contingency planning workgroups, system contingency coordinator, team leaders, business process owners, and management. The contingency planning coordinator should work closely with system technical managers to ensure the viability of the <Facility/System> contingency plan. The contingency plan coordinator manages contingency teams that are not system specific (see section 5.2). It is recommended that the individual(s) appointment(s) be documented in writing and that specific responsibilities be identified and included in their job descriptions.

5.1.3 System Contingency Coordinators

A coordinator and an alternate should be appointed for *each system* under ownership or controlling authority of the <Facility/System> by <Facility> management and system owners. Their primary task is to monitor and coordinate the <Facility/System> contingency planning, training and awareness, exercises, and testing. Additionally, this person manages contingency teams (see Section 5.2) that are assigned specifically to their system and report directly to the contingency plan coordinator. It is recommended that the individual(s) appointment(s) be documented in writing, and that specific responsibilities be identified and included in their job descriptions.

5.1.4 Incident Notification

The facilities managers for the locations where the critical components of the <Facility's> systems are located should be provided with the telephone numbers of <Facility/System> emergency response team members. Upon notification, the team meets in a location to be announced for the purpose of conducting initial incident assessment and issuing advisory reports of status to the <Facility/System> and <Name> management. If the facilities manager, emergency response personnel, or <Facility> emergency response team leader has determined that the building cannot be entered, the alternate meeting place will be announced.

5.1.5 Internal Personnel Notification

The <Facility/System's> emergency notification procedure, or a modified version thereof, should be developed and used for notification of the crisis management team and other disaster recovery teams regarding specific response actions taken during response operations. Within the personal contact database, a single-source personal information table should readily be available that includes home addresses, contact telephone phone numbers, and emergency contact information. In the event of a disaster, a lack of specific personal data, including home addresses, cell phone numbers, pager numbers, and alternate contact information, could result in the inability to locate and contact key personnel and team members. This automated personnel database should be maintained and updated continuously. This database may be maintained internally or somewhere else within the department, as long as the information contained therein remains current and accessible.

5.1.6 External Contact Notification

The <Facility/System's> emergency notification procedure, or a modified version thereof, should be developed and used for notification of its contingency plan service providers, <Name> agencies, external contacts, vendors, suppliers, and so on.

5.1.7 Media Releases

All incident-related information (printed or spoken) concerning the <Name> is coordinated and issued through the department or component office of public affairs.

5.1.8   Alternate Site(s)

Include location of prepositioned information technology assets for activation in a contingency operation mode. It is suggested that local sites for facility- or system-specific contingencies be maintained, such as a "tech hotel," where the contingency planner rents space and information technology equipment.

Additional local alternatives could be in the form of reciprocating MOAs and/or MOUs with <Name> or other organizations for the utilization of space for the installation of equipment, connectivity infrastructure, and personnel accommodations, should the need arise.

An alternate site with a distance of at least 100 miles should be considered. Should a regional event take place that renders <Facility> systems ineffective and thereby unable to be physically accessed, a relocation site would serve the needs for contingency operations.

5.2   Teams

The following are suggested teams that will be assigned to execute the contingency plan. Some teams may not be necessary depending on the system. If this is the case you should simply remove the heading and table. Certain teams will be replicated for each system and placed under the system contingency coordinator given the vast differences in hardware, software, and external communications for each system. Each team has a roster and task list of actions and responsibilities generated by the IMS database that is included in an appendix.

5.2.1   Damage Assessment Team

The damage assessment team is a technical group responsible for assessing damage to the <Facility/System> and its components. It is composed of personnel with a thorough understanding of hardware and equipment and the authority to make decisions regarding the procurement and disposition of hardware and other assets. This team is primarily responsible for initial damage assessment, accounting of damage assessment, loss minimization, and salvage and procurement of necessary replacement equipment and interfaces. This team should include vendor representatives.

The damage assessment team enters the facility as soon as they have received permission to do so from emergency services. A written detailed account should be made of the general status of the work area, with specific attention to the condition of hardware, software, furnishings, and fixtures. Recommendations should be made that all damaged equipment, media, and documentation be routed immediately to disaster recovery and restoration experts for a determination as to its ability to be salvaged or restored.

5.2.2   Operations Team

The operations team consists of operators responsible for running emergency production for critical systems, coordinating with both the backup team to ensure that applications system data and operating instructions are correct and with the liaison team to advise on the production status and any unusual problems requiring assistance. Data input/control teams can be separate groups or subgroups of the operations team. Also, the PC support team under the operations recovery team is responsible for reestablishing microcomputer operations at the backup site or remote sites and for assisting with reinstating PC applications.

5.2.3 Communications Team

The communications team is composed of <Facility/System's> communications specialists responsible for restoring voice, data, and video communications links between users and the computers, regardless of location in the event of a loss or outage. Communication vendor (carrier) input in designing and implementing the recovery plan is very important. Influential factors in developing recovery procedures for this team include: the type of network, the time requirement for restoration, percentage of the network to be recovered, and budget considerations.

5.2.4 Data Entry and Control Team

The data entry and control team is responsible for entering data as it is restored. They ensure that the data is the best available backup and meets validation for the system.

5.2.5 Off-Site Storage Team

The off-site storage team is responsible for retrieving backup copies of operating systems, applications, systems, applications data, and ensuring security of the data, backup facilities, and original facilities. The team is composed of members of <Facility/System> familiar with vital records archival and retrieval.

5.2.6 Administrative Management Team

The administrative management team coordinates primary and alternate site security and specialized clerical and administrative support for the contingency plan coordinator and all other teams during disaster contingency proceedings. The administrative team may also assist groups outside the information resources area as needed. The administrative team is responsible for reassembling all documentation for standards, procedures, applications, programs, systems, and forms, as required at the backup site. The administrative team is responsible for arranging for transportation of staff, equipment, supplies, and other necessary items between sites.

5.2.7 Procurement Team

The Procurement team consists of persons knowledgeable about the information resources and supplies inventory and the budgetary, funding, and acquisition processes responsible for expediting acquisition of necessary resources.

5.2.8 Configuration Management Team

The configuration management team is composed of individuals with teleprocessing skills. They work closely with the communications teams in establishing voice and data communication capabilities.

5.2.9 Facilities Team

The facilities team is responsible for arranging for the primary and backup facilities and all components.

5.2.10 System Software Team

The system software team consists of system software programmers responsible for providing the system software support necessary for production of critical applications systems during recovery.

5.2.11 Internal Audit Team

The internal audit team is responsible for observation and oversight participation in the recovery effort.

5.2.12 User Assistance Team

The user assistance team is composed of individuals with application use knowledge. The team is made up of major user area managers, production control, and applications lead analysts responsible for coordination and liaison with the information resources staff for applications recovery and restoration of data files and databases. Under the general leadership of the user assistance team, technical applications specialist and database administration subteams perform necessary application restoration activities. Setting priorities for applications recovery is a primary influence on procedures for this team and its subgroups.

5.3 Data Communications

Depending on the location of the cabling, a cable cut by a backhoe could render a <Facility/System> and associated buildings without connectivity. Oftentimes, redundant cabling can mean two fiber-optic cables laid in the same trench for failover connectivity. Although this may be adequate for routine telecommunication interruptions, it represents a single point of failure for communications and connectivity.

The level of data connectivity required is determined pending the final decision regarding the disaster declaration. Data communications specifications should be documented in Appendix H, "Communication Requirements," in this plan and should be stored in the secure off-site storage location or <Name>, in the event that a permanent replacement facility is required.

5.4 Backups

The most important physical asset in any facility or system is its data and information. Data and information processing are a major reason for the existence of <Name>. Moreover, all of the <Name> systems are dependent on the preservation of data, including software manuals and documentation. To minimize the impact of a disaster, it is extremely important to protect the sensitivity or confidentiality of data, to preserve the authenticity and accuracy of data, and to maintain the availability of data. These three goals are commonly defined as "confidentiality, integrity, and availability." The protection of the confidentiality, integrity, and availability of data is of singular importance in information security and disaster recovery planning. Confidentiality, integrity, and availability of data are intrinsic to disaster recovery planning.

Effective procedures to perform full data backups on a regular weekly basis must be implemented. A copy of the weekly backups should be securely transported on a weekly basis and stored off-site in an environmentally controlled storage facility, preferably outside the immediate regional area. Frequent backups should be implemented to ensure the recovery of the most current data version and to increase the likelihood of usable media in a postevent scenario.

5.4.1 Vital Records/Documentation

Vital records and important documentation should be backed up and stored off-site. Vital records are any documents or documentation that is essential to the operations of an organization, such as personnel records, software documentation, legal documentation, legislative documentation, benefits documentation, and so on.

Documentation of all aspects of computer support and operations is important to ensure continuity and consistency. Formalizing operational practices and procedures in detail helps to eliminate security lapses and oversights, gives new personnel detailed instructions on how to operate equipment or do a particular task, and provides a quality assurance function to help ensure that operations are performed correctly and efficiently every time.

Security documentation should be developed to fulfill the needs of those who use it. For this reason, many organizations separate documentation into policy and procedures for each user level. For example, a functional security procedures manual should be written to inform end users how to do their jobs securely, and a technical and operational security procedures manual should be written for systems operations and support staff focusing on system administrations concerns in considerable detail.

There should be at least two copies of current system security documentation. One copy should be stored on-site and be immediately accessible. A backup copy must be stored off-site and should include documents such as system security plans (SSP), contingency plans, risk analyses, and security policies and procedures. Additional copies may be necessary for some documentation, such as contingency plans, which should be easily accessible in the event of a disaster. It is recommended that copies of the contingency plan be distributed to the <Facility/System> contingency plan coordinator, executive management, and team leaders for safekeeping.

Documentation should be duplicated either in hard copy or compatible media format and stored at the off-site storage or the (recovery site) location. The original primary on-site unit retains the original copies of all information. Updates to documentation should be rotated on an as-required basis, under the control of the responsible team. Off-site documentation should include technical and operational documentation.

Many of the below listed documents may be found in the completed certification and accreditation package (the system security authorization agreement [SSAA] and appendices). If the information is in the SSAA, keep it current and maintain a copy off-site.

The following documentation should be maintained off-site:

- Security-related information technology (IT) policy and procedure memorandum, circulars, publications

- Department or component mission statement

- Letters of delegation for key information system security personnel

- Complete hardware and software listings

- Internal security and information system audits

- Detailed IT architecture schematics (logical/physical, network, devices)

- Network cable routing schematics (on floor overlay)

- System testing plans and procedures

- Review and approval of plans and procedures

- System configuration

- Review and approval of proposed configuration

- Changes made to the system configuration

- Evaluation of changes for security implications

- Technical standards for system design, testing, and maintenance to reflect security objectives

- Contingency plans for incident response procedures and backup operations

- Data backup/restoration procedures and procedures for storage, transportation, and handling of backup tapes

- Reports of security-related incidents

- Sensitivity and criticality determination

Appendix B

- Baseline security checklist for each system

- Software licensing information

Additionally, it is recommended that <Facility/System> management personnel develop detailed procedural manuals specifying how their functional responsibilities are to be discharged in the event of their unavailability. This is especially important for key personnel. Copies of these manuals should be kept off-site with other documentation.

5.5 Office Equipment, Furniture, and Supplies

Although the current strategy is for office equipment, furniture, and supplies to be ordered on an "emergency as required" basis at the time of the disaster, it is recommended that <Facility/System> management review supply needs and coordinate with the local procurement office to develop a revolving emergency inventory of work space and survival supplies for immediate use in the event of a disaster. The revolving inventory of work space supplies should include not only basic essential work space supplies such as pens, pencils, note pads, and paper, but also <Facility and System>-specific forms and templates. Additionally, a revolving inventory of survival supplies should be maintained, including bottled drinking water, personal products, and food rations, in the event personnel cannot be evacuated or are temporarily prevented from leaving the confines of the building because of weather conditions.

5.6 Recommended Testing Procedures

The <Facility/System> contingency plan should be maintained routinely and exercised or tested at least annually. Contingency procedures must be tested periodically to ensure the effectiveness of the plan. The scope, objective, and measurement criteria of each exercise is determined and coordinated by the <Facility or System> contingency plan coordinator on a per-event basis. The purpose of exercising and testing the plan is to continually refine resumption and recovery procedures to reduce the potential for failure.

There are two categories of testing: announced and unannounced. In an announced test, personnel are instructed when testing will occur, what the objectives of the test are, and what the scenario will be for the test. Announced testing is helpful for the initial test of procedures. It gives teams the time to prepare for the test and allows them to practice their skills. Once the team has had an opportunity to run through the procedures, practice, and coordinate their skills, unannounced testing may be used to test the completeness of the procedures and sharpen the team's abilities. Unannounced testing consists of testing without prior notification. The use of unannounced testing is extremely helpful in preparing a team for disaster preparation because it focuses on the adequacy of in-place procedures and the readiness of the team. Unannounced testing, combined with closely monitored restrictions, help to create a simulated scenario that might exist in a disaster. This more closely measures the teams' ability to function under the pressure and limitations of a disaster. Once it has been determined whether a test will be announced or unannounced, the actual objective(s) of the test must be determined. There are several different types of tests that are useful for measuring different objectives.

A recommended schedule for testing is as follows:

- Desktop testing on a quarterly basis

- One structured walk-through per year

- One integrated business operations/information systems exercise per year

The contingency plan coordinator, contingency system coordinators, and team leaders, together with the <Facility> office management and <System Owners>, determine end-user participation.

6   Recommended Strategies

The following information represents potential recommendations to the <Facility/System> director and other technical management positions as appropriate. These should be considered as solutions that potentially may assist in the continued development of their recovery capabilities in a postdisaster situation.

6.1   Critical Issues

6.1.1   Power

The <Facility> technology director should work to develop power requirements necessary to provide uninterrupted service for the <Facility or System> data center. After the determination of power requirements has been developed for the continuous operability of the <System> the <Facility> should follow the standard procurement process to obtain, install, test, and maintain such a system. It should be noted that the standard life cycle for the amortization of a diesel-powered backup generator is 20 years.

6.1.2   Diversification of Connectivity

As it stands, the current connectivity configuration represents a single point of failure to the entire <System>. The dedicated connectivity from all the regional offices converges in the <System> data center. A single occurrence of fire, power failure, terrorist act, or civil unrest could completely disrupt e-mail and Internet-based connectivity between the building and the regions. Additionally, <System> users rely upon Internet connectivity to provide outside e-mail availability to the department and the regions therefore, based upon any of the aforementioned scenarios that function, would also cease to function.

6.1.3   Off-site Backup Storage

The current schedule implemented for the transfer of backup tapes to the off-site storage facility is inconsistent with the objectives of contingency planning. The schedule has the

<System> staff maintaining the most current backup tapes onsite in the building for a 30-day period prior to transfer to the off-site storage facility. Thus, all data extracted from office backup tapes will be more than 30 days old. In today's data-intensive environment this provides stale information to the <System> end users. This is especially critical in view of the fact that the only time the staff must rely on the off-site backup media is when the system has failed and any incremental backups are ineffective and/or inefficient to resolve the situation. The loss of 30 days of work and data based on the impact of a disaster is not acceptable.

The schedule controlling this process should be revisited and modified to reflect a more frequent transfer timeline. The accepted standard is the transfer of backup media to the offsite storage on a weekly basis to establish a continuously current flow of data into the backup copies. This allows the staff to execute restorations utilizing the most updated information available. This is particularly true regarding the e-mail systems.

7   Terms and Definitions

The following is a comprehensive list of terms that are important in contingency planning and recovery operations. Add any <Facility>-specific and system-specific terms with definitions relevant to the contingency plan in the appropriate alphabetical positions.

ABC fire extinguisher — Chemically based devices used to eliminate ordinary combustible, flammable liquid, and electrical fires.
Acceptable level of risk — Typically refers to the point at which the level of risk is more acceptable than the cost to mitigate the risk (in dollars or effect on computer system function).
Access — The ability to do something with a computer resource. This usually refers to a technical ability (such as read, create, modify, or delete a file; execute a program; or use an external connection); admission; entrance.
Access control — The process of limiting access to the resources of an IT system only to authorized users, programs, processes, or other IT systems.
Accountability — The property that enables activities on a system to be traced to individuals, who may then be held responsible for their actions.
Actuator — A mechanical assembly that positions the read/write head assembly over the appropriate tracks.
Activation — When all or a portion of the recovery plan has been put into motion.
Adequate security — Security commensurate with the risk and magnitude of the harm resulting from the loss, misuse, or unauthorized access to, or modification of, information. This includes assuring that systems and applications used by <Name> operate effectively and provide appropriate confidentiality, integrity, and availability through the use of cost-effective management, personnel, and operational and technical controls.
Alert — Notification that a disaster situation has occurred and to stand by for possible activation of disaster recovery plan.

Alternate site — A location, other than the normal facility, used to process data and/or conduct critical business functions in the event of a disaster. Similar terms: alternate processing facility, alternate office facility, alternate communication facility.

Application — The use of information resources (information and information technology) to satisfy a specific set of user requirements.

Application program — A software program comprising a set of statements, defining certain tasks.

Application recovery — The component of disaster recovery that deals specifically with the restoration of business system software and data, after the processing platform has been restored or replaced. Similar term: business system recovery.

Array — An arrangement of two or more disk drives: may be in redundant array of independent disks (RAID) or daisy-chain fashion.

Asset — A value placed on goods owned by an organization.

Assumptions — Basic understandings about unknown disaster situations that the disaster recovery plan is based on.

Assurance — A measure of confidence that the security features and architecture of an automated information system accurately mediate and enforce the security policy.

Asynchronous Transfer Mode (ATM) — A network architecture that divides messages into fixed-size units (cells) and establishes a switched connection between the originating and receiving stations; enables transmission of various types of data (video, audio, and so on) over the same line without one data type dominating the transmission.

Audit system — An independent review, examination of the records, and activities to access the adequacy of system controls to ensure compliance with established policies and operational procedures. The audit system is an essential tool for the determination and recommendation of necessary changes in controls, policies, or procedures.

Audit trail — A series of records of computer events about an operating system, an application, or user activities.

Auditing — The review and analysis of management, operational, and technical controls.

Authentication — Proving (to some reasonable degree) a user's identity. It can also be a measure designed to provide protection against fraudulent transmission by establishing the validity of a transmission, message, station, or originator.

Authorization — The permission to use a computer resource. Permission is granted, directly or indirectly, by the application or system owner.

Automated — Means *computerized* for the purpose of this document.

Availability — The property of being accessible and usable, upon demand by an authorized entity, to complete a function. The information technology system or installation contains information or provides services that must be available on a timely basis to meet mission requirements or to avoid substantial losses. Controls to protect the availability of information are required if the information is critical to the <Name>'s activity's functions. Access to some information requires <Name> to ensure the availability of that information within a short period of time.

Back office location — An office or building used by the organization to conduct support activities that is not located within an organization's headquarters or main location.

Backbone — The underlying network communication conduit or line by which all main servers and devices are connected; backbone devices are typically servers, routers, hubs, and bridges; client computers are not connected directly to the backbone.

Backup — Means either procedures or standby equipment that are available for use in the event of a failure or inaccessibility of normally used equipment or procedures or to make a copy of data or a program in case the original is lost, damaged, or otherwise unavailable.

Backup agreement — A contract to provide a service that includes the method of performance, the fees, the duration, the services provided, and the extent of security and confidentiality maintained.

Backup position listing — A list of alternative personnel who can fill a recovery team position when the primary person is not available.

Backup strategies (recovery strategies) — Alternative operating method (such as platform or location) for facilities and system operations in the event of a disaster.

Bandwidth — The amount of data that can be transmitted via a given communications channel, as between a hard drive and the host PC, in a given unit of time.

Block — A portion of a volume usually 512 bytes in size; often referred to as a *logical block*.

Burst mode — A temporary, high-speed data transfer mode that can transfer data at significantly higher rates than would normally be achieved with nonburst technology; the maximum throughput a device is capable of transferring data.

Bus — The main communication avenue in a computer; an electrical pathway along which signals are sent from one part of the computer to another.

Business continuity planning (BCP) — An all-encompassing umbrella term covering both disaster recovery planning and business resumption planning. Also see disaster recovery planning and business resumption planning.

Business impact analysis (BIA) — The process of analyzing all business functions and the effect that a specific disaster may have upon them.

Business interruption — Any event, whether anticipated (such as a public service strike) or unanticipated (a power blackout) that disrupts the normal course of business operations at a corporate location.

Business interruption costs — The costs or lost revenue associated with an interruption in normal business operations.

Business recovery coordinator — See disaster recovery coordinator.

Business recovery process — The common critical path that all companies follow during a recovery effort. There are major nodes along the path that are followed regardless of the organization. The process has seven stages: (1) immediate response, (2) environmental restoration, (3) functional restoration, (4) data synchronization, (5) restore business functions, (6) interim site, and (7) return home.

Business recovery team — A group of individuals responsible for maintaining and coordinating the recovery process. Similar term: recovery team.

Business resumption planning (BRP) — The operations piece of business continuity planning. Also see: disaster recovery planning.

Business unit recovery — The component of disaster recovery that deals specifically with the relocation of key organization personnel in the event of a disaster and the provision of essential records, equipment supplies, work space, communication facilities, computer processing capability, and so on. Similar term: work group recovery.

Byte — The fundamental data unit for personal computers, comprising eight contiguous bits.

Cache — A large bank of random access memory used for temporary storage of information.

Computer-aided design (CAD) — The use of a computer in industrial design applications such as architecture, engineering, and manufacturing.

Call back — A procedure for identifying a remote terminal. In a call back, the host system disconnects the caller and then dials the authorized telephone number of the remote terminal to reestablish the connection. Synonymous with *dial back*.

Central office — A secure, self-contained telecommunications equipment building that houses servers, storage systems, switching equipment, emergency power systems, and related devices that are used to run telephone systems.

Certified disaster recovery planner (CDRP) — A CDRP is certified by the Disaster Recovery Institute, a not-for-profit corporation that promotes the credibility and professionalism in the DR industry.

Checklist test — A method used to test a completed disaster recovery plan. This test is used to determine if the information such as phone numbers, manuals, equipment, and so on in the plan is accurate and current.

Clustered servers — The concept of combining multiple host computers together through a private communication line, such as Ethernet backbone, to form a ring of host computers; this ring of host computers acts as a single entity, capable of performing multiple complex instructions by distributing the workload across all members of the ring.

Clustered storage — The concept of combining multiple storage servers together to form a redundant ring of storage devices; clustered storage systems typically perform multiple read and write requests through parallel access lines to the requesting computer.

Cold site — An alternate facility that is void of any resources or equipment except air-conditioning and raised flooring. Equipment and resources must be installed in such a facility to duplicate the critical business functions of an organization. Cold sites have many variations depending on their communication facilities, uninterruptible power source (UPS) systems, or mobility (relocatable shell). Similar terms: shell site, backup site, recovery site, alternative site.

Command and/or control center (CAC/CNC/CCC) — A centrally located facility having adequate phone lines to begin recovery operations. Typically it is a temporary facility used by the management team to begin coordinating the recovery process and used until the alternate sites are functional.

Commerce service provider (CSP) — A company that provides e-commerce solutions for retailers.

Commercial off-the-shelf (COTS) — Commercially available products that can be purchased and integrated with little or no customization, thus facilitating customer infrastructure expansion and reducing costs.

Competitive local exchange carrier (CLEC) — A long-distance carrier, cable company, or small startup local exchange carrier that competes for business in a local telephone market. Many CLECs also offer Internet services.

Computer virus — A program that "infects" computer systems in much the same way as a biological virus infects humans. The typical virus "reproduces" by making copies of itself and inserting them into the code of other programs—either in systems software or in application programs.

Appendix B

Communications failure — An unplanned interruption in electronic communication between a terminal and a computer processor, or between processors, as a result of a failure of any of the hardware, software, or telecommunications components composing the link. (Also refer to network outage.)

Communications recovery — The component of disaster recovery that deals with the restoration or rerouting of an organization's telecommunication network or its components in the event of loss. Similar terms: telecommunication recovery, data communications recovery.

Computer recovery team (CRT) — A group of individuals responsible for assessing damage to the original system, processing data in the interim, and setting up the new system.

Confidentiality — The assurance that information is not disclosed to unauthorized entities or processes. The information technology system or installation contains information that requires protection from unauthorized or inappropriate disclosure. Some information must be protected from unauthorized or accidental disclosure. <Name> is required to prevent some information from release to persons without the proper qualifications. Information requiring protection from unauthorized disclosure includes classified information, information related to military operations and equipment, confidential commercial business information, confidential <Name> business information, Privacy Act information, law enforcement confidential information, procurement-sensitive information, budgetary information, and information exempt from disclosure under the Freedom of Information Act (FOIA).

Configuration control — The process of controlling modifications to the system's hardware, software, and documentation that provides sufficient assurance that the system is protected against the introduction of improper modifications before, during, and after system implementation.

Configuration management (CM) — The management of changes made to a system's hardware, software, firmware, documentation, tests, test fixtures, and test documentation throughout the development and operational life of the system.

Consortium agreement — An agreement made by a group of organizations to share processing facilities and/or office facilities if one member of the group suffers a disaster. Similar terms: reciprocal agreement.

Contingency plan — A plan for emergency response, back-up operations, and postdisaster recovery for information technology systems and installations in the event normal operations are interrupted. The contingency plan should ensure minimal impact upon data-processing operations in the event the information technology system or facility is damaged or destroyed.

Contingency plan — A plan that addresses how to keep an organization's critical functions operating in the event of any kind of disruptions. See disaster recovery plan.

Contingency planning — See also disaster recovery planning.

Controller — A unit or circuitry that manages the information flow between storage disks and the computer.

Cooperative hot sites — A hot site owned by a group of organizations available to a group member should a disaster strike. Also see hot site.

Cost-benefit analysis — The assessment of the costs of providing data protection for a system versus the cost of losing or compromising a system.

Cost of ownership — The purchase price of equipment plus the cost of operating this equipment over its projected life span.

Countermeasure — Any action, device, procedure, technique, or other measure that reduces the vulnerability of or threat to a system.

Crate and ship — A strategy for providing alternate processing capability in a disaster via contractual arrangements with an equipment supplier to ship replacement hardware within a specified time period. Similar terms: guaranteed replacement, quick ship.

Crisis — A critical event that if not handled in an appropriate manner may dramatically impact an organization's profitability, reputation, or ability to operate.

Crisis management — The overall coordination of an organization's response to a crisis in an effective, timely manner with the goal of avoiding or minimizing damage to the organization's profitability, reputation, or ability to operate.

Crisis simulation — The process of testing an organization's ability to respond to a crisis in a coordinated, timely, and effective manner by simulating the occurrence of a specific crisis.

Critical functions — Business activities or information that could not be interrupted or unavailable for several business days without significantly jeopardizing operation of the organization.

Critical records — Records or documents that if damaged or destroyed would cause considerable inconvenience and/or require replacement or re-creation at considerable expense.

Cryptography — The principles, means, and methods for rendering information unintelligible and for restoring encrypted information to intelligible form.

Damage assessment — The process of assessing damage following a disaster to computer hardware, vital records, office facilities, and so on and determining what can be salvaged or restored and what must be replaced.

Data center recovery — The component of disaster recovery that deals with the restoration, at an alternate location, of data centers services and computer processing capabilities. Similar term: mainframe recovery.

Data center relocation — The relocation of an organization's entire data processing operation.

Declaration fee — A one-time fee charged by an alternate facility provider, to a customer who declares a disaster. Similar term: notification fee. *Note*: Some recovery vendors apply the declaration fee against the first few days of recovery.

Decryption — The process of taking an encrypted file and reconstructing the original file. This is the opposite of encryption.

Dedicated line — A preestablished point-to-point communication link between computer terminals and a computer processor, or between distributed processors, that does not require dial-up access.

Departmental recovery team — A group of individuals responsible for performing recovery procedures specific to their department.

Dial backup — The use of dial-up communication lines as a backup to dedicated lines.

Dial-up line — A communication link between computer terminals and a computer processor, which is established on demand by dialing a specific telephone number.

Digital audio tape (DAT) — A digital magnetic tape format originally developed for audio recording and now used for computer backup tape; the latest DAT storage format is DDS (Digital Data Storage).

Digital linear tape (DLT) — A serpentine technology first introduced by Digital Equipment Corporation and later developed by Quantum for tape backup/archive of networks and servers; DLT technology addresses midrange to high-end tape backup requirements.

Disaster — Any event that creates an inability on an organization's part to provide critical business functions for some predetermined period of time. Similar terms: business interruption, outage, catastrophe.

Disaster prevention — Measures employed to prevent, detect, or contain incidents that, if unchecked, could result in disaster.

Disaster prevention checklist — A questionnaire used to assess preventive measures in areas of operations such as overall security, software, data files, data entry reports, microcomputers, and personnel.

Disaster recovery — The ability to respond to an interruption in services by implementing a disaster recovery plan to restore an organization's critical business functions.

Disaster recovery administrator — The individual responsible for documenting recovery activities and tracking recovery progress.

Disaster recovery coordinator — The disaster recovery coordinator may be responsible for overall recovery of an organization or unit(s). Similar term: business recovery coordinator.

Disaster recovery period — The time period between a disaster and a return to normal functions during which the disaster recovery plan is employed.

Disaster recovery plan (DRP) — The document that defines the resources, actions, tasks, and data required to manage the business recovery process in the event of a business interruption. The plan is designed to assist in restoring the business process within the stated disaster recovery goals.

Disaster recovery planning — The technological aspect of business continuity planning; the advance planning and preparations that are necessary to minimize loss and ensure continuity of the critical business functions of an organization in the event of disaster. Similar terms: contingency planning, business resumption planning, corporate contingency planning, business interruption planning, disaster preparedness.

Disaster recovery software — An application program developed to assist an organization in writing a comprehensive disaster recovery plan.

Disaster recovery teams (business recovery teams) — A structured group of teams ready to take control of the recovery operations if a disaster should occur.

Disk array (see array) — An arrangement of two or more hard disks, in RAID or daisy-chain configuration, organized to improve speed and provide protection of data against loss.

Distributed computing environment — A set of middleware standards that defines the method of communication between clients and servers in a cross-platform computing environment. It enables a client program to initiate a request that can be processed by a program written in a different computer language and housed on a different computer platform.

Dynamic growth and reconfiguration (DGR) — A Dot Hill technology that allows the system administrator to quickly and easily add capacity or change RAID levels while the system is in use.

Electromagnetic interference (EMI) — What occurs when electromagnetic fields from one device interfere with the operation of some other device.

Electronic Industries Association (EIA) — A trade association that establishes electrical and electronics-oriented standards.

Electronic vaulting — Transfer of data to an off-site storage facility via a communication link rather than via portable media. Typically used for batch or journaled updates to critical files to supplement full backups taken periodically.

Emergency — A sudden, unexpected event requiring immediate action because of a potential threat to health and safety, the environment, or property.

Emergency preparedness — The discipline that ensures an organization's or community's readiness to respond to an emergency in a coordinated, timely, and effective manner.

Emergency procedures — A plan of action to commence immediately to prevent the loss of life and minimize injury and property damage.

Employee relief center (ERC) — A predetermined location for employees and their families to obtain food, supplies, financial assistance, and so on in the event of a catastrophic disaster.

Encryption — The process of coding a message to make it unintelligible.

Enterprise storage network (ESN) — An integrated suite of products and services designed to maximize heterogeneous connectivity and management of enterprise storage devices and servers; a dedicated, high-speed network connected to the enterprise's storage systems, enabling files and data to be transferred between storage devices and client mainframes and servers.

Environment — The aggregate of external procedures, conditions, and objects that affect the development, operation, and maintenance of a system.

Ethernet — A local area network standard for hardware, communication, and cabling.

Extended outage — A lengthy, unplanned interruption in system availability due to computer hardware or software problems or communication failures.

Extra expense coverage — Insurance coverage for disaster-related expenses that may be incurred until operations are fully recovered after a disaster.

Facilities — A location containing the equipment, supplies, voice, and data communication lines, to conduct transactions required to conduct business under normal conditions. Similar terms: primary site, primary processing facility, primary office facility.

Failover — The transfer of operation from a failed component, such as a controller or disk drive, to a similar, redundant component to ensure uninterrupted data flow and operability.

Fault tolerance — The ability of a system to cope with internal hardware problems, such as a disk drive failure, and still continue to operate with minimal impact, such as by bringing a backup system online.

Appendix B

Fiber channel-arbitrated loop (FC-AL) — A fast serial bus interface standard intended to replace SCSI on high-end servers. A fiber channel implementation in which users are attached to a network via a one-way ring (loop) cabling scheme.

Fiber channel — A high-speed storage/networking interface that offers higher performance, greater capacity and cabling distance, increased system configuration flexibility and scalability, and simplified cabling.

Fiber channel community (FCC) — An international nonprofit organization whose members include manufacturers of servers, disk drives, RAID storage systems, switches, hubs, adapter cards, test equipment, cables and connectors, and software solutions.

Fiber Distributed Data Interface (FDDI) — A 100 Mbps ANSI standard LAN architecture, defined in X3T9.5. The underlying medium is optical fiber (though it can be copper cable, in which case it may be called CDDI) and the topology is a dual-attached, counterrotating token ring.

File backup — The practice of dumping (copying) a file stored on disk or tape to another disk or tape. This is done for protection in case the active file gets damaged.

File recovery — The restoration of computer files using backup copies.

File server — The central repository of shared files and applications in a computer network (LAN).

Footprint — The amount of floor space that a piece of equipment (e.g., a rackmount enclosure) occupies.

Form factor — The physical size and shape of a device; often used to describe the size of disk arrays in a rack mount enclosure.

Forward recovery — The process of recovering a data base to the point of failure by applying active journal or log data to the current backup files of the database.

Full recovery test — An exercise in which all recovery procedures and strategies are tested (as opposed to a partial recovery test).

Generator — An independent source of power usually fueled by diesel or natural gas.

Gigabyte — Approximately one billion bytes, 1024 megabytes.

Host bus adapter (HBA) — A hardware card that resides on the PC bus and provides an interface connection between a SCSI device (such as a hard drive) and the host PC.

Halon — A gas used to extinguish fires; effective only in closed areas. Currently being phased out due to environmental concerns.

Heat, ventilation, and air conditioning (HVAC) — The system that provides and maintains a controlled environment with conditions conducive to continuous and uninterrupted computer operations.

High-priority tasks — Activities vital to the operation of the organization. Similar terms: critical functions

Home page — The main page on a Web site that serves as the primary point of entry to related pages within the site and may have links to other sites as well.

Host-attached storage — A storage system that is connected directly to the network server; also referred to as server-attached storage.

Hot site — An alternate facility that has the equipment and resources to recover the business functions affected by the occurrence of a disaster. Hot sites may vary in type of facilities offered (such as data processing, communication, or any other critical business functions needing duplication). Location and size of the hot site is proportional to the equipment and resources needed. Similar terms: backup site; recovery site; recovery center; alternate processing site.

Hot spare — A backup component, such as a disk or controller, that is online and available should the primary component go down.

Hot swappable — The ability to replace a component, such as a disk drive, controller, fan, or power source, while the system is online, without having to power down; also referred to as hot-plug removable.

Hierarchical storage management (HSM) — A storage system in which new, frequently used data is stored on the fastest, most accessible (and generally more expensive) media (RAID) and older, less frequently used data is stored on slower, less expensive media (tape).

Hub — A device that splits one network cable into a set of separate cables, each connecting to a different computer; used in a local area network to create a small-scale network by connecting several computers together.

Human threats — Possible disruptions in operations resulting from human actions such as a disgruntled employee, terrorism, and so on.

Identification — The process that enables, generally by the use of unique machine-readable names, recognition of users or resources as distinguishable to those previously described to the automated information system.

Information system — The organized collection, processing, transmission, and dissemination of information in accordance with defined procedures, whether automated or manual.

Information technology installation — One or more computer or office automation systems, including related telecommunications, peripheral and storage units, central processing units, and operating and support system software. Information technology installations may range from information technology installations, such as large centralized computer centers, to individual stand-alone microprocessors, such as personal computers. A *sensitive information technology installation* means an information technology installation that contains or provides processing for a sensitive information technology system.

Information technology system — An information system that is automated or is an assembly of computer hardware and software configured for the purpose of classifying, sorting, calculating, computing, summarizing, transmitting and receiving, storing and retrieving data with a minimum of human intervention. The term includes single application programs that operate independently of other program applications. A *sensitive information technology system* means an information technology system that contains sensitive information.

Infrastructure — (1) the physical equipment (computers, cases, racks, cabling, and so on) that composes a computer system; (2) the foundational basis that supports the information management capabilities, including the telecommunications and network connectivity.

Initiator — A small computer system interface (SCSI) device that requests another SCSI device (a target) to perform an operation. Usually a host computer acts as an initiator and a peripheral device acts as a target.

Institute of Electrical and Electronics Engineers (IEEE) — The largest technical society in the world, consisting of engineers, scientists, and students; has declared standards for computers and communications.

Appendix B

Integrity, data — That attribute of data relating to the preservation of (1) its meaning and completeness, (2) the consistency of its representation(s), and (3) its correspondence to what it represents. The information technology system or installation contains information that must be protected from unauthorized, unanticipated, or unintentional modification or destruction, including detection of such activities. Integrity is important to all information because inaccuracy compromises the value of the information system. Law enforcement, mission- and life-critical, and financial information are examples of information requiring protection to preserve integrity.

Integrity, system — That attribute of a system when it performs its intended function in an unimpaired manner, free from deliberate or inadvertent unauthorized manipulation of the system.

Interface — A connection between hardware devices, applications, or different sections of a computer network.

InterFacility Contingency Planning Regulation — A regulation written and imposed by the Federal Financial Institutions Examination Council concerning the need for financial institutions to maintain a working disaster recovery plan.

Interim organizational structure — An alternate organization structure that is used during recovery from a disaster. This temporary structure typically streamlines chains of command and increases decision-making autonomy.

Internal hot sites — A fully equipped alternate processing site owned and operated by the organization.

Internet — A worldwide system of linked computer networks.

Internet service provider (ISP) — A company that provides Internet access services to consumers and businesses. ISPs lease connections from Internet backbone providers. Although most ISPs are small companies that service a local area, there are also regional and national ISPs (such as America Online).

Interoperability — The ability of one computer system to control another, even though the two systems are made by different manufacturers.

Interruption — An outage caused by the failure of one or more communications links with entities outside of the local facility.

Intranet — A computer network, based on Internet technology, that is designed to meet the internal needs for sharing information within a single organization or company.

Input/output (I/O) — Reception (read) or transmission (write) of computer signals; the entire connection path between the CPU bus and the disk drives.

I/Os per second (IOPS) — A measure of performance for a host-attached storage device or RAID controller.

Just a bunch of disks (JBOD) — A disk array without a controller.

Kernel — The core of an operating system such as Windows 98, Windows NT, Mac OS or UNIX; provides basic services for the other parts of the operating system, making it possible for it to run several programs at once (multitasking), read and write files, and connect to networks and peripherals.

LAN recovery — The component of disaster recovery that deals specifically with the replacement of LAN equipment in the event of a disaster and the restoration of essential data and software. Similar term: client/server recovery

Leased line — Usually synonymous with *dedicated line*.

Legacy — A computer, system, or software that was created for a specific purpose but is now outdated; anything left over from a previous version of the hardware or software.

Line rerouting — A service offered by many regional telephone companies allowing the computer center to quickly reroute the network of dedicated lines to a backup site.

Line voltage regulators — Also known as surge protectors. These protectors/regulators distribute electricity evenly.

Linear tape open (LTO) — A new standard tape format developed by HP, IBM, and Seagate.

Local area network (LAN) — A LAN consists of personal computers that are connected together through various means, so that they can communicate with each other. A network of computers within a limited area, such as a company or organization; computing equipment, in close proximity to each other, connected to a server that houses software that can be accessed by the users. This method does not utilize a public carrier. See also WAN.

Logic bomb — A computer code that is preset to cause a malfunction at a later time when a specified set of logical conditions occurs. For example, a specific Social Security number in a payroll system is processed and the logic bomb is activated, causing an improper amount of money to be printed on the check.

Logical unit number (LUN) — An addressing scheme used to define SCSI devices on a single SCSI bus.

Loss — The unrecoverable business resources that are redirected or removed as a result of a disaster. Such losses may be loss of life, revenue, market share, competitive stature, public image, facilities, or operational capability.

Loss reduction — The technique of instituting mechanisms to lessen the exposure to a particular risk. Loss reduction is intended to react to an event and limit its effect. Examples of loss reduction include sprinkler systems.

Machine-readable media — Media that can convey data to a given sensing device, such as diskettes, disks, tapes, and computer memory.

Magnetic ink character reader (MICR) equipment — Equipment used to imprint machine-readable code. Generally, financial institutions use this equipment to prepare paper data for processing or for encoding (imprinting) items such as routing and transit numbers, account numbers, and dollar amounts.

Mainframe computer — A high-end computer processor, with related peripheral devices, capable of supporting large volumes of batch processing, high performance online transaction processing systems, and extensive data storage and retrieval. Similar term: host computer.

Malicious software — Any of a family of computer programs developed with the sole purpose of doing harm. Malicious code is usually embedded in software programs that appear to provide useful functions but, when activated by a user, cause undesirable results.

Mean swaps between failure (MSBF) —A statistical calculation used to predict the average usefulness of a robotic device, such as a tape library, with any interruption of service.

Mean time between failure (MTBF) — A statistical calculation used to predict the average usefulness of a device without any interruption of service.

Mean time to repair (MTTR) — The average amount of time required to resolve most hardware or software problems with a given device.

Media transportation coverage — An insurance policy designed to cover transportation of items to and from an EDP center, the cost of reconstruction, and the tracing of lost items. Coverage is usually extended to transportation and dishonesty or collusion by delivery employees.

Megabyte — Approximately one million bytes, 1024 kilobytes.

Mirroring — A method of storage in which data from one disk is duplicated on another disk so that both drives contain the same information, thus providing data redundancy.

Mission critical — Any computer process that cannot be allowed to fail during normal business hours; some computer processes such as telephone systems must run all day long and require 100 percent uptime.

Mobile hot site — A large trailer containing backup equipment and peripheral devices delivered to the scene of the disaster. It is then hooked up to existing communication lines.

Modulator demodulator unit (modem) — Device that converts data from analog to digital and back again.

Monitoring — An ongoing activity that checks on the system, its users, or the environment.

Multi-platform — The ability of a product or network to support a variety of computer platforms such as IBM, Sun, and Macintosh; also referred to as *cross-platform*.

Natural threats — Events caused by nature causing disruptions to an organization.

Network — The Open Systems Interconnect (OSI) seven-layer model attempts to provide a way of partitioning any computer network into independent modules from the lowest (physical) layer to the highest (application) layer. Many different specifications exist at each of these layers. The network is composed of a communications medium and all components attached to that medium whose responsibility is the transference of information.

Network architecture — The basic layout of a computer and its attached systems, such as terminals and the paths between them.

Network-attached storage (NAS) — A disk array storage system that is attached directly to a network server rather than to the network server (host attached). It functions as a server in a client/server relationship; has a processor, an operating system or microkernel; and processes file I/O protocols such as SMB and NFS.

Network outage — An interruption in system availability as a result of a communication failure affecting a network of computer terminals, processors, or workstations.

Network service provider (NSP) — A company that provides the national or international packet-switching networks that carry Internet traffic; also called a backbone operator.

Node (or network node) — Any device that is directly connected to the network, usually through Ethernet cable; nodes include file servers and shared peripherals; the name used to designate a part of a network. This may be used to describe one of the links in the network, or a type of link in the network (for example, host node or intercept node).

Nonessential function/data — Business activities or information that could be interrupted or unavailable indefinitely without significantly jeopardizing critical functions of an organization.

500

Nonessential records — Records or documents, which, if irretrievably lost or damaged, would not materially impair the organization's ability to conduct business.

NT (Microsoft Windows NT) — An operating system developed by Microsoft for high-performance processors and networked systems.

Off-host processing — A backup mode of operation in which processing can continue throughout a network despite loss of communication with the mainframe computer.

Off-line processing — A backup mode of operation in which processing can continue manually or in batch mode if the online systems are unavailable.

Off-site storage facility — A secure location, remote from the primary location, at which backup hardware, software, data files, documents, equipment, or supplies are stored.

Online systems — An interactive computer system supporting users over a network of computer terminals.

Open systems network — A network composed of equipment that conforms to industry standards of interoperability between different operating systems such as UNIX and Windows NT).

Operating software — A type of system software supervising and directing all of the other software components plus the computer hardware.

Operating system — The master control program, such as Windows, that manages a computer's internal functions and provides a means of control to the computer's operations and file system.

Organization chart — A diagram representative of the hierarchy of an organization's personnel.

Organization-wide — A policy or function applicable to the entire organization.

Original equipment manufacturer (OEM) — A company that manufactures a given piece of hardware (unlike a value-added reseller, which changes and repackages the hardware).

Outage — See systems outage.

Outsourcing — The transfer of data-processing functions to an independent third party.

Owner — The individual designated as being responsible for the protection of IT resources. The owner generally falls into two broad categories: custodial and owner. For example, the *owner* of the resources, may be the manager of that facility. Resources located within user areas may be *owned* by the manager of those areas. To assist with the determination of ownership, individual system boundaries must be established. A system is identified by logical boundaries being drawn around the various processing, communications, storage, and related resources. They must be under the same direct management control with essentially the same function, reside in the same environment, and have the same characteristics and security needs. Ownership of information and/or information-processing resources may be assigned to an organization, subordinate functional element, a position, or a specific individual. When ownership is assigned to an organizational or functional element, the head of the unit so designated is considered the resource owner. Some, but not necessarily all, factors to be considered in the determination of ownership are listed below:

    1. The originator or creator of data

    2. The organization or individual with the greatest functional interest

    3. Physical possession of the resource

Appendix B

Parallel test — A test of recovery procedures in which the objective is to parallel an actual business cycle.

Parity data — A block of information mathematically created from several blocks of user data to allow recovery of user data contained on a drive that has failed in an array; used in RAID levels 3 and 5.

Password — A string of alphanumeric characters chosen by an individual to help ensure that their computer access is protected. Passwords are changed frequently to minimize the risk of unauthorized disclosure. Additional passwords may be assigned by the user to particular files or data sets.

Peripheral equipment — Devices connected to a computer processor that perform such auxiliary functions as communications, data storage, printing, and so on.

Personal computer interconnect (PCI) — An industry-standard bus used in servers, workstations, and PCs.

Petabyte — 1024 terabytes.

Physical safeguards — Physical measures taken to prevent a disaster, such as fire suppression systems, alarm systems, power backup and conditioning systems, access control systems, and so on.

Platform — A hardware standard, such as IBM, Sun, or Macintosh.

Portable shell — An environmentally protected and readied structure that can be transported to a disaster site so equipment can be obtained and installed near the original location.

Procedural safeguards — Procedural measures taken to prevent a disaster, such as safety inspections, fire drills, security awareness programs, records retention programs, and so on.

Proprietary — Privately developed and owned technology.

Protocol — A standard that specifies the format of data and rules to be followed in data communication and network environments.

Rackmount — The cabinet that houses a server/storage workstation (also referred to as a server rack); to mount equipment into a cabinet.

RAID advisory board (RAB) — An organization of storage system manufacturers and integrators dedicated to advancing the use and awareness of RAID and associated storage technologies. Started in 1992, RAB states its main goals as education, standardization, and certification.

Real time — Immediate processing of input or notification of status.

Reciprocal agreement — An agreement between two organizations with compatible computer configurations allowing either organization to utilize the other's excess processing capacity in the event of a disaster.

Record retention — Storing historical documentation for a set period of time, usually mandated by state and federal law or the Internal Revenue Service.

Recovery action plan — The comprehensive set of documented tasks to be carried out during recovery operations.

Recovery alternative — The method selected to recover the critical business functions following a disaster. In data processing, some possible alternatives would be manual processing, use of service bureaus, or a backup site (hot or cold site). A recovery alternative is usually selected following a risk analysis, business impact analysis, or both. Similar terms: backup site, backup alternative.

Recovery capability —This defines all of the components necessary to perform recovery. These components can include a plan, an alternate site, change control process, network rerouting, and others.

Recovery management team — A group of individuals responsible for directing the development and on-going maintenance of a disaster recovery plan. Also responsible for declaring a disaster and providing direction during the recovery process.

Recovery planning team — A group of individuals appointed to oversee the development and implementation of a disaster recovery plan.

Recovery point objective (RPO) — The point in time to which data must be restored in order to resume processing transactions. RPO is the basis on which a data projection strategy is developed.

Recovery procedures — The actions necessary to restore a system's processing capability and data files after a system failure.

Recovery team — See business recovery team.

Recovery time — The period from the disaster declaration to the recovery of the critical functions.

Redundant array of independent (or inexpensive) disks (RAID) — A collection of storage disks with a controller (or controllers) to manage the storage of data on the disks.

Redundant data path (RDP) — Dot Hill's software technology that creates an alternate data path between the server and the storage system in the event of system component failures to ensure continuous access to data.

Relocatable shell — See portable shell.

Risk — A combination of the likelihood that a threat will occur, the likelihood that a threat occurrence will result in an adverse impact, and the severity of the resulting adverse impact.

Risk analysis — A formal systematic approach to assessing the vulnerability of an information technology system or installation. Risk analysis is the process of analyzing threats to and vulnerabilities of an information system to determine the risks (potential for losses). The resulting data is then analyzed. The analysis is used as a basis for identifying appropriate and cost-effective measures to counter the identified threats and vulnerabilities. The risk analysis identifies threats, quantifies the potential losses from threat realization, examines the cost-benefit of applying alternative measures to counter the identified threats and reduce potential loss, and defines or documents the degree of acceptable risk. Similar terms: risk assessment, impact assessment, corporate loss analysis, risk identification, exposure analysis, exposure assessment.

Risk management — The process of the identification, measurement, control, and minimization of security risk in information systems. Also, it means to assess risk, take actions to reduce risk to an acceptable level, and maintain risk at that level. Inherent in this definition are the concepts that risk cannot be completely eliminated, and the most secure computer system is the one that no one uses.

Router — An electronic device that connects two or more networks and routes incoming data packets to the appropriate network.

Safeguards — The protective measures and controls that are prescribed to meet the security requirements specified for a system.

Salvage and restoration — The process of reclaiming or refurbishing computer hardware, vital records, office facilities, and so on following a disaster.

Salvage procedures — Specified procedures to be activated if equipment or a facility should suffer any destruction.

Sample plan — A generic disaster recovery plan that can be tailored to fit a particular organization.

Satellite communication — Data communications via satellite. For geographically dispersed organizations, it may be a viable alternative to ground-based communications in the event of a disaster.

Scalable — The ability of a product or network to accommodate growth.

Scan — To examine computer coding or programs sequentially, part by part. For viruses, scans are made for virus signatures or potentially unsafe practices, such as changes to an executable file, direct writes to specific disk sectors, and so on.

Scope — Predefined areas of operation for which a disaster recovery plan is developed.

Secure — In terminology, such as *secure LAN* or *secure device*, means that the routing addresses on the network are monitored and allowed to proceed only for authorized users. This network traffic monitoring and authorization process is referred to as <Name>'s *firewalls*. Systems and devices not being monitored are referred to as being outside of <Name>'s secure firewall and the term *nonsecure* is applied.

Security features — These are controls that protect against the identified vulnerabilities, such as fire and water alarms, passwords and other access protection, use of removable media for data storage, data validation controls, audit trails, uninterruptible power sources (UPS) to protect against electrical outages, personnel screening, computer security awareness training of users, and so on.

Security infraction — The failure to follow applicable laws and regulations and established <Name> policies and procedures pertaining to the protection of <Name> information and computer resources. Henceforth, *infraction* and *violation* are to be used interchangeably throughout this document.

Security policy — The set of laws, rules, and practices that regulate how an organization manages, protects, and distributes sensitive information.

Security specification — A detailed description of the security requirements and specifications necessary to protect an information technology system or installation.

Sensitive information — Information that requires a degree of protection due to its nature, magnitude of loss, or harm that could result from inadvertent or deliberate disclosure, modification, or destruction. This includes the following types of information:

    1. Mission critical, meaning that loss or harm would be such that an <Name> office could not perform essential functions.

    2. Should not be disclosed under the Freedom of Information Act, such as proprietary data and economic forecasts. Proprietary data includes trade secrets, commercial, or financial data obtained in the course of government business, from or relating to a person or persons outside the government, not generally available to the public, and which is privileged, would cause competitive harm if released, or impair the ability of the government to obtain data in the future.

    3. Complies with OMB Circular A-127 Financial Management Systems.

4. Complies with the Privacy Act of 1974. Data, which pertains to a specific individual by name, Social Security number or by some other identifying means, and is part of a system of records as defined in the Privacy Act of 1974.
5. Classified

Serial storage architecture (SSA) — A high-speed method of connecting disk, tape, and CD-ROM drives, printers, scanners, and other devices to a computer.

Server — A computer that stores application and data files for all workstations on a network; also referred to as a file server.

Shadow file processing — An approach to data backup in which real-time duplicates of critical files are maintained at a remote processing site. Similar term: remote mirroring

Simulation test — A test of recovery procedures under conditions approximating a specific disaster scenario. This may involve designated units of the organization actually ceasing normal operations while exercising their procedures.

Skills inventory — A listing of employees that lists their skills that apply to recovery.

Small computer system interface (SCSI) — An interface that serves as an expansion bus that can be used to connect hard disk drives, tape drives, and other hardware components.

Spindle — Mechanism inside a hard disk drive that moves the heads into place; the axle on which a disk turns.

Stand-alone processing — Processing, typically on a PC or midrange computer, that does not require any communication link with a mainframe or other processor.

Storage area network (SAN) — A network infrastructure of shared multihost storage, linking all storage devices as well as interconnecting remote sites.

Striping — A method of storage in which a unit of data is distributed and stored across several hard disks, which improves access speed but does not provide redundancy.

Structured walk-through test — Team members walk through the plan to identify and correct weaknesses.

Subscription — Contract commitment providing an organization with the right to utilize a vendor recovery facility for recovery of their mainframe processing capability.

Super-user — A system account that has full systemwide administrative privileges. Most UNIX machines have a log-on account called *root* that acts as the super-user.

Sustained mode — The measured transfer rate of a given device during normal operation.

Switch — A network traffic-monitoring device that controls the flow of traffic between multiple network nodes.

System — A generic term used for its brevity to mean either a major application or a general support system. A system is identified by logical boundaries drawn around the various processing communications, storage, and related resources. They must be under the same direct management control (not responsibility), perform essentially the same function, reside in the same environment, and have the same characteristics and security needs. A system does not have to be physically connected.

System outage — An unplanned interruption in system availability as a result of computer hardware or software problems, or operational problems.

System security plan (SSP) — A plan to be developed by <Name> in accordance with OMB and NIST guidelines implementing the Computer Security Act of 1987, to safeguard the security of its information technology systems and installations.

Appendix B

Systems downtime — A planned interruption in system availability for scheduled system maintenance.

Systems integrator — An individual or company that combines various components and programs into a functioning system, customized for a particular customer's needs.

Target — A SCSI device that performs an operation requested by an initiator.

TCQ — Tag command queuing; a feature introduced in the SCSI-2 specification that permits each initiator to issue commands accompanied by instructions for how the target should handle the command. The initiator can either request the command to be executed at the first available opportunity, in the order in which the command was received, or at a time deemed appropriate by the target.

Technical threats — A disaster-causing event that may occur regardless of any human elements.

Telco — Abbreviation for a *telecommunications company*.

Temporary operating procedures — Predetermined procedures that streamline operations while maintaining an acceptable level of control and auditability during a disaster situation.

Terabyte — Approximately one trillion bytes, 1024 gigabytes.

Test plan — The recovery plans and procedures that are used in a systems test to ensure viability. A test plan is designed to exercise specific action tasks and procedures that would be encountered in a real disaster.

Test scenarios — Are descriptions of the tests to be performed to check the effectiveness of the security features. They may include validation of password constraints, such as length and composition of the password, entry of erroneous data to check data validation controls, review of audit information produced by the system, review of contingency plans and risk analyses, and so on.

Threat — Any circumstance or event with the potential to cause harm to a system in the destruction, disclosure, modification of data, and/or denial of service.

Throughput — Measures the number of service requests on the I/O channel per unit of time.

Time bomb — Computer code that is preset to cause a later malfunction after a specific date, time, or a specific number of operations. The Friday the 13th computer virus is an example. This virus infects the system several days or even months before and lies dormant until the date reaches Friday the 13th.

Topology — Geometric arrangement of nodes and cable links in a local area network, may be either centralized or decentralized.

Transfer rate — The number of megabytes of data that can be transferred from the read/write heads to the disk controller in one second.

Trap door — A set of instruction codes embedded in a computer operating system that permits access while bypassing security controls.

Trojan horse — A program that causes unexpected (and usually undesirable) effects when willingly installed or run by an unsuspecting user. A Trojan horse is commonly disguised as a game, a utility, or an application. A person can either create or gain access to the source code of a common, frequently used program and then add code, so that the program performs a harmful function, in addition to its normal function. These programs are generally deeply buried in the code of the target program, lie dormant for a preselected period, and are triggered in the same manner as a logic bomb. A Trojan horse can alter, destroy, disclose data, or delete files.

Turnkey — A product or system that can be plugged in, turned on, and operated with little or no additional configuring.

Uninterruptible power supply (UPS) — A backup power supply with enough power to allow a safe and orderly shutdown of the central processing unit should there be a disruption or shutdown of electricity.

UNIX — An operating system that supports multitasking and is ideally suited to multi-user applications (such as networks).

Uploading — Connecting to another computer and sending a copy of program or file to that computer. See also downloading

Useful records — Records that are helpful but not required on a daily basis for continued operations.

User — A person or a process accessing an automated information system, either by direct or indirect connection.

User contingency procedures — Manual procedures to be implemented during a computer system outage.

User ID — A group of characters and/or numbers that uniquely identifies an individual and are used to gain valid access to a computer system. A user ID is normally coupled with a password that is set by the owner of the user ID.

Value-added reseller (VAR) — A business that repackages and improves hardware manufactured by an original equipment manufacturer.

Virus — A code segment that replicates by attaching copies of itself to existing executable programs. This is usually done in such a manner that the copies will be executed when the file is loaded into memory, allowing them to infect still other files, and so on. The new copy of the virus is executed when a user executes the new host program. The virus may include any additional "payload" that is triggered when specific conditions are met. For example, some viruses display a text string on a particular date. There are many types of viruses including variants, overwriting, resident, stealth, and polymorphic. Viruses often have damaging side effects, sometimes intentionally, sometimes not.

Virus detection software — Software written to scan machine-readable media on computer systems. There are a growing number of reputable software packages available that are designed to detect and remove viruses. In addition, many utility programs can search text files for virus signatures or potentially unsafe practices.

Virus signature — A unique set of characters that identify a particular virus. This may also be referred to as a virus marker.

Vital records — Records or documents, for legal, regulatory, or operational reasons, that cannot be irretrievably lost or damaged without materially impairing the organization's ability to conduct business.

Voice recovery — The restoration of an organization's voice communications system.

Vulnerability — A weakness in an information system or component (such as security procedures, hardware design, or internal controls) that can be exploited, attacked, or fail. Vulnerabilities include susceptibility to physical dangers, such as fire or water; unauthorized access to sensitive data; entry of erroneous data; denial of timely service; and fraud.

Wide area network (WAN) — A network that uses high-speed, long-distance communications technology (such as phone lines and satellites) to connect computers over long distances. Similar to a LAN except that parts of a WAN are geographically dispersed, possible in different cities, or even on different continents. Public carriers are included in most WANs; very large WANs may incorporate satellite stations or microwave towers.

Warm site — An alternate processing site that is only partially equipped, as compared to a hot site that is fully equipped.

Web cache — A Web cache fills requests from the Web server, stores the requested information locally, and sends the information to the client; the next time the Web cache gets a request for the same information, it simply returns the locally cached data instead of searching over the Internet, thus reducing Internet traffic and response time.

Web site — A location on the World Wide Web that is owned and managed by an individual, company, or organization, usually containing a home page and additional pages that include information provided by the site's owner, and may include links to other relevant sites.

World Wide Web (WWW) — A global hypertext system operating on the Internet that enables electronic communication of text, graphics, audio, and video.

Worm — A complete program that propagates itself from system to system, usually through a network or other communication facility. A worm is similar to a virus. It is able to infect other systems and programs usually by spawning copies of itself in each computer's memory. A worm differs from a virus, in that a virus replicates itself, while a worm does not. A worm copies itself to a person's workstation over a network or through a host computer and then spreads to other workstations. A worm might duplicate itself in one computer so often that it causes the computer to crash. Sometimes written in separate segments, a worm is introduced surreptitiously into a host system, either for fun or with intent to damage or destroy information. It can easily take over a network, as the "Internet" worm did. The "Internet" worm was intentionally released into the ARPANET (predecessor to the Internet) by Robert Morris in 1976 as an experiment. Unlike a Trojan horse, a worm enters a system uninvited.

XOR engine: Process or set of instructions that calculates data bit relationships in a RAID subsystem.

8 Appendices

All the items in this section should receive a separate appendix. In many cases information will be generated from the IMS database. Frequent updates and reviews should be made for this data. A printed copy should be made for inclusion in the contingency plan. However, as this is the dynamic information, the official record should be the IMS. Access to the IMS should be available from outside the <Facility's> normal operation location. IMS data should be stored in a location geographically separate from <Facility's> offices. A means to access this data from alternate locations should be in place and tested.

Appendix A — Contingency Plan Contact Information

This appendix should include all points of contact of positions described in the contingency plan and key organizational personnel. Include home and mobile telephone numbers. Include emergency location assignments. Include a telephone tree that lists the order of contact when a contingency situation or disaster is declared.

The contact list should indicate the system and organization within the <Facility> with which each individual is associated.

A reference list of emergency services and public utilities should be included.

Appendix B — Emergency Procedures

Include emergency procedures for <Name> and the <Facility>. Describe actions to be taken by employees emphasizing personnel safety. Address potential scenarios including fire, bomb threat or event, and civil disorders. Include evacuation procedures.

Appendix C — Team Staffing and Taskings

Include a roster and list of actions and responsibilities for each team created by <Facility> in Section 5.2. The following is an example of two tables for each team:

Role	Name
Contingency plan coordinator (team leader)	
Facilities representative (to coordinate closely with facility engineer)	
Technical representative (s)	

Precontingency
Action 1
Action 2
Disaster contingency immediate response
Action 1
Action 2
Postcontingency
Action 1
Action 2

Appendix D — Alternate Site Procedures

This appendix should include detailed procedures on setting up the selected alternate site(s). Include contact individuals and numbers, maps for reaching the facility, equipment on-site that should be brought online, equipment required for procurement, and telecommunications providers for contact. There should be separate procedures based on the <Facility's> maintained availability of a hot site and a cold site.

Appendix E — Documentation List

Include a list of all <Name>, <Facility>, and system documentation pertinent to the operation and maintenance of each system. This list should include but is not limited to system architecture, operating manuals, system security plans, risk assessments, MOUs, MOAs, SLAs, testing procedures and results, system interdependencies, asset inventory, hardware inventory, software inventory, backup procedures, configuration guidelines, alternate site status and inventory, and standard operating procedures.

Documentation must be developed, updated, and modified to reflect the most current information and then entered into an automated DRP relational database. A copy should then be stored at the off-site storage facility. This data should be reviewed and modified as changes occur within the environment.

Appendix F — Software Inventory

This appendix should be populated with the most current data that directly reflects the current software, software being tested and evaluated, software that is operational in the acceptance environment pending final review, software implemented in production, software that is owned, whether on-site or off-site, and software that is deployed by the <Facility>. This should include the licensing agreements. A copy of this data should be stored at the off-site storage facility along with the contingency plan. An automated tool could assist with the development and implementation of this type of product.

Appendix G — Hardware Inventory

This appendix should be populated with the most accurate data reflective of the hardware assets currently owned and deployed by the <Facility>. In addition, the inventory of the alternate site hardware assets should be included. The purchase and implementation of an automated tool could assist in this effort.

Appendix H — Communications Requirements

This appendix should include the most accurate data associated with the data and voice communications in place for <Facility>. It should include an inventory of all communications equipment, diagrams, and uniquely identified data WAN and LAN circuits, data network backup alternatives, and voice network specifications.

Appendix I — Vendor Contact Lists

This appendix should be populated with the listing of all vendors and contractors that currently provide support or will provide support in a postdisaster environment. Additionally, any service-level agreements (SLAs) that have been executed and all subsequent modifications should be included with accurate points of contact (POCs) and emergency contact information.

Appendix J — External Support Agreements

This appendix should include documentation for service and emergency maintenance agreements with manufacturers, data storage facilities, telecommunications providers, and staff transportation providers. It should include points of contact and authorization procedures for delivery of services.

Appendix K — Data Center/Computer Room Emergency Procedures and Requirements

This appendix should include additional emergency procedures for all secured data center or computer room facilities hosting <Facility> systems. Information on fire, smoke, water, and intrusion alarms should be included. Procedures for turning off power should be included. Facility layout, power requirements, cable diagrams, and media connection outlets should be included. A data center inventory should be extracted from Appendixes F, G, and H and included in this appendix.

Appendix L — Plan Maintenance Procedures

This appendix should include the frequency of review for the plan. It can be divided into static information and dynamic information. This responsibility should be assigned to an individual associated with the contingency plan and included in their official job description.

Appendix M — Contingency Log

This appendix should include the assessments and results of any exercise or real contingency operations. It should be written from available documentation after recovery and restoration. Include comprehensive lessons learned documenting unanticipated difficulties, staff participation, restoration of system backups, permanent lost data and equipment, and shutdown of temporary equipment used for the resumption, recovery, and restoration.

CRISIS MANAGEMENT PLAN FOR HIERARCHICAL ACCESS, LTD.

This example is derived from a number of sources, most notably McMaster and Lewis and Clark Universities.[1, 2]

PURPOSE

This crisis management plan is designed to maximize the protection for personnel in the event of a crisis. Immediately following a crisis, this plan is to be placed into effect by the senior management present. Safety of personnel, life and limb, is paramount, and supersedes any efforts to protect property. All employees are responsible for becoming familiar with this plan and for following their associated duties in the event of its activation.

CRISIS MANAGEMENT PLANNING COMMITTEE

HAL's crisis management planning committee consists of the chief executive officer, vice president of operations, director of human resources, and the chief information security officer, whoever they may be.

The planning committee meets annually to review the crisis management plan and schedule appropriate training and exercises.

CRISIS TYPES

For the purposes of this plan there are three categories of crises. The first, although serious, should not require the implementation of this plan.

The CM team leader or his or her appointed representative assesses the elements of the crisis and determines what level of crisis HAL faces based on the following criteria:

Category 1: Minor damage to physical facilities or minor injury to personnel; addressable with on-site resources or limited off-site assistance. Category 1 events are of a limited duration and have little or no significant impact on personnel safety or organizational operations. Examples of category 1 events include the following:

- Small building fire
- Power outage
- Minor flooding due to plumbing failure or excessive precipitation

- Individual personal accident, illness, or injury, including heart attack or stroke
- Assault or battery incident
- Vehicle accident
- Alcohol-related incident
- Employee suicide

Category 2: Major damage to physical facilities requiring considerable off-site assistance. Category 2 events are of longer duration than category 1 events and may impact more than a few personnel. Category 2 events may escalate depending on crisis conditions and require implementation of the crisis management plan. Sample category 2 events include the following:

- Moderate building fire
- Widespread public health issue such as a flu or cold
- Power outage
- Excessive flooding due to excessive precipitation
- Isolated suspected terrorist attack, such as a chemical or biological agent or explosive
- Hostage or sniper incident
- Vehicle accident
- Alcohol-related incident
- Minor earthquake, hurricane, or tornado damage
- Riots or demonstrations

Category 3: Organization-wide crisis requiring evacuation of organizational facilities, if possible, and/or cessation of organizational functions pending resolution of the crisis. Category 3 crises represent the highest level of impact on the organization and may occur in conjunction with local, state, or federal emergency relief efforts. Some examples of a category 3 crisis include:

- Public health epidemic or outbreak
- Terrorist attack or explosion
- Other explosion (chemical, natural gas, or other)
- Major chemical or biological agent spill or release
- Widespread fires or wildfires
- Massive flooding, mudslides, or landslides requiring regional evacuation
- Massive earthquake, hurricane, or tornado damage

CRISIS MANAGEMENT TEAM STRUCTURE

The crisis management team has the following purpose:

- To develop and maintain awareness of the crisis or emergency situation for HAL management
- To coordinate support and assistance for crisis and emergency responders

HAL's crisis management team consists of the following individuals:

- Team leader: Current director of human resources or appointed representative. The team leader is responsible for overseeing the actions of the crisis management team and for coordinating all crisis management efforts in cooperation with disaster recovery and business continuity planning as needed.
- Communications coordinator: To be appointed by the team leader.
- The communications coordinator is responsible for managing all communications between the CM team, HAL management, employees, and the public, including the media.
- Emergency services coordinator: To be appointed by the team leader.
- The emergency services coordinator is responsible for contacting and managing all interaction between HAL management and staff and any needed emergency services, including utility services.
- Other personnel as needed

RESPONSIBILITY AND CONTROL

The chief executive officer is primarily responsible for the implementation and control of the crisis management plan. In the event of his or her unavailability or incapacitation, the vice president of operations serves as the second in command. The remainder of the chain of command flows based on seniority within the organization from the vice president team. If all vice presidents are unavailable or incapacitated, the crisis management team leader serves as the executive-in-charge.

Once the responsible individual has received notification of a crisis category event, they make the determination as to whether or not to implement the crisis management plan, along with any other needed plans, such as disaster recovery or business continuity. The crisis management team then begins work to minimize the threat to personnel safety and to identify any potential loss of life or health.

IMPLEMENTATION

The crisis management team leader is responsible for implementing the automatic notification system once the crisis management plan is activated.

Assumptions

- If the physical building is not at risk or damaged, it can serve as the base of operations.
- If available, corporate security provides security assistance and assists in the coordination of emergency services.
- Each department establishes and maintains an emergency alert roster and communications plan containing the home, mobile, and alternate phone numbers of all employees.
- The organization's automated notification system, if operational, serves as the primary means of communicating with all employees.

- The organization keeps all information confidential, with all official communications coming through the CM communications officer. No names are released.
- If telephone services are functional, either land line or mobile:
  1. Crisis management team leader receives authorization from the executive-in-charge to activate the CM plan.
  2. CM team leader notifies CM team and begins building evacuation or quarantine procedures if needed. If building evacuation or quarantine is not needed, the CM team leader establishes an operations center in the executive conference room. If the building is uninhabitable, the CM team leader identifies a suitable alternate location from local merchants or other regional facilities. He or she then notifies the CM team and executive management as to this location.
  3. CM team communications coordinator updates automatic notification system to advise employees as to their next course of action. This could include some of the following:
     a. Stay at home.
     b. Find nearest shelter.
     c. Report your status.
     d. Contact your supervisor.
     e. Report to work immediately.
     f. Report to alternate work site (in most instances this is Contingencies, Inc., 221 Industrial Park Drive).
     g. Seek medical attention immediately.
     h. Notify local law enforcement of the details of the incident.
  4. CM team emergency services coordinator notifies the appropriate emergency services of the CM team's activation and its contact information. If the appropriate services have not already been deployed, then the ES coordinator requests them. Emergency services requested could include:
     a. Fire department
     b. Police at the local, state, or federal level
     c. Bomb squad
     d. Search and rescue
     e. Health department or U.S. Centers for Disease Control and Prevention
     f. Ambulance or medivac
     g. Power provider
     h. Natural gas/propane provider
     i. Telephone provider
     j. Water provider
     k. Sewer provider
     l. Post Office in the event of a postal-based attack
     m. Internet/data communications provider
     n. Appropriate emergency management agency (FEMA or state emergency management agency)

      o.   Animal control in the event of a potentially infectious (for example, rabid) animal

      p.   Road services department, state or local

      q.   Towing or crane operation company

5.   CM team communications service coordinator then monitors incoming communications for additional information.

6.   All team members monitor the situation using available television, telephone, and Internet services and make additional decisions, briefing executive management as needed.

- If telephone services are not functional:

7.   Crisis management team leader checks in with the executive-in-charge as soon as a crisis is suspected, to receive authorization to activate the plan.

8.   CM team leader leaves word at the front gate for all team members to check in to the operations center at the executive conference room or at the designated alternate site immediately upon reporting to the office.

9.   If possible, CM team communications coordinator updates any automatic notification system to advise employees as to their next course of action; if not, word is left at the front gate to the facility.

10.   Remainder of CP plan is executed as best possible, using physical notifications and/or runners to convey communications.

In the event of a major crisis or emergency, the crisis management plan is implemented as follows:

Crisis Management Protocols

   a.   Medical Emergency

      Steps:

      Person identifying situation

      1. Notify security services and indicate medical emergency. They contact emergency services and ambulances, if necessary.

      2. Be available to provide information to the emergency services team or security about the situation.

      Corporate security services

      3. Security services contacts crisis management team.

      4. Security services contacts the health authority, if necessary (or police department).

      Crisis management team

      5. Set up crisis command center.

      6. Arrange for temporary accommodations and relocations, if necessary.

      7. Prepare for appropriate communication.

      8. Arrange for hotline, if necessary, for employees and families.

   b.   Violent Crime or Behavior

      Steps: (crime is in progress)

      Person experiencing situation

      1. Stay calm, give money, or meet demands if possible.

2. Notify security services as soon as possible. Dial x 9999. Security services contacts local police if required.
3. Dial 911 if security services are not immediately responsive.
4. Secure the area or move to a safe environment.

Security services

5. Security services contacts the crisis management team.
6. Notify police if required.

Crisis management team

7. Initiate communication plans.
8. Set up crisis command center if required.
9. Arrange counseling or victim services for victims and affected individuals.

Steps: (discovery of violent crime after the fact)

Person discovering the situation

10. Notify security services. They notify emergency services if required.
11. Go to a safe place and wait for security. Report anything noted of relevance to security services.

Security services

12. Security services contacts the police department.
13. Security services contacts the crisis management team.

Crisis management team

14. The crisis management team contacts other required personnel.
15. Arrange for counseling or victim services for those affected.
16. Prepare media response as required.
17. Notify family if required.
18. Arrange memorial services if required.
19. Send a representative to the funeral if required.
20. If required, assist family with packing belongings.
21. Facilitate refunds if required.

   c.   Political Situations

Steps: (riots or demonstrations)

Person identifying situation

1. Notify security services. They notify emergency services and the police if required.
2. Move to a safe environment.

Security services

3. Secure the area with assistance of police.
4. Notify the crisis management team.

Crisis management team

5. Initiate communication plans.
6. Set up crisis command center if required.
7. Arrange counseling or victim services for victims and affected individuals.
8. Coordinate media communications.

d. Accidents Outside Organizational Facilities Involving Employees
    1. Notify a member of the crisis management team.
    2. The crisis management team contacts required personnel.
    3. Prepare press release, if required.
    4. Arrange counseling, if required.
    5. Arrange memorial service, if required.
    6. Identify member of organization to attend funeral, if required.
    7. Assist family with belongings, insurance, and benefits, if required.
e. Environmental or Natural Disaster and Evacuation
    Steps:
    Person discovering the situation
    1. Pull fire alarm and follow procedures to evacuate the area.
    2. Notify security services.
    Security services
    3. Security services initiates communication with crisis
       management team.
    4. Fire department is called, if not already on premises.
    5. Police department is called, if required.
    Crisis management team
    6. Set up crisis command center.
    7. Emergency shelter is notified.
    8. Hotline initiated if needed.
    9. Press release is prepared, if required.
    10. Provide emergency funds as required.
f. Bomb Threats
    Steps:
    Person identifying situation
    1. Notify security services.
    Security services
    2. Assess situation and notify police, if necessary.
    3. Follow evacuation procedures.

If the crisis occurs during working hours, the CM team leader receives direct notification from the on-site executive-in-charge. If the crisis occurs after hours, the CM team leader receives notification as the on-site security officer notifies their security organization, which in turn notifies executives in accordance with their established policies, based on the available alert roster.

CRISIS MANAGEMENT PLAN PRIORITIES

The crisis management team concentrates efforts on the following priority 1 objectives until these objectives are substantially met. Priority 2 and 3 objectives are addressed as resources become available. The crisis management team creates and maintains a log of all events and activities as they occur.

Priority I Objectives

a. Communication network: Establish a communication network using existing resources.
   1. Telephone—land line or mobile
   2. Automated notification system
   3. Intranet
   4. E-mail
   5. Runners

b. Medical assistance: Provide medical assistance to injured or ill individuals.
   1. 911 emergency services
   2. First aid kits in emergency packs—CM teams and executive management
   3. Transportation by personal vehicles to regional health clinic or hospital by volunteers

c. Fire suppression: Provide assistance to minimize damage by local fires.
   1. 911 emergency services
   2. Building fire suppression releases are manned by CM team.
   3. Local fire extinguishers are manned by volunteers.

d. Search and Rescue: Provide searches for unaccounted personnel and transport to medical assistance as needed.
   1. 911 emergency services
   2. Corporate security officers
   3. Supervisors and managers

e. Utilities Survey: Evaluate condition of services and disable or enable as appropriate.
   1. 911 emergency services
   2. Utility service providers
   3. CM team members
   4. Priority to power/electric
   5. Priority to natural gas/propane
   6. Priority to water/sewer

f. Hazardous substance control: Evaluate presence of or threat from possible radiological, chemical, or biological hazards.
   1. 911 emergency services
   2. Local health officers
   3. CM team members

Priority II Objectives

a. Facility survey: Determine occupancy during and after crisis.
   1. 911 emergency services
   2. Local health officers
   3. DR team members
   4. CM team members
   5. Priority of occupancy is to data center, help center, and administrative offices.

b. Shelter: Identify suitable shelter during or after crisis for personnel safety.
   1. Basement of primary facility is rated as storm shelter.
   2. Basement of merchant shops across Main Street is also rated as storm shelter; it is a converted industrial mill.
   3. City auditorium and town hall are also rated as storm shelters.
c. Food and drinking water: Identify source for emergency sustenance and arrange for support.
   1. Work rooms in building to be stocked with multiple cases of drinking water and emergency rations at all times.
   2. Merchant shops across Main Street include several snack, coffee, and restaurant facilities.
   3. Support buildings around main offices are stocked with emergency water.
d. Sewer system: Determine primary and alternate facilities to support employee biological functions.
   1. Restrooms in primary office building
   2. Merchant shops across Main Street include facilities.
   3. Support buildings around main offices equipped with facilities.
   4. Construction support company two miles away rents portable facilities.
e. Communications: Establish a communication system with the campus community, and advise everyone regarding availability of basic services.
   1. Automated notification system
   2. Telephone—land line or mobile
   3. Intranet
   4. E-mail
   5. Door-to-door runners
f. Criminal activity control: Establish a security patrol system to control crime.
   1. 911 emergency services
   2. Corporate security officers
   3. Supervisors and managers
g. Psychological assistance: Establish a system to deal with cases of emotional distress. Local health center or counseling center can provide counseling as needed. Red Cross also provides assistance in this area if the crisis is widespread.

Priority III Objectives

a. Valuables material survey: Identify, survey, and secure valuable materials within the organization.
   1. 911 emergency services
   2. Corporate security officers
   3. DR team
   4. Supervisors and managers

b. Information survey: Identify, survey, and secure all organizational records. This is performed by the appropriate DR teams with the support of available IT personnel.

 1. First priority is to data center electronic information and backups.
 2. Second priority is to accounting electronic information and backups.
 3. Third priority is to help desk electronic information and backups.
 4. Fourth priority is to all remaining local machines and hard copy information.

c. Supplies and equipment: Develop system to renew flow of supplies and equipment from outside resources. CM will coordinate with available DR and BC teams as needed for supplies and equipment.

The executive-in-charge, based on the recommendations of the CM team leader determines when to deactivate the crisis management plan.

AFTER THE EMERGENCY

Immediately following conclusion of the crisis and deactivation of the CM plan, all affected parties will meet at the operations center for debriefing. Within 48 hours of the crisis, an after-action review will be held at a location to be determined by the executive-in-charge.

Any needed memorial services, notification of next-of-kin, completion of legal or insurance documentation, or other post-emergency functions will be coordinated by the CM team leader with the assistance of the executive team and corporate council.

Updated and approved by CM team and executive management on February 10, 2008.

Acceptance   In contrast to mitigation, acceptance of risk is a choice to do nothing to protect a vulnerability and to accept the outcome of its exploitation. This may or may not be a conscious business decision.

Access control lists (ACLs)   Lists, matrices, and capability tables governing the rights and privileges of a particular user to a particular system.

Active scanning   Collecting information about computers by sending traffic and observing what traffic returns as a result; must be used in conjunction with enumeration.

Advance party   Includes members or representatives of each major business continuity team.

After-action review (AAR)   A detailed examination of the events that occurred from first detection to final recovery from an incident.

Alarm   An indication that a system has just been attacked or continues to be under attack.

Alarm clustering   The consolidation of almost-identical alarms into a single higher-level alarm.

Alarm compaction   Alarm clustering that is based on frequency, similarity in attack signature, similarity in attack target, or other similarities.

Alarm filtering   The process of classifying the attack alerts detected by an intrusion detection system to more efficiently distinguish or sort false positives from actual attacks.

Alert   An indication that a system has just been attacked or continues to be under attack.

Alert message   A scripted description of the incident; it consists of just enough information so that each responder knows what portion of the incident response plan to implement without impeding the notification process.

Alert roster   Document containing contact information for the individuals that need to be notified in the event of an actual incident.

Assembly area   A designated area where individuals should gather in the event of a specific type of emergency to facilitate a quick head count.

Asset   An organizational resource that is logical, such as a Web site, information, or data; or physical, such as a person, computer system, or other tangible object.

Attack   An intentional or unintentional attempt to cause damage to or otherwise compromise information or the systems that support it.

Attack profiles   Description of a typical attack, including its methodology, indicators of an attack, and broad consequences.

Attack scenario end case   A document that estimates the cost of the best, worst, and most likely outcomes from an attack.

Attack scenarios   Descriptions of typical attacks, including methodology, indicators of an attack, and broad consequences.

Auxiliary phone alert and reporting system
A secondary automated phone system, located offsite at a secure service provider's location.

Availability   Ensuring that authorized users—persons or computer systems—are able to access information without interference or obstruction, and to receive it in the required format.

Avoidance   A risk control strategy that attempts to prevent the exploitation of the vulnerability. This is the preferred approach, and is accomplished by countering threats, removing vulnerabilities in assets, limiting access to assets, and adding protective safeguards.

Bare metal recovery   Method of data recovery where the affected system is rebooted from a CD-ROM or other remote drive, and the operating system is quickly restored by images backed up from a known stable state.

Baselines   Normal, expected levels of network, system, and application activity.

Behavior-based IDS   A network intrusion detection system that collects statistical summaries by observing traffic that is known to be normal in order to establish a performance baseline.

Black bag operation (op)   A search in which the suspect never knows a search occurred, because the scene is restored to its original state.

Business continuity (BC)   The final response of the organization when faced with any interruption of critical operations.

Business continuity (BC) plan   A document that expresses how an organization ensures that critical business functions continue at an alternate location while the organization recovers its ability to function at the primary site if a catastrophic incident or disaster occurs.

Business continuity plan (BCP)   A process used to create plans for the resumption of critical business functions in the event the primary site(s) and/or people are not able to be used.

Business disaster recovery policy   A policy for the direction and guidance of any and all disaster recovery operations.

Business impact analysis (BIA)   An investigation and assessment of the relative value and importance of the various business units and their functions to determine the potential for risk and magnitude of losses due to the threat and vulnerability environment. It is used to develope strategies for disaster recovery and business continuity. One of the assumptions made in the BIA is that all parts of the organization are important to the continuation of an organization, but that some are more crucial than others.

Business resumption (BR) plan   A document that describes an approach that merges the capabilities of both the disaster recovery plan and business continuity plan.

Business resumption planning (BRP)   A process used to create plans for the resumption of business activities, including recovery at the primary site (DRP) and, when necessary, continuation of functions at alternate sites (BCP).

C.I.A. triangle   An industry standard for computer security, the C.I.A. triangle is based on three critical characteristics of information: confidentiality, integrity, and availability.

Cabling system   Network of wiring that interconnects data networking or telephone equipment.

Chain of command   The list of officials ranging from an individual's immediate supervisor through the top executive of the organization.

Chain of custody   *See* chain of evidence.

Chain of evidence   A log of everyone who has had access to or possession of evidentiary material from its collection to its presentation during legal proceedings. Sometimes called chain of custody.

Champion A high-level manager with influence and resources that can be used to support the project team, promote the objectives of the contingency planning project, and endorse the results that come from the effort—ideally, a CIO or CEO.

Clearing Closing down the organization's presence at the alternate business continuity site.

Clipping level A measurement of activity outside the performance baseline determined by a stat IDS or behavior-based IDS.

Cold site Provides only rudimentary services and facilities, essentially an empty room with standard heating, air conditioning, and electrical service.

Computer forensic software Specialized software designed to analyze disk images for evidence of an incident.

Computer forensic workstations and/or backup devices Equipment to create disk images, preserve log files, and save other relevant incident data.

Computer forensics The preservation, identification, extraction, documentation, and interpretation of computer media for evidentiary and/or root cause analysis.

Confidence value A value associated with an intrusion detection system's ability to detect and identify an attack correctly.

Confidentiality Ensures that only those with the rights and privileges to access information are able to do so.

Configuration rules Specific configuration codes entered into security systems to guide the execution of the system when information is passing through it.

Contact information May include phone numbers, e-mail addresses, public encryption keys for encryption software, and instructions for verifying the contact's identity.

Contingency plan The plan prepared by the organization to anticipate, react to, and recover from events that threaten the security of information and information assets in the organization, and, subsequently, to restore the organization to normal modes of business operations.

Contingency planning (CP) The process of preparing an organization to anticipate, react to, and recover from events that threaten the security of information and information assets in the organization, and, subsequently, to restore the organization to normal modes of business operations.

Contingency planning management team (CPMT) A group assembled to define the scope of the contingency planning project and identify the resources to be used.

Control Security mechanisms, policies, or procedures that can successfully counter attacks, reduce risks, resolve vulnerabilities, and generally improve the security within an organization.

Countermeasure Security mechanisms, policies, or procedures that can successfully counter attacks, reduce risks, resolve vulnerabilities, and generally improve the security within an organization.

Crisis A significant business disruption that stimulates extensive news media coverage.

Crisis management (CM) Actions taken by an organization in response to an emergency situation in an effort to minimize injury or loss of life.

Cross-training The process of ensuring that every employee is trained to perform at least part of another employee's job.

Cryptographic hashes A calculated unique data value computed based on a much larger set of data to be used to determine if the larger set of data has been altered.

Cyberterrorists   People who hack computer systems to conduct terrorist activities through a network or Internet pathways.

Data classification scheme   A data protection method that requires information owners to classify the information assets for which they are responsible.

Database shadowing   The storage of duplicate online transaction data, along with the duplication of the databases at the remote site to a redundant server.

De facto standards   Informal but widely accepted standards.

De jure standards   Formal standards that may be published, scrutinized, and ratified by a group.

Degraded mode   Operating under adverse conditions such as loss of power or lighting, or loss of communications (phone or network).

Differential backup   The storage of all files that have changed or been added since the last full backup.

Disaster recovery (DR) plan   A plan designed to reduce the impact of a disaster and shorten the time needed to recover from a disaster whether natural or man-made.

Disaster recovery planning (DRP)   The preparation for recovery from a disaster, whether natural or man-made.

Disk   Hard disk, a computer storage device, usually employing magnetized disks.

Disk mirroring   A process of using two disk drives to simultaneously record the same data to provide an immediately available backup in the event of a failure.

Disk striping   Not a form of redundant storage, striping creates one larger logical volume across several available hard disk drives, and stores the data in segments, called stripes, across all the disk drives in the array.

DNS cache poisoning   A type of attack in which the DNS tables of a DNS server are compromised to enable network traffic to be routed to a destination of the attacker's choosing.

Easily portable printer   Used in war room to print copies of log files and other evidence from non-networked systems.

Electronic vaulting   The bulk transfer of data in batches to an off-site facility.

Encryption software   Specialized software designed to scramble data. It often includes mechanisms to manage the keys necessary for the process as well.

Enterprise information security policy (EISP)   A policy that is based on and directly supports the mission, vision, and direction of the organization and sets the strategic direction, scope, and tone for all security efforts.

Enumeration   The process of identifying what resources are publicly available for exploit; must be used in conjunction with passive or active scanning.

Events   Unexpected activities identified and addressed by the incident response plan.

Evidence-gathering accessories   May include hardbound notebooks, digital cameras, audio recorders, and chain-of-custody forms. Evidence storage bags and tags and evidence tape are also needed to preserve evidence for possible legal actions.

Evidentiary material   Information, graphics, images, or any other physical or electronic item that could have value as evidence of guilt (or innocence) in a legal proceeding, whether criminal or civil.

Executive-in-charge   The ranking executive on-site when the crisis or emergency arises who is authorized to initiate the crisis management plan.

Exploit   Illegal use of a system or information. It is also a targeted solution to misuse a specific hole or vulnerability, usually in software, that an attacker creates to formulate an attack.

Facilitated data-gathering session   Group of individuals from a particular business area, along with their managerial team, who gather to brainstorm the answers to the questions needed to complete the business impact analysis process.

False attack stimulus   An event that triggers alarms and causes a false positive when no actual attacks are in progress.

False negative   The failure of an intrusion detection system to react to an actual attack event. Of all failures, this is the most grievous.

False positive   An alarm or alert that indicates an attack is in progress or that an attack has successfully occurred, when in fact there was no attack.

Focus group   Group of individuals from a particular business area, along with their managerial team, who gather to brainstorm the answers to the questions needed to complete the business impact analysis process.

Forensics   The application of methodical investigatory techniques to collect and preserve data for use in criminal, civil or administrative investigations.

Full backup   A full and complete backup of the entire system, including all applications, operating systems components, and data.

Hacker   A person who gains access to information by circumventing controls or by misusing information systems. In the past this term was associated with dedicated and persistent users who often pushed the limits of systems to learn as much as possible about them. A preferred term for those who attempt to bypass controls is an attacker.

Head count   Verifying the location of all individual persons within a building or organization. An essential step in emergency situations.

Hierarchical roster   An alert roster that requires that the first person call certain other people on the roster, who in turn call other people, and so on.

Honeynet   A simulated network or subnet configured to resemble a production network. Appears as a valuable target to attackers.

Honeypot   Devices configured to resemble production systems appearing to offer valuable information. If an attacker takes the bait, alarms are triggered.

Honeypot farm   A network of honeypots configured to resemble a production network.

Honeytoken   Similar to a honeypot but at the file level. Any interaction with a honeytoken most likely represents unauthorized or malicious activity. An example would be a simulated record placed into a database, and monitored by the system.

Horizontal job rotation   The movement of employees between positions at the same organizational level, rather than through progression and promotion.

Host-based IDS (HIDS)   A network intrusion detection system that resides on a particular computer or server, known as the host, and monitors activity only on that system.

Hot site   A fully configured computer facility with all services, communications links, and physical plant operations that is capable of establishing disaster recovery operations at a moment's notice.

Hot swappable   Devices that can be replaced without taking down the entire system. Often used in reference to disk drives.

Incident candidates   Possible security incidents to be evaluated, for example, the presence of unfamiliar files, unfamiliar processes running, or an unusual use of computer resources.

Incident classification The process of evaluating circumstances around organizational events, determining which events are possible incidents, and then determining whether or not the event constitutes an actual incident.

Incident reporting mechanisms Phone numbers, e-mail addresses, and online forms that users can use to report suspected incidents; at least one mechanism should permit people to report incidents anonymously.

Incident response (IR) The set of procedures that commence when an incident is detected.

Incident response (IR) plan A document describing actions an organization can and perhaps should take while the incident is in progress.

Incident response planning (IRP) The process used to prepare an organization to detect and respond to incidents that threaten the security of the organization and its information.

Incremental backup A backup that archives files that have been modified that day, and thus requires less space and time to create than the differential backup.

Information security (InfoSec) The protection of the confidentiality, integrity, and availability of information, whether in storage, during processing, or in transmission through the application of policy, training, education and technology.

Information security policy A document that provides rules for the protection of the information assets of the organization.

Integrity Information has integrity when it is whole, complete, and uncorrupted.

Intellectual property The ownership of ideas and control over the tangible or virtual representation of those ideas. Use of another person's intellectual property may or may not involve royalty payments or permission, but should always include proper credit to the source.

Intrusion detection system (IDS) A network burglar alarm designed to be placed in a network to determine whether or not the network is being used in ways that are out of compliance with the policy of the organization.

Intrusion prevention systems (IPS) Intrusion management systems that take a more reactive approach, built on the ability to respond to known methods of attack and to create adaptive responses to previously unknown attacks.

IR duty officer Person responsible for scanning the organization's information infrastructure for signs of an incident.

Issue-specific security policy (ISSP) A policy that addresses specific areas of technology, requires frequent updates, and contains a statement on the organization's position on a specific issue.

Job rotation The movement of employees from one position to another so they can develop additional skills and abilities.

Knowledge-based IDS A network intrusion detection system that examines data traffic in search of patterns that match known signatures—that is, preconfigured, predetermined attack patterns.

Likelihood The probability that a specific vulnerability within an organization will be successfully attacked.

Malware Software components or programs designed to damage, destroy, or deny service to target systems. Common instances of malicious code (malware) are viruses and worms, Trojan horses, logic bombs, and back doors.

Mirrored site The ultimate in hot sites, it is identical to the primary site, and includes live or periodic data transfers. As such, it is capable of immediate operations.

Mission   A written statement of an organization's purpose.

Mitigation   A control approach that attempts to reduce the impact caused by the exploitation of vulnerability through planning and preparation.

Mutual agreement   A contract between two organizations for each to assist the other in the event of a disaster.

Need-to-know   An additional restriction on a security clearance. Regardless of security clearance, employees are not allowed to view any and all data that falls within their level of clearance. Before someone can access a specific set of data, an additional need-to-know requirement must be met.

Network port   An equipment interface for communicating with a computer program over a network.

Network-Attached Storage (NAS)   Commonly a single device or server that attaches to a network, and uses common communications methods, such as Windows file sharing, NFS, CIFS, HTTP directories, or FTP, to provide an online storage environment.

Network-based IDS (NIDS)   Monitors traffic on a segment of an organization's network. A NIDS looks for indications of ongoing or successful attacks and resides on a computer or appliance connected to that network segment.

Noise   Ongoing activity from alarm events that are accurate and noteworthy but not necessarily significant as potentially successful attacks.

On-call information   *See* alert roster.

Packet sniffers and protocol analyzers   Equipment designed to capture and analyze network traffic that may contain evidence of an incident.

Passive scanning   Collecting information about computers by listening to network traffic; must be used in conjunction with enumeration.

Policy   A plan or course of action used by an organization to convey instructions from its senior-most management to those who make decisions, take actions, and perform other duties on behalf of the organization.

Port lists   List of commonly used network ports and ports exploited by Trojan horses.

Primary site   The location or group of locations at which the organization executes the functions of the organization.

Rapid onset disasters   Disasters that occur suddenly, with little warning, taking the lives of people and destroying the means of production, for example, earthquakes, floods, storm winds, tornadoes, or mud flows.

Reaction force   Individuals that are needed to quickly respond to each particular incident.

Recovery phase   The recovery of the most time-critical business functions—those necessary to reestablish business operations and prevent further economic and image loss to the organization.

Recovery point objective (RPO)   The point in the past to which the recovered applications, systems, and data at the alternate infrastructure will be restored, e.g., as of 2:00 a.m. yesterday.

Recovery time objective (RTO)   The period of time within which systems, applications, or functions must be recovered after an outage, for example, one business day.

Redundant array of independent disks (RAID)   Technology that uses several hard drives to distribute information across multiple drive units for operational redundancy.

Redundant personnel   Individuals hired above and beyond the minimum number of personnel needed to perform a business function.

Remote journaling (RJ)   The transfer of live transactions to an off-site facility.

Residual risk   The risk that remains to an information asset even after a control has been applied.

Response phase   The phase associated with implementing the reaction to a disaster facing the organization and focused on those actions designed to control or stabilize the situation, if possible.

Risk assessment   Assigning a risk rating or score to each information asset; useful in gauging the relative risk to each vulnerable information asset and facilitating development of comparative ratings later in the risk control process.

Risk control   The process of applying controls to reduce the risks to an organization's data and information systems.

Risk identification   The process of applying controls to reduce the risks to an organization's data and information systems.

Risk management   The process of identifying vulnerabilities in an organization's information systems and taking carefully reasoned steps to ensure the confidentiality, integrity, and availability of all the components in the organization's information system.

Root cause analysis   The determination of the initial flaw or vulnerability that allowed the incident to occur by examining the systems, networks, and procedures involved.

Safeguard   Security mechanism, policy, or procedure that can successfully counter attacks, reduce risk, resolve vulnerabilities, and generally improve the security within an organization.

Scanning utilities   Tools used to identify which computers are active on a network, as well as which ports and services are active on the computers, and what function or role the machines may be fulfilling.

Secure storage facility   Location for securing evidence and other sensitive materials.

Security clearance   An authorization level assigned to each user of data to indicate the level of classified information he or she is authorized to view.

Sequential roster   An alert roster that requires a contact person call each and every person on the roster.

Service agreements   Contractual documents guaranteeing certain minimum levels of service provided by vendors.

Service bureau   A service agency that provides physical facilities in the event of a disaster.

Signature matching   A process used by network intrusion detection systems. It looks for attack patterns by comparing measured activity to known signatures in the knowledge base to determine whether or not an attack has occurred or may be underway.

Signature-based IDS   A network intrusion detection system that examines data traffic in search of patterns that match known signatures—preconfigured, predetermined attack patterns.

Single point of failure   A critical element of a system or process that can halt the entire system or process.

Site policy   The rules and configuration guidelines governing the implementation and operation of intrusion detection systems within the organization.

Site policy awareness   The intrusion detection system's ability to dynamically modify its site policies in reaction or response to environmental activity.

Six-tape rotation   A method of backup that uses a rotation of six sets of media. It uses five media sets per week and offers roughly two weeks of recovery capability.

Slow onset disasters Disasters that slowly deteriorate the capacity of an organization to withstand their effects. Examples include droughts, famines, environmental degradation, desertification, deforestation, and pest infestation.

Smoldering crisis Any serious business problem not generally known within or without the company that may generate negative news coverage if or when it goes "public."

Standards Detailed statements of what must be done to comply with policy.

Statistical anomaly-based IDS (stat IDS) A network intrusion detection system that collects statistical summaries by observing traffic that is known to be normal to establish a performance baseline.

Storage Area Networks (SANs) An online storage environment that uses Fiber-channel direct connections between the systems needing the additional storage and the storage devices themselves.

Strategic planning The process of moving the organization toward its vision.

Succession planning A process that enables an organization to cope with any loss of personnel with a minimum degree of disruption to the functionality of the organization.

Sudden crisis A disruption in the company's business that occurs without warning and is likely to generate news coverage and may adversely impact employees, investors, customers, suppliers, and other stakeholders.

Switched port analysis (SPAN) port An output port on a switch that provides a consolidated stream that copies all data sent to or from the designated ports on the switch. When used with an IDS the SPAN port will be programmed to include all data processed by any port on the switch.

Systems diagramming A method of analysis used to understand the operation of systems and to chart process flows and interdependency studies for both manual and automated systems.

Systems-specific security policies (SysSPs) Policies that are frequently codified as standards and procedures to be used when configuring or maintaining systems.

Task rotation Similar to job rotation, involves the rotation of a portion of a job, rather than the entire position.

Threat A category of objects, persons, or other entities that pose a potential risk of loss to an asset.

Threat assessment Examination of the current environment to assess it for likely threats to establish the likelihood of experiencing a loss.

Threat-agent A specific and identifiable instance of a general threat.

Time-share A disaster recovery site leased in conjunction with a business partner or sister organization.

Transference A control approach that attempts to shift the risk to other assets, other processes, or other organizations through rethinking how services are offered, revising deployment models, outsourcing to other organizations, purchasing insurance, or implementing service contracts with providers.

Trap and trace An automated response to an attack that uses a combination of resources to detect an intrusion and then to trace the intrusion to its source.

Trigger The circumstances that cause the incident response team to be activated and the incident response plan to be initiated.

True attack stimulus An event that triggers alarms and causes an intrusion detection system to react as if a real attack is in progress.

Vertical job rotation In an industry where there is a clear career progression from a lower level position to a higher one, a person who has progressed through the ranks could be called on to perform lower-level jobs.

Vision A written statement of what an organization would like to accomplish.

Vulnerability A weakness or fault in the protection mechanisms intended to protect information and information assets from attack or damage.

War game A simulation that uses a subset of response plans in place to create a realistic test environment.

War room A location for central communication and coordination. If a permanent war room is not necessary, the team should create a procedure for procuring a temporary war room when needed.

Warm site Similar to a hot site, but typically software applications are either not included, not installed, or not configured.

Well-known vulnerabilities Vulnerabilities that have been examined, documented, and published.

B

I

X

Z